# Rock and Roll
## Its History and Stylistic Development

### Fifth Edition

## Joe Stuessy
Texas State University—San Marcos

## Scott Lipscomb
Northwestern University

**PEARSON**
Prentice
Hall

Upper Saddle River, New Jersey, 07458

**Library of Congress Cataloging-in-Publication Data**

Stuessy, Joe.
   Rock and roll : its history and stylistic development / Joe Steussy, Scott Lipscomb.—5th ed.
      p. cm.
   Includes discography (p.  ), bibliographical references (p.  ), and index.
   ISBN 0-13-193098-2
  1.  Rock music—History and criticism.   I.  Lipscomb, Scott David   II.  Title.
   ML3534.S83 2006
   781.66'09—dc22

2005014032

**Editor in Chief:** Sarah Toubourg
**Editorial Assistant:** Evette Dickerson
**Executive Marketing Manager:** Sheryl Adams
**Senior Managing Editor:** Lisa Iarkowski
**Production Liasion:** Fran Russello
**Manufacturing Buyer:** Ben Smith
**Cover Design:** Kiwi Design
**Cover Illustration/Photo:** Kurt Steir/CORBIS
**Image Permission Coordinator:** Carolyn Gauntt
**Composition/Full-Service Project Management:** John Shannon/Pine Tree Composition
**Printer/Binder:** Courier Companies, Inc.

Credits and acknowledgments borrowed from other and sources and reproduced, with permission, in this textbook appear on the appropriate page and on page xii.

Pearson Education LTD, London
Pearson Education Singapore, Pte. Ltd.
Pearson Education, Canada, Ltd
Pearson Education—Japan
Pearson Education Australia PTY, Limited

Pearson Education North Asia Ltd
Pearson Educatión de Mexico, S.A de C.V.
Pearson Education Malaysia, Pte. Ltd.
Pearson Education, Upper Saddle River,
  New Jersey

10  9  8  7  6  5  4  3
**ISBN: 0-13-193098-2**

Dedicated with love
to my wife, Chris;
to my children Debbie and Kevin;
and to the memory
of my parents.

—Joe Stuessy


Dedicated with love
to my wife, Jordana;
to my children
Kevin, and Sterling;
and to my parents, Dixie and A. D. Petrey
and Dave and JoAnn Lipscomb.

—Scott Lipscomb

# Contents

# Acknowledgments

Even rock and rollers grow older. Some of the key figures in the early chapters of this book are now in their sixties (or deceased). The remaining Fab Four and the Bad Boys of Rock are over sixty years old. I began playing in rock and roll bands in about 1957, at the age of fourteen. Some quick math reveals that I, too, crossed the mid-century mark over a decade ago. While creating the Third Edition of this book, it became obvious that a new chapter was needed on recent trends in rock. I feared that my appreciation for and knowledge of most post–1980s rock left much to be desired. My attitude toward much of this recent music was that of a crusty curmudgeon. The need for a more sympathetic (but still critical) approach was apparent.

Dr. Scott Lipscomb has, I believe, admirably filled the need in the third and subsequent editions. I certainly appreciate his contributions as will, I predict, our readers.

I also want to thank Dr. Charles Eagle, former professor of music at Southern Methodist University. Over the past twenty-five years, he has greatly influenced my growth as a musician, scholar, and person. He has helped me see beyond the trivial, think beyond the obvious, and feel beyond the immediate.

I have taught a course in rock music for over 30 years. From the more than 9,000 students in these classes, I have learned a great deal about how nonmusic majors interact with music. Many of these students—at Southern Methodist University, the University of Texas at San Antonio, and Texas State University—have made helpful comments, asked provocative questions, offered loans of tapes and recordings, and shared important pieces of information. I am grateful to all of them for their help and interest.

Special thanks go to the many people at Prentice Hall who helped see this project through to its completion. I also would like to thank the following reviewers: Robert Bonora, Community College of Southern NV and John Turk, Youngstown University.

Finally, I want to thank my family for their unswerving support. My parents, Mr. and Mrs. C. J. Stuessy, never gave less than their total support, whether I was playing a piano concerto with the Houston Symphony or "Rock Around the Clock" with my teenage rock and roll combo. My wife Chris has injected a whole new spirit into my life and work. Her unwavering love and support are appreciated more than I can say. And my kids—Debbie and Kevin—have shown continuing interest in and appreciation of the fact that Dad would be writing a book about rock and roll!

*—Joe Stuessy*

Many individuals played an important role in the preparation of this text. I am extremely fortunate to have benefited greatly over the years from the knowledge of my many students . . . at the University of California, Los Angeles, The University of Texas at San Antonio, and now at Northwestern University. I arrive in the classroom every day, well-prepared for the purpose of filling the fertile minds of my students with the wonders of music . . . and yet my students manage to teach me something new during every session. Particularly important to more recent developments referenced in Chapters 13 through 18 of this text was the substantial amount of assistance received from several gifted students at Northwestern University. Sarah Williams, Jennifer Walshe, Michael Gaertner, and Kristin Bird were extremely helpful in providing an additional (i.e., "younger") perspective regarding current groups, artists, and musical trends. Without their input, the more recent evolutions evident in popular music would not have been covered with near the depth or insight that you will find in these pages. I would also like to express my appreciation to Chelsea Valenzo-Duggan and Alissa Yatcko for their assistance with a variety of research- and library-related tasks. Additionally, as many scholars working in the field of popular music have found, the research of Joel Whitburn and his published compilations of dates, lists, and statistics derived from the *Billboard* Charts was indispensable to our work. His kind and unhesitating willingness to assist personally with a couple of requests is greatly appreciated by both authors. Likewise, *The Rolling Stone Encyclopedia of Rock & Roll* (3rd edition) was a valuable and oft-used resource. The Web site of the Recording Industry Association of America (riaa.com) was indispensable in finding up-to-date information on Gold and Platinum certification of various artists' recordings. And, of course, a special thanks to my co-author Joe Stuessy, our editor Chris Johnson, and Prentice Hall for allowing me the privilege of participating in the release of this fifth edition text.

Most important, I want to acknowledge the essential role my family plays in every aspect of my life and the patience they have shown as I spent many late nights and weekends burning the midnight oil to complete this labor of love. I would like to express my heartfelt appreciation to my loving wife, Jordana, and our children J. D., Kevin, and Sterling.

*—Scott Lipscomb*

## *LYRIC PERMISSIONS*

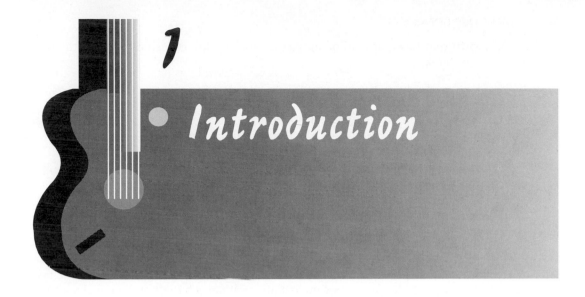

# Introduction

## WHY STUDY ROCK?

Let us begin with the question, Why study rock and roll? One might reply somewhat flippantly, "Because it's there!" But the question deserves a more thoughtful answer than that.

First we must realize that rock and roll is basically and primarily a musical style. It utilizes the same musical elements (rhythm, pitch, dynamics, form, timbre, etc.) found in all styles of music. How these ingredients are combined, in what proportions and with what characteristics, defines rock as a distinct musical style.

As with all musical styles, there are some "good" examples, some "bad" examples, and a lot in between. It is as inaccurate to say that all rock is bad as to say that all classical music is good. Such musical value judgments should rest not on a total style per se but upon how creatively and skillfully the musical creator uses the musical resources appropriate to the specific style.

But rock and roll is more than just a musical style. It is an extremely important and influential social factor. When the final figures are in from the second half of the twentieth century, rock will undoubtedly prove to be the single most potent economic factor in the multibillion-dollar music industry. Musically, rock has influenced the music we hear on television, in films, and in commercials. It has influenced jazz, church music, classical music, and even its own ancestors, rhythm and blues and country and western. Socially, the rock culture's influence has been witnessed in hairstyles, clothing, language, lifestyles, and politics. In other words, any historian of the last half of the twentieth century must devote significant consideration to rock and roll being one of the primary forces in our society as a whole (socially, culturally, economically, politically, and musically).

Any force that has that kind of impact on society deserves study. That is the purpose of this book.

## WHY THIS BOOK?

Certainly there is no lack of written material on the subject of rock and roll. Over 200 books have been written on Elvis Presley alone. Several books also deal effectively with the general history of rock and roll. So why this book?

Obviously, one driving motivation for any author who sets out to write a book is that there is a need for that new book—specifically that it will either cover new areas of the general topic or cover previously discussed areas in a new way. This study of rock hopes to bring to the reader the history of rock and roll with the following four guiding principles in mind:

1. *Don't let the trees get in the way of the forest.* Many books on rock and roll make the admirable attempt to discuss virtually every rock-and-roll performer who ever plugged in a guitar or stepped up to a microphone. That is not the purpose of this study. Rather, we have attempted to determine major trends and primary influential performers, thus painting the history of rock and roll in broad brush strokes. The result is that many performers in the history of rock are only briefly mentioned in these pages, or not mentioned at all.

   To write a study of contemporary (or recent) history in this way is to engage in a continuing exercise in self-control. When we approach the history of the sixteenth century, for example, we have an easier time identifying the main trends, most influential ideas, and principal characters. Our vantage point from 500 years away allows us to take that perspective. We have the advantage of 20/20 hindsight and know with assurance what really proved to be important in light of subsequent human experience.

   But when we look at our own times, our temporal closeness, although it is an advantage in some ways, is also our worst enemy. Our perspective is cluttered with details; we know too much! Therefore, we must repetitively force ourselves to ask questions like, Was this really important in light of what followed? Or, Was this so-called new style or idea really a significant departure from that which preceded it?

   It is hoped, then, that this study will provide the reader with a feeling for the evolution of rock and roll over a fifty-year period, not through a recitation of each and every detail along the way but by means of a broader representation of the general flow of styles, people, and ideas.

2. *Try to "tell it like it is."* Another pitfall of being too close to a subject is that one's personal biases may creep into the writing and prejudice the reader's perspective. As much as possible, we hope that histories are objectively written. But again, our closeness to the subject makes such objectivity difficult (for author and reader). It is fairly easy to be objective about some phenomenon of the fifteenth century, but we often have strong feelings about ideas, events, and people in our own lifetime. We are hard-pressed to remain objective about something (such as music) that interacts with us at a very personal level.

   Nevertheless, there has been a conscious attempt in this study to outline the history of rock as fairly as possible. Of course, any author is a distinct human being and, therefore, cannot totally escape his or her own particular perspective. Thus, there is always some amount of the author's personality and philosophy reflected in his or her work, no matter how honest the attempt to achieve complete objectivity. Indeed, we should expect the historian to have subjective opinions about his or her subject. Such opinions, in fact, might prove especially insightful to the reader. In the case of this book, such personal reflections have been stored up to be presented all in one chapter, clearly labeled as such (see Chapter 19, "An Overview and an Editorial"). If the comments contained therein prove provocative or instructive, so be it; if not, perhaps they will prove interesting or at least entertaining.

3. *Rock and roll is, first and foremost, music.* Rock and roll is many things: It is show biz; it is money; it is record contracts, Top 40 radio, and role models; it is all this and much more. But strip all that away and one still comes to one inescapable fact: Rock and roll is a musical style. Many books speak of performers' lives, tell amusing anecdotes, reveal sales statistics, chronicle albums and songs, and analyze lyrics but neglect to describe what is fundamental to all of the above: the music. Although the current study will include the foregoing elements, it also will address the basic question, What, musically speaking, is rock and roll? It is assumed that most readers will not be conversant with the technical aspects of music (if so, all the better!). Thus each chapter includes a section that discusses a specific aspect of the music of rock and roll. These sections, called musical close-ups, focus on a particular aspect of the music itself. (The organization of Chapter 2, "The Roots of Rock," is a bit different; it has three musical close-ups—one following each of the three main topic areas.) In some of the musical close-ups, various elements of the music are discussed (for example, rhythm, melody, form, or texture). In other close-ups, related musical topics are addressed (for example, improvisation or lyrics); and in Chapters 11 and 12, specific pieces of music are analyzed in detail.

It is hoped that this approach will remind the reader that the person who is knowledgeable about rock music must know more than album titles, song lyrics, sales charts, and performers' lives. Whereas understanding the social, economic, and political implications of rock and roll is of great importance, understanding the music is fundamental.

4. *Rock and roll is an important part of society.* Rock and roll has not existed in a vacuum. Quite the contrary, it has had a vital and an active interrelationship with the general society. Various aspects of this interrelationship (social, economic, and political) will be discussed as appropriate within each chapter. But in addition to that, each chapter begins with an overview. These overview sections provide a general introduction to each chapter's topic, setting the scene for what is to follow. As appropriate, the overview section may discuss where a particular style came from, how it fits into a broader historical perspective, and how it interrelates with other aspects of society.

## BEFORE WE BEGIN: A LIBERAL VIEW OF ROCK HISTORY

When we speak of "musical snobs," many people immediately think of the stereotyped classical musician or classical music lover. But, in fact, musical snobs come in many forms. For example, there are several varieties of jazz snobs. One variety feels that jazz is the "only true American music," dismissing rock, for example, as being a rather decadent musical corruption and a mindless glob of musical nonsense. Even within jazz there are specialists in snobbery. Some, for instance, feel that the early Dixieland was "the only true and classic jazz," with all that follows being a declining aberration of a once-pure style. Others feel that the "bop" style of the mid- and late 1940s was the apex of jazz history, viewing all that preceded it as being preparatory and that which followed as being a subsequent decline. Some look at a very popular jazz style such as swing (the big band era music) and vehemently assert that "it isn't jazz at all!"

Similarly, in rock and roll we have our resident snobs. Like jazz fans, they identify one particular style (such as the Beatles, or Jimi Hendrix, or the Presley–Little Richard style) as the "real" rock and roll and dismiss most other styles with words of damnation, such as "soft rock," "wimp rock," "bubblegum rock," or (worst of all) "commercial junk!" Usually comments such as these reveal more about the person making the statement than about the music being discussed. Perhaps an accurate translation of these lofty statements would be, "The style I like is real rock; other styles are not." This is, to say the least, a very narrow-minded and egocentric view of musical style. Perhaps a better perspective is to say, "I prefer this particular style, but I recognize that there are many other legitimate styles that others may prefer."

This study opts for the latter, rather liberal, view. Rock is interpreted here as a broad generic term under which a diverse subsystem of styles can legitimately exist. The list of substyles is mind-boggling: rockabilly, country rock, folk rock, jazz rock, hard rock, soft rock, punk rock, heavy metal rock, Latin rock, progressive rock, disco, fusion, new wave, reggae, glitter rock, art rock—the list could go on and on. Many such labels are simply the artificial creations of the media and the public relations persons who must somehow promote yet another rock band as being somehow "new" and "different." Often there is little or nothing new, different, or significant, and the stylistic label has virtually no musical meaning. To give too much credence to this myriad of ministyles would lead to utter bewilderment on the part of the student of rock history. Therefore, we shall propose a very broad organizational pattern for the history of rock.

As we shall see in Chapters 2 and 3, "The Emergence of Rock and Roll," the early formation of rock resulted from the flowing together (in unequal proportions) of three preexisting styles: pop, country and western, and rhythm and blues. Somewhat later a second infusion came from jazz, folk music, gospel, and classical music (again in unequal proportions). These, then, are the seven basic styles that have flowed into the creation and development of rock.

In some instances, these tributaries flowed together into an integrated mainstream in which the individual donors lost their distinct identities in the mixture known as rock and roll. But, in other cases, elements of one of the tributaries retained a distinctive presence and created a shading of rock and roll closer to the tributary's original identity. As an example of this, consider pop music (discussed in Chapter 2). In some ways, pop elements were absorbed into early rock and roll. But we must also note that there has always been a softer side of rock that favors one of its direct ancestors: pop.

In this way, rock is very much like a child as related to parents and grandparents. To a large extent, the child is a blend of characteristics (in unequal proportions) of all of these direct ancestors. The child has his or her own distinct look and personality; he or she is not a carbon copy of any one ancestor but is an indefinable mixture. Nevertheless, as he or she develops, there are certain characteristics and behaviors that occasionally remind us very distinctly of one of the parents or grandparents. For example, as the child reaches adolescence, he or she may develop a body build much like Dad's, or display a natural talent for music, reminding us of his or her maternal grandmother.

Two colossal entities will appear in this history of rock music. In some ways they are similar, but they serve very different purposes. The first, Elvis Presley, was able to bring together the three tributary streams that led to rock and roll and embody them all within himself. At times, he was the indefinable mixture; at other times, he set one or another of rock's ancestors into clear relief. He was the master chef who blended the ingredients into a new dish without, however, allowing the distinctiveness of each ingredient to be destroyed.

As with Presley, the incalculable value of the Beatles was their musical breadth. Through their leadership, they pulled rock together one last time and slung it into the future in a variety of fragmented quantities. They were like the boy playing in the snow, who gathers up a huge handful of snow, compresses it into a simple ball, and then hurls it into the air, only to see it fragment into dozens of pieces.

Let us begin in the early 1950s—a time when almost no one had heard the term *rock and roll*, or had any idea of the musical and social revolution that was about to occur.

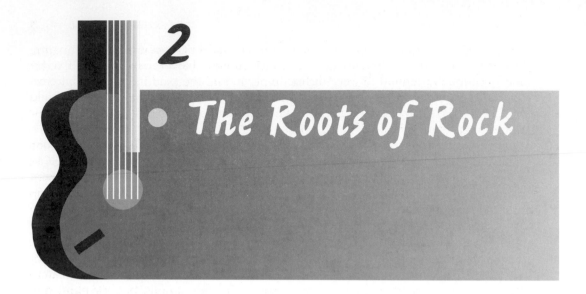

2

# The Roots of Rock

## OVERVIEW: THE EARLY FIFTIES

### The General Society

Compared with the decades that preceded and followed, the decade of the 1950s was a good one. The late 1920s to mid-1930s were years of extreme financial pressure. The early 1940s were consumed by the most destructive war the world has ever known. And in the late 1940s, the United States was involved in a "police action" (war) in Korea. The decade following the 1950s was one of the most turbulent in our nation's history, a time of social and political unrest as well as war (Vietnam).

Preceded and followed by turbulent decades, the 1950s seem serene and comfortable. Certainly no decade is trouble free. Even the 1950s witnessed several dramatic issues: Senator Joe McCarthy stirred up considerable controversy regarding the invasion of American society by communism. The Supreme Court issued a landmark decision in 1954 that declared the policy of "separate but equal" education for blacks and whites to be unconstitutional. A lingering fear of "the bomb" caused many people to build bomb shelters in their backyards and prompted schools to hold weekly air raid drills.

But, in general, things were relatively good. General Dwight Eisenhower was inaugurated as president in 1953. The economy stabilized with little or no inflation. There was a feeling of well-being throughout the nation. After years of war and depression, American society was finally able to settle down and go on with the business of progress. Families looked forward to a stable and relatively predictable future. The game plan was clear: Do well in school; go to college; marry and raise a

6

family somewhat more affluently than you were raised. The plan called for men to follow their careers and provide well for their families; women were to keep a stable and decent environment functioning at home. If one followed the game plan, personal happiness and professional success were the inevitable rewards.

Gradually economic affluence sifted down to middle-class families, who were now able to own their own home, buy a new car, take a vacation, and purchase a newcomer to the entertainment scene: a television set. The fascination with television was overwhelming. There were those who would watch a test pattern if nothing else was on! The programming was good, clean family entertainment: variety shows, family comedies, westerns, children's shows, news, cartoons, drama, sports, and music *(Your Hit Parade)*.

The popular music of the early 1950s fit the pattern perfectly. Most of the nation was listening to a style of music we shall refer to as pop. This style of music was a continuation of the popular styles of earlier decades. The lyrics typically dealt with innocent boy–girl love; the lyrical and musical content was nonthreatening. Like society in general, pop music sought to be comfortable, pleasant, and righteous. Excess was avoided. Musically, it seemed to express a society's desire to be left alone to enjoy the good life, unthreatened by the turmoil, controversy, and ugliness endured in previous decades.

## Subcultures

Of course we oversimplify when we speak of "society." Although we may use the term to represent the majority of average citizens, we must also recognize a number of subcultures that showed characteristics quite different from the norms of society in general. To begin our study of rock and roll, we must focus on two of these subcultures.

The black culture of the early 1950s was quite distinct from the general white middle-class society. Racial segregation was the norm, especially in the South and the Southwest. It is hard for us to realize today that it was just over fifty years ago that blacks were required to sit in the last three or four rows of city buses. Public areas usually had separate drinking fountains and bathrooms for "colored" and "white." Blacks were routinely barred from many public accommodations, such as hotels and restaurants. And, of course, separate housing districts and schools existed for blacks and whites (even after the 1954 Supreme Court decision barring segregation in public schools).

With such strict segregation, it is only natural that the segregated culture would maintain its own distinct characteristics, such as speech, dance, religion, dress, and music. Among the musical styles associated with the black culture were jazz (in a variety of substyles), gospel (a religiously oriented style), and rhythm and blues.

Rhythm and blues (R & B) is of great importance in our story of the development of rock and roll. Various blues styles had developed during the twentieth century. Related to jazz and the spiritual and gospel styles, R & B grew as a distinct style unto itself. Just as blacks were segregated from white society, so R & B music existed separately from the pop music market. R & B had its own performers, record companies, and consumers. R & B records, often referred to as "race" records, sold

within their own distinct market. An R & B performer or record rarely crossed over into the national pop market (conversely, pop music rarely infiltrated the R & B market).

A second subculture was identified with country and western (C & W) music. The poorer whites of the South developed a style of folk music often referred to as "hillbilly." As time passed and the style spread, variations inevitably occurred (e.g., bluegrass and western swing). The generic term *country and western* may be used to encompass these and other variant styles. As with R & B, the C & W market was quite distinct from the larger pop market. Appealing primarily to poorer rural whites in the South, Midwest, and Southwest, C & W maintained its own performers, record companies, and consumers. Pop songs rarely crossed over into the C & W market. However, a few C & W performers and songs managed to break into the national pop scene (more about that later).

Each of these three markets—pop, R & B, and C & W—contributed in varying degrees to the formation of rock and roll. R & B was by far the heaviest musical contributor; C & W also made its contribution; pop music contributed the least, but must not be overlooked. Let us take a closer look at each of rock's primary ancestors: pop, C & W, and R & B.

## POP MUSIC

### Tin Pan Alley

To appreciate the tremendous impact of rock and roll, one must first understand the nature of the popular music the nation listened to in the early 1950s. Pop music was derived from the long Tin Pan Alley tradition, with influences from the old swing period of the 1930s and early 1940s, Hollywood movie music, and Broadway show tunes. Tin Pan Alley is the name given to an area of New York City that became the center of popular music publishing from the late 1800s to the late 1950s. Tin Pan Alley songs were generated primarily by white professional songwriters. Although the style changed over the decades, certain general characteristics were constant.

Typically the lyrics were nonoffensive, noncontroversial, and most often dealt with simple boy–girl romantic love. Usually Tin Pan Alley songs had a very straight, uncomplicated rhythm, with four (or sometimes three) beats to each measure. The rhythm was kept in the background of the musical fabric. Melodies were very important; they were usually rather easy to remember, so the average person could sing or whistle them after hearing them a few times. The melodies were "pretty" in the traditional sense; they usually moved freely within one octave (sometimes a little more) and moved stepwise or with small leaps. The melodic contours were interesting, much like a gently undulating curve. The musical material was symmetrically organized into units of four measures (called phrases). Tempos were usually moderate to slow; faster tunes were typically bouncy and cute, often with light or humorous lyrics. Usually the songs were recorded by professional singers with fine voices and were accompanied by a full orchestra and small chorus.

This Tin Pan Alley tradition was still very much alive in the pop songs of the early 1950s. Songs from Broadway shows and Hollywood movies conformed to the popular style and provided a wealth of material. Table 2–1 shows twenty-one of the top fifty songs from 1950 to 1954, with a brief description of each.

## Table 2–1

| Title | Artist | Date of Peak Popularity | Comments |
|---|---|---|---|
| "Goodnight Irene" | Gordon Jenkins and the Weavers | Aug.–Nov. 1950 | slow, lush, romantic ballad |
| "Third Man Theme" | Anton Karas | May–July 1950 | instrumental; movie related |
| "Mona Lisa" | Nat "King" Cole | July–Aug. 1950 | slow, romantic ballad |
| "Music, Music, Music" | Teresa Brewer | March–April 1950 | upbeat, cute; about music |
| "Tennessee Waltz" | Patti Page | Jan.–Feb. 1951 | moderate tempo; about joys of life |
| "Be My Love" | Mario Lanza | March 1951 | semioperatic love song |
| "Too Young" | Nat "King" Cole | June–July 1951 | slow, romantic ballad |
| "Because of You" | Tony Bennett | Sept.–Oct. 1951 | moderate tempo; love song |
| "Cry" | Johnnie Ray | Jan.–March 1952 | an early "screamer"; lost love |
| "Wheel of Fortune" | Kay Starr | March–May 1952 | moderate to slow; ballad |
| "Blue Tango" | Leroy Anderson | May–June 1952 | instrumental; moderate tempo |
| "Delicado" | Percy Faith | July 1952 | instrumental; moderate tempo |
| "Till I Waltz Again with You" | Teresa Brewer | Feb.–March 1953 | moderate; sad love song |
| "Doggie in the Window" | Patti Page | March–May 1953 | upbeat; cutesy-pie novelty song |
| "Song from Moulin Rouge" | Percy Faith | May–July 1953 | instrumental; movie theme |
| "I'm Walking Behind You" | Eddie Fisher | July–Aug. 1953 | slow; rejected love |
| "Vaya con Dios" | Les Paul and Mary Ford | Aug.–Oct. 1953 | slow; love song |
| "Oh My Papa" | Eddie Fisher | Jan.–Feb. 1954 | slow; emotional tearjerker |
| "Secret Love" | Doris Day | Feb.–March 1954 | lush, slow love song; movie related |
| "Wanted" | Perry Como | April–May 1954 | slow; lonely-for-love song |
| "Hey There" | Rosemary Clooney | Sept.–Oct. 1954 | slow love song; Broadway show |

Notice that all but two of the songs in Table 2–1 are in a slow to moderate tempo; most are love oriented; several are pure instrumentals. Two of the songs deserve additional comment. Nat "King" Cole's "Too Young" is a rather rare example of an early 1950s pop song that speaks directly to youth. Specifically, it commiserates with a person who is told that he or she is too young to really be in love. Johnnie Ray's "Cry" is unusual because of the vocal style, which, due to Ray's very emotive performance, almost approaches the "shouting" level of some early rockers. Note also that only one of the artists listed in Table 2–1, Nat "King" Cole, was black (there were a few other black pop performers, such as the Mills Brothers and the Ink Spots).

Note also that most of the songs held their peak popularity for about two months. Usually there was a period of rising popularity that lasted about four weeks and an equal period of declining popularity. Thus, a top song would exist on the charts for sixteen to twenty weeks, sometimes as long as twenty-five weeks.

## The Majors

Another facet of the early 1950s pop market was the complete domination by a handful of major recording companies known as the majors—RCA Victor, Columbia, Capitol, Mercury, and Decca. In 1954, of the fifty top-selling discs, forty-two were produced by the five majors. Although the majors' biggest income came from pop music, they also produced classical, jazz, and some C & W.

These major companies held a large number of artists under contract. Their promotion and distribution systems were sophisticated and effective. Thus, when a new record was to be released, a nationwide promotion campaign was launched and the product was distributed through a network of middlemen to retail outlets throughout the nation. Several of these major companies also produced phonographs, were tied to radio and television networks and stations, and had subsidiary sheet music publish-

Nat "King" Cole, Eddie Fisher, Tony Bennett, and Frank Sinatra (*Source:* Michael Ochs Archive, Ltd.)

ing operations. They truly seemed to have a stranglehold on the popular music industry.

The huge resources of these companies were used to create a very professional product. Professional composers and arrangers created the songs. The written arrangements were placed in the hands of professional musicians. Typically, large musical forces were used—a full orchestra and small chorus. All of these musicians read their music; there was virtually no improvisation. The lead singers were pros: They read music and had fine voices, with excellent range, superb control, and good voice quality.

The popular music market was national in its scope. Over a period of four to eight weeks, a song's popularity would peak in every regional market. Furthermore, it was not uncommon to have multiple versions of a given hit song. Thus, if an artist on Columbia had commercial success with a particular song, the other companies would quickly produce a version of the same song featuring one of their artists.

Two final characteristics of considerable importance must be underscored. First, the pop music market was adult oriented. Although the 1950s were years of increasing affluence, the adults still controlled the money in the early years of the decade. The recording companies were controlled by adults; the professional songwriters, performers, and consumers were adults. Teens simply listened to and accepted their parents' music. There seemed to be no real alternative; in fact, most teens saw nothing unusual about the situation.

Finally, the pop music market of the early 1950s was almost exclusively white. Again, the record company personnel, the songwriters, the performers, and the consumers were predominantly white. As with most aspects of the music industry, the basic reason had to do with the pocketbook. The adult whites were the primary consumers; thus the recording industry aimed its product squarely at that market.

Neither the pop music consumer nor the recording industry could have anticipated that within a few years the music market would experience a total revolution—one that would reverse almost every one of the foregoing characteristics!

## MUSICAL CLOSE-UP: THE ELEMENTS OF MUSIC

To fully understand any musical style, one must be able to analyze the various elements of music as they exist in that particular style. In this first musical close-up, we shall briefly describe these elements of music. In subsequent musical close-ups, we shall examine one or another of these elements in greater detail as it pertains to a given style or topic.

### Rhythm

We begin with rhythm because it is basic to all music. *Rhythm* refers to the interrelationship between music and time. Music, even in its simplest form, exists in time. Whether we are speaking of Beethoven's Ninth Symphony or just one note, there is a beginning, a duration, and an ending. Although we often compare music and art, they are dissimilar in at least this one respect. When you look at a painting, your eye sees it all at once. Music is more like dance, plays, books, movies, and even baseball games. All of these develop through time. We cannot listen to Beethoven's Ninth Symphony, read *War and Peace,* or watch the seventh game of the World Series in an instant. We must allow each to unfold over its own appropriate period of time. Furthermore, each has an *internal* pace of activity, with moments of exciting activity alternating with moments in which the action subsides.

In music, the composer must determine the rhythmic nature of his or her creation. In the broadest sense, the composer must determine how long he or she wishes the piece to be. At a middle level, he or she can control the rhythmic flow of the piece. For example, the piece might have a slow-moving, rather uncomplicated opening, followed by a sudden flurry of activity; then it may build to a busy and fast climax, allowing the rhythmic tension to dissipate in the final section. And at the closest level, the composer must determine the exact length of each note and how it relates to the length of the other notes sounding before, after, and simultaneously. All of this results in how the music exists in time—its rhythm.

However, usually when we speak of rhythm, we mean the specific rhythmic patterns produced by the varying lengths of notes. The following two patterns, because the notes relate to each other differently in time, produce different rhythmic effects.

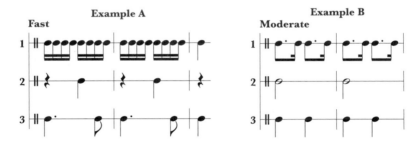

Notice the words *fast* and *moderate.* They describe how fast all of the notes are moving through time (example A therefore moves faster than example B). This is called tempo and is a part of the total rhythmic aspect of a song.

Study examples A and B closely. You will see that at a given moment (within each beat), there are simultaneous occurrences of long notes, short notes, and sometimes silence. If possible, perform these rhythms in class (using hand claps, nonsense syllables, or numbers). Each example has a totally different effect as a result of the differing rhythms.

It is not so terribly important that you understand everything about the rhythmic patterns in examples A and B. What is important is that you realize that the rhythmic element of a piece is made up of many notes, each with different lengths compared with the others. These must be determined and performed rather exactly for the rhythmic part of the piece to make sense.

You participate in the rhythm of a piece when you tap your foot, clap to the beat, or dance. Such reactions are natural and help explain why strongly rhythmic pieces have such appeal. In Chapter 3's musical close-up, we shall review some of these comments about rhythm and see how they apply to the early styles of rock and roll.

## Melody

When a vibrating body (e.g., a guitar string, a piano string, or a saxophone reed) is put into motion fast enough, we begin to perceive that a pitch or tone is created. The faster the vibration, the higher the pitch seems to be. Thus, if a string vibrates 100 times per second, we hear a very low pitch; if it vibrates 12,000 times per second, we hear a very high pitch. When we hear two or more pitches in succession, we begin to think of a melody or tune.

If you whistle or hum four to six notes (pitches) in succession, you will have created a short melody. Melodies are very important in music. Although we may physically *feel* the rhythm of the music, usually what we remember about a song is the tune (and sometimes the words associated with that tune).

When discussing melody, we shall encounter several new terms. The *range* of a melody describes how high and how low the melody goes. Melodies that move from very low to very high notes have a wide range; those that move up or down very little have a narrow range.

The terms *conjunct* and *disjunct* tell us whether a melody is moving gradually from its lower pitches to its higher pitches (conjunct) or whether it is jumping from high to low (disjunct). Examples C and D show what we mean by *conjunct* and *disjunct*.

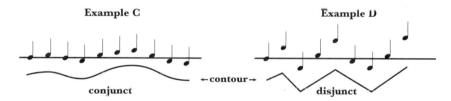

Notice that the *contours* of these two melodies are very different. One smoothly moves up and down (conjunct); the other is jagged and angular (disjunct). Melodic contours are similar to the contours of landscapes: softly rolling hills versus angular mountain ranges.

Sometimes melodies are repetitive. In a repetitive melody, a short melodic pattern (*motive*) might be repeated over and over. This is quite different from the kind of melody that seems to spin itself out continually, rarely repeating itself.

Finally, we should note briefly that sometimes melodies are combined with other melodies simultaneously. This is an important idea and will be discussed further when we speak of texture.

## Harmony and Tonality

If melody is the combination of notes in *succession,* harmony is the combination of notes *simultaneously.* If a friend sings a certain note and you join in with a higher or lower note, you are harmonizing. When three or more notes are sounded simultaneously, we have a *chord.* If you place your entire forearm down on a piano keyboard, the resulting sound will be a chord—not a particularly pretty chord, but a chord nevertheless.

Over the centuries, musicians have developed a way of creating chords that sound a bit better than the one you and your forearm just created. The most basic traditional chord consists of the minimum number of notes—three—and is called a *triad*. But as you might guess, a traditional triad is not just any three notes. There is a system for creating a good-sounding traditional triad.

Musicians work with seven pitches, named according to the first seven letters of the alphabet: A, B, C, D, E, F, and G (there are also other notes known as sharps and flats, but we really do not need to worry about them yet). To create a traditional triad, one starts on any of the seven basic pitches, skips the next one, plays the third one, skips the fourth one, and plays the fifth one.

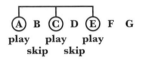

Now the notes A, C, and E have created a triad. We call it the A triad because A is its basic or "root" pitch. If one used C as the root of a triad, the three notes would be C, E, and G. The musical alphabet repeats up and down the pitch spectrum as follows:

The distance from a given note to its next occurrence in the musical alphabet is called an *octave*.

Chords are extremely important in music. If all we had were melody and rhythm, music would sound rather empty. Harmony is used to accompany melodies and to fill out the sound of the music. Effective harmonic practice is not a simple matter. For now, be sure you understand the concept of the traditional triad. More complicated chord structures will be explained as necessary.

Closely related to harmony is the concept of tonality. You have no doubt heard musicians speak of the "key" of B-flat or the "key" of E. For most traditional music, the words *key* and *tonality* are interchangeable. Perhaps the easiest key to understand is the key of C. When lined up starting on C, the seven notes of the musical alphabet result in the key of C.

The note C is the beginning and ending note, so we call this entire key "C." Also of great importance are the fourth and fifth notes of the key, F and G.

Each note in the key of C can have its own triad:

```
G   A   B   C   D   E   F /G \
E   F   G   A   B   C   D |E  |
Ⓒ   D   E   Ⓕ   Ⓖ   A   B |Ⓒ /
```

Other keys have a different lineup of notes; for example, the key of E-flat has these members:

```
B♭  C   D   E♭  F   G   A♭/B♭\
G   A♭  B♭  C   D   E♭  F |G  |
Ⓔ♭  F   G   Ⓐ♭  Ⓑ♭  C   D |E♭/
```

Don't worry about the flats (♭) in this example; just understand that a different collection of notes creates a different key. And again notice that the first, fourth, and fifth notes are the most important, and that the name of the key comes from the name of the first and last note.

We will have more to say about keys and chords in a later musical close-up in this chapter.

### Timbre

Next we must consider the exact quality of the sounds being produced. After all, pianos do not sound like clarinets, and clarinets do not sound like guitars. The difference in the sound quality of these instruments involves *timbre*—the tone quality of sound. Have you ever thought about how many different voices you recognize? Even if they were all speaking exactly the same words, you would probably recognize the voices of your parents, your siblings, quite a few close friends, several movie and television stars, and even some politicians. Each voice has a distinctive sound quality or timbre (pronounced "tam-burr").

Composers must decide whether a melody is to be played on a trumpet or saxophone and whether a chord is to be played by piano, banjo, or guitar. Shall the bass be an acoustic string bass, a tuba, or a bass guitar? Decisions like these have a great effect on how the final piece of music sounds. Elvis's "Hound Dog" would not be the same if it were played by a marching band, even if the melody, harmony, and rhythm were exactly the same. Certain timbres are associated with certain styles of music. Dixieland music sounds best when played by a small ensemble of trumpet, clarinet, trombone, tuba, banjo, and drums (and maybe a piano); rock and roll requires several electric guitars and drums; swing bands need trumpets, saxophones, trombones, piano, bass, and drums.

In the last few decades the recording industry and rock and roll have added considerably to the world of timbre. For one thing, there is now a huge arsenal of electronic instruments to be considered. Some are basically acoustic instruments whose sound is electronically amplified, like guitars. However, in most cases, the sound itself is electronically produced and modified (most notably, the synthesizer). Also, the contemporary recording studio can do much to change the timbre of the musical product. With today's technical resources for mixing, overdubbing, and editing (plus echo, phase shifting, etc.), the competent studio engineer can dramatically alter the sound of the basic raw material. This too is an aspect of timbre.

### Texture

One of the factors that makes a given piece of music sound the way it does is its *texture*—the way the various musical lines function in relation to each other. There are three basic possibilities: monophony, homophony, and polyphony.

Monophony is the simplest musical texture. Monophonic texture exists when there is one and only one musical line. Thus, one singer, without any accompaniment, singing a solo line is an example of monophony. The essential point is not how many *singers* (or players) there are but how many *musical lines*. Thus, ten singers all singing exactly the same melodic line are still creating monophony.

Homophony is a bit more complex. With a homophonic texture one musical line predominates, but other lines are also present in a subservient role. One of the most common types of homophony is the melody-and-accompaniment texture. Here one line is clearly the melody and all other musical sounds serve as accompaniment. A folk singer accompanied by a guitar is an example of homophony. Perhaps you have heard quartets where the top line is the primary melodic line and the other three lines simply harmonize the top line. This is another type of homophony, but again, one line predominates and the other lines are subservient.

In polyphony, we find two or more independent lines of approximately equal importance. If you have ever sung a round like "Row, Row, Row Your Boat," you have participated in a polyphonic texture. One singer begins the song, and then a second singer begins four beats later; and if a third singer is available, he or she begins four beats after the second singer. Each singer is singing the tune rather independently; each is just as important as the others. Music that is polyphonic can be a bit difficult to listen to at first, because it sounds so busy. There are, after all, multiple melodic lines to try to hear, rather than just one.

Sometimes we speak of texture as being thick or thin. In this sense, texture may be perceived as a continuum. Two singers singing a duet would be on one end of the continuum—a very thin texture. On the opposite end, we might find a song with several vocal melodic lines, a full orchestra with the high brass playing fanfarelike material, the strings playing scale passages, the woodwinds playing frilly ornaments, the low brass playing a powerful countermelody, and the percussion playing frenziedly. Add a background chorus and some synthesizer chords and we have a very thick texture.

Most popular music, including rock and roll, utilizes the melody-and-accompaniment texture, a type of homophony. On occasion, however, some musically creative minds have explored other textures; we will take special note of such cases as we encounter them.

### Volume

When a vibrating body is displaced a little, it produces a relatively quiet sound; when it is displaced a lot, it produces a louder sound. If you barely touch a piano key, the hammer inside touches the string and hardly moves it. A very soft sound is produced.

If you give the key a sharp whack, the hammer pops against the string, setting it into violent motion. A louder sound is produced. Technically, this is called the *amplitude* (amount of displacement) of a vibrating body. Usually, though, we call it volume or loudness.

Most rock and roll is loud, but we will study some styles and songs that use a variety of volume levels. As with any of the elements of music, the constant, unchanging use of a certain element leads to boredom. *Dynamics* is the term musicians use to describe the various fluctuations in amplitude. The creative mind skillfully manipulates all of the available musical elements—including dynamics.

## Form

Form is the organizational structure of a piece of music. It is the result of *changes* in some or all of the musical elements.

Think for a moment about one of your favorite television shows. Possibly there is a short "teaser," or introduction, that gives you a hint of what is to come and sets the scene. After a commercial there is a series of scenes that set forth the primary and secondary characters and problems in that particular episode. Following another commercial, another series of scenes introduces more complications and conflicts. After another commercial, a series of scenes leads to a turning point of some kind that suggests that the end is in sight and all will be well. A final scene shows the happy participants basking in the glow of another successful escapade. Your television show, which exists over a period of time (e.g., thirty minutes), is organized into sections and subsections. The sections and subsections are delineated by changes, as characters appear and disappear, as complications arise and are resolved, and as settings change.

So it is with a musical composition. Often a song begins with an introduction; then there is a section that introduces a main melody and the lyrical topic. This section may be repeated with new lyrics. Next there may be a section with new music and new lyrics. Subsequent sections may repeat earlier music with new or repeated lyrics. Usually there is an instrumental section near the middle of the piece and a "fade-out" section at the end. We can chart this organizational structure as follows:

In the foregoing diagram, the repeating A shows that the music is repeated; the superscripts (′ or ″) indicate new lyrics. What tells us when a section is ending and a new section is beginning? Change—change in one or more of the musical elements. From one section to the next, there may be a change in the rhythm, melody, key, texture, or lyrics. At any juncture in the musical form, there are a limited set of options: The musicians can (1) repeat previous material, (2) play new material, or (3) play something based upon earlier material, but not an exact repetition (we call this last one variation or development). This may sound complicated, but you will be surprised how easy it is to "feel" the changes from section to section.

### A Word about Words

Technically speaking, the lyrics of a song are not an integral part of the music. Thus, although "Yesterday" by the Beatles certainly has words (lyrics), there are many purely instrumental arrangements that are entirely recognizable, even though no lyrics are sung or spoken. Nevertheless, lyrics are intimately associated with the music of most popular songs.

People are funny where lyrics are concerned. Many people say, "Oh, I don't really pay attention to the words; I just like the music (or the beat)." Yet they can often sing the words along with an instrumental arrangement or "mouth" the words as the song is being played on the radio. If the music suddenly stops, they continue singing the tune by themselves, words and all.

Too often we think *only* of lyrics and forget about the music. For example, if asked to write a paper about the music of a 1960s folk singer or group, one usually tells all about the protest songs, the antiwar sentiments, the pleas for racial equality, the love songs, the symbolism, and so on. But often little is said about the melodic lines, harmonies, forms, and other musical elements.

Lyrics are, of course, verbal expression; music is nonverbal expression. Frequently we listen closely to songs with lyrics, but find our minds wandering when listening to pure instrumentals. Perhaps this is because the average nonmusician understands the verbal language of the lyrics but does not understand the nonverbal language of the instrumental. Similarly we can usually identify groups by ear when one or more voices are singing words. But it is more difficult to identify purely instrumental groups.

But, music too, is a language. The trained musician has learned to communicate using that language. It is just as intelligible, and probably more powerful, than verbal language. Although it is not the purpose of this book to make the reader an accomplished musician, it is hoped that it will enhance his or her appreciation of, and ability to understand, some aspects of this nonverbal language.

One final word about words. Just as with the other aspects of rock and roll, the lyrics have undergone dramatic stylistic changes through the five decades of rock's history. At times, the lyrics have been the subject of derision, and at other times, the subject of heated controversy. Our study will comment on the verbal aspects of rock as one part of the total picture, distinct from the music yet intimately associated with it.

## COUNTRY AND WESTERN

Unlike the huge pop market, the C & W market had a relatively small and regionally well-defined audience. Although there were C & W radio stations, performers, and recording companies all over the nation, by the early 1950s the South, Southwest, and Midwest had become the real centers of development for this style. The most influential C & W-oriented radio show was *The Grand Ole Opry*, broadcast from

Nashville's WSM. In the late 1940s and early 1950s, the Opry attracted more and more C & W songwriters and performers to Nashville.

Led by the Acuff–Rose publishing house, publishers flooded to Nashville. The recording industry was not far behind. The C & W market had been served largely by small independent record companies scattered throughout the South, Southwest, and Midwest. Each of these small companies (called "indies," short for "independent") was a low-budget operation with a few artists under contract. Each specialized in a certain "sound" it hoped would make its products recognizable. They usually produced singles rather than albums, because that is what they and their consumers could afford. Unlike the major companies, the indies' distribution system was simple and unsophisticated—often just a guy in a pickup truck with a box of records. But to promote a new record they did not need to blanket the country as the majors did. They could hit a definable list of radio stations in a specific list of cities in a certain geographic region. The system worked well.

This is not to say that the majors had no interest in C & W. Indeed, the majors produced a number of prominent C & W acts, often on subsidiary labels. First Decca and then Capitol, Columbia, and RCA established Nashville offices. The popularity of the cowboy western movies in the 1930s and 1940s and cowboy television shows in the late 1940s and early 1950s had promoted a national market for the singing cowboy (e.g., Gene Autry, Roy Rogers and Dale Evans, and Tex Ritter). This created a receptivity within the national pop market for the C & W style. As a result, a number of major artists were able to escape the smaller C & W market and become national stars (e.g., Eddy Arnold and Hank Snow).

Like the pop market, the C & W market consisted of white adults. Not generally a very affluent market, what money did exist in the C & W subculture belonged to the adults.

The music of the C & W market showed both similarities and dissimilarities to pop music. As with pop music, C & W's melodies and lyrics were of prime importance. The lyrics were often love oriented (usually tales of unrequited love or the jilted lover). The harmonies were usually simpler than those of pop music. The form of the typical C & W song was similar to that of the Tin Pan Alley pop song.

C & W rhythm was simple and straightforward and usually more prominent than was typical of pop music. There were usually three or four beats per measure with little or no subdivision, thus creating a very simple square-cut sound. There was usually a lead singer, often with a vocal trio or quartet in the background. The musicians often performed their own original material, although there was also a repertoire of traditional songs handed down from earlier generations. Generally the music was not notated; arrangements were worked out in rehearsal and, once set, were performed according to that plan. When instrumental solo breaks occurred, the solos stayed very close to the established melody rather than wandering into intricate flights of fancy, as they might in jazz.

Perhaps the most recognizable characteristic of C & W music of the early 1950s was its timbre, much of which emanated from two specific sources: the vocalist and the steel guitar. C & W vocalists often sang with a rather nasal quality. Instead of carefully intoning each melodic pitch, they would slide from note to note. A number of male C & W singers developed the ability to yodel—a vocal device (used by earlier C & W and folk singers) in which the singer "cracks" his voice, allowing it to move into a female range (called falsetto).

The steel guitar entered the C & W picture from a rather unlikely source: Hawaii. After Hawaii became a U.S. territory in 1900, the mainland was swept with a fascination for the exotic island culture. By the 1920s, the steel guitar's popularity was set. In 1931, the Electro String Instrument Company of California (Rickenbacker guitars) developed the first electric Hawaiian steel guitar. Later developments included placing the instrument on a stand, adding the double-neck feature, and adding pedals. Being a rather conservative culture, the C & W music market was slow to include some of these innovations, especially electronic amplification.

By the early 1950s, the typical C & W band included a vocalist, a vocal backup group, electric pedal steel guitar, piano, violin, bass (acoustic or "stand-up" bass), and acoustic and electric guitars. Note the obvious omission: drums. Although there were a few nonconformists, most traditional C & W bands avoided drums until the mid-1950s. The rhythm was set by the bass player, who "slapped" his strings on the accented beats, and by the guitars and piano, which reinforced all the beats.

## MUSICAL CLOSE-UP:
### INSTRUMENTATION IN ROCK AND ROLL

When we think of rock and roll we usually think of electric guitars, drums, and singers. These are, in fact, the essential ingredients for a rock-and-roll band from the early 1950s to today. But there have been changes in the nature of these instruments, and some styles have added other instruments to the rock-and-roll ensemble. In this musical close-up we shall briefly survey the instrumentation of rock from 1955 to today, and then take a closer look at specific instruments.

The typical 1950s rock-and-roll band consisted of four to six players. The usual ingredients included drums, bass (acoustic), two electric guitars (one rhythm and one lead), piano (acoustic), and saxophone (alto or tenor). Some bands, of course, varied from this basic ensemble. Thus, Bill Haley's Comets used a steel guitar instead of a piano, reflecting their C & W background. Buddy Holly's Crickets used only drums, an acoustic bass, and two guitars. Elvis Presley's early Sun recording used only two guitars and a bass (remember that drums were traditionally avoided in C & W music). Jerry Lee Lewis's early hits also used a trio—piano, guitar, and drums. Little Richard's recording sessions for his big hits on Specialty used various instrumental lineups, but usually included piano, bass, drums, guitar, and several saxophones.

The 1960s saw a greater diversification in rock instrumentation. The Beatles' lineup of three guitars (lead, rhythm, and bass) and drums was widely imitated. If any instrument was added to this basic foursome, it was usually piano (increasingly in its electronic form and with its various electronic spin-offs). The folk movement of the 1960s went back to basics, using acoustic guitar, harmonica, banjo, acoustic bass, and sometimes bongo drums. The Motown sound featured a vocal group plus full orchestral instrumentation. Finally, the jazz-rock trend near the end of the decade added a "horn line" consisting of trumpet(s), woodwinds (saxes or flute), and trombone.

The 1970s and 1980s witnessed the expansion of electronic instruments. Every few months a new synthesizer appeared that rendered its predecessors outmoded. The piano player of the old rock bands became the "keyboard player," confronted with a dazzling array of instruments: synthesizer, string synthesizer, electric piano, organ, clavinet, and acoustic piano. Other than this electronic expansion, the basic instrumentation of the 1960s was simply carried forward. The ensemble of three or four guitars and drums remained basic to hard rock and heavy metal. Some black groups continued to use horn lines; disco utilized full orchestral instrumentation. The electronic explosion has continued with increasing use of guitar synthesizers, drum synthesizers, and computer-interfaced keyboards.

Let us now take a closer look at each of the principal components of the rock ensemble.

## Guitar

Guitars, the basic instruments of all rock and roll, come in two basic varieties: acoustic and electric. Some early rock and rollers (Elvis Presley, for example) started with the acoustic guitar. But most quickly learned that the unamplified acoustic guitar was no match for the electric guitars, piano, saxophone, and drums of the rock ensemble. Some guitarists stayed with their acoustic instrument, merely adding electronic amplification by a contact microphone, a fairly common practice since the mid-1930s. However, except for the folk- or country-influenced rock performers, rock guitarists quickly adopted the true electric guitar as the basic instrument.

Electric guitars have electromagnetic pickup devices placed below the steel strings. The vibration of the string disturbs the magnetic field of its individual pickup, resulting in a signal that is sent through an amplifier and on to a loudspeaker. Various controls operated by the hands or feet can control volume, tone, and equalization, and can add special effects such as reverberation, "fuzz tones," "wah-wah," and phase shifting. Because electric guitars do not require the wooden sound chamber of the acoustic guitar, they may be made of metal or wood, have hollow or solid bodies, and take on a variety of shapes.

In 1954, Leo Fender introduced the Stratocaster, an update on his earlier electric guitar called the Telecaster (and before that, the Broadcaster). It became the model for electric guitars in rock and roll for many years. Also, the Gibson company, a leading guitar manufacturer since the early part of this century, had introduced a Les Paul solid body electric guitar in 1952. Among the important developments in recent years has been the wireless electric guitar, which broadcasts its electric signal to an amplifier without the use of wires. This has had important ramifications for onstage performance, allowing some of the more acrobatic acts to run, jump, roll, and cavort all over a huge and elaborate stage setting without fear of entangling themselves in wires.

Over the years there have been various experiments with the basic guitar sound of rock and roll. There have been double-necked guitars and twelve-string guitars (the usual guitar has six strings); exotic cousins of the guitar, such as the sitar, have found their way into rock. In the early 1950s, Leo Fender introduced the solid body electric bass guitar. The early rock-and-roll bands continued to prefer the acoustic bass, but by the end of the decade more and more players had switched to the electric instrument. By the 1960s, the old stand-up bass was gone, except in some folk- or country-influenced bands. The electric bass was much more portable and provided powerful bass lines that could match the volume level of the drums, electric guitars, and electric pianos.

Through the late 1970s and early 1980s, the synthesizer technology, once the province of the keyboard player, became available to the guitarist. The sounds of a synthesizer are triggered by electrical impulses. Historically, these impulses have been triggered by means of keyboards. However, the same electronic impulse can be triggered by picking a guitar string—hence the guitar synthesizer of the 1980s. Thus, the basic synthesizer settings, controlled by hand or foot, respond to the notes performed by the guitarist. Although the guitarist appears to be playing a typical electric guitar, he is really sending a series of electrical impulses to a synthesizer, which in turn translates the notes into the timbre of a flute, trumpet, and so on.

### Voice

Let us not forget one of the most basic and essential instruments of all: the human voice. Although there are a number of purely instrumental rock hits, the vast majority contain vocals. When asked to name rock stars, we will almost invariably name stars who are primarily known as singers (some, of course, may have also been instrumentalists—usually guitarists or keyboard players).

In the early 1950s, the ideal pop singer was the "crooner," who was at his best singing soft, slow love songs—so-called ballads. The crooner (usually male) had a pleasant voice quality in the traditional sense: He sang perfectly in tune and had a wide range and excellent control of his voice. This ideal carried over into the softer side of rock with singers like Pat Boone, Paul Anka, Frankie Avalon, the Carpenters, and Barry Manilow.

On the opposite end of the continuum from the crooners were the "shouters" or "screamers." There is little precedence for this style in white music prior to rock and roll. However, R & B singers had developed a "shouting" style several decades before rock and roll. R & B stars like Joe Turner, Big Mama Thornton, Wynonie Harris, and Elmore James half sang, half yelled their songs. There was usually a harsh, raspy quality to the voice. The general melodic contour was followed, but exact melodic pitches were only approximated. This shouting style carried over into the harder styles of rock and roll, best exemplified in the early days by Little Richard and later by Janis Joplin, James Brown, and a host of the hard rock and heavy metal bands of the 1970s and 1980s.

In between the crooners and the shouters was a wide variety of vocal styles. Characterized by a harder and more powerful vocal quality than the crooners, these mainstream singers still adhered to the correct melodic pitches but were prone to provide strong vocal accents, bend some pitches, and add various vocal embellishments to their rhythmically driving songs. This large middle ground between crooners and shouters is exemplified by such diverse singers as Jerry Lee Lewis, Fats Domino, the Beach Boys, and a good many of the Motown singers of the 1960s and later.

Of course, some of the more versatile performers can convincingly sing two or three styles. Using Presley as an example, consider these songs: "Hound Dog," "Jailhouse Rock," and "Hard-Headed Woman" (shouter); "Love Me Tender," "Don't," and "Can't Help Falling in Love" (crooner); "All Shook Up," "Don't Be Cruel," and "Heartbreak Hotel" (in between).

Although the terms *crooner* and *shouter* may prove useful in describing some singers, let us not erroneously force a label on a given voice—truly the most personal and unique of all musical instruments.

### Drums

If rhythm is the heart of rock and roll, drums must be the central ingredient in the rock band. Except for a few very early rock recordings (from the C & W background) and some folk music of the early 1960s, drums have been an integral part of the rock music scene.

The typical rock drum set (sometimes called trap set, or traps) is played by one person and consists of a bass drum (played by a foot pedal), a snare drum, a tenor drum, a tom–tom, a sock cymbal, a ride cymbal, a pair of hi-hat cymbals, and a cowbell. There may be a variety of mallets: soft mallets, hard sticks, and wire brushes.

Drum sets remained relatively constant until the late 1970s. From 1975 to 1985, however, several innovations occurred. The traditional acoustic drum requires a hollow-sounding chamber to shape and color its sound (thus, the big bass drum and the narrower, smaller snare drum). But innovators realized that the sound of a drumhead being struck by a stick could be produced electronically. Thus, the advent of the compact solid body drums. For example, Simmons made a drum set in which the drumheads (or pads) have electronic pickups that sense how hard the pad is struck. Resulting pulses are then sent to a control unit that fires analog or digitally recorded sounds. Each drum is just a few inches deep. With such systems, an entire drum set can be packed into a relatively small case and easily transported. Drummers like that.

What drummers do not like is the development of electronic drum machines. The various drum sounds (snare, bass, cymbal, etc.) are among the easiest sounds to artificially reproduce electronically. Thus, we now have "drum boxes" or "drum machines" that do a remarkably good job of replacing the drummer. A typical drum box may be no more than 16 inches long, 4 inches high, and 8 inches deep. The user can program a steady bass drum beat and a variety of subdivisions on a snare drum, a tenor drum, and cymbals; he or she can even add accents on a cowbell or "hand claps." The machines are easy to use and reproduce a very believable drum sound with absolute technical accuracy. Most can store about 100 patterns and ten full-length songs in memory for instant recall.

### Keyboards

In the beginning, there was the simple, old upright piano with two or three pedals and eighty-eight keys. But since rock's early days, there has appeared a bewildering catalog of keyboards of every size, shape, and description. About the time that the

A drum Kit (Source: C Squared Studios / Getty Images Inc./ PhotoDisc, Inc.)

performer has invested in and mastered his or her shiny new keyboard, a newer and shinier one is marketed that makes the former one seem old-fashioned. Our purpose here will not be to describe every keyboard modern technology has developed, but to discuss a few of the principal models from which the others are derived.

One of the problems pianists faced was that they were at the mercy of the instrument they found at the job site. If the piano was not properly maintained, pedals failed to work, some of the keys did not play, or the instrument was out of tune. The electric piano solved all of this. In the mid- to late 1960s, it gradually replaced the old acoustic piano in most rock bands. At least the performer could be sure the piano was in tune, all its notes played, and it could be placed anywhere on stage.

Even though electric pianos had shortened keyboards (usually only sixty-four notes) and did not sound exactly like the acoustic piano, practicality triumphed and the electric piano became the standard keyboard for rock and roll. Soon there were variations on the basic electric piano. For example, the clavinet allowed the pianist to switch between two different timbres; RMI made an instrument that allowed a similar switch between a piano and a harpsichord sound.

This turn to electronics launched a revolution in rock-and-roll keyboards. New electronic keyboard instruments appeared that attempted to imitate a wider variety of instruments. An early example was the Mellotron, an instrument that used tapes of prerecorded tones by various instruments. The popular Mellotron 400 contained a rack of tapes with three tracks, each of which provided a different timbre (e.g., brass, strings, flute). By selecting one of these three timbres and then pressing a key, one obtained the actual sound of a particular instrument playing a particular note. Although a number of groups experimented with the Mellotron, its sound became especially identified with the Moody Blues.

At about the same time (late 1960s and early 1970s), synthesizers were being developed that were practical to use in performance. Basically synthesizers do two things: (1) They generate sounds by means of oscillators, and (2) they modify sounds by means of various devices such as filters, envelope shapers, and ring modulators. With the synthesizer, the keyboard player could produce an entire range of sounds by mastering a complex of knobs, buttons, slides, and patch cords. It required some retraining, but the result was worth the trouble.

As the synthesizer revolution advanced, newer, easier-to-use models poured into the market. Some specialized in string sounds, whereas others allowed for a variety of preprogrammed sounds, each available at the touch of a button. Add-ons were developed, such as the sequencer, which allowed the user to set up a series of pitches, rhythms, timbres, and volumes that could be set into motion at the flip of a switch. Some newer synthesizers allow the user to devise all of the settings and then assign them to the synthesizer's memory for later recall. And, of course, the inevitable linkage between the computer and the synthesizer has been made with the development of Musical Instrument Digital Interface (MIDI).

Electronic organs, instruments that predate the beginnings of rock and roll, added still other sounds to the rock keyboard player's resources. Laurens Hammond introduced the electronic organ in 1939. As rock musicians discovered the sound of the electronic organ in the 1960s (most notably the Hammond B-3 model), other companies (e.g., Farfisa and Vox) entered the market in competition with Hammond.

The keyboard player of the 1970s and 1980s was typically surrounded by four to six keyboards, each with a specialized role to play. The most elaborate electronic keyboardists (e.g., Keith Emerson and Rick Wakeman) confronted racks of instruments that resembled the cockpit of a 747.

### Saxophone

There are five basic saxophones: soprano, alto, tenor, baritone, and bass. All of the saxophone family members have the same basic shape (except for the soprano, which comes in two different shapes: the normal curved shape like its siblings, and the straight shape, which more closely resembles a clarinet). The fingering among all of the saxes is similar, so if a player can play one, he or she can generally play them all.

The saxophone (sax) became a favorite in the jazz of the 1930s and 1940s, crossing over into rhythm and blues as well. The black bluesmen particularly favored the versatility and sensuality of the tenor sax. Thus, it was natural that the early rock-and-roll bands, which borrowed so much from R & B, often included the saxophone. Fats Domino's songs usually included not only a saxophone accompaniment but frequently a sax solo at the instrumental break. Little Richard's bands contained up to three or four saxophones. Even Bill Haley's Comets, in spite of their primarily C & W background, included a saxophone.

Since then saxophones have alternately appeared and disappeared in various rock styles. The Motown sound of the 1960s utilized the saxophone, especially the baritone sax, which doubled bass lines and occasionally played solos. The jazz rock sound of the late 1960s and early 1970s incorporated various saxophones. The sound of the soprano sax became particularly popular in the early 1970s, with groups such as Weather Report and Chuck Mangione's. In the years 1975 to 1985, occasional specialty songs featured the sax, and many black groups—such as Earth, Wind, and Fire—continued to rely upon its sound.

## RHYTHM AND BLUES

The last of the three main tributaries leading to rock and roll, R & B, is also, by far, the most important. So direct is the line from R & B to early rock and roll that one may listen to certain R & B tunes from the 1945 to 1955 period and be convinced that one is hearing 1958 vintage rock and roll.

Unlike either the pop or the C & W market, the R & B market was black. The performers and consumers were black. The R & B market was served, almost exclusively, by small, independent record companies—"indies"—and there were many of them, most owned and administered by whites.

Like C & W, R & B had a limited but well-defined audience. The basic center of R & B's development was the South; however, as the black population spread throughout the Southwest, the Midwest, and into the major metropolitan centers, R & B went along. Thus, although most R & B singers traced their roots back to New Orleans, the Mississippi Delta, Alabama, Georgia, Tennessee, and Florida, by the 1930s and 1940s many had relocated to other parts of the country. The small, independent R & B record companies located where there was talent and a market. Chicago, New York City, and Los Angeles became three leading centers for R & B recording. From a long list of such companies, the following were formed in the late 1940s and went on to have considerable impact in the 1950s: Atlantic (New York), Chess (Chicago), Speciality (Los Angeles), and Imperial (Los Angeles). The records produced by these and other indies for the R & B market served only their well-defined pattern of consumers. They rarely, if ever, expected sales in either the pop or C & W market, and, conversely, they expected no competition in their market from pop or C & W records.

The music of R & B was quite different from pop and C & W. A large percentage of R & B songs were based on a set musical scheme known as the twelve-bar blues. (The next musical close-up will provide a detailed description of the twelve-bar blues.) The music was rarely notated; as with C & W, it was usually worked out in rehearsal and then performed according to a loosely predetermined plan. Although it did not approach the complexity of the finest jazz of its time, R & B improvisation allowed for considerable freedom and spontaneous invention. Although some traditional songs were passed from generation to generation, most R & B songs were originals created by the performer. Many expressed personal sentiments related to love, jobs, "hard knocks," and general philosophies of life.

A typical R & B combo might consist of some or all of the following instruments: guitars (electric or acoustic or both), bass (acoustic), piano, drums, saxophone, and harmonica. As its name implies, R & B was characterized by a hard-driving, prominent rhythm. The harmonies are those of the twelve-bar blues: just three basic chords with occasional variations. Although the words were important, the melody got minimal creative attention, generally seeming to be little more than a vehicle to carry the lyrics. In fact, there is great similarity among blues melodies, only partially because they usually conformed to the structure of the twelve-bar blues.

The power of R & B resided in the strong, insistent rhythm, the personally expressive lyrics, and the vocal performance style (which was often of the "shouting" variety). Some outstanding R & B performers from earlier decades include Big Bill Broonzy, Bessie Smith, "Howlin' Wolf" (Chester Burnett), "Muddy Waters" (McKinley Morganfield), Lightnin' Hopkins, Ma Rainey, Joe Turner, Memphis Slim, T-Bone Walker, Elmore James, Otis Spann, and B. B. King. Listening to many of these stars, one can hear elements of 1950s rock and roll up to three decades before "Heartbreak Hotel." For example, Memphis Slim's "All by Myself" hints at the later style of Fats Domino. In "Roll 'em Pete" by Joe Turner and Pete Johnson, one can hear the beginnings of the 1950s rock piano style and harbingers of "Bony Moronie." In Elmore James's "Sunnyland," one hears hints of Chuck Berry's guitar style. And in Otis Spann's "Bloody Murder," there are fragments of bass lines that are exactly replicated in 1950s rock and roll. Although pop music and C & W played their respective roles in the creation of rock, it is black R & B that leads most directly and powerfully into rock and roll.

## MUSICAL CLOSE-UP: THE TWELVE-BAR BLUES

The term *blues* is used many different ways in music: One hears of urban blues, rural blues, country blues, jump blues, talkin' blues, rhythm and blues, and more. It is a vague and loosely used word. However, in one of its usages, it is rather definite. Much of the music of the early blues singers and rhythm-and-blues players followed a similar musical scheme. Specifically, three or four common patterns evolved using eight-measure, twelve-measure, sixteen-measure, and occasionally ten-measure forms, with a rather consistent usage of three basic chords. Over the years, one of these forms came to be quite standardized: the twelve-measure form. By the late 1920s, when musicians referred to the "blues progression," they meant the standard twelve-measure blues. That form became the basis for most boogie-woogie jazz of the 1930s, a large percentage of R & B of the 1930s and 1940s, and much of the upbeat rock and roll of the 1950s. Although used less frequently, it still appeared occasionally in the rock of the 1960s and beyond. For any one musical formula to be so durable and omnipresent, it must have considerable appeal to performers and listeners alike. It is so basic that we must study it more closely.

As any rock fan knows, music has *beats*. These are simply rhythmic pulses put into the music by the composer or performer and heard and felt by the listener.

Musicians group these beats into units called measures or bars. One blues chorus consists of forty-eight beats. Because the beats are usually grouped into measures of four beats each, there are twelve measures in a standard blues chorus. This is shown below.

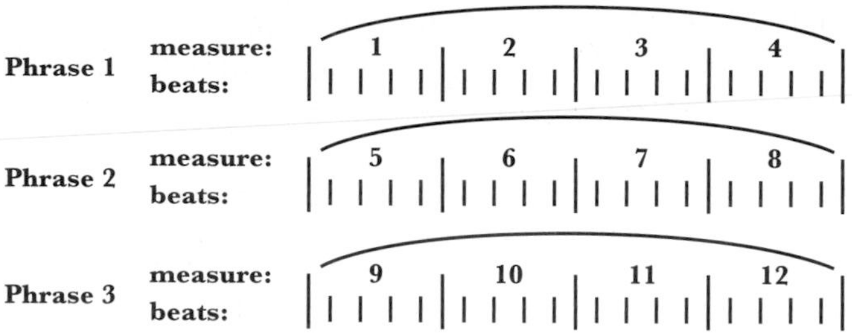

This one blues chorus is comparable to a sentence in English. As with most sentences, our twelve-bar "sentence" divides into smaller units called phrases (a term common to both music and English). In the standard twelve-bar blues, each phrase is four bars long. In music, we indicate phrases by large, curving lines over the measures (note the preceding example).

Recall that a key is like a family of seven different notes, each of which can have its own triad (three-note chord). The triads in the key of C are shown below.

**triads on each note**

| | | | | | | | | |
|---|---|---|---|---|---|---|---|---|
| | **G** | **A** | **B** | **C** | **D** | **E** | **F** | **G** |
| | **E** | **F** | **G** | **A** | **B** | **C** | **D** | **E** |
| **Notes in the key of C:→** | **C** | **D** | **E** | **F** | **G** | **A** | **B** | **C** |
| | **I** | **II** | **III** | **IV** | **V** | **VI** | **VII** | **I** |

For ease of reference, we can number these chords with Roman numerals, as shown in the preceding example. For the basic twelve-bar blues, we can concern ourselves with only three of these chords: the I, IV, and V. These three chords are distributed in the twelve-bar blues form as shown below.

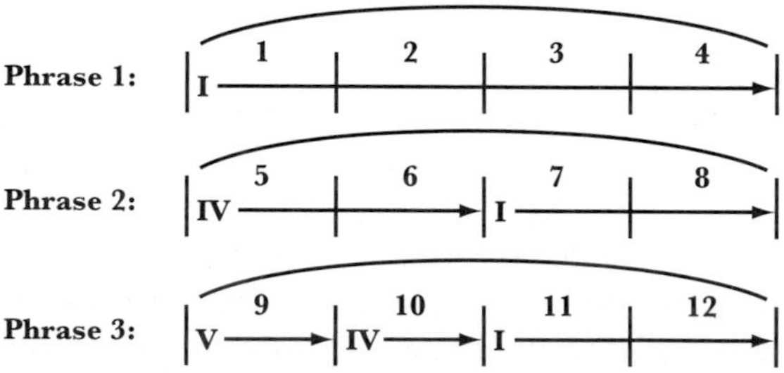

Now let us add the melody and lyrics. The words used in a twelve-bar blues are usually in the form of a couplet—that is, two lines that rhyme. At this point, you may perceive a potential problem. We have two rhyming lines of text, but three phrases of music. Something has to give! The blues singer's solution is to repeat the first line of the couplet, thus creating an A-A-B scheme. The melody of the first phrase is also repeated for the second phrase. The second line of the couplet is therefore delayed until the third phrase of the music; the melody carrying this second line of the couplet is usually slightly different from the melody used in the first two phrases.

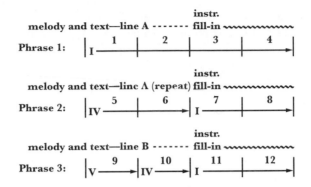

One final point: In the traditional twelve-bar blues, each line of text consumes about half the musical phrase (about two measures). The last two measures of each phrase are filled in by the instrumentalists (see the preceding example).

Now let us apply this scheme to a real rock-and-roll record. Listen to Elvis Presley's version of "Hound Dog."

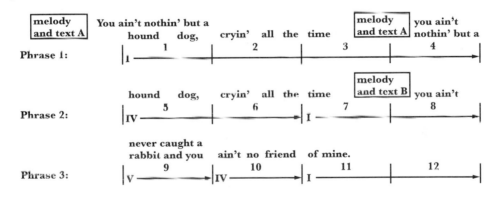

Elvis cheats a little by beginning each line of text a little before the downbeat of the phrase. But other than that, this song follows the scheme nicely. You can actually count along by enunciating each beat ("1, 2, 3, 4"), keeping track of which measure you are in by counting the measure numbers on each downbeat: 1–2–3–4, 2–2–3–4, 3–2–3–4, 4–2–3–4, and so on. Listen several times until you really "feel" the form. On one listening, focus on the background singers. They are singing the I, IV, and V chords, so you can hear them change at the appropriate moments.

This basic twelve-bar blues has been used for thousands of songs for at least a hundred years (probably more). Although there are many examples that follow our twelve-bar blues scheme perfectly, there are many more that modify one or more aspects of it. Some performers have changed some of the chords; others have eliminated the instrumental accompaniment for a few measures; and still others have varied the melodic and text schemes. There are almost as many variations as there are songs and performers. Still, the basic twelve-bar blues comes through. It is a very resilient concept.

The serviceability of the twelve-bar blues is truly remarkable. If no singer is present, instrumentalists can still improvise a twelve-bar blues. Professional musicians know and feel the twelve-bar blues almost as well as they know their own names. All any professional needs to say to another is, "Let's do a blues in B-flat," and everything that needs to be said is said. Someone counts off four beats to set the tempo and off they go. The basic scheme is adaptable to any style of rock and roll, jazz, country and western, and, of course, R & B. There are even examples of classical uses of this basic scheme!

One last point: Lest you think we have just described one of the shortest songs in history—only twelve measures long—understand that the twelve-bar chorus is repeated any number of times. If it is a vocal blues, the text normally changes with each chorus. Some jazz recordings repeat the chorus some forty to fifty times. With each chorus, the instrumentalist who has the "lead" improvises on a new musical idea—thus providing variety and interest to what would otherwise be a rather boring situation.

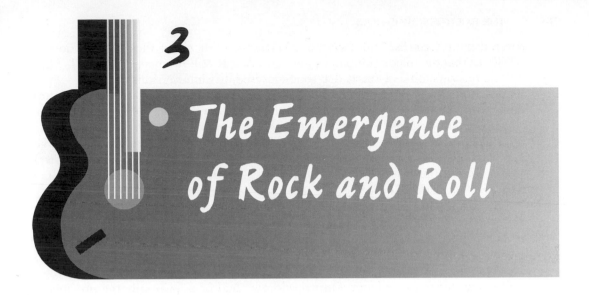

**3**

# The Emergence of Rock and Roll

## OVERVIEW: CROSSOVERS AND COVERS

Pop, C & W, and R & B coexisted in the early 1950s as three separate and distinct markets, as if separated by tall brick walls. But in a short three-year period (roughly 1954 to 1956), individual bricks were removed until the "walls came tumbling down." What emerged from the ruins was a new giant on the musical scene: a style that came to be known as rock and roll.

To understand how these bricks began to be removed, we must understand the related phenomena of "crossovers" and "covers." Crossovers were records that originated in one market but succeeded in another. Although there had been a few crossover hits before the 1950s, they became more frequent in the early 1950s. Typically the early 1950s crossover was an R & B song that sold enough to appear on the lower end of the pop charts. Among the early crossover hits were "Lawdy Miss Clawdy" (Lloyd Price), "Gee" (the Crows), and "Earth Angel" (the Penguins). "Cryin' in the Chapel" (the Orioles) is a particularly good example because in July 1953, while holding the top position in the R & B market, it also climbed to number eleven in the pop charts, thus narrowly missing the Top 10.

Observing this new interest in crossover R & B hits, the major companies moved quickly to produce their own popularized versions of R & B originals. The result of this process is called a cover version, that is, a subsequent version of an original song. Of course, multiple versions of hits were common within the pop market long before the 1950s. Much has been written about white artists covering the songs of black musicians, but in reality the practice worked both ways. For example, Doris Day's pop hit "Secret Love" was covered by the Moonglows; and "Crying in the Chapel" was originally a C & W ballad before being covered by the Orioles, who in turn were covered by at least five more versions. What was new about the cover versions of 1954 was that the major companies were covering R & B originals. Table 3–1 (Shaw 1982, 97) shows some of the R & B songs covered by white versions in 1954.

These pop covers usually equaled or exceeded the sales of the original hits. Sometimes both the original version and the pop cover version coexisted on the pop charts (a good example is "Ain't That a Shame," original version by Fats Domino, cover version by Pat Boone). In addition to crossovers and covers, the pop market made an attempt at creating its own originals in a style similar to the new R & B cover sound. Thus Eddie Fisher, a pop singer, sang "Dungaree Doll," and Kay Starr recorded "Rock and Roll Waltz."

To say that 1954 and 1955 were years of turmoil and confusion in the pop music industry would be a considerable understatement. The crossover sales, the R & B cover versions, and the pop "soundalikes" indicated that something new was happening. Specifically, the increasing popularity of these new sounds reflected an important new phenomenon: the emergence of a distinct youth culture.

Prior to this time the entertainment industry had been primarily the province of adults. After all, the dollars were in the adults' pockets and those dollars were what interested the entertainment industry. But in the mid- and late 1950s, some of those dollars gradually flowed down into the pockets of the youth. Movies appeared that were aimed at a teenage audience. James Dean starred in a movie called *Rebel without a Cause;* Sidney Poitier and Glenn Ford starred in *Blackboard Jungle.* If, as psychologists tell us, youth is inherently and naturally a time of rebellion, the typical 1955 youth had a problem: what to rebel against! *Rebel without a Cause* portrays that question as well as anything could. Dean portrayed a sullen, brooding teenager who feels an internal anger and rebellion, but has no real targets at which to unleash his feelings. In *Blackboard Jungle,* the teenagers strike out at whatever is around: parents, the educational system (teachers), and each other.

An image began to form: the rebellious teenager, sullen, brooding, rebelling against his or her environment, often with little justifiable reason. The model

## Table 3–1

| Song | R & B Original (chart position) | Pop Cover (chart position) |
|---|---|---|
| "Earth Angel" | Penguins (8) | Crew Cuts (3) |
| "Goodnight Sweetheart" | Spaniels (24) | McGuire Sisters (7) |
| "Heart of Stone" | Charms (15) | Fontaine Sisters (1) |
| "Shake, Rattle, and Roll" | Joe Turner (*) | Bill Haley (7) |
| "Sh-Boom" | Chords (5) | Crew Cuts (1) |
| "Sincerely" | Moonglows (20) | McGuire Sisters (1) |
| "Two Hearts" | Charms (8)** | Pat Boone (16) |
| "Tweedle Dee" | La Vern Baker (14) | Georgia Gibbs (2) |
| | *did not chart | |
| | **R & B chart only | |

became the "juvenile delinquent"— black leather jacket, shirt open, collar upturned, hair slicked back into a "ducktail" or "duck's ass," long sideburns, spit curl in front, sneer permanently planted on the lips. A Tough Guy and a Swinging Chick—cool, but ready to lash out at any moment.

A new youth identity emerged. No longer were youth simply the miscellaneous offspring of adult society, content to await the passage of time until they grew old enough to be admitted to society as adults. They coalesced into a society of their own and increasingly identified with their own movies, their own role models, their own dress code, slang, hairstyles, behavior, and of course, their own music.

What music? That question was answered best by the movie *Blackboard Jungle*. The sound track included an earlier rock-and-roll release by Bill Haley called "Rock Around the Clock." If there was ever any doubt, this firmly underscored the intimate association between the new youth culture and rock and roll.

## BILL HALEY AND THE COMETS

If the early emergence of rock and roll can be symbolized by any one artist, that person would have to be Bill Haley. Haley was born in Detroit in 1927, and his musical career swept across the three music markets (pop, C & W, R & B), thus representing what rock and roll as a genre did in the mid-1950s.

Haley's primary early identification was with C & W. His band was called the Saddlemen, and it consisted of the usual C & W instrumentation (including steel guitar) plus the drum set and saxophone from the R & B tradition.

Haley was familiar with and admired R & B music. Even when playing typical C & W jobs, he and his band would slip in the occasional R & B song in a C & W style that would not offend his patrons. After changing his group's name to the

Bill Haley and the Comets (*Source:* © 1956 Columbia Pictures Corporation. All rights reserved. Courtesy of Columbia Pictures)

Comets, Haley made a serious attempt to achieve national attention with his unique combination of R & B and C & W. In 1952 came "Crazy, Man, Crazy," followed in 1954 by "Shake, Rattle, and Roll" (an original R & B hit by Joe Turner). Also in 1954 came Haley's version of an R & B hit, "Rock Around the Clock" (originally recorded by Sonny Dae). Only mildly successful at first, its association with the popular movie *Blackboard Jungle* put it over the top in 1955.

With the huge success of "Rock Around the Clock," the walls between R & B, C & W, and pop began to crumble. Here was a white C & W band singing their version of an R & B song and seeing that song move up the pop charts until it peaked at number 1 in July 1955, a position it held for two months. According to *Cash Box,* "Rock Around the Clock" was the top-selling record in 1955. To be sure, Haley's "Shake, Rattle, and Roll" (1954) eventually sold over one million copies and was among the top five for nearly five months. But it was "Rock Around the Clock" that had the most dramatic impact on the nation's consciousness. Haley followed with "Dim, Dim the Lights" (1955), which crossed over to appear on the R & B charts, a particularly unusual phenomenon because "white" records rarely appeared on the R & B charts.

In that crucial year of 1955, Haley and his Comets seemed to represent the raucous new style called rock and roll. His popularity continued into 1956 (and beyond) with his film *Rock Around the Clock* (an early prototype of the teen rock film, which still exists today) and several more hits, including "See You Later, Alligator," "Corrine, Corrina," and "Green Door." But Haley simply was not the person needed to personify the continuing development of the new youth-oriented rock and roll. Haley was nearly forty years old and had a rather round, innocent baby face with a receding hairline (in spite of his 1950s-style "spit curl" in front). His "straighter" C & W background was all too evident.

A new figure was needed to be the "front" man for rock and roll—someone younger, someone whose image was closer to the brooding and sullen James Dean image and the juvenile delinquent image of *Blackboard Jungle,* someone who could project an image of raw power and slightly menacing rebellion. As so often happens, the right person appeared in the right place at the right time.

## ELVIS PRESLEY

Elvis Presley was unique, and that is what made him the central figure in the early development of rock and roll. He popularized the new style, disseminating it throughout society in a way no other individual could. It is probably not too great an overstatement to suggest that without Presley rock may well have proven to be the musical fad its detractors claimed it to be, falling into the same category as the hula hoop and the Davy Crockett coonskin cap—sensations of American culture that consume our attention for a period of time, only to disappear into the realm of nostalgia.

### A Summary of Presley's Life and Career

Elvis Aron Presley was born in Tupelo, Mississippi, in 1935. In a nation that rigidly observed racial segregation (especially in the Deep South), it is hard to imagine how the black culture and the white culture could ever mix. But Presley's childhood and youth provide an answer to that dilemma. The Presleys were very poor. In southern white society, those at the very bottom of the socioeconomic scale were called poor white trash and were considered to be on a par with the blacks. This was more than simply an abstract social stratification; it was manifested in the reality of life. "Poor white trash" lived "on the other side of the tracks" in many southern towns, sometimes intermingled, or at least juxtaposed, with "nigger town."

Thus, a poor white southern boy like Elvis was in a position to absorb a real variety of musical influences, including R & B, white and black gospel, C & W, bluegrass, western swing, and pop. From the radio, which brought the young Elvis both pop music and various forms of C & W, and from the very real influences inherent in his living circumstances, which brought him the R & B and gospel sounds, the musical Elvis became, in effect, racially integrated.

The Presleys' economic fortunes did not improve significantly after their move to Memphis in 1948. They lived in a federally funded housing project, and Elvis attended L. C. Humes High School, a school whose population was drawn from predominantly lower income levels. Naturally surrounded by white musical influences (pop and C & W), Elvis sought out the black musical sounds with which he had become familiar in Tupelo. It is reported that Elvis hung out around the Beale Street area, a musical hotbed of black music.

Elvis's life at Humes High seems to have passed rather unremarkably. He was merely an average student; he was not a member of the popular "in" crowd. He just seemed "different." Some of that difference may again be traced to the biracial influences in his early life. In the racially segregated South of the early 1950s, it was important that racial identities be preserved. Elvis crossed those lines of identity. He wore loud and "outrageous" clothes and liked and sang black-style music. He dressed like a "hood," which meant black leather jackets, open shirts, and upturned collars. He wore long sideburns with his hair greased back into a "ducktail." Thus, his image was not that of the typical mid-1950s white middle-class teenager, but a combination of black and lower-class white.

His one point of popularity was his singing. His peers at Humes enjoyed his musical performances, such as the one at the 1952 school variety show. Shortly after his graduation in 1953, Presley went to a small local recording company called the Memphis Recording Service to make a record as a gift to his mother. Although Sam Phillips, owner of the Memphis Recording Service and Sun Records, was not present at this first recording session, Marion Keisker was. It was she who brought Presley's unique musical style to the owner's attention upon his return. Phillips had recorded a number of black artists in the R & B style. His more successful market, however, was C & W. He is reputed to have said, "If I could find a white man who had the Negro sound and the Negro feel, I could make a billion dollars" (Hopkins 1972, 56). When he heard Presley's tapes, he knew he had his man. Presley's contract with Sun Records was signed in July 1954.

Elvis went on to release five singles on the Sun label between mid-1954 and the end of 1955. The first Sun release underscores the biracial nature of rock and roll's roots and its most famous practitioner. On one side of the single was "That's All Right (Mama)," an R & B song by Arthur "Big Boy" Crudup. On the flip side was "Blue Moon of Kentucky," a C & W standard by Bill Monroe. Backed by Scotty Moore (guitar) and Bill Black (bass), Presley's first record became a regional hit, eventually selling about 20,000 copies. Interestingly enough, some white radio stations refused to play Elvis's early releases because they assumed he was of mixed racial blood.

By the time of his fifth and final Sun release ("Mystery Train" and "I Forgot to Remember to Forget"), Presley had become an important figure in the C & W world, as evidenced by his being named the number 1 "up and coming" C & W artist in a Billboard disc jockey poll (1955). Over this same year and a half, his reputation also spread by means of personal appearances, primarily on the "Louisiana Hayride" show, which regularly toured the C & W geographic market promoting new artists as well as more established stars.

His appearances on such shows were a harbinger of things to come. After all, Elvis was not the typical C & W act. His vocal and musical style was heavily influenced by R & B and black gospel. His appearance was a mixture of black fashion and the teenage hood. His performance style included a good bit of active body movement, much of it sexually suggestive. Traditional C & W performers just didn't do that. Whenever a package show (a show including a roster of artists) included Elvis, promoters noticed that the audience included more and more teenagers, especially females. They screamed and cried for Elvis and barely tolerated the more traditional performers. The other artists and their adult fans became increasingly irritated with this new phenomenon. They could hardly be expected to realize that they were witnessing the beginnings of a major musical, social, and economic revolution.

Near the end of 1955 and the beginning of 1956, two related events occurred that would set into motion the national impact of Elvis Presley. First, "Colonel" Tom Parker took over the personal management of Presley from former manager Bob Neal. Shortly thereafter, Parker negotiated Presley's release from Sun Records and subsequently sold his contract to RCA Victor. The Colonel had shopped around

for an advantageous contract for Elvis. Atlantic Records, a small company at that time, offered $25,000, which represented big dollars for such a company in 1955. Giant RCA easily exceeded that offer with a $35,000 sales price, plus a $5,000 signing bonus for Elvis. In retrospect, the purchase of Elvis Presley for a total of $40,000 stands as one of the best business deals since the purchase of Manhattan from the Indians for a few trinkets.

With the release of "Heartbreak Hotel" in 1956, Presley was off and running (as was rock and roll). His first national hit sold more than one million copies in a matter of months. A

Elvis and his parents, Gladys and Vernon (*Source:* Reproduced by permission of the Estate of Elvis Presley. Courtesy of Elvis Presley Enterprises, Inc.)

Elvis as a young rock and roller (*Source:* Reproduced by permission of the Estate of Elvis Presley. Courtesy of Elvis Presley Enterprises, Inc.)

subsequent release, "Hound Dog"/"Don't Be Cruel," sold over three million copies in one year. Sales orders for "Love Me Tender" exceeded one million before its release. In 1956, Presley's record sales went over the ten million mark. If some of these figures fail to impress today, one must understand that these were mind-boggling statistics in the mid-1950s.

Another amazing phenomenon was that both sides of a Presley single often achieved popularity. Normally the "A" side is promoted for chart sales; the backup, or "B" side, is a throwaway. "Hound Dog" and "Don't Be Cruel" (two sides of the same single) both reached number 1 on the charts; "Don't" and "I Beg of You" both reached the Top 10, as did "One Night"/"I Got Stung" and "A Fool Such As I"/"I Need Your Love Tonight."

It should also be noted that Presley continued to cover C & W and R & B songs, thus continuing the biracial musicality that brought him to national prominence. Among his R & B covers for RCA were "Hound Dog" (Big Mama Thornton), "Shake, Rattle, and Roll" (Joe Turner), "Lawdy Miss Clawdy" (Lloyd Price), "Cryin' in the Chapel" (the Orioles), and a host of Little Richard songs ("Tutti Frutti," "Long Tall Sally," "Rip It Up," and "Ready Teddy"). There were also C & W covers (the most famous being "Blue Suede Shoes" by Carl Perkins) and even pop covers (e.g., "Blue Moon" by Richard Rodgers, 1934).

The crumbling of the walls between the C & W, R & B, and pop markets was also evidenced by the number of Presley's crossover hits. "Heartbreak Hotel" reached number 1 on both pop and C & W charts and number 3 on the R & B charts. "Don't Be Cruel," "Hound Dog," "Teddy Bear," "Jailhouse Rock," and "All Shook Up" hit number 1 on all three charts. "Love Me Tender" reached number 1 on pop, number 3 on C & W, and number 4 on R & B charts. Even as late as 1960 "Are You Lonesome Tonight?" made all three charts.

In 1958 Presley was inducted into the army. Two life-altering events occurred during Elvis's service period. First, his mother Gladys died during his first year of service. The effect on Elvis was profound. His love for and dedication to his mother were very real. He bore a striking physical resemblance to her (which became even more evident in Elvis's later years). Second, it was during his service years that he met Priscilla Beaulieu, an encounter that would also have far-reaching effects.

Upon his return from Germany in 1960, Elvis's career resumed with a movie called *G.I. Blues*. It exploited his return and, of course, his identification as a soldier. This was far from the first film starring Elvis Presley. Beginning with *Love Me Tender*

Elvis as a teen idol (*Source:* Reproduced by permission of the Estate of Elvis Presley. Courtesy of Elvis Presley Enterprises, Inc.)

in 1956, Elvis made some thirty-three films over the next sixteen years. Most were teen rock exploitation films of little dramatic merit. Elvis longed for more substantial dramatic roles, but Colonel Parker preferred the glitzy, insubstantial films, apparently feeling that more serious roles were not in keeping with the Presley image.

As rock and roll moved on to newer styles in the 1960s, the frequency and impact of Elvis's single hits declined. Among his more successful hits from the mid-1960s until his death in 1977 were the following: "Suspicion" (1964), "In the Ghetto" (1969), "Suspicious Minds" (1969), "Don't Cry Daddy" (1970), "The Wonder of You" (1970), "Burning Love" (1972), "Promised Land" (1974), and "Way Down" (1977). However, Elvis began to pull back from live performances in the early 1960s, and from about 1962 to 1968 was rarely seen in person. It was a time of withdrawal and seclusion (except for the movie career and the resulting sound track albums). He did produce several fine gospel albums during these years (*His Hand in Mine* and *How Great Thou Art*). He surrounded himself with a group of loyal "good old boys" known as the Memphis Mafia and retreated to his Memphis home, Graceland, which he had purchased and renovated years earlier for his family.

In 1967 Elvis married Priscilla Beaulieu; a daughter, Lisa Marie, was born nine months later. Beginning with a television special in December 1968, Elvis returned to live performances. He found that he still retained a tremendous appeal, especially

to audiences in the thirty-year-old-plus age group (his original fans). Colonel Parker successfully marketed him in Las Vegas and on tour to major cities as well as minor sites that rarely had the opportunity to host live concerts by big-name acts. A high point came in 1973 with another television special, "Aloha from Hawaii," the first television show to be transmitted internationally by satellite. An audience estimated at one billion viewed Elvis's Hawaiian special.

However, personal problems that began to surface in the 1960s became more exagger-

Elvis and Priscilla (*Source:* Reproduced by permission of the Estate of Elvis Presley. Courtesy of Elvis Presley Enterprises, Inc.)

Elvis in the 1970s (*Source:* Reproduced by permission of the Estate of Elvis Presley. Courtesy of Elvis Presley Enterprises, Inc.)

ated in the 1970s. Elvis developed a weight problem that detracted from his image as a rock sex symbol. When "off the road," his weight would balloon to well over 200 pounds. Facing the beginning of a tour, he would go on a crash diet program, complete with pills, and lose twenty to thirty pounds in a matter of weeks. Following the tour, the weight returned. This extreme up-and-down weight pattern and an increasing reliance on drugs played havoc with his mental and physical health. His divorce from Priscilla in October 1973 and the resulting loss of Lisa Marie was a devastating personal shock. His personal life and his health continued to deteriorate throughout the 1970s. He finally died of heart-related problems in Memphis on August 16, 1977 (he was forty-two years old).

After his death, Elvis's recording of "My Way," a song written by Paul Anka and popularized by Frank Sinatra, was released and became a big seller. Since then, millions of Presley albums (some old, some elaborately repackaged) have been sold. In 1981, a remix of "Guitar Man" (1968) reached number 1 on the country music chart. His movies continue to appear on television, and numerous books about his life have appeared. Graceland has become a major tourist attraction.

**The Importance of Presley**

Although various persons vehemently argue that others, such as Buddy Holly, Bill Haley, and Little Richard, were truly the central influences in the early development of rock and roll, the consensus is that Elvis Presley really was "the King." Many reasons for this could be cited, but let us focus on a few of the most important ones.

1. *Presley was "the King" because he was the musical personification of what rock and roll was.* Rock and roll developed as a biracial music, and more than any other major star of the time, Presley's musical style genuinely reflected those biracial influences. The styles of Berry, Domino, and Little Richard derived primarily from the black R & B tradition; Haley and Holly sounded thoroughly white. Perhaps the only one to approach Presley's biracial style was Jerry Lee Lewis. But his short-lived career as a rock-and-roll artist did not hold a candle to Presley's overall success.

2. *His multifaceted personality and his musical versatility meant that his appeal could be broadened beyond that of the typical rock-and-roll star.* Elvis was many things to many people. If one wanted a sex symbol, Elvis's good looks, sneer, and bodily movements filled

the bill. If one wanted the teenage "hood" image, one could find it in Elvis's side-burns, black jacket, open shirt, upturned collars, and greasy ducktail. If one valued respect for God, Elvis was your man. He was unashamedly religious and, in fact, recorded many hymns, Christmas songs, and gospel albums. If you liked patriotism in your stars, you had to like Elvis: he willingly served in the military and always paid his income taxes without the usual tax dodges practiced by so many millionaires. If you were impressed by respect for elders, you were impressed by Elvis. He never lost the politeness his mother Gladys instilled in him as a young southern boy. Even at the age of forty, he addressed his elders (and others) as "Mr." or "Mrs." and always said "Yes, sir" and "No, ma'am." If your musical tastes ran toward shoutin' rock and roll, softer rock, romantic ballads, hymns, gospel, country, patriotic anthems, social commentary, escapism, or tearjerkers, you could find an Elvis song to your liking. How could one person fill so many contradictory demands and still succeed? The music industry would love to know. It tried to create Elvis clones, but such attempts just did not work. He was unique.

3. *Elvis's commercial success was overwhelming.* By the time of Elvis's death, at least five hundred million copies of Presley records had been sold. Record sales since his death and on into the future will multiply that staggering figure. Presley holds the record for the most charted albums, the most hits in the Top 10, the most two-sided hit singles, the most consecutive Top 10 records, and the most total weeks in the number 1 position (eighty weeks). Perhaps the most revealing statistic is that he holds the record for the most consecutive years on the charts (including posthumous albums): twenty-seven. This is just over a quarter of a century.

## Final Reflections on Presley

Let us return for just a moment to the second of the foregoing points (Elvis's versatility and multifaceted appeal). One will frequently read that Presley began as a true rock and roller but disintegrated into a rather bland, somewhat pathetic pop star after about 1960. Rock historians typically denigrate his music following that point.

Such a viewpoint can be successfully argued, especially when considering the rather embarrassing movies and resulting sound tracks of the 1960s. However, one should also consider that what is sometimes portrayed as a weakness may, in fact, be a strength. Presley assimilated many preexisting styles into his unique musical style. It is only natural that the resulting Presley style would at times show an integration of these styles; but at other times, one or another of these ingredients would come to the fore, leaving the others in the background. Thus, even among his early hits was a shouting rock-and-roll song like "Hound Dog," a sultry song like "Don't Be Cruel," and a romantic pop ballad like "Love Me Tender." In spite of the movies and sound tracks of the 1960s, the original musical roots were still alive in Elvis, as evidenced by his NBC television special of December 1968. Rejoined by members of his original group and clad in black leather, he gave a powerful demonstration that the original rock and roll, raw and basic, was still alive and well within the King.

His versatility and multifaceted appeal is what made him the most influential and successful proponent of rock and roll of his time. Only with those characteristics could he take rock and roll and make it a phenomenon that affected society in general, not just a small hard-core subculture. Had Presley stayed in a narrow style of "real rock and roll," the new musical style might well have remained a subculture music like C & W, R & B, and gospel, appealing only to a small slice of the general population. Instead, largely because of Elvis's pivotal impact, rock and roll moved out of its identity as "teen music" to become the popular musical style of the last half of the twentieth century.

## MUSICAL CLOSE-UP:
### RHYTHM IN EARLY ROCK AND ROLL

Rhythm is perhaps the most basic of all of the musical elements, because all sound must have a beginning, a duration, and an end—that is, an existence in time. By rhythm, we mean how sound is ordered in time.

Music psychologists believe that human beings respond naturally to the beat or rhythmic aspect of music because our own body is, in fact, a complex of periodic vibrations and beats (pulses). Perhaps this is why when we hear a strongly rhythmic piece of jazz or rock we cannot resist tapping our feet, clapping our hands, moving our bodies, or dancing.

Although rhythm is *always* there no matter what the musical style, it is true that in some styles the rhythm is more strongly perceived than in others. For example, in Debussy's *Prelude to The Afternoon of a Faun*, the beat is very slow and is purposely deemphasized. The music seems to float through time. In contrast, in Elvis Presley's "Hound Dog" the beat and rhythm are very much in evidence; the rhythm is "right up front."

There are four basic observations that we can make about the rhythm in almost any piece of music. These are as follows:

1. *How fast is the beat?* The musical term for the speed of the beat is *tempo*. Elvis's "Hard-Headed Woman" has a fast tempo, "Return to Sender" has a moderate tempo; "Love Me Tender" has a slow tempo. We can measure the tempo accurately and objectively by use of a metronome, a device that measures the number of beats per minute. Table 3–2 shows some of Elvis's songs and their tempos.
2. *How are the beats organized?* As we saw in our discussion of the twelve-bar blues, pop musicians usually organize beats into groups of four. The technical term for this organizational grouping of beats is *meter*. Thus, *quadruple meter* is the organization of beats into groups of four; *triple meter* is the organization of beats into groups of three; and so on, with duple meter, quintuple meter, et cetera. The vast majority of rock and roll is in quadruple meter. Most of the music discussed in this book is in quadruple meter; as we encounter the exceptional examples that are not, we will call that to your attention. Recall from Chapter 2 that each grouping of beats is called a measure or bar. So if we speak of eight bars of quadruple meter, we are referring to a total of thirty-two beats organized into eight groups of four.
3. *How strong are the beats?* The beat is an emphasized aspect of rock and roll. Most people can "feel" the beat in a rock piece and can demonstrate that beat by tapping their feet, snapping their fingers, or clapping their hands.

| Table 3–2 | | |
|---|---|---|
| **Song** | **Description** | **Metronome Tempo** |
| "Hard-headed Woman" | fast | 195 beats/minute |
| "Long Tall Sally" | fast | 192 beats/minute |
| "I Got Stung" | fast | 190 beats/minute |
| "Hound Dog" | fast | 180 beats/minute |
| "Don't Be Cruel" | moderately fast | 172 beats/minute |
| "Jailhouse Rock" | moderately fast | 162 beats/minute |
| "Return to Sender" | moderate | 132 beats/minute |
| "Are You Lonesome Tonight?" | slow | 75 beats/minute |
| "Love Me Tender" | slow | 72 beats/minute |

All of the beats in a measure are not equally strong. Traditionally, the first beat (the "downbeat") is the strongest beat; the next strongest is the third beat; the second and fourth are relatively weak. However, many rock songs emphasize beats two and four—just the opposite of the traditional approach. When this occurs, the music is said to have a strong *backbeat*.

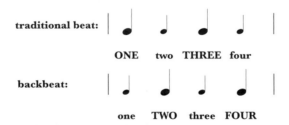

Again, music psychologists have suggested that the excitement and intense rhythmic appeal of rock may be partially due to this backbeat rhythm, which is in conflict with, or sets up a tension against, our traditional expectations.

Some rock emphasizes all four beats equally. For example, listen to the opening section of Chicago's "Saturday in the Park." The piano's introductory measures emphasize all four beats equally; however, when the drummer enters, he accents beats two and four. Or listen to the Beatles' "Why Don't We Do It in the Road?"; here again, the piano part emphasizes all four beats equally, but the drum part clearly accents beats two and four.

4. *How are the beats subdivided?* Rhythm would be a pretty simple matter if it consisted only of beats. But the real rhythmic interest (and complexity) of most music is determined by what happens "inside" or between the beats. Each beat is usually subdivided into smaller parts. For our purposes, we shall concentrate on the subdivision of the beat into two, three, and four parts.

Faster rock and roll of the 1950s used a duple subdivision of the beat. Listen to the bass line of Elvis's "Jailhouse Rock" and you will hear a very clear duple subdivision of the beat.

Slower, softer songs were more likely to have a triple subdivision of the beat. For example, listen to the Platters' "The Great Pretender," or the Flamingos' "I Only Have Eyes for You." Notice especially the piano's repeating chords, three per beat:

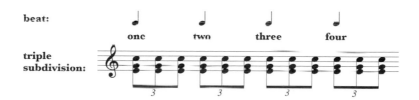

An interesting combination of the backbeat and a duple subdivision is found in some 1950s (and later) rock songs. Try the following exercise and make your own rock beat.

Listen to "Sweet Nothings" by Brenda Lee or "Short Shorts" by the Royal Teens for clear examples of this combination.

We shall frequently refer to the rhythmic characteristics of various rock styles and certain rock pieces. We may speak of the tempo, the meter, the backbeat, or the sub-division pattern. It is hoped that this brief introduction will provide a basis for understanding these later comments.

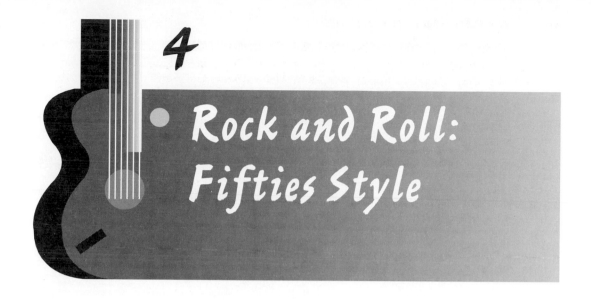

# 4

# Rock and Roll: Fifties Style

## OVERVIEW: THREE BASIC TRENDS EMERGE

If one looks a step below the all-pervasive presence of Elvis Presley, one finds a small collection of major figures who helped establish the three basic trends that characterized early rock and roll. This chapter will take a closer look at these performers, survey some of the minor figures who fill out the total picture, and examine the changes brought about in the music industry by rock and roll. First, however, we must examine briefly the three basic trends of early rock and roll: mainstream rock, rockabilly, and soft rock.

### Mainstream Rock

Of rock's three primary ancestors (pop, C & W, and R & B), it was R & B that provided the heaviest influence. In fact, there are those who would argue, with some justification, that rock and roll is essentially a newer, updated continuation of R & B, other styles merely being offshoots of this main line of development.

However one chooses to conceptualize it, it is true that the harder "mainstream" styles of 1950s rock and roll show a definite lineage back to R & B. First there was the heavy reliance upon the twelve-bar blues form. A majority of upbeat (fast), hard-driving 1950s rock songs were based upon the twelve-bar blues. Following is a list of some examples, some of which are "pure" (adhering closely to all of the aspects of the twelve-bar blues pattern), whereas others modify one or more of the pattern's characteristics. For example, "Jailhouse Rock" expands to a sixteen-bar blues; several songs change the traditional lyric pattern; and a few move to a middle section not related to blues. But all use the basic twelve-bar blues as the point of departure.

| | |
|---|---|
| Elvis Presley | "Hound Dog" |
| | "Hard-Headed Woman" |
| | "I Got Stung" |
| | "Jailhouse Rock" |
| | "Teddy Bear" |
| Little Richard | "Jenny, Jenny" |
| | "Lucille" |
| | "Tutti Frutti" |
| | "Long Tall Sally" |
| | "Good Golly Miss Molly" |
| Chuck Berry | "School Days" |
| | "Johnny B. Goode" |
| Bill Haley | "Rock Around the Clock" |
| | "Shake, Rattle, and Roll" |
| Fats Domino | "Ain't That a Shame" |
| Buddy Holly | "Oh Boy" |
| Jerry Lee Lewis | "Whole Lot of Shakin' Going On" |
| Ray Charles | "What'd I Say" |
| Danny and the Juniors | "At the Hop" |
| Bobby Day | "Rockin' Robin" |

The preceding list is by no means exhaustive. It represents only a fraction of the total number of 1950s rock songs based upon the twelve-bar blues.

Another characteristic of R & B that carries over into the harder 1950s rock-and-roll songs is the vocal performance style. Just as there had been R & B shouters, there were rock-and-roll shouters. Perhaps the best example is Little Richard. Listen to any of his songs from the preceding list. There is a distinct difference in voice production when one changes from a "pure" tone to a "shout." Try speaking your name loudly. Then really yell it. Feel the difference? The shout has a harder sound, usually with a raspiness to it. Presley approaches the shouting style in "Jailhouse Rock," "Hard-Headed Woman," and "Hound Dog." But not all R & B singers were shouters. Some belted out a song with a strong, hard vocal style that stopped short of shouting. So, too, many 1950s rock singers belted out their songs without actually shouting. Most of the songs of Chuck Berry, Fats Domino, and Jerry Lee Lewis fall into this category.

Like R & B, most 1950s mainstream rock was not notated. The lyrics, melody, and chords for one chorus might be sketched. From there the total arrangement was worked out without notation. Also, the instrumentation of the typical rock-and-roll band was similar to that of the old R & B band: guitars, piano, drums, and saxophone.

Another important characteristic of 1950s rock that was derived from earlier R & B was the bass line. R & B bass lines were more melodic than the bass lines of pop and C & W. The purpose of most bass lines is to provide the bottom of the harmony (the root). In much C & W and pop, the required bass note was played on each beat or every other beat. But in R & B, a more active bass line was preferred. It was closer in concept to the old bass lines of boogie-woogie. Thus, the bass would provide not only the root of the chord but also devise a short melodic pattern that would outline all three or four notes of the chord, sometimes with a few added pitches. For example:

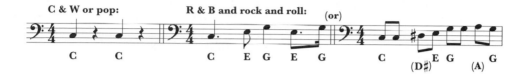

A large variety of such patterns was devised. Adding such a melodic pattern to the bass also added to the overall rhythmic activity of the song. Listen to the bass part of some 1940s R & B (e.g., Otis Spann's "Bloody Murder") and you can hear the predecessors of the bass lines of much 1950s rock.

Finally, the rhythmic aspect of R & B carried over to the harder styles of early rock and roll. Unlike in C & W and pop, rhythm was one of the most prominent elements of R & B. The drummer was not just there to provide a quiet rhythmic structure or play a simple beat; he was an integral part of the music, equal to the other members of the band. The basic rhythm of the song was also emphasized in the piano and guitars. It was a strong, heavy beat. These characteristics carry over into 1950s mainstream rock with a few slight changes. For one thing, the beat became faster. Also, the emphasis on the second and fourth beats (the backbeat) became stronger as rock developed its own rhythm. That extra accent on the second and fourth beats, including hand claps in many cases, can be heard in many 1950s rock songs.

## Rockabilly

Although most of the leading performers of early mainstream rock were black, there were a few white mainstream rockers. This was particularly true where the white performer had grown up with a heavy dose of R & B in his environment (e.g., Elvis Presley and Jerry Lee Lewis). But more often the white rock-and-roll performer's background leaned toward C & W. These white performers, usually southerners, applied their C & W styles to the R & B-oriented mainstream rock, thus creating a style known as rockabilly. Generally the effect was to lighten and clean up the hard-driving, more basic mainstream style. To some, rockabilly made rock more acceptable; to others it seemed to be a regrettable dilution of a purer style.

Bill Haley's background was C & W, but when he took R & B material and modified it with a C & W sound, he not only laid the foundation for rock and roll, in general, but for rockabilly specifically. Nonetheless, the real center for the early development of the rockabilly style was Sam Phillips's Sun Studios in Memphis. Presley's success encouraged many other southern white C & W musicians to trek to Memphis in the hope of finding success with the new rockabilly sound. In the years that followed (approximately 1955 to 1959), Sun released recordings by Carl Perkins, Jerry Lee Lewis, Johnny Cash, and a host of less significant artists. Perkins will be remembered for his one national hit, "Blue Suede Shoes." This song, released late in 1955, became a Top 10 hit on the C & W, R & B, and pop charts in 1956. Other companies quickly jumped on the rockabilly bandwagon. With Bill Haley already on its roster, Decca added Buddy Holly and the Crickets and the Johnny Burnette Trio (all on the subsidiary Coral and Brunswick labels). Capitol signed Gene Vincent ("Be-Bop-a-Lula" and several less successful follow-up songs); Chess released "Susie Q" by Dale Hawkins on its subsidiary Checker label; Liberty Records countered with "Summertime Blues" by Eddie Cochran, a Presley look-alike.

One of the most influential rockabilly acts was the Everly Brothers (Phil and Don). Their parents were C & W musicians; the boys toured with them and appeared on their radio show, thus absorbing a strong C & W background. With Presley as a model, they turned toward the rockabilly sound, creating their own personal mixture and becoming immensely popular. Between 1957 and 1960 (inclusive), they placed eleven hits in the Top 10, including four number 1 songs. "All I Have to Do Is Dream" (1958) was the only song by someone other than Presley to reach the number 1 position on the pop, R & B, and C & W charts.

One of the few nonsoutherners to be associated with rockabilly, Rick Nelson developed a softer, more pop-oriented style of rockabilly. Using his preestablished recognition as a member of the Nelson family of the very popular *Ozzie and Harriet* television sitcom, Nelson had a series of hits beginning in 1957 and continuing through 1972. Between 1957 and 1960 (inclusive), he placed eleven songs in the Top 10. Nelson died in a plane crash in 1986.

The musical style of rockabilly is difficult to identify in precise terms. Rockabilly singers stopped short of the shouting style (in slower songs, sometimes approaching a crooner's style). They usually sang clearly and cleanly on pitch; the lyrics were enunciated distinctly. The instrumentation was close to that of the mainstream style, except there was less emphasis on saxophone and acoustic guitars were used more often. Drums, not part of the traditional C & W sound, were added, reflecting the R & B influence. Although electric bass was used by later rockabilly groups, the earliest groups used acoustic bass, which was "slapped" to add a percussive beat. The following songs exemplify the rockabilly style.

The Everly Brothers (*Source:* Photograph courtesy of the Country Music Foundation, Inc.)

| Buddy Holly | "Maybe Baby" |
|---|---|
| | "Peggy Sue" |
| | "Not Fade Away" |
| | "That'll Be the Day" |
| | "Oh Boy"* |
| The Everly Brothers | "Wake Up, Little Susie" |
| | "Bird Dog"* |
| | "Bye Bye Love" |
| Jerry Lee Lewis | "Whole Lot of Shakin' Going On"* |
| | "Great Balls of Fire" |
| Carl Perkins | "Blue Suede Shoes"* |
| Bill Haley | "Rock around the Clock"* |
| Gene Vincent | "Be-Bop-a-Lula"* |
| Dale Hawkins | "Susie Q" |
| Buddy Knox | "Party Doll" |

Although some rockabilly songs are based, at least in part, on the twelve-bar blues (e.g., the titles marked with an asterisk [*]), most follow the eight-bar or sixteen-bar forms typical of C & W and pop songs.

In some cases the rockabilly rhythm approached that of mainstream rock. But normally the beat was lighter, with less of the hard-driving, heavy beat of the R & B-influenced mainstream. Even so, to help identify rockabilly as a rock style, the back-beat on the second and fourth beats was often present. The boogie-oriented bass lines of mainstream rock were less frequent in rockabilly, except for the "hardest" examples.

Rockabilly provided a more acceptable alternative for those who were drawn to the new rock-and-roll style but were not quite ready to accept the harder mainstream sound. It offered the excitement and appeal of rock without the raucous, unrefined musical style of the mainstream and without its racially objectionable (to some) associations.

## Soft Rock

As we have discussed, pop music was one of the ancestors of rock and roll. From the beginning, there has been a vital market for a softer style of rock that reflected that heritage by combining elements of rock with elements

Rick Nelson (*Source:* Michael Ochs Archive, Ltd.)

of pop music. Many rock purists deny that soft rock is a legitimate style of rock. They seem to perceive it as being the illegitimate offspring of an unholy alliance between pop and rock, dismissing it with such derisive phrases as "schlock rock," "schmaltz," and other terms better left unmentioned here. Such purists typically dismiss this style with a condescending sniff or an incredulous "You call that rock?!"

In spite of these reactions, two facts seem incontrovertible: (1) Much of this music contains clearly identifiable elements of rock, and (2) this style has had a broad and consistent appeal (market) from the beginning of rock to the present day. Apparently there is a need within society to balance the harder mainstream rock with a softer, less raucous alternative while still maintaining some essential elements of the rock style.

From the beginning, rock music was dance music. Whether at the high school prom or the Friday afternoon sock hop in the school gym, teens liked to dance to their new music. But dancing for four hours to "Tutti Frutti" and similar songs would be monotonous, nerve-wracking, and physically exhausting. Teens in the 1950s liked to "slow dance." With sociosexual mores being far more conservative than they later became, close dancing was a vital part of the developing boy/girl relationship. After all, holding hands and dancing in a close physical embrace was socially acceptable if done under the guise of "dancing." Many a relationship developed during the slow tunes played as the dance evening moved into its final hours.

Two rather distinct tracks may be discerned in the soft rock of the 1950s: (1) the white soft rock developed by Elvis, Pat Boone, and the good-looking teen idols modeled after them, and (2) the black soft rock developed by the numerous vocal groups referred to now (not then) as "doo-wop" groups. As with so many of the developments of rock, Elvis Presley established a model for the white soft rock style. From the beginning of his RCA output, Elvis recorded soft, slow ballads such as "I Want You, I Need You, I Love You," "Love Me Tender," "Anyway You Want Me," "Loving You," "Don't," and "Don't Ask Me Why" (all 1956 to 1958 releases). The softer pop side of Elvis continued and even increased during the balance of his career. Some of these songs are pure pop, bearing no real relationship to rock; others, however, contain clearly identifiable elements of rock.

Perhaps no one better exemplifies the softer pop rock style of the 1950s than Pat Boone. He was a young, handsome, and talented singer whose clean-cut appearance, performance style, and lifestyle provided a useful alternative to the more menacing styles of rock. Boone's career began by making commercially successful covers of R & B and mainstream rock originals, including "I'll Be Home" (Flamingos), "Two Hearts, Two Kisses" (Otis Williams and the Charms), "Ain't That a Shame" (Fats Domino), "Tutti Frutti" and "Long Tall Sally" (Little Richard), "At My Front Door" (El Dorados), "Chains of Love" (Joe Turner), and "I Almost Lost My Mind" (Ivory Joe Hunter). But beyond the covers, Boone also did the original popular versions of some upbeat songs such as "Why Baby Why" and "Wonderful Time Up There," and some slow to moderate tempo songs such as "Sugar Moon," "April Love," "Love Letters in the Sand," "Don't Forbid Me," and "Moody River." Many accounts of rock history deny that Boone sang rock and roll and omit him entirely. After all, he did not fit the desired image of the rebellious, countercultural rock star. However, if one listens objectively to some of his performances (e.g., a national television performance of "Tutti Frutti"), one must admit that he did sing rock and roll.

Pat Boone (*Source:* Michael Ochs Archive, Ltd.)

The vocal style is not as hard and raucous as Little Richard's, of course, but all the same basic rock elements are there.

It is also true, of course, that many of Boone's recordings are in a pure pop ballad style, derived from the Tin Pan Alley and Hollywood traditions, containing no pretense of rock. Boone has been criticized on the grounds that through his cover versions he capitalized on the original work of many black R & B artists. However, through his recordings he brought many of these songs to national prominence when, given the society and marketplace of the 1950s, they otherwise would have languished in obscurity.

If Elvis could include soft rock and pure pop ballads in his repertoire, others could legitimately specialize in this field. In the late 1950s and early 1960s, a large list of such performers achieved significance. Most were similar to Pat Boone and the softer side of Elvis in that they were attractive, young, talented, and rather wholesome in their appearance. The list would include Paul Anka, Frankie Avalon, Bobby Rydell, Bobby Vee, Bobby Darin, Tommy Sands, and female counterparts Connie Francis and Brenda Lee (although the latter tended toward a soft form of rockabilly).

For the predecessors of black soft rock, we look not toward Elvis Presley but further back, into the 1940s and early 1950s, to groups such as the Mills Brothers and the Ink Spots. Black vocal ensembles of three to six singers (most often four or five) were increasingly popular in the early 1950s. Such groups usually included a particularly talented lead singer and a backup vocal ensemble who provided good close harmony. To add rhythmic activity, the backup vocalists often sang rhythmic patterns using nonsense syllables. Although some were very simple ("doo-wah," and "doo-wop"), some became quite complex ("oodly-pop-a-cow, pop-a-cow, pop-a-cow-cow"  Frankie Lymon and the Teenagers, 1956 [Miller 1980, 83]). Their acts were tightly choreographed, so that the singers turned sideways, pivoted, kicked one foot, and tugged their shirt cuffs with coordinated precision. Groups such as the Ravens, the Orioles, and the Crows developed the style in the early 1950s. Landmark records were "Crying in the Chapel" (Orioles, 1953), and "Gee" (Crows, 1954). In 1954, the Chords released "Sh-Boom," which reached number 5 on the pop charts (number 3 on the R & B charts). A cover version by the Crew Cuts also reached the Top 10 just one week later. Further covers of "Sh-Boom" were recorded by Billy Williams, Sy Oliver, and even country artist Bobby Williamson. The song also cracked the Top 20 in England. The popularity of the "doo-wop" (or more accurately, the "sh-boom") song was established.

Still in 1954, the Penguins released "Earth Angel," which rose to number 8 nationally (number 1 on the R & B charts). Again, a cover by the Crew Cuts proved successful, also achieving a number 8 ranking. By 1955, the floodgates were opened,

The Crew Cuts (*Source:* Michael Ochs Archive, Ltd.)

and the bird groups (Crows, Falcons, Penguins, Flamingos, etc.), car groups (Imperials, Impalas, El Dorados, Fleetwoods, Edsels, etc.), and other doo-wop groups poured into the market. Most of these groups achieved one or two successful hits and disappeared. Few rock styles boast such a long list of one- or two-shot artists. Following is a select list of representative hits:

"Why Do Fools Fall in Love?" (Frankie Lymon and the Teenagers)
"In the Still of the Night" (Five Satins)
"Come Go with Me" (Dell-Vikings—a racially integrated group)
"Silhouettes" (Rays)
"Get a Job" (Silhouettes)
"The Book of Love" (Monotones)
"Little Darlin'" (Diamonds—a white group singing in a black "doo-wop" style)
"Come Softly to Me" (Fleetwoods)
"Since I Don't Have You" (Skyliners)
"I Only Have Eyes for You" (Flamingos)
"Tears on My Pillow" (Little Anthony and the Imperials)
"Blue Moon" (Marcells)
"A Thousand Miles Away" (Heartbeats)
"Daddy's Home" (Shep and the Limelites)

The Platters (*Source:* Michael Ochs Archive, Ltd.)

Notable exceptions to the one-shot syndrome were the Platters and the Coasters. Consisting of four males and one female, the Platters released a formidable string of hits, including the first duo-wop song to achieve number 1 status on the pop charts, "The Great Pretender." Other Platter hits include "Only You," "The Magic Touch," "My Prayer" (a remake of an earlier hit by the Ink Spots), "Twilight Time," and "Smoke Gets in Your Eyes." In a very different way, the Coasters also defied the one-shot syndrome. Their hits included "Searchin'," "Youngblood," "Yakety Yak," "Charlie Brown," "Along Came Jones," and "Poison Ivy." Whereas the Platters sang songs of romantic love in beautiful harmony, with the talented solo voice of Tony Williams soaring over the top, the Coasters took a humorous approach to teen life with a less polished sound and an emphasis on the spoken bass part (e.g., "Why's everybody always pickin' on me?" from "Charlie Brown").

## LITTLE RICHARD

The purest prototype of hard, mainstream rock was Little Richard. Elvis's multifaceted musical style included not only mainstream rock but also rockabilly and soft rock. But in Little Richard may be found, in one self-contained package, the embodiment of the type of mainstream rock that leads to the Rolling Stones, Jimi Hendrix, Alice Cooper, James Brown, David Bowie, and Prince, among others.

Although various accounts disagree about his actual birth date, his mother reports it as December 5, 1932. Born Richard Wayne Penniman, in Macon, Georgia, he was the third of twelve children. His father worked in the construction industry and "handled" moonshine (White, *Little Richard*, 1984, 3). Although a simple but sincere belief in God was a part of the Penniman household, Richard was recalcitrant and a troublemaker. This basic conflict between hell-raising and piety was to typify Richard's life and career. But more than that, this dichotomy is clearly manifested in the music. In his biography of Little Richard, Charles White notes that Richard "twice discarded super-stardom for the church, typifying the conflict between sacred and secular music which is built into the black culture" (White, *Little Richard*, 1984, xiii). A further conflict arose due to Richard's homosexuality. After leaving home at the age of fourteen, he learned a variety of styles, including pop, gospel, and R & B; his experiences ran from a traveling medicine show to black blues bands. Several early recordings led nowhere.

After his father was shot and killed outside of a local tavern, Richard became the main breadwinner of the family. He continued to play and sing throughout the South and even released several gospel-oriented R & B recordings for the Houston-based Peacock Records. Returning to the Georgia area, Richard started a new band and began listening to the music of Fats Domino, Chuck Berry, and Lloyd Price. At Price's suggestion, he sent an audition tape to Specialty Records in Los Angeles. After many months had elapsed, Specialty responded with a contract.

Specialty Records was a moderately successful gospel and R & B label. Its biggest success had been Lloyd Price's "Lawdy, Miss Clawdy" in 1952. Owner Art Rupe wanted "a big band sound expressed in a churchy way" (White, *Little Richard*, 1984, 44). As Specialty's producer Robert "Bumps" Blackwell said, he wanted "a gospel singer who could sing the blues" (White, *Little Richard*, 1984, 46). Blackwell had been involved in the early careers of Ray Charles and Quincy Jones. Now he was to supervise a recording session for Little Richard in New Orleans. After taping four rather uninspired songs by a somewhat intimidated Little Richard, the group broke for lunch. While at lunch, Richard went to a piano and launched into a raucous version of an off-color song called "Tutti Frutti." Blackwell knew it was what he wanted. He quickly got the local songwriter, Dorothy La Bostrie, to clean up the lyrics; they returned to the studio and in fifteen minutes had what was to become a rock-and-roll classic on tape.

The chorus of "Tutti Frutti" is a twelve-bar blues. The verses also follow the twelve-bar form, but with a modification in the third phrase to lead smoothly to the chorus. Added to Richard's pounding boogie-style piano is guitar, bass, tenor sax, baritone sax, and drums. Richard's shouting style and falsetto "woo's" set the style for many to follow. The musicians were professional recording session men from New Orleans who had also backed Fats Domino. The lyrics of the chorus are classics of 1950s nonsense:

Awop-Bop-a-Loo-Mop Alop Bam-Boom
Tutti Frutti, Aw Rootie; Tutti Frutti, Aw Rootie
Tutti Frutti, Aw Rootie; Tutti Frutti, Aw Rootie
Tutti Frutti, Aw Rootie, Awop-Bop-a-Loo-Mop Alop Bam-Boom

"Tutti Frutti" is the model for most of Little Richard's hits. The characteristics noted earlier apply in varying degrees to his other hits: "Long Tall Sally," "Slippin' and Slidin'," "Rip It Up," "Ready Teddy," "The Girl Can't Help It," "Lucille,"

"Jenny, Jenny," and "Good Golly Miss Molly." Although "Tutti Frutti" sold about 500,000 copies and appealed to both black and white teens, for some, Little Richard's style was a bit too raucous and noisy. In spite of its importance in the history of rock, "Tutti Frutti" rose only to number 21 on the pop charts (number 2 on the R & B charts). It was quickly covered by both Elvis Presley and Pat Boone, as was "Long Tall Sally." "Rip It Up," backed with "Ready Teddy," reached number 27 (number 1 on the R & B charts), and again both were covered by Presley (Buddy Holly also recorded "Rip It Up"). Although some teens preferred the cover versions, it is not true that the Presley, Holly, or Boone recordings overshadowed Little Richard's. In fact, only two of these covers reached the Top 40 (Boone's versions of "Tutti Frutti" and "Long Tall Sally").

Little Richard's performance style was frenetic. He sang, shouted, danced, gyrated, and sweated profusely. He became the symbol for wild, unrestrained rock and roll. The parallel between his performance style and his long-held ambition to be a preacher, exhorting his congregation into frenzied expressions of praise and self-confession, reminds us of the ironic link between the southern black religious experience and the Little Richard style of rock and roll. It is reported that participants in his postconcert orgies sometimes awakened to Richard's sincere readings of the Bible. This dichotomy ruptured in 1957, when he renounced his show business career and turned toward religion.

In fact, Richard gave Bible college a try and even married a young Washington, D.C., secretary named Ernestine Campbell. But neither the marriage nor the religious education lasted. He released several gospel albums and gradually found himself pulled back toward show business. In 1962, he launched his comeback with a tour of England. While in England he met two aspiring British rock groups: the Beatles and the Rolling Stones. Mick Jagger insightfully describes Richard's performance style as "hypnotic, like an evangelistic meeting where, for want of a better phrase, Richard is the disciple and the audience the flock that follows. I couldn't believe the power of Little Richard on stage. He was amazing" (White, *Little Richard*, 1984, 119). Back in the United States, Richard released songs on Specialty, Vee Jay, and Okeh Records, but these barely entered the Top 100.

By the late 1960s, Richard had slipped into a pattern of self-parody, complete with outrageous costumes, homosexual hype, and old rock and roll. His style had passed on, and this camp act seemed to be the only thing that worked. Through the early 1970s, he pursued his perpetual "comeback" but succeeded only in becoming hopelessly involved with drugs and alcohol. As a result of several personal tragedies, he once again abandoned his wild lifestyle and turned toward religion. His lifelong internal battle is revealed in the following remarks:

I felt that my singing was like . . . Billy Graham giving a message. I gave a message in song to help people . . . to know the way. There was always that little beam of light, of love. . . . I decided to come back and teach goodness in this business. To teach love, because music is the universal language. (White, *Little Richard*, 1984, 165)

My true belief about Rock 'n' Roll . . . is this: I believe this kind of music is demonic. I have seen the rock groups and the punk-rock people in this country. And some of their lyrics is demonic. They talk against God. . . . I believe that kind of music is driving people from Christ. It is contagious. (White, *Little Richard*, 1984, 197)

Little Richard (*Source:* Michael Ochs Archive, Ltd.)

Author Charles White's comments suggest similarities and contrasts between Richard's preaching style and his rock performance style.

> The immaculately suited figure of Richard Penniman strode down the aisle of the church. His build was that of an athlete. His face was that of a man nearer his twenties than his fifties. Could this be the posturing, flamboyant Little Richard of just three years before who dressed in gaudy satin jump-suits and garish, glittering robes? Who peacocked around the stage in pancake makeup, mascara, and a foot-high wig? Who threw his clothes into fighting audiences after reducing them to a frenzy with his mind-crunching Rock 'n' Roll?
>
> Yes. Those large flashing eyes that had mesmerized screaming audiences for more than twenty years were not dimmed at all. The charisma was still there. And above all, that magnificent voice was in better form than ever as it soared above the congregation singing the introductory hymn, "He Is Lord." (White, *Little Richard,* 1984, 203)

Perhaps Little Richard was not the King of Rock and Roll he claimed to be. But he was one of the most influential figures in rock history. He was egotistical, controversial, dynamic, original, and unpredictable. Although his influence would last as long as there was rock and roll, his own personal musical style was out of date. There would be no "comeback." Still, as he recalls his friends Elvis, Buddy Holly, Jimi Hendrix, Janis Joplin, Sam Cooke, and so many others, he can say, "I have God to thank that I'm a living legend and not a dead one" (White, *Little Richard,* 1984, 196).

## FATS DOMINO

Antoine "Fats" Domino (born on February 26, 1928, in New Orleans) represents an interesting contrast to Little Richard. Certainly there were similarities: Both were southern blacks who played piano and sang; both came from the R & B tradition; both became very popular rock-and-roll stars of the 1950s. Beyond those rather basic similarities, they were more different than alike.

Fats came from a musical family. He quit school at the age of fourteen to go to work as a factory worker by day and a club musician by night. Among his musical jobs, he played with a prominent New Orleans band headed by Dave Bartholomew. Bartholomew, local representative for Imperial Records, arranged for a recording session at the J&M studio (where Little Richard's "Tutti Frutti" session would take place five years later). Owner and chief engineer Cosimo Matassa was a master at creating the New Orleans R & B sound. From this session came Fats's first hit, "The Fat Man," released in 1950.

Before 1955 drew to a close, Fats had placed twelve hits on the Top 10 of the R & B charts, beginning with "The Fat Man" and including a number 1 hit, "Goin' Home" (1952). Fats changed very little of his successful R & B style as he was transformed into a rock-and-roll star of the mid- and late 1950s. Listening to that first hit, "The Fat Man," one quickly perceives the R & B lineage of 1950s rock and roll. His use of the falsetto voice is particularly interesting. Unlike Little Richard's occasional falsetto "woo's," Fats actually sings an entire sixteen-bar solo with falsetto "wah-wah's"—approximating the sound of a harmonica solo. The form of "The Fat Man" is that of an eight-bar blues (a modification of the traditional twelve-bar blues). Fats preferred the eight-bar forms even in his rock-and-roll songs. The instrumentation of "The Fat Man" is similar to the R & B-oriented rock band of the 1950s: saxes, guitar, bass, drums, and piano. Most noticeable, however, is the piano style. It is a boogie-woogie style piano that is less flamboyant and more refined than Little Richard's style.

Fats's first hit to cross over to the pop charts was "Ain't That a Shame." Released in 1955, it became number 1 on the R & B charts and rose to number 10 on the pop charts. A cover version by Pat Boone reached number 1 in September 1955. "Ain't That a Shame" is a twelve-bar blues, typical of R & B-oriented rock hits of the 1950s but an exception to Fats's usual eight-bar blues.

Subsequent Domino releases continued to do well on the R & B charts, and he placed more and more hits on the pop charts. The Domino sound was essentially unchanged in "I'm in Love Again" (1956), "Blueberry Hill"

Fats Domino (*Source:* Michael Ochs Archive, Ltd.)

(1956), "Blue Monday" (1956), "I'm Walkin'" (1957), "Whole Lotta Loving" (1958), and "I Want to Walk You Home" (1959).

Not all 1950s rock hits were newly composed. With hits rising and falling faster than ever before, there was a tremendous demand for material. A common practice was to resurrect old pop favorites from previous decades and recast them in the new rock style. This usually involved adding a rock bass line and a recognizable rock beat. Fats Domino was particularly successful at this. "Blueberry Hill," for example, had been popularized back in the 1940s by white big bands. "My Blue Heaven" (1956) is even older, dating back to 1927. These Tin Pan Alley songs conform to the thirty-two-bar pop song form, with four phrases of eight bars each.

Near the end of the 1950s, many people, including performers and recording company executives, assumed that rock and roll was a fad and would not last. A particular concern was that a performer would be narrowly "typed" as a rock-and-roll performer only; when the fad died, the star would die with it, leaving the recording company stuck with an anachronistic "has-been." To counter this possibility, some performers attempted to move toward a pop style in hopes of establishing themselves as "legitimate" artists capable of continued appeal after rock disappeared and pop music settled back into "business as usual." The continued appeal of Elvis Presley in a variety of styles seemed to confirm this strategy.

By 1960 the typical mainstream rock-and-roll style was indeed beginning to fade. Fats's hits were becoming less frequent. The sound of "Walking to New Orleans," released in 1960, was pop oriented. Strings were added; the old boogie-woogie rock piano disappeared; there were no rocking saxophone solos. The lyrics seemed to be an attempt to elicit a nostalgic reaction from the listener by referring to earlier hits ("Ain't That a Shame," "I'm Walkin'," and "I Want to Walk You Home"). "Walkin' to New Orleans" proved to be Fats's last Top 10 hit. Except for a minor hit in 1968 (the Beatles' "Lady Madonna"), Fats's career after the early 1960s revolved around nostalgia tours and Las Vegas appearances.

Fats Domino's style was less flamboyant, less hysterical, and less threatening than the pounding, raucous style of Little Richard. Fats seemed more refined and controlled. He actually sat on a piano bench, playing and singing his repertoire without the histrionics of Little Richard or Jerry Lee Lewis. As one surveys 1950s rock from the vantage point of history, Fats's music seems uncomplicated and enjoyable and his lifestyle rather free from controversy and trauma. He remains a lovable reminder of less troubled times.

## CHUCK BERRY

Electric guitar has become the central instrumental ingredient in rock and roll. Out of the "big six" of 1950s rock (Presley, Richard, Lewis, Holly, Berry, and Domino), it is surely Chuck Berry whose influence was most strongly felt on rock guitar styles until the appearance of Jimi Hendrix a decade later.

Charles Edward Anderson Berry was born in St. Louis in 1926. He sang in the Baptist church choir and learned to play guitar while in high school. His roots were squarely in the black R & B tradition, although he was not from the South, as were Little Richard and Fats Domino. After spending three years in reform school for attempted robbery, he worked for a time in local R & B clubs and in the General

Motors plant (a parallel to Fats Domino's situation) in order to support a wife and two children.

While playing at the local Cosmopolitan Club, the Chuck Berry Trio was heard by famed bluesman Muddy Waters, who suggested that the group go to Chicago and audition for Chess Records. Leonard and Phil Chess's record company was an independent company, not unlike Imperial, Specialty, and Sun. Chess and its subsidiary Checker had recorded some of the biggest names in R & B (Muddy Waters, Howlin' Wolf, Jimmie Rodgers, Sonny Boy Williamson), as well as the new rock and rollers (Bo Diddley, Dale Hawkins, the Moonglows, the Flamingos). Chess was also well connected to influential disc jockey Alan Freed, who was willing to promote R & B music and black rock and rollers.

Berry's group auditioned with a song named "Ida Red," actually a C & W song made popular by Bob Wills and His Texas Playboys. Leonard Chess renamed the song, modified the lyrics, and issued it as "Maybelline." In return for the consideration of being listed as coauthor, Alan Freed agreed to promote the record. By subsequent Chuck Berry standards, "Maybelline" is rather basic and unimpressive, both from musical and technical production perspectives. Nevertheless, with Freed's help it hit the charts in 1955, eventually rising to number 5 (number 1 on the R & B charts).

After several intervening hits, Chuck made the pop charts again with "Roll Over Beethoven" (1956). "Too Much Monkey Business" and "Brown-Eyed Handsome Man" achieved R & B success in 1957 before "School Days," "Rock and Roll Music," "Sweet Little Sixteen," and "Johnny B. Goode" all landed in the Top 10 in 1957 and 1958. Subsequent hits in the 1950s ("Carol," "Sweet Little Rock and Roll," "Almost Grown," and "Back in the U.S.A.") placed more toward the middle of the Top 100.

In late 1959, Berry was arrested for violation of the Mann Act. He had picked up a fourteen-year-old girl in El Paso who worked as a waitress and prostitute. She joined his tour, traveling through New Mexico, Arizona, Colorado, and Missouri.

Reaching St. Louis, Chuck put the girl to work as a hatcheck girl in his club. Shortly thereafter, he fired her and presumably sent her home. Instead she filed a complaint with the police. Berry was convicted in a 1960 trial, but the conviction was overturned on appeal. A second trial resulted in a three-year sentence and a fine. He was eventually released in 1964 (White, *Rock Stars*, 1984, 42–44).

After his release, Berry managed several hits, including "No Particular Place to Go" (number 10, 1964). Remarkably he had his only number 1 pop chart hit ("My Ding-a-Ling") in 1972, at the age of forty-six.

Chuck Berry (*Source:* Michael Ochs Archive, Ltd.)

Like Domino, Berry stopped short of Little Richard's shouting style. His enunciation is generally clearer than most blues-oriented singers, even though it retains a recognizable black quality. Berry's friend Johnny Johnson adds an effective piano style to many Berry recordings (e.g., listen carefully to "Sweet Little Sixteen," "Almost Grown," "Johnny B. Goode," "Back in the U.S.A.," "Rock and Roll Music," and "Reelin' and Rockin' "). Berry's lyrics speak to the newly emerging teen society about the everyday concerns of their lives: cars, girls, school, rock music, and the problems of growing up. Frequently the songs develop a story or idea ("School Days" and "Johnny B. Goode").

Generally, Berry's lyrics are far superior to the "walk-talk" and "arms-charms" clichés and nonsense syllables of many 1950s rock songs. "School Days" is a particularly good example. It moves through the typical teenager's day, including getting up and going to school, lunch time, the classroom experience, dismissal, and the after school, malt shop social. The feeling is one of understanding and support—as if Chuck were putting his arm around the teenager and saying, "Yeah, life can be a drag sometimes, but we all get through it okay! Hang in there!"

But Berry's biggest contribution was setting the model for the rock-and-roll guitar style. For him, the guitar was more than an accompanying prop hanging off his shoulders. It was a frontline instrument, often on a par with the lead vocal. Notice the alternation of voice and guitar in the chorus of "Johnny B. Goode," and also in "School Days" and "No Particular Place to Go." The statement-and-answer technique in which the guitar mimics the just-completed vocal line is related to the two-bar or four-bar "trade-offs" found in jazz. It is as if Berry and his guitar are doing a duet.

Several of Berry's guitar introductions became famous per se and were widely imitated. Compare the intros to "Back in the U.S.A.," "Roll Over Beethoven," and "Johnny B. Goode." The double note playing in his solos, the alternating chords of his rhythmic accompaniments (similar to some rock piano styles) set models to be followed for years.

Most of Berry's rock hits were in the standard twelve-bar blues form. His stage act was not as hysterical as Little Richard's, but it was more animated than Fats Domino's. Even though he was the oldest of the major rock stars of the 1950s, he developed his famous "duck walk" across the stage. Unlike some other 1950s rock stars, Berry never modified his style to appeal to a broader "legitimate" pop audience. Throughout his career, he stayed with the style that made him one of the biggest stars of rock and roll.

## JERRY LEE LEWIS

Jerry Lee Lewis is the white counterpart to Little Richard. As one compares their lives and musical styles, one perceives an uncanny number of parallels and relatively few differences. Like Richard, Jerry Lee was born into a rather poor family in a small southern town (Ferriday, Louisiana). In both cases, the mother was the dominant influence, the father's influence being negated due to complications resulting from bootleg whiskey transactions. Whereas Bud Penniman was shot outside of a tavern, Elmo Lewis was incarcerated while Jerry Lee was a young child. Both Jerry Lee and Little Richard endured an ongoing internal battle between their religious faith and their hell-raising rock-and-roll lifestyles. Like Little Richard, Jerry Lee's career as a rock-and-roll hit maker ended prematurely, although it was not a voluntary interruption as was Richard's. A primary difference was that many of Jerry Lee's problems resulted from his active heterosexuality—quite the opposite of Richard's sexual lifestyle.

Musically there were also many similarities. Both were pianists and were heavily influenced by gospel music and black R & B. Young Jerry Lee and his cousin Jimmy Lee Swaggart attended evangelist meetings conducted by musician/preacher Brother Janway, whose piano style included a pounding bass line and simple right-hand melodies (Lewis 1982, 15). But Jerry Lee was also captivated by the R & B musicians, including B. B. King and Muddy Waters, who played at Haney's Big House in the Chocolate Quarters of Ferriday (Lewis 1982, 15). In their mature rock-and-roll style, both Lewis and Richard played twelve-bar blues with pounding, boogie-derived bass lines and improvised right-hand figures, including glissandi, repeating chords, and boogie patterns. They were best in hard, fast, rocking songs; their performance styles were flamboyant, including lots of physical movement while playing the keyboard in every imaginable position.

Jerry's marital escapades (which would finally have a major effect on his career) began in 1951, when he married a preacher's daughter named Dorothy. She was seventeen and in the eleventh grade; Jerry was sixteen and in the eighth grade (he had been repeatedly held back in the seventh grade). To assuage parental objections, Jerry enrolled in Southwestern Bible Institute (Waxahachie, Texas) with the goal of becoming a preacher. In a matter of months, Dorothy filed for divorce and Jerry Lee was invited to leave the Institute.

Having found a new love named Jane Mitcham (a high school junior), Jerry remarried before the divorce from Dorothy was finalized. Such disregard for the finer points of the law (and his preference for younger women) would eventually contribute to Jerry's downfall. The marriage to Jane was a rough one. After several years, the marriage had deteriorated to the point of no return.

While visiting his cousin Jay Brown, Jerry met Myra Gail, Jay's twelve-year-old daughter. Something more than a family relationship developed, and in September 1957, Jerry filed for a divorce from Jane. A bitter battle ensued during which it was revealed that the legality of Jerry's second marriage was questionable, owing to his failure to properly divorce Dorothy. To Jerry it seemed unnecessary to legally end a marriage that probably never even existed legally. So he dropped his legal action against Jane and in December 1957 married Myra Gail.

In 1956, while Jerry was still married to Jane, Jay Brown (Jerry's older cousin, bass player, and soon-to-be father-in-law) persuaded Jerry to come to his home in Memphis and visit Sam Phillips's Sun Records. After Sam's success with Elvis Presley (not to mention Carl Perkins, Johnny Cash, Roy Orbison, and Conway Twitty), almost any aspiring young southern rock and roller figured that the path to fame and fortune began at Sam Phillips's front door. Jerry Lee had tried Sun Records once before but had left with a "don't-call-us-we'll-call-you" answer.

This time things turned out better. Jerry Lee recorded "Crazy Arms" and several other country songs. Phillips was impressed and signed Jerry Lee to a contract. Late in 1956, Sun released "Crazy Arms," and it became a mild success. It was on December 4 of that year that the so-called "Million Dollar Quartet" met, rather by accident, at the Sun studios. Jerry Lee had gone to the studio to meet Carl Perkins, but as he entered the studio, he heard a familiar voice singing "Blueberry Hill." It was Elvis Presley, accompanying himself on piano. Shortly, the three were joined by Johnny Cash. The four played and sang a series of church songs and gospel hits before breaking up to go their separate ways.

Sun Records saw Jerry as another rockabilly star, but Jerry had other ideas. A pounding mainstream rock-and-roll song called "Whole Lot of Shakin' Going On" had been particularly successful on his most recent tour. Jerry's recording of "Whole Lot of Shakin'," a cover version of a song released two years earlier by the Commodores, became a smash hit in 1957, reaching the top position on both the C & W and R & B charts and number 3 on the pop charts.

In late 1957, Sun Records released "Great Balls of Fire," written by Jack Hammer and Otis Blackwell. The flip side was Hank Williams's country tune "You Win Again." Blackwell had written several major hits for Elvis Presley ("Don't Be Cruel" and "All Shook Up") and Little Richard ("Good Golly Miss Molly"). Aided by an appearance on Steve Allen's show and a promotional film called *Jamboree,* Jerry Lee reached the number 2 spot on the pop charts with "Great Balls of Fire" (number 3 on the R & B charts and number 1 on the C & W charts). Blackwell also wrote Jerry Lee's third major hit, "Breathless," released in February 1958, shortly after Jerry's marriage to Myra. His last major hit was "High School Confidential," the title song from an MGM movie in which the Jerry Lee Lewis Trio made a cameo appearance.

Sun's Million Dollar Quarter—Jerry Lee Lewis, Carl Perkins. Johnny Cash, and Elvis Presley (*Source:* Michael Ochs Archive. Ltd.)

Jerry Lee Lewis (*Source:* Michael Ochs Archive, Ltd.)

"Whole Lot of Shakin' Going On" and "Great Balls of Fire" had been Top 10 hits in England. Thus, Jerry embarked on his first overseas tour to the mother country, where his arrival was enthusiastically anticipated. Against better advice, he took his new thirteen-year-old bride (and cousin) along. No sooner had the entourage disembarked than an inquisitive reporter discovered Myra. A subsequent interview with the loving couple gave the reporter all he needed. Headlines screamed the news of Jerry Lee's child bride. The British were outraged. Some tour dates were canceled; others were played to half-empty halls and to jeering, taunting audiences. An editorial in the *Daily Sketch* suggested that "there is a limit to the amount of private misbehavior which the public will put up with in performers' private lives" (Lewis 1982, 177). One can only speculate as to the editor's reaction to the antics of the Rolling Stones and other British rock groups just a few years later.

Jerry Lee, staggered by the British reaction, expected more tolerance upon his return to the United States. However, he met with a similar response. "High School Confidential" quickly dropped from the charts, and many concerts were canceled. Jerry Lee's days as a rock-and-roll star were over. Repeated "comebacks" failed; he returned to the C & W sound from whence he had come. Between 1961 and 1975, he placed over twenty songs on the country charts, including eleven in the Top 5.

Post-rock-and-roll life has not been kind to Jerry Lee. His marriage to Myra ended in divorce in 1970 (Jerry has had three more marriages since then). Two of his sons died tragically, as did two of his wives. There have been problems with alcohol, drugs, tax evasion, shootings, fist fights, automobile wrecks, arrests, extramarital affairs, and debilitating physical illness.

Jerry Lee Lewis, in his brief moment of stardom, had a disproportionate impact on rock and roll. His unique blend of C & W and R & B, and his piano style, vocal style, and lifestyle, influenced many of his contemporaries and many who would follow. Although he longed to be known as the King of Rock and Roll, he must settle for his lifelong nickname: the Killer.

## BUDDY HOLLY

Charles Hardin (Buddy) Holley did not fit the mold of the other early rock and rollers. Born in Lubbock, Texas, in 1936, his musical background was almost exclusively C & W oriented. Black R & B and gospel were not significant factors in the culture of western Texas, so Buddy grew up without the biracial musical influences that characterized Elvis's and Jerry Lee's backgrounds.

His country-style band signed a contract with Decca Records and during 1956 released several straight country songs, including an early version of "That'll Be the Day." None was successful, and Decca released Buddy from his contract.

In early 1957, Buddy and his band (the Crickets) journeyed to the Clovis, New Mexico, recording studio owned by Norman Petty. Among the songs recorded at that session was a punched-up version of "That'll Be the Day." Petty took the demo tape to New York where, after several rejections, it was accepted by the Coral–Brunswick label. Holley's Decca contract had inadvertently dropped the "e" from his name; Buddy retained the misspelling as his professional name. Petty became Holly's manager, and the Crickets' personnel and instrumentation solidified: Niki Sullivan on guitar; Joe Mauldin on acoustic bass; Jerry Allison on drums; and, of course, Holly on guitar.

By August 1957, "That'll Be the Day" had risen to number 1. In the next year and a half, Holly and the Crickets released eight more singles, including "Peggy Sue," "Oh Boy!" "Maybe Baby," "Rave On," "Think It Over," "Early in the Morning," and "Heartbeat." Because separate contracts had been signed, some of these songs were released under the name of Holly on the Coral label, and some were released under the name of the Crickets on Brunswick.

In the summer of 1958, Buddy married Maria Elena Santiago, a Puerto Rican girl from New York. Supposedly at her suggestion, questions arose regarding Norman Petty's handling of Buddy and the band, especially concerning Petty's listing as coauthor of several Holly songs. Finally in late 1958, Holly split from both Petty and the Crickets. He recruited new sidemen, planned a tour, and initiated a recording session. The recording session was oriented toward a soft rock sound, utilizing the Dick Jacobs orchestra. Before this new Holly sound had a chance to be released, Buddy's new quartet (including bassist Waylon Jennings) set out on a tour with Dion and the Belmonts, Ritchie Valens, and the Big Bopper (J. P. Richardson). Following a concert at Clear Lake, Iowa, on February 2, 1959, Holly, Valens, and Richardson were killed in a plane crash in the wee hours of the next morning. Coral subsequently released a song from that last pop-oriented recording session—a Paul Anka tune with the ironic title "It Doesn't Matter Anymore." It rose to number 13 and was, of course, Holly's last hit.

Buddy Holly was different from the other 1950s rock pioneers. R & B was not really a significant factor in his musical background. The R & B influence upon his essentially C & W sound apparently came secondhand through his idol, Elvis Presley. Buddy did not look like most 1950s rock stars. He was tall and thin, wore thick horn-rimmed glasses, and typically performed in a dark suit and bow tie. He emanated none of the sexuality of Presley or the flamboyance of Little Richard or Jerry Lee Lewis.

Like Chuck Berry, vocalist/guitarist Holly wrote most of his own material, thus helping to establish a trend that would characterize the rock of the following decades. His instrumental lineup was also forward-looking, consisting of lead guitar, rhythm guitar, bass, and drums—a basic rock instrumentation for years to come. Unlike most other early rock and rollers, Holly pursued a more conservative lifestyle. He was not known as a drinker, womanizer, or druggie. In many ways, he was less

Buddy Holly with Jerry Allison (left) and Joe Mauldin (center) (*Source:* Michael Ochs Archive, Ltd.)

like the typical rock-and roll sex symbol and more like the average middle-American teenager of the 1950s. His lyrics were almost exclusively about uncomplicated boy/girl romance. Again, somewhat like Chuck Berry, they reflect the rather innocent, fun-loving, teenage lifestyle of the 1950s, uncluttered by the sexual undertones typical of Presley, Lewis, and Little Richard, and the social heaviness and angry rebellion of later rock.

Holly's serious approach to his music also led him into the world of production and technology, such as it was in 1957 and 1958. He experimented with double tracking his voice and guitar ("Words of Love") and paid close attention to the technical side of his recordings. His turn toward a softer sound in his last recording sessions has prompted much speculation. Holly's late 1958 releases had not fared particularly well; thus it is possible that he was attempting to broaden his reputation from that of a narrow rock and roller to that of a legitimate pop artist (recall Fats Domino's similar turn about one year later with "Walkin' to New Orleans").

No discussion of Buddy Holly would be complete without mentioning his unique vocal characteristics. Holly's "hiccup" style (technically, the glottal stop) is derived most directly from Elvis Presley, who frequently transformed one syllable into at least two (for example, in Presley's "Mystery Train," listen to "comin' rou-ound the li-ine"). Holly carries such divisions to new heights with his treatment of "my

Pe-eggy Su-ue-ue-ue-ue-e-ue-ue" and the words "over you-e-ou" in "It Doesn't Matter Anymore." Another Holly trademark is his habit of changing the color (or timbre) of his voice in midphrase. At times he sings in a dark, husky, Presley-like voice; then gradually he changes to a thin, almost effeminate sound. This progression is very noticeable in the lines, "There's no use in me a cryin', I've done everything and now I'm sick of tryin'" in "It Doesn't Matter Anymore." The thin voice changing to the more normal voice is evident in sections of "Peggy Sue." It is almost as if Holly is running his voice through an electronic filter without the aid of a filter!

Perhaps because he was the first rock star to die suddenly and unexpectedly, an almost cultlike following emerged for Buddy Holly. Certainly Don McLean's song "American Pie," with its reference to "the day the music died," enhanced the Buddy Holly mystique. In 1959, rock and roll was a vital, dynamic new force, and its proponents were young, vigorous, and invested with the assumed immortality of youth. The shock of Holly's death was exaggerated by its lack of precedence. A very real pall was cast over the new rock-and-roll generation for weeks and months after his death. It was the first rock-and-roll death; it was far from the last.

## OTHERS IN THE 1950S

Between July 1955 and December 1960 there were 81 number 1 hits. Of these, only sixteen were recorded by the major artists discussed in Chapters 3 and 4 (Haley, Presley, Lewis, Holly, Domino, Berry, and Little Richard). In fact, fourteen of those sixteen were by Elvis Presley (the others were by Bill Haley and Buddy Holly). Together, Lewis, Holly, Domino, Berry, and Little Richard placed only twenty-five hits in the Top 10, from 1955 through 1960. This means that there were a host of other performers providing hits for the charts in the last half of the 1950s. In this section we will survey some of the other aspects of the 1950s music scene, pointing out some of the more significant artists.

### R & B- and Gospel-Derived Rock

Several artists whose background lay in R & B or gospel found success in the late 1950s. Lloyd Price had enjoyed several R & B hits in the early 1950s, including the crossover hit "Lawdy Miss Clawdy." With relatively little change in style, he moved into the rock market with songs such as "Stagger Lee" (1959) and somewhat softer hits such as "Personality" and "I'm Gonna Get Married."

Ray Charles started as a jazz crooner in the style of Nat "King" Cole; but through the

Ray Charles (*Source:* Michael Ochs Archive, Ltd.)

Sam Cooke (*Source:* Michael Ochs Archive, Ltd.)

early 1950s, his style reflected more R & B influences. In 1955, he added a strong gospel element in "I Got a Woman." An unrestrained, emotional vocal delivery over a pounding, rocking accompaniment characterized this and later R & B hits. Charles finally crossed over to the national pop charts in 1959 with the classic "What'd I Say," his first million seller. Between 1959 and 1963, he placed nine more songs in the Top 10, including the C & W-oriented "I Can't Stop Loving You." Ray Charles died in 2004 at the age of 73.

The blending of gospel and blues is also evident in the style of Sam Cooke. In the early 1950s, Cooke was the lead singer with the Soul Stirrers, a popular black gospel group. His crossover to the pop market came in 1957 with "You Send Me" (number 1). The combination of the softer sound with the gospel-flavored vocal had enormous appeal. The extended vocal melismas (extending one syllable over many notes) and the soulful interpolations on "I know, I know, I know" and "whoa-oh-oh-and-whoa-oh-oh-oh" seemed like a whole new world to white fans of soft rock. Cooke's voice was emotional, but not raspy and raucous. Follow-up hits included "For Sentimental Reasons," "Only Sixteen," "Wonderful World," "Chain Gang," and "Twistin' the Night Away." Sam Cooke died in 1964 from gunshot wounds.

## Rockabilly

The importance of Sun Records in Memphis in the early development of the rockabilly style has already been mentioned. Carl Perkins, Elvis Presley, and Jerry Lee Lewis were all products of Sun Records. Another early hit maker for Sun Records was Johnny Cash. Cash was born in 1932 in Arkansas, and his first release, "Cry, Cry, Cry," was a moderate country hit. In 1956, however, "I Walk the Line" rose to number 17 on the national charts. Cash's low voice and decidedly country-style delivery set him apart from the more R & B-influenced rockabillies. Following several more Top 20 hits, Cash moved to Columbia Records, where he continued to score Top 40 hits, including "Ring of Fire" (1963) and "A Boy Named Sue" (1969). He died on September 12, 2003 at the age of 71.

In addition to those already mentioned, many other rockabillies enjoyed brief moments in the limelight, only to fade after a few hits. The following list summarizes some of them:

| Gene Vincent | "Be-Bop-a-Lula" (1956) |
|---|---|
| Guy Mitchell | "Singing the Blues" (1956) |
| | "Heartaches by the Number" (1959) |
| Marty Robbins | "A White Sport Coat" (1957) |
| | "El Paso" (1960) |
| Buddy Knox | "Party Doll" (1957) |
| Eddie Cochran (died, 1960) | "Summertime Blues" (1958) |
| Conway Twitty | "It's Only Make Believe" (1958) |
| Johnny Horton (died, 1960) | "The Battle of New Orleans" (1959) |
| | "Sink the Bismarck" (1960) |
| | "North to Alaska" (1960) |

## Soft Rock

One of the most talented young singer/songwriters of the 1950s was Paul Anka, a Canadian whose first hit "Diana" came in 1957 when he was only sixteen years old. From 1958 through 1960, Anka had six more Top 10 songs, including "Lonely Boy" and "Put Your Head on My Shoulder." He continued to produce hits through the 1960s and 1970s, including a number 1 hit in 1974 "(You're) Having My Baby." He also composed "My Way"—a hit for both Frank Sinatra and Elvis Presley.

Bobby Darin (born Walden Robert Cassotto) produced his first hit "Splish Splash" on Atco Records, a subsidiary of Atlantic Records, in 1958. Starting with this genuine rock sound (even affecting something of black enunciation), Darin gradually softened his style in later hits. "Dream Lover" (1959) and subsequent hits such as "Mack the Knife," "Beyond the Sea," "Clementine," and "Won't You Come Home Bill Bailey" are closer to a swinging pop style. In 1973, he died of a heart condition at the age of thirty-seven.

Philadelphia was to become a center for the handsome-male-teen-idol syndrome. With the national publicity afforded by Dick Clark's American Bandstand television show, a number of young Philadelphians achieved major success. Typical of these smooth young singers was Frankie Avalon. Chancellor Records, a Philadelphia company, persevered through several flops with Avalon until "Dede Dinah" (1958), a cute, upbeat tune that rose to number 7. The eighteen-year-old Avalon followed with several modest hits before hitting number 1 with "Venus." Although Avalon's songs were aimed at, and consumed by, a young audience, they were very pop oriented, bearing little or no relationship to rock and roll. Other teen idols from Philadelphia and elsewhere followed Avalon's success:

| Tommy Sands (Houston) | "Teen-Age Crush" (1957) |
|---|---|
| Fabian (Philadelphia) | "Turn Me Loose" (1959) |
| | "Tiger" (1959) |
| Neil Sedaka (Brooklyn) | "Calendar Girl" (1960/1961) |
| | "Breaking Up Is Hard to Do" (1962) |

| Bobby Rydell (Philadelphia) | "Wild One" (1960) |
| | "Swingin' School" (1960) |
| | "Volare" (1960) |
| Mark Dinning (Grant County, Okla.) | "Teen Angel" (1960) |
| Bobby Vee (Fargo, N.D.) | "Devil or Angel" (1960) |
| | "Rubber Ball" (1960/1961) |
| | "Take Good Care of My Baby" (1961) |
| | "Run to Him" (1961) |
| Bobby Vinton (Canonsburg, Penn.) | "Roses Are Red" (My Love) (1962) |
| | "Blue on Blue" (1963) |
| | "Blue Velvet" (1963) |
| | "There! I've Said It Again" (1963) |
| | "Mr. Lonely" (1964) |

White vocal groups ranged from the rock-oriented style of Danny and the Juniors and Dion and the Belmonts to the pop-style sounds of the Teddy Bears ("To Know Him Is to Love Him"), the Fleetwoods ("Come Softly to Me" and "Mr. Blue"), and the Browns ("The Three Bells"). The Philadelphia group Danny and the Juniors' song "At the Hop" reached number 1 in early 1958 and has become a rock-and-roll

Teen Idols—Fabian, Tommy Sands, Paul Anka, Bobby Darin, and Frankie Avalon (*Source:* Michael Ochs Archive, Ltd.)

Johnny Mathis (*Source:* Michael Ochs Archive, Ltd.)

classic. Their follow-up hit, "Rock and Roll Is Here to Stay," made the top 20 and continues to be a rock-and-roll anthem. Somewhat softer than Danny and the Juniors were Dion and the Belmonts. Dion DiMucci and his three friends came from the Bronx and made several modest hits before releasing "A Teenager in Love" in 1959. The follow-up "Where or When" (1960) moved to a softer pop sound. Dion himself achieved several major hits in the early 1960s, most notably "Runaround Sue," a number 1 hit in 1961.

Among the most popular black solo singers were Johnny Mathis and Tommy Edwards. Stylistically a pop crooner, Mathis was recognized for his flawlessly expressive voice and remarkable range. In 1957, Mathis released four ballads that reached the Top 20, including the number 1 hit "Chances Are." The unprecedented success of his *Greatest Hits* album (1958) started a trend for collected hits albums; it remained on the *Billboard* album charts for some 490 weeks (that's almost ten years!).

Tommy Edwards was somewhat older than the typical late-1950s pop star. When "It's All in the Game" reached number 1 in 1958, Edwards was thirty-six years old. This song (music written by Charles Dawes, vice president under Calvin Coolidge) had been released originally in 1951, at which time it had risen to number 18. From 1958 through 1960, Edwards placed five more songs in the Top 40.

Female singers were rather rare in the late 1950s rock scene. Those who did achieve success did so in the soft rock style. Connie Francis (Concetta Franconero) produced a remarkable list of some thirty-five Top 40 songs from 1958 through 1964. Her style ranged from cute, up-tempo songs ("Stupid Cupid" of 1958 and "Lipstick on Your Collar" of 1959) to soft rock ("Who's Sorry Now" of 1958), to a pure pop style ("Where the Boys Are" of 1961).

Brenda Lee (Brenda Mae Tarpley) came from a C & W musical background and was only eleven years old when she signed a contract with Decca Records. After several modest hits in 1956 and 1957, she gained national attention with "Sweet Nothin's" (number 4, early 1960) and "I'm Sorry" (number 1). Brenda continued to place occasional songs in the Top 10 through the early 1960s.

**Instrumental Groups**

Although singers have dominated the rock scene, the purely instrumental song has enjoyed constant, though infrequent, popularity. Typically, a group would achieve major chart success with a particularly catchy instrumental, then fade from view. The public apparently finds it easier to identify and become attached to a vocalist than to recognize the stylings of an instrumentalist. Certainly the verbal appeal of a song lyric is more direct than the more subtle appeal of purely instrumental music.

One of the first successful rock instrumentals was "Honky Tonk" (1956), by Bill Doggett, a jazz and R & B player from the 1930s and 1940s (born in 1916). The hard blues and boogie-derived sound of "Honky Tonk" featured a honking saxophone lead similar to Rudy Pompilli's sound on "Rock Around the Clock"; it was an exciting "new" sound to the rock-and-roll-infatuated teenagers of 1956. A similar sound was produced in 1957 with "Raunchy" by Bill Justis, a studio musician and producer for Sun Records. His growling, gutsy saxophone lead sounded like the title of the song—"Raunchy." Another instrumental featuring a "dirty" saxophone lead became a number 1 hit in 1958: "Tequila" by the Champs. It featured a "hook" that consisted of the spoken song title.

Inevitably, the instrumental was bound to focus on the electric guitar. Two such instrumentals achieved major success in 1958: "Rumble" by Link Wray (number 16) and "Rebel-Rouser" by Duane Eddy (number 6). Eddy broke the pattern in several ways. He was a handsome youngster (barely twenty years old) who managed to achieve a series of hits. His "twangy" guitar sound was recognizable and widely imitated. Among his fifteen Top 40 hits were two other Top 10 hits: "Forty Miles of Bad Road" (1959) and "Because They're Young" (1960). Table 4–1 shows other instrumentals that gained popularity in the late 1950s and early 1960s.

**Novelties**

Throughout the history of popular music there have appeared musical oddities known as novelty songs. Usually humorous or whimsical songs with a catchy musical or lyrical hook, these songs are sometimes in the prevailing popular style, but more often they run counter to it, thus offering a simple relief from the norm. In other cases they are so bad, they are good. Novelties frequently have a sort of "camp" appeal—meaning that they are so out of the prevailing style that they catch on. It is almost impossible to predetermine the success of a novelty song. They seem to happen by accident, unpredictably catching the public's fancy.

| | Table 4–1 | |
|---|---|---|
| **Song** | **Performer** | **Featured Instrument** |
| "Rawhide" | Link Wray | guitar |
| "Crossfire" | Johnny and the Hurricanes | guitar |
| "Red River Rock" | | guitar |
| "Walk Don't Run" | Ventures | guitar |
| "Sleep Walk" | Santo and Johnny | guitar |
| "Topsy II" | Cozy Cole | drums |
| "White Silver Sands" | Bill Black Combo | piano |
| "The Happy Organ" | Dave "Baby" Cortez | organ |
| "Last Date" | Floyd Cramer | piano |
| "On the Rebound" | | piano |
| "San Antonio Rose" | | piano |

**Table 4–2**

| Song | Chart Position | Comments |
|---|---|---|
| "The Purple People Eater" (Sheb Wooley) | No. 1, 1958 | Hook: "a one-eyed, one-horned, flying purple people eater" (using speeded-up voice). |
| "Itsy Bitsy Teenie Weenie Yellow Polka-Dot Bikini" (Brian Hyland) | No. 1, 1960 | Seemingly risqué lyric; hook line reveals girl in bikini is only two years old. |
| "Alley-Oop" (Hollywood Argyles) | No. 1, 1960 | Nasal, off-key vocal tells of comic-strip caveman; "so-bad-it's-good" category. |
| "Ahab the Arab" (Ray Stevens) | No. 5, 1962 | Another "so-bad-it's good" song. |
| "The Monster Mash" (Bobby [Boris] Pickett and the Crypt-Kickers) | No. 1, 1962 | Ditto. A parody of TV monster shows and the dance craze. |

The 1950s had the normal dosage of novelty songs. Typically, the popularity of such songs is short-lived and their creators rarely produce subsequent titles. An exception to this rule is David Seville (born Ross Bagdasarian). Seville hit the charts first in April 1958 with "Witch Doctor," a humorous song with a catchy nonsense hook: "Oo-ee, oo-ah-ah, ting-tang, walla-walla bing-bang." The novel sound of the human voice speeded up on tape (as used in "Witch Doctor") inspired Seville to create "The Chipmunk Song" later that year. In this number 1 hit, Seville used a speeded-up vocal trio for his three little characters, whose popularity continued into the 1980s, even after his death in 1972.

Most other novelty hits and artists enjoyed nothing close to the longevity of the Chipmunks' appeal. Table 4–2 shows some of the successful novelty hits of the 1950s and early 1960s.

## THE INDUSTRY

The rock revolution of the mid-1950s was more than a musical revolution. The popular music industry, which had followed rather well-entrenched, comfortable practices for decades, was literally turned upside down. The Big Five recording companies went from producing forty-two of 1954's top fifty recordings to only seventeen of 1956's top fifty. This is a drop of 60 percent in two years. The other thirty-three top discs of 1956 were released by twenty-five different companies. A well-controlled, orderly, and predictable market had become chaotic.

The music publishing industry was also in turmoil. With the coming of rock and roll, sheet music sales dropped dramatically. In the older pop music tradition, published sheet music was an important aspect of any song's popularity. But the rock and rollers of the mid-1950s were teenagers, the vast majority of whom played by ear. They simply listened to the record and imitated it. Rock and roll grew primarily from the aural tradition of R & B and C & W, not from the written tradition of pop and Tin Pan Alley.

Furthermore, sheet music did not accurately reflect the sound of the recorded song. With earlier sheet music, the written melody, chords, and rhythms were a simplified but reasonably accurate approximation of the recorded version. But the printed page could not begin to approximate the real sounds of Presley, Little Richard, or Jerry Lee Lewis. Finally, there was also the problem of the short-lived rock hit. By the time it became clear that a given rock song was headed for popularity, it was too late to print, distribute, and sell ample copies before the song's popularity had peaked and it faded into oblivion. This trend away from published sheet music is evident from *Variety*'s Sheet Music Best Seller lists. In 1955 and 1956, most of the popular recordings were not even on the *Variety* lists.

The effects of the rock revolution were also felt throughout the rest of the music industry. Established singers, instrumentalists, arrangers, orchestrators, copyists, and conductors found themselves out of the mainstream, with reduced demand for their talents. Much is often said about society's protests against early rock and roll on religious, moral, musical, and racial grounds. But it is often overlooked that one of the earliest and strongest reactions against rock and roll came from the established music industry itself. *Variety* magazine, the entertainment world's trade journal, ran frequent antirock articles and editorials throughout 1955 and 1956. Industry representatives from the president of MGM Records to pop star Frank Sinatra condemned the new style. Although their remarks were often couched in musical and moralistic terms, one suspects that underlying much of the vehemence was sheer economic distress. The music industry began to realize that the old rules no longer held; it was a new ball game. The reaction was convulsive.

## Radio

Most of the traditional music industry saw rock and roll as a monstrous menace, but one segment of the business viewed the new style as its savior. Television had put a serious dent in the popularity of radio. In the early 1950s it was reasonable to believe that radio had been superseded by television in much the same way that the automobile had superseded the horse and buggy. After all, why just listen to entertainment when you could listen and watch?

Rock and radio formed an early alliance: The quickest, easiest, and cheapest way for a small independent record company to promote its new rock star was to obtain radio airplay. Rock and roll generally did not have access to the national television networks, which were aligned with the major record companies. *Your Hit Parade* was a popular weekly television show, but it was associated with the pop tradition. Each week, the *Your Hit Parade* staff singers and orchestra performed live "covers" of the previous week's Top 10 pop songs. But from 1955 on, these pop singers and instrumentalists were faced with an increasing number of rock-and-roll hits in the Top 10. Their live cover versions were, at best, pale pop-style imitations of the original rock hits. The show's traditional adult audience gradually lost interest because of the increasing frequency of rock-and-roll songs, and the teenagers were not interested in Snooky Lanson's pop version of "Hound Dog." By 1958, *Your Hit Parade* had disappeared from the air. Except for brief segments on variety shows such as those hosted by Ed Sullivan and Steve Allen, it was not until the advent of Dick Clark's *American*

*Bandstand* (beginning in the fall of 1957) that television offered a show specifically focused on teen rock and roll; otherwise, there was little rock and roll on television.

Not so with radio, however. Although network radio stations tended to stay with pop music broadcasts, dramas, and serials, the smaller independent stations programmed recorded music. Many specialized in the specific styles (like C & W or R & B) that were favored in their particular locale. The announcers who played the records began to develop a personality of their own. Thus, Alan Freed, one of the first white disc jockeys to play black music for a predominantly white audience, began playing black R & B and rock and roll on his radio shows in Cleveland and later in New York City. Similar programs appeared in Los Angeles, New Orleans, Memphis, and Nashville. The successful music and news format of the independent stations spread, as many were converted into "chain" ownership—one owner or set of owners controlling stations in a series of cities. The format, known as Top 40 radio, consisted of frequent rotation through the Top 40 lists, fast-talking personalities as disc jockeys, and an hourly newscast. It was fast paced and well suited to the new musical style of rock and roll. Catering to the teen audience, the stations competed for ratings with contests, promotional stunts, and personality-oriented disc jockeys. Disc jockeys such as Wolfman Jack (Bob Smith), Dick Clark, and (later) Murry the K would establish national reputations. By the late 1950s, radio was the medium for promotion and dissemination of rock. The AM dial was simply a series of competing personalities hyping the same songs in the Top 40 format. Radio was alive and well, thanks to rock and roll.

## Payola

But there was an inherent problem in this partnership between the record industry and radio. Largely because of rock and roll, record sales exploded from $213 million in 1954 to $603 million in 1959 (Gillett 1983, 39). However, the majority of this increase went to small independent companies and subsidiaries, hundreds of which vied for the public attention needed to propel their unknown act to number 1 status. Radio play was the sine qua non of the process. If a record got radio play, it stood a chance; if not, it was dead. Thus, the radio stations and the popular disc jockeys found that they had a life and death hold on the new rock-and-roll record industry.

Engulfed in a sea of new promotional discs each week, stations had to make decisions as to which would be played and which would not. For the most part, stations blindly followed the *Billboard* charts to create their playlists. But major Top 40 stations in large markets could introduce a new record locally and start it on its journey up the charts. For the promotional representatives of the record companies, vying each week with all of the other "next Elvises," it was essential to obtain airplay. One could rely upon the quality "in the grooves," or one could "assist" the evaluation process by offering certain advantages to disc jockeys, program directors, and station managers. Such inducements might include cash, "promotional weekends" in the Bahamas, or partial ownership in the song, the artist, or even the record company itself.

During the period of 1959 to 1960, action was taken by government on several fronts. The Federal Trade Commission charged several record companies and distributors with unfair trade practices. Almost simultaneously, the district attorney of New York initiated grand jury hearings related to charges of commercial bribery against various disc jockeys, including Alan Freed. Freed was eventually convicted in 1962 of two counts of commercial bribery. Finally, in February 1960, the U.S. House of Representatives Legislative Oversight Committee expanded its investigation of rigged television game shows to include payola practices in the music industry. During testimony, a number of disc jockeys admitted to taking cash, gifts, and royalty payments in return for promoting certain records. Dick Clark was questioned extensively. He owned rights to over 150 songs but claimed that he had never "consciously" promoted them. He admitted that he had a personal interest in 27 percent of the music played on *American Bandstand* but argued that these would have been played anyway because of their popularity. Eventually the House committee recommended amendments to the Federal Communications Act that would prohibit payments of cash or gifts in exchange for airplay. The amendments became law in September 1960 (Miller 1980, 102–103). Such legislation would seem to make for a cleaner industry and fairer competition. Indeed, radio stations have centralized the control of record selection in the hands of one program (or music) director, thus removing such discretion from individual disc jockeys. But reports of varying forms of payola, including drugs, prostitution, and "promotional" vacations, have intermittently surfaced throughout the history of rock and roll. Perhaps this is because one basic fact has not changed: Radio airplay (and its more contemporary extension, television videos) is just as much a life-and-death factor now as it was in the 1950s. As long as this is true, payola, in one form or another, is likely to persist.

## MUSICAL CLOSE-UP:
### IS SOFT ROCK REALLY ROCK?

Do songs like "All I Have to Do Is Dream," "Only You," "Love Letters in the Sand," and "In the Still of the Night" belong on rock-and-roll record anthologies and in rock history books? After all, our image of "true" rock and roll is that of raucous, noisy, rebellious singers screaming lyrics over a sea of drums and guitars while jumping and dancing on stage. But sometimes idealized images only partially reflect the situation as it really was (or is). Although rock music does include some indefinable spiritual qualities and some musically unnotatable nuances, many of its musical elements can be quite clearly analyzed and defined. When these elements are found in a song, the result is a type of rock. We can then go on to describe the specific style of rock; for example, soft rock, rockabilly, or mainstream. In this musical close-up we shall examine the soft rock style of the 1950s and identify the musical elements that link the style to its pop parentage, as well as its sibling rock styles.

Most soft rock songs have a slow to moderate beat. One of the slowest examples is "Daddy's Home" (Shep and the Limelights), which has about 45 beats per minute. Quicker tempos may be heard in "Little Darling" by the Diamonds (145 beats per minute); "Runaround Sue" by Dion and the Belmonts (155 beats per minute); and "Wonderful Time up There" by Pat Boone (185 beats per minute). These last three songs have fast enough tempos to move from the category of soft rock to mainstream, but tempo is not our only consideration in categorizing a song. Most soft rock songs do not have a strong backbeat (accents on the second and fourth beats of each measure). Boone's "Wonderful Time up There" has a light backbeat, but again, other factors suggest its retention in the soft rock category.

Perhaps the most noticeable rhythmic factor in soft rock is the triple division of the beat. This division is often most clearly heard in the piano part, which consists of repeating right-hand chords in the middle or upper keyboard range. The list of examples of this three-notes-per-beat phenomenon would be a long one indeed. Listen to selections from the following list:

"I Only Have Eyes for You" (The Flamingos)
"I Want You, I Need You, I Love You" (Elvis Presley)
"Love Letters in the Sand" (Pat Boone)
"Earth Angel" (The Penguins)
"Only You" (The Platters)
"Sh-Boom" (The Crew-Cuts)

*Note:* In "Sh-Boom," Listen for a vocal example of the triple subdivision on "ya-da-da, da-da-da, da-da-da, da-da-sh."

Like its pop music parent, soft rock places considerable emphasis on beautiful melodies. The tunes are often conjunct and have greater range than those found in other rock styles. But like other rock styles, the singers often use blue notes and various vocal interpolations derived from R & B and gospel music. Falsetto is quite common in soft rock (e.g., "In the Still of the Night" by the Five Satins, or "The Duke of Earl" by Gene Chandler). Lyrics are generally love oriented and similar to those of the pop music tradition. However, the nonsense syllables of R & B-derived rock and roll are often included, usually to create a rhythmic vocal background (e.g., "There's a Moon out Tonight" by the Capris; "Sincerely" by the Moonglows; and "In the Still of the Night" by the Five Satins). The vocal style of the black groups is closer to the old R & B sound, whereas the soft rock of white performers like Boone, Presley, and the Everly Brothers is closer to the pop tradition.

Along with the triple division of the beat, the most recognizable element of many soft rock songs is the harmony. Almost as common as the twelve-bar blues progression is the following series of chords:

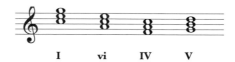

For want of a better label, we shall call this the I-vi-IV-V progression.* This series of chords forms the basis for countless soft rock songs. There are variations on this

---

*In some cases, the middle note of the triad is lowered one half step; this changes a "major" triad into a "minor" triad. Traditionally, we use uppercase Roman numerals for major triads and lowercase Roman numerals for minor triads.

series, especially where the harmonic rhythm (speed of the chord changes) is concerned. Thus, in some cases, each chord lasts for two beats; in other songs, each chord holds for an entire measure (four beats); and sometimes each chord sustains through two measures (eight beats). Another common variation is to substitute the ii chord for the IV. To hear this progression with each chord strummed and held, listen to the introduction to "Runaround Sue" (Dion and the Belmonts). For other examples of the I-vi-IV-V progression, listen to some of the following songs:

**Two Beats per Chord:**
"Earth Angel" (Penguins)
"A Thousand Miles Away" (Heartbeats)
"Sh-Boom" (Crew Cuts)
"Silhouettes" (Diamonds)
"You Send Me" (Sam Cooke)
"Gee" (Crows)
"All I Have to Do Is Dream" (Everly Brothers)
"Daddy's Home" (Shep and the Limelights)
"There's a Moon Out Tonight" (Capris)

**Four Beats per Chord (one measure per chord):**
"In the Still of the Night" (Five Satins)
"Maybe" (Chantels)

**Eight Beats per Chord (two measures per chord):**
"Little Darling" (Diamonds)
"Runaround Sue" (Dion and the Belmonts)
"The Duke of Earl" (Gene Chandler)

*Note:* The verse of this song reverts to four beats per chord.

The timbre of soft rock is related to other rock styles. Usually there is a lead singer with backup vocals (trio or quartet). Instrumental accompaniment includes guitar, piano, drums, and often saxophone. Vocal timbres vary from the black sound of the "doo-wop" groups to the C & W-oriented sound of the Everly Brothers, to the pop-oriented sound of Pat Boone, Paul Anka, and Frankie Avalon. The bass line suggested by the I-vi-IV-V progression may be sung by a bass voice, often to nonsense syllables; for example:

Doo - be-doo - be   Doo - be-doo,   Shoo-be - doo
I          vi          IV         V

Other songs have bass lines similar to mainstream rock. For example, listen to the bass lines of the following songs:

> "Sixteen Candles" (Crests)
> "Only You" (Platters)
> "Sugar Moon" (Pat Boone)
> "Love Letters in the Sand" (Pat Boone)

Pat Boone's "Wonderful Time Up There" makes a melodic line out of a boogie-woogie-derived rock bass line:

The form of most soft rock songs is borrowed from the pop and Tin Pan Alley tradition. A common form in this tradition is a thirty-two-bar chorus divided into four internal sections, each of which is eight bars long. We represent this form with

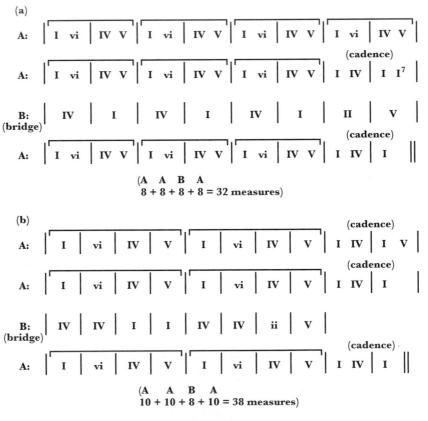

**Figure 4.1**

the letters AABA because the music of the first eight measures is repeated (some-times with minimum alteration) for the second eight measures. Then comes a new eight measures (called the "bridge"), followed by a return to the first eight measures. Most of the songs mentioned in this musical close-up follow this formal scheme. A common variation is to add two measures to the eight-measure sections to close out ("cadence") the harmonic progression. Figure 4.1 (on page 78) shows two thirty-two bar schemes that typify many soft rock songs of the 1950s.

To hear examples of the two progressions shown in Figure 4.1, listen to "Earth Angel" by the Penguins (a), and "Maybe" by the Chantels (b). Next to the twelve-bar blues progression, the I-vi-IV-V progression cast into the thirty-two bar AABA form is the most commonly encountered formula in 1950s rock.

### Summary

Early soft rock included the pop-oriented style of Presley, Boone, Anka, and Avalon; the black-oriented sounds of the Platters and the "doo-wop" groups; the C & W-oriented styles of the Everly Brothers and Ricky Nelson; and the mainstream-oriented styles of Danny and the Juniors and Dion and the Belmonts. Softer rock was very popular and set a trend that would coexist with the "harder" rock styles up to the present day. Is soft rock really rock and roll? Well, by elimination, it is not pure pop, nor is it C & W, R & B, gospel, classical, or jazz. Judging by its musical elements, it is a form of rock, albeit a softer style musically and in terms of image. To parallel a familiar song title, "Soft rock and roll is here to stay."

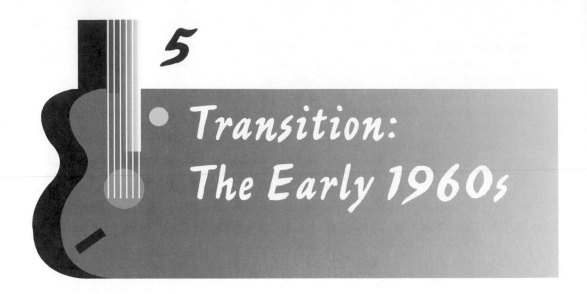

5

# Transition: The Early 1960s

## OVERVIEW: THE FRAGMENTATION OF THE MARKET

By the turn of the decade, much of the power of the first rock-and-roll shock wave had dissipated. Little Richard had turned toward religion; Jerry Lee Lewis's rock-and-roll career was over because of his marital scandals; Chuck Berry was in jail; Buddy Holly was dead. There seemed to be declining interest in hearing yet another twelve-bar blues or I-vi-IV-V song. The payola hearings had put a serious damper on the promotional activities of many small independent record companies. The market seemed to fragment into a variety of directions, no one of which could achieve real domination.

A review of the seven best-selling records of 1961 gives a hint of the remarkable variation in the market (see Table 5–1).

An examination of the charts from 1960 through 1963 fails to suggest any dominant trend; it was a period of transition. There were still vestiges of the old styles as they faded from their positions of dominance, and there were undeveloped seeds of new styles, several of which would eventually mature into major trends. And as is typical of a fragmented market, each of these coexisting styles was entirely distinct from, indeed in almost direct opposition to, all of the others. It was a confusing time.

Out of this indistinct collection of artists, songs, and styles we can identify four conflicting trends: (1) vestiges of the 1950s, (2) the emerging folk music trend, (3) surfing music, and (4) the dance craze. Because it is "old business," we will briefly summarize the first of these four in this overview. Then we will discuss the other three styles in greater detail.

## Table 5–1

| Song | Artist | Comments |
| --- | --- | --- |
| 1. "Exodus" | Ferrante and Teicher | movie theme; instumental (duo piano); pseudoclassical style |
| 2. "Calcutta" | Lawrence Welk | instumental; pop style |
| 3. "Will you Still Love Me Tomorrow?" | Shirelles | black female vocal group |
| 4. "Tossin' and Turnin' " | Bobby Lewis | 1950s rock style |
| 5. "Wonderland by Night" | Bert Kaempfert | instrumental (trumpet solo); pop style |
| 6. "Are You Lonesome Tonight?" | Elvis Presley | pop-style ballad |
| 7. "Travelin' Man" | Ricky Nelson | soft rockabilly |

### Vestiges of the Fifties

The early 1960s saw the continuation of two of the basic trends cited in Chapter 4, "Rock and Roll: Fifties Style," rockabilly and soft rock. Instrumentals and novelty hits also appeared intermittently. But one is hard-pressed to find genuine examples of mainstream rock as established by Presley, Little Richard, Lewis, Berry, Domino, and Holly.

Rockabilly singers whose first hits came in the 1950s continued to have success in the early 1960s. This would include Marty Robbins, the Everly Brothers, Brenda Lee, Roy Orbison, Johnny Cash, and Ricky Nelson. Even Ray Charles released a successful C & W oriented album that produced the hit single "I Can't Stop Loving You" (1962). These early 1960s rockabilly songs tended toward the soft side.

Indeed, the early 1960s witnessed the triumph of the softer sounds. These ranged from the soft rock sounds of the late 1950s to the pure pop style of the early 1950s. In the pure pop category were songs like "Surrender," "Now or Never," and "Are You Lonesome Tonight?" by Elvis Presley, and "Moody River" by Pat Boone. Traditional pop stars returned to favor with vocals such as Steve Lawrence's "Go Away Little Girl" (1963); pop-style instrumentals by Percy Faith, Acker Bilk, David Rose, Bert Kaempfert, and Lawrence Welk became big hits. The only number 1 instrumental reminiscent of the 1950s rock instrumental was "Telstar" by the Tornadoes, the first British group to have a number 1 hit on the U.S. charts. They were not the last.

The soft rock of the teen idols continued with hits by Bobby Vee, Bobby Vinton, Bobby Rydell, and Neil Sedaka. Sedaka was one of several talented young songwriters from New York City's Brill Building group who would have continued success through the 1960s and beyond.

In the early 1960s, the black male vocal groups were joined by a host of black female vocal groups. Continuing a line that began in the 1950s with the doo-wop groups, these groups formed a link to the later Motown style. Table 5–2 shows some of the early 1960s vocal groups whose success lay in their appealing soft rock styles.

One of the most successful vocal groups in the early 1960s was the Four Seasons. Originally called the Variatones, the group and its lead singer Frankie Valli (born Francis Castelluccio) had tried since 1955 to place their ensemble and solo recordings on the charts. Valli's strong falsetto voice, backed with tight, good vocal harmonies, finally caught the public's attention with "Sherry" in 1962. The vocal sound was a precursor of the later harmonies of the Beach Boys and other surfing groups. The Four Seasons went on to release a series of hits throughout the 1960s, including "Big Girls Don't Cry" (1962), "Walk Like a Man" (1963), and "Dawn (Go Away)" (1964). They scored a number 1 hit as late as 1976 with "December 1963 (Oh, What a Night)."

The early 1960s also found more female solo singers achieving success. Even as Connie Francis and Brenda Lee continued to have hits, new female singers appeared, such as Lesley Gore ("It's My Party," 1963), Shelley Fabares ("Johnny Angel," 1962), and Little Peggy March ("I Will Follow Him," 1963).

Finally, the early 1960s saw a steady stream of novelty songs. In 1960 there was Johnny Preston's "Running Bear" and Larry Verne's "Mr. Custer." In 1961 the Tokens sang "The Lion Sleeps Tonight," a South African folk song with the repeating African title, "wimoweh," sounding for all the world like another variation of doo-wop. The year 1963 was even more bizarre, with one hit by a Japanese pop

## Table 5–2

| Group | Description | Sample Hits | Year |
|---|---|---|---|
| Shirelles | black female quartet | "Will You Still Love Me Tomorrow?" | 1960 |
| | | "Dedicated to the One I Love" | 1961 |
| | | "Soldier Boy" | 1962 |
| Drifters | black male quintet | "There Goes My Baby" | 1959 |
| | | "Save the Last Dance for Me" | 1960 |
| | | "On Broadway" | 1963 |
| | | "Under the Boardwalk" | 1964 |
| Marvelettes | black female quartet | "Please Mr. Postman" | 1961 |
| | | "Playboy" | 1962 |
| Marcels | black male quintet | "Blue Moon" | 1961 |
| Crystals | black female trio | "He's a Rebel" | 1962 |
| | | "Da Doo Ron Ron" | 1963 |
| Chiffons | black female quartet | "He's So Fine" | 1963 |
| Ruby and the Romantics | black female lead w/ black male quartet | "Our Day Will Come" | 1963 |
| Angels | white female trio | "My Boyfriend's Back" | 1963 |
| Maurice Williams and the Zodiacs | black male trio | "Stay" | 1960 |

singer singing in Japanese ("Sukiyaki" by Kyu Sakamoto) and one by five Catholic nuns singing about the founder of the Dominican order ("Dominique," by Sister Luc-Gabrielle, known as the Singing Nun).

These vestiges of the late 1950s enjoyed their last big heyday before the social and musical revolutions of the mid- and late 1960s. But even as Percy Faith's "Theme from A Summer Place" was on its way to becoming the second most popular recording of the 1960s (Whitburn, *Top 40 Hits*, 1996, 809) the seeds of new sounds were germinating.

## THE BEGINNINGS OF THE FOLK MUSIC TREND

In the purest sense, a true folk song is one that has been handed down (by ear) from generation to generation and whose composer or author and exact time and place of origin are unknown. So technically speaking, it is as impossible for someone to sit down today and compose a folk song as it would be for a carpenter to go to his shop this afternoon and build an antique.

Thus, most "folk music" in the 1960s was not true folk music but actually was music composed in the style of traditional folk music. The model was the Appalachian folk ballad, a style that used various acoustic guitar or guitarlike instruments to accompany one or more singers singing highly personalized lyrics that told of the real issues of life: money, jobs, love, death, and so on. Compared to the typical lyrics of pop music or early rock and roll, folk lyrics were rather serious. Some folk lyrics dealt with national phenomena that closely affected people's lives, such as war, the labor movement, or legal and social injustices.

The roots of the 1960s folk music trend lie in the 1940s. Early in that decade a quartet was formed called the Almanac Singers, which included Pete Seeger and Woody Guthrie. Guthrie had a long history of writing songs that reflected his experiences during the Great Depression, the dust bowl days, World War II, and the union movement. An outspoken political and social critic, he wrote columns for the *Communist Daily Worker* and *People's World*. Among his 1,000-plus published songs is the anthem "This Land Is Your Land." The Almanac Singers recorded several albums before reorganizing as the Weavers (without Guthrie) in the late 1940s. They actually hit the pop charts in 1950 with "Goodnight, Irene" and "Tzena, Tzena." Like the Almanac Singers, they were associated with left-wing causes and organizations, and at the height of the McCarthy era, they were blacklisted as being subversive. The group disbanded in 1963; however, original member Pete Seeger continued his activities as a solo singer. His songs "If I Had a Hammer," "Where Have All the Flowers Gone," and "Turn, Turn, Turn" became important hits in the folk music movement of the 1960s.

Generally, the music industry of the 1950s believed (correctly) that folk music's appeal was to a small subculture. However, in 1957, a briefly popular musical phenomenon appeared that hinted that there might be a wider audience for folk styles. Calypso, a style of folk music from the Caribbean area, made a brief but powerful appearance on the charts, due primarily to singer Harry Belafonte. Born in New York City, Belafonte had spent much of his youth in Kingston, Jamaica. In the early weeks of 1957, Belafonte's "Jamaica Farewell" reached the Top 20, and later that year "The Banana Boat Song (Day-O)" reached the Top 5. The music featured

Belafonte's gentle, lyrical voice and a distinct Jamaican-English lyric. There was a hint of soft Latin bongo drum rhythms and acoustic guitars. Although considered a novelty at the time, calypso, in retrospect, takes its place in the series of steps that laid the groundwork for the folk music trend of the 1960s.

### The Kingston Trio

In 1957 (the year of Belafonte's hits), college students Dave Guard, Bob Shane, and Nick Reynolds formed a vocal trio in Stanford, California, known as the Kingston Trio (note the calypso connection in the group's name). Their first hit, "Tom Dooley" (number 1, 1958), was an adaptation of a Blue Ridge Mountain folk tune from the Civil War days. It was about a mountaineer named Tom Dula who was hanged for murder in 1868 (Bronson 1988, 45). It was a folk song according to the purest definition and may be considered the first real hit in the folk music trend.

"Tom Dooley" was a serious song compared to other hits of the time. Its spoken introduction sets the story into the historic tradition of the eternal love triangle. The song sings of murder, questionable justice, and hanging. The musical accompaniment consists exclusively of acoustic instruments—string bass, guitar, and banjo. The image of the Kingston Trio was also very different from the popular rock image. They were white, clean-cut college boys with close-cropped hair, button-down shirts, and dress slacks (the so-called Ivy League look). These characteristics set a style that would influence countless other folk groups.

Although the Kingston Trio eventually placed ten songs in the Top 40, no single after "Tom Dooley" reached higher than number 8. However, their albums sold very well—another harbinger of things to come. Their first seven LPs (long-playing albums) (excluding reissues) were certified as gold albums (they eventually released over thirty albums). One of the other Kingston Trio hits—"M.T.A." (1959)—offered another hint of things to come. In its own lighthearted way, it was a protest song—a forerunner of more serious protest songs to follow. Like "Tom Dooley," "M.T.A." begins with a spoken introduction, this time a tongue-in-cheek monologue (accompanied only by a string bass) about the citizens of Boston rallying to the defense of human rights. The "burdensome tax" in this case is not a tax on tea but a subway fare increase. It is a gentle, humorous introduction for the general public to the protest lyric so common in earlier folk songs and a central characteristic of the folk songs of the 1960s.

The trend that was launched by the Kingston Trio has been called the urban folk trend. The music was produced primarily not by authentic backwoods country folk, but by

The Kingston Trio (*Source:* Michael Ochs Archive, Ltd.)

sophisticated, well-educated collegians in or around urban centers. For example, the Brothers Four ("Greenfields," number 2 in 1960) were fraternity brothers at the University of Washington. In 1961, the Highwaymen, a group of five Wesleyan University students, had major hits with "Michael" and "Cotton Fields." Other groups to follow the trend included the Rooftop Singers, the New Christy Minstrels, the Smothers Brothers, the Limeliters, the Journeymen, and the Whiskey Hill Singers.

### Peter, Paul, and Mary

Representing the next stage in the developing folk music trend was another vocal trio: Peter, Paul, and Mary. Unlike most of their predecessors, they produced an impressive list of hit singles while maintaining a strong popularity on LPs and in live performance. Seven of their first eight albums were certified gold, and they placed a dozen songs in the Top 40 from 1962 through 1969.

Peter, Paul, and Mary's image was in contrast with the clean-cut Ivy League look of earlier folk groups. Peter Yarrow and Paul Stookey had mustaches and beards; Mary Travers had long, straight hair. There was a gentle hint of the intellectual-revolutionary "folknik," a type that already existed at the hard-core center of the folk movement. But in 1962, the country was not quite ready for the harder protests of Baez, Dylan, and others. Peter, Paul, and Mary provided a softer, more commercial version suitable for popular consumption.

The tone of the new folk countermovement was set in Peter, Paul, and Mary's first album. The printed album notes included key words such as "sincerity," "authenticity," "*Truth*," "*Good*," "virtue," and "honesty." The listener was promised "no gimmicks" and told that "mediocrity has had it" and "hysteria is on the way out" (Belz 1972, 84). This music was not for the teenybopper but for the older, more thoughtful college student and young adult, who were discovering that politics and government were not just the business of gray-haired, balding old men but of a vigorous, dynamic, and youthful new generation. At the age of forty-three, John F. Kennedy had just been elected the youngest president of the United States. It was

Peter, Paul, and Mary (*Source:* Michael Ochs Archive, Ltd.)

the time of the New Frontier and the youth-oriented peace corps. The college-age youth and young adults began to believe that they could make a difference in the world. The lyrics of earlier rock seemed frivolous. The flamboyance and hysteria of Jerry Lee Lewis and Little Richard seemed childish and mindless. The new sociopolitically conscious youth wanted music with a message. An entire subculture began to grow within and around the college campuses. Students gathered in nearby coffeehouses to listen to campus poets and singers dispense meaningful philosophies to the accompaniment of guitar and bongo drums. This was not music to dance to; it was music to *think* to.

These socially aware young people did more than listen passively to the new music. They acted out the messages. They organized to fight for social causes of all kinds—major and minor—from racial prejudice and war to fraternity hazing and freshman dormitory hours. They organized sit-ins, walk-ins, lay-ins, marches, and freedom bus rides. The concept of social disobedience was considered a viable form of social protest against the establishment.

The music was a central part of this new campus-oriented subculture. Peter, Paul, and Mary's second single (and first Top 10 hit) was "If I Had a Hammer," coauthored by Pete Seeger. It spoke of striking a blow for "justice," "freedom," and "love between the brothers and the sisters all over this land." In this case they were not singing of romantic love but of a higher order of Love that ideally should exist between all people. Their follow-up hit "Puff, the Magic Dragon" (1963) spoke wistfully of the lost pleasures and innocence of childhood.

Later, in 1963, came two cover versions of songs written and recorded by Bob Dylan—"Blowin' in the Wind" (number 2) and "Don't Think Twice, It's All Right" (number 9). Peter, Paul, and Mary's more polished style was more acceptable to a wider audience in 1963 than the rawer Dylan originals. The first of these two songs deserves particular attention. As much as any other song of 1963, "Blowin' in the Wind" expressed the sentiments of the folk-oriented youth culture:

> . . . how many times must the cannon balls fly
> before they're forever banned?

> . . . how many years must some people exist
> before they're allowed to be free?

After asking these and other similar questions, the song suggests optimistically that the answers are "blowin' in the wind." In other words, the youth knew the questions and had the answers. Their new spirit of activism and involvement seemed to suggest that positive changes would be forthcoming. "Blowin' in the Wind" and other similar songs not only *reflected* the thinking and attitudes of an already committed segment of the youth generation, they *spread* these thoughts and attitudes effectively to others whose energies could be sparked to join the new youth revolution. The new Kennedy administration seemed receptive and sympathetic to these attitudes and stimulated hope that, indeed, the youth might "change the world."

Peter, Paul, and Mary's sound was commercially viable enough to sell well nationally, yet their philosophy and sentiments were those of the new youth movement. Their image was midway between the conventional Ivy League look of their predecessors and the more revolutionary look of the hard-core folkniks who would follow.

They were an important link in the evolution of the folk movement of the 1960s. Their hits continued until 1969, when "Leaving on a Jet Plane" (by John Denver) became their only number 1 hit. The group disbanded shortly thereafter.

## Musical Characteristics

Folk music was quite different than the mainstream and rockabilly styles of the 1950s. First, there was none of the shouting style of R & B and mainstream rock. Generally the folk vocal style involved good voices in the traditional sense, singing perfectly on pitch, with good vocal control. Lyrics were clearly enunciated—after all, they carried the all-important message. Soloists sang in a very pure vocal tone, sometimes even purging their voices of any vibrato (that "wiggle" in the pitch that classical and pop singers cultivated). Duo, trio, and quartet harmonies were correctly voiced in the traditional sense. The melodic lines were similar to those of the C & W and pop styles—that is, they had interesting contours, normal to wide ranges, and traditional symmetrical forms.

Folk song harmonies were simple and diatonic (all within a given key) but avoided the twelve-bar blues progression of R & B and mainstream rock and the I-vi-IV-V progression of pop and soft rock. Each song seemed to have originated as a lyric with melody, the harmonies being the result of adding chords to accompany the melody.

With the slower ballads, rhythm was very much in the background: felt, but not emphasized. In the faster tunes, the rhythm was provided by the strummed guitar (or banjo) chords. If a string bass was present, it reinforced the basic beat. But there was none of the forceful rhythm or backbeat of R & B, mainstream rock, or rockabilly.

## Summary

With the folk trend of the early 1960s, we see the first of the external influences that would have an impact on the history of rock and reshape its future. As with any live and growing entity, rock was susceptible to such new external influences as it developed. Were this not so, it would have stagnated rather than become the dynamic, constantly evolving phenomenon it has shown itself to be. Let us reiterate some of the main characteristics of the early folk music trend.

1. *Lyrics.* There was a new sense of seriousness in the lyrics. Songs spoke of major issues of social and political importance. The writers and singers sought not only to reflect the thinking within their subculture but to foster similar attitudes and provoke action in a wider audience. Key issues were peace, racial equality, and love.
2. *Demographics.* The rock and roll of the 1950s had been considered "young people's" music. No real differentiation was made between the "teenybopper" and the upper-teen and college-age youth. But folk music's appeal was principally to the older end of the youth spectrum. The music industry realized that they were not dealing with one demographic group, but two: the eighteen-to-twenty-four age group, and the seventeen-and-below age group. Although music's appeal is never as clearly defined as these demographic groupings suggest, there was little doubt that folk music was primarily by and for the eighteen-to-twenty-four demographic group.
3. *Albums.* The seriousness of the lyrics and the greater financial capacity of the eighteen-to-twenty-four age group combined to make the LP the primary medium of folk

music. Increasingly, albums replaced singles as the biggest share of the market. Folk groups, for all of their popularity, did not produce many hit singles. Since the introduction of the LP in 1948 by Columbia Records, the long-play format had appealed to an older, more conservative audience. Between 1954 and 1957, the exact years of rock's first explosion, the 45-rpm single had replaced the older 78 rpm as the most popular record format. The two-and-a-half-minute single became the primary medium of early rock. Harry Belafonte was perhaps the first singer to achieve popularity primarily through LP sales (nine Top 10 albums, but only one Top 10 single). With the popularity of the folk-oriented LP, the 45-rpm single became identified more with the teenage market and the LP with the college-age and young-adult market.

4. *Acoustic instruments.* The folk musician abhorred the electronic artificiality of electric guitars and elaborate studio production techniques. Remember Peter, Paul, and Mary's 1962 album notes: This was to be the "real thing," real people playing real instruments without artificial assistance from electronics, echo chambers, overdubbing, and multitracking. Honest and simple, that was the key.

In late 1963 and early 1964 the initial phase of folk music's popularity absorbed several traumatic blows. We shall resume our look at folk music in Chapter 8, "Folk Music and Folk Rock." In the meantime, much will have changed.

## SURFING MUSIC

The fragmentation of the early 1960s market resulted in a variety of trends, some of which were diametrically opposed to one another. If the key words of the folk music trend were "honesty," "authenticity," "sincerity," "freedom," and "brotherhood," the key words of surfing music were those found in the title of the 1964 Beach Boys hit, "Fun, Fun, Fun." Seemingly almost every characteristic cited earlier for the folk movement is exactly inverted for surfing music. The folkies avoided the artificiality of electric instruments; the surfers had no problem with electricity. The folkies disliked the "gimmickry" of recording studio techniques; the surfers, on the other hand, exploited echo effects, overdubbing, and extensive editing. The folkies sang of heavy topics—love, peace, racial harmony—in a serious way; the surfers sang of cars, girls, beach parties, and big waves. The folkies became involved in social action designed to raise the national consciousness regarding social and political injustices; the surfers appeared to be completely indifferent to such things.

Just as folk music was at the center of a subculture, with its norms of dress, language, and behavior, so surfing music was at the heart of its own subculture. The geographic center was southern California. As the popularity of the music spread across the country, would-be surfers (whether in Iowa, Tennessee, or Maine) acquired deep tans, bleached their hair blond, put on their sandals and cutoffs, waxed down their surfboards, and revved up their Impalas, T-birds, or Corvettes. The fact that the largest nearby body of water may have been the county swimming pool was hardly a consideration. Unlike the folkers, the surfers' deepest social concern was whether the local drugstore would run out of suntan lotion.

Beach-oriented movies highlighting the carefree southern California lifestyle began as early as 1959, when *Gidget* initiated a series of "sun-and-surf" movies.

Youthful, attractive stars such as Sandra Dee, Frankie Avalon, Cliff Robertson, Annette Funicello, and James Darren scored major successes in these movies.

One of the first performers to become associated with the surfing subculture was Dick Dale. Enjoying regional (southern California) popularity with his live performances and early recordings, Dale released an album in 1962 called *Surfer's Choice*, but it failed to make any national impact.

Far more successful were Jan and Dean. Jan Berry, Dean Torrence, and Arnie Ginsberg had formed their band in high school and had early success with "Jennie Lee" (number 8, 1958), released under the name of Jan and Arnie. Under the name of Jan and Dean, they had further successes with "Baby Talk" (1959) and a doo-wop version of "Heart and Soul" (1961). The peak of Jan and Dean's popularity came in 1963 and 1964. "Surf City," a song by Beach Boy Brian Wilson, became their first (and only) number 1 hit. They eventually placed fifteen songs in the Top 40. Their career ended when Jan was nearly killed in an automobile wreck in 1966.

**The Beach Boys**

When one refers to surfing music, one normally refers specifically to the music of the Beach Boys, indisputably the trendsetters in this genre. The group originated in Hawthorne, California, in 1961 with brothers Brian, Carl, and Dennis Wilson, their cousin Mike Love, and friend Al Jardine. After an early local label hit, "Surfin'," they went on to Capitol Records, where they eventually logged over thirty Top 40 hits, including eight in the Top 5. The musical style of the Beach Boys will be discussed in some detail in the musical close-up at the end of this chapter; here we shall simply chronicle their history and briefly describe two distinct phases of their work.

Their notoriety began with "Surfin' Safari" (number 14, 1962), the song that initiated their "surfing music phase," and the follow-up release, "Surfin' U.S.A." (number 3, 1963). These first two songs were rockers, with "Surfer Girl," the Beach Boys showed that their sound could be adapted to the slow ballad. Subsequent hits that consistently exemplify the Beach Boys' surfing sound include "Little Deuce Coupe" (number 15, 1963), "Be True to Your School" (number 6, 1963), "Fun, Fun, Fun" (number 5, 1964), "I Get Around" (number 1, 1964), "Help Me Rhonda" (number 1, 1965), "California Girls" (number 3, 1965), "Barbara Ann" (number 2, 1966), and "Sloop John B" (number 3, 1966).

The surfing style of the Beach Boys was largely determined by Brian Wilson, the oldest of the Wilson brothers. In addition to being the musical mentor of the group, Brian became increasingly conversant with the technical aspects of the recording studio. Somewhat more serious and introverted than the others, Brian hardly fit the "sun-and-fun" carefree Beach Boy image. Nevertheless, his musical and technical leadership of the group was beyond question.

Following a nervous breakdown in 1964, Brian stopped touring with the group and devoted himself to the creation of a new, more serious style. The result was an album released in mid-1966 called *Pet Sounds*. Using up-to-date studio techniques and extra musicians, this Beach Boys' album, which hinted at a stylistic change, was critically acclaimed but did not sell as well as previous albums.

The real move into their second phase—the post-surfing music phase—came with the release of "Good Vibrations" in late 1966. Had the Beach Boys stopped

The Beach Boys in the 1960s (*Source:* Michael Ochs Archive, Ltd.)

prior to "Good Vibrations," they might be remembered only as a good rock-and-roll band of the early 1960s who had spearheaded the pleasant and carefree sounds of surfing music. Brian Wilson, Mike Love, and the rest of the band worked for over six months on "Good Vibrations." It was literally pieced together from ideas committed to tape at four different studios. After over ninety hours of studio time, eleven versions, and some $50,000 in production costs, "Good Vibrations" was released. It not only hit the number 1 position but became a million seller.

"Good Vibrations" was a milestone in the development of rock. Musically and technically, it was more sophisticated than any rock hit up until its time. Only the Beatles were experimenting in similar ways at that time. Prior to this it was assumed that a rock hit should last about two minutes and thirty seconds, and once the tempo, beat, key, and texture were established, they should not change. "Good Vibrations" did not follow the formula. As Brian Wilson said, in its "three minutes and thirty-five seconds . . . it had a lot of riff changes. It had a lot of movements . . . changes, changes, changes. Building harmonies here, drop this voice out, this comes in, bring the echo chamber in, do this, put the theremin here, bring the cello up a little louder here. I mean it was a real production. The biggest production of our life" (Leaf 1985, 90).

The success of "Good Vibrations" encouraged Brian to pursue further experimentation. He began to plan an album, to be called *Smile*, that would expand upon many of the ideas first tried in *Pet Sounds* and "Good Vibrations." He was moving away not only from the old surfing music but from the rest of the Beach Boys as well. His new friends, such as Van Dyke Parks, were more associated with the new hip, spiritualistic, free-thinking, and drug-oriented culture. Brian poured his heart and soul into *Smile*. When the rest of the Beach Boys came off tour to record the new material, there were problems. Some of the group feared that Brian's new creativity was commercially risky. Hurt and confused, Brian dropped the *Smile* project. Eight of the twenty songs were eventually released, including a Van Dyke Parks–Brian Wilson collaboration called "Heroes and Villains" (1967). Although there are reports of longer, even more creative versions of this song, the version eventually released was a suitable follow-up to "Good Vibrations." Like its predecessor, "Heroes and Villains" avoided rock formulas and involved frequent changes in texture, rhythm, and timbre. The album that was released in place of the aborted *Smile* album was called *Smiley Smile*. Sales did not go well, and *Smiley Smile* marked the beginning of the decline of the Beach Boys' popularity. In 2004, Brian Wilson, with the help of original collaborator Van Dyke Parks, officially released *Smile* and promoted the release with a national tour, bringing this "teenage symphony to God" (Wilson's description) back from extinction.

After the release of the Beatles' *Sgt. Pepper* album in 1967, a new world of rock exploded. Ironically, the Beach Boys were actually closely paralleling the creative growth of the Beatles. But to the public, they were still associated with the old surfing sound, hopelessly naive and innocent sounding by 1967 standards. In spite of continued efforts by Brian, Carl, and the others, they were "typed," and their greatest successes in the 1970s and early 1980s would lie in the realm of nostalgia. In 1988, they hit the charts again with "Kokomo." One can only speculate that had *Smile* been released at or about the same time as *Sgt. Pepper*, the story of the Beach Boys might have been very different.

The Beach Boys (*Source:* Michael Ochs Archive, Ltd.)

Chubby Checker (*Source:* Michael Ochs Archive, Ltd.)

### *THE DANCE CRAZE*

From its beginnings, rock and roll has been associated with dancing. Teen dances in the 1950s
usually fell into two categories: slow and fast.
With slow dances couples held each other close
and moved slowly around the dance floor in a
type of box step. Fast rock-and-roll dances usually took the form of the jitterbug, a holdover
from the big band swing of the 1930s and 1940s.
Again, couples touched, if only by hand, and
engaged in a variety of fast steps that could
include considerable virtuosity and gymnastics.

In 1959, Hank Ballard and the Midnighters
recorded a song called "Teardrops on Your Letter." The flip side of the single was a song called
"The Twist." When it began to catch on, a cover
version was released by Cameo–Parkway
Records (Philadelphia). Their new artist, Ernest
Evans, was adept at imitating other singers (such
as Hank Ballard and Fats Domino). Using the
name Chubby Checker (compare with Fats
Domino), Evans recorded "The Twist," thus initiating an explosion of dance-oriented records.
"The Twist" is unique in rock history, having achieved the number 1 position on two
separate occasions (September 1960 and January 1962). It eventually appeared on
the Top 100 charts for a total of over thirty-eight weeks, a record that still stands.

Checker and "The Twist" were popularized on *American Bandstand*. The song and
the dance became a national fad, spinning off countless twist records for Checker
and others.

| | |
|---|---|
| "Let's Twist Again" | Chubby Checker |
| "Slow Twistin' " | Chubby Checker |
| "Twist It Up" | Chubby Checker |
| "Twist and Shout" | Isley Brothers; Beatles |
| "The Peppermint Twist" | Joey Dee and the Starlighters |
| "Twistin' the Night Away" | Sam Cooke |
| "Twistin' U.S.A." | Danny and the Juniors |
| "Twist, Twist Senora" | Gary "U.S." Bonds |
| "Twistin' Mathilda" | Jimmy Soul |

As the dance spread beyond a teenage phenomenon to the adult crowd, the teens moved off the twist and on to other dances, and there was certainly no lack of alternatives. Chubby Checker himself followed with "Pony Time" (1961), "The Fly" (1961), the "Limbo Rock" (1962), "Popeye the Hitchhiker" (1962), "Let's Limbo Some More" (1963), and "Let's Do the Freddie" (1965). Other artists, led by black artists from Philadelphia, often on the Cameo–Parkway label, invented a seemingly endless string of new dances (see Table 5–3).

There was a sameness to many of the dance records. Most often relying on the twelve-bar blues structure, the songs usually contained lyrics that provided instructions on how to do the given dance. Sometimes the teens invented their own variations without aid of any "instruction song." Most of these dances were, in effect, individual dances. The partners faced each other without actually touching, sometimes drifting several feet apart. Sociologists may speculate that this individualized form of dancing was a harbinger of the self-oriented, "do your own thing" mentality that flourished in the 1960s. Certainly these dance records kept black music on the charts in the face of the folk trend, the surfing trend, and the coming British invasion. The dance craze of the early 1960s also served as a precursor of disco (1970s) and break dancing (1980s).

### Summary

The 1960s rock scene splintered into many directions. There were pop-oriented teen idols, female groups in the doo-wop tradition, novelty songs, folk singers, surfers, and twisters. No one style predominated. Rock seemed to be losing its direction in a hopeless fragmentation of the market. Was it possible to pull this diverse musical perspective together and send the seemingly dissipating energies of rock into a new direction? The answer was yes. In Chapter 6, "The Beatles," we shall discuss the far-reaching revolution that was about to take place.

### Table 5–3

| Song Title | Artist and Year | Label |
|---|---|---|
| "Continental Walk" | Hank Ballard and the Midnighters (1961) | King |
| "The Fish" | Bobbly Rydell (1961) | Cameo |
| "Bristol Stomp" | Dovells (1961) | Parkway |
| "Wah Watusi" | Orlons (1962) | Cameo |
| "Mashed Potato Time" | Dee Dee Sharp (1962) | Cameo |
| "Bongo Stomp" | Little Joey and the Flips (1962) | Joy |
| "Do the new Continental" | Dovells (1962) | Parkway |
| "Loco Motion" | Little Eva (1962) | Dimension |
| "Surfers' Stomp" | Marketts (1962) | Liberty |
| "Hully Gully Baby" | Dovells (1962) | Parkway |

*(continued)*

| Table 5–3 (cont.) | | |
|---|---|---|
| "Wiggle Wobble" | Les Cooper and the Soul Rockers (1963) | Everlast |
| "Do the Bird" | Dee Dee Sharp (1963) | Cameo |
| "The Bounce" | Olympics (1963) | Tri Disc |
| "The Hitch Hike" | Marvin Gaye (1963) | Tamla |
| "Monkey Time" | Major Lance (1963) | Okeh |
| "Do the Boomerang" | Jr. Walker and the All Stars (1965) | Soul |
| "Do the Clam" | Elvis Presley (1965) | RCA |
| "Do the Freddie" | Freddie and the Dreamers (1965) | Mercury |
| "The Jerk" | Larks (1965) | Money |
| "The Shake" | Sam Cooke (1965) | RCA |
| "The Cool Jerk" | Capitols (1966) | Karen |

## MUSICAL CLOSE-UP:
### MUSICAL TEXTURE AND THE BEACH BOYS

Musical texture has to do with how the various layers of musical sounds relate to each other. If we conceive of a kind of musical "space"—from the very lowest pitch to the very highest—the question becomes, how do we fill that space? We can use one note or musical line, or many. If there is more than one, how do they interact? Because the Beach Boys were one of the first rock groups to explore a variety of textures, it seems appropriate to take a closer look at their style, with a particular emphasis on texture. First we will discuss their surfing style, then we will examine their more mature style, using "Good Vibrations" and "Heroes and Villains" as our models.

### The Surfing Style

The surfing style of the Beach Boys shows two particular influences. Brian Wilson was particularly fond of the Four Freshmen, a white pop group of the early 1950s. Their clean, sophisticated, jazz-influenced harmonies became an early model for Brian, who would spend hours singing along with their records. He especially liked the high tenor voices of the Freshmen and the Hi-Los, another 1950s male vocal group. Brian learned to sing in a high male voice as well as in a true falsetto.

Carl Wilson, of course, absorbed these same influences. But he preferred the new sounds of 1950s rock and roll—especially Chuck Berry. It should not be surprising, then, that even in their early surfing hits, these two influences—the quartet harmonies of the Four Freshmen and the rock-and-roll style of Chuck Berry—would manifest themselves.

Listen first to "Surfin' U.S.A." The most obvious influence, of course, is Chuck Berry. The music is that of Berry's "Sweet Little Sixteen," with lyrics rewritten by Brian to fit the surfing theme. After a short Berry-like guitar introduction, Mike Love's lead vocal is sung in multitracked unison. The vocal harmonies (on the words "ooh" and "inside, outside, U.S.A.") are both above and below the midrange lead line. At the words "everybody's gone surfin'," the lead changes to high voice and the background vocal stops. The title line ("Surfin' U.S.A.") is sung in low unison (again, no background vocal). If we were to draw a picture of this general scheme (an approximation at best), it might look like the figure below.

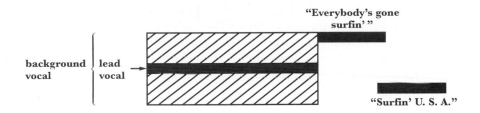

With "Surfer Girl," the texture is slightly different. In the introduction there are background vocal harmonies under a high lead line. In the first section of the song (A), all voices move together on block chords; the top voice is the lead and the others are harmonizing. All are singing the same words and rhythms; there is no independence for any one voice. The harmony is spread widely over the available musical space—from the high lead to the bass—and is filled in nicely in the middle. This sound shows a reference back to the Four Freshmen and the Hi-Los. At the end of this section the voices split, with the high voice moving independently, while the lower vocal harmony sings "surfer girl, my little surfer girl." After repeating the A section, the bridge (B) features a midrange lead voice accompanied by background vocals ("aah"); at the words "everywhere I go," the voices join again in block chords with the highest voice predominating.

With "Fun, Fun, Fun," the Berry influence is particularly obvious, especially in the guitar introduction (compare with Berry's intro to "Johnny B. Goode"). The A section begins with midrange voices in unison. This monophonic texture is sustained until the title words "Fun, Fun, Fun," when a full homophonic texture develops covering a very full pitch spectrum from high voice to bass. On the word "away," the high voice is sustained, while the other voices harmonize a rhythmic pattern on "fun, fun, fun till her Daddy takes the T-bird away." For the repeat of the A section (new words), the midrange unison returns to take the lead but is accompanied by background vocals sustained from the end of the previous section. In subsequent sections of the repeated A section, the midrange voice sings the lead, accompanied by background vocals on "ooh" and "you walk (look/drive) like an ace now." Skip to the end of the song (the fade section). Here, a new texture develops; the high falsetto pattern zooms off on its own, while the accompanying voices sing a repeating pattern on "fun, fun, fun now that Daddy took the T-bird away."

Listen to other Beach Boy surfing hits and you can find examples of monophony (unison line), homophony (all voices moving together), and polyphony (several independent lines). With five voices, the Beach Boys can have one solo line (often multitracked) and still have full four-voice harmony for accompaniment. Sometimes the lead is high, accompanied by voices below; at other times the lead is midrange, with accompanying voices surrounding it above and below. The frequency of change in these textures, sometimes within one phrase, adds variety and interest to the music.

But compared with later Beach Boys' works, these early surfing sounds seem to be only elementary exercises. Let us look at two later works.

### "Good Vibrations"

"Good Vibrations" (fall 1966) was the most creative and innovative single to be released in rock music up until that time. The song begins with high voice (multitracked unison) with heavy echo. It is accompanied by repeating organ chords, one per beat, and a bass pattern that repeats every two measures. The first eight measures are repeated with the addition of percussion. The snare drum reinforces the first three notes of the bass pattern, followed by a tambourine shake on beat four of each odd-numbered measure and a snare drum on beat four of each even-numbered measure. In the sixteenth measure, the snare plays a triple division of each beat to drive the music into the next section.

Suddenly the lead vocal shifts to the low range ("I'm pickin' up good vibrations"). The triple division of the beat is picked up by cellos, while the drums play a simple four-beat rhythm (tambourine on the backbeat). The swooping sound is made by a theremin. This electronic instrument was invented in 1924 by Leon Theremin. It consists of a small box with a metallic rod protruding. As the player moves his hand around the rod, a continuous tone is emitted that follows the up-and-down hand movements, thus producing higher and lower pitches.

As this texture continues, background vocals are added in a repeating pattern ("ooh, bop, bop, good vibrations"). Shortly, yet another layer of vocals is added with high voice on top ("good, good, good, good vibrations"). By this time we have a multilayered instrumental accompaniment (drums, tambourine, cellos, theremin, and bass), plus three layers of voices, all interacting perfectly.

After repeating this entire progression, a new section provides a marked contrast. A piano modified to sound like an old barroom piano plays solid chords alternately with the bass. Color is added by drums and tambourine. To this texture are added voices, first an almost inaudible humming, that progress to another multilayered vocal texture. Suddenly this "wall of sound" is broken and we are left only with an organ playing sustained churchlike chords to the accompaniment of shakes on maracas and other percussion. A unison vocal line (midrange) enters with the words "Gotta keep those good vibrations a-happenin' with her." On the repetition, bass is added plus vocal harmonies above the previous line. On the third and final repetition a single line in the upper organ register enters as an accompanying counterpoint. On this repetition, the voices fade out, leaving only the instrumental accompaniment. As this texture is about to end, one jazzlike vocal chord is superimposed and sustained. After a moment of silence, an earlier section returns (where we had three vocal layers, cellos, etc.). The voices end after only two repetitions, leaving the instrumental accompaniment to finish the section.

Next we encounter an exercise in polyphony. With heavy echo and only a bass accompaniment, a rising falsetto line enters, to be joined shortly by a second line whose first five notes descend in opposition to the upper voice. Finally, other voices enter with pitches to intertwine with the preexisting lines. This texture gives way to the theremin, cellos, drums, and tambourine, playing their earlier accompaniment. This sound fades to end the song.

"Good Vibrations" goes well beyond the Beach Boys' earlier surfing style, yet, in spite of its complexity, preserves the basic Beach Boys' sound. It is one of the milestones in the history of rock.

### "Heroes and Villains"

Listen to "Heroes and Villains" and see whether you can discern the many sectional changes and multiple layers of instrumental and vocal sounds within each section. Let us call your attention to several of the more interesting spots.

As the first section closes, the rhythm stops and there is a pause while the voices slide into a chord that is dissonant (does not harmonize traditionally) with the instrumental chord. Both the break in the rhythm and the dissonance were "no-no's" in rock music prior to this. The following section has at least two vocal layers. One sings the line "heroes and villains" while another sings a "bomp-bomp-bomp" accompaniment over sustained organ bass notes. The voices fade and only the organ remains.

After the "la-la" section, another multilayered vocal ("doo, doo, doo") takes place that contains considerable complexity; it pulls together just at the end of the section. This section (and several subsequent sections) is *a cappella*, that is, without instrumental accompaniment. In the "my children were raised . . . " section, note the method of producing the vocal accompaniment tones: a hard glottal attack followed by a decay. The subsequent section removes all accompaniment and echo, resulting in an old barbershop quartet sound.

Do not be discouraged if you are unable to separate all of the various sound layers in "Heroes and Villains." Get what you can and try to appreciate the complexity involved in conceptualizing and producing this song. Although the Beatles had a greater impact on rock history, Brian Wilson and the postsurfing Beach Boys were doing work just as creative, if not more so, at about the same time (1966 to 1967). And to a large extent, Brian "did it himself"; he had no George Martin. But then, that story awaits us in Chapter 6.

**6**

# The Beatles

## OVERVIEW: REVOLUTION WITHIN A REVOLUTION

The coming of rock and roll turned both music and the music industry upside down. The pop sounds of Perry Como, Eddie Fisher, and Doris Day yielded to the rocking sounds of Elvis Presley, Little Richard, and Jerry Lee Lewis. An industry dominated by five major record companies was now populated with hundreds of successful, small independent companies. A well-ordered succession of predictable hit records, each sustaining its popularity for months at a time, was replaced by a dizzying sequence of hits and artists, many of whom zoomed to popularity only to fade to obscurity within a few weeks. Even the general society felt the changes. A white adult-oriented society was transformed into a youth-oriented society with a growing acceptance of, and even fascination with, the black culture. And all of this flip-flopping took place in the space of about three years. Rock and roll was a revolution.

By the beginning of 1964, rock was ready to enter its second decade. Much of the power of that original thrust had dissipated. Music was in a state of confusion. Fans listened alternately to Elvis, the teen idols of soft rock, the silly novelty tunes, the female (and male) doo-wop groups, the increasingly serious folk groups, the equally "unserious" surfers, and to a plethora of twists and other dance records. What was rock and roll in the early 1960s? One could give half a dozen equally valid answers.

Society, too, was in a state of disarray. The 1960s had begun as the Kennedy years, as America entered a New Frontier (Kennedy's name for his overall political program). The folk singers sang of peace, racial justice, and the "love between the brothers and the sisters all over this land." There was a new kind of optimism "blowin' in the wind." But as the shots echoed through Dealey Plaza in Dallas on November 22, 1963, the dream shattered. America's youngest president, the symbol of this new hope for a utopian future and the youth culture's philosophical leader, was killed by an assassin's bullet. The hope, optimism, and faith of the youth movement was simultaneously staggered by that same bullet.

The nation's emotional reaction is difficult for today's youth to comprehend. Since 1963, the list of prominent political and social figures who have been the targets of violence is long and varied. Our society has become accustomed (and comparatively desensitized) to political violence. But in November 1963, the shock of John Kennedy's assassination sent the nation into a prolonged period of depression and self-doubt. The United States was a civilized nation; things like that just did not happen here!

But no matter how hard we tried to deny it, we could not. Were we a sick society? What was wrong with American culture that could allow such an assassin to emerge from within it; and then, to our horror, there was even an assassin of the assassin! The liberals blamed the conservatives; the conservatives blamed the liberals. The Communists did it; the anti-Communists did it. And so on and so forth. Even today many people can tell you exactly where they were and what they were doing on November 22, 1963, when they first heard that shocking news—Kennedy's been shot!

The United States has always been a nation with a cultural inferiority complex. "Real" culture came from Europe. Americans considered their indigenous cultural products to be unsophisticated at best, and downright embarrassing at worst. Not until the early years of the twentieth century did classical composers begin to create a uniquely "American" style. Previously they had merely based their style on European models. When classical performers aspired to the concert stage, it was obligatory that they journey to Paris, Rome, Vienna, or London for study. Similarly, many music scholars enthusiastically studied and wrote about the folk music of Europe or the Far East, but rarely considered the folk music of America worthy of serious academic pursuit.

Jazz was perhaps the most embarrassing of all (until rock and roll, of course). Although Americans viewed jazz (arguably America's most significant musical contribution to world culture) as just fun music (or worse), not worthy of being taken seriously, many important European composers included elements of jazz in their "serious" compositions. Soon jazz was no longer a strictly American phenomenon. After all, it had traveled to Europe and had been taken seriously by European composers, and there were fine European jazz performers playing "our" music. It must be okay! Today, high schools and universities offer jazz ensembles, jazz history courses, and even jazz degrees.

Rock and roll was an even bigger embarrassment than jazz. No one could take *that* seriously! It was just noisy American teenage music (heavily black-oriented besides). To be legitimized, it would need to receive the European "seal of approval," as jazz had done decades earlier.

With the Kennedy assassination generating national self-doubt, our cultural inferiority complex reached an all-time low; we were vulnerable to a cultural invasion. With that invasion, rock and roll, itself an American revolution, would experience its own revolution. The rules were about to be rewritten. Things would never be the same again.

## THE EARLY BEATLES

### The Formative Years

Volumes have been written on the Beatles, as a group and as individuals. Lengthy film and television documentaries have been produced (the BBC did a thirteen-hour documentary on them). We shall not attempt to include here every detail nor tell every anecdote of Beatledom (see the bibliography for more exhaustive studies). Instead we shall describe how the group originated, what their early style was, and how Beatlemania hit America. We shall then discuss a middle period of expansion and tentative experimentation. Finally, we shall examine their mature period in which, even as they were beginning to come apart, their work redefined the perimeters of rock and roll and sent music in new directions.

John Winston Lennon was born in Liverpool, England, on October 9, 1940. His mother Julia was a fun-loving and carefree soul who, within a year of John's birth, left her husband to live with another man. John's father was a ship's steward and frequently had been absent from home for extended periods. Increasingly, John was left in the care of his Aunt Mimi (Julia's sister) and Uncle George. Unlike John's natural parents, Mimi and George made John the center of their lives; they became his substitute parents.

From his earliest days in primary school, it was obvious that John was bright. He loved to read and frequently created poems, short stories, and drawings. Equally obvious was a streak of impishness that gradually progressed through mischievousness into a mild form of delinquency. After Uncle George's sudden death in 1955, John became more and more of a burden to Aunt Mimi; his grades dropped and his rebellion became more troublesome. In 1956, John first heard Elvis Presley's recordings; he was mesmerized. Julia shared her minimal knowledge of banjo with John, who had obtained an inexpensive guitar. Although the BBC declined to play rock and roll, Radio Luxembourg did, and John listened constantly. He adopted the rebellious "teddy-boy" image: greasy hair, ducktail in back, a pointed slide of hair in front, and tight "drainpipe" pants.

What finally moved John to action was a smash hit (in Britain) by Lonnie Donegan, "Rock Island Line." It was in the "skiffle" style—a simple, three-chord style featuring an easily accessible instrumental lineup of guitar or banjo, or both, and homemade instruments such as a washboard (played with thimble-capped fingers) and "bass" made from a broom handle, wooden chest, and a tightly strung wire. John organized his own skiffle group, first named the Blackjacks but soon becoming the Quarry Men (John attended Quarry Bank High School). Working wherever they could find jobs, the Quarry Men played both skiffle and rock and roll, imitating Presley, Haley, Little Richard, and others. In July 1957, they were playing a garden party in Woolton when band member Ivan Vaughan introduced his friend from Liverpool Institute to John. After several days, John invited Ivan's friend Paul McCartney to join the Quarry Men.

The Quarry Men (*Source:* Michael Ochs Archive, Ltd.)

James Paul McCartney was born on June 18, 1942. Paul, like John, was naturally bright, excelling in English composition and art. But unlike John, Paul enjoyed his success at school and created an impressive scholastic record. By 1955, the McCartneys had moved to a home only one mile from Mimi Smith's home in Woolton. When Paul was fourteen, the family was staggered by the death of Mary McCartney, Paul's mother. Jim McCartney, Paul's father, gathered his strength and determined to carry on the stable, orderly, and loving home his wife had helped to create.

Jim McCartney had run a rather successful society band (The Jim Mac Jazz Band) in the 1920s. His musical background was an influence in the McCartney home. When the skiffle rage hit Britain, Paul was determined to get a guitar. His father, happy to encourage musicality in his son, obliged. Although right-handed in every other way, Paul found it more natural to play his new guitar left-handed. He had the guitar restrung in reverse order and taught himself to play. He imitated the vocal and guitar styles of Presley, Little Richard, Carl Perkins, and the Everly Brothers. By the summer of 1957, he had become quite proficient. At the Woolton garden party when he first heard the Quarry Men, he amazed John Lennon and the others with his authentic renditions of Little Richard songs.

Once Paul became a member of the Quarry Men, he and John became close friends. They shared a passion for guitars and rock and roll; both were quick-witted and fascinated with language and art. But in many ways, they were vastly different. John was rebellious and iconoclastic; he fought any form of authority or inhibition. He could be rude and callous, reveling in "cruelty jokes" and deprecatory remarks about the physically handicapped, Jews, and other minorities. Nevertheless, he was generous to a fault. Paul, on the other hand, was practical to the point of being downright stingy. He strove for the approval of authority figures and consciously fostered an image of the good boy. He viewed the upper levels of society not with John's disdain, but with envy. In their commonalities lay the foundation of one of the most successful songwriting teams and entertainment acts in music history. In their differences lay the seeds of the eventual disintegration of the act and also, in some ways, the dual directions British rock would take from the mid-1960s to the present day.

By 1957, John had flunked out of Quarry Bank School. Yielding to pressure from Aunt Mimi, he enrolled in Art College in Liverpool. The skiffle style had run its course, and now the Liverpool groups, including the Quarry Men, were free to concentrate solely on rock and roll. It was in late 1957 that a young (fourteen-year-old) friend of Paul's started hanging around the Quarry Men. His name was George Harrison.

George (born February 25, 1943) attended Dovedale Primary School, near Penny Lane, at the same time John was there, although George was two grades behind John. In 1954, George went on to Liverpool Institute where he found a new friend named Paul who shared his interest in guitar, skiffle, and rock and roll. Like John, George resented formal education and did not do well in school. He too adopted the rebellious teddy-boy look and was easily hooked by the skiffle sound of Lonnie Donegan in 1956.

George's mother bought him a guitar, and he began to teach himself to play, copying the chords and bass lines from American rock-and-roll records, especially those by Buddy Holly. When Paul finally introduced him to the other members of the Quarry Men, he demonstrated a few of the patterns he had learned and sat in with the group whenever possible. John looked condescendingly upon this quiet fourteen-year-old, who was even then rather somber and introverted; nevertheless, he was tolerated as a friend of Paul's.

In July 1958, John's mother Julia was struck and killed by a car near Aunt Mimi's house. John continued his studies at Art College, where he met Cynthia Powell—the future Mrs. John Lennon. Meanwhile, the Quarry Men, often without a drummer, continued playing odd jobs here and there, whimsically calling themselves Johnny and the Moondogs, the Rainbows, and the Nurk Twins.

One of the most talented students at Art College was Stu Sutcliffe. Gifted but antisocial, he looked, dressed, and acted the part of the countercultural brooding artist. It was only natural that he and John Lennon would become friends. Stu saw John and his rock-and-roll image as a valuable addition to his young rebel image. Although he had no idea how to play, he bought a bass guitar, determined to join John's group.

Through local club owner Alan Williams (later to become their first manager), the group was booked on shows and even a Scottish tour. Tour promoter Larry Parnes suggested a name change; Stu suggested the name "Beetles," a reference to Buddy Holly's Crickets. Feeling that such a name was less than appealing, the group extended it to Silver Beetles, and for a while, Long John and the Silver Beetles. John, who had a never-ending fascination with spelling and language, suggested the misspelling that was to become a legend: Beatles.

The Scottish tour was a low-budget, second-rate tour that found them backing up some of Parnes's less impressive acts. But the Silver Beatles, by all contemporary accounts, were hardly a sophisticated musical act themselves. Paul was clearly the most competent; by this time, John was playing well enough; George was barely more than a beginner. Stu could hardly play at all and he knew it; he frequently played with his back to the audience to disguise his ineptness. The group had no coordinated stage costumes, no image, and no set act. To be frank, in May 1960, the Silver Beatles were not very good.

Back in Liverpool, Alan Williams contacted a club owner from Hamburg, Germany, named Bruno Koschmider. The latter had used British groups at his Kaiserkeller club before, and they had done well. Now Koschmider wanted a Liverpool group for another of his clubs, the Indra. Unable to secure one of the more prominent Liverpool groups like Rory Storm and the Hurricanes or Gerry and the Pacemakers, Koschmider accepted the ill-prepared, drummerless Beatles (during the summer of 1960, they decided to drop the "Silver"). To solve one problem, Paul McCartney approached local drummer Pete Best about joining the Beatles for a two-month booking in Hamburg. Pete promptly agreed and he and his glittering new drum set were in the Beatles.

Hamburg in 1960 was an attractive, clean German city, having been largely rebuilt after the destruction of World War II. Its entertainment district, known as the Reeperbahn (somewhat comparable to "the strip" in Las Vegas) was well-known throughout northern Europe for its free, hedonistic lifestyle, which offered alcohol, drugs, and sex to its fun-seeking patrons. The Kaiserkeller was a large, thriving club in the midst of this entertainment mecca. The Indra, however, where the Beatles were booked, was at the "wrong" end of the Reeperbahn. It was, to be charitable, a "dive."

Faced with the necessity of performing four and a half hours per night, night after night, week after week, the group began to forge a set repertoire and at least the beginnings of a stage act. Through fellow musicians at other clubs, they were introduced to the after-hours nightlife of the Reeperbahn—including large quantities of beer, free and easy sex, and "Prellys" (Preludin, a German diet pill that, in effect, was an "upper").

Good news came when Herr Koschmider decided to move the Beatles to the Kaiserkeller, where they would share the stage alternately with another band. Pete Best, although his drumming was certainly adequate for the Beatles, was otherwise rather distinct from the other four. The female segment of the audiences would stare right past John, George, and even Paul, and "make eyes" at Pete, whose athletic good looks upstaged the others. Furthermore, he did not join in the increasingly outrageous stage antics of John and Paul, nor in the off-hours revelries.

It was at the Kaiserkeller that Stu Sutcliffe met Astrid Kirchherr, a beautiful blond from an upper-class German family, whose talents were in art and photography. She befriended all of the Beatles, but developed an increasingly close relationship with Stu. She convinced Stu to let her cut his hair in a "French cut"—short, with hair down on his forehead. One by one, George, Paul, and John converted to the new hairstyle. Only Pete retained his greased pompadour.

When a new music club—the Top Ten—opened in direct competition with the Kaiserkeller, the Beatles defected, leaving Herr Koschmider in a rage. Possibly through Koschmider's suggestion, the German police discovered George was underage and deported him back to Liverpool. Shortly thereafter, Paul inadvertently set some curtains on fire and found himself on the wrong side of the German police. Soon, all of the Beatles decided to follow George home.

The Silver Beatles—Pete Best, George Harrison, Paul McCartney, and John Lennon (*Source:* Michael Ochs Archive, Ltd.)

The Cavern Club, literally a cellar below a warehouse near the Liverpool docks, had been a jazz club since opening in 1957. Realizing the growing popularity of the new "beat" sound, owner Ray McFall gradually included some local rock groups among the bands to be presented there. He hired the Beatles for his noontime shows and soon was attracting a large clientele of office and shop workers (mostly female). The Cavern Club was not opulent; it consisted of a small, crowded room with a small bandstand against one wall. The acoustics were poor, and the atmosphere was stifling. But the Beatles began to create a loyal Liverpool following.

In mid-1961, they returned to Hamburg to play at the Top Ten Club, alternating sets with singer Tony Sheridan. Trouble emerged as Paul became increasingly critical of Stu's unarguable lack of musical ability. Stu, in the meantime, was becoming more and more serious about his painting and about Astrid, gradually losing his interest in rock and roll. He was also suffering from severe headaches and his moods fluctuated wildly. Except for occasional performances for "old times' sake," he dropped out of the Beatles, allowing an eager Paul to move over to bass guitar.

On this second trip to Hamburg, the Beatles made their first commercial recording. Bert Kaempfert's Polydor label was primarily interested in Tony Sheridan. The Beatles, using the name "the Beat Brothers," served as Sheridan's backup band. Sheridan recorded "My Bonnie Lies over the Ocean" and "When the Saints Go Marching In." The Beat Brothers recorded "Ain't She Sweet" and an instrumental called "Cry for a Shadow." The Sheridan recording was released in Germany and was a fair success. The Beat Brothers' record remained in Polydor's vaults. John, Paul, George, and Pete headed back to Liverpool and the Cavern Club.

## Brian Epstein

Disc jockey Bob Wooler had been particularly interested in the Beatles for some time, and whenever he emceed a local dance, he encouraged the teens to ask their favorite record shop for "My Bonnie" by the Beatles. Sure enough, in October 1961, several of them went to one of the largest and most successful local record stores and asked the manager, Brian Epstein, for the new Beatles record.

Epstein knew nothing of the Beatles, the Cavern Club, or for that matter, rock and roll. The son of an upper-middle-class Jewish family, Brian was a sophisticated businessman whose passions were clothing design, theater, and classical music. A meticulous and organized man, he had taken over the record department of his family's large store, called NEMS. Brian took pride in the fact that through his connections in the record business he could fulfill any customer's request, no matter how obscure. Nevertheless, he searched unsuccessfully for "My Bonnie" by the Beatles. Since the teenage customers had said the group was from Liverpool and was playing at the Cavern Club just a few hundred yards from his store, Brian decided the easiest way to locate the record was to visit with the group itself.

The Cavern Club was hardly Brian's cup of tea; however he was fascinated with the four rough boys who nonchalantly tossed off song after song with a defiant disregard for their audience or the accepted standards of good taste. For the next month or so, Brian continued to visit the Cavern Club and even had several formal meetings with the Beatles. He had been quietly learning from his friends in the industry what it was like to manage a rock band. Against all advice, he finally proposed to the Beatles that he become their manager. To his surprise and delight, they accepted.

Although 1962 was to be a big year for the Beatles, it did not begin well. Brian's first priority was to obtain a recording contract. He started at the top with Decca, EMI, Philips, and Pye Records. In early January, the Beatles recorded some fifteen songs (including three originals) in Decca's London studios. Their nerves got the best of them and their performance was not impressive. Having decided to sign only one new "beat" band at that time, Decca elected to go with Brian Poole and the Tremeloes instead of the Beatles. When Brian Epstein heard of their decision, he was outraged. After an unsuccessful attempt to change their minds, he stomped out of their offices, warning the Decca executives that one day his group would be bigger than Elvis Presley. The executives smiled knowingly; they had heard that line before. More bad news came in April. As the Beatles landed in Germany for a booking at Hamburg's Star-Club, they were greeted with the news that Stu Sutcliffe had died that very day (the cause was subsequently diagnosed as a brain tumor).

## George Martin and Parlophone

The Beatles were ready for some good news. It came soon enough. In early June 1962, the Beatles returned to London to audition for Parlophone Records. Parlophone was a subsidiary label in the huge EMI family. To be accurate, among EMI's various component labels, Parlophone was at the bottom of the totem pole. Its normal fare included spoken comedy and some "light" music groups. The head of Parlophone was a knowledgeable, sophisticated musician named George Martin. He had ambitions of bringing Parlophone to a more competitive and respectable status in the industry. The new "beat" sound seemed to be one way to achieve this improved status; so he listened with interest to the demo tape Brian Epstein sent him in April. In June he listened to John, Paul, George, and Pete in person as they played through their repertoire. George liked the Beatles both personally and musically, sensing the hidden potential for a new and fresh sound. In July he offered Brian the minimum EMI contract: one year and four songs, at a royalty of one penny per double-sided record.

Things started moving fast. In August it was agreed that Pete Best was not fitting in personally or musically. George Martin had been using a session drummer for recording purposes, reserving Pete for public appearances. The boys gave Brian the job of informing Pete that he was being dropped. It was a crushing blow for Pete, a two-year Beatle veteran, coming just as they had finally secured a recording contract.

Richard Starkey was born on July 7, 1940, in Liverpool, in the midst of German bombing raids. In spite of a broken home and poor economic resources, Ritchie (as he was called) was a cheerful child. A series of illnesses took their toll on his education and his physical health. Because of many long absences from school, he was only minimally competent at reading and writing when he was discharged from school at the age of fifteen. Complications from appendicitis had left him with a delicate stomach; pleurisy had affected one of his lungs; even at fifteen he was showing signs of premature graying. After a brief experience in a skiffle band, Ritchie joined Rory Storm and the Raving Texans (later called the Hurricanes). Because he wore so many rings, he earned the nickname "Rings" and later "Ringo." Finally, "Starkey" was shortened to "Starr." The band established a strong reputation around Liverpool and Hamburg. They were certainly well ahead of the rough-edged Beatles. In Hamburg, Ringo hung around the Beatles on their off-hours binges, while Pete went his own way.

In August 1962, the Beatles invited Ringo to join them. He acquired a Beatle haircut, shaved his beard, and said good-bye to Rory Storm. The last of the six major pieces of what would become the Beatle legend (John, Paul, George, Ringo, Brian, and George Martin) was finally in place.

In September 1962, the Beatles recorded "Love Me Do" and "P.S. I Love You" for release by Parlophone. Ringo was replaced by a session drummer on their first recording. The record was released on October 4 but was given minimal publicity by EMI. Through some airplay on Radio Luxembourg and very minimal airplay on the BBC, "Love Me Do" eventually climbed to number seventeen by December 1962.

In late November, George Martin set up another recording session. Upon hearing the final version of "Please, Please Me," he assured the Beatles that it was destined to be number 1. Television appearances on *Thank Your Lucky Stars* and a radio appearance on the BBC's *Saturday Club* helped George's prediction come true. On March 2, 1963, the *Melody Maker* charts showed the Beatles' second release as number 1. They were the heroes of Liverpool.

George Martin wisely followed immediately with a full album of newly recorded songs from the Beatles' live performance repertoire. It was a mix of Lennon–McCartney songs (e.g., "I Saw Her Standing There" and "Do You Want to Know a Secret?") and cover versions (most notably the Isley Brothers' "Twist and Shout"). Brian busily arranged radio, television, and tour appearances, not only to

The Beatles with George Martin (*Source:* Michael Ochs Archive, Ltd.)

publicize the group and its record releases but also to ensure adequate revenue should the record successes prove to be of the flash-in-the-pan variety.

The third Parlophone release, "From Me to You," hit number 1 in late April 1963. By then, Gerry and the Pacemakers, old friends from Liverpool, had joined the Beatles on the charts. People began to speak of the "Liverpool sound" or the "Mersey sound" (the Mersey River ran through Liverpool).

As "From Me to You" was peaking in popularity, Cynthia Lennon, married exactly one year, gave birth to a son (April 23, 1963). John named the baby Julian, after his mother Julia. Meanwhile, Brian added several more Liverpool groups to his NEMS-based agency, and promoters and record companies flocked to Liverpool to sign any group that combed their hair forward, wore high-buttoned coats, and could hold a guitar. By midsummer, Brian was managing the number 1, 2, and 3 acts on the British charts: the Beatles, Gerry and the Pacemakers, and Billy J. Kramer and the Dakotas.

The Beatles' fourth big hit, "She Loves You," fared even better than its predecessors, zooming to number 1 on the basis of advance orders and holding that position for two months. In September, the *Melody Maker* poll showed the Beatles as the top British pop group. Their most notable television appearance of the year came in October with *Sunday Night at the London Palladium,* before a viewing audience estimated at fifteen million. In late October came a successful tour of Sweden; and in

The Beatles at the peak of British Beatlemania—1963 (*Source:* Michael Ochs Archive, Ltd.)

November came an appearance as a part of the 1963 Royal Command Performance for an exclusive audience that included the Queen Mother and Princess Margaret. It was at this show that John made his famous quip, "Will the people in the cheaper seats clap your hands? All the rest of you, if you'll just rattle your jewelry. . . ."

Late 1963 saw the British version of Beatlemania in full swing. Newspapers overflowed with Beatle interviews and articles portraying them as lovable, innocent, charming, witty lads; Beatles products were rampant. Their second LP, *With the Beatles*, was successful, as was their fifth single, "I Want to Hold Your Hand" (number 1). Parlophone, EMI's poor relation just a year earlier, had held the number 1 position for thirty-seven weeks out of the past fifty-two. And the Beatles, who just eighteen months earlier had been thrilled to see the inside of a real recording studio, now held seven out of the Top 20 positions on the British charts. But if British Beatlemania surpassed their wildest dreams, they "hadn't seen nothin' yet."

## BEATLEMANIA—AMERICAN STYLE

In 1963 everyone knew that real rock and roll was exclusively American music. Any other country's "rock" was merely a pale imitation. So when George Martin approached EMI-owned Capitol Records in the United States about releasing a Beatle record, he was virtually ignored. The fact that the record "Please, Please Me" was number 1 in Britain did not impress Capitol's American executives. After all, other British acts, such as Cliff Richard, had bombed miserably in the United States. George finally persuaded a small Chicago record company, Vee Jay, to release "Please, Please Me" and later, "From Me to You." Neither song reached the

Top 100. He also convinced Swan Records to release "She Loves You," and again, it failed to make the Top 100.

In November 1963, Brian Epstein flew to New York to try to break down the barriers. After much hesitation, Capitol agreed to release "I Want to Hold Your Hand" in January 1964. Brian also convinced promoter Sid Bernstein to present the Beatles in concert at Carnegie Hall. Finally, he contacted Ed Sullivan, host of a CBS television variety show that had aired for some twenty years. Sullivan, on a recent trip to England, had seen Beatlemania firsthand; he booked the group for two shows in February—as a novelty act. With considerable misgivings, the Beatles hoped to do what no previous British group had done: crack the American pop–rock scene. There was no way anyone could have foreseen that they would not only "crack" it but blow it wide open.

When several U.S. disc jockeys began playing privately obtained recordings of "I Want to Hold Your Hand," Capitol moved its release date up to December 26, 1963. By the time the Beatles stepped off the airplane in New York, their song had been number 1 for one week.

Beatlemania—American style—had begun. The American public was beginning to emerge from the tragic aftermath of the Kennedy assassination. Suddenly here were four lads who could not deliver a straight line if their lives depended upon it. Their happy-go-lucky music proposed nothing more than wanting to hold your hand! The right people in the right place at the right time.

With the success of "I Want to Hold Your Hand," other record companies began to cash in on the Beatles. Vee Jay rereleased "Please, Please Me," and Swan did the same with "She Loves You." MGM quickly obtained the rights to "My Bonnie," the record made by Tony Sheridan and the Beat Brothers back in Hamburg. Tollie Records issued "Twist and Shout." Later in 1964, Atco issued "Ain't She Sweet," another of the Hamburg recordings.

A crowd estimated at 5,000 awaited the Beatles at the airport. There were 50,000 applications for seats at the Ed Sullivan show; the auditorium seated 700. The nation's disc jockeys played Beatle records nonstop, pausing only to announce "Beatle time" and "Beatle temperature." All America watched the press conference to see what these strange, mop-haired people were like. The quick-witted charm came through strongly.

> *Reporter:* Was your family in show business?
>
> *John:* Well, me Dad used to say me Mother was a great performer.
>
> *Reporter:* What do you think of the campaign in Detroit to stamp out the Beatles?
>
> *Paul:* We've got a campaign of our own to stamp out Detroit. (Norman 1982, 279)

The lines were delivered with good humor, posing no threats to anyone (except possibly Detroit). The Beatles were intelligent, yet fun; they were talented rock and rollers, yet nonthreatening. America went wild.

It was estimated that the Beatles' first Ed Sullivan appearance was seen by some seventy million people—approximately 60 percent of the viewing audience. The Beatles were the subject of magazine and newspaper articles and radio and television special reports. The *Wall Street Journal* estimated that some $50 million worth of Beatle products would be sold in 1964. Unfortunately, Brian had not foreseen this

The Beatles with Ed Sullivan
(*Source:* Michael Ochs Archive, Ltd.)

potential market and had signed over 90 percent of the profits from such sales to an independent company called Seltaeb (Beatles spelled backwards), a company originally formed through Brian's attorney's firm.

The Beatles packed the Washington Coliseum sports arena and New York's Carnegie Hall. They returned to Britain having done more than they ever expected to accomplish with their American "invasion." By April 1964, the American pop charts had been Beatle-ized. With Capitol, Vee Jay, Swan, and others all issuing Beatle records, the market was glutted. "I Want to Hold Your Hand" hit number 1 on February 1 and stayed there for seven weeks. On March 21, it yielded the number 1 position to "She Loves You." Two weeks later, "She Loves You" gave way to "Can't Buy Me Love." A glance at the Top 5 for the week of April 4, 1964, is staggering:

1. "Can't Buy Me Love"
2. "Twist and Shout"
3. "She Loves You"
4. "I Want to Hold Your Hand"
5. "Please, Please Me"

In December 1956, Elvis Presley had placed nine singles in the Top 100 in one week. That incredible feat was surpassed on March 28, 1964, when the Beatles placed ten singles in the Top 100. By mid-April, there were fourteen Beatle singles in the Top 100 (Bronson 1988, 145). Granted, much of this chaos resulted from five record companies releasing Beatle records as fast as possible, but it is also true that people were buying them. It is estimated that 60 percent of the singles sold in the first quarter of 1964 were Beatle recordings (Belz 1972, 145).

The Beatles began to spread out to other ventures. John published some of his drawings, verses, and prose musings as *In His Own Write*. Later, in 1965, he published *A Spaniard in the Works*, which, like the earlier work, exemplified his whimsical fascination with the English language.

The Beatles' first movie, *A Hard Day's Night* (released in the summer of 1964), was a huge commercial success. The Beatles toured Scandinavia, Holland, Australia, and the Far East. In August they returned to the United States, where they found Beatlemania to be even greater than before. They performed in twenty-three cities, attended at every stop by total bedlam. The mobs at airports, hotels, and concerts engulfed them. Girls hid in hotel air conditioning shafts; fans were injured in the mad rush of the crowds; kids fell from overhead beams, balcony rails, and elevated walkways; they climbed onto the wings of the Beatles' airplane; often the Beatles escaped concerts in armored trucks. The anecdotes of Beatlemania are endless.

By early 1965 the multimillion dollar rock lifestyle was in full swing for the Beatles. There were elaborate new cars, new homes for themselves and their families, and steady girlfriends, along with the dizzying array of one-nighters. Marijuana became a regular habit in 1964; by 1965 their pill popping had spread to a regular rainbow: French Blues, Purple Hearts, Black Bombers, and Yellow Submarines. Finally, George and John were introduced to LSD—one of the most mind-altering of drugs. Meanwhile, the new government of Britain, headed by Prime Minister Harold Wilson, awarded the Beatles the MBE—Membership of the Most Excellent Order of the British Empire—an honor previously reserved for war heroes (which they were not), members of titled families (which they were not), and the very wealthy (which they were).

Their second movie, *Help!*, was as successful as *A Hard Day's Night*. A third tour to the United States began in August 1965 with a concert at Shea Stadium. Some 55,000 screaming fans nearly drowned out the sound of the music. By now, the Beatles had placed twenty-three songs in the American Top 100 (in eighteen months). Most of the songs were Lennon–McCartney creations and were relatively consistent in musical style. They tended to be pleasant, upbeat rock-and-roll tunes, easy to listen to, dance to, and enjoy. In these eighteen months a rather predictable Beatles style had become familiar to all. These were good, solid rock-and-roll songs, but not revolutionary and certainly not profound. In September 1965 it was reasonable to believe that the Beatles were nothing more than a delightful and incredibly successful rock-and-roll band with a distinctive but not shockingly creative sound.

## THE MIDDLE PERIOD: EXPERIMENTATION

By late 1965 the Beatles were in a position enjoyed by few stars in any field: They could do no wrong. Whatever they did it was, by definition, the Right Way. Usually once pop artists establish a successful style they cling to it desperately, for to experiment with new sounds is to risk loss of aural identity and fans. But the Beatles were in the unique position of being able to do whatever struck their fancy. Such freedom can be bewildering. It is easier when there are rules and guidelines, dos and

The Beatles at Shea Stadium (*Source:* Michael Ochs Archive, Ltd.)

don'ts, and accepted and proven precedents to follow. But the creative mind strikes out into the new and uncharted territory, always with a burning question, "What if I try this?"

The Beatles had that spark of creativity. Given the security of their position and the resulting freedom, they began to experiment. It was at this time that the basic differences between Paul McCartney and John Lennon began to emerge in serious ways, as their muses led them in different directions. Paul was rather conservative, sentimental, anxious to please, willing to conform, and extremely talented in a musically traditional way. John was rebellious, aggressive, bitterly cynical, linguistically adept, and less musically talented. Both, within the constraints of their very different personalities, possessed creative minds.

### "Yesterday"

In the spring of 1965 Paul approached George Martin with a song he had written called "Yesterday." He intended it to be a vocal solo for himself, accompanied only by his own acoustic guitar. It was a song with a beautifully flowing melody, an unusually sophisticated chord pattern (for pop–rock music), and a sensitive set of lyrics. Martin suggested that such a refined song should be set to strings—possibly a string quartet. At first, Paul reacted negatively. After all, what would people think of the world's most successful rock band singing to the accompaniment of a string quartet—the medium used by Mozart, Haydn, and Beethoven for their most eloquent musical statements. Nevertheless, Paul and George worked out an arrangement and recorded it. "Yesterday" was released on the *Help!* album in Britain and as a single in the United States. It not only climbed to number 1 in the United States, but also eventually became the Beatles' most recorded song, with over 2,500 cover versions (Bronson 1988, 185). Predictably, John hated the song. A soft love ballad with sentimental lyrics was not his style.

"Yesterday" is not a rock song. It is pure pop music. Thus, the song itself did not initiate a new style of rock. However, it did serve notice that the Beatles were no longer a predictable rock band content to grind out a string of hits according to a proven formula. If "Yesterday" had not been followed by more surprises, it would simply be another example of a rock group occasionally straying into the "legitimate" pop field (remember Presley, Domino, and Holly). But in light of what followed for the next five or six years, "Yesterday" takes its place as the first hint of what was to come.

### Rubber Soul

In late 1965, the first of three important Beatle albums appeared. These three albums would show a gradual increase in experimentation, providing a transition from the "yeah, yeah, yeah" early period to the mature style of the Beatles. *Rubber Soul* even *looked* different. The front cover showed the slightly distorted faces of the four Beatles; nowhere on the front cover could be found the magical words "The Beatles." It was an arty cover; somewhat surreal, it gave a hint of what would later be called psychedelic. Gone too were the "yeah, yeah, yeah" songs. John had discovered the lyrics of Bob Dylan. George Harrison had discovered the sitar. All four had heard the new folk rock from America. Four-track recording replaced the older two-track technology. As a result, rhythm, voices, and instrumentals could be recorded, erased, rerecorded, and mixed separately. Putting together a song became a constructive process, not unlike creating a fine painting, layer by layer. New ideas for

The Beatles on the *Rubber Soul* album cover (*Source:* Michael Ochs Archive, Ltd.)

sounds were contributed by Paul, John, and George, and then refined by George Martin. Sometimes Martin would propose new ideas or changes himself. It was a dynamic creative process.

During a tour to India, George Harrison had been introduced to the sitar by David Crosby of the Byrds. Anxious to integrate the unique sound of this exotic instrument into rock, Harrison found the perfect opportunity in John's new song "Norwegian Wood." Thus the experimentation with timbres new to rock (string quartet and now sitar) continued.

In "The Word," John's lyrics take a turn from the usual boy–girl Beatle songs toward his emerging philosophy of love as the answer to world problems. He says that the Word can set you free and that the "Word is Love." Again, this is a hint of things to come ("All You Need Is Love"). Paul's song "Michelle" is more traditional, being a song in praise of a woman. But its harmonies are not so traditional. As with "Yesterday," Paul creates a fascinating melody and a sophisticated sequence of chords. The bilingual lyrics (English and French) were not without precedent in pop music but were distinctly unusual for an American or a British rock group.

"In My Life" is generally a good song, but what is particularly interesting is the instrumental break. According to the "formula," somewhere in the middle of the song there should be a brief "break" that features an instrumental lead—usually a guitar. But the Beatles do not do the usual. Instead, there is what sounds like a harpsichord solo in a polyphonic texture more closely associated with Bach than the Beatles. The peculiar sound is actually a piano played by George Martin at half speed and an octave lower than desired. When mixed back in at double speed, it sounds at the proper octave and proper tempo. But this process alters the timbre of the piano to approximate that of a harpsichord. All of this extra creative effort was not necessary. The song would have been fine with the usual guitar solo. But that extra touch of creativity is what increasingly began to set the Beatles apart from other rock bands.

### Yesterday and Today

The next album, *Yesterday and Today*, was released only in the United States. "Nowhere Man" reveals a new kind of Beatle lyric. Previous Beatle lyrics dealt with boy–girl romance or other matters lacking in profundity. "Nowhere Man" is a social commentary, showing an awareness of the more serious, "relevant" lyrics of the folk and folk rock movement. The song describes the sort of person who refuses to "get involved," who wanders down the middle of life's road, voicing no opinions, supporting no vital causes, and never speaking his mind. The song urges him to change, get off dead center, and contribute to the dynamics of society. The heavier, socially oriented lyric was to become more common in subsequent Beatle songs.

Also on *Yesterday and Today* was "I'm Only Sleeping," with its guitar sounds mixed in backward (again, a device to be called upon many times later). Yet another hint of things to come was the song "And Your Bird Can Sing," with its obtuse, surrealistic lyrics (e.g., "You say you've seen seven wonders, and your bird is green, but you don't see me"). Beatle fans quickly came to recognize these kinds of songs as the work of John Lennon.

One of the more controversial examples of the Beatles' use of their new freedom was the cover design for the original *Yesterday and Today* release. Now known as "the butcher cover," it showed the four Beatles amidst large pieces of red, raw meat and decapitated baby dolls. After public cries of protest, Capitol recalled three-quarters of a million albums and provided replacements. As distasteful as it may have been in this case, we must again note the Beatles' ability to presage later trends (e.g., Alice Cooper and punk rock).

### Revolver

The third album in this transitional period was *Revolver*. Its release in August 1966 was coordinated with yet another tour to the United States (their last). The Beatles arrived to find themselves in the midst of the biggest Beatle controversy yet. Back in February, John had given an interview to an English reporter, which said, in part,

> Christianity will go. It will vanish and shrink. I needn't argue with that; I'm right and I will be proved right. We're more popular than Jesus now; I don't know which will go first—rock 'n' roll or Christianity. (Coleman 1984, 312)

The British public, accustomed to John's iconoclastic remarks, took the comments in stride. However, when *Datebook*, an American teen magazine, quoted the interview, there was a burst of outrage. Starting in the South, the reactions spread across the United States and eventually reached Spain, the Vatican, and South Africa, where Beatle records were subsequently banned for five years. But the most serious problem was in the United States. Over thirty radio stations banned Beatle records; there were protest marches and record-burning sessions. The public, which two and a half years earlier had fallen in love with the witty, charming Beatles, now found that that same cocky attitude had a negative side.

Brian Epstein attempted to offer the press "clarifications" and "explanations" aimed at taking the sting out of John's remarks. The gist of these apologies was that John was bemoaning the apparent decline of Christianity's influence as illustrated by the regrettable fact that the Beatles were more popular than Jesus. A certain percentage of the public, anxious to have their cute, lovable Beatles back, accepted such dubious explanations. But the pressure still mounted for an apology from John himself. Yielding to the pressure, the usually articulate John stumbled uncharacteristically through an "apology" of sorts at a press conference in Chicago. Gradually the furor died away.

Seemingly anxious to avoid a similar controversy, the media and the public ignored several potentially inflammatory remarks made by John about the Vietnam War. The American tour was a success, but the Beatles were tiring of the drudgery of live performance. Though no one knew it at the time, the Beatles' appearance on August 29, 1966, at San Francisco's Candlestick Park would be the group's last live concert ever. One of the problems was that the increasingly experimental nature of their recorded music made its exact replication in live concert virtually impossible.

The new album, *Revolver*, continued the trend of experimentation. The cover took the *Rubber Soul* cover one step further. Again, the group's name appeared nowhere on the front. The black-and-white cover showed sketches of the four famous faces; flowing up to the top of the cover was a montage of photos of the individual Beatles. The trend of the arty album covers thus established what would continue through the present day. The album itself contained more Indian-influenced sounds ("Love You Too"). There was a mainstream rocker ("Got to Get You into My Life") with added trumpets and saxes. And there was "Tomorrow Never Knows," with its tape sounds mixed in backward and at varying speeds, along with John's continuing love theme ("love is all and love is everyone").

Two songs stand out as further indicators of what would become the Beatles' mature style. Paul's "Eleanor Rigby" carries the string quartet idea of "Yesterday" a step further (this time a string octet). The song's lyrics focus on two lonely persons—Eleanor Rigby and Father McKenzie—who find themselves out of life's mainstream. In many ways this song seems to be a precursor of the subsequent *Sgt. Pepper* album. The nihilism of "Nowhere Man" ("making all his nowhere plans for nobody") is carried forward in "Eleanor Rigby" ("writing the words of a sermon that no one will hear" and similar lines). And lines like "Eleanor Rigby puts on a face that she keeps in a jar by the door" shows that Paul is not far behind John in his ability to turn the English language to his needs.

The other song of particular interest is "Yellow Submarine." Drug-oriented lyrics were creating controversies throughout the music industry. Such songs were usually written with liberal use of double entendre: lines that had two possible interpretations, one drug oriented and the other non–drug oriented. When challenged, the performers could innocently provide the "straight" interpretation; but to the initiated, the drug-oriented message was understood. The Beatles, though by this time into marijuana, pills, and LSD, had previously avoided this particular controversy. Yellow subs were a type of pill, and the lyrics described a dreamlike fantasyland. The sounds included bubbling sounds, gushing water, tinkling ice, and a military band. Heard at one level, it was what would later be called psychedelic. However, on

The Beatles on the *Revolver* album cover (*Source:* Michael Ochs Archive, Ltd.)

another level, it could be heard as an amusing childlike cartoon, much like the Beatles themselves—innocent, lovable, and cute. The double entendre and eventually the overt drug reference would also become a factor in the later Beatles' style.

### "Penny Lane" and
### "Strawberry Fields Forever"

In late 1966, the Beatles drifted in different directions. When they all regrouped in December, they began work on what would be a double-sided single: "Penny Lane" and "Strawberry Fields Forever." "Penny Lane" is a nostalgic look back to Liverpool, specifically the area where the Quarry Men had begun. Paul had heard a piccolo trumpet (a small trumpet often used for the high trumpet lines in baroque music) and asked George Martin if the instrument could be included in his song. Together they worked out the trumpet countermelody that characterizes "Penny Lane."

John's "Strawberry Fields Forever" was also a nostalgic look back to Liverpool—and much more. Strawberry Field was a Salvation Army home not far away from Aunt Mimi's house. But the lyrics convey more of an impression of nostalgia than anything specific. The words continue the surrealistic trend evident earlier in "And Your Bird Can Sing."

> No one I think is in my tree,
> I mean it must be high or low,
> that is you can't, you know, tune in,
> but, it's all right.
> That is, I think it s not too bad.

Two versions of "Strawberry Fields Forever" were recorded: one with a heavy guitar sound and a second with the softer sound of cellos and brass. The two versions were also played in different tempos and different keys. When John heard the two versions, he could not decide between them. He liked the beginning of one and the ending of the other. A simple splice would not work because of the different tempos and keys. With considerable technical skill and almost unbelievable good luck, George Martin managed to modify the tape speeds enough to bring the two versions together. The result is a very eerie sound that, with John's stream-of-consciousness lyrics, creates a purely psychedelic impression. Further coloration was added by mixing in (backward and at varying speeds) pieces of tape with the sounds of piano runs and arpeggios. John, who was sinking more and more into an LSD-oriented lifestyle, had created (with George Martin's help) a real musical drug trip.

Released in February 1967, "Penny Lane" and "Strawberry Fields Forever" both reached the Top 10 ("Penny Lane" hit number 1). The two songs revealed the increasing differences between Paul's and John's musical styles and lifestyles.

That year, 1967, was to be a pivotal one not only for the Beatles but for the history of rock music. The "Fab Four" were to experience several life-altering changes, and they would produce an album in which they would "put it all together," launching them into their most impressive period of musical productivity, while simultaneously revolutionizing popular music.

## THE LATER BEATLES: REVOLUTION

Paul McCartney summed it up well: "We're so well established that we can bring our fans with us and stretch the limits of pop" (Schaffner 1977, 53). With *Rubber Soul, Yesterday and Today, Revolver,* "Penny Lane," and "Strawberry Fields Forever," the Beatles (with the essential participation of George Martin) had tried a little of this and a little of that. They had pushed, pulled, poked, and tugged at the outer walls of rock and roll. In 1967, they would gather all of their creative forces, synthesize all of the experimental bits and pieces from their middle period, and produce one massive effort that would become the classic rock album in the history of rock and roll: *Sgt. Pepper's Lonely Hearts Club Band.*

### Sgt. Pepper's Lonely Hearts Club Band

If the decade of the 1960s was the century's most interesting decade (as many would argue), 1967 was that decade's most interesting year. For the Beatles the winds of change had begun shortly before the new year. On November 9, John had attended a preview of an art exhibit opening at the Indica Gallery. Both puzzled and fascinated by the avant-garde exhibition, he was approached by a small woman dressed in black. She silently handed him a card that contained one word: "Breathe." She was the artist whose works were being exhibited—Yoko Ono.

Early in 1967 Brian Epstein attempted suicide (he had tried once before). Brian was a tormented soul. When the Beatles decided to stop touring, Brian felt that he was no longer needed. George Martin produced their records. They hardly needed publicity any longer! And they had grown so independent that they paid little attention to Brian's advice anyway. His personal life was in turmoil, owing to his homosexuality and formidable drug habit. On August 27, 1967, he finally succumbed to

The Beatles and their manager Brian Epstein (*Source:* Getty Images Inc.)

an apparently accidental drug overdose. From a dapper, fastidious record shop manager in 1961 to a deeply troubled, suicidal drug addict in 1967, Brian Epstein ironically was Beatlemania's creator and, at the age of thirty-two, its first victim. But Brian had underestimated his importance to the Beatles. Without his sometimes unwanted and certainly unappreciated guidance, the Beatles' personal and corporate lives began to come unglued.

On August 4, 1967, the Beatles attended a lecture on spiritual regeneration given by an Indian guru, the Maharishi Mahesh Yogi. Fascinated by his words, they accompanied the Maharishi to Bangor, North Wales, for further indoctrination. They were there when the telephone call about Brian's death reached them.

Meanwhile, the *Sgt. Pepper* album had been released (June 1, 1967) and had begun its 168-week stay on the charts. It had begun as a whimsical song (by Paul) called "Sgt. Pepper's Lonely Hearts Club Band." The idea grew to become a unifying theme for a whole album. The Beatles would actually become Sgt. Pepper's band, presenting a series of "acts" in a psychedelic concert atmosphere. As work progressed, George Martin and the Beatles were energized by the gradual awareness that they were creating something truly innovative and unique—a revolutionary masterpiece.

The album begins with crowd noises; the music enters and Sgt. Pepper's band is introduced. The sound mix includes brass band music and crowd reactions. Next we are introduced to Billy Shears (Ringo) who moves directly into "A Little Help from My Friends." A simple and catchy song, it contains drug-oriented double entendres ("I get high with a little help from my friends") and the dialogue between Billy and a Greek-like chorus.

"Lucy in the Sky with Diamonds" is one of the album's most interesting songs. The initials, L., S., and D. send a fairly clear signal that the song is drug related. But, as usual, an alternative explanation was offered: John said that the song was inspired by a drawing made at school by his four-year-old son Julian. Certainly the lyrics evoke an LSD trip through fantasylike images (e.g., "tangerine trees and marmalade skies," "newspaper taxis," "Plasticine porters with looking-glass ties"). Musically, there is a shift of meter from the triple meter of each verse to the quadruple meter of the choruses. This is a first for rock and roll. After all, such meter changes almost destroy the song's danceability. Experimentation with timbre also contributes to the overall effect (e.g., the modified organ sounds near the beginning; the echoless voice at the beginning, which is then doubled only to return to solo voice, but with heavy echo).

Paul's song, "She's Leaving Home," draws on several earlier experiments. As with "Yesterday" and "Eleanor Rigby," the accompaniment is provided by a string ensemble, this time with harp added. The triple meter negates any rock feeling. Paul begins the story as a narrator; in the first chorus, falsetto voices comment as outsiders, while regular voices play the role of the parents. This pattern continues through subsequent verses and choruses. Internal ironies abound in lines like "She's leaving home after living alone for so many years." Similarly, no sooner have the parents said "how could she do this to me" than they say that they "never thought of themselves." Overall, the story allows a sympathetic insight into both the girl's problems and the parents' perspective. It was a common story in 1967 when thousands of teenagers ran away from home to hippie communes in San Francisco and elsewhere.

The lyrics of John's "Being for the Benefit of Mr. Kite!" came almost directly from an old theater bill he had purchased in an antique shop. The interest here lies in the instrumental sections at the words "Henry the Horse dances the waltz!" and "Mr. Kite is topping the bill"; both are accompanied by a dazzling blend of steam organ sound effects that were cut into irregular lengths and then mixed in at different speeds, sometimes backward, sometimes distorted—all over a steady simple waltz beat.

Side two opens with a sitar and other Indian instruments, announcing George Harrison's song "Within You Without You." The trancelike effect couches a philosophic discourse drawn from George's readings in Eastern theology. One hardly perceives a regular meter in this song, partially because of changes from quadruple to quintuple to triple meter, but also because of the irregular phrase lengths, which tend to obscure any strong metrical effect. Seemingly incongruous crowd noises yank us out of this otherworldly sound experience into the totally different sound world of "When I'm Sixty-Four." Paul has traveled back in time to evoke a musical style more typical of the 1930s than of a 1960s rock band. In tribute to his Dad, who had recently turned sixty-four, Paul may have been imagining what the old Jim Mac Jazz Band might have sounded like. The square beat and symmetrical form are throwbacks to the older pop style; the bridge sections (e.g., at "you'll be older too") break the symmetry and otherwise antique sound of this song.

Following "Lovely Rita," a crowing cock signals that we are in for another of John's somewhat eccentric treats: "Good Morning, Good Morning." The lyrics seem to comment on the emptiness of the average person's day-to-day life—going through the motions, issuing meaningless pleasantries, and fantasizing an exciting escapade. Unlike the old-fashioned clarinet sounds of Paul's "When I'm Sixty-Four," the heavier sound of saxes is used for John's accompaniment. The bridge section ("Everybody knows there's nothing doing," etc.) includes saxes playing a bass line drawn from earlier R & B-inspired rock and roll. The song ends with more barnyard noises.

Finally, the musical potpourri ends with a reprise of the *Sgt. Pepper* theme, thanking us for our attention and closing out the album's story line. But we are not really finished. With no break, we are pulled into a song called "A Day in the Life." John begins with a tale gleaned from his habitual newspaper reading. As the lyrics become more disjointed, John delivers the line, "I'd love to turn you on." This line (referring to drugs, music, sex, or spirituality?) is followed by a building wall of sound made by some forty musicians hired for this session. Their starting and ending points were established, and in between they improvised. As instruments are added and the notes climb in range, a seething yet stationary musical wall is erected. Suddenly near its peak it is cut off, and Paul enters with a new section ("Woke up, fell out of bed," etc.). As he describes going to the upper deck (smoking section) of the double-decker bus, he goes into a dream (marijuana cigarette?). As his voice floats rather aimlessly on the syllable "aah," heavy echo is added and the voice fades behind a steadily louder unison line, which finally takes over and moves with a transitional cadence into the next section. John returns to the same music with which the song began. Again he ends with the line, "I'd love to turn you on," followed by the building wall of sound. This time, however, the wall is not curtailed until it reaches its peak. A dramatic silence follows, and then a huge chord is struck; the chord is allowed to decay (diminish in volume) until it disappears into silence. The total decay time is some forty-five seconds. It is, to say the least, a strange way to end an album. What is the purpose of this chord? Although we are unable to say for sure, it is fun to speculate. There is no doubt that the Beatles knew they had produced a monument in rock and roll. It would have been discouraging for them to have invested over four months (and some 700 hours) of creativity into an album only to have their listeners pay casual attention to the record and, the second it ends, give it no further thought, moving right on to another record or to other activities. The ending chord of *Sgt. Pepper* does hold us up for what seems to be an interminable forty-five seconds. It almost forces us to reflect. Perhaps that is the point.

*Sgt. Pepper* was a success both commercially and critically. Virtually every phase of the pop industry recognized it immediately as being a revolutionary album. There were complaints, of course, about the drug messages (some real and some imagined). In an interview with Alan Aldridge, Paul admitted that "A Day in the Life" contained intentional drug references but denied that any of the other songs were drug related. He said that everyone seemed to find drug references in their songs, so they finally decided to go ahead and write a flagrantly drug-related song (Eisen 1969, 145). His apparent candor added to the confusion. Why admit a drug reference in one case and deny it in another? In interpreting Paul's remarks, we must remember the Beatles' delight in confusing and "putting on" the public.

Beatles *Sgt. Pepper's Lonely Hearts Club Band* album cover
(*Source:* Michael Ochs Archive, Ltd.)

Almost as important as the music itself was the revolutionary *Sgt. Pepper* album cover. Folding like a book, it was more elaborate than any previous pop or rock album. Every detail of the front cover has been scrutinized and analyzed. In addition to the Beatles in their Sgt. Pepper costumes, there are some sixty other familiar faces (including Stu Sutcliffe's). On the back cover are the complete lyrics (another new idea for rock albums) and the four Beatles with Paul's back to the camera (more about that later). Along with the record came a cutout sheet with sergeant's stripes, a picture card, a mustache, two badges, and a stand-up cutout. After *Sgt. Pepper*, elaborate album packaging became the norm.

The idea of unifying the entire album with one thematic concept also became widely imitated. The term *concept album* became a chic catchword in the industry. It suddenly seemed that every group was producing concept albums (sometimes the concept was more imagined than real). Frequently a specific "theme song" opened and closed such albums, as was suggested by the Sgt. Pepper theme and its reprise.

And 1967 was not yet over. Later in June the Beatles appeared as British representatives on an international television special beamed to hundreds of millions of viewers via satellite. They sang "All You Need Is Love." Their huge successes were followed by their first flop. Paul's idea for a film called *Magical Mystery Tour* revolved around the Beatles and a weird entourage of "friends" touring the British countryside in a psychedelically painted bus. Everything possible went wrong. Their fans and the media surrounded them at every stop. There were endless traffic jams and overlooked practicalities (such as hotel reservations and studio time). The enthusiasm of the Beatles waned, but Paul persisted. After being shown on British television on December 26, the film was massacred by the critics. And for once the public agreed. The days of "the Beatles can do no wrong" were over. Insiders agreed that if Brian had still been around to shepherd his headstrong foursome, this disaster might have been averted.

Fortunately the *Magical Mystery Tour* album was a successful follow-up to *Sgt. Pepper*. The American release contained the six songs from the movie plus other collected singles. Of particular note are "The Fool on the Hill," a simple yet beautiful ballad by Paul, and "I Am the Walrus," an eccentric song by John. In the latter, John creates more wordplays and surrealistic combinations, based loosely on Lewis Carroll's *Through the Looking Glass*. There are orchestral instruments playing traditional sections and then sliding from one pitch to another, adding the psychedelic touch. There is a chanting chorus mixed in, various verbal interpolations, and even a reading of Shakespeare's *King Lear*.

Yet another post-Brian disaster awaited the Beatles. In December 1967, they opened their Apple Boutique. Within eight months, the boutique had failed; the Beatles created chaos when they closed the store with the sale to end all sales: They simply gave away their remaining inventory.

In February 1968, the Beatles announced that they were giving up drugs now that they had discovered a better way to obtain their spiritual goals. They followed the Maharishi to Rishikesh, India, for a full-fledged immersion into the guru's theology. There was fasting, chanting, mass prayer, and meditation. Ringo and his wife Maureen left after ten days; Paul and his girlfriend Jane Asher soon followed. Finally, even John and Cynthia and George and Pattie became disillusioned with the validity of the guru's teachings. After almost two months of indoctrination, they also left.

The Beatles with friends visit Maharishi Mahesh Yogi (*Source:* Getty Images Inc.)

During the two months in India, John had been corresponding with Yoko Ono. He was intrigued by her iconoclasm and the apparent profundity of her art works and writings. At times he made fun of her artsy eccentricity; but he also felt that she could lead him into intellectual and philosophical realms he had only imagined. John had previously confessed to Cynthia his innumerable infidelities. Now he began to flaunt his developing relationship with Yoko Ono before Cynthia's eyes. The other Beatles became increasingly aware of Yoko Ono during mid-1968. She sat beside John in the recording studio during sessions; she attended their business lunches and meetings; she seemed omnipresent and intrusive. Their resentment grew as they realized that Yoko was not simply John's latest fling but a permanent addition to the Beatle family.

The public became aware of Yoko Ono's relationship with John in June 1968. The Beatles' fans were even less amused than the other Beatles. Wherever they went, John and Yoko were greeted with catcalls and racial slurs; hate mail arrived regularly. For years Cynthia had endured John's sharp tongue, his endless touring, his inability to handle liquor, his LSD trips, and his persistent infidelity. To the utter amazement of all, John sued Cynthia for divorce on grounds of adultery. Flabbergasted and hurt, Cynthia countersued on the same grounds. John and his lawyers righteously denied the charges until it became obvious that Yoko Ono was pregnant; this weakened their argument considerably. Cynthia was granted a divorce in November 1968; she retained custody of Julian.

### *The Beatles* (the "White Album")

The most important Beatle album to come out in 1968 was simply entitled *The Beatles*. It has become known as the "White Album" because its cover is completely white and devoid of any print or graphics except on the spine and a number on the front cover representing the order of production. Having launched an explosion of garish, elaborate album art with *Sgt. Pepper*, the Beatles now went to the opposite extreme with the ultimate in plain simplicity.

The White Album was a double album (previously rare in pop music except for special collections) and contained thirty songs. Beatle fans consider it either their heroes' best or worst album! The controversy arises from the extreme eclecticism of the music: There is a bewildering variety of styles on this album. Although the reason for this eclecticism was not apparent to all at the time, it has since become obvious. The White Album was not so much the work of one group but of four individuals, each of whom was heading in a different direction. The album seems to telegraph the message that the breakup of the Beatles was imminent. The sessions that produced *The Beatles* were characterized by tension, bickering, resentment, and egocentricity. John's songs were harsh, eccentric, avant-garde, and purposely uncommercial. Paul's contributions seemed (at least to John), sentimental, bland, and overly commercial. George added four songs to the White Album, but tried to stay out of the escalating Lennon–McCartney tug-of-war. Ringo, musically the most conservative of the group, seemed beaten down by the battles; he even resigned, leaving the sessions for several weeks before being talked into returning. These problems would have been enough to doom the average rock group and their album. But the White Album somehow managed to emerge as a very successful album musically and commercially. It reached number 1 on the album charts and held that position for nine weeks (144 weeks in the Top 200).

There may be a secondary, more subtle reason for the extreme variety of style on the White Album. Jan Wenner, in *Rolling Stone* magazine, said "The Beatles is the history and synthesis of Western music" (Schaffner 1977, 113). Although that might be an overstatement, it nonetheless contains an element of truth. By 1968, the Beatles were the personification of the old cliché: They were legends in their own time. And they knew it. They also knew that their life expectancy as a group was limited. Throughout the White Album there are musical and verbal references to a wide variety of preexisting musicians and styles, each of which had contributed in one way or another to the musical fabric from which the phenomenon known as the Beatles had grown. Whether it was consciously done or not, the White Album seems to pay tribute to the Beatles' musical predecessors—to the many influences that had to have been there first for there to have been Beatles. Their tributes are genuine and authentic.

Although we could randomly select almost any six songs from *The Beatles* to exemplify the eclecticism of this album, let us look closely at these six:

"Back in the U.S.S.R."
"Why Don't We Do It in the Road?"
"Honey Pie"
"Revolution 9"
"Good Night"
"Rocky Raccoon"

The Beatles in the late 1960s
(*Source:* Michael Ochs Archive, Ltd.)

Listening objectively to these six songs, it is hard to imagine that these songs were done by the same group, much less on the same album. Once again, the Beatles had revolted against themselves. This is the exact opposite of the concept album trend they themselves had begun with *Sgt. Pepper.*

"Back in the U.S.S.R." is a straight-ahead mainstream Beatles rock song. The overall concept derives from Chuck Berry's "Back in the U.S.A." At the bridge the Beatles play musical and verbal tribute to the Beach Boys. The historic connection of Berry and the Beach Boys is particularly appropriate (recall "Surfin' U.S.A.").

The Beatles were not given to the use of the old twelve-bar blues. Some British bands were basing their entire approach on the historic twelve-bar form. The Beatles' interest, however, was in breaking new ground by creating new forms and harmonic progressions in rock and roll. But the White Album contains three 12-bar blues: "Yer Blues," "Birthday," and "Why Don't We Do It in the Road?". This last song is just about as basic as a twelve-bar blues can be. There are no complications, no tricks, no gimmicks. The basic harmonies are pounded out on the piano, and the lyrics are shouted in true R & B tradition. Whereas we might have expected the Beatles to produce a sophisticated, modified interpretation of the blues, instead we get the raw, authentically performed genuine article.

The same is true of "Honey Pie." Picking up where he left off with "When I'm Sixty-Four," Paul creates a genuine replica of the old pop song style of the 1920s. Imitating the sound of a scratchy old 78-rpm record, Paul begins with a verse section without a regular beat. The verse sets the scene for the chorus, which is accompanied by a regular quadruple beat. The instrumental backing is a perfect representation of the old bands of the preswing era, with their emphasis on the clarinet ensemble. A hint of Charleston rhythm is added; and there is even a brief tongue-in-cheek reference to Tiny Tim, a musical curiosity of the late 1960s who sang old songs of the 1920s in a high, vibrating falsetto accompanied by ukulele. Again the form, melody, harmony, and timbre combine to recreate the earlier style with perfect authenticity.

If the varying styles of other White Album cuts seem surprising, John's "Revolution 9" provides a real shock. It offers over eight minutes of miscellaneous sounds welded into a musical montage. There are bits and pieces of various conversations, musical segments backward and forward, and sound effects at various speeds. Intermittently a voice clearly enunciates "number 9, number 9." There is hysterical laughter, radio distortion, and some moaning and heavy breathing, speeded up to sound like the gurgling sounds of a baby. The other Beatles and George Martin pleaded with John not to include the "song" on the album, but his determination was unswerving. A poll of fans by the *Village Voice* revealed "Revolution 9" to be the most unpopular of all Beatle works (Schaffner 1977, 115). Although the piece may have mystified Beatle fans, it was nothing new to the classical avant-garde. Composer John Cage had worked for years with musical montages of this type. His *Variations IV* is actually quite similar to "Revolution 9," except that Lennon's essay added the rather attractive unifying device of the recurring "number 9." John and Yoko both knew and admired Cage's work, so in that sense "Revolution 9" fits in nicely with the other works on the album, which authentically reflect the work of other musical predecessors and contemporaries. John's obsession with the number 9, by the way, derived from the fact that the number had been an uncanny part of almost every significant aspect of his life.

After the seemingly mindless cacophony of "Revolution 9," we are dumped into the pop world of the early 1950s with John's "Good Night" (sung by Ringo). Again, it is a perfectly authentic representation of the pop style described in Chapter 2, "The Roots of Rock," of this book. There is the lush orchestral accompaniment, the background choir, the lyrical melody, the beautiful harmonies, and the subdued rhythms that typify this style. Yet the performance does not seem to be a parody but an authentic rendering of another musical predecessor of the Beatles.

"Rocky Raccoon" is a humorous narrative that seems to poke gentle fun at the folk ballad style. Paul is accompanied by acoustic guitar and harmonica, bringing to mind the pre-1965 Bob Dylan. Paul even allows his voice to slump off pitch, especially at the end of phrases, just like Dylan (e.g., listen to the phrase "booked himself a room in the local saloon"). "Rocky" pays good-natured tribute to Dylan, albeit with tongue planted firmly in cheek.

Other songs on the album reinforce the notion that the individual Beatles were heading in very different directions and that the album contains references to the groups' predecessors, contemporaries, and influences. John's "Happiness Is a Warm Gun" begins with typical Lennon-style surrealistic lyrics; but midway, the music turns to a late 1950s doo-wop style, complete with I-vi-IV-V progression, doo-wop backup on the words "bang-bang-shoot-shoot," and vocal falsetto. In "Julia," John writes a beautiful, sentimental song in loving memory of his mother. His "Yer Blues" is a raucous rock song in the style of many contemporary British blues-based bands. He refers to the Maharishi in "Sexy Sadie," with lyrics directly critical of the guru, although John thought better of specifically naming him and substituted the new title. Paul's "Blackbird" gives hints of his views of the shaky status of the group and suggests his own ambitions ("take these broken wings and learn to fly; all your life you were only waiting for this moment to arise"). "Savoy Truffle," by George, uses a horn section reminiscent of earlier Beatle songs and Harrison songs to come. "Long, Long, Long" delivers George's religio-philosophical theme of love, whether the man-to-woman type of love or the love of God.

The White Album was released on the new Apple Records label. The idea of the Apple Boutique had gradually expanded into other ventures, such as Apple Music, Apple Films, Apple Publicity, Apple Records, and Apple Electronics, all under the aegis of Apple Corps, Ltd. Not the least of the new organization's components was the Apple Foundation for the Arts, an agency that would provide money and other resources for struggling, unknown artists in all fields. But Apple Foundation was soon submerged in a sea of tapes, musical manuscripts, novels, paintings, plays, and so on. It was a nice idea, but also a highly impractical one.

That music can have a remarkable effect on human behavior is a fact that has been known for centuries. A regrettable example arose in mid-1969 when Charles Manson led his communal family on a bloody binge that resulted in the gruesome murder of actress Sharon Tate and others. Manson viewed the Beatles as prophets, and his interpretation of songs like "Helter Skelter," "Blackbird," "Revolution 9," and "Piggies" convinced him that his heroes were instructing him to commit bloody atrocities upon wealthy white society. The scenes of his crimes were adorned with titles of Beatle songs written in the blood of his victims. As Brian Epstein had learned earlier, and John Lennon would experience later, Beatlemania had its darker side.

Apple Records' first single release proved to be the Beatles' biggest seller of all time: "Hey Jude" backed with "Revolution" (not the same as "Revolution 9"). "Hey Jude" (number 1 for nine weeks) was slightly over seven minutes long—nearly three times the length of the normal Top 40 song. Beginning only with Paul's piano and vocal, the song builds steadily by adding more and more vocal and instrumental accompaniment. Once the peak level is reached, it builds even more impact by constant repetition; the fade-out line lasts some four minutes. With "Revolution," John attempted to clarify his role within the youth revolution; specifically, he agreed that the world needed change, but he felt that a line should be drawn short of destructive revolution. The song naturally created controversy. To the more radical youth it sounded like a sellout—a namby-pamby revolutionist who espoused revolution only to the extent that it remained comfortable. However, to most, it seemed a responsible statement of the ideal of constructive change. John and Yoko's philosophy of idealistic nonviolence would become their main theme in the years to come.

Several other Beatle productions occurred in 1968. A cartoon feature film called *Yellow Submarine* featured caricatures of the Beatles in a psychedelic fantasyland adventure. George Harrison issued a solo album, *Wonderwall Music*, half of which featured Eastern-derived sounds, the other half, Western-style songs. As implied by the symbolic wall on the cover with only one brick missing, *Wonderwall Music* suggests the minimal musical interchange between East and West.

Far more controversial was John's album *Two Virgins*. Created with Yoko Ono, the album contains a collection of sounds typical of the late 1960s avant-garde:

screams, squawks, and blowing noses. But the real controversy surrounded the cover, which showed John and Yoko in a full frontal nude photograph. The general reaction, even among devoted Beatle fans, was that John had allowed his eccentricity to get a bit out of hand.

There were few bright spots for the Beatles in 1969. A single, "Get Back," proved successful, rising to number 1 in the spring. Tensions had developed over the management problem. After Brian's death, the Beatles had tried to manage their empire on their own. It had become a chaotic disaster. John wanted New Yorker Allen Klein to become the Beatles' new manager. Klein had managed numerous rock acts off and on, including the Rolling Stones. Paul advocated hiring Lee Eastman, father of his new bride, Linda Eastman McCartney. George and Ringo lined up with John, possibly fearing the consequences of nepotism in a McCartney–Eastman arrangement. Klein became the new manager and began to put Apple's house in order. But the inherent problems were overwhelming, and the inevitable end was not far off.

After Paul and Linda's high-society wedding in March, and John and Yoko's marriage the same month, fans were beginning to wonder if there would ever be another Beatle album. John and Yoko seemed to be drifting further into eccentricity. They spent their honeymoon in the Amsterdam Hilton with some fifty reporters in attendance. They stayed in bed for a week, growing their hair for peace. In April, the Lennons held another "happening." This time they concealed themselves under a bag on top of a table. Such a posture, said John, promoted honest communication and would encourage world peace.

### Abbey Road

The best thing to come from the Beatles in 1969 was the *Abbey Road* album. This album continued the level of excellence achieved by *Sgt. Pepper* and *The Beatles*. The album title refers to EMI's Abbey Road studios, where the Beatles had been recording throughout most of their career. Even as the group was disintegrating, they managed to "Come Together" (the album's opening song) one more time, literally and musically, at and in Abbey Road (the studio and the album). Even though each Beatle contributed individual songs, the entire group played and sang on almost every track.

Perhaps the most interesting feature is George's emergence as a first-rate songwriter. His contributions to the White Album had shown considerable promise. But with "Something" and "Here Comes the Sun," Harrison achieved qualitative, if not quantitative, equality with Lennon and McCartney. "Something," with its clever harmonic progressions (especially its instantly recognizable cadence) and double time shifts, has become a standard. Similarly, "Here Comes the Sun" contains effective shifting accents in the chorus and changing meters in the instrumental break. These two songs are among *Abbey Road's* most attractive songs.

John was going in two opposite musical directions at the same time. There were the avant-garde experiments with Yoko Ono, but there were also genuine rock songs in which he seemed to be going back to basics. "Come Together," for example, is a throwback to basic rock and roll (although the lyrics are typical Lennon). "I Want You (She's So Heavy)" is a more modern example of the harder mainstream rock of the late 1960s. Almost eight minutes long, "I Want You" builds up to a powerful ending, with a unison instrumental riff in the midst of electronic distortion.

The Beatles *Abbey Road* album cover (*Source:* Michael Ochs Archive, Ltd.)

Paul's "Oh! Darling" is a slow rock song whose lyrics are screamed by the usually more lyrical Paul. It is also a throwback to earlier rock, complete with 1950s bass lines and chord progressions. "Because" is an effective song, using jazzlike vocal harmonies in which the Beatles' voices unite in a surprisingly sophisticated blend. Harpsichord adds color to the accompaniment; the result is a beautifully delicate texture.

The album concludes with a series of songs unified into a set. Lyrics and instrumental fragments unite the songs, which otherwise display considerable variety. Beginning with Paul's "You Never Give Me Your Money," the set moves to "Sun King" by John. Almost a variation of George's "Here Comes the Sun," the song recalls the sophisticated harmonies and textures of "Because." "Golden Slumbers" alternates with "Carry That Weight," a rock riff that leads to a strong example of the Beatles' guitar work. The beautiful and majestic "The End" closes the album on the recurring Beatle theme of love.

*Abbey Road* was the Beatles' biggest-selling album, holding the number 1 position for eleven weeks. Subsequent albums consist of reissues, unreleased songs, or specially recorded single tracks. Never again would the Beatles gather for the purpose of recording an entire album.

## The "Death" of Paul and the Breakup
## of the Beatles

Near the end of 1969 the famous "Paul-is-dead" hoax became an international rage. Charles Manson was not the only person who carefully studied Beatle lyrics, music, and album covers for hidden meanings and universal truths. Especially with Lennon's enigmatic lyrics, it became a challenge to analyze every line for the "real message." Fans found hidden messages in "Strawberry Fields Forever" ("I buried Paul") and backward messages in "Revolution 9" ("turn me on, dead man"), and between "I'm So Tired" and "Blackbird" ("Paul is dead; miss him; miss him") (Schaffner 1977, 127). The inclusion of backward messages ("backmasking") on records was not a hoax: The practice definitely exists. And indeed, if one listens to the aforementioned spots, the suspected messages do seem to be there.

The Paul-is-dead hoax spread like wildfire. Assiduous Beatle fans discovered numerous "clues" to confirm their suspicions. The theory developed that Paul had been killed in an automobile accident in 1966 (when the Beatles stopped touring) and that the first hints had appeared in *Sgt. Pepper* (e.g., Paul's armband on the inside cover reads O.P.D.—"Officially Pronounced Dead"). Reinforcing clues were found on *Magical Mystery Tour*, the White Album, and *Abbey Road*. The personal appearances of Paul McCartney did little to lessen the convictions of the believers. They were convinced that an impostor had taken his place. As of this writing, it appears to be a safe conclusion that the rumors of Paul's death were greatly exaggerated (in 1993, he released an album entitled *Paul Is Live*).

The death of the Beatles as a group was no hoax, however. In the summer of 1969, John and Yoko released a single called "Give Peace a Chance." The record was credited to the Plastic Ono Band, which was simply a group gathered hastily for this recording. In September, John and Yoko traveled to Toronto for a rock revival concert. John's real musical and spiritual life was now outside the Beatles. By 1970, it was clear that the Beatles were each going separate ways. In January, John and Yoko released an album from their Toronto Plastic Ono Band concert. In May, Ringo released a solo album (*Sentimental Journey*), as did Paul (*McCartney*). George quietly joined Eric Clapton's band on tour and prepared his own solo album, *All Things Must Pass*, to be released in December.

Paul's album included a "press interview" that, in effect, indicated that Paul was withdrawing from the Beatles. John, having agreed months earlier to keep his own plans to resign private, was furious with Paul for making such a public declaration. In April 1970, the Beatles' new film *Let It Be* was released. The record album of the same name was released to coincide with the movie. It consisted of tracks recorded a year earlier. The four Beatles were no longer interested in the *Let It Be* album project, so Allen Klein brought American producer Phil Spector in to sift through the various tracks and edit and remix them. Spector added strings, chorus, and layers of sound to the basic Beatles' songs. Though the songs are consistent with the Beatles' late-1960s works, Spector's production work seems overdone when compared to the more refined and understated ideas of previous Beatle albums. The album does contain an earlier Beatle single "Get Back," which is a good basic Beatle rock tune. And, of course, there is the title song, which in many ways sums up the Fab Four's attitude, not only toward the album but also to the ending of the legendary Beatles. Perhaps it was also their best advice to their many distraught fans: Let it be.

## Summary

When one thinks of rock's first five decades in the broadest sense, one is inclined to think of pre-Beatles and post-Beatles rock. They were the watershed. Their influence on the music is undeniable. But there were other influences: on clothing, hairstyles, lifestyles, and philosophies. As with Presley, they covered the entire spectrum of pop and rock. Within their work, there are examples of hard mainstream rock, avant-garde rock, psychedelic rock, symphonic rock, and lighthearted rock ditties. They had gathered together the first ten years of rock's development, molded it to their concept, added their own creative innovations, and then slung it into the future. It would fragment into a bewildering variety of styles and trends, as others would pick up and develop one or another of the stylistic fragments. Album art would never be the same again; there would be hundreds more "concept albums" and double albums. There would be more backmasking and hidden messages. No longer was rock simply fun music; it was serious. Scholars would analyze the music and lyrics; there would be university courses in rock music (unthinkable in 1962). The Beatles' legacy, some of it good and some of it dubious, would influence rock, and therefore people, for decades to come.

The four Beatles continued to produce individually after the group ended in 1970. George Harrison's *All Things Must Pass* was a boxed triple album and contained the single hit "My Sweet Lord," a song whose similarities to "He's So Fine" by the Chiffons (1963) earned George a lawsuit. In 1971, he sponsored a benefit concert to raise money for victims of the Pakistani civil war; appearing with him were Ringo, Eric Clapton, Bob Dylan, and others. He continued to produce albums reflecting his Indian theology and musical style. Harrison's albums in the 1970s and early 1980s experienced moderate sales. He died of cancer in 2001.

Ringo Starr followed his *Sentimental Journey* with a country-oriented album called *Beaucoup of Blues*. He stayed with a gentle, uncomplicated style of rock in subsequent albums and in the early 1970s had several hit singles ("Photograph" and "You're Sixteen"). He turned to an acting career in a number of rather average movies. Unlike John, Ringo strove for commercial success and uncontroversial popularity; unlike George, he was not selling any heavy theological messages or trying to save the world; unlike Paul, he preferred simple, uncomplicated music to sophisticated experimentation.

Paul McCartney emerged as the most successful ex-Beatle. With Linda McCartney, he formed Wings and produced several albums that were musical and commercial successes (e.g., *Ram* in 1971 and *Band on the Run* in 1973). Beginning with *Red Rose Speedway* (1973), he produced five consecutive number 1 albums. His *Tug of War* album (1982) included a hit single "Ebony and Ivory," sung with Stevie Wonder, and his next album, *Pipes of Peace* (1983), included "Say, Say, Say," sung with Michael Jackson. His movie *Give My Regards to Broad Street* was a reasonable success. By the 1970s, Sir Paul McCartney had become an elder statesman of music. Among other things, he turned his energies to large-scale pop-rock-classical efforts such as *Standing Stone* (1997).

John Lennon and Yoko Ono (*Source:* Michael Ochs Archive, Ltd.)

For John Lennon, the 1970s were difficult times. He and Yoko moved to the United States in 1971. For a while they involved themselves in politics and various social causes. When their visas expired, they began a four-year battle to avoid deportation. Although prior drug arrests were cited as the cause for deportation, there is some reason to suspect that the couple's outspoken espousal of unpopular causes did not endear them to the authorities. From 1973 to 1975, they were separated, with John moving to Los Angeles. Life began to clear up after his return to New York. In late 1975, John and Yoko's first child was born—on John's birthday.

In spite of all the personal difficulties, John had some success in his career. His *Imagine* album (1971) was a huge success, as was the hit single of the same name. Subsequent albums in the early 1970s also reached the Top 10. But in 1976, he retired from the music business to become a full-time husband and father. It was not until the autumn of 1980 that he and Yoko returned to the studio to cut an album of songs that would reflect the new John Lennon. There were no drugs and no alcohol at the sessions. The songs spoke of family relationships, clean living, and a very simple kind of love. The resulting album, *Double Fantasy,* pointed toward a new direction in rock music. But events were to leave that new direction undeveloped.

John had long been superstitious about the number 9. He and his son Sean were both born on October 9. Brian first met the Beatles on November 9; John met Yoko Ono on November 9. There were many other significant occurrences of the number 9 throughout his life and work (recall "Revolution 9"). He had even changed his name to John Ono Lennon, happily noting that there were now nine o's in his and Yoko's full names. In December 1980, John was shot by Mark David Chapman, a Beatle fan since the early days. He murdered John not long after obtaining his autograph! John died at 10:50 P.M. on December 8, 1980, in Roosevelt (9 letters) Hospital on Manhattan's Ninth Avenue. Because of the time difference, back in Liverpool, where it had all begun, it was December 9.

Over a quarter of a century after the Beatles disbanded, their recordings continued to sell. *Live at the BBC,* featuring fifty-six performances from the early 1960s, reached number 3 on the album charts in 1994. *Anthology 1, Anthology 2, and Anthology 3* were released in 1995–1996 and all reached the number 1 position. "Free as a Bird" and "Real Love" were "new" songs based on two John Lennon demos from the late 1970s. "Real Love" reached number 11 and became the Beatles' twenty-third gold single (the most of any group thus far). In 2000, the Beatles had sold over 113 million albums, more than any previous recording artists. An anthology of the band's number 1 hits (appropriately entitled *1*) became their nineteenth number 1 album. By 2001, this album had sold over twenty million copies. One can only wonder if and when Beatlemania will ever end.

## MUSICAL CLOSE-UP:
### THE TECHNICAL SIDE OF THE BEATLES' MUSIC

Before 1966, everyone knew what rock and roll was: simple, enjoyable music that was loud and usually fast, with a strong 4/4 beat (and backbeat); it had silly words, uninventive melodies, and three-chord harmonies; the songs lasted for about two and a half minutes, and the simple forms contained lots of repetition. Many songs still fit the old model. But by the last half of 1967 the boundaries had been pushed back. By the end of the 1960s, there were basically no limits to what a rock band could do, assuming that they were creative and talented enough to utilize the new freedom. Although others contributed to this revolution, the real impetus came from the Beatles. Certainly their early songs revealed moments of creativity, but it was with "Yesterday" in late 1965 that the Beatles began a revolution within rock and roll that would leave no parameter of music untouched and would redefine what rock and roll could be.

### Rhythm and Meter

If there were one fundamental "given" of early rock and roll (other than the twelve-bar blues, perhaps), it was the beat. The rhythmic underpinnings of mainstream rock were its insistent 4/4 meter, the moderate to fast tempos, the heavy backbeat, and the duple division of each beat. Slower tempos and triple division of the beat were reserved for soft rock styles. The Beatles challenged these "givens" and freed rock and roll from the tyranny of 4/4 meter.

One of the least disruptive metric changes in a 4/4 song is a single measure of 2/4. A quadruple measure is, after all, basically a combination of two duple measures. So by adding an extra pair of beats one does not disrupt the alternating flow of strong and weak beats. For example, listen to "Revolution" from the White Album. The song is basically in 4/4 meter, but there is a 2/4 measure inserted in the first two phrases. You can count along by counting two measures of 4/4 (eight beats), then two extra beats, and then resume counting two measures of 4/4. You should land on beat 1 on the word "world."

| "Say want re | well | know | world" |
|---|---|---|---|
| ↓ ↓ ↓ | ↓ | ↓ | ↓ |
| \| 1 - 2 - 3 - 4 \| 1 - 2 - 3 - 4 \| | 1 - 2 \| | \| 1 - 2 - 3 - 4 \| 1 - 2 - 3 - 4 \| | 1 |

For another example of the 2/4 measure inserted into a 4/4 song, listen to "Golden Slumbers" (*Abbey Road*). After counting seven measures of 4/4 (beginning on the words "Once, there was a way"), insert one 2/4 measure and everything works out fine.

Triple meter (e.g., 3/4 time) represents a completely different metrical world when compared with duple and quadruple meter. Triple meter is more typically associated with the waltz than with rock and roll. But in "Lucy in the Sky with Diamonds" each verse is in 3/4. One measure before the entrance of each chorus, there are four strong beats played by Ringo, signaling the change to 4/4 meter. As the song alternates verse and chorus the meter changes from triple to quadruple. "She's Leaving Home" is in triple meter throughout. In some songs the Beatles toss in one or more measures of triple meter. For example, listen to "Back in the U.S.S.R." On the second time through the opening section (beginning with "Been away so long I hardly knew the place"), the meter shifts to 3/4 for two measures at the words "Back in the U.S., Back in the U.S." (Alternately, one could hear these measures as continuing in quadruple meter with an extra duple measure added on the words "U.S.S.R.") "Blackbird" begins with a guitar introduction of seven beats (a measure of triple and a measure of quadruple). The verse follows this metric system:

$$\left| \frac{3}{4} \right| \frac{4}{4} {\longmapsto\!\!\!\longrightarrow} \left| \frac{6}{4} {\longmapsto\!\!\!\longrightarrow} \right| \frac{4}{4} \left| \frac{6}{4} \right|$$

The chorus also moves between measures of three, four, and six beats. Another interesting example is "All You Need Is Love." In the "Love, love, love" opening, there is an alternation of quadruple and triple meter. The verse follows this metric scheme:

$$\left| \frac{4}{4} \right| \frac{3}{4} \left| \frac{4}{4} \right| \frac{3}{4} \left| \frac{4}{4} {\longmapsto\!\!\!\longrightarrow} \right| \frac{3}{4} \right|$$

The Beatles occasionally experimented with five beats per measure. The introduction to "Good Morning, Good Morning" is in 4/4; but as the verse begins ("Nothing to do to save his life"), the meter switches to quintuple. After three measures of 5/4 (quintuple), there is a measure of 3/4 and a measure of 4/4. The verse continues to shift between triple, quadruple, and quintuple meters before the chorus settles into a more normal 4/4. Can rock have five beats per measure? Listen and see.

"Strawberry Fields Forever" introduces still another metrical shift. In simple meters (e.g., 4/4 and 2/4), there are two eighth notes (e) per beat. But there is another metrical structure called compound meter, in which there are three eighth notes per beat. If the eighth notes are of equal duration in both cases, the beat in compound meter is slower because each beat must accommodate three eighth notes instead of two. Study the diagram of the rhythmic structure of five measures from "Strawberry Fields Forever."

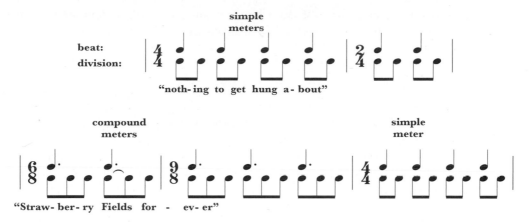

Notice that if the eighth note divisions move at a steady pace, the beat gets further apart (slower). In the section where John sings "Living is easy with eyes closed," there are three notes put into the space (two beats) where four eighth notes normally go. This confuses the metrical feeling even more.

Accenting notes irregularly also confuses one's perception of meter. In the middle section of "A Day in the Life," listen to the piano after Paul sings "dragged a comb across my head." Each beat is divided neatly into four equal parts (called sixteenth notes). But the accents fall off the beat, thus confusing the meter.

Needless to say, when songs have three or five beats per measure, when accents are irregular, and when the speed of the beat is shifting, the old rock-and-roll backbeat is nullified. Although most Beatle tunes retain the rock backbeat, some do not. For example, in John's "Give Peace a Chance," not only is the backbeat not present, but first and third beats are heavily accented—just the opposite of the rock backbeat.

Finally, the Beatles even challenged the concept that "real" rock and roll should have a moderate to fast tempo and soft rock should have a slower tempo. "Come Together" moves at about eighty beats per minute; that is just slightly faster than Presley's "Are You Lonesome Tonight" (seventy-five beats per minute). Yet "Come Together" is hardly a soft rock ballad. Consider also the songs "Golden Slumbers" and "Carry That Weight." Paul begins "Golden Slumbers" in a soft rock style; the tempo is about eighty beats per minute. Gradually Paul's voice hardens, and we move imperceptibly into "Carry That Weight"—certainly not a soft rock song, but still at the same tempo. Or, for the best example, consider the coda of "I Want You (She's So Heavy)." Using compound meter, the beat slows to about forty-five per minute. That is much slower than Elvis's "Love Me Tender" (seventy-two beats per minute), but no one has ever accused "I Want You" of being soft rock. In fact, one author suggests that this song is an early example of heavy metal (Schaffner 1977, 125).

### Melody

It has long been recognized that Lennon, Harrison, and especially McCartney were talented songwriters. Prior to the Beatles, mainstream rock melodies were generally repetitive and rather unimaginative. Melodic writing had not been an impressive aspect of R & B, and because much early mainstream rock was derived from R & B, rock melodies were similarly uninteresting. However, even in the early Beatle songs, melodies were unique and showed hints of real melodic flair (e.g., "And I Love Her"). But by the time their talents had matured, Lennon and McCartney (and later Harrison) were composing melodies that exploited a large range, combined stepwise movement with melodic leaps effectively, and were specifically designed to suit a particular song; each melody was an individual entity, not to be confused with another Beatle tune.

Sometimes, Beatle tunes move steadily up or down an entire scale. For example, "Norwegian Wood" begins on the fifth scale degree (above the key center, or tonic note) and gradually moves down the scale to the fifth degree below tonic. Conversely, "Yesterday" begins on the first and second scale degrees and then moves up the scale to the tonic note an octave higher before beginning a gradual descent back down the scale. Compare the melodic contours of these two songs, as shown below.

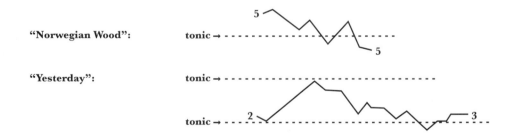

Other tunes are less scalar; they move by small leaps to outline chords. For example, "Got To Get You into My Life" begins by outlining the notes of the tonic chord (scale degrees 1, 3, and 5). Thus, the melody moves through scale degrees 5–3–3–3–1–5–5–5–3–3–3-(4)-3-(2)-1 before ending with a large leap from scale degrees 2 to 8.

The appeal of many Beatle tunes cannot be fully explained through technical analysis. Some writers simply have an instinctive feel for creating tunes that catch our attention and stay in our mind. The melodies for "Hey Jude" and "Yellow Submarine" are not particularly sophisticated; they are simple enough to be remembered and sung or whistled by the average listener, but different enough to be distinguishable from the other songs that clamor for our attention. The same can be said for the beautifully lyrical melodies of "Yesterday," "Michelle," and "Something." The association of words, rhythms, and melody makes a very powerful impression on our minds.

The Beatles were quite skillful at creating melodic lines whose rhythm successfully reflects the rhythm of the text. Their poetry often did not have the singsong regularity that allows for simple melodic writing. For example, consider the words from "Being for the Benefit of Mr. Kite!":

> For the benefit of Mr. Kite
> There will be a show tonight on trampoline.
> The Hendersons will all be there,
> late of Pablo Fanques fair, what a scene.
> Over men and horses, hoops and garters,
> Lastly through a hogshead of real fire!
> In this way Mr. K will challenge the world!

The rhythm in the melody of this song fits this text perfectly, and the melodic line is varied and interesting enough to carry us smoothly from beginning to end. This rather irregular text is set to music quite naturally, with no awkwardness.

The adaptability of Beatle tunes is exemplified by the number of cover versions of their songs. Indeed, one can hardly go through a day of hearing piped-in music in grocery stores, doctors' offices, shopping malls, and elevators without hearing "Eleanor Rigby," "Let It Be," "Hey Jude," and all of the others being played by a million and one strings.

## Harmony and Tonality

With the possible exception of the Beach Boys, there had been little real creativity in harmonic or tonal aspects of rock music prior to the Beatles. There had been hundreds of twelve-bar blues and an almost equal number of I-vi-IV-V progressions. Melodies and chords were drawn almost exclusively from the major scale or the old blues scale. Once a song was determined to be in a certain scale, the chords stayed close to just those notes. The technical term for this practice is *diatonic*—that is, adhering to the notes of a given scale. The opposite of diatonic is *chromatic*—using notes outside of the prevailing scale. For rock's first ten years, diatonic harmonies prevailed.

But the Beatles did not want to sound like everyone else. With very few exceptions, they avoided the twelve-bar blues and the I-vi-IV-V formulas. Their refusal to fall into the easy acceptance of rock clichés led them into some interesting harmonic territory.

Even with the early Beatles there are chord progressions that are surprises. "I Saw Her Standing There" begins normally enough, but after the words "So how could I dance with another" there are falsetto voices on "oh." The chord at this moment is a major triad whose root is the lowered sixth scale degree. This chord is found in neither the major scale nor the blues scale. We symbolize it as ♭VI: it is a "chromatic" harmony—meaning a chord outside of the normal scale. Several years later, the same chord appeared in "Penny Lane." This song begins as if it will be a I-vi-IV-V progression. But after going through the formula once, Paul takes us in a different direction. The second phrase begins with I and vi but then moves to a minor chord on tonic (the song is in a major key, so the I chord "should" be major). The bass line then moves to the sixth scale degree, but instead of the diatonic vi chord, we get a chromatic chord on vi (technically it is called a half-diminished seventh chord). As the bass line descends one half step to ♭ VI, we encounter the same chord we heard in "I Saw Her Standing There." Finally, the bass line moves down to the fifth scale degree, harmonized diatonically as V, and the verse is repeated. The middle section of "Penny Lane" moves to a new tonal center on ♭ VII. This sort of thing is old business in classical music, but it is rather adventuresome for a pop rock song.

The use of chromatic chords is one reason the Beatles' music sounded different. For example, in "Back in the U.S.S.R." the verse moves from the tonic chord (I) to the IV chord. But then to harmonize a "blue third" (flattened third scale degree) in the melody, the Beatles build a major triad using the blue note as the root of the chord. This same chord (♭ III) is used in the middle section of "Birthday." Here the chord alternates with ♭ VII so persistently that the song seems to change keys. Although a complete listing of all such chromatic chords used by the Beatles is well beyond the scope of this discussion, please note in the analyses that follow that when you see a Roman numeral with a flat or a sharp (flat ♭ or ♯) in front of it, the chord is a chromatic chord.

There has developed over the centuries a set of normal chord progressions with diatonic chords. We have become accustomed to hearing a certain chord (e.g., ii) normally progress to another chord (ii usually moves to V). Many Beatle songs depart from the "normal" traditions of chord progression. In some cases, nontraditional chord progressions are combined with chromatic chords. The result is a truly unique harmonic style. The following examples show some Beatle songs that include nontraditional progressions (indicated by a bracket) and chromatic chords (indicated by an asterisk).

"Help!"—published key: G major

$$| \ \text{ii} \ | \ \text{ii} \ | \overset{*}{\flat\text{VII}} | \overset{*}{\flat\text{VII}} | \ \text{v}^7 \ | \ \text{v}^7 \ | \ \text{I} \ | \ \text{I} \ ||$$

$$| \ \text{I} \ | \ \text{I} \ | \ \text{iii} \ | \ \text{iii} \ | \ \text{vi} \ | \ \text{vi} \ | \text{IV} \ \overset{*}{\flat\text{VII}} | \ \text{I} \ ||$$

"In My Life"—Published Key: G major

$$| \ \text{I} \ | \ \text{vi} \ \overset{*}{\text{I}^7} \ | \ \text{IV} \ \overset{*}{\text{iv}} \ | \ \text{I} \ | \ \text{(repeat 4 measures)} \ |$$

$$| \ \text{vi}^7 \ | \ \text{IV} \ | \overset{*}{\flat\text{VII}} | \ \text{I} \ | \ \text{vi}^7 \ | \overset{*}{\text{II}^7} \ | \overset{*}{\text{iv}} \ | \ \text{I} \ |$$

*Note:* With chords such as I7, iv, and II7, the root of the chord is diatonic, but at least one of the upper notes of the chord is chromatic.

"Michelle"—published key: D minor

$$| \ \overset{*}{\text{I}} \ | \ \text{iv}^7 \ \text{VI} \ | \overset{*}{\flat\text{VII}} \ \overset{*}{\sharp\text{VI}} \ | \ \overset{*}{\text{VI}^7} \ | \ \text{v} \ \text{VI} \ | \ \text{v} \ |$$

"Being for the Benefit of Mr. Kite!"—published key: D minor

$$\left|\ \overset{*}{\flat vii}\ \overline{\overset{*}{iv^+}\ (\textbf{augmented})}\ \right|\ VI\ i\ \left|\ \overset{*}{IV^7}\ \right|\ \overset{*}{IV^7}\ \left|\right.$$

$$\left|\ \overset{*}{\flat vii}\ \overline{\overset{*}{iv^+}}\ \right|\ VI\ i\ \left|\ V^7\ \right|\ i\ \overset{*}{i^7}\ \left|\right.$$

$$\left|\ VI\ V^7\ \right|\ i\ VI\ i\ \overline{\left|\ VI\ V\ \right.}\ \left|\ i\ \right|$$

*Note:* This song begins with so many chromatic chords that the actual key is ambiguous. Even though it settles in D minor, the opening measures emphasize C minor.

"Strawberry Fields Forever"—published key: A major

$$\left|\ I\ \right|\ I\ \left|\ \overset{*}{v}\,min7\ \right|\ \overset{*}{v}\,min7\ \left|\ \overset{*}{VI^7}\ \right|\ \overset{*}{VI^7}\ \left|\ IV\ V\ \overset{*}{VI}\ \right|\ \overset{*}{VI}\ \left|\ \overset{*}{IV}\,maj7\ V\ \right|\ I\ \left|\right.$$

An ambiguity of keys exists in a number of Beatle songs. Even in an early song such as "Can't Buy Me Love," the introduction and choruses are in major, but the verses, which are really twelve-bar blues, lie in minor. Similarly, "Come Together," which is basically in minor throughout, turns to major on the words "Come together."

Another song that contains some tonal ambiguity is "She Loves You." Although this song is basically in E-flat major (published key), there is considerable emphasis on C minor, a key that is closely related to E-flat because it shares the same key signature. The song begins on a C minor chord, and there is an important cadence on C minor at the words "and you know that can't be bad." The final cadence of each verse is also interesting as it moves from a minor iv chord (a chromatic chord) to the diatonic V chord.

The Beatles rarely resorted to the old twelve-bar blues form. But with "Yer Blues" the Beatles modify the form to suit their needs. For every 4/4 measure of the standard blues form, the Beatles substitute two measures of 3/4, as shown below.

$$\tfrac{3}{4}|\ I\text{---}|\text{----}|\text{----}|\text{----}|\text{----}|\text{----}|\text{----}|\text{----}|\ \textbf{(8 bars)}$$

$$|\ IV\text{---}|\text{----}|\text{----}|\text{----}|\ I\text{---}|\text{----}|\text{----}|\text{----}|\ \textbf{(8 bars)}$$

$$|\ \flat III\text{--}|\text{----}|\tfrac{4}{4}V\text{----}|\text{----}|\tfrac{3}{4}\ I\ |\ IV\ |\ I\text{---}|\text{----}|\ \textbf{(8 bars)}$$

Of course, one could also hear this as twelve measures of 6/4 instead of twenty-four measures of 3/4. Notice also the chromatic chord that begins the third phase and the meter change to 4/4 for two measures in that same phrase. This is the blues, Beatles style.

Much has been said about the "modality" of the Beatles' melodies and harmonies. This is because many of their tunes and chord progressions seem to be based upon *modes*—a system of scales that predates our major and minor scales. Many of these modal references contain the lowered seventh scale degree, or the lowered third degree, or both. These notes may suggest several older modes, but are also part of the blues tradition. It seems more likely that the Beatles' use of these scale degrees was guided by the blues tradition than by the pre-seventeenth-century Greek modes.

The tune of "Eleanor Rigby" has often been cited as a use of the Dorian mode—a scale that is like our minor scale but uses a raised sixth scale degree. Indeed, in this tune, although the minor scale predominates, the sixth scale degree is sometimes raised (as it would be in the Dorian mode) and sometimes not. But these modal references are probably the result of harmonic considerations: using the raised sixth in association with the diatonic i chord and the lowered sixth as the root of the diatonic VI chord.

Much more could be said about the Beatles' use of harmony and tonality. Later songs such as "Because" and "Sun King" (with its surprising eleventh chord initiating a new key) show creative musical minds at work. To keep these harmonic practices in perspective, however, we must remember that what seemed fresh and innovative in rock was, in fact, old business in classical music, jazz, and even in more sophisticated types of older pop music (for example, in Broadway show tunes). Nevertheless, if rock was ever to move beyond the mundane simplicity of three or four chords, simple rhythms, and unimaginative melodies, someone had to lead the way.

## Timbre

Although the Beatles' experiments with rhythm, melody, and harmony were important, perhaps innovations most obvious to the average listener were in the area of timbre—the new sound colors they brought to the world of rock and roll. The ensemble known as the Beatles consisted of voices accompanied by three guitars and drums. But as any Beatle fan can tell you, that was only the beginning. Where sound color was concerned, George Martin truly became the "fifth Beatle." Sometimes the ideas were his; at other times he refined the ideas proposed by the group.

Let us begin with the group and with the most basic instrument at their disposal: the voice. As with Presley and Holly, Paul McCartney was especially capable of a variety of vocal timbres. At times he could project a soft, lyrical voice, as in "Yesterday" or "The Long and Winding Road." But at other times he could use the shouting style of the old R & B tradition, as in "Why Don't We Do It in the Road?" and "Oh! Darling." In "Golden Slumbers" Paul begins as a crooning ballad singer; but as the song progresses his voice becomes more harsh and distorted. Finally he reverts to the softer sound before moving into "Carry That Weight." Such changes in vocal timbre are accomplished naturally by the singer. However, there are also instances where the Beatles used electronics to modify the voice; for example, listen to the electronically modified vocal effects in "Honey Pie."

The guitar was also subjected to timbral modification in some Beatle recordings. The opening of "I Feel Fine" (1964) uses intentional electronic feedback. In "I'm Only Sleeping" the guitar sound is subjected to electronic filtering (removing certain frequencies, thus resulting in a change of timbre).

Beyond these timbral experiments within their own instrumentation, the Beatles added a variety of other instruments and ensembles to their recordings. Many were mentioned in the earlier sections of this chapter (e.g., the string ensembles in "Yesterday," "Eleanor Rigby," and "She's Leaving Home"). In various songs we hear flutes ("You've Got to Hide Your Love Away"), harpsichord ("Because"), piccolo trumpet ("Penny Lane"), brass and saxes ("Got to Get You into My Life"), sitar ("Norwegian Wood"), brass band ("Yellow Submarine"), organ and bass harmonica ("Being for the Benefit of Mr. Kite!"), clarinets ("Honey Pie"), full orchestra ("A Day in the Life"), and a little bit of everything in "Strawberry Fields Forever." In "Within You Without You" we hear tabla (drums) and dilruba (a long-necked Indian lute).

The addition of sound effects, although not new in pop and rock (e.g., "409" by the Beach Boys), is a technique commonly found in Beatle recordings. Examples include the airplane sounds in "Back in the U.S.S.R.," the various sound effects in "Yellow Submarine," animal sounds in "Good Morning, Good Morning," and the alarm clock in "A Day in the Life."

Still another category of timbral experimentation is that of tape effects. This would include the speeded-up piano solo in "In My Life," the remarkable mixing of two versions of "Strawberry Fields Forever," the spliced-together and overdubbed fragments that conclude "Being for the Benefit of Mr. Kite!", and the tape-generated and manipulated sounds of "Tomorrow Never Knows." The end of the middle section of "A Day in the Life" (the "dream" section), with its heavily echoed and fading vocal line against the increasingly predominant unison string and brass line, is a particularly effective manipulation of sound. There are examples of backward instrumental segments ("Tomorrow Never Knows") and backward verbal "messages." And, of course, there is the tape montage of "Revolution 9." Beyond these experiments are the avant-garde essays of John and Yoko in their *Unfinished Music* albums (*Two Virgins* and *Life with the Lions*).

The examples previously cited are only a small sample of the timbral experiments made on various Beatle records. Choose almost any song from the *Revolver* album on and you will hear (1) an uncommon use of a common instrument, (2) the addition of an uncommon instrument, (3) the addition of external sound effects, and/or (4) the electronic manipulation or modification of sounds. Imagine the purchaser's excitement as he or she placed each new Beatle album on the turntable to discover what new rainbow of sound had been cooked up *this* time.

## Form

The Beatles led the way in rock music toward expanded and irregular forms. Most pop and rock songs from the 1950s and early 1960s conformed to one of several patterns, two of which are shown below.

**Typical twelve-bar blues pattern:**

| | 12-bar | 12-bar | | Instrumental | 12-bar | | Fade- |
| Intro | chorus | chorus | *(etc.)* | break | chorus | *(etc.)* | out |

**Typical AABA pattern:**

| Intro | A | A | B (bridge) | A | Instrumental break | B | A | Fade-out |

Internal phrases were typically four measures long; total song length was around two minutes and thirty seconds. Although exceptions may be found, these were the generally accepted norms for successful pop and rock hits.

The Beatles' most obvious challenge to these norms came in the area of length. Although many of their songs conform to the Top 40 two-and-a-half-minute "rule," a significant number of songs go well over that time frame. Examples include "Yer Blues" (four minutes), "Helter Skelter" (four and a half minutes), "While My Guitar Gently Weeps" (four minutes), "A Day in the Life" (five minutes), "Hey Jude" (seven minutes), "I Want You (She's So Heavy)" (over seven and a half minutes), and "Revolution 9" (eight minutes).

Of course, anyone can make a long song simply by repeating a short song ad nauseam. And in fact "Hey Jude" and "I Want You (She's So Heavy)" do use considerable repetition to create length. But some songs achieve their length by comprising a variety of sections that gradually build to the total length. As an example, consider "A Day in the Life" (see below).

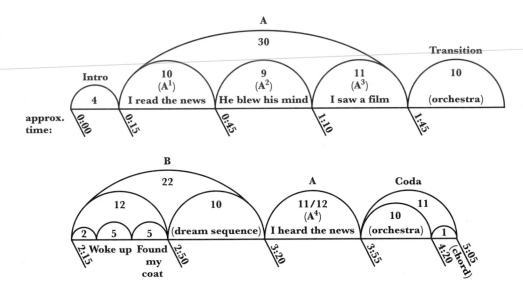

This form is unique. There probably is not another song in the world with exactly the same structure. It is not a reproduction of some preestablished formula. (*Note:* The measure numbers and sectional divisions are approximate because of changing meters and some overlap of sections.) Notice that none of the sections are the usual four- or eight-bar lengths. For example, the first section ("I read the news today," etc.) sounds as though it might be a regular eight-measure section, divisible into two four-measure phrases; but there are two measures added to the end ("I saw the photograph") to create the extended ten-measure length. Such irregular phrase lengths abound in Beatle songs. Examples include early songs such as "Love Me Do" (thirteen-measure sections) and "Do You Want to Know a Secret" (fourteen-measure section created by two six-measure phrases plus a two-measure extension); middle period songs such as "Michelle" (six-measure phrases and a bridge of ten measures) and "Yesterday" (seven-measure phrases); and later songs such as "I Am the Walrus"

(three-measure phrases) and "Hello Goodbye" (a fifteen-and-a-half-measure section, divided into phrases of four, four and a half, three, and four measures each).

Beyond matters of microform (phrase lengths, internal sections, etc.) are considerations of macroform—the structure of groups of songs and entire albums. The innovativeness of the concept album (e.g., *Sgt. Pepper*) has already been mentioned. Even the eclectic White Album has some interesting balances between songs. There is "Revolution 1" and "Revolution 9"; there is "Honey Pie" and "Wild Honey Pie"; there is a song about a weeping guitar followed by a song referring to the happiness of a warm gun; there is a sequence of "Blackbird," "Piggies," and "Rocky Raccoon" (and later a song referring to a monkey); after the harsh avant-gardism of "Revolution 9," the album ends with the soft nostalgia of "Good Night." The *Abbey Road* album ends with a series of songs and fragments woven together into a kind of multimovement suite. The Beatles were obviously thinking of larger structures.

## Texture

The Beatles' contributions in the area of texture were less impressive. The overwhelming majority of Beatle songs are homophonic, with the emphasis on the melody-and-accompaniment format. Where vocal polyphony exists, it is rather simple. For example, in the chorus of "She's Leaving Home," the lead vocal sings a slow-moving upper line ("She is leaving home") while a lower line moves in faster note values ("We gave her most of our lives," etc.). Sometimes a countermelody is devised to operate against the lead vocal. For example, in "Help!" there is a slow-moving countermelody below the melody; this counterline follows the harmonic progression and is more a part of the accompaniment than a true polyphonic line equal to the main melody. A brief example of vocal polyphony is found in the a cappella (without accompaniment) sections of "Paperback Writer." A vocal falsetto above the lead line adds to the texture, but again this line seems more an extension of the harmonic accompaniment. A cappella sections are rather rare in the Beatles' songs (as they are in most rock and pop styles); examples include "Nowhere Man" and "Paperback Writer."

Of course with the added instrumental components in so many songs (e.g., strings and brass), a thicker and more interesting texture is a natural result. In the quasiclassical moments (e.g., the instrumental break of "In My Life" and the string accompaniments of "Yesterday," "Eleanor Rigby," and "She's Leaving Home") there are varying amounts of polyphony (often the contribution of George Martin). The piccolo trumpet line in "Penny Lane" adds a refreshing touch of polyphony to the texture of that song.

## Lyrics

Beatle lyrics have been analyzed, reanalyzed, and probably overanalyzed. Hidden messages, backward messages, social profundities, and global prophecies have been found in the words of Beatle songs. The lyrics have inspired everything from the stark tragedy of the Manson murders to the silly hype of the Paul-is-dead hoax. Although we should not downplay the Beatles' skills in lyric writing, we cannot claim for them the role of innovators of the meaningful rock lyric. That award lies in the area of the folk music trend and with Bob Dylan in particular.

Early Beatle lyrics, although well written, were fairly typical of most pop rock texts. Most were boy–girl love songs, complete with hand-holding, letter writing, and lots of "yeah, yeah, yeahs." It was in 1964 that the Beatles met Bob Dylan and became acquainted with his songs. Within the next year, subtle differences became apparent in Beatle lyrics. For example, Dylan's 1964 song "My Back Pages" speaks of the "black-and-white" false self-assuredness of youth compared to the greater willingness to consider the "gray" aspects of issues that comes with maturity. In 1965, "Help!" says:

When I was younger, so much younger than today,
I never needed anybody's help in any way.
But now those days are gone, I'm not so self-assured,
And now I find I've changed my mind, I've opened up the doors.

From mid-1965, Beatle lyrics became increasingly thoughtful and thought provoking. The sensitive lyrics of "Yesterday," the social commentary of "Nowhere Man," and the poetic images and turns of phrase in "Eleanor Rigby" showed that the Beatles were capable of growing beyond the simple lyrics of boy–girl romance to concerns about major social issues, the socially disaffected individual, the more sensitive aspects of mature relationships, and, of course, drugs. In the 1967 to 1970 albums and singles there is considerable variety in lyrics, but in addition to the subjects just noted, there is more emphasis on nostalgia ("Penny Lane" and "Get Back"), personal criticism ("Sexy Sadie"), surrealism and nonsensical stream-of-consciousness texts ("I Am the Walrus"), and love and peace ("All You Need Is Love" and "Give Peace a Chance").

Dylan used imagery, metaphor, and symbolism throughout his lyrics. From 1965 on, so did the Beatles. Much of this symbolism is obvious; some is obscure and subject to interpretation. It is a short step from obscure symbolism to meaningless surrealism. But accustomed to finding the meaning of the obscure symbol, fans were determined to find specific meaning in the surreal. This led to the fascination with detecting the hidden meanings in meaningless lyrics and the questionable individual interpretations of Charles Manson and the Paul-is-dead fans.

The role of the double entendre in drug-related songs was discussed earlier in this chapter. Here again, fans became accustomed to deciphering the deliberate drug references and sometimes carried this practice forward into songs that happened to make innocent or meaningless use of words which, if the context were sufficiently contorted, could be construed as drug references.

Certainly the Beatles' lyrics were extensive in their subject matter, and they were skillfully written. Because of their position as trendsetters and spokesmen for a generation, their influence on subsequent pop and rock lyrics was great. However, in this aspect of their music, they themselves had been significantly inspired by an earlier revolutionary: Bob Dylan.

## Summary

It might seem reasonable to conclude that each of the Beatles' experiments in rhythm, melody, harmony, timbre, and form led to copious imitations and established new norms. The truth is that some did, but most did not. To expect each and every Beatle innovation to establish a new trend is to put too fine a point on the argument. In a broader sense, they created an environment of creativity, experimentation, and innovation. No longer did rock need to be subject to proven formulas and strict norms. Thus, even though a given artist or group might not directly imitate a specific Beatle device, they could allow their minds to wander creatively and discover their own innovation or experimental combination. No longer bound to "traditional" instrumentation, established forms, or trite lyrics, truly creative artists could give their musical minds a freer rein. This establishment of a climate of freer musical creativity is of greater importance than any single Beatle innovation or experiment.

Another point that must be made is that the average Beatle fan was not attracted to the music as a result of a conscious appreciation of their technical innovations. It is highly doubtful that upon hearing a new Beatle song teenager A telephoned teenager B to report with excitement the Beatles' use of the Dorian mode in a five-measure phrase accompanied by a ♭III chord. However, it is likely that many fans sensed that there was something "different" about the Beatles' music. It simply did not sound like other rock and roll. The technical devices explained in this musical close-up are the reasons why the music sounded "different"; but it should not be concluded that the fans' conscious awareness of these devices was the reason for their fascination with the music.

Finally, it must be admitted that what we have described as "innovations" were not really "firsts" in the truest sense of the word. Precedence for almost every device cited in this chapter can be found in classical music, jazz, and even Broadway tunes. However, they do seem innovative within the world of rock music. But even there it is possible to cite some prior examples. However, to have a truly innovative influence, one must be in a position to have an impact on a general society. Thus it may be true, for example, that David Crosby and the Byrds were the first to perceive the usefulness of the sitar in rock. But it was Harrison and the Beatles who first issued a major hit illustrating that usage ("Norwegian Wood," late 1965). The Byrds' "Eight Miles High" did not become known until the late spring of 1966. Admittedly, this beclouds the issue of innovativeness. Who is the true innovator, the one with the idea or the one who brings the idea to public attention first or with the most impact? Although such arguments over the Beatles' innovativeness have raged for years (and will continue to do so), it seems fair to conclude that because of their very visible position as trendsetters, they brought to the world of rock many new ideas (whether they were literally their own original ideas or not) and had a major influence on the direction of rock and roll for years to come.

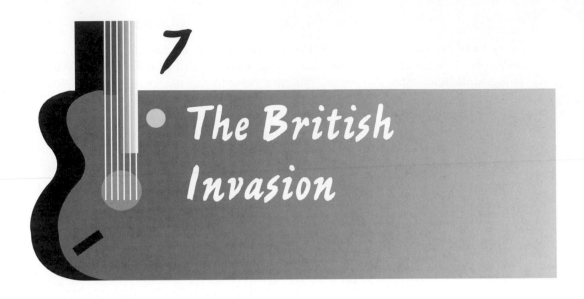

# 7

# *The British Invasion*

## OVERVIEW: THE BRITISH ARE COMING!

The Beatles were responsible for initiating many new ideas in rock and roll. But perhaps none was more significant than their initiation of "the British invasion." Indeed, beginning in 1964, a major geographical shift occurred that continues to the present day. Prior to 1964, rock and roll was an American product, exported to other parts of the globe to varying degrees. The British, especially, loved the American product, and they provided lucrative record sales, tour sites, and even "second homes" for U.S. rock stars like Buddy Holly, Little Richard, Gene Vincent, Eddie Cochran, and Jerry Lee Lewis (until his "great scandal"). British youth imitated these American stars and their 1950s-oriented styles. Many British rock stars attained popularity in their own country but were unable to export their success back to the United States. Only the Tornadoes, Lonnie Donegan, and Cliff Richard had made brief appearances on the U.S. charts.

But in 1964, beginning with the Beatles, British rock groups became the rage in rock-and-roll's homeland. Of the twenty-three number 1 hits in 1964, nine were by British artists (six by the Beatles). In 1965, the score was dead even, with thirteen out of twenty-six number 1 songs being of British origin (five by the Beatles). Although the trend abated slightly in 1967 and thereafter, a new premise had been established: Rock and roll was no longer an exclusive American product. From 1964 on, British and American rock artists competed more or less equally in the market. As we shall see, several important trends were initiated or cofounded by British rock artists.

As important as this geographic shift is, we must not succumb to the tendency of popular history to exaggerate facts. It has frequently been said that after the Beatles hit the United States in 1964, the British dominated the charts, and it was almost impossible for American groups to sneak in a hit in the last half of the 1960s. In fact, of the 124 number 1 hits from 1964 through 1969, only thirty-five were by British artists. This is certainly a dramatic change from the pre-1964 charts (two British number 1 hits in the ten years from 1954 through 1963), but it hardly constitutes the kind of exclusive domination sometimes reported.

With the British invasion came a split in rock's mainstream—a duality that would weigh heavily on subsequent decades of rock and roll. The seed of that duality was contained within the Beatles in the persons of Paul McCartney and John Lennon. Although history may view them as a songwriting team, they were, in fact, less of a team than two opposite individuals who cooperated (sort of) in a highly successful corporate venture. Paul was more refined, more traditionally talented musically, and more compliant to societal norms. John was iconoclastic, rebellious, and inclined to nonconformity. Paul tended toward the elegant, the nostalgic, and the sentimental. John leaned toward the raw, the raucous, and the shocking. This tension is reflected in albums like the White Album and in double-sided hits like "Penny Lane" and "Strawberry Fields Forever."

The dichotomy within the Beatles themselves is the prototype for an even larger division within the British invasion as a whole. The British groups that constitute that "invasion" seem to split rather neatly into two camps: the softer, more refined, less rebellious bands on the one hand, and the hard, raw, basic R & B-oriented mainstream rock bands on the other. In spite of their own internal duality, the Beatles became the representatives of the former trend (probably because of their early image as being cute and lovable, and their later reputation as being eclectic experimenters); the personification of the latter trend was the Rolling Stones. Most rock fans of the later 1960s could identify themselves as either Beatle fans or Rolling Stones fans. Rarely was anyone an equal fan of both. The difference was musical to some extent, but it also involved image, lifestyle, and personality type. One could quickly assess a new acquaintance as a friend or foe with one basic question: "Are you a Beatle or a Stone?"

Although we risk oversimplification, it is useful to perceive this basic split in British rock as an important model for post-1964 rock. Many of the trends we observe in rock after 1964 seem to fall in line behind the Beatles or the Stones. The softer British groups discussed later in this chapter, the jazz rock groups of Chapter 11, "Jazz Rock," the art rock of Chapter 12, "Art Rock," and several of the other trends of the 1970s and 1980s owed much, directly or indirectly, to the Beatles. The harder British groups, many San Francisco groups, and later the hard rock, punk, and heavy metal groups owed much (again, directly or indirectly) to the Rolling Stones. To guard against oversimplification, we must understand that there are still other influences to be considered, as well as individual innovations and stylistic variations. And, of course, our earlier basic trends—mainstream, rockabilly, and soft rock—and the folk influence persisted through the 1970s and 1980s.

Having discussed the initiators of the British invasion in some detail in Chapter 6, "The Beatles," it is now important that we cross to the other side of the street and meet the Rolling Stones.

## THE ROLLING STONES

### The Years Before "Satisfaction"

The Beatles' formative years were influenced by American rock and roll of the 1950s: Presley, Holly, and Little Richard. But the Rolling Stones' earliest influences went further back to the roots of rock and roll: black R & B. Young Michael Jagger (born on July 26, 1943) and several friends formed what can loosely be called a band (they had no equipment and never performed in public), just for the fun of playing and singing their favorite R & B songs, as well as some 1950s rock tunes (especially those by Chuck Berry). To make their R & B roots clear, they called themselves Little Boy Blue and the Blue Boys. Jagger lived in Dartford, Kent, in a middle-class home and attended the respectable London School of Economics (LSE). Living several blocks away in Dartford was Keith Richards (born on December 18, 1943), a young guitarist who sometimes sat in on rehearsals with the Blue Boys. Unlike Jagger, Richards had not been successful in his educational career. He was expelled from Dartford Technical School and ended up in Sidcup Art College in 1958 (the same year the recalcitrant John Lennon entered Liverpool Art College).

There was an active subculture of R & B aficionados in London. One of the most ardent was Alexis Korner, who led his own R & B-oriented band called Blues Incorporated and eventually opened his own club, the Earling Club. On occasion, Korner used a drummer named Charlie Watts (born June 2, 1941), who was a fairly accomplished jazz drummer but also enjoyed R & B. Also hanging around Korner and his club was a young blues enthusiast named Brian Jones (born February 28, 1942). Brian played piano and clarinet and had an enviable record in his studies. But at the age of thirteen, he had heard jazz (especially saxophonist Charlie Parker) and suddenly lost interest in everything else. At the age of fourteen, he dropped out of school and began playing sax in jazz and R & B bands. At Korner's Earling Club, Brian tried to catch on as a guitarist, calling himself Elmo Lewis. (This was an interesting pseudonym, which apparently contained a reference to blues artist Elmore James with Brian's first name and his father's name: Lewis; coincidentally, it is also the name of Jerry Lee Lewis's father: Elmo Lewis.)

The Blue Boys often attended the sessions at the Earling Club, hoping for a chance to perform. Jagger was given an occasional opportunity to sing with Korner's band but did not make a positive impression. Nevertheless, the Blue Boys and "Elmo Lewis" became acquainted and decided to join forces. Their debut was as an intermission band at the Marquee Club (another R & B and jazz club) on July 12, 1962. The group consisted of Jagger, Richards, "Elmo Lewis," Ian Stewart, Dick Taylor, and Mike Avory. Taking their name from a song by blues singer Muddy Waters, they called themselves the Rolling Stones.

The jazz-oriented audience at the Marquee Club thought the Stones were too close to rock and roll. Brian Jones was sufficiently irritated by the criticism to write a letter to *Jazz News* that revealed a rather thoughtful assessment of the situation.

[A] pseudo-intellectual snobbery . . . unfortunately contaminates the jazz scene. . . . It must be apparent that Rock 'n' Roll has a far greater affinity for R & B than the latter has for Jazz, insofar that Rock is a direct corruption of Rhythm and Blues whereas Jazz is Negro music on a different plane, intellectually higher but emotionally less intense. (Norman 1984, 70)

For the balance of 1962, the Rolling Stones played wherever work could be found.

When bassist Dick Taylor quit the group, he was replaced by Bill Wyman (born William Perks on October 24, 1936), an "older" man of twenty-six years. Also in 1962, Charlie Watts began playing occasionally with the Stones. By 1963, he became their regular drummer, although he continued to prefer his first musical love, jazz.

It was in 1963 that a nineteen-year-old public relations agent for Brian Epstein's NEMS determined that he wanted to manage his own rock group instead of being a small cog in the growing Epstein–Beatles machine. Thus, Andrew Loog Oldham approached the Rolling Stones about becoming their manager. Brian Jones signed a management contract with Oldham and a more established agent named Eric Easton. Jones also saw to it that he was given an extra salary as leader of the Rolling Stones.

Decca Records' Dick Rowe had become known as the man who turned down the Beatles in favor of Brian Poole and the Tremeloes. Needless to say, he was anxious to offset that disastrous decision by signing a truly successful group. Thus, when George Harrison recommended to Rowe that he sign a new group called the Rolling Stones, he jumped at the chance. In May 1963, the Rolling Stones made their first recording. "Come On," a Chuck Berry song, was the A side; the flip side of the single was an R & B song called "I Want to Be Loved." To promote their new record, the group appeared on the television show *Thank Your Lucky Stars*, uncharacteristically dressed in coordinated suits, Beatles' style. Shortly thereafter, Ian Stewart was dropped from the performance lineup; he served as their road manager from then until his death in 1985.

"Come On" reached number 26 on the British charts. The Stones began the arduous grind of performing and touring in hopes of building a following. Everywhere they went they were confronted with British Beatlemania; irked and resentful, they dropped the Beatlelike coordinated suits, electing to appear in street clothes. Their second release, "I Want to Be Your Man" (ironically, a Lennon–McCartney song) rose to number 3 in late 1963.

Through 1964, the Stones gradually formed their counterimage to the Beatles. Their stage act became more sexually suggestive; they allowed their hair to grow longer and to attain a scruffy, unkempt look. Oldham purposely built the image of "surliness, squalor, rebellion, and menace" (Norman 1984, 113).

Brian continued to think of himself as the group's leader, taking his extra salary and claiming the better hotel rooms. He thought that the others were unaware of his preferred contractual position, but he was mistaken. Meanwhile, Oldham was insisting that Jagger and Richard (Keith had dropped the *s* from his name) become a songwriting team like Lennon and McCartney. Their early attempts were unsuccessful, except for one song called "Tell Me (You're Coming Back)"—a Beatlelike tune complete with some "whoa, yeahs." This original song was included on their first LP, released in April 1964. The album's other cuts are either R & B-oriented mainstream rock (e.g., covers of songs by Bo Diddley and Chuck Berry) or actual R & B songs by older black artists like Jimmy Reed and Willie Dixon. The sexually

The early Rolling Stones (*Source:* Michael Ochs Archive, Ltd.)

oriented "I'm a King Bee" suggests the Jagger image that would be so successfully exploited over the next three decades.

The time had come for the Stones to join the British invasion of America. Their first U.S. and Canadian tour was launched in June 1964. "Not Fade Away," backed with "I Wanna Be Your Man," had barely made the U.S. charts. Their arrival at Kennedy Airport drew hundreds instead of the thousands the Beatles had drawn. Unlike the Beatles' Ed Sullivan television appearance, the Stones were hosted by Les Crane on an obscure late-night talk show, and on Dean Martin's *Hollywood Palace,* where their host paid them little attention, except to make fun of them. In Omaha, 600 fans "jammed" an auditorium seating 15,000; in San Antonio, they performed in a 20,000-seat arena to a few hundred listeners. The Stones' first attack on American Beatlemania was largely unsuccessful, except for their final concerts at a sold-out Carnegie Hall in New York City.

While in the United States, the Stones stopped by the Chess studios in Chicago, where so much of the early R & B had been recorded. There they met Muddy Waters, Chuck Berry, and Willie Dixon. While at Chess they recorded "It's All Over Now," which when released later that year rose to the Top 10 in Britain and number 26 in the United States.

The balance of 1964 was spent on a European tour and a second more successful American tour. On the latter, they enjoyed a more respectable reception at Kennedy Airport and actually appeared on Ed Sullivan's show. The studio audience tore up the studio as the Stones performed, causing Sullivan to promise that he would never offer the Stones a return engagement on his show (he did, however). It was on this second U.S. tour that Jagger saw James Brown perform. Fascinated and impressed, Jagger set out to imitate Brown's dancing form and incorporate his moves into the Rolling Stones' act.

### "Satisfaction"

In January 1965, the Stones' second album, *12 × 5,* was released. Again, it leaned heavily on the R & B sound that was the foundation of the group's sound. "Time Is on My Side" reached the number 6 position in the United States; the Stones thus cracked the American Top 10 for the first time. Another single, "The Last Time," reached number 1 in England and number 9 in the United States. By spring of 1965, the Rolling Stones had the top single, the top EP (extended play–a 33⅓ rpm album, usually containing four songs on a seven-inch disc), and the top LP in Britain. And they were only months away from finally topping the U.S. charts.

During their third U.S. tour (spring 1965) the Stones made a return appearance on the *Ed Sullivan Show* and appeared on the youth music–oriented *Shindig.* While resting in a motel room, Keith began playing a guitar pattern that he thought sounded catchy. Mick improvised some words to Keith's riff, and the result was "(I Can't Get No) Satisfaction." They recorded the song and released it in the United States before releasing it in England. It zoomed to number 1 in the summer of 1965. Controversy surrounded the song because of its ambiguous lyrics. Some argued that it referred to masturbation; others thought it was about sex in general. Jagger, following the old double entendre script we have discussed previously, said it referred to the general lack of any kind of satisfaction (sexual, artistic, spiritual, etc.) obtainable when a rock group was touring in a foreign country.

We first mentioned Allen Klein when he became the Beatles' manager in 1969. The Rolling Stones' biographer, Philip Norman, in describing Klein, says that "a

The Rolling Stones (Source: Michael Ochs Archive, Ltd.)

piranha might conceivably have the edge in politeness" (Norman 1984, 155). Klein was known for his habit of ferreting out the soft spots in his clients' recording contracts, with the intent of breaking the contracts or obtaining more dollars for his clients. He relished lawsuits, having sued everyone from the Diner's Club to the Internal Revenue Service. His client list was impressive: Steve Lawrence, Eydie Gorme, Bobby Darin, Sam Cooke, Buddy Knox, the Dave Clark Five, the Animals, Donovan, and Herman's Hermits. Klein offered to become Andrew Oldham's "business manager," thus leaving Oldham free to pursue the purely creative aspects of the Stones' career. Oldham accepted. His partner, Eric Easton, who objected, was edged out (amidst lawsuits, of course).

The Stones rushed out a new album called *December's Children (and Everybody's)* just in time for Christmas 1965. It contained another number 1 hit "Get Off My Cloud." This song had been promoted during their fourth U.S. tour in the fall of 1965. This tour found Brian Jones adopting the new Swinging London look, complete with capes, furs, and high-heeled boots. In Los Angeles, he met and began dating Anita Pallenberg; he and Keith also tried an exciting (and dangerous) new drug: LSD.

In fact, Brian's alcohol and drug intake was becoming quite a problem. He had missed the "Satisfaction" recording session because he was stoned on booze and pills. He reportedly downed two bottles of whiskey and handfuls of pills each day. He had hash and grass lying all over his house. He seemed frustrated that he was unable to compose songs as successfully as the Jagger–Richard team. His paranoia led him to think that the other Stones were "out to get him." When LSD was added to this picture, matters got worse. Once he refused to enter a recording studio because he was convinced that the studio was crawling with black beetles.

The year 1966 began with yet another successful single, "19th Nervous Breakdown," an unsympathetic portrait of upper-class party girls. The flip side contained "As Tears Go By," accompanied by a string ensemble and acoustic guitars. It sounded like a rather blatant imitation of McCartney's "Yesterday." The Stones' fourth album, *Aftermath* (April 1966), contained only songs by Jagger and Richard. On the album Brian played sitar ("Mother's Little Helper"), a stringed folk instrument called a dulcimer ("Lady Jane" and "Waiting"), and marimba ("Under My Thumb" and "Out of Time"). The song "Paint It Black" hit number 1 in the United States. Meanwhile, the Stones' touring schedule was fierce: Australia, New Zealand, and Europe in the first half of 1966, and Great Britain in the fall. Their live performances were met with increasingly wild behavior and outright violence on the part of their fans—but more on that later.

Andrew Oldham formed Immediate Records as an alternative creative outlet for himself and the Stones. Keith Richard produced "Today's Pop Symphony," featuring an orchestral medley of Jagger–Richard songs, possibly intended to show the world that their tunes were as solid and adaptable as Lennon and McCartney's.

The year 1967 was a year of scandal and increased controversy about the Rolling Stones. The album *Between the Buttons* contained two hit singles, "Ruby Tuesday" (number 1 in the United States) and "Let's Spend the Night Together." The latter, especially, seemed to be another blatant step into overtly sexual lyrics. The press began digging out all sorts of drug and sex stories about the Stones. Although such reports were generally based on fact, some specifics were inaccurate. For example, one report linked Mick Jagger with LSD use. Actually Jagger had resisted LSD and was rather concerned about Brian's and Keith's increasing habit. Although he angrily denied the report, by the end of the year he too had become an LSD user. During the year, Jagger, Richard, and Jones were arrested on drug charges, disgusting Andrew Oldham to the extent that he washed his hands of them, leaving them to the care of Allen Klein.

The release of *Sgt. Pepper* was a shock. It clearly gave the lead to the Beatles in the Beatles–Stones race. The Stones promptly went into the studio to record what they hoped would be an appropriate response. Unfortunately, Brian was incapable of participating in any meaningful way. He sat among his guitars and stands, sleeping. When he played, he played so badly that the others quietly disconnected his amplifier leads. When it was finally released in December, *Their Satanic Majesties Request* was a gross disappointment. Even the Stones themselves realized that they had failed to "out Beatle" the Beatles. They had tried earlier in 1967 with "We Love You," an attempt to answer the Beatles' "All You Need Is Love." The Stones' song was even accompanied by a promotional film, similar to the pioneering film produced for the Beatles' monster hit.

In spite of the apparent competition between the two leading British rock groups, they were actually rather good friends. In fact, when the Beatles traveled to Bangor, North Wales, in August 1967 to absorb the Maharishi's wisdom, they were accompanied by Mick Jagger and Marianne Faithfull, who had begun living together in late 1966.

The Rolling Stones "Their Satanic Majesties Request" album cover (Source: Michael Ochs Archive, Ltd.)

Seemingly having learned their lesson, the Stones' next single, "Jumpin' Jack Flash," was a basic R & B-oriented mainstream rock-and-roll song, unclouded by efforts at Beatlelike sophistication or chic psychedelia. It was the kind of basic, raw rock and roll the Stones did best.

In 1968, Brian was arrested again on drug charges. His physical and emotional health were deteriorating rapidly. Into this picture came a fervent Stones fan named Kenneth Anger, a filmmaker, student of the occult, and disciple of Aleister Crowley. Anger envisioned Jagger as a modern-day Lucifer and Richard as his attendant devil. He proposed a film for them called *Lucifer Rising*. Anita Pallenberg, originally Brian's girlfriend but now living with Keith, was heavily into the occult and had turned Keith on to black magic and witchcraft. Marianne Faithfull had recently read Mikhail Bulgakov's *The Master and Margarita*, a book about a smooth-talking Satan who visits Russia to assess the effects of the Revolution. The story inspired Mick and Keith to write a song called "Sympathy for the Devil." They recorded the song and included it on their late 1968 album, *Beggar's Banquet*. The album also contained the single "Street Fighting Man," which was suppressed in the United States because it was already a powder keg of street violence. The National Democratic Convention had been marred by street rioting; race riots and the assassination of Robert Kennedy were still too fresh in the minds of Americans.

The time had come for the Stones to be rid of Brian Jones. They were preparing for another U.S. tour, and there was no chance of Brian's obtaining a U.S. work permit with two drug convictions on his record. Furthermore, his mental and physical condition had deteriorated badly. He was no longer an asset and would have to be fired. Mick, Keith, and Charlie Watts softened the blow by hinting that the separation was temporary. They offered to buy him out for 100,000 pounds. Brian, in turn, pretended to be elated at the prospect of solo work or work with other British groups.

At the age of fourteen, Mick Taylor had substituted for Eric Clapton in John Mayall's Bluesbreakers. At seventeen, he became Mayall's lead guitarist, remaining with the group for four years. In May 1969, he sat in on the Stones' *Let It Bleed* recording sessions and was subsequently hired not as a member of the Rolling Stones but as their employee. A nonsmoker, nondrinker, and vegetarian, he seemed an odd choice on the personal level, but he was an excellent guitarist. His public debut was planned for July 5 at a free concert to be given by the Stones at Hyde Park in London.

But before that debut could take place, tragedy struck. On July 2, 1969, Brian and three friends were sitting around his swimming pool drinking brandy, vodka, and whiskey. Brian had taken a number of "downers" and gone swimming. The water was warmed to 80 degrees. Left alone in the pool for a few minutes, he had drowned. An autopsy showed that Brian's liver was twice its normal size and "in an advanced state of degeneration." His heart was distended; his system contained large quantities of alcohol and "an amphetamine substance." The official explanation of the death was "death by misadventure" (Norman 1984, 301–302).

The Hyde Park concert went on as planned. Some 250,000 fans attended. Films of the occasion reveal that the Stones played very badly, possibly as a result of Brian's death, their lack of recent public performances, or the presence of a new guitarist. More trauma awaited the Stones. In July, Marianne Faithfull, who had lost the baby she had been carrying, attempted suicide by taking a massive overdose of pills. Her romance with Mick had worn off; her looks had deteriorated badly as she, Keith, and Anita had become heavily involved in hash, speed, cocaine, and heroin.

## Altamont

In mid-1969, the Rolling Stones were at the peak of their career, yet they were almost flat broke. They had made a lot of money but had spent it as fast as they made it. Allen Klein, who had finally edged Oldham and Easton out, had become increasingly infatuated with his new wards, the Beatles. So the Stones turned to Klein's nephew, Ronnie Schneider, who with everyone's blessing became their new manager. They promptly released two albums, a greatest hits album called *Through the Past Darkly,* and the just completed *Let It Bleed* album. The latter was released to coincide with their upcoming U.S. tour in late 1969. Designed to highlight the group's R & B roots, the American tour was to feature artists such as B. B. King and Ike and Tina Turner as warm-up acts.

As the 1969 American tour progressed, it attracted more and more negative publicity. Ticket prices were unusually high, and the Stones' habit of showing up hours late compounded the problems. The tour was being filmed in hopes of creating a full-length documentary. Jagger decided that what was needed to turn things around was a big finish. Earlier in 1969, a huge free outdoor concert had been presented in Woodstock, New York. It had attracted many top-name rock acts and had been nearly violence free. Woodstock was being described as the biggest and most positive event in rock's tumultuous decade of the 1960s. Jagger decided that the big finish for their American tour would be a free outdoor concert on the West Coast—one that would be considered "Woodstock West." After several other sites were considered and dropped, an offer was accepted to use the Altamont Raceway near Livermore, California (about forty miles southeast of San Francisco). This decision was made on Friday, December 3; the concert was to be on Saturday, December 4! For a security force, Jagger invited various California chapters of Hell's Angels, motorcycle gangs known for their violence and disruption of similar events. If the idea was to "put the arsonist in the fire station" in hopes of avoiding violence, it did not work.

By Saturday morning, the crowd had already reached 100,000. The Angels appeared armed with their lead-weighted pool cues and other more conventional weapons. By early afternoon, fights were breaking out all over the grounds. There were beatings, and many members of the crowd were already stoned on cheap drugs. As Santana began to play, violence erupted around the stage. The Angels punched, kicked, and bludgeoned everyone, from cameramen to stoned nudists. When the Jefferson Airplane took the stage, their male vocalist, Marty Balin, was slugged in the face. As the Rolling Stones stepped out of their helicopter, a freaked-out youngster punched Jagger in the face amidst a torrent of profanity and threats. As Crosby, Stills, Nash, and Young performed, the violence approached riot proportions.

Finally, the Rolling Stones took the stage. Mayhem abounded as pool cues, fists, and boots flew in all directions. As Jagger began "Sympathy for the Devil," all hell broke loose. After a few phrases, Mick stopped the music and pleaded for people to "cool out." The Stones started the song again with no change in audience behavior. Again, the music stopped. Keith Richard threatened to enter the melee personally. Jagger pathetically pleaded for sanity. They finished "Sympathy" and began the

Violence at Altamont (*Source:* Michael Ochs Archive, Ltd.)

calmer "Under My Thumb." Suddenly a fight erupted between the Angels and an eighteen-year-old black youth named Meredith Hunter. The Angels grabbed him and plunged a knife into his neck and back and then stomped him in the face. Unaware that a murder was taking place right before his eyes, Jagger called for a doctor—"someone's been hurt." The concert continued, largely because the Stones were afraid of what might happen if they cut their set short. Finally, Jagger thanked everyone for a wonderful time and expressed appreciation to the Angels for helping out! The Stones made a rapid getaway in their helicopter.

Hunter was not the only casualty at Altamont. Two other youths were killed as a car ran over them while they lay sleeping on the ground. Another youth drowned in an irrigation ditch. Yet another had jumped from a traffic overpass and sustained multiple injuries. No one knows the number or severity of the multiple beatings and bad drug trips experienced that day. The documentary film of the tour was more than anyone could have expected. *Gimme Shelter*, with its climactic footage of a silver blade descending on Hunter's back, is a sobering film. The rock community was disheartened by the violence at Altamont. Even *Rolling Stone* magazine, in a major article published some six weeks later, suggested that the real blame for Altamont lay with the rock band whose name the publication shared.

For those who doubt that music affects behavior, watch *Gimme Shelter* (it is available for rental in most video stores). As Mick Jagger said onstage that night, "We always have something funny happen when we start that number." The Stones did not perform "Sympathy for the Devil" for some six years after Altamont. Interestingly, as the band tried to calm the crowd, they turned to the relatively tame "Under My Thumb," revealing an instinctive realization that music has the capacity to affect behavior. But at Altamont, the flow of events had gone too far. Nothing could have defused the disastrous situation that rolled to its inevitable conclusion on that grisly Saturday night.

## After Altamont

Altamont created considerable resentment toward the group for their apparently callous attitude toward the tragedies that had occurred there. But it also seemed to spur on even more violence in subsequent concerts. The Stones' European tour in the fall of 1970 was accompanied by extreme violence.

Meanwhile, Mick, Keith, and Bill Wyman were in deep tax trouble. To escape payment, they moved to France. In 1971, the Stones signed with Atlantic Records; they would produce records on their own label—Rolling Stones Records—but the manufacture and distribution would be through Atlantic. To head their new label, they selected Marshall Chess, son of Leonard Chess of Chess Records in Chicago.

In April 1971, *Sticky Fingers* was released. It contained "Brown Sugar," a song whose lyrics were widely condemned as being both sexist and racist; it became the Stones' sixth number 1 hit in the United States. Most of the other songs on the album were drug related.

The year 1972 found the Stones returning to America for yet another tour. Their album *Exile on Main Street* was number 1 in the United States. Mick hoped for smaller concert sites and tightly controlled circumstances, to avoid another Altamont. But the Stones were victims of their own creation. As biographer Philip Norman puts it, "It was too late for the Stones to beat the economics they themselves had largely invented. [They were doomed to] performing in vast spaces like the one they had barely escaped from with their lives, to audiences among whom it was now commonplace to snort cocaine and throw bottles at the band" (Norman 1984, 360).

For an opening act, the Stones used Stevie Wonder, again presumably to emphasize their black musical roots. Jagger's act became even more sexually provocative. The crowd reactions were predictable and normal for Stones concerts. Violence and arrests abounded.

Recorded in Jamaica, *Goat's Head Soup* was released in 1973. It contained another number 1 single, "Angie." Personally, things were no more stable than usual. Anita and Keith were arrested several times for possession of everything from marijuana to heroin to unlicensed weapons. Meanwhile, Mick and his new wife Bianca lived the high life, bouncing between the United States, France, and England—largely to avoid paying taxes. They argued frequently and furiously. Bianca, a successful model, was especially appalled by the squalor and heroin-addicted lifestyle of Keith and Anita, who by now had had their second child.

In 1974, Mick Taylor quit the Rolling Stones. This nonsmoking, nondrinking vegetarian was by now a heroin addict. He decided to get out while he still could. Ronnie Wood, a former guitarist with Rod Stewart's band Faces, took Taylor's place. Through the mid-1970s, Keith was in such a heroin-induced fog that Mick had to try to carry the band. The resulting albums, including *It's Only Rock and Roll, Made in the Shade, Metamorphosis*, and *Black and Blue*, were disappointing. The Stones had no Top 10 hits in 1974 and no Top 40 hits in 1975. For their 1975 tour, Mick had a stage prop that caused still more controversy. It was a huge inflatable rubber phallus, which he rode, hit, and otherwise pummeled to the sexually explicit song, "Star, Star." In August 1976, the Stones were to be a part of a rock festival in England. Some 200,000 fans showed up, and so did the Stones—four hours late. They were not well received. The end seemed near.

Keith and Anita finally separated, and Keith began to pull out of his heroin habit. *Some Girls* was released in 1978 and contained the Stones' first number 1 hit ("Miss You") in five years. The album seemed to announce the return of the typical Rolling Stones music. The albums *Tattoo You* (1981) and *Undercover* (1983) continued in the vein of *Some Girls*. In 1983, the Stones separated from Atlantic and signed with CBS. The first album on their new label was released in 1985, and ironically it was a solo album by Mick Jagger. Keith bitterly resented Mick's solo venture. Nevertheless, they subsequently released a group album called *Dirty Work*, which contained a hit called "Harlem Shuffle."

The Stones toured the United States in 1981 and 1982. As Mick Jagger did more solo work and Keith Richards (he added the *s* back to his name) played with other bands, rumors spread that the Rolling Stones were finally breaking up. To be sure, their real heyday had been the 1960s and 1970s. After all, by 2000, Jagger, Richards and Watts were nearing sixty years old, and Bill Wyman was in his mid-sixties. Nevertheless, as the new century dawned, the Rolling Stones were still performing to huge sellout audiences. Albums, too, continued to sell very well. *Voodoo Lounge* (1994) reached number 2 and won a Grammy. *Bridge to Babylon* (1997) reached number 3 and was the band's nineteenth platinum album. A live album, *Live Licks,* was released in 2004 and added a few guest artists plus bassist Daryl Jones (replacing Bill Wyman).

## The Bad Boys of Rock

The preceding discussion of the Rolling Stones contained little analysis of their music; that will be reserved for the musical close-up at the end of this chapter. Of equal or greater importance to the history of rock and roll is the image of the

The Rolling Stones in the 1970s
(*Source:* Michael Ochs Archive, Ltd.)

Rolling Stones. There can be no doubt that Presley, Berry, Lewis, and Little Richard were less than cherubic choirboys. And certainly the lovable Beatles had created considerable controversy, especially from *Sgt. Pepper* on. But many of the less socially acceptable escapades of these and other rock stars were kept deliberately quiet. Certainly none of them had consciously provoked public displeasure and condemnation, except possibly the recalcitrant John Lennon, who sometimes enjoyed controversy for controversy's sake.

The Rolling Stones, however, were the first significant rock group to foster an overtly negative image. Although Oldham consciously hyped their bad-boy image, not much hype was really needed. They projected the image quite naturally by just being themselves. The image of the Stones as representatives of the more rebellious, surly, antisocial side of rock was fostered in two ways: (1) through their personal lives (more specifically, those of Brian Jones, Mick Jagger, and Keith Richard; Charlie Watts and Bill Wyman were more conservative and stayed out of the negative limelight), and (2) through the outrageous antics of their fans. Let us examine both aspects more closely.

Brian Jones had encountered trouble as early as 1958, when at the age of fourteen he was named as the responsible party by a female classmate who was pregnant. By the age of twenty he had fathered two sons by two different girlfriends; he provided no support for either son—both of whom he had named Julian. By 1965 Brian had taken up with Anita Pallenberg. Their relationship was characterized by drugs, alcohol, and some rather bizarre behavior. Anita soon moved on to Keith Richard.

In May 1967 Brian was arrested on a drug charge. He eventually received a sentence of three years' probation and a small fine, plus psychiatric treatment. Brian celebrated his victory with an orgy of drinks and pills that put him into a hospital two days later.

The Rolling Stones (*Source:* Michael Ochs Archive, Ltd.)

In May 1968 Brian was arrested for drugs again. Although pronounced guilty, he was cited for his sincere efforts to kick the habit and was fined fifty pounds and court costs. Among his escapades around this time were a suicide attempt and a fight with Mick that ended when Brian threatened Jagger with a knife. Brian's death in 1969 was hardly a shock to those who knew him well.

Keith Richard had started on drugs while a student at Sidcup Art College. In 1967, he, Mick and Marianne, George and Pattie Harrison, and assorted friends were enjoying a relaxing weekend when the police raided Redlands, Keith's country home. A considerable amount of drugs and paraphernalia was confiscated. However, the main drug supplier managed to escape with a briefcase full of LSD. At a trial in June, Keith was found guilty and sentenced to one year in prison and a five hundred pound fine. On appeal, the conviction was overturned.

By 1971, Keith and Anita were undergoing treatment for heroin addiction. The treatment failed. They were buying heroin in consignments that cost four thousand pounds and using it up in about a month. Keith experienced three more drug arrests in 1976 and 1977.

Mick Jagger was also arrested in the Redlands raid of 1967. He was sentenced to three months in prison and a fine of two hundred pounds. Eventually his conviction was upheld, but the sentence was changed to a one-year conditional discharge. The judge addressed Mick as follows:

> . . . you will have to be of good behavior for twelve months. . . . If in that time you do commit another offense, you will not only be punished for that offense, but brought back and punished for this one also. . . . You are, whether you like it or not, the idol of a large number of the young in this country. Being in that position, you have very grave responsibilities. If you do come to be punished, it is only natural that those responsibilities should carry higher penalties. (Norman 1984, 236)

The second factor in creating the bad-boy image was the concert behavior at Rolling Stones concerts. Granted, kids had rushed the stage at Elvis's performances; and Beatle fans were capable of all sorts of silliness. But Stones concerts brought fan

misbehavior to a whole new level. In 1966, Paris police used clubs and tear gas to subdue 3,000 rioters. In Marseilles, a chair was thrown at Jagger, opening a two-inch cut above his eye. A concert in Lynn, Massachusetts, was stopped by police after only a few minutes. In Vancouver, there were thirty-six casualties, ranging from minor wounds to broken bones and concussions. In London, a concert was stopped after three minutes when Jagger was attacked by three girls, thus starting a tidal wave toward the stage.

By the late 1960s, the love-and-peace generation had been transformed into the drug-and-violence generation. First there was the crushing blow of the first Kennedy assassina-

Mick Jagger (*Source:* Michael Ochs Archive, Ltd.)

tion. Then many youth transferred their allegiance to young Robert Kennedy. But just as he appeared to be in a position to become the Democratic presidential nominee in 1968, he too was gunned down. That same year, Dr. Martin Luther King Jr., yet another hero of the youth movement, was assassinated. Also in 1968, the presidential candidate youth perceived to be more likely to end the war, Hubert Humphrey, was defeated by Richard Nixon. These events, coupled with violence at the Democratic National Convention and in so many metropolitan ghettoes, gave an aura of violence to the late 1960s.

More than any other rock group, the Rolling Stones, with their bad-boy image, became the musical rallying point for antisocial violence. Stones' biographer Philip Norman refers to the *Let It Bleed* album of 1969 as a "sound track to the new barbarism" (Norman 1984, 321). He notes further that "the Stones had made destruction cool and the Devil a rock star; they had sold a million copies of an exhortation to slaughter. They were the household gods of every spaced-out, subterranean screwball in America" (Norman 1984, 321–322). The Stones were greeted in 1969 with the following published message:

> Greetings and welcome Rolling Stones; our comrades in the desperate battle against the maniacs who hold power. The revolutionary youth of the world hears your music and is inspired to even more deadly acts. . . . We will play your music in rock 'n' roll marching bands as we tear down the jails and free the prisoners, as we tear down the State schools and free the students, as we tear down the military bases and arm the poor, as we tattoo 'burn, baby, burn' on the bellies of the wardens and the generals and create a new society from the ashes of our fires. (Norman 1984, 322)

The Stones' 1972 tour showed no change in concert behavior. In Vancouver, 2,000 non–ticket holders rushed the entrance throwing rocks and iron. In Montreal, an equipment truck was dynamited, and there was rioting by some 3,000 victims of ticket forgers. In Tucson, some 300 fans were arrested. In Rhode Island, Keith, Mick, Marshall Chess, and a bodyguard were arrested following a scuffle.

Between the well-publicized personal lifestyle of the individual Stones and the outrageous behavior of their fans, the group became the personification of the most rebellious, most antisocial, most hedonistic side of rock. They, more than any other rock group, initiated a path within rock that would lead through the hard rock of the 1970s, the punk rock of the late 1970s and early 1980s, the heavy metal of the 1980s, and the gangsta rap of the 1990s.

### Are You a Stone or a Beatle?

There can be little doubt that the Beatles and the Stones were the leaders of the British invasion. They both sprang from the same musical soil: a fascination with 1950s rock and roll and its R & B roots. But the Stones were more interested in basic R & B for its own sake. They were the most prominent among the bands referred to as the British blues bands. With only a few side excursions along the way, they continued to develop their R & B-influenced mainstream rock style. The Beatles, on the other hand, struck out into new territory, developing precedents for new variants of rock and roll and pushing back the boundaries of the style.

Yet the two groups were not on an exactly equal footing. The Beatles were considered *the* group, and the Stones were considered their foremost challengers. As a result, it is not surprising that although the Stones were, at times, jealous and resentful of the Beatles' success, they sometimes expressed "the sincerest form of flattery": imitation. Consider the following comparisons:

| | |
|---|---|
| **1963:** | The Stones appear on *Thank Your Lucky Stars* dressed in coordinated suits, just as the Beatles had done in 1962. |
| | The Stones' first Top 10 hit is their second release, "I Wanna Be Your Man"—by Paul McCartney and John Lennon. |
| **1964:** | Jagger and Richard try to compose their own songs; their efforts produce one mild hit, "Tell Me (You're Coming Back)"—very similar to the Lennon–McCartney style. |
| | *England's Newest Hit Makers: The Rolling Stones*, their first album, has a cover reminiscent of *With the Beatles*, released six months earlier. |
| | The Stones hope for a Beatlelike reception at Kennedy Airport for their first U.S. tour (four months after the Beatles arrived in New York); they are greeted by hundreds, not thousands. |
| | The Stones finally land an *Ed Sullivan Show* appearance on their second U.S. tour—eight months after the Beatles' first appearance with Sullivan. |
| **1965:** | "Get Off My Cloud" uses a chord progression very similar to that of "Twist and Shout"—a Beatles hit in 1964. |
| **1966:** | "As Tears Go By," a sedate, soft ballad accompanied by strings and acoustic guitar, is very similar to "Yesterday," released by the Beatles in 1965. |
| | *Aftermath* includes sitar and other instruments not normally associated with rock; the Beatles' "Norwegian Wood," with its sitar accompaniment, was included on *Rubber Soul*—released in late 1965. |
| | Keith Richard produces "Today's Pop Symphony," an orchestral medley of Stones' tunes, similar to so many pop covers of Lennon–McCartney songs. |
| **1967:** | *Their Satanic Majesties Request* is generally acknowledged to be an attempt to respond to *Sgt. Pepper*, released six months earlier. Even the album art is similar. |
| | "We Love You" is similar in spirit to "All You Need Is Love," by the Beatles. The Stones even make a promotional film, just as was done for the Beatles' song. |
| **1968:** | The Stones attempt a BBC television special called *The Rolling Stones Rock and Roll Circus* (never actually shown); it is similar in concept to the Beatles' *Magical Mystery Tour* television preview a year earlier. |

This comparison, which could be extended, should not be surprising. After all, the Beatles were clearly the most successful rock-and-roll act of their time, so it was only natural for other acts to emulate their formulas for success. However, the eventual success of the Rolling Stones did not lie with their Beatle simulations. Their reputation and successes were based on their contrasts with the Beatles. Perhaps it finally took the disappointment of *Their Satanic Majesties Request* to show them that they would need to let the Beatles be the Beatles and allow themselves to be the Rolling Stones.

## Summary

The Rolling Stones hold an important position in the history of rock and roll. To be sure, they were not musical creators and innovators like the Beach Boys and the Beatles. Nor were they talented musicians in the traditional sense. When Andrew Oldham approached Eric Easton about co-managing the Stones, Easton's only reservation was that they needed to replace Mick Jagger with someone who could sing. Since Easton's original assessment in 1962, a number of other people have pondered the same thought! So why are they important? Consider the following possibilities:

1. Since the end of the 1950s, rock had gradually moved away from its R & B roots. Indeed, mainstream rock had seemed on the verge of extinction in the early 1960s. There was soft rock, folk music, surfing music, and dance songs, but very little real, raw, basic rock and roll. The British invasion brought with it the return of mainstream rock, with the Beatles on the gentler side of the mainstream and the Stones on the harder side. As the Beatles generally veered toward a more sophisticated style of rock, the Stones stimulated a rebirth of more basic R & B-derived mainstream rock.
2. This fundamental split within the ranks of the British invasion, the fork in the road created by the Beatles and the Stones, is central to the history of rock since the mid-1960s. As with any such fork, the two groups had a common stem in the 1950s rock style of Berry, Holly, Presley, and Little Richard. But they eventually veered off from each other, in close proximity at first but with widening separation as their styles developed. This fork in rock's mainstream not only determined much about subsequent British rock but also much about rock and roll in general.
3. Since its beginnings, rock had always had a seamier underside. Many of the 1950s rockers led less than angelic lives; occasional songs had sexual undercurrents; the payola hearings revealed that the rock industry sometimes involved questionable ethics. But the Rolling Stones blatantly shoved the darker side of rock into the open, capitalizing on, and reveling in, their reputations as bad boys. Drugs, sex, violence, the occult, suicide—the whole range of the Stones' antisocial behavior—was flaunted as part of their image. Their fans responded in kind, bringing new levels of violence and misbehavior to the rock scene. Again, the Stones were not necessarily the first to be the way they were; but they were the first to carry such characteristics to such an extreme and flaunt them. Thus was set into motion a trend that persists to the present, as some rock groups fall all over themselves trying to out shock and out repulse their predecessors.
4. Finally the Stones deserve an important place in rock history simply because of their longevity. Since 1962 they have persevered through changing styles and all manners of personal adversity. No other group in history has held a comparable position of importance for so long a time.

## ALL THE OTHERS

In the wake of the Beatles and the Rolling Stones came a tidal wave of English rock groups. They achieved considerable success in 1964 to 1966 before the first wave dissipated, leaving only the Beatles and Stones as consistent hit makers. Then in the late 1960s there was a second wave that would have its primary effect in the early 1970s and beyond. We will deal with the groups of the second wave in subsequent chapters.

The first-wave British groups often were identified by their geographic origin: the Mersey groups (Liverpool), the Manchester groups, the Tyneside groups (Newcastle), the London groups, and so on. But for our purposes, it is more useful to think of them as they line up stylistically behind the Beatles or the Stones. The most numerous and commercially successful were the Beatlelike groups. Table 7–1 summarizes some of the more successful of these groups.

When discussing the Rolling Stones, we noted that they were a blues-based band. Their general sound, basic harmonic vocabulary, shouting vocal style, and use of the blues scale suggest their derivation from the older R & B style. A significant number of first-wave British invasion groups followed the lead of the Stones as they veered away from the Beatles' image and musical style.

Actually the real initiator of the British blues trend was John Mayall, whose group, the Bluesbreakers, never enjoyed a Top 40 hit in the United States and remains relatively unknown. Mayall's Bluesbreakers really were a blues band (as opposed to a blues-based rock-and-roll band). Encouraged by Alexis Korner, whose band, Blues Incorporated, was actively promoting the R & B style in the Soho district clubs in London, Mayall organized his Bluesbreakers in 1962. Playing the Marquee Club as well as the other blues-oriented clubs in the area, Mayall used a

number of young musicians who would go on to other significant British rock bands (e.g., Mick Taylor of the Rolling Stones, John McVie and Mick Fleetwood of Fleetwood Mac, and Eric Clapton of the Yardbirds and Cream).

The Bluesbreakers played an authentic style of basic R & B, using the old twelve-bar blues progression, the blues scale, the shouting vocal style, and even adopting a black-sounding vocal timbre and enunciation. If you can find a Mayall album such as *Looking Back* (1969), listen to a sampling of Mayall's work from 1964 to 1967. "Stormy Monday," for example, features outstanding guitar work by Eric Clapton and a blues vocal by Mayall that would convince even the most discerning listener that the singer was black (until he ends the song with a very clipped British-sounding, "Thank you very much indeed").

John Mayall (*Source:* Michael Ochs Archive, Ltd.)

## Table 7–1

| Group | Geographic Origin | Top Hits | Comments |
|---|---|---|---|
| Dave Clark Five | London | "Glad All Over" (no. 6, 1964); "Bits and Pieces" (no. 4, 1964); "Over and Over" (no. 1, 1965) | Clark was drummer and manager; group used guitars, drums, and tenor sax; "Bits and Pieces" was slightly harder than most of their songs. |
| Searchers | Liverpool | "Needles and Pins" (no. 13, 1964); "Love Potion No. Nine" (no. 3, 1965) | Sang many covers of American hits; a softer style; sophisticated and pleasant. |
| Peter and Gordon | London | "A World Without Love" (no. 1, 1964) | Peter Asher and Gordon Waller; had hits with several McCartney songs; Asher became a producer for Apple Records; later an important U.S. producer (for James Taylor and Linda Ronstadt, among others). |
| Billy J. Kramer and the Dakotas | Manchester | "Little Children" (no. 7, 1965); "Bad to Me" (no. 9, 1964) | Followed Beatles' pattern (managed by Epstein, Hamburg appearances, Parlophone recordings produced by Martin); recorded many Beatle songs; more popular in England than in the United States. |
| Gerry and the Pacemakers | Liverpool | "Don't Let the Sun Catch You Crying" (no. 4, 1964); "Ferry Across the Mersey" (no. 6, 1965) | Popular in England along with the Beatles in 1963; followed the Epstein–Hamburg–Martin pattern; soft, sophisticated style. |
| Freddie and the Dreamers | Manchester | "I'm Telling You Now" (no. 1, 1965); "Do the Freddie" (no. 18, 1965) | Successful in England prior to American hits; the "Freddie" capitalized on the U.S. dance craze; lovable and humorous. |
| Wayne Fontana and the Mind-benders | Manchester | "Game of Love" (no. 1, 1965); "A Groovy Kind of Love" (no. 2, 1966) | Slightly harder sound. |
| Herman's Hermits | Manchester | "I'm into Something Good" (no. 13, 1964); "Can't You Hear My | The most popular of these groups; lead singer was Peter Noone; if the Beatles were |

*(continued)*

**Table 7–1 (cont.)**

| Group | Geographic Origin | Top Hits | Comments |
|---|---|---|---|
| | | Heartbeat" (no. 2, 1965); "Mrs. Brown You've Got a Lovely Daughter" (no. 1, 1965); "I'm Henry VIII, I Am" (no. 1, 1965); "There's a Kind of Hush" (no. 4, 1967) | lovable, Herman's Hermits were downright squeezable. |
| Hollies | Lancashire (debut in Manchester) | "Bus Stop" (no. 5, 1966); "Stop Stop Stop" (no. 7, 1966) | Group's name derived from Buddy Holly; numerous personnel changes; they continued through the 1970s and into the 1980s. |

The blues purity of Korner's Blues Incorporated and Mayall's Bluesbreakers was converted into a blues-based rock style by the Rolling Stones and their followers in the first wave of British invasion groups. Table 7–2 summarizes some of these bands.

If one is looking for a direct line from these blues-based bands to the hard rock and heavy metal bands of the 1970s and 1980s, one can look to the Yardbirds. Growing out of the same London R & B scene that produced Korner's Blues Incorporated, Mayall's Bluesbreakers, and the Rolling Stones, the Yardbirds found their initial success with a song called "For Your Love" (number 6 in the United States in 1965). A quintet, the Yardbirds claimed a series of lead guitarists who would have a significant impact on later rock: Eric Clapton (earlier a member of the Bluesbreakers and later a founder of Cream), Jimmy Page (Led Zeppelin), and Jeff Beck.

Prior to that first hit, the Yardbirds played straight R & B. But with "For Your Love" and the follow-up "Heart Full of Soul" (number 9 in 1965), they moved to the newer blues-based rock sound being popularized by the Stones and the Animals. Their third hit, "I'm a Man," recorded earlier by Muddy Waters and Bo Diddley, is closer to the traditional blues style. By the time of these hits, Clapton had been replaced by Jeff Beck and Jimmy Page. The next hit, "Shapes of Things," contains a guitar instrumental break that sounds way ahead of its time—closer to the sounds of the hard rock groups of the 1970s. Clapton, when he was with the Yardbirds in the early days, had initiated such improvisatory breaks, calling them "rave-ups"; they could go on for as long as thirty minutes and were the forerunners of the lengthy instrumental solos that typified the San Francisco bands in the later 1960s. The Yardbirds' last U.S. Top 40 hit, "Happenings Ten Years' Time Ago," featured both Beck and Page as lead guitarists; this song also presages the hard rock and heavy metal sounds of the 1970s and 1980s. In 1968, the Yardbirds disbanded; Jimmy Page tried at first to organize a group known as the New Yardbirds, but finally changed the name to Led Zeppelin.

## Table 7–2

| Group | Geographic Origin | Top Hits | Comments |
|---|---|---|---|
| Animals | Newcastle upon Tyne | "House of the Rising Sun" (no. 1, 1964); "We Gotta Get Out of This Place" (no. 13, 1965); "Don't Let Me Be Misunderstood" (no. 15, 1965) | Lead singer: Eric Burdon; notice his half black, half British accent; occasionally used a shouting vocal style. |
| Manfred Mann | Johannesburg, South Africa | "Do Wah Diddy Diddy" (no. 1, 1964); "Sha La La" (no. 12, 1965); "Pretty Flamingo" (no. 29, 1966); "Mighty Quinn (Quinn the Eskimo)" (no. 10, 1968) | Mann (Michael Lubowitz) attended Juilliard School of Music; originally a blues-based band (listen to "Why Should We Not," "Got My Mojo Working" and "Hoochie Coochie"); drifted toward folk-oriented style ("With God on Our Side") and soft rock ("Sha La La"). |
| Kinks | London | "You Really Got Me" (no. 7, 1964); "All Day and All of the Night" (no. 7, 1965); "Tired of Waiting for You" (no. 6, 1965) | Organized by Ray and David Davies; built an image not unlike the Rolling Stones both onstage and offstage; also, like the Stones, survived into the 1980s (although with less success). |
| Zombies | St. Albans | "She's Not There" (no. 2, 1964); "Tell Her No" (no. 6, 1965); "Time of the Season" (no. 3, 1969) | Like Manfred Mann, their style varies; "She's Not There" and "I Want You Back" have the harder blues-based sound; "Tell Her No" moves closer to the Beatles. |
| Troggs | Wiltshire | "Wild Thing" (no. 1, 1966); "Love Is All Around" (no. 7, 1968) | Began by trying to out Stone the Stones; but their third U.S. hit ("Love Is All Around") was a softer ballad. |

In his article on the British invasion in *The Rolling Stone Illustrated History of Rock and Roll,* Leslie Bangs poses a reasonable question: "It might legitimately be asked whether more than a handful of British invasion bands would have made the States, and rock history, if they hadn't ridden in on the Beatles' coattails" (Miller 1980, 176). There is probably considerable truth to that proposition. However, the fact remains that all of the bands discussed in the aforementioned survey (and more) did cross the Atlantic in the Beatles' and Stones' wake. In doing so, they reinforced the directions indicated by the Beatles and the Stones and thus laid the groundwork for many more British rock groups that would follow in a second wave in the late 1960s and throughout the 1970s.

## MUSICAL CLOSE-UP:
### THE MUSICAL STYLE OF THE ROLLING STONES

The key words in considering the musical style of the Rolling Stones are *simplicity* and *repetition.* In this musical close-up, we will briefly examine a dozen or so Stones songs and then take a more detailed look at two of their most famous songs, "Satisfaction" and "Sympathy for the Devil."

In their many hits of the mid- and late 1960s, the Stones preserved the general feeling of the blues, the shouting vocal style, and the blues scale. But they rarely adhered to the traditional twelve-bar blues form and its prescribed chord pattern. An exception is "19th Nervous Breakdown." It begins with what sounds like a traditional twelve-bar blues. However, it is extended by two extra measures of the IV chord and two extra measures of I (plus one connecting measure of I). This extended sixteen-bar blues chorus plus an eight-measure bridge forms the basis of the song.

Introduction (2 measures)
A (12-bar blues plus 4-bar extension and 1-bar connection)
A (12-bar blues plus 4-bar extension)
B (8-bar bridge)
A (12-bar blues plus 4-bar extension)
Instrumental Break (3 bars)
B (8-bar bridge)
A (12-bar blues)
Fade-out on repeated I-chord riff

"Heart of Stone" is actually based on a twelve-bar form, but the chords do not follow the traditional blues progression.

$$\left|\ \text{I}\ \left|\ \text{IV}\ \left|\ \overset{*}{\text{II}}\ \left|\ \text{V}\ \right|\right.\right.\right.$$

$$\left|\ \text{vi}\ \left|\ \text{vi}\ \left|\ \text{vi}\ \left|\ \text{vi}\ \right|\right.\right.\right.$$

$$\left|\ \text{IV}\ \left|\ \text{V}\ \left|\ \text{vi}\ \left|\ \text{I}\ \ \text{V}\ \right|\right.\right.\right.$$

*Note:* The asterisk indicates a chromatic chord (i.e., one that is outside the prevailing key).

This chorus is repeated three times, followed by a fade-out that repeats the last two measures. Remember the key words: simplicity and repetition.

"Paint It Black" uses only two progressions, each four bars long, that alternate until near the end of the song.

| i | | i | | V | V |(repeat 4 bars)|

| i VII | III iv | V | V |(repeat 4 bars)|

For the fade-out, the first four bars (i and V) are repeated over and over.

"Under My Thumb" is a sixteen-bar cycle as follows:

| vi | V | IV | IV | (repeat 4 bars) |

| I | I | IV | II* | vi | V | I | I |

This sixteen-bar cycle is repeated until the fade-out, which consists of a repeating I chord.

As the foregoing analyses suggest, the Stones tended to stay with diatonic chords (i.e., chords within the prevailing scale), set into traditional formal units of four, eight, twelve, and sixteen measures. The following analyses show the basic harmonic and formal schemes of a number of other Rolling Stones hits.

"Get Off My Cloud" (the two harmonic schemes repeat alternately throughout the song):

| I IV | V IV | (repeated 7 more times = 16 bars)

| I iii | IV V | (repeat 2 more times) | ♭VII | V | (= 8 bars)

"Time Is on My Side" (formal scheme A A B A A):

A=  | I | IV V | I | IV V | ⎫
                               ⎪
    | vi | V | vi | II* | ⎬ 16 bars
                               ⎪
    | V | IV | V | IV | ⎪
                               ⎪
    | V | IV | V | V | ⎭

B=  | IV | I | IV | I | ⎫
                           ⎬ 8 bars
    | IV | vi | II* | V | ⎭

*Note:* The asterisk indicates a chromatic chord (i.e., one that is outside the prevailing key).

"As Tears Go By" (the following sixteen-bar scheme is repeated throughout):

$$\left.\begin{array}{l} |\ \text{I}\ |\ \overset{*}{\text{II}}\ |\ \text{IV}\ |\ \text{V}\ |\ \text{(repeat}\ 4\ \text{bars)}\ | \\ |\ \text{IV}\ |\ \text{V}\ |\ \text{I}\ |\ \text{vi}\ |\ \text{IV}\ |\ \text{IV}\ |\ \text{V}\ |\ \text{V}\ | \end{array}\right\}\ \text{16 bars}$$

"Jumpin' Jack Flash" (the following basic sixteen-bar scheme is repeated throughout, until the fade-out):

$$\left.\begin{array}{l} |\ \text{I}\ |\qquad\quad\text{(repeat}\ 7\ \text{more times)}\qquad\quad| \\ |\ \overset{*}{\flat\text{III}}\ |\ \overset{*}{\flat\text{VII}}\ |\ \text{IV}\ |\ \text{I}\ |\ \text{(repeat}\ 4\ \text{bars)}\quad| \end{array}\right\}\ \text{16 bars}$$

"Honky Tonk Woman" (A B A B A [instrumental] B B):

$$\text{A=}\ \left.\begin{array}{l} |\ \text{I}\ |\ \text{I}\ |\ \text{IV}\ |\ \text{IV}\ |\ \text{I}\ |\ \overset{*}{\text{II}}\ |\ \text{V}\ |\ \text{V}\ | \\ |\ \text{I}\ |\ \text{I}\ |\ \text{IV}\ |\ \text{IV}\ |\ \text{I}\ |\ \text{V}\ |\ \text{I}\ |\ \text{I}\ | \end{array}\right\}\ \text{16 bars}$$

$$\text{B=}\ |\ \text{I}\ |\ \text{IV}\ |\ \text{I}\ |\ \text{I}\ |\ \text{(repeat}\ 4\ \text{bars)}\quad|\ \Big\}\ \text{8 bars}$$

"Gimme Shelter" (sixteen-bar cycle repeated throughout):

$$\left.\begin{array}{l} |\ \text{i}\ |\qquad\quad\text{(repeat}\ 7\ \text{more times)}\qquad\quad| \\ |\ \text{i}\ |\ \text{VII}\ |\ \text{VI}\ |\ \text{VI}\ |\ \text{i}\ |\ \text{VII}\ |\ \text{VI}\ |\ \text{VI VII}\ | \end{array}\right\}\ \text{16 bars}$$

"You Can't Always Get What You Want":

$$|\ \text{I}\ |\ \text{IV}\ |\text{(repeat 2 bars)}|\text{(repeat 2 bars)}|\text{(repeat 2 bars)}|$$

$$|\ \text{I}\ |\ \text{IV}\ |\text{(repeat 2 bars)}|\text{(repeat 2 bars)}|\ \overset{*}{\text{II}}\ |\ \text{IV}\ |\ \underbrace{\ \text{I}\ |\ \text{IV}\ |\text{(repeat 2 bars)}|}_{\text{4-bar extension}}$$

"Brown Sugar" (eight-bar verse, eight-bar chorus, and four-bar bridge, which is repeated for an instrumental break):

| verse: | | I | I | IV | | IV | I | I | ♭VII* | I | | (8 bars) |

| chorus: | | V | V | I | | I | V | V | I | I | | (8 bars) |

| bridge: | | ♭III* | I | ♭VI* | ♭VII* | I | | | | | | (4 bars) |

*Note:* The asterisk indicates a chromatic chord (i.e., one that is outside the prevailing key).

The foregoing series of brief analyses provide a fairly representative sample of the Stones' treatment of harmony and form. The chord progressions are simple and repetitive. Chromatic chords are used infrequently, the major chord on the second scale degree (II) being the most common. Also encountered are the ♭VII and ♭III, both of which are not uncommon in blues-related styles inasmuch as they are simply major triads built on the "blue" seventh and "blue" third scale degrees. The four-bar, eight-bar, and sixteen-bar units are simply repeated to create the total song length.

Similarly, there is little rhythmic variance from the norms established by earlier rock styles. The Stones adhere to quadruple meter; the backbeat on the second and fourth beats is usually present. Most Stones songs divide each beat into duple divisions; a few slower songs (e.g., "Time Is on My Side" and "Heart of Stone") use a triple division of the beat.

The normal timbre of the Stones is modified occasionally by the use of additional instruments. Thus, there is marimba on "Under My Thumb," some fine saxophone work on "Brown Sugar," and a variety of instruments on "Ruby Tuesday" (recorder, cello, and piano) and "You Can't Always Get What You Want" (French horn, organ, piano, and chorus).

The vocal timbre of Mick Jagger is derived from the old shouting blues style (listen to "Get Off My Cloud" for a good illustration). Jagger lacks a rich vocal quality and is often slightly off pitch. He frequently adds spoken improvisations and interpolations like "Oh, my, my, my," "Easy, baby," and "Yes, it is." Listen to "Time Is on My Side" for a good example of Jagger's spoken interpolations (including an affected black style of enunciation). There is occasional use of vocal falsetto.

The Stones' melodies are not as sophisticated as those by Lennon and McCartney (or Harrison). Melody was not a particularly important parameter in R & B, nor is it with the Stones. Like their harmonic style, their melodic style usually adheres to the prevailing scale and is rather repetitive. Use of the blues scale is common (e.g., "Gimme Shelter"). It is not accidental that relatively few of the Stones' tunes have been covered in pop versions (as happened constantly to Beatle tunes). Taken out of their blues-based rock context, they do not seem to lend themselves to other stylistic interpretations.

Before leaving the Stones, let us take a close look at two of their most popular works, "Satisfaction" and "Sympathy for the Devil."

"Satisfaction" has as its nucleus a sixteen-bar chorus consisting of four 4-bar phrases:

| phrase A: | | I | I | IV | IV | |
|---|---|---|---|---|---|---|
| phrase A (repeated): | | I | I | IV | IV | |
| phrase B: | | I | V | I | IV | |
| phrase C (riff): | | I | ♭VII* | I | ♭VII* | |

*Note:* The asterisk indicates a chromatic chord (i.e., one that is outside the prevailing key).

Phrase 2 is a repetition of phrase 1; phrase 3 is contrasting; phrase 4 is the famous guitar riff from which is derived the other sections of the song.

The entire song consists of the sixteen-bar chorus alternating with the verses based on this guitar riff. The diagram below shows the formal scheme of the song.

*Note:* **Phrase C = guitar riff (R)**

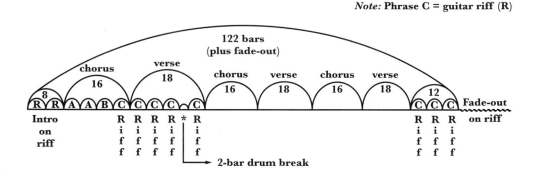

The verses consist of four repetitions of the four-bar guitar riff interrupted between the third and fourth repetitions by a two-bar drum break, thus creating an eighteen-bar section.

"Sympathy for the Devil" never reached the Top 40, but most Stones fans consider it one of the group's most representative songs from the 1960s. It consists of two 4-measure progressions that are repeated throughout the song's six-minute length.

Thus, the basic harmonic vocabulary is limited to four chords: I, IV, V, and ♭VII. Each chorus consists of six phrases: four repetitions of pattern A and two repetitions of pattern B. On the fourth occurrence of pattern A, the last measure is repeated, creating a five-bar phrase.

Following a ten-bar drum introduction, the chorus occurs five times, the first three and the fifth having lyrics, and the fourth being primarily an instrumental break. The closing section repeats pattern A about thirteen times before finally fading out. Thus, the entire formal structure is as shown below.

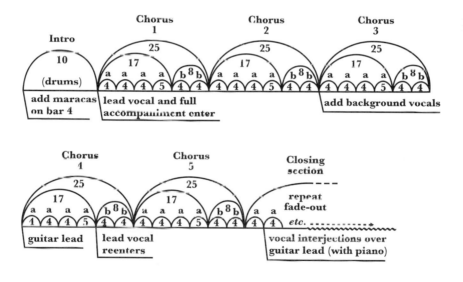

The 4/4 samba beat, once initiated, undergoes little or no change after the beginning of the first chorus. Maracas are added in the fourth measure of the introduction and remain throughout. The lead vocal, piano, bass, and guitar accompaniment enter at the first chorus. The only subsequent timbral changes are the addition of backup vocals in the third chorus and the guitar lead in the fourth chorus.

Judging by the musical parameters (harmony, rhythm, melody, form, texture, and timbre), "Sympathy for the Devil" is really rather simple, basic, and repetitive. Its appeal, via its insistent rhythm and repetitive melodic and formal units, is visceral rather than to the musical mind. For example, compare the last analysis to the one of Blood, Sweat, and Tears' version of the same song (Musical Close-Up, Chapter

11). The greater sophistication of that arrangement is reflected in the more complex analysis required. But it is the Stones' simplicity and repetitiveness that are at the heart of their appeal to so many listeners—fans who do not wish to be bothered by innovativeness and complexity. Certainly the Stones represent a marked contrast to the Beatles, with all the latter's creativity and musical experimentation. Starting from similar positions, these two British groups diverged onto different paths, each leading the way to very different styles of rock and roll.

# 8 Folk Music and Folk Rock

## OVERVIEW: THE YOUTH GENERATION OF THE 1960S

When we examined the early phases of the folk music movement, we spoke of a new sense of optimism as the youth felt an opportunity to redirect society under the leadership of the Kennedy administration. The tragic events of November 22, 1963, burst that optimism; the national mourning over Kennedy's assassination may have been a prelude to the subsequent overreaction known as Beatlemania. By the end of the decade, disillusionment, violence, drugs, and generally antisocial behavior (as at Altamont) seemed to prevail. Between these various points, however, there is much left to be filled in. Before discussing the folk music movement of the 1960s, let us pause to understand more fully what the youth of the 1960s were like.

The 1950s were dominated by a Republican administration and tended to be years of political and social conservatism. The 1960s, in contrast, were liberal years dominated by Democratic administrations. Social issues, particularly those related to minorities and the disadvantaged, were stressed from the outset. One of the first issues to be taken up by the youth was that of racial integration—the civil rights movement. Young people participated in a variety of demonstrations intended to focus attention on racial segregation and discrimination. There were lunch counter sit-ins, freedom bus rides, and protest marches. The movement achieved an important milestone in 1965 with the passage of major civil rights legislation. Impressed with their ability to have a measurable impact and to effect change, the youth tackled another major problem: the Vietnam War. This one proved to be an even bigger challenge.

The military draft had existed for years. The youth rebelled against the selective service system and the growing involvement of the United States in the escalating military conflict in Vietnam. As American involvement grew and more youth were

175

drafted into participation in a war of which they disapproved, the protests grew more adamant. Some fled to Canada; others burned their draft cards and went underground. The youth protesters demanded peace; the peace symbol, ☮, was seen everywhere; friends and strangers greeted each other with the old World War II victory sign, now converted to the peace sign, and the words "Peace, brother (sister)." But the youth were less successful in this campaign than they had been in the civil rights campaign. The war escalated throughout the 1960s and did not end until the early 1970s. The frustration resulting from their inability to effect policy change in this regard may be a partial explanation for the growing domestic violence that erupted in the late 1960s.

Another cause of importance to the youth was ecology. There was a growing concern that unrestrained population growth and industrial expansion would eventually deplete or foul the natural resources of the nation. Air and water were being polluted; oil and gas resources were dwindling; forests were being used up at an alarming rate. These concerns led to a new consciousness of the value of natural products. Natural foods became an important trend. Along with a fascination with nature and its preservation came a deep suspicion of technology, from the air-polluting, gas-guzzling automobile to the newly evolving computer industry.

Such noble ideals led to some interesting inconsistencies, however. The concern for the rights and well-being of others was counterbalanced by a growing concern for the self. Thus, there was a new fascination with "getting to know one's self." In searching for a path to the inner self, a variety of spiritual vehicles was tried, such as Zen Buddhism, transcendental meditation, and various spiritual gurus, from the Reverend Sun Myung Moon to the Maharishi Mahesh Yogi. And there were more mundane vehicles, specifically drugs, including barbiturates, amphetamines, LSD, cocaine, heroin, and, of course, marijuana. The coexistence of the drug trend and the natural health food trend was one of the odd contradictions of this period.

Still more inconsistencies emerged as the peace-conscious youth found that to make their point they would need to resort to violence. Political violence in the name of peace and human rights flared at the universities across the nation, culminating in 1968 with riots at the Democratic National Convention and the killings at Kent State University (1970). Undoubtedly, such violence was related to the frustration caused by the assassination of such youth heroes as Robert Kennedy and Martin Luther King Jr.

As an expression against "the establishment" (parents, government, schools, churches, and the military-industrial complex), many youth just "dropped out." They grew their hair longer and longer, dressed in ever more outlandish styles, and ran away to communes in San Francisco and other points west. Increasingly, cultural heroes were not good-looking, righteous, "knights on white horses" but antiheroes. In sports, there was Joe Namath, who projected a "buck-the-system," hard-living, hard-playing "Broadway Joe" image; and there was Muhammad Ali (Cassius Clay), who adopted the Muslim religion and then defied the draft. Movie heroes were often bums, prostitutes, and general ne'er-do-wells. And rock-and-roll groups made up of physically unattractive, drug-abusing, womanizing bad boys (see Chapter 7, "The British Invasion") were admiringly accepted.

Finally, there was the sexual revolution. Sex was brought out into the open. Old role models were questioned. Women began to be seen as sexual equals and as partners in throwing off the sociosexual stereotypes of the past. Skirts were shortened to well above the knee; all female fashions became daringly revealing. Cohabitation and communal living were considered as alternative lifestyles. The slogan "Freedom Now" referred not only to the end of racial discrimination but also to the loosening of the sexual mores of earlier generations.

The 1960s were turbulent, troublesome, exciting, tragic, and revolutionary. Much was gained; much was lost. We probably must wait for future historians, blessed with the greater perspective of further intervening decades, to provide a final evaluation of the 1960s. Indeed, some of the changes initiated in the 1960s are still unwinding, and we cannot be sure whether the eventual effects on human society will be for better or for worse.

What we can be sure of is that music was a central ingredient in the 1960s landscape. The music of the 1960s reflected much of society's concerns and feelings, but it also reinforced attitudes and beliefs and helped modify value systems, spreading the changes to an ever-widening segment of the population. Many were motivated by music to act. If one suspects such statements as possible exaggeration, one should ask someone who was part of the 1960s youth generation what it would have been like without the music. No Beatles, no Dylan, no Stones; no soul music; no acid rock. The possibility is so bewildering that it is difficult to formulate a coherent answer.

## BOB DYLAN

The youth movement of the early 1960s was closely identified with the folk music styles of the Kingston Trio and Peter, Paul, and Mary. These serious, socially conscious youth shunned rock and roll as being mindless commercial junk. The result seemed to be an irreparable split between the "folkies" and the "rockers." But from within the folk movement came a singer who would bring together the two cultural and musical factions and have an important revolutionary impact on the nature of rock and roll. His name was Bob Dylan.

Robert Zimmerman (Bob Dylan) was born in Duluth, Minnesota, on May 24, 1941. Six years later, he and his family moved to the small town of Hibbing. He attended the University of Minnesota for several months but dropped out late in 1960. He hung around the coffeehouses and small clubs, singing and playing guitar whenever he was allowed. In this atmosphere he absorbed a good dose of folk music, especially songs by his hero Woody Guthrie. Hearing that Guthrie was dying of Huntington's disease in a New York City hospital, Dylan (his newly adopted "professional" name) decided to leave Minnesota, seek fame and fortune in the big city, and meet and visit Guthrie.

After moving to New York City in 1961, Dylan visited with Guthrie on numerous occasions and, through Guthrie, was welcomed into the folk culture of New York City, centered to a large degree in the Greenwich Village area. Accompanied only by his own acoustic guitar and harmonica, Dylan auditioned for Columbia Records' John Hammond. Among the songs Dylan sang at that audition was "You're No Good," an old folk song by Jesse Fuller. If you can, listen to that song (on the *Bob Dylan* album) and honestly decide whether you would have recommended Mr. Dylan for a major label recording contract.

The young Bob Dylan (*Source:* Michael Ochs Archive, Ltd.)

For whatever reasons, John Hammond foresaw a future for this scruffy, raw, and untrained singer. Dylan's first album was released in March 1962. It contained traditional folk songs and blues plus two original songs by Dylan: "Song to Woody," a tribute to his hero, and "Talkin' New York." The latter song was in the "talking blues" style developed by blues singer Huddie Ledbetter (Leadbelly) and popularized by Woody Guthrie. In this type of song, a story is half spoken, half sung (or intoned) to a simple chordal accompaniment. Dylan's "Talkin' New York" is autobiographical as it tells of his leaving the "Wild West" to settle in New York City. Even in this early song, there are hints of Dylan's primary talent: the ability to write lyrics with artistic skill. The song also reveals the dry wit and sarcasm that would be heard in many other Dylan songs.

The follow-up album, *The Freewheelin' Bob Dylan* (March 1963), contained all original material and caught the attention of the folk community. It contained one of Dylan's most important songs, "Blowin' in the Wind." This song was covered by Peter, Paul, and Mary, who converted it into a number 2 hit. It became an anthem of the youth movement and expressed the optimism and confidence inherent in the youth movement prior to the gunshots in Dallas. But the *Freewheelin'* album also contained one of Dylan's most bitter songs, "Masters of War." It condemns the military-industrial complex, and even goes so far as to rejoice in its hoped-for death (whether Dylan is referring to individuals or to the complex as a whole is not really clear). The album also contains "Don't Think Twice, It's All Right," also covered successfully by Peter, Paul, and Mary. This song is typical of many of Dylan's "love songs." Rather sarcastically, Dylan tells his girlfriend, "You just kinda wasted my precious time, but don't think twice, it's all right." Finally, there is the sheer poetic beauty of "A Hard Rain's a-Gonna Fall," which somewhat vaguely refers to the whole spectrum of humanity's disregard for itself. All in all, Dylan's second album was a strong indication of the greatness that resided in this young artist.

With *The Times They Are a-Changin'* (January 1964), Dylan emerged as a major star of the folk movement. Still accompanied only by his acoustic guitar and harmonica, he sang songs about war (the sarcastic "With God on Our Side") and racial prejudice ("The Lonesome Death of Hattie Carroll"). There is also the "Ballad of Hollis Brown," a song about a mass murder on a South Dakota farm; it ends with the vague lines, "There's seven people dead on a South Dakota farm; somewhere in the distance there's seven new people born." Does he mean that the seven are spiritually reborn in an afterlife? Or is it a comment on our callous attitude toward the death of those not close to us? As is often the case with Dylan's lyrics, we cannot be sure. The title song, "The Times They Are a-Changin'," is another youth anthem in the vein of "Blowin' in the Wind." Compared to the earlier anthem, however, this song has a rougher edge to it. Dylan warns the establishment that there is a new force in the nation and that they had better adapt to it or they'll "sink like a stone" in the floods of change.

In the summer of 1963, Dylan appeared at the Newport Folk Festival. Introduced by Joan Baez, he brought the crowd to an emotional climax with "Blowin' in the Wind." Joining Baez, Peter, Paul, and Mary, Pete Seeger, Theodore Bikel, and other folk stars, he sang the civil rights anthem "We Shall Overcome." He was firmly fixed as the messiah of the youth-folk movement.

Following this success, the next album, *Another Side of Bob Dylan*, was a bit of a surprise. He seemed to pull back from the leading edge of protest and appeared to be more mellow and contemplative. It was only the first of several twists and turns in Dylan's career. Dylan seemed to dislike being stereotyped; as soon as he felt his image was becoming too stabilized, he shifted to a new direction. In "My Back Pages" he appears to question the self-assuredness of his earlier statements, characterizing them as the overromanticized "musketeering" of youth; he saw himself as too cocky, too certain, and too simplistic in his judgments. Note the last two lines, which are both enigmatic and ironic:

Yes, my guard stood hard when abstract threats
Too noble to neglect
Deceived me into thinking
I had something to protect
Good and bad, I define these terms
Quite clear, no doubt, somehow.
Ah, but I was so much older then,
I'm younger than that now.

If *Another Side* was a mild surprise to Dylan's protest-oriented followers, the single that hit the charts in May 1965 was even more unsettling. "Subterranean Homesick Blues" only rose to number 39 but started a ripple that would become a tidal wave within a matter of months. This time it was not the lyrics that caused consternation; the problem was the music. It used a drum set and electric guitars; in fact, it sounded suspiciously like rock. The album, *Bringing It All Back Home*, used electric instruments on half of its songs. The folkies's worst fears were confirmed in July at the 1965 Newport Folk Festival. Dylan's much-anticipated appearance created a near riot as he strolled onto the stage with an electric guitar and proceeded to perform to the accompaniment of the Paul Butterfield Blues Band. Amidst the booing and hissing, few realized that a new style had been born: "folk rock." To Dylan's horrified followers, it seemed that he had "sold out" and "gone commercial."

Actually the Byrds had adapted Dylan's "Mr. Tambourine Man" to their rock style and released it as a single back in March 1965. However, it did not break into the charts until early June, achieving number 1 status on June 26. So who invented "folk rock," the Byrds or Dylan? Dylan's "Subterranean Homesick Blues" hit the charts first; but the Byrds' single hit number 1, whereas Dylan's barely cracked the Top 40 (and then only for one week). Let us just say that the Byrds and

Dylan hit upon the folk rock style at about the same time and can share the credit (or blame).

As if to further confound his fans, Dylan released another electrified single called "Like a Rolling Stone" (August 1965). This six-minute song (included on the *Highway 61 Revisited* album) became his first major hit, rising to the number 2 position and breaking the radio industry's two-and-a-half minute norms.

"Like a Rolling Stone" was rock music with folklike (or at least Dylanlike) lyrics. Therein lay the basis of the new folk rock style. Dylan's next album, *Blonde on Blonde* (summer 1966), continued the new combination style. It was rock's first double album, preceding *The Beatles* by about two and a half years. Of particular note is "Rainy Day Women #12 and 35," a number 2 hit (Dylan himself has never had a number 1 hit). The song seems to be an answer to his critics—those hard-core folkies who saw him as a traitor to the cause. He nonchalantly notes that people will criticize you ("stone you") no matter what you do or how good you try to be. He tosses off the criticism with a double entendre: "Everybody must get stoned." This hook line can mean that everybody must endure criticism (getting "stoned" in the biblical sense) or that one is best advised to shrug off criticism and simply get "stoned" (i.e., with drugs or alcohol). Either way, Dylan seems generally unimpressed by his critics' disapproval.

In the summer of 1966, Bob Dylan, at the height of his career, seemed to disappear. For a year and a half there were no new albums (except for a collected hits album) and no tours. Speculation and rumors ran rampant. It turned out that he had had a very serious motorcycle accident in late July 1966. He retreated to upstate New York to recuperate from the accident. Joining him was a Canadian group known simply as the Band. During much of 1967, Dylan and the Band rehearsed and recorded a series of new songs (eventually released as *The Basement Tapes* in 1975).

In January 1968, Dylan released his first album since the accident. *John Wesley Harding* seemed different somehow. The voice was more mellow and pleasing; there was little of the old anger and protest against world problems. Nor was there the heavy folk rock of *Highway 61 Revisited* or *Blonde on Blonde*. The jacket notes are surrealistic and almost impossible to decipher logically. A brief excerpt will suffice to demonstrate this.

> There were three kings and a jolly three too. The first one had a broken nose, the second a broken arm, and the third was broke. "Faith is the key!" said the first king. "No, froth is the key!" said the second. "You're both wrong," said the third, "The key is Frank!" (Dylan 1973, 255)

The "story" goes on from there, and just as one has the feeling that he or she is just one phrase away from comprehending the message, the story takes another befuddling turn. Dylan's lyrics followed this same surrealistic pattern. For example, "All Along the Watchtower" seems to be an interesting story, but we are never exactly sure what it is about. Dylan set a very interesting scene.

> Outside in the distance a wildcat did growl,
> Two riders were approaching, the wind began to howl. (Dylan 1973, 259)

The only difficulty is that this scene is set at the end of the poem, rather than at the beginning.

Dylan's last album of the 1960s was *Nashville Skyline* (1969). Once again he surprised fans with another unexpected turn, this time toward a country sound. Among the others on the album were Charlie Daniels, Johnny Cash, and Chet Atkins. The presence of steel guitar made the country sound obvious. A number 7 hit, "Lay Lady Lay," came from this album.

Although our main concern here is the Dylan of the 1960s, we can briefly survey Dylan's later career. He became a model for the singer/songwriter trend of the 1970s. Perhaps his most interesting album of the seventies was *Blood on the Tracks,* a number 1 album in 1975. Speaking with great insight, he sang "Tangled Up in Blue" about the contradictory confusions and pains that accompany a broken relationship. Dylan had married back in 1965, and at the time of *Blood on the Tracks* he was recovering from the dissolution of that marriage. There are other fine songs on this album, such as "Simple Twist of Fate" and the long Western ballad, "Lily, Rosemary, and the Jack of Hearts."

In a series of San Francisco concerts in 1979, Dylan again shocked his fans by turning to a Christian message. A subsequent album, *Slow Train Coming,* contained a collection of "born again" messages. Dylan was as convincing with this new message as he had been some sixteen years earlier with his social protests. Two more Christian-oriented albums, *Saved* and *Shot of Love,* were released in the early 1980s. His 1983 album, *Infidels,* seemed to withdraw back into Dylanesque vagueness; some felt it was a move away from his born again message, but others argued that it was simply a more subtle statement of that same philosophy. It seems that with Dylan the arguments never cease. Whether the thrust is civil rights, war, folk rock, country rock, surrealism, broken relationships, or Christian faith, Dylan and his obtuse lyrics are at the center of controversy.

Before leaving Dylan we must underscore once again his most significant contribution to the history of rock. His lyrics, with their symbolism, internal ironies, sarcasm, thought-provoking messages, dry wit, surrealism, and graceful flow, were the most influential and sophisticated since the beginning of rock and roll. Through his influence on the Beatles, especially on John Lennon, the Dylanesque lyric found its way into the very heart of 1960s rock. Inevitably, there have been many since who have tried to sound heavy and profound, in hopes of being taken as seriously as Dylan; very often they end up sounding merely pretentious. It is safe to say that because of this eloquent spokesman for the 1960s youth generation, rock lyrics have not been the same since.

Bob Dylan (*Source:* Michael Ochs Archive, Ltd.)

## THE BYRDS

The story of the Byrds is one of remarkable potential that was only partially fulfilled. They possessed the creativity and musicianship to achieve a status comparable to that of the Beach Boys, Dylan, and maybe even the Beatles, but were undone by a curse that sometimes affects rock bands: constant personnel changes. The constant shifting of personnel is debilitating for several reasons. Not only is the band's popularity undermined as fans follow departing members into new bands, but there is a loss of the musical "ESP" that naturally evolves as the same musicians work together over a number of years. Regrettably, the Byrds were unable to maintain a set membership for any significant length of time. Even so, they managed to have a significant, though brief, impact on the history of rock.

The central figure in the Byrds was Jim McGuinn. Born in Chicago, McGuinn's background was with folk music; he was a backup musician for the Limelighters, and after working as a solo act in Greenwich Village he joined the Chad Mitchell Trio. In 1964, McGuinn met Gene Clark, a young Missourian who had learned his folk style as a member of the New Christy Minstrels. David Crosby, a product of Los Angeles, had some five years' experience as a folk singer with Les Baxter's Balladeers. Chris Hillman, also from Los Angeles, had played bluegrass-style mandolin in his own group, the Hillmen. Crosby introduced the group to a drummer from New York named Mike Clarke. By 1964, the quintet was formed.

Their first Columbia album contained four songs by Bob Dylan, including "Mr. Tambourine Man." The single was released in March 1965 but did not enter the charts until early June. The idea of setting a Dylan song to electric rock-oriented accompaniment was new at the time. The new folk rock style was born with this recording and Dylan's "Subterranean Homesick Blues" and *Bringing It All Back Home* album. By June 26, the Byrds's version of "Mr. Tambourine Man" was number 1.

Using some original material and two more Dylan songs, the Byrds recorded their second album, *Turn, Turn, Turn.* Folk singer Pete Seeger had created the title song by adapting the words from the Book of Ecclesiastes in the Bible and setting them to music. "Turn, Turn, Turn" moved to the number 1 position by December 1965. With two number 1 hits within nine months, there was every reason to believe that the Byrds were on the road to success.

In early 1966, Gene Clark left the group. Deciding to remain a quartet, the Byrds prepared their third album, *Fifth Dimension* (summer 1966). This album produced their third (and most controversial) hit, "Eight Miles High" (number 14). Musically the song is quite adventuresome for mid-1966, paralleling some of the things the Beatles were doing about this time. There are unusual chord progressions and use of the Dorian mode (like a minor scale but with its sixth note raised one half step). There is a predominant bass line, interesting close three-part harmony, and good twelve-string guitar work by McGuinn. It was widely believed that the lyrics referred to the effects of LSD, but the Byrds denied the drug association, claiming the song simply celebrated the joys of airplane flight (remember the pre-1967 double entendre syndrome).

The Byrds' drift toward increased musical sophistication continued in their next album, *Younger than Yesterday* (March 1967). However, before 1967 was over, disagreements between McGuinn and Crosby had become intolerable. Crosby left (later to form Crosby, Stills, and Nash).

Once again, McGuinn's decision was not to replace the departed member. The remaining trio (McGuinn, Hillman, and Clarke), plus various outside musicians, created *The Notorious Byrd Brothers*, possibly the most interesting album of the Byrds' career. Certainly it is an eclectic album. There is "Artificial Energy," with its amphetamine references and electronically modified brass sounds; and there are the folk rock sounds of "Goin' Back," with its reminiscences of childhood, and "Draft Morning," an effective protest song. The latter contains some particularly effective lyrics ("no hurry to learn to kill and take the will from unknown faces"). Note also the mixed-in sound effects (war sounds) and a militarylike trumpet call. The trumpet call is an effective touch per se; but its effect is enhanced because its notes are dissonant against the prevailing harmonies, nicely reinforcing the message that the military concept is in conflict with the Byrds' antidraft sentiments.

There are several songs on *The Notorious Byrd Brothers* that have a country sound (e.g., "Change Is Now," "Wasn't Born to Follow," and "Old John Robertson"). These country sounds are intermingled with the electronic sounds more typical of rock. The result began to be called country rock, a style that the Byrds would develop further on their next album.

*The Notorious Byrd Brothers* also contains experiments in meter, such as "Get to You," which alternates sections with five beats per measure and sections with six beats per measure. Similarly, "Tribal Gathering" moves from a very jazzlike quintuple meter to a more normal quadruple meter. Strings are used in various spots throughout the album, often subjected to electronic modification, such as filtering (e.g., "Natural Harmony") and phase shifting (e.g., "Old John Robertson"). Phase shifting, or "phasing," is an electronic manipulation that shifts the positive and

The Byrds (*Source:* Michael Ochs Archive, Ltd.)

negative phases of the sound waves so that there is a modification of the timbre of the original sound. The most effective use of phasing is in the string section of "Old John Robertson." Note also the polyphonic texture in this section.

As we listen to *The Notorious Byrd Brothers,* with its experiments with odd meters, polyphony, external sound effects, and electronic manipulations, we are reminded of the Beatles' experimentation. Indeed, this album suggests that the Byrds had the potential to achieve comparable status as innovators in rock. But shortly after the release of this album, more personnel problems hit the band. Mike Clarke left and was replaced by Hillman's cousin, Kevin Kelly. The group became a quartet again with the addition of Gram Parsons. Parsons favored the country rock sound, and this influence is felt in the next album, *Sweetheart of the Rodeo.* Here the country rock style dominated and became a prototype for later country-oriented rock groups. The personnel problem hit dead bottom in mid-1968, when Parsons and Hillman left to form the Flying Burrito Brothers. This left McGuinn as the only remaining member of the original Byrds. Changing his first name to Roger when he joined the Subud faith, he continued to release Byrds albums using a variety of players. But these simply did not measure up to the 1965 to 1968 Byrds. In 1973, McGuinn finally disbanded the Byrds. Ironically, it was in 1973 that the five original members got together one last time to record an album, *Byrds.*

There is little doubt that the 1965 to 1968 Byrds were one of rock's most talented and creative bands. They were cofounders of folk rock (with Dylan); they led the way to the country rock sound that became popular in the 1970s; "Eight Miles High" has the questionable distinction of being one of the first drug songs in rock; and they were certainly one of the most innovative groups of their time in the use of electronic sound manipulation. One wonders what their position in rock history would have been had the original five members stayed together for eight to ten years.

## THE MAMAS AND THE PAPAS

*Folk rock* is a vague and generalized term. Following the example set by the Byrds and Dylan, scads of folk rock groups suddenly appeared. For the most part, such groups were the folkies of the early 1960s; now they added drums and converted to electric guitars and called themselves folk rockers. One of the most successful of these groups was The Mamas and the Papas. Whereas the Byrds had blended the folk style with a harder rock sound, the Mamas and the Papas tended toward a softer rock style. In the two-year period from early 1966 through late 1967, they placed nine singles in the Top 40, including six Top 10 hits.

John Phillips was from South Carolina; he had followed a fairly typical folk music path, having performed in Greenwich Village with several groups. Cass Elliot (real name Ellen Cohen) was from Baltimore, Maryland. By 1964, Elliot and her husband James Hendricks had joined with Denny Doherty and Zal Yanovsky (both from Canada) to form the Mugwumps.

In early 1965, Doherty and Elliot joined with John Phillips and his wife Michelle to form yet another folk group. Soon they had all moved to Los Angeles and obtained a contract with Dunhill Records. Calling themselves the Mamas and the Papas, they adopted the popular new folk rock sound. Using top-rate Los Angeles backup musicians and excellent production work by Dunhill owner Lou Adler, they released their first album, *If You Can Believe Your Eyes and Ears,* in early 1966.

The album zoomed to number 1, and two singles, "California Dreamin'" and "Monday, Monday," hit the Top 10 (the latter song became their first and only number 1 song). Some of their success was probably due to the general rage for the new folk rock style. But beyond that, the Mamas and the Papas had an appealing sound. John Phillips was a talented writer and arranger; the four-part vocal harmonies were absolutely solid and musical. The technical production and instrumental backup were first-rate. A second album, *The Mamas and the Papas* (issued in late 1966), was another success, yielding two Top 10 singles, "I Saw Her Again" and "Words of Love."

The successes continued in 1967 with two more albums and three singles: "Dedicated to the One I Love" (a cover of a 1961 hit by the Shirelles), "Creeque Alley" (a clever autobiography of the group), and "Twelve-Thirty (Young Girls Are Coming to the Canyon)." Also in 1967, John Phillips and Lou Adler organized the Monterey International Pop Festival, an early example of the type of rock festival that would become so popular in the later 1960s (and beyond). Among the future stars presented there were Jimi Hendrix, Janis Joplin, and the Who.

The year 1968 was the beginning of the end for the Mamas and the Papas. "Glad to Be Happy" went only as high as number 26 and became the group's last Top 40 hit. By mid-1968, the Mamas and the Papas had disbanded.

Cass Elliot went on to moderate success as a solo act and television performer. She died in 1974 from what was variously reported as a heart attack or choking on a sandwich or a chicken bone. John and Michelle Phillips divorced in 1970. John briefly tried a solo career but succumbed to an increasingly serious drug habit. Recovered from his addiction, he and his daughter from a previous marriage, Mackenzie Phillips, toured the country in the mid-1980s promoting the antidrug

The Mamas and the Papas
(*Source:* Michael Ochs Archive, Ltd.)

message. John died in 2001. Michelle Phillips turned to a moderately successful acting career.

The emphasis with the Mamas and the Papas was on their solid and effective vocal harmonies. With echo and some overdubbing, the quartet could sound like a full chorus. The folk aspect of their folk rock blend was derived more from their image than from anything else. They rarely engaged in protest songs about the war, the draft, or civil rights. But with the men's goatees and mustaches and the women's long, straight hair, and their multicolored shirts, they looked like soft-core folkniks ("hippies"). The rock side of their folk rock blend was a softer style of rock, lacking the harshness of Dylan or the hard beat and grinding electric guitar work of McGuinn and the Byrds. The Mamas and the Papas created a pleasing commercial version of folk rock and are remembered with a nostalgic smile by their many 1960s fans.

## SIMON AND GARFUNKEL

In 1957, two fifteen-year-old school chums, modeling themselves after the Everly Brothers, recorded a song called "Hey Schoolgirl." The song peaked at number 49 and secured them an appearance on *American Bandstand*. Using the pseudonyms Tom and Jerry, they released several more singles (that flopped) before giving up on show business and returning to school. The boys' real names were Paul Simon and Art Garfunkel.

Simon and Garfunkel first met when both boys were eleven years old and attending school in Forest Hills, New York. After attending college, they pursued separate careers in the music business. Paul wrote songs and worked as a song promoter. He released several more unsuccessful recordings under various pseudonyms. Garfunkel recorded as Artie Garr on Warwick Records.

The young men joined forces again and auditioned for Columbia Records as a folk singing duo. They were awarded a contract and in late 1964 released their first album, *Wednesday Morning 3 A.M.* The album contained some Dylan songs, a few traditional folk songs, and some original Paul Simon songs. One of these was "The Sounds of Silence." It was recorded with voices and acoustic guitars, as was the rule for folksingers in 1964. The album went nowhere, and so the discouraged duo went their separate ways again. Meanwhile the folk rock revolution of mid-1965 had happened. Tom Wilson, the Columbia producer of *Wednesday Morning*, went back to "The Sounds of Silence" tape and remixed it with electric bass, electric guitars, and drums. The result: folk rock.

In this new version, "The Sounds of Silence" skyrocketed to number 1 on New Year's Day, 1966. There is no clearer demonstration of the shift from folk to folk rock than to compare "The Sounds of Silence" from *Wednesday Morning 3 A.M.* with the later popular version. The voice tracks are the same; the difference lies in the rhythm tracks: the bass line and the electric guitar accompaniment.

Quickly a new folk rock album was recorded and released. *Sounds of Silence* included the title hit plus another Top 10 hit, "I Am a Rock." The latter song has a typical folk rock sound; the lyrics stress the aggressive alienation of the loner who refuses to risk contact with others. It was a logical follow-up to "The Sounds of Silence," also a song about loneliness. Simon's ability to write lyrics appropriate to the Dylan-inspired folk rock movement is evident in lines like "people talking with-

Simon and Garfunkel (*Source:* Michael Ochs Archive, Ltd.)

out speaking; people hearing without listening; people writing songs that voices never share."

In late 1966, *Parsley, Sage, Rosemary and Thyme* was released and contained yet another Top 10 hit, "Homeward Bound." A series of singles in 1966 and 1967 seemed to indicate a slight erosion in Simon and Garfunkel's popularity. But the tremendously successful film *The Graduate*, with sound track by Simon and Garfunkel, propelled the duo back into the limelight. The sound track album held the number 1 position for nine weeks. It contained the folklike "Scarborough Fair/Canticle," "The Sounds of Silence," and "Mrs. Robinson." This last song, with its sarcastic portrait of the movie's Mrs. Robinson, became Simon and Garfunkel's first number 1 single since "The Sounds of Silence."

The 1968 album *Bookends* shows the effects of *Sgt. Pepper.* As with that album, *Bookends* includes the complete lyrics on the outside back cover and is, in part, a concept album. It opens with an instrumental song that is heard again at the end of the first side, with vocals added. The concept deals with time and the various stages in human lives. Thus the opening song refers to a child who is threatening to commit suicide by jumping from a building's ledge. "America" seems to be about a young couple who set out together to see America. Apparently their search is not successful ("I'm empty and aching and I don't know why"). "Overs" seems to be about a married couple for whom life together has become dull and routine. In spite of their unfulfilling relationship, they really cannot break apart.

A particularly remarkable track is "Voices of Old People." Garfunkel had visited several homes for the elderly and recorded various remarks and segments of conversation. These are combined into a montage that provides effective insights into the problems and loneliness of old age. This montage is followed by "Old Friends," a song that reflects upon the desperately solitary existence of many senior citizens. Lines like "Old friends sat on their park bench like bookends" and "can you imagine us years from today, sharing a park bench quietly? How terribly strange to be seventy" were sobering reminders to the "don't trust anyone over thirty" generation!

Side 1 ends with the "Bookends Theme," a wistful commentary on the inevitable passage of time. The symbolism of bookends is effectively carried out by the theme, which is at both "ends" of side 1, by the image of the old people on opposite ends of the park bench, and by the allusion to our life cycle, with its remarkable similarities between infancy and old age.

Side 2 includes "Mrs. Robinson" and a strong folk rock tune, "A Hazy Shade of Winter." Overall, the album shows the new freedom creative artists were experiencing in the post-*Sgt. Pepper* days. For example, neither "Voices of Old People" nor "Old Friends" shows any relation to rock. (The latter is accompanied by a large orchestra that builds to a climax near the end—reminiscent in concept to "A Day in the Life" from *Sgt. Pepper.*) But the old rules were gone; the more creative artists were free to ignore the old formulas and to express themselves with whatever means seemed most effective. It was exciting to buy albums like *Bookends* in those days, not knowing exactly what to expect—from the folk rock of "A Hazy Shade of Winter" to the montage of "Voices of Old People," with a wide variety of styles in between.

Simon and Garfunkel lost none of their appeal as the decade of the 1970s dawned. *Bridge over Troubled Water* (1970) yielded no fewer than three Top 10 singles. Rather surprisingly, the duo decided to go their separate ways. Paul Simon, who had done most of the songwriting for the team, had continued success through the 1970s, with albums and singles consistently hitting the Top 10. Simon also appeared frequently on television and in several movies, including his own production, *One-Trick Pony.* In the mid-1980s, he showed some of the old folksinger's flair for social and political concerns by basing an album on his feelings regarding the difficulties in South Africa (*Graceland*).

Art Garfunkel's solo career has been less illustrious. Several early albums and one single fared well, but subsequent albums revealed declining impact. The duo reunited for a highly successful concert in Central Park in September 1981. The resulting album reached number 6 in 1982 and contained a moderate hit, "Wake Up Little Susie," originally recorded by Tom and Jerry's role models, the Everly Brothers.

Simon and Garfunkel's success stemmed largely from Paul Simon's undeniable skills at lyric writing and tune writing. Just for fun, listen to "A Simple Desultory Philippic" from *Parsley, Sage, Rosemary and Thyme.* It pokes gentle fun at Dylan, folk rock, and even Simon and Garfunkel themselves. If you can identify every name and reference contained in this song, you score an "A+" for your knowledge of the 1960s. One hint: The pathetic "I've lost my harmonica, Albert" at the end of the song refers to Dylan's manager, Albert Grossman.

## OTHER FOLK ROCKERS

To accommodate the wide variety of post-1965 folk rockers, the definition of the term *folk rock* must be very generalized indeed. After all, the Mamas and the Papas, Dylan, and Simon and Garfunkel do not sound alike. Each artist who melded the lyrical profundities and tunefulness of folk music with the electrification, bass line, and hard beat of rock found a unique recipe to achieve the combination. And, as always, the purists on both sides were righteously indignant. The pure folkies felt that their music had been corrupted by the crass commercialization and mindless noise of rock; the pure rockers resented the invasion of their basic good-time music by the self-conscious profundities of the folkies. But, in between, a vast new audience relished the opportunity to have somewhat more thought-provoking and intelligent lyrics served up to them in a musical context they enjoyed.

### Joan Baez and Judy Collins

Joan Baez held out against folk rock as long as possible. She appeared at the 1959 Newport Folk Festival and soon became a well-known figure in the early 1960s folk scene. Her first album, *Joan Baez* (1960), set a pattern that would hold for over a decade. The album contained traditional American and English folk songs sung in a clear voice with perfect pitch and excellent enunciation. It sold well but contained no hit singles. Such was to be her fate throughout the 1960s. Her fourth album, *Joan Baez in Concert, Part 2* (1963), contained a live version of "We Shall Overcome," a civil rights anthem of the 1960s with which she would forever be identified.

When Dylan turned to folk rock in mid-1965, Baez, a close friend of Dylan's, refused to go along. Instead, she stayed with her pure acoustic, socially oriented style. Her social involvement was not only musical; she often marched and sang at civil rights demonstrations and student protest meetings.

It was not until the 1970s that Baez finally relented to the pressures of musical style by softening her approach and adding the electrification of folk rock. She found considerable success writing her own songs. *Diamonds and Rust* (1975) was a monster album commercially and musically. The title song—only her second single hit—seems to be a rather bitter complaint about a certain "legend" who is "so good with words and with making things vague." She takes another shot at Dylan in her version of his "Simple Twist of Fate." For one sarcastic chorus, she does a perfect imitation of his unique, off-pitch vocal style, complete with the falling pitches at the end of each phrase.

The central position of Joan Baez in the 1960s folk music scene inspired other female vocalists to follow. Judy Collins's first two albums contained standard folk material, but beginning with her third album, she joined the Baez–Dylan trend of contemporary protest songs. Like Baez, her albums sold well enough, but there were few hit singles. Her most enduring hit was Stephen Sondheim's "Send in the Clowns," which was number 36 in 1975 but returned to the charts in 1977 (number 19). Yet another female singer to follow the Baez–Collins lead was Joni Mitchell. Because her primary impact was in the 1970s, we will discuss her career in more detail in Chapter 14, "The Continuing Fragmentation of Rock."

### Sonny and Cher

Sometimes associated with the folk rock trend of the late 1960s were Sonny and Cher. Indeed, Cher's first hit, "All I Really Want To Do" (number 15 in 1965), was a Dylan song. Salvatore "Sonny" Bono and Cherilyn Sarkisian were married in 1963 and began recording as Caesar and Cleo, and finally as Sonny and Cher. They produced a number of hits as a duo from 1965 through 1972 but also released solo recordings. Cher, whose solo success was considerably greater, eventually charted some twelve Top 40 hits, including three number 1 songs. In the early 1970s, the duo became major television personalities thanks to their own CBS series. In spite of (or because of?) Cher's risqué clothing styles, the pair found a wider pop audience and gradually lost their folk rock identification. Sonny Bono died in 1998. He had served as a member of the U.S. House of Representatives from California.

### Buffalo Springfield

As was previously mentioned, stylistic labels such as "folk rock" are often inadequate indicators of a group's real style. Such is the case with the Buffalo Springfield. They first gained national attention in early 1967 with a song that was in the folk protest vein, "For What It's Worth" (number 7 in 1967). Consequently, they were immediately typed as another folk rock group. But, in fact, the Buffalo Springfield covered a wide stylistic range. They were a quintet consisting of Stephen Stills, Neil Young, Richard Furay, Dewey Martin, and Bruce Palmer. Most had experience in folk-oriented groups. Their first album, *Buffalo Springfield* (early 1967), revealed the versatility and solid musicianship of the quintet. Using material written by Stills and Young, the album contained strong rock songs like "Sit Down, I Think I Love You" and a prototype of the country rock style developed later by the Byrds, Dylan, and others, "Go and Say Goodbye."

Released in late 1967, *Buffalo Springfield Again* revealed a somewhat harder sound in songs such as the psychedelic "Mr. Soul" (note the "Satisfaction"-like guitar riff), "Bluebird" (complete with shouting vocal style and hard guitar solos), and "Hung Upside Down" (listen to the guitar solo in the middle). There is still a touch of country in Richie Furay's "A Child's Claim to Fame"; and there is a more elaborate experimental song called "Broken Arrow," which alternates between triple and quadruple meters, adds external sound effects, and ends with a very convincing jazz piano solo. The folk rock style was virtually gone by the time of the second album.

The third and last album (excluding compilations) was *Last Time Around* (1968). By this time Jim Messina had replaced Bruce Palmer. The country sound continued with "Kind Woman"; a light Latin influence can be felt on "Pretty Girl Why" and "Uno Mundo"; and straight-ahead rock is heard in "Special Care" and "Questions."

In 1968, Messina and Furay left to form a country rock band named Poco. Stills joined with David Crosby (the Byrds) and Graham Nash (the Hollies) to form Crosby, Stills, and Nash. They were soon joined by Neil Young, thus reuniting two members of the defunct Buffalo Springfield. Several ex-Springfield members eventually found their way into later groups, such as the Southern-Hillman-Furay Band and Loggins and Messina.

## Donovan

Another artist whose original identification was with the folk style but who moved on to other things is Donovan Leitch. Born in Glasgow, Scotland, Donovan seemed like a British Bob Dylan. Indeed, he wore a denim cap, played harmonica and acoustic guitar, and sang folklike songs. His first single, "Catch the Wind," managed to achieve the number 23 position on the U.S. charts. However, his early 1966 tour to America was not successful.

Returning to England, Donovan underwent a dramatic change of image and sound. His next single, "Sunshine Superman," was a smash hit, rising to the number 1 position. It initiated a new phase in Donovan's career: the mystical flower power period. Following quickly with the number 2 hit "Mellow Yellow," Donovan returned to the United States as a flower-bedecked hippie. The new psychedelic image sold well; his *Sunshine Superman* album (number 11) contained the hard-rocking "Season of the Witch." After a series of moderate hits, Donovan made the Top 5 again in 1968 with "Hurdy Gurdy Man," a good example of late-1960s psychedelia, with its electronically modified vocal track and its heavily distorted guitar solo.

By 1968, the folk rock explosion had fizzled. Dylan was recuperating from his motorcycle accident; the Byrds were turning toward country rock; the Mamas and the Papas were disbanding; Buffalo Springfield had moved away from folk rock before disbanding; Donovan had gone psychedelic; and Sonny and Cher had turned more toward commercial pop rock. Only the sounds of Simon and Garfunkel lingered on. But in its two- to three-year heyday, folk rock had brought together two important and seemingly antithetical styles of music. Some excellent new music had been produced. And from these beginnings would grow some important trends in the subsequent decade—namely the singer–songwriter trend and the country rock trend (see Chapter 14).

---

## MUSICAL CLOSE-UP:
## THE SONG STYLE OF BOB DYLAN

Thus far we have mentioned three basic types of organizational structure for songs: the twelve-bar blues, the AABA form, and a unique approach to song form in which a new and different form is created for each song. This last is sometimes called the through-composed form; that is, for each new section of text, new music may be composed. This form has had considerable appeal for classical composers because it means that the music can respond to variations in mood, images, and situations in the lyrics as one proceeds through the total length of the text. This is a very different approach from one that sets each and every verse to the same music, regardless of the verbal contents of each verse. That approach is called strophic and is very typical of folk music. Which brings us to Bob Dylan.

If you sing hymns in church, you are familiar with strophic song form. Recall that the music is printed just one time through; but below the music are the words to verses 1, 2, 3, 4, and so on. So it is with most early folk songs. Bob Dylan grew up admiring this folk song tradition, and his basic approach to song form reflects this influence. Many old folk ballads consist of four lines of text, each one of which is set to a four-measure phrase, thus creating a sixteen-measure strophe. This sixteen-measure strophe is simply repeated for each new stanza of text.

As we have seen, a large percentage of early rock followed either the twelve-bar blues form (in its own way a very specific kind of strophic form) or the AABA pattern. With the Beatles, a new freedom emerged regarding form, and often each song would have its own unique form (e.g., "A Day in the Life"), somewhat like the concept of the through-composed song. With Dylan and the other folk-oriented singers, the strophic form typically prevailed. Sometimes Dylan adhered rather closely to the old folk pattern; other times he used the strophic form as a general organizing structure but took considerable freedom within each strophe. In this musical close-up, we shall examine a few representative examples of Dylan's songs to see how they illustrate the strophic principle. We can begin by finding a sort of norm and then going from there.

Let us start with "Blowin' in the Wind." Each of the three stanzas of this song contains four lines. The first stanza can serve as a model.

How many roads must a man walk down before you call him a man?
Yes, 'n' how many seas must a white dove sail before she sleeps in the sand?
Yes, 'n' how many times must the cannon balls fly before they're forever banned?
The answer, my friend, is blowin' in the wind, the answer is blowin' in the wind. (Dylan 1973, 33)

Each of the aforementioned lines is given a four-measure melody, resulting in a sixteen-measure strophe. The first three melodic phrases are very similar, and the fourth is contrasting. Thus, the musical form inside each strophe is AAAB. The same music is then used for the second and third strophes. This is a good example of the strophic song form.

"Don't Think Twice, It's All Right" is quite similar except that the first two musical phrases are parallel, with the third and fourth phrases having new melodies. Thus the internal pattern would be AABC. As you are listening to this song, note that each four-measure phrase breaks into two half phrases or subphrases (e.g., "It ain't no use to sit and wonder why, babe/It don't matter, anyhow"). This is fairly common even in the four-measure phrases of classical music. "Don't Think Twice" has four strophes, each sixteen measures long.

"My Back Pages" follows a similar pattern. Its six stanzas are all set to the same music; each strophe is sixteen measures long, consisting of four four-measure phrases. The internal melodic scheme is like that of "Blowin' in the Wind" (AAAB).

Using these three songs as our basis, we can find some interesting variations. For example, "Positively 4th Street" consists of twelve short stanzas, each of which is set to the same two four-measure phrases (AB). This is unusually short for Dylan, who generally prefers the sixteen-measure length. What is more, each eight-measure strophe ends "up in the air" rather than on a solid I chord. This is what theorists call a "half cadence" (ending on the V chord); it propels us forward from one stanza into the next rather than solidly closing off each one.

"The Times They Are a-Changin'" is another strophic song, this time with five stanzas. But these do not follow the traditional 4 + 4 + 4 + 4 form. Instead, there are basically six lines per stanza; for example:

Come senators, congressmen/Please heed the call
Don't stand in the doorway/Don't block up the hall
For he that gets hurt/Will be he who has stalled
There's a battle outside/And it is ragin'.
It'll soon shake your windows/And rattle your walls
For the times they are a'changin'. (Dylan 1973, 85)

The first and third lines are set to a five-measure melody; the other lines are set to four-measure melodies. Thus, we have a twenty-six measure strophe. Granted, it is irregular, but Dylan makes it work.

Rather unusually, Dylan sets each of the five stanzas of "Rainy Day Women #12 and 35" to the traditional twelve-bar blues form. Moreover, "Subterranean Homesick Blues" is based loosely upon the sixteen-bar blues (like twelve-bar blues except there are eight measures of I instead of four at the beginning of each verse). A comparison of the sixteen-bar form and the variation found in "Subterranean Homesick Blues" follows:

| Sixteen-Bar Blues | Subterranean Homesick Blues |
|---|---|
| Phrase 1: 4 bars of I | 4 bars of I |
| Phrase 2: 4 bars of I | 4 bars of I |
| Phrase 3: 2 bars of IV; 2 bars of I | 2 bars of IV; 4 bars of I |
| Phrase 4: 2 bars of V; 2 bars of I | 2 bars of V; 2 bars of I |

As you can see, there is a two-measure extension of the third phrase (two extra bars of the I chord). Thus, we have an eighteen-bar form. Furthermore, strophes 3 and 4 are varied slightly.

Finally, we should look at two songs that use the verse-and-chorus form. In this approach, there is a chorus whose words and music are always the same; this chorus alternates with a series of verses, each of which has the same music but different words. The verse for "Like a Rolling Stone" contains five musical phrases, each four measures long, thus creating a twenty-bar form. The chorus ("How does it feel," etc.) is normally twelve measures long (three four-bar phrases). This chorus alternates with the four verses as follows:

| | |
|---|---|
| Verse 1: | 20 measures ("Once upon a time") |
| Chorus: | 10 measures ("How does it feel") |
| Verse 2: | 20 measures ("You've gone to the finest school") |
| Chorus: | 12 measures ("How does it feel") |
| Verse 3: | 20 measures ("You never turned around to see") |
| Chorus: | 12 measures ("How does it feel") |
| Verse 4: | 20 measures ("Princess in the steeple") |
| Chorus: | 12 measures ("How does it feel") |

Note that the first chorus is shortened by two measures (one subphrase of music is skipped over). This verse-and-chorus form is related to the strophic concept, inasmuch as the same musical sequence is repeated four times with new words for each verse.

"Mr. Tambourine Man" also follows the verse-and-chorus approach. Here the song opens and closes with the chorus. Each verse begins with a four-measure phrase that divides into two two-measure subphrases. The music of the second subphrase (e.g., "has returned into sand") can be repeated to new words, thereby internally extending the basic length of the verse. Thus, the first verse is essentially a sixteen-bar form with four four-measure phrases; but the second subphrase of the first and third phrases is repeated (with new words) to produce a twenty-bar verse. The diagram below may help clarify this:

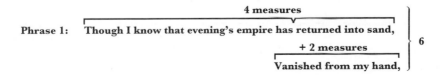

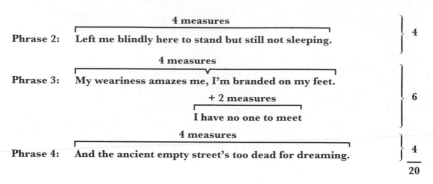

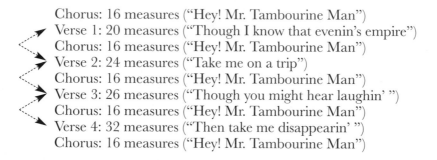

Similarly, the second verse extends the structure even further; this time the second subphrase of the first phrase is repeated three times (each time with new words) before moving on to the second phrase. With this and subsequent extensions, this second verse grows to a total length of twenty-four measures. The third verse is extended to twenty-six measures, and the fourth and final verse becomes a thirty-two bar form. The relatively simple chorus (four four-bar phrases) is the same each time. This progressive internal growth within each verse results in an interesting overall form.

Chorus: 16 measures ("Hey! Mr. Tambourine Man")
Verse 1: 20 measures ("Though I know that evenin's empire")
Chorus: 16 measures ("Hey! Mr. Tambourine Man")
Verse 2: 24 measures ("Take me on a trip")
Chorus: 16 measures ("Hey! Mr. Tambourine Man")
Verse 3: 26 measures ("Though you might hear laughin' ")
Chorus: 16 measures ("Hey! Mr. Tambourine Man")
Verse 4: 32 measures ("Then take me disappearin' ")
Chorus: 16 measures ("Hey! Mr. Tambourine Man")

Whether Dylan is setting a series of stanzas to the same music or repeating verse-and-chorus combinations, the strophic concept prevails. Strophic song form is a rather simple idea; but Dylan's creativity with lyrics leads to some complex variations within the form. As a result of the influence of the folk movement, the strophic song form joined the twelve-bar blues form of R & B and the AABA form of Tin Pan Alley and soft rock as relatively standardized forms to be used by rock musicians for decades to come. The through-composed song, as exemplified by some Beatle songs, is much less commonly encountered than these other three forms.

# 9

# Soul and Motown

## OVERVIEW: SOUL MUSIC: ITS DEFINITION AND HISTORY

"Soul" in music is like love: You know when it is there, and you know when it is not. But soul, as a musical genre, defies accurate definition. Listening to the music is only a partial answer because, as Arnold Shaw has written, "Soul has almost as many strains in it as there are artists" (Shaw 1982, 365).

Some of the biggest names in soul music have tried to define soul, but their definitions do not provide much clarification. For example, consider the following (Hirshey 1984, 51, 339, 77, 228):

Soul ain't nothin' but a feelin'.

—Wilson Pickett

For a singer, soul is total vocal freedom.

– Don Covay

I am not a blues singer or an R & B singer, I'm a soul singer. We go into the studio without anything prepared, just record what come out. That's soul—the way you feel.

—Otis Redding

(Soul) is what comes from within; it's what happens when the inner part of you comes out. It's the part of playing you can't get out of the books and studies. In my case, I believe that what I heard and felt in the music of my church. . . was the most powerful influence on my musical career. Everyone wants to know where I got that funky style. Well, it comes from the church. The music I heard was open, relaxed, impromptu—soul music.

—Milt Jackson

Soul to me is a feeling, a lot of depth and being able to bring to the surface that which is happening inside. . . . It's just the emotion, the way it affects other people.

—Aretha Franklin

The first three definitions imply that soul has something to do with the rather free expression of feelings. But that could apply to a number of musical styles. Milt Jackson's comments provide a useful hint: that there is a relationship between soul music and black church music. Aretha Franklin confirmed this when she said, "Now there's a plain bare fact. Soul came up from gospel and blues. That much you can write down" (Hirshey 1984, xiii).

We know that the blues has some very definite musical characteristics. And we can identify some rather specific characteristics of gospel music (especially its vocal style). Therefore, if we *combine the characteristics of R & B and gospel, and then allow the performer to utilize these elements with enough freedom to express his or her innermost feelings,* we may come remarkably close to understanding that elusive term, *soul.* In the musical close-up at the end of this chapter, we shall look more closely at how the vocal style of gospel music is carried over into the soul singer's style.

Blues, gospel, jazz, R & B, and rock and roll all have their roots in the South. To understand where soul music came from, we must start in the black southern church. Aretha Franklin and Milt Jackson were correct in their remarks about the importance of the gospel music of the black church. We have noted before the relationship between black secular music and black religious music. At the same time that the sacred and the secular seem to be pulling in opposite directions (virtually pulling someone like Little Richard apart), ironically they also blend together in musical expression. A gospel song and a shouting blues may be musically identical, except that in one case the lyrics say "love my Jesus!" and in the other, "love that woman!"

From the Mississippi Delta area and the black southern church (most often Baptist), blues and gospel music, respectively, expanded northward. The expansion of the blues from the Delta to the North began back in the 1920s. Black workers were flowing to the northern industrial centers in hopes of finding jobs. For example, by 1943, nearly 200,000 blacks had come to Detroit for work. With this northward migration from the 1920s to the 1940s came black music, especially the blues. In the meantime, various substyles developed, such as electric blues, urban blues, and of course, rhythm and blues. In the 1940s, the new sound of "blues" was almost a happy sound; it was up-tempo, aggressive, and electrified. Performers like B. B. King, Muddy Waters, and Howlin' Wolf represented this new "jump blues."

Because of the central importance of the church in the life of the southern black, gospel music also moved northward as the black southerners migrated. Gospel singers like Sister Rosetta Tharpe came from Arkansas to Chicago and eventually to Harlem, in New York City. Mahalia Jackson, born in New Orleans but transplanted to Chicago, was the most successful popularizer of gospel, attracting a significant following even among whites.

Thomas Dorsey was one of the biggest names in gospel. Composer and performer, his gospel work dates back to the 1920s. When the word "soul" was appropriated by the 1960s black generation, Dorsey noted that it was really nothing new.

It was first in the Negro church. When I was a little boy, the churches couldn't afford an organ and the sisters sat in the amen corner and kept rhythm by clapping their hands. There is no need for some fellow born yesterday to come up and tell me now that soul is something new. At church, they do more foot tapping and hand clapping than they ever did. (Hirshey 1984, 27)

In the 1940s, a number of independent record companies were formed and went about popularizing black blues and gospel. Savoy and Apollo (both formed about 1942), Specialty (1945), Chess (1947), Atlantic (1948), Peacock (1949), and Vee Jay (1953) were typical of such companies.

The expansion of black music into the white market began in the 1950s. Alan Freed was an influential champion of black music. By 1951, Freed was playing R & B in a white radio market. He sponsored citywide dances in Cleveland that featured an all-black roster of entertainers. Meanwhile, youngsters formed singing groups in the black areas of Detroit, Cincinnati, Chicago, Cleveland, Philadelphia, and New York City (Harlem).

Some of these would-be stars were born in these cities; but most had moved with their families from the South. Gospel coaches like Billy Ward in New York City worked with the youngsters, teaching them the finest nuances of gospel and R & B singing. From his knowledge of these young singers, Ward pulled the cream of the crop together into a group called the Dominoes (about 1950). For a lead singer he tapped a seventeen-year-old named Clyde McPhatter (originally from Durham, North Carolina). After McPhatter left the group in 1953, he was replaced by Jackie Wilson. McPhatter went on to a recording contract with Atlantic Records and formed his own group, the Drifters. They hit the R & B charts with "Money Honey." After military service, McPhatter continued as a solo act, scoring a big hit in 1958 with "A Lover's Question." He died in 1972 in Houston of heart, liver, and kidney complications. He was thirty-nine years old.

Meanwhile, in 1959, the Drifters had reorganized with lead singer Ben E. King. They scored a number 2 hit in 1959 with a Leiber and Stoller song "There Goes My Baby." In 1960, they had hits with "This Magic Moment" and "Save the Last Dance for Me" (their only number 1 hit). King also went solo, achieving hits with "Spanish Harlem" (number 10 in 1961) and a secular version of an old gospel song, "Stand by Me" (number 4 in 1961). The Drifters continued to have hits through the early 1960s.

Groups like the Dominoes and Drifters gathered, rehearsed, and performed in the streets. Often they started as church groups and could be found singing in front of stores or local Baptist churches. Their vocal roots were with the close harmony gospel quartets of the 1930s and 1940s, possibly with the additional influence of pop groups such as the Ink Spots and the Mills Brothers. Certainly one of the most influential models was the Soul Stirrers. Formed in Texas in the 1930s by R. H. Harris, the Stirrers were a traveling quartet, appearing all over the country. When Harris retired in 1950, nineteen-year-old Sam Cooke became the lead singer. As author Gerri Hirshey wrote, "His voice transfigured the sound of quartet gospel and, as early as 1950, in his gospel work, heralded the sound of soul" (Hirshey 1984, 47). Cooke's move to the pop side with "You Send Me" in 1957 became a model for other gospel singers to cross over to the white market. After all, R & B, through its offspring rock and roll, had proven successful with whites. By the late 1950s, other gospel artists rushed to make whatever adjustments were necessary to achieve the same crossover success.

Yet another model was Ray Charles. The early influence of the church on Ray Charles is obvious when he speaks of his early years in Greenville, Florida: "You went to church every Sunday. So naturally I was around church music. The preacher would say a couple of lines and then the church would sing what he said. It was very ad-lib" (Hirshey 1984, 49). In Charles's early recording sessions, he simply ad-libbed secular words to familiar gospel songs; often a bit of jazz and blues got mixed in as well. "I Got a Woman," his 1954 hit for Atlantic, combines the heavy chords of church piano, a strong R & B-oriented band, and, as Hirshey so aptly says, "a vocal that bounced between the bedroom and the blessed" (Hirshey 1984, 50). That blues and gospel mix, the secular–sacred dichotomy, was evident in the no-holds-barred falsetto shrieks and vocal groans. When "What'd I Say" hit the Top 10 in 1959, with Charles's call-and-response moans and verbal interactions with the Raelettes (his backup vocal group), he successfully brought the fiery combination of gospel and R & B to the national market. It was soul music.

This new success for black music led to a new kind of black pride and an interest in black roots. At first, that elusive quality of blackness—a combination of earthiness, emotionalism, and spirituality—was called "funk." But the term *soul* also began to be applied to much the same quality. Thus, there was "A Bit of Soul" in 1955 and "Hornful of Soul" in 1957, both by Ray Charles. The aforementioned Milt Jackson recorded "Plenty, Plenty Soul" in 1957. Ray Charles and Milt Jackson combined on a 1957 album called *Soul Brothers*.

The famous Apollo Theater in Harlem launched many rock and roll, R & B, and soul careers. On amateur night in the 1950s, the Apollo was throbbing with "bird" groups, "car" groups, "royalty" groups, and "romance" groups singing the umpteenth version of "Gee," or "Earth Angel," or "Sincerely." Most of these groups had male singers only. Exceptions like the Teen Queens and the Chantels ("Maybe," 1958) were harbingers of the female groups of the 1960s. In the all-male groups there was a ganglike machismo. As Ben E. King says,

> My buddies and I would walk from 116th Street to 129th. And in those blocks alone you'd find anywhere from three to five groups. We'd stop and listen, and if we felt that we were better, we would challenge them. It was territorial, you know. (Hirshey 1984, 35)

Thus, as the 1960s dawned, the southern-rooted suffering and pain of the blues had joined with the joyful and unrestrained celebration of gospel. But soul music would probably be merely a footnote to rock history if it had not been for one record company, which by the end of the decade would be almost synonymous with soul music. We need to discuss Atlantic Records and meet two men—Ahmet Ertegun and Jerry Wexler.

## ATLANTIC AND STAX

Ahmet Ertegun, the son of a Turkish ambassador to the United States, was enthralled with the music of black America. In 1947, he and Herb Abramson formed a new company called Atlantic Records. It was a small independent company dedicated to black music—primarily R & B. In the beginning, most of

Ahmet Ertegun (*Source:* Michael Ochs Archive, Ltd.)

Atlantic's performers did not write their own songs; it was Ertegun who did. The first hit for the fledgling company came in 1948 with "Drinking Wine, Spo-Dee-O-Dee" by Stick McGhee.

Nevertheless, true success was slow in coming. By 1950, Atlantic had placed only three songs in the R & B Top 10. But thanks to hits by Clyde McPhatter, Ray Charles, La Vern Baker, and Chuck Willis, Atlantic steadily increased its impact on the R & B market, and by 1956 claimed seventeen out of that year's eighty-one Top 10 hits. Some of these hits (e.g., La Vern Baker's "Tweedle Dee") were finding success in the pop market via cover versions. Atlantic's growing success was partially due to the addition of a talented producer named Jerry Wexler, who had joined Atlantic in 1953.

The crossover phenomenon of the mid-1950s began to benefit little Atlantic Records and its hopeful young stars. La Vern Baker's "Tweedle Dee" hit number 14 on the pop charts in 1955; by 1959, she hit the Top 10 with "I Cried a Tear." McPhatter had three moderate pop chart hits before "A Lover's Question" made the Top 10 in 1958–59. Chuck Willis's "C.C. Rider" rose to number 12 in 1957, and his "What Am I Living For" made the Top 10 in 1958. Breaking with the black tradition, Ertegun signed Bobby Darin to a contract and was rewarded with a long string of major hits through 1962 on the subsidiary Atco label. Further success came though the popularity of the Coasters and the songwriting talents of Jerry Leiber and Mike Stoller. By the end of the 1950s, Atlantic had moved from a small indie with moderate R & B success to a very successful independent in the pop market. In the 1960s, Jerry Wexler steered it in the direction of soul music, resulting in even greater success. Thanks to the soul movement, Atlantic would become a major label by the late 1960s.

Soul singer Wilson Pickett had his own description of how he achieved his sound.

> You harmonize; then you customize. . . . You look around for a good, solid used chassis. This be your 12-bar blues. R & B ain't nothin' if it ain't the 12-bar blues. Then you look around for what else you got. And if you come up like most of us, that would be gospel. (Hirshey 1984, 46)

Pickett combined his blues and gospel into an R & B hit in 1962, "I Found a Love." But his greatest success came in 1965, and afterward, when Jerry Wexler took him back down south to record in Memphis and Muscle Shoals, Alabama. In 1966, Pickett had his biggest hit, "Land of 1,000 Dances," with its listing of previous songs and dances and its "na-na-na-na-na" chorus. The idea of recording down south proved successful in more ways than one. Wexler discovered that by returning to southern recording studios, he found an unusual blend of blues, gospel, and C & W in the racially mixed studio bands. Some of Atlantic's finest recordings, with artists like Pickett and Aretha Franklin, were made in these southern studios. Among the other soul artists Wexler produced in the 1960s were Solomon Burke, the Sweet Inspirations, King Curtis, Percy Sledge, and Joe Tex.

A fortuitous outcome of Wexler's travels to the South was the relationship established with a Memphis recording company called Stax Records. For the past century and a half, Memphis has produced a variety of black and white musicians who mixed musical styles from blues to hillbilly to gospel. In the mid- to late 1950s, the result was Sun Records' rockabilly sound. In the 1960s, it was the southern soul sound of Stax and its subsidiary, Volt. If Motown called itself "Hitsville, U.S.A.," Stax could legitimately claim the name "Soulsville, U.S.A."

Back in 1959, Jim Stewart and Estelle Axton started a small record company named Satellite Records. By 1961, they had changed the company's name to Stax and signed a distribution agreement with Atlantic Records. With this agreement the two companies found moderate success with performers such as the MarKeys, Carla Thomas, and Booker T. and the MGs.

For the next few years, the Atlantic–Stax partnership flourished. Between Stax's own artists and the Atlantic artists who recorded there, a strong sound of southern soul emerged. In addition to the Atlantic artists mentioned earlier, there were Stax–Volt artists like Otis Redding, Sam and Dave, and Isaac Hayes.

Redding was born in Little Richard's hometown of Macon, Georgia, in 1941. He absorbed a variety of musical influences, from the country sounds of his favorites Eddy Arnold and Hank Williams to the R & B-oriented rock and roll of hometown hero Little Richard. And, of course, Otis sang in the choir at the Mount Ivy Baptist Church, where his father led the congregation. So all of the pieces of the musical puzzle were in place. Like so many gospel and soul singers, he particularly admired Sam Cooke. In 1965, he hit the pop charts with "I've Been Loving You Too Long (to Stop Now)." He followed up with his own composition, "Respect," which did very well on the R & B charts but was only a mild success on the pop charts (number 35). Redding's unique blend of blues, gospel, rock, country, and pop made a tremendous impact at the 1967 Monterey International Pop Festival. Unfortunately, he was killed on December 10, 1967, in an airplane crash. The posthumously released single "(Sittin' on) The Dock of the Bay" became his only number 1 pop chart hit (early 1968).

Sam Moore and Dave Prater recorded one of the soul anthems of the 1960s, "Soul Man" (number 2 in 1967), composed by Isaac Hayes. Sam was a gospel-trained deacon's son and the grandson of a Baptist preacher; Dave was from Ocilla, Georgia. After signing with Atlantic, Sam and Dave were sent by Jerry Wexler to Memphis to record for Stax. "Soul Man" was followed by another Top-10 hit, "I Thank You." By 1968, Sam developed a nearly fatal drug addiction, and Dave was experiencing severe personal problems. They drifted apart personally, but after Sam's recovery from drugs they continued to perform together.

Isaac Hayes represents Stax's final years of success. After several moderate hits, he released the "Theme from *Shaft*" (number 1, 1971). The song won an Oscar, and Isaac Hayes became the act for Stax. However, after the success of "Shaft," things changed. As Isaac says, "Life got beautiful. And then it got weird" (Hirshey 1984, 355). Somewhere the soul sound got lost. The catchy wah-wah guitar effects in "Shaft" and the simple, repetitive, insistent dance beat evolved into disco (Isaac is sometimes called the father of disco). He left Stax in 1974 and later recorded the first of several albums that seemed to confirm his move from soul to disco, *Disco Connection* (1976).

The early 1970s were tough times for Stax. The same year that Otis Redding died, Stax's agreement with Atlantic ended. The cooperation had already soured by 1966; Stax had closed its doors to outside producers like Atlantic. Finally, in 1975, Stax filed for bankruptcy.

By the mid-1970s, soul music had run its course. Stax was gone, the old R & B label, Chess, had folded in 1968; Motown moved to Los Angeles in 1971; Otis Redding was dead, and most of the other big soul stars had lost their status. Jerry Wexler left Atlantic in 1975 to become a vice president of Warner Brothers; Ahmet Ertegun retreated to Atlantic's administrative boardroom. But before we leave the story of soul, we must take a close look at two of its most dominant personalities: Aretha Franklin and James Brown.

## ARETHA FRANKLIN

The Reverend C. L. Franklin was known as the Man with the Million-Dollar Voice. After leading congregations in Memphis, where his daughter Aretha was born in 1942, and Buffalo, he moved to Detroit to become pastor of the New Bethel Baptist Church. His rich, booming voice and his "brimstone with a beat" preaching style earned him such a reputation that Chess Records recorded over seventy of his sermons.

Aretha was deeply involved in the church and frequently heard gospel singers like Clara Ward and Mahalia Jackson perform at her father's church. By age eight or nine, Aretha was singing in church too. Having noted Sam Cooke's success in crossing from the gospel style to the national pop market, the seventeen-year-old Aretha recorded some demo records (happily paid for by her proud father).

It was John Hammond who heard Aretha sing and decided that she could follow Cooke's path into the pop market. Hammond had a knack for spotting raw talent and for converting it into a commercially successful product. He had been instrumental in the recording careers of blues singers Bessie Smith and Billie Holiday, as well as in that of folksinger Bob Dylan.

For six years in the early 1960s, Aretha tried to be a pop singer for Columbia Records. Hammond had foreseen a more blues-oriented direction for her, but Columbia's A and R head Mitch Miller saw her as a pop singer. Aretha, perhaps remembering

Aretha Franklin (*Source:* Atlantic Records)

Sam Cooke, seemingly agreed. She sang show tunes and jazz-flavored commercial pop. Her four Columbia albums fared poorly.

Atlantic's Jerry Wexler had long coveted the opportunity to tap Aretha's gospel roots and develop her into a soul singer like so many others that he and Atlantic were successfully marketing in the 1960s. So when Aretha's contract with Columbia expired, Wexler signed her to Atlantic Records (1967). Following the successful pattern he had used with Wilson Pickett and others, Wexler took Aretha to Rick Hall's Fame Studios in Muscle Shoals, Alabama. The magical mixture of the finest black and white southern studio musicians and the long overdue gospel/soul voice of Aretha Franklin were dynamite. The first Atlantic album, *I Never Loved a Man the Way I Love You,* went to number 2 on the album charts. The title song became a Top 10 hit, and "Respect," an Otis Redding song, became Franklin's first (and only) number 1 song. Lady Soul was finally on her way.

Aretha proceeded to place seven out of her next eight singles in the Top 10, all before 1968 was over. She went on to win Grammy awards for best R & B performance by a female artist eight years in a row. If Atlantic was the soul label, Aretha was surely that label's top artist. Whereas most of the soul artists discussed in this chapter appealed primarily to black audiences and were heard mostly on black radio stations, enjoying only the occasional crossover hit, Aretha found consistent success with both black and white audiences, while retaining her gospel/soul sound.

Jerry Wexler has provided real insight into how Aretha worked.

> In general, the sessions went like cream. She'd take the song—she found most of them—or she'd write it. And she would work out a layout, working at home with her little electric piano and the girls. So you had three major ingredients: first of all, you had the arrangement implicit in the piano bars, you had the lead vocal, and you had the vocal background leads. She brings all this into the session. She'd sit at the piano and start to line it out, and the girls might or might not be there. So she might sing their parts, too. Then all we did was start to shade in drums, bass, guitar. We might make small changes, but it would always be by agreement with her. You know, change a bass line here and there. But those records were so damned good because she took care of business at home. (Hirshey 1984, 243–244)

Aretha did songs by some of the finest songwriters, soul and otherwise: "Respect" (Otis Redding), "Spanish Harlem" (Jerry Leiber and Phil Spector), "Eleanor Rigby" (Lennon/McCartney), "Bridge over Troubled Water" (Paul Simon), "Say a Little Prayer" (Burt Bacharach and Hal David), "Chain of Fools" (Don Covay), and "A Natural Woman" (Carole King and Gerry Goffin).

The *Lady Soul* album (1968) reached number 2 on the album charts and contained three Top 10 singles. *Soul '69* was also a strong album, utilizing a stellar jazz-oriented backup band. In this album the incredible versatility and range of Aretha's voice is obvious. From twelve-bar blues to Glen Campbell's "Gentle on My Mind" to Sam Cooke's "Bring It on Home to Me," Aretha displays remarkable vocal agility, from a sultry low contralto voice to a gospel-shouting soprano.

Another fascinating album is *Amazing Grace* (1972). For this one, Aretha returned to her pure gospel roots. Atlantic set up shop in the New Temple Missionary Baptist Church in Los Angeles. Joined by Reverend James Cleveland and his Southern California Community Choir, plus a "live" congregation on two successive nights, Aretha sang traditional songs like "What a Friend We Have in Jesus" and the title song (a truly remarkable version extending to almost eleven minutes). There is "How I Get Over" by her childhood idol Clara Ward, "Wholy Holy" by Marvin Gaye, and even "You'll Never Walk Alone" by Rodgers and Hammerstein. Particularly interesting is the combination of two songs into one arrangement: Thomas Dorsey's "Precious Lord, Take My Hand" and Carole King's "You've Got a Friend" (providing a whole new interpretation of the latter).

As is often the case with superior musical talents, Aretha was anxious to adapt her abilities to a variety of musical styles (one thinks of people like Elvis Presley, Bob Dylan, and the Beatles). Often such artists are accused of "selling out," of being inconsistent or uncommitted, and (most damning of all) of going "commercial." But it seems only natural that talented musicians should be interested in applying their talents to a variety of good songs, no matter what the stylistic point of origin. When Aretha sings a song, whether a traditional gospel song or a tune by Rodgers and Hammerstein (Broadway composers), the song becomes Aretha's. Such a practice reveals not a lack of musical identity but, quite the contrary, a forceful and secure identity that can be applied to almost any song with no loss of individuality.

With Jerry Wexler gone and disco and harder rock styles predominating in the last half of the 1970s, Aretha left Atlantic Records, signing with Arista Records in 1979. She continued to be regarded as one of the most important artists on the music scene.

## JAMES BROWN

As noted earlier, the term *soul music* includes a wide variety of styles. This becomes particularly evident when one considers that the two most prominent representatives of soul music were as different as day and night. Aretha Franklin was known as Lady Soul; she was the model for the female soul singer. James Brown was called the Godfather of Soul and Soul Brother Number 1 (also Mr. Dynamite, the Hardest-Working Man in Show Business, and Mr. Sex Machine); he was the model for the male soul singer. Yet these two leading soul singers seem to be almost exact opposites. Aretha has total vocal control, allowing her to execute intricate melodic and rhythmic nuances with precise control of pitch and timbre. Her voice is clear and strong; she has a remarkable range and uses it to express a wide range of emotions. Brown's voice is raspy and strong (in the latter respect they are alike). He typically shouts a raw and basic vocal line devoid of any hint of sophistication. Franklin's arrangements are often quite complex and sophisticated; Brown's songs are among the simplest and most basic in all of popular music. Franklin is rather shy and introverted. Brown is flamboyant, egotistical, and aggressive; he thrives in the spotlight.

James Brown's style has been called southern soul. This may seem a curious designation inasmuch as all soul must trace its roots to the R & B and gospel styles of the South. However, many soul singers, although their roots may have been in the South, developed in the major cities of the Midwest and Northeast. Although Brown had to go north to be heard, he has remained deeply, loyally, and thoroughly southern. Among the record companies identified with soul music (Atlantic, Chess, Specialty, Peacock, Vee Jay, Savoy, and Apollo), possibly the most strongly connected with pure southern soul was King Records in Cincinnati. In Gerri Hirshey's words, "From 1956 to 1971, King served as a pipeline for the loudest, the rawest, the most fundamental in-your-face soul ever pumped up from the green hills of Georgia" (Hirshey 1984, 260). And that describes James Brown.

Brown was born on May 3, 1933, in Augusta, Georgia. He was naturally musical from an early age, teaching himself keyboards, drums, and bass. Around Augusta, James tried all of the usual odd jobs, seemingly headed nowhere or worse. In 1949 he was arrested and sent to jail for three and a half years for breaking into automobiles. So by the ripe old age of twenty, he was hardly a candidate for "the boy most likely to succeed."

But by the early 1950s he had also realized his interest in music. He formed a small gospel group; with R & B sounds beginning to cross over to national popularity, the group moved toward R & B and called themselves the Famous Flames. They recorded a demo record with the song "Please, Please, Please." King Records liked the sound and signed them to a contract. The song was rerecorded and released on King's subsidiary label, Federal, in 1956, and became a regional R & B hit (number 6). A 1958 follow-up hit, "Try Me (I Need You)," actually went to number 48 on the national charts and hit the top of the R & B charts. These songs were not far from the "doo-wop" sound; the newly popular rock-and-roll sound is more evident in 1959's "Good Good Lovin'" and 1960's "Think" (Brown's first Top 40 hit).

During the early 1960s, Brown toured the country with his James Brown Revue, including forty singers, dancers, and musicians. It was during this period that Brown developed his overpowering stage act. The show was programmed down to the last detail. There were reportedly fines levied by Brown if one of his musicians missed a note. His dancing became the model for performers from Mick Jagger to Michael Jackson, and he became known as the Hardest-Working Man in Show Business. At the end of the show, with sweat pouring off his face, he would launch into "Please, Please, Please," sinking to his knees and appearing to collapse prostrate on the stage.

James Brown (at the drums) and the Original Flames (*Source:* Michael Ochs Archive, Ltd.)

Several of the Famous Flames would help him off the stage, draped in a colorful cape; but he would always return for another round of "Please, Please, Please," followed by more collapses and capes. After several "last" rounds, the audience was in a frenzy. As his boyhood friend Leon Austin tells it,

> He's not gonna come out there and be cool, and he ain't gonna have on this pretty suit that ain't gonna get dusty. He gonna wallow. He's gonna just be splittin', dancin', fallin'; he'd jump outta a air-o-plane, I swear. Mess up his knees so he can't work the next job. Or he may scream so hard he can't sing the next night. But he ain't gonna worry about that. (Hirshey 1984, 283)

As Brown moved toward the mid-1960s, there seemed to be a change in style. The voice became even rawer, with a more raspy shouting style. There were hints of the new style in his versions of "Night Train" (1962) and "Out of Sight" (1964). In 1965 the new sound took shape in two 12-bar blues, "Papa's Got a Brand New Bag" and his biggest hit of all, "I Got You (I Feel Good)." There is a choppy feeling to these songs; the horns punctuate Brown's phrases with short bursts; bass and drums play short, tightly coordinated accompanying patterns called "riffs." In some cases, there are only two or three chords in the entire song. The band "vamps" (repeats the accompanying riff) on one chord, while Brown seemingly improvises his declamatory phrases. At a certain moment, all move to a second chord, establishing a new riff. Finally, the song returns to the original chord and riff. If possible, listen to "There Was a Time" (1967), "Sex Machine" (1970), or "Make It Funky" (1971) for good examples of this style. This is almost as simple and repetitive as music can get. The music is more of a social experience. Brown's live performance antics and dancing were the main points. As Hirshey writes, "James Brown's funk works its best mojo from the neck down. You love it or hate it; it's magic or it's just screams" (Hirshey 1984, 289). Certainly it is very different from the sophisticated soul of Aretha Franklin or the commercialized black sound of Motown.

By 1967, Brown was at the height of his career and was truly "Soul Brother Number 1." That year he performed before about three million concertgoers and sold some fifty million records. Between 1967 and 1972, he placed thirty songs in the Top 40. Most were number 1 hits on the R & B charts but typically placed well below the Top 10 on the pop charts. He became a worldwide symbol of blackness. Leon Austin says that in Africa, Brown and his entourage were greeted by people who emerged from their mud shacks carrying James Brown albums, even though they had no electricity and no phonograph. But they knew James Brown.

Brown is not the shy, retiring type. His flamboyant performance style is described firsthand by Doon Arbus in the article "James Brown Is Out of Sight" (Eisen 1969, 286–297). In his heyday, Brown reportedly owned some 500 suits, 300 pairs of shoes, miscellaneous diamonds and cars, a personal jet, and a funky home in Queens. His ego is legendary. He insisted that onstage performances be note for note like the recorded performances. Says Brown, "I had a lot of problems with my musicians, you know. A lot of times they thought they were doing it themselves. I wanted them to know it wasn't them doin' it" (Hirshey 1984, 276). As Leon Austin says, "He's selfish and he can't help it. If you try to overpower him, then he'll show you how much he don't need you. And then, when you do somethin' for him, he'll come back and fall on his knees and thank you" (Hirshey 1984, 281).

Brown's close identification with the black cause led him to the edge of politics at times. His song, "Say It Loud—I'm Black and I'm Proud," was interpreted by some as a call to black militancy; but most heard it as Brown apparently intended it—as an encouragement of black pride. In his concerts, Brown advocated a positive, non-violent approach to racial change. His slogans "Don't terrorize, organize!" and "Don't burn, learn!" suggest a constructive attitude.

We have repeatedly remarked that music affects behavior. One related phenomenon is the effect that entertainers have as role models. A close friend of Brown's, Reverend Al Sharpton, has remarked that "black entertainers . . . become substitute fathers. We learn how to dress from watchin' a star; we learn how to walk. We look at James Brown and we say, 'Hey, that's how I'm gonna be a man'" (Hirshey 1984, 277).

By the mid-1970s, changing styles had begun to push Brown to one side. Blacks were dancing to disco beats. These were tough years for Brown, filled with severe financial and personal problems. Perhaps most traumatic was the death of his son Teddy. He was also upset by the death of his friend of some twenty years, Elvis Presley. At the funeral, a teary-eyed James Brown stared into the coffin, stroked Elvis's arm, and was heard to say, "Elvis, how you let this happen? How you let it go?" (Hirshey 1984, 278). By 1978, Brown had hit bottom.

From 1977 to 1985 there were no Top 40 hits; albums, including a disco album and several live albums, did not fare well. His appearance in the popular movie *The Blues Brothers* sparked some interest in a younger generation. That appearance also suggested the historically accurate connection between black R & B, gospel and soul, and the black church experience.

Brown stayed with the simplified, repetitive, and percussively rhythmic style he developed in the mid-1960s. He apparently preferred the simplicity because he felt it had commercial appeal. As he told *Downbeat* magazine in 1968,

I tried the heavy approach two or three times, and every time I tried, I got stopped. Just have to keep coming back and simplifying it. It's a funny thing. You make a little three-finger chord on the guitar and they'll sell a million copies, and the minute the cat spreads his hand out across the neck, you can't give the record away. (Hirshey 1984, 289)

## Soul Summary

Nowhere was the peculiar relationship between the secular and the sacred in black society more evident than in soul music: Like two "ends" of a circle, they were as far apart as possible, yet adjacent. James Brown has been known to close his shows with the Lord's Prayer. Gerri Hirshey paraphrased dancer Lola Love's description of a performance as follows: There were "no fewer than twenty-

James Brown. (*Source:* Getty Images Inc.)

four splits before James Brown shook the boogie out and dropped to his knees in prayer" (Hirshey 1984, 58).

There were many soul singers in the 1960s, each with a slightly different approach to the music.

Other than Franklin and Brown, who predominated in the soul genre, and the Atlantic–Stax artists discussed previously, we must mention several other important soul performers. Jackie Wilson, for example, was from Detroit and was the replacement for Clyde McPhatter after the latter left the Dominoes. After singing lead with the Dominoes for three years, he moved to a successful solo career. Finding himself hounded by a young songwriter named Berry Gordy Jr., Wilson finally agreed to record his song "Reet Petite." It was a mild hit in 1957. Subsequent songs written by Gordy and sung by Wilson fared better. "To Be Loved" became Wilson's first Top 40 hit (1958), and the follow-up, "Lonely Teardrops," hit the Top 10. By the end of 1961, Wilson could claim seventeen Top 40 hits. However, it was during that year that Wilson was shot by a woman in a hotel room. He recovered, but his career slowed dramatically. He managed to place seven more hits in the Top 40 between 1962 and 1968 before permanently dropping off the charts. In 1975, he was hospitalized for a heart condition; after spending eight years in a nursing home, he died in 1984 at the age of forty-nine.

Somewhere between the pop commercial sound of Motown and the true soul sound was a group known as the Impressions. Formed in the late 1950s, they had their first hit in 1958 with "For Your Precious Love" (number 11). Attributed to Jerry Butler, a member of the Impressions, the song was the work of fellow Impression Curtis Mayfield. Butler left the group in about 1960 to begin a moderately successful solo career. Mayfield stayed with the Impressions throughout the 1960s and did most of the songwriting for the group. They eventually placed fourteen songs in the Top 40, including Top 10 hits "It's All Right" (1963) and "Amen" (early 1965). In the late 1960s, Mayfield's songs became increasingly identified with black pride and social consciousness.

Ike Turner had played piano and guitar for Sam Phillips's Sun Records. He also recorded with his own group, the Kings of Rhythm, who scored an early R & B success on Chess Records with "Rocket 88" (1951). By 1957, Ike had decided to add his girlfriend to the band as lead singer. Her name was Annie Mae Bullock, later known as Bonnie Turner, and finally as Tina Turner. Ike was from Clarksdale, Mississippi; Tina was from Brownsville, Tennessee. They married in 1958 and first hit the Top 40 with "A Fool in Love" (number 27 in 1960). They developed a blatantly suggestive stage act, complete with veiled orgasms and sexually provocative comments between Ike and Tina. Her miniskirts were as "mini" as they could get. Restricted to black audiences and R & B stations and charts, they finally broke onto the national pop scene beginning with their appearance at Altamont with the Rolling Stones in late 1969. Shortly thereafter, they enjoyed their first Top 5 hit, "Proud Mary" (early 1971). The duo recorded for several labels through the 1960s and 1970s. After their divorce in 1977, Tina went on to a successful career in the 1980s, including the number 1 hit, "What's Love Got to Do with It?" While Tina became one of the hottest acts of the 1980s, Ike faded from public attention.

As one contemplates James Brown sobbing, squealing, panting, wailing, and sweating through "Please, Please, Please," one must remember that most true soul music flourished within an all-black market. Many soul artists toured the so-called chitlin' circuit of southern black concert sites and urban ghettos. Their records were promoted on radio stations adhering to a black format, and their greatest chart successes were on the R & B charts. Granted, there were occasional breakthroughs by Brown, Redding, Sam and Dave, Pickett, and most notably by Franklin. But the most overwhelming success on the pop charts was reserved for a small company that grew into a monster. That brings us to the story of Motown.

## MOTOWN

Ahmet Ertegun, founder of Atlantic Records and son of a Turkish ambassador to the United States, was enthralled by the black musical tradition of R & B and gospel. Berry Gordy Jr., a native-born American black man, was rather embarrassed by it. Gordy's preference was for jazz, a far more sophisticated style of popular music whose roots were also black. In 1953, Gordy opened his 3-D Record Mart in Detroit and tried to specialize in a jazz-oriented inventory. But the kids kept asking for the music of Fats Domino and the early doo-wop groups. Gordy's store was forced to close in 1955.

In 1960, the thirty-one-year-old Gordy borrowed $700 and started his own record company, Tammie Records (soon changed to Tamla Records). At first, Tamla simply distributed records such as Barrett Strong's "Money" for Gordy's sister's label, Anna. But in late 1960, Tamla released its own record, "Shop Around," by the Miracles, a group led by singer/songwriter William "Smokey" Robinson. Against all odds, the record went to number 2 on the pop charts. What followed is an amazing story; the tiny independent label became a major power in the music industry in an incredibly short period of time. Just seven years later, Gordy's record empire, including Motown Records and subsidiary labels Tamla, Gordy, and Soul, sold more singles than any other company, independent or major. This empire was profiled by *Fortune* magazine and the *New York Times*. Not bad on $700 of borrowed money.

Motown began in a blue-trimmed white frame house at 2648 West Grand Avenue in Gordy's hometown, Detroit. Gordy's entire family pitched in to make it as professional a facility as possible. The recording studio itself was no larger than a suburban living room.

In 1960, Detroit had the fourth largest black population in the United States—over half a million. They liked, played, sang, and bought music. But generally, if they wished to record,

Berry Gordy Jr. (*Source:* Michael Ochs Archive, Ltd.)

they had to go to Chicago, Philadelphia, or New York. Within that black Detroit population was a gold mine of talent. With a combination of reliable musical instincts and a strong business sense, Gordy managed to obtain some of that talent for his new company. He knew exactly what he wanted Tamla and the newly created Motown Records to do, and he knew how to do it.

The music market had resegregated in the early 1960s. The rock-and-roll explosion of the mid-1950s had integrated music at a time when the rest of society was largely segregated. But in the 1960s, even as society moved closer to real integration, and as the folk singers were singing out for racial equality, the music industry ironically moved back toward segregation. The early 1960 teen idols, the surfers, the folkies, and the British were all white. Only the dance craze of the early 1960s kept black music on the pop charts. The soul trend, with its gospel and R & B orientation, found its primary acceptance in a purely black market. Typically, soul records climbed to the top of the R & B charts but wallowed in the bottom half of the pop charts. Berry Gordy's intention was to bring a style of black music to prominence in both the black and white markets. To do this, he knew he had to have talented black musicians whose roots were in gospel, R & B, or doo-wop, but who understood that those styles had to be "stylized" to become more commercially successful with a wider audience. Finally, to make the formula work consistently, there had to be absolute control, allowing for little or no variation from the established patterns.

### Smokey Robinson

One of the first real "finds" was Smokey Robinson. Smokey was a talented songwriter who had started a group called the Matadores. Changing their name to the Miracles, they auditioned for Berry Gordy in the pre-Motown days. Gordy used his connections to get the Miracles a release on End Records in New York. Their recording of "Got a Job" (1958) went to number 1 on the R & B charts. When Gordy started Tamla, he signed the Miracles and released "Shop Around," which hit the Top 5 in early 1961 and put Tamla–Motown on the map, initiating the incredible success story.

Smokey Robinson became one of the important building blocks for the new record company. His work as lead singer of the Miracles was a major part of his value. The Miracles were a consistent success throughout the 1960s, registering over two dozen Top 40 hits (including five in the Top 10). Their last Top 40 hit was "Love Machine (Part I)" in late 1975 and early 1976; it was a disco-flavored song and was made by the "new" Miracles without Robinson, who had left the group in 1971. Robinson's strong falsetto voice, with a smoothness and expressiveness reminiscent of Sam Cooke, was a major asset to Motown throughout the 1960s. But of equal importance was his songwriting ability. In 1962, he wrote three Top 10 songs for Motown's first female star, nineteen-year-old Mary Wells. Later, Smokey wrote Mary's only number 1 hit, "My Guy" (1964); Smokey also wrote major hits for other Motown stars, including the Temptations and Marvin Gaye.

### Female Groups

The prototypes for the Motown female groups of the 1960s were the Marvelettes. Their song "Please Mr. Postman" became Tamla's first number 1 song, confirming that Gordy's formula could work. "Please Mr. Postman" was later recorded by the Beatles and the Carpenters, the latter version also hitting number 1 in 1975. The Marvelettes had nine more Top 10 hits for Tamla through 1968, including two Top 10 hits, "Playboy" and "Don't Mess with Bill" (the latter being another Smokey Robinson song).

Another big Motown female group was Martha and the Vandellas. Martha Reeves had attended New Liberty Baptist Church as a young girl; there she heard a black singer named Della Reese (whose first name was later incorporated into the name Vandellas) and began to picture herself as a successful vocal performer. Martha formed her own group, the Delphis, and when Gordy's new record company opened, the group promptly auditioned. They were not accepted immediately. In fact, Martha was hired as a secretary at Motown. She also did various parts in recording sessions as needed, ranging from hand claps to backup vocals. Finally, in 1962, Berry Gordy signed Martha's vocal trio (now called the Vandellas) to a recording contract and released "Come and Get These Memories" in the spring of 1963. It barely broke the Top 30. But the follow-up song, "Heat Wave," moved to the number 4 position, and the Vandellas were a success. Recording on the Gordy label, the group (with numerous personnel changes) eventually placed a dozen hits in the Top 40 before disbanding in 1971. Their biggest hit came in 1964 with "Dancing in the Street." As happened with a number of young Motown stars, Martha eventually began to question the exact distribution of money from the company to the performers. Gordy perceived such questioning as disloyalty, and Martha fell out of favor. She left Motown in 1972, recording for several other labels through the 1970s with no real success.

### Marvin Gaye

Another success story in Motown's early days was Marvin Gaye. Unlike the other Motown stars, Gaye was not from Detroit. He played organ and sang in his father's Washington, D.C., church before taking up piano and drums. Berry Gordy spotted him while he was performing in Detroit and signed him to his new label. At first, Gaye was used as a session drummer and on tour with the Miracles. His first solo release came in late 1962 with "Stubborn Kind of Fellow." Through the 1960s, Gaye placed seventeen songs in the Top 40 and joined with four of Motown's female singers (Diana Ross, Mary Wells, Kim Weston, and Tammi Terrell) for a dozen more Top 40 hits in a duet format. Gaye's biggest solo hit was "I Heard It through the Grapevine" (number 1 in 1968–69). A talented musician, he proved to be a successful songwriter and producer. His success continued through the 1970s with two number 1 songs and several important albums.

In the late 1970s, troubled times began for Gaye. A bitter divorce action with Anna Gordy Gaye (Berry's sister and seventeen years older than Marvin) resulted in a strange double album called *Here, My Dear*, with numerous songs full of irony, contradictions, and sarcasm. Following the divorce, there were problems with the IRS, involvement with drugs, and a bankruptcy action. Changing to Columbia Records, he managed a Top 5 hit in early 1983 called "Sexual Healing," but in 1984 he was shot and killed at the age of forty-four by his own father.

Like so many others, Gaye's career illustrates the old dichotomy between the secular and the sacred in the life of the black musician. His father was a Pentecostal preacher, and Marvin's early vocals have a distinct gospel sound. But like Sam Cooke, he wished to show that the black gospel sound could be transferred to the pop style. From the heavier sentiments of *What's Going On?* (about ecology, nuclear war, and inner-city poverty), he moved to one of Motown's most sexually oriented albums, *Let's Get It On*. An embittered man, several of his last recordings for Columbia were quite explicit in their violent references to sex (e.g., "Masochistic Beauty").

### H-D-H and the Formula for Success

Gordy struck another gold mine when he hired Eddie Holland as a songwriter and producer. Soon Gordy added Eddie's brother Brian and singer/songwriter Lamont Dozier to the Motown staff. Between 1963 and 1967, Holland, Dozier, and Holland (H-D-H) teamed up to provide songs and production for the majority of Motown's hit singles. They were the musical creators behind numerous hits by Martha and the Vandellas, the Miracles, Marvin Gaye, the Four Tops, and the Supremes. After logging nearly thirty Top 20 hits, H-D-H demanded an accounting of their royalties. A series of lawsuits ensued; the end came in 1972 by means of an out-of-court settlement. Together and separately, the songwriting team scored moderate hits throughout the 1970s for themselves and other artists.

When H-D-H stopped creating hits for Motown in 1968, morale dropped perceptibly. Most of the Motown artists were not songwriters or producers (Robinson,

Lamont Dozier, Eddie Holland, and Brian Holland (*Source:* Michael Ochs Archive, Ltd.)

Gaye, and Stevie Wonder were exceptions). Without the help of Holland, Dozier, and Holland, many were left "high and dry." Typically, Eddie Holland had worked with the vocal leads in the various groups; Lamont Dozier had helped with vocal backgrounds and instrumental tracks; Brian Holland handled overall composition and assisted with backup tracks. Without this musical foundation, sales dropped right along with morale.

In a way, Berry Gordy's secret of success was also nearly his undoing. He insisted on total control; he established a pattern or formula, saw that it worked, and then allowed little or no deviation. By sticking with a few songwriters–producers (namely Robinson and H-D-H), he guaranteed a consistency of musical style. Although that worked beautifully, when H-D-H left, that consistency was threatened. It was not unlike an athletic team that relies heavily on one or two outstanding players; when one of those players is hurt, disaster can strike.

Gordy's rigid control was evident throughout the Motown operation. For example, he hired Cholly Atkins as choreographer. Cholly's routine was similar with all of the groups. He started rehearsals with forty-five minutes of floor exercises; then he taught the physical routines to go with each song. Once learned, the routine was never to vary. The emphasis was on synchronized precision. Contrast this with the freely exuberant boogying of a soul artist like James Brown.

Gordy liked the businesslike concept of quality control. As the decade of the 1960s progressed, his standards became more rigid. He tightened up the funkier leanings of some groups, almost purging any vestiges of gospel or true soul sound; there were no raw R & B edges left. Nothing was left to chance. His use of the same basic backup band—the so-called Funk Brothers—on hundreds of recordings helped provide a consistency of sound. Note how many Motown recordings emphasize baritone sax, vibes, organ, and hand claps.

Through the uproarious 1960s, Motown's lyrics studiously avoided controversy and any heaviness beyond boy–girl romance. Only after about 1968 did songs like "Love Child" and "I'm Livin' in Shame" (Supremes), "War," "Ball of Confusion," and "Don't Let the Joneses Get You Down" (Temptations), or "Livin' in the City" (Wonder) begin to come from Motown. Some of Marvin Gaye's work in the 1970s carried Motown far beyond its previous boundaries with respect to lyrics.

Gordy employed an etiquette coach to teach the female performers how to get in and out of a car, how to apply makeup and style their hair, and how to walk, talk, and behave in public. There was also a vocal coach descended from the old gospel coach tradition in Harlem. The choreographer, the piano accompanists, the etiquette, makeup, and wardrobe people, and the vocal coach were all parts of the Artist Development Department. There was not to be the slightest change in any act without Gordy's approval. He even oversaw the individual performers' finances and laid down strict rules of conduct while on tour. There would be no fraternizing with fans. The concept was that of a family: one for all and all for one. Thus, Marvin Gaye played on the Vandellas' recordings; Martha Reeves sang and clapped on Gaye's recordings; Robinson wrote songs for almost everyone. And personal relationships developed within the "family": Smokey Robinson married Claudette Rogers of the Miracles; Marvelette Wanda Young married Miracle Bobby Rogers; Marvelette Katherine Anderson married the Temptations' road manager Joe Schaffner; Marvin Gaye married Anna Gordy.

## The Four Tops and the Temptations

A second wave of major stars hit Motown in the mid-1960s. The Four Tops had sung together since the mid-1950s, recording briefly on Chess, Columbia, and Riverside Records. Gordy discovered the four Detroit natives singing in a black resort area in Michigan. Starting as a backup group, they had their first release ("Baby I Need Your Loving") in late 1964. Their third release, "I Can't Help Myself," hit number 1 in mid-1965. Before moving to ABC–Dunhill Records in 1972, the Tops placed seventeen hits in the Top 40 for Motown. Most of these were Holland-Dozier-Holland songs, featuring the distinctive and polished sound of lead vocalist Levi Stubbs. More recent hits include "When She Was My Girl" (number 11 in 1981) and "Indestructible" (number 35 in 1988).

Certainly the most popular Motown male group of the 1960s was the Temptations. They sang well, dressed well, and danced. The dual lead singer format (Eddie Kendricks and David Ruffin) was straight out of the earlier black groups like the Soul Stirrers and the Ravens. Kendricks had a strong falsetto voice, whereas Ruffin was a smooth baritone. Atypically this quintet did not consist of Detroit natives; various members came from Alabama, Texas, and Mississippi. As one might expect, this group of transplanted southerners had strong gospel roots. As Ruffin said, "I heard gospel before I could think" (Hirshey 1984, 204). Their first hit was "The Way You Do the Things You Do," coauthored by Smokey Robinson. After several moderate hits, they hit number 1 in 1965 with "My Girl" (again coauthored by Robinson). Thereafter, the Temptations poured out a steady stream of hits through the late 1960s and early 1970s (thirty-five Top 40 hits, to be exact, including four number 1s). Changes began in 1968 when David Ruffin left the group. Also, Paul Williams's increasingly serious drug problem caused poor health and missed performances. By 1970, he had to drop out of the Temptations. In 1973, owing some $80,000 in back taxes, Williams drove to a spot not far from the old Motown offices and shot himself. He was thirty-four years old.

In 1971, Eddie Kendricks left the group. Even with all of these personnel changes, the group continued its success. In the late 1960s, they changed from the typical Motown style to a more modern style set by Sly and the Family Stone; the Temptations' first hits in the new style, sometimes called psychedelic soul, were "Cloud Nine" and "Run Away Child, Running Wild" in 1969. Some of their early 1970s hits led toward the disco style of that decade.

## Gladys Knight and the Pips

Continuing in the more traditional Motown style was Gladys Knight and the Pips. Gladys (born in Atlanta in 1944) was singing gospel music as early as 1952, when a family singing group was formed with her as the central attraction; thus, the Pips were born. In those early years, they toured with Jackie Wilson and Sam Cooke and recorded with moderate success for various labels.

In 1965, Gladys Knight and the Pips signed with Motown's Soul label, and in late 1967 they hit the number 2 position with "I Heard It Through the Grapevine" (Marvin Gaye's Tamla recording went to number 1 a year later). From then until 1973, the group scored a dozen more hits, including two more Top 10 songs.

In spite of their success, Knight and the Pips felt they were not being treated as a priority Motown act; thus, they switched to Buddah Records in 1973. Whereas many ex-Motowners flopped after leaving the company, Knight and the Pips flourished, at least initially. The debut Buddah album, *Imagination* (number 9 in 1973), yielded three Top 5 hits, including their first number 1 song, "Midnight Train to Georgia." However, from the mid-1970s on, album sales declined and single hits stopped.

### Stevie Wonder

Back in 1960 when it became known that a local man was starting a record company, Detroit parents flocked to West Grand Avenue with their young geniuses in tow, sure that theirs would be the next Sam Cooke or Chuck Berry. Most were far from it. However, ten-year-old Steveland Morris was different. He amazed Berry Gordy by playing the piano, the organ, the drums, and anything else he could find in the small Motown studio. Young Mr. Morris was promptly signed to the Tamla label and given a new professional name: Little Stevie Wonder. His fourth release, "Fingertips–Part 2," went to the number 1 position in 1963. It was the young company's second number 1 hit and the first number 1 hit for Wonder. His live performances on the Motortown Reviews were so successful that Gordy decided to release a live recording. The live seven-minute version of "Fingertips" was too long for a single, so it was divided into two parts and released as part 1 and part 2. The first live single to hit number 1, "Fingertips" is a mainstream, rocking song with Wonder playing solo on the first instrument he had learned as a young boy: the harmonica. Combining Wonder's twelve-year-old voice and harmonica with a strong instrumental backup, the song generated real excitement. It launched the career of an artist whose singles charts accomplishments would rank him fourth in the history of rock, behind only Elvis Presley, the Beatles, and Elton John (Whitburn, *Top 40 Hits*, 1996, 805).

Although Wonder had a string of sixteen Top 40 hits in the 1960s (over half reached the Top 10), it was not until the beginning of the 1970s that his full potential began to be realized. In 1970, he released his first self-produced album *Signed, Sealed, and Delivered*. It was his highest-ranking album (number 25) since his very first Tamla album, *Little Stevie Wonder / The 12 Year Old Genius*, a number 1 album. Next he turned to synthesizer and other electronic keyboards in *Where I'm Coming From*. In 1971, he turned twenty-one and demanded an accounting of his royalties. Stevie received his accounting; he took $250,000 of his $1 million trust and set up his own forty-track studio. He began production of his own album, refusing to submit to Motown's control. Finally, Berry Gordy made him an unprecedented offer (for Motown). The company would distribute his album and split songwriting royalties fifty-fifty; Wonder would do his own production and have his own publishing company. In effect, he had full artistic control.

The first album under this new contract was *Music of My Mind* (1972). It did well, but Stevie's next album, *Talking Book*, was a smash-hit album, peaking at number 3 and remaining on the charts for 109 weeks. *Talking Book* contained two number 1 hits, "Superstition" and "You Are the Sunshine of My Life." "Superstition" reflects Stevie's admiration of the psychedelic soul sound of Sly and the Family Stone, tempered by the more sophisticated style of Earth, Wind, and Fire. "You Are the Sunshine of My Life" suggested jazz–rock fusion in its harmonies and horn line.

Little Stevie Wonder (*Source:* Michael Ochs Archive, Ltd.)

*Innervisions* (1973) moved to more socially conscious lyrics than had previously come from Motown (e.g., "Higher Ground" and the Top 10 hit "Living in the City"). In mid-decade, Wonder negotiated a new contract with Motown; guaranteeing him thirteen million dollars over seven years, the contract was the biggest single artist contract in rock history's first twenty years. The 1976 album *Songs in the Key of Life* became the first American album to enter the album charts at number 1.

Years in preparation, *Journey Through the Secret Life of Plants* (1979) was more sophisticated than any previous Wonder album. "Send One Your Love" revealed a definite drift toward jazz-oriented harmonies and melodic concepts. The line of development that began in 1963 with "Fingertips" and culminated with the 1979 *Plants* album is one of the most impressive in the history of rock music.

As Wonder moved into his third decade in the music industry, he appeared to lose no momentum. The sound track album to *The Lady in Red* (1984) produced another number 1 hit, "I Just Called to Say I Love You." There can be no doubt that Little Stevie is one of the giants. Starting with *Talking Book*, every Stevie Wonder album since 1972 (except one 1960s compilation album) has landed in the Top 5. Meanwhile, he recorded a dozen more Top 10 singles, including nine number 1 hits.

Motown's rise from a small, local, independent company in 1960 to an industry giant in less than ten years is truly remarkable. Berry Gordy knew what he wanted, knew how to do it, and then did it. His ability to spot and utilize talents such as Smokey Robinson, Holland-Dozier-Holland, Marvin Gaye, and Stevie Wonder explains a large measure of his success. His absolute control led to both success and problems. Although many Motown artists were grateful for Gordy's formula for success, they also bucked against it at various points. Among those who have left the Motown "family" are some big names: Holland, Dozier, and

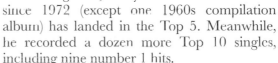

Stevie Wonder (*Source:* Michael Ochs Archive, Ltd.)

Holland, the Miracles, the Contours, the Spinners, Diana Ross, the Isley Brothers, Martha Reeves, Gladys Knight and the Pips, and the Four Tops. In some cases, Motown owned the group names, so when the individuals left, Gordy simply trotted out some new members under the old name.

Although the 1960s Motown sound shared common roots with soul music, namely gospel and R & B, it was not the same as soul music. Remember how that word "freedom" came up in almost every definition of soul? Motown's 1960s style was anything but free. There was little or no improvisation vocally or instrumentally. The raw and rough edges of soul were not to be found in Motown. It was slick, professional, polished, and precisely coordinated. The sound was popular with blacks and whites; but it should not be confused with real soul music.

Motown Records left Detroit in 1971 for a high-rise building on Sunset Avenue in Los Angeles. Motown's success continued with names like the Jackson Five, the Commodores, Stevie Wonder, and Diana Ross. Berry Gordy Jr., was still the kingpin; and millionaire vice president Smokey Robinson divided his time between the company and his family, consisting of former Miracle Claudette and their two children, Tamla and Gordy. In June 1988, however, Motown was purchased by MCA Records, Inc., thus bringing to an end its distinction as the largest black-owned-and-operated company in America.

## DIANA ROSS AND THE SUPREMES

On the basis of all of the other Motown stars of the 1960s, the company would certainly have been successful; but the difference between Motown's being successful and its becoming an industry giant was Diana Ross and the Supremes. In terms of chart performance in the decade of the 1960s, they rank third behind the Beatles and Elvis Presley. From 1964 through 1969, they rolled up twelve number 1 hits plus eleven Top 40 hits. They are the only American group to have five consecutive number 1 singles (they later had four consecutive number 1s).

While in high school, Diana Ross was asked to join a female vocal group that would be a "sister" group to the Primes. As the Primes evolved into the Temptations, the Primettes evolved into the Supremes. While still the Primettes, Diana, Florence Ballard, and Mary Wilson (originally from Mississippi) won a high school talent contest and began pestering Berry Gordy Jr., for an audition with his new record company. Finally, a former neighbor of Diana's, Smokey Robinson, arranged for their audition. They signed with Motown in 1962 and began recording as the Supremes. They endured several flops before Gordy put H-D-H on their case. That did it.

"When the Lovelight Starts Shining Through His Eyes" rose to number 23 in early 1964. They started the Dick Clark Cavalcade of Stars tour as the opening act; but during the tour, "Where Did Our Love Go" was released and moved up the charts to number 1. By the end of the tour, they had the prestigious closing spot on the show. Before 1965 was over, the Supremes had registered six number 1 songs ("Where Did Our Love Go," "Baby Love," "Come See About Me," "Stop! In the Name of Love," "Back in My Arms Again," and "I Hear a Symphony") and one number 11 hit. All were H-D-H compositions.

By the mid-1960s, the Supremes were Motown's biggest act. Naturally they got the whole quality control treatment: H-D-H songs and production, Cholly Atkins choreography, the etiquette coach, and so on. Compared to some of the male groups, the Supremes' stage act was less athletic; for them, Cholly Atkins designed graceful and (of course) precisely synchronized hand movements.

The series of hits continued unabated in 1966. But problems began to arise. Some say the problems began when Diana Ross started showing up at social functions arm in arm with Berry Gordy. Gradually, she was becoming more than just the lead singer of a trio; she was becoming "the act," with Florence and Mary serving as backup vocalists. After 1967 began with another number 1 hit ("Love Is Here and Now You're Gone"), things changed. The next release, "The Happening" (also number 1), was credited to "Diana Ross and the Supremes." Florence began missing performances because of "illness." Although the exact circumstances have never been clarified, she either left the group or was expelled in 1967 (replaced by Cindy Birdsong). Florence tried to make it as a solo act on ABC Records but had no luck. She endured a bewildering series of personal and professional disasters through the 1970s. By 1976, she weighed 198 pounds and had high blood pressure. That same year she died of cardiac arrest at the age of thirty-one.

The Supremes' hits kept coming in 1967, 1968, and 1969. Finally, Diana Ross, with Gordy's encouragement, left the group to begin her career as a solo performer. "Someday We'll Be Together" was ironically Diana's last recording with the Supremes; it became the group's last number 1 hit. Diana was replaced by Jean Terrell, and the group endured numerous personnel changes throughout the 1970s.

The Supremes (*Source:* Michael Ochs Archive, Ltd.)

Diana Ross (*Source:* Michael Ochs Archive, Ltd.)

Mary Wilson was the only constant member of the Supremes from the beginning until they faded from sight in the late 1970s. As Florence had done earlier, Mary sued Motown in 1977 for money she felt she was owed from the early days. Eventually she received 50 percent usage and interest in the name Supremes. Mary eventually published a biography of her life with Motown.

Diana Ross went on to become a major figure in the music industry. She became a successful star on television, in Las Vegas, and in films such as *Lady Sings the Blues, Mahogany,* and *The Wiz.* She left Motown in 1981 for what was reported to be a $20 million contract with RCA and EMI. In 1983, she reunited with ex-Supremes Mary Wilson and Cindy Birdsong for the finale of a two-hour television special saluting Motown's twenty-fifth anniversary.

The music of the 1960s Supremes is now classic and typifies the famed "Motown sound." There is the lead singer with vocal backup; there is the strong, professional orchestration, using strings, brass, sax, keyboards, and percussion. Note especially the frequent reliance on baritone saxophone (doubling the bass line and providing solo breaks) and vibraphone (listen to "My World Is Empty Without You Babe" as a good example). The beat is always strong, with a heavy backbeat often reinforced by hand claps. A trademark is the rather predictable modulation (change of key) that occurs about two thirds to three quarters through the song. The music abruptly shifts from one key (e.g., C major) to a key one half step higher (e.g., D-flat major); for an obvious example, listen to "Baby Love" (the modulation occurs about one minute and thirty-five seconds into the song). And, of course, there is no real improvisation or deviation from the predetermined arrangement. These were all elements in "the formula"; millions of record sales proved it worked.

## MUSICAL CLOSE-UP:
### MELODY AND THE SOUL SINGER

Most descriptions of soul singing abound in subjective terms like *freedom, feelings,* and *emotion.* Such words are fine when describing the general impression of a vocal style; but if we are really trying to understand a musical style, we must consider the objective, relatively precise elements of music, such as rhythm, timbre, melody, harmony, and form. Even though the art of soul singing would seem to be a very elusive phenomenon, we must at least attempt to analyze, in objective musical terms, what there is about the finest soul singers that makes their style what it is.

As noted earlier, soul singing is derived primarily from the gospel-singing tradition of the southern black church. The previous discussion has indicated that many soul singers (1) were originally from the South and (2) had their earliest musical experiences as singers in the church. Quite a few (e.g., Cooke, Gaye, and Franklin) were offspring of clergymen.

Perhaps, then, it would be instructive to listen to a bona fide soul singer singing gospel. That should give us some real insights. We can find just what we are looking for in Aretha Franklin's *Amazing Grace* album. To simplify our task, let us take an uncomplicated and well-known tune: the hymn "What a Friend We Have in Jesus." Aretha turns this straightforward hymn into a gospel song. The basic hymn tune follows.

This tune has a familiar form: sixteen measures, divided into four equal phrases, each four measures long. Furthermore, note that the first, second, and fourth phrases are almost alike (the familiar AABA pattern). The rhythm is quite uncomplicated. Every note is within the scale of F major except the F♯ in the ninth measure. Now let us see what Aretha does to this simple little hymn.

First, there is the matter of form. Aretha turns this tune into a six-minute piece. To do this she subdivides each of the four-measure phrases into two halves and then elongates each half into a full four-measure phrase of its own.

Thus, she has turned a sixteen-bar song into a thirty-two bar song. But then she repeats the first half of the song (original phrases A and A) before going on to the second half, which she also repeats. So now the sixteen-bar tune has become sixty-four bars long. But on the final occurrence of the original fifteenth measure, she "gets off" on the word "everything," repeating that measure over and over before finally resolving on a cadence. After adding the instrumental introduction, the doubling of the form, the repetition of each half, and the extension on "everything," the sixteen-bar tune has become a four-and-a-half-minute song. But she is not finished yet. After a short pause, Aretha hums and sings through the last half of the tune one more time, complete with the repetitive extension on the final "everything." The six-minute result begins to suggest what is meant by the word "freedom" when it is applied to the musical element of form.

But what is even more important is how Aretha fills that elongated form with a combination of pitches and rhythms, that is, with melody. Compare the first two measures of the original tune with Aretha's first phrase:

To be sure, the basic pitches of the tune are there, but there are notes added and the rhythms are significantly modified, with some notes falling behind where they "should" be and others coming ahead. Even the notation in the previous example does not exactly replicate the fine pitch variations of Aretha's voice (e.g., the extra pitch inflections on "have" in the second measure). The gospel/soul singer's vocal freedom is further illustrated the next time she sings these same measures:

This is still more different from (and more complex than) the earlier example. Again, standard notation cannot effectively capture every nuance of pitch and rhythm she sings. Note the arrow in the second measure of the foregoing example; this is a good example of a "blue note"—a pitch that is unstable, vacillating between A and A♭ (what the blues singers called "worrying" the pitch).

Although we cannot compare every measure of the original tune with Aretha's version, we can point out a few other places to notice. Frequently the gospel/soul singer adds short vocal phrases ("interpolations") as a sort of emotive commentary on the text. For example, note such phrases as "Oh, yes we do," "Oh-oh," "Oh, yeah," and "Let's do that one more time"—sung in the same style as the main melody. Also, there is the freedom to add words like "what a privilege (it is) to carry," or repeat words like "we often, we often, forfeit." The best examples in "What a Friend" are the extensions on "everything"—repeated for nearly one full minute with a different melodic phrase each time. If you can listen to the entire performance while following the original tune, you will be able to see what freedom of pitch and rhythm means to the soul singer.

One of the most pronounced characteristics of the gospel/soul singer is the melisma: a technique in which one syllable is extended over two or more pitches. As Wilson Pickett said, soul singers "put ten, maybe twenty notes to one word, like Sam Cooke done, and Jackie Wilson and all them" (Hirshey 1984, 51). Look back at the first example and the one that follows it and notice where words like "have" and "friend" are extended over three or four notes each. If you have access to the *Amazing Grace* album, listen to the title song (extended to almost eleven minutes); it contains many examples of extended melismas (e.g., Aretha's repetitive melismas on the word "through," about four minutes and ten seconds into the song).

Finally, there is the matter of vocal timbre. The soul singer employs a wide variety of vocal timbres. These range from the shout (in "What a Friend," listen to Aretha on the words "and what needless pain" or you can hear many shouts in "Amazing Grace") to a very breathy tone (listen to the second occurrence of the title line from Aretha's "I Never Loved a Man"). Other vocal timbres used in soul music include the raspiness of James Brown and the male falsetto voice so often used by male backup groups. The soul singer moves with dizzying speed through a full range of such timbres.

Soul's roots in the black southern church are clear. In that sacred experience, there was freedom to react vocally to the preacher's message or to an inner stirring of the spirit. Impromptu phrases were shouted out or moaned. So it is with the gospel singer. As gospel merged with R & B (similar roots) and the new kid on the block—rock and roll—soul music was born. Although the beat got harder, the instrumentation became more electric, and the overall forms grew more patterned, the soul singer still retained that freedom of expression—freedom of form, timbre, pitch, and rhythm—learned so long ago in a little white wood-frame church somewhere in the heart of the South.

# 10

## San Francisco

## OVERVIEW: AMERICA COUNTERS
## THE BRITISH INVASION

New York City has been described as America's great melting pot. But for the last half of the 1960s this epithet seemed to better describe San Francisco. A bewildering kaleidoscope of styles, musical and cultural, blended together into an almost indescribable mixture. In the words of Jefferson Airplane member Paul Kantner,

> There was an interweaving of the rock and roll world and the political world, the world of labor unions and the armed forces and kids and hippies and yippies and weathermen and democrats, mods and rockers, policemen worlds and the drug world, artists, craftsmen, Sierra Clubs and Hell's Angels, women's movements and Black Panthers, gurus, Jesus freaks, punks, lawyers, doctors, and Indians—you get the picture, I hope. (McDonough 1985, vii)

How and why did such an unlikely mixture come together in San Francisco at just this time? The disillusionment of the youth movement seemed to deepen with the coming of the Johnson administration; with LBJ, the youth sensed a return to "politics as usual" and the death of the Kennedy dream. The Vietnam War escalated as each new step pulled the nation deeper into involvement in Southeast Asia. Kids began "dropping out and turning on." Where does one go when one drops out of one's own family and society? Northern California seemed to be the answer. Almost any other geographic area of the country seemed to represent either conservatism or the hated "establishment." The West Coast was "new America," representing new thought, new ways, and alternative lifestyles. Countercultural thought had flowed from the University of California at Berkeley, San Francisco State University, Stanford University, Mills College, and numerous small colleges in the area.

Youth from all over the nation, from every conceivable cultural background, hitchhiked their way to the youth mecca of the mid-to-late 1960s: San Francisco. Although they would eventually land wherever they could find shelter and food, many made it to the exact epicenter of the psychedelic–flower power world, the Haight–Ashbury neighborhood. Central to this scene were drugs, free sex, the love–peace philosophy, and music.

By 1967, the San Francisco scene reached its zenith. It has been estimated that there were between 500 and 1,500 local bands operating in the Bay Area at that time. By 1970, the wave had begun to lose its power, and the youth moved into the new mentality of the 1970s. But the most influential of the San Francisco bands would leave their mark on the history of rock in several important ways.

To coalesce the disparate fragments of this eclectic society, several catalysts were necessary. One came in the form of rock concert halls. The history of several of these ballroom music halls reached back to the swing era of the 1930s and early 1940s. In late 1965, concert promoter Bill Graham began presenting concerts at the Fillmore Auditorium and later at the Fillmore West and the Winterland Arena. Graham booked hundreds of rock acts into his various sites over the next five years, featuring big-name acts and virtual unknowns. By the turn of the decade, the rock festival phenomenon (such as Woodstock and Altamont) had created audiences too large and unruly for more "intimate" presentation (the Winterland, for example, seated about 5,400 and was one of the largest of these concert halls). Concerts gradually moved to stadiums and sports arenas seating 50,000 and more. But for a time, Graham's concert halls in San Francisco, as well as others like the Avalon and the Longshoremen's Hall, pulled the new San Francisco youth society together to share a common musical experience.

A second coalescing factor was radio. The key figure here was Tom Donahue. As a viable radio alternative, FM was just beginning to expand. For years it had been the home of classical music and easy listening styles. Prohibited from merely replicating AM programming, stations such as New York's WOR-FM began a "contemporary music" format that featured album tracks, lengthy sets, and a calmer, more sophisticated style of disc jockey chatter. The format was called progressive rock, and later, AOR (album-oriented rock).

In 1967, Tom Donahue was hired by an almost down-and-out San Francisco FM station, KMPX. There he tried the new "progressive" format; it sold. Soon KMPX's advertising revenues quintupled. In 1968, Donahue moved to a station that had been broadcasting classical music, KSFR; changing its call letters to KSAN and its format to "progressive rock," the station soon became the mainstay of the new San Francisco rock scene.

If the new youth culture of San Francisco was a bewildering mixture, so was the music. Although one occasionally hears about the "San Francisco sound," in fact it is almost as indistinct a term as "folk rock" or "soul." In Charles Perry's words, "Musically, the meaning is hard to pin down. . . . The boundaries of the San Francisco sound become impossibly vague" (Miller 1980, 271). Many of the musicians who populated the San Francisco groups cut their musical teeth in earlier folk groups. Quite a few of these bands also admired the old R & B style. So when the British blues-based bands, such as the Stones, hit this country with their harder mainstream rock, many of the San Francisco bands blended elements of the folk style with the R & B-derived rock style of their British counterparts. The result was a hard-driving style of rock that was really the only American style of the time that could counter the harder styles of the British bands.

We can point to a few characteristics that, to varying degrees with various bands, typify most of the San Francisco bands:

1. Drugs were an important element in the music and lifestyles of these groups. Sometimes this music is called "psychedelic rock" or "acid rock." Certainly there had been drug references before (e.g., "Eight Miles High" and "Lucy in the Sky with Diamonds"). But with the San Francisco bands, drugs became a dominant theme. By 1967, the old double entendre trick was discarded, and the lyrics became blatantly and explicitly drug oriented. Beyond the lyrics, certain aspects of the music itself were identified with drugs. The long instrumental improvisations and the electronic experimentation (points 3 and 4) became associated with acid rock. San Francisco was considered the psychedelic capital of the nation. The bands and their fans were assumed (not always correctly) to be stoned-out, freaked-out acid eaters. The whole scene was psychedelic, from the music to the clothing to the brightly painted Volkswagen minibuses. Hair was long, stringy, and greasy. Clothing ranged from Jesus look-alikes to Superman outfits—the freakier the better. Psychedelic posters advertised upcoming concerts at the Fillmore and other concert halls.

2. Volume levels at live concerts reached a new high. Rock and roll had never been quiet music, but most groups had managed to get by with tinny-sounding public address systems. But an explosion of sound technology through the 1960s now permitted groups to amplify their sound with tremendous power through walls of speakers. It is said that the Grateful Dead carried twenty-three tons of sound equipment with them for a major concert. The decibel level at such concerts annihilated any form of communication; one's attention was riveted on the band because one had no choice. The vibrations literally could be felt in the rib cage; the ringing in the ears lasted for hours after the concert had ended.

3. Up until this point, the singer had dominated the rock scene. But the San Francisco groups often placed considerable emphasis on the instrumentalists, especially the guitarists. Long improvisations, often lasting twenty to thirty minutes, were common at live concerts. Such improvisations were old hat in the jazz scene but were new to rock (except for some British blues-based bands, such as the Yardbirds). To the psychedelically oriented rock fans, such long-winded flights of fancy seemed to be musical "trips," possibly inspired by drugs.

4. The same explosion of electronic technology that allowed for more sophisticated sound reproduction also placed an expanding arsenal of sound-producing gadgets at the disposal of rock musicians. They soon learned that electricity could generate sound. Especially fascinating was the phenomenon of electronic feedback. Electronically produced music had been around for several decades in the classical field, but again, to the acid rockers, these "new" sounds were "far out." And, again, there was the association of these freaky sounds with the drug experience.

# THE JEFFERSON AIRPLANE

The first San Francisco band to get a recording contract with a major label (RCA) was the Jefferson Airplane. The group had been formed in 1965 by male lead singer Marty Balin, a member of a folk group called the Town Criers. In 1965, he took over a small club on upper Fillmore Street; he renamed the club The Matrix and recruited guitarists Paul Kantner and Jorma Kaukonen and vocalist Signe Toly to join him as the house band. Calling themselves the Jefferson Airplane, they went through several bassists and drummers before settling on Jack Casady and Skip Spence, respectively. Playing a mixture of folk rock and Beatle-like tunes, they were signed to an RCA contract in 1965 and released their first album, *Jefferson Airplane Takes Off,* in 1966. The album did not fare well.

Following the release of that album, female lead singer Signe Toly Anderson left the band, as did Spence, who went on to join Moby Grape. Spence was replaced by Spencer Dryden. For a new female lead singer, the band chose Grace Slick, a member of another local band called the Great Society. This new lineup—Slick, Balin, Kantner, Kaukonen, Casady, and Dryden—recorded the Airplane's second album, *Surrealistic Pillow* (1967). It placed number 3 on the album charts and yielded two hit singles (the Airplane's only Top 40 singles), "Somebody to Love" (number 5) and "White Rabbit" (number 8). The disillusionment of the youth generation is suggested by the opening lines of "Somebody to Love": "When the truth is found to be lies/And all the joy within you dies." "White Rabbit," appearing in the same powerful summer as *Sgt. Pepper,* casts aside any pretense of double entendre: "One pill makes you larger, and one pill makes you small/And the ones that Mother gives you don't do anything at all." The lyrics evoke images of a psychedelic *Alice in Wonderland,* including the hook line "Go ask Alice," which would become the title of an antidrug movie years later. Musically, "White Rabbit" is very well done, utilizing a bolero-type beat, beginning quietly and steadily building to a strong finish.

With this album, Grace Slick became the first real female rock star. Previously, female singers had been associated either with soft rock, including the doo-wop style, or the Motown female group image. But with the Airplane, Grace Slick became a legitimate mainstream rock lead singer.

In late 1967, the Airplane issued *After Bathing at Baxter's.* Although the album reached the Top 20, there were no single hits. This was not unusual for the San Francisco groups. In fact, many of these groups were quite disdainful of Top 40 hits and considered chart success a rather unbecoming embarrassment.

Gradually, Slick and Kantner took greater control of the Airplane, reducing Balin's role as they did so. *Crown of Creation* (1968) contained an interesting variety of styles. The title song, by Kantner, was a mainstream rock song; Slick's "Lather" sounds like a latter-day folk rock song, complete with externally mixed sound effects and obscure lyrics. Of particular interest is "Chushingura," a haunting and tasteful example of the type of electronic experimentation referred to in this chapter's overview. In addition to the natural sounds of piano and acoustic guitar, there is electronic feedback and other electronically generated sounds; the asymmetric clicking sounds were reportedly made by a row of suspended steel balls, such as those that may be found in shopping mall gift shops.

The Jefferson Airplane (*Source:* Michael Ochs Archive, Ltd.)

After touring Europe in 1968, the group released a live album, *Bless Its Pointed Little Head.* A strong cut on this album is the live version of "Plastic Fantastic Lover," first issued on *Surrealistic Pillow.* It features a shouting lyric and good instrumental improvisation. The Airplane's last 1960s album was *Volunteers,* released in 1969. It contained songs with sociopolitical messages ("We Can Be Together" and "Volunteers") and strong vocal and instrumental work.

Personnel problems began to plague the Airplane in the early 1970s. Dryden and Balin left. Meanwhile, Kaukonen and Casady had formed Hot Tuna. (Other late-1960s "edible" rock groups included Vanilla Fudge, Moby Grape, the Flying Burrito Brothers, the Strawberry Alarm Clock, and even the Ultimate Spinach.) Forming their own independent label, Grunt Records, the Airplane released several more albums before ceasing to exist.

From the ruins of the Jefferson Airplane arose a new band. Back in 1970, *Blows Against the Empire* had been released under the name of the Jefferson Starship. That album was recorded by Kantner, Slick, Casady, and others (including Jerry Garcia, David Crosby, and Graham Nash). Writing in *BAM* (Bay Area Music) magazine, Blair Jackson said, "The Starship is the rock world's longest-running soap opera" (McDonough 1985, 145). Indeed, trying to keep track of Airplane–Starship personnel after 1970 is mind-boggling. Let us restrict ourselves to a few high points. One of the more interesting additions was that of "Papa" John Creach, born in Beaver Falls, Pennsylvania, in 1917. Papa John, a black violinist, had been involved in the blues scene for decades; he had amplified his violin back in the mid-1940s. He began to sit in on Jefferson Airplane performances in 1970 and became a member of the Airplane–Starship throughout the 1970s.

Marty Balin rejoined the group in 1975, helping them attain their first number 1 album, *Red Octopus,* and a number 3 single, "Miracles." Thereafter, Slick and Balin dropped out of the group, leaving Kantner as the only remaining original member. But by 1982 Slick had rejoined the Starship. Several moderately successful albums emerged in 1982 and 1984. In the latter year, Paul Kantner left the Starship; as a result of his lawsuit, the band was required to drop the name Jefferson, thus becoming simply the Starship. As the Starship, the band enjoyed continued success into the late 1980s (including three number 1 hits), until they temporarily disbanded in 1990.

In the early 1990s, Kantner, Creach, Casady, Balin, and others reformed as Jefferson Starship. By 2000, Balin, Kantner, and Casady began touring as Jefferson Airplane's Volunteers. There was also a separate band named Starship led by Mickey Thomas. We warned you that it was mind-boggling!

## THE GRATEFUL DEAD

Elvis's fans tore at his clothes, screamed and cried, and, years later, fainted as he lay in state at Graceland. Beatlemania was a kind of cultural hysteria that sociologists have yet to explain fully. And there are Stones fans who refuse to hear even the slightest criticism of their heroes. But few fans are as devoted, persevering, and tolerant as "the Deadheads"—the relatively small but unswervingly loyal following of the Grateful Dead.

The Dead seem to be the archetypal San Francisco band of the late 1960s, combining all of the major characteristics of that style. Yet, they are also different from most of the other bands of that time. Like so many others, their roots were in the folk era of the early 1960s.

Jerry Garcia was born in San Francisco in 1942. His family moved around the Bay Area a great deal, and Jerry, although unquestionably bright, never settled into a successful school routine. By fifteen, he was in constant trouble for fighting, drinking, and smoking marijuana. He finally dropped out of school at seventeen and joined the army. Following several courts-martial and a series of AWOLs, the army decided it would struggle along without Jerry's services; he was discharged.

Returning to civilian life, he found that folk music was the rage in the San Francisco of the early 1960s. He became fascinated with bluegrass music and, having learned to play the five-string banjo, began playing in local coffeehouses. Several of the other future Dead members were playing in bands in the Bay Area at the same time. Inevitably their paths crossed. Ron "Pigpen" McKernan was the son of San Francisco disc jockey Phil McKernan, who had hosted a blues show on station KRE in the late 1950s. Pigpen absorbed his father's enthusiasm for the blues and, after dropping out of school, learned to play harmonica and joined the Bay Area club–musician scene. Along with several others, Garcia, McKernan, and Bob Weir formed Mother McCree's Uptown Jug Champions. Thanks to the Beatlemania of 1964, the jug band decided to go electric and play rock and roll. McKernan switched from harmonica to organ; they added drummer Bill Kreutzmann and changed their name to the Warlocks. Soon, Phil Lesh, a classically trained violinist and serious avant-garde composer, was invited to join the Warlocks.

One of the more colorful aspects of mid-1960s life in San Francisco was author Ken Kesey (*One Flew over the Cuckoo's Nest*) and his free-thinking band of cohorts, the Merry Pranksters. Kesey was known for throwing wild and weird parties, which included, among others, Kesey's intellectually liberated friends, the less intellectual but equally countercultural Hell's Angels, and the Warlocks. Anything and every-thing went on at these freely structured party–happenings (called Acid Tests). The only predictable constants were drugs (especially LSD), weird costumes, and loud rock music by the Warlocks. As Garcia later said, "The Acid Tests were thousands of people, all hopelessly stoned, all finding themselves in a roomful of other thousands of people, none of whom any of them were afraid of" (Jackson 1983, 55).

In such an atmosphere, the Warlocks were able to experiment freely. Their music got louder, harder, more improvisatory, and longer. Playing with all sorts of electron-ically generated sounds, from distortion to feedback, they were met with enthusiastic approval by the party-goers. But by mid-1966, the Acid Tests had ended. Kesey had been charged with drug possession and had fled to Mexico. The dance–concert scene at halls like the Fillmore and the Avalon offered more structure than the free-form Acid Test format.

Changing their name to the Grateful Dead, the band moved into an old Victo-rian structure in the Haight–Ashbury neighborhood. Their music at this time con-sisted of blues material, Motown and soul songs, and Dylan songs. There were extended improvisations worked into these songs and continuing experimentation with sound alterations, such as guitar fuzz, feedback, and tremelo bar. In late 1966,

The Grateful Dead (Photograph by Herb Greene) (*Source:* © Herb Greene 1966. Courtesy Robert Koch Gallery, San Francisco)

the Dead signed a record contract with Warner Brothers. Unfamiliar with the structured environment of the recording studio, the band turned out a rather unimpressive first album, *The Grateful Dead* (number 73 in 1967).

Many groups say they are not seeking commercial success in order to preserve their countercultural image, but they then sign lucrative record contracts and do everything possible to achieve top-of-the-chart success. But the Dead seemed to practice what they preached. Even during the peak of their popularity (late 1960s), they did not have a Top 40 hit. Their albums have sold well but not spectacularly. Their real emphasis was on live performance. They were a concert, not a studio, band. They have played five-hour concerts, free concerts, and even hauled their equipment to Egypt at a cost (to them) of $500,000 to play a benefit concert at the foot of the Great Pyramids (1978). They considered themselves and their Deadhead followers to be an extended family; their best work was done when that family gathered for a live concert.

After the release of that first album, the band added drummer Mickey Hart and lyricist Robert Hunter. The next two albums, *Anthem of the Sun* (1968) and *Aoxomoxoa* (1969), fared only moderately. Finally, they released a live double album, *Live/Dead*, in late 1969. Most Deadheads consider this to be the group's best album of the 1960s; indeed, a group whose main emphasis is on live performance should fare best on a live album. If one includes various compilations and reissues, well over half of the Dead's releases are live albums; that is an unusually high percentage of live albums, but it does make sense.

Several cuts on *Live/Dead* deserve comment. For example, the twenty-one minute version of "Dark Star" illustrates the lengthy instrumental improvisation that typifies the Dead and other San Francisco groups. The Dead were known for taking half an hour to tune up and decide what to play. Indeed, the opening of "Dark Star" seems to grow from out of nowhere, as if the band were simply trying to get into a groove. But the playing is technically proficient and musically inventive. For an example of typical San Francisco electronic experimentation, listen to "Feedback"—which is exactly what the title suggests. "Saint Stephen" is a fun-loving rock song; "Turn On Your Lovelight" is a good illustration of both the blues-based rock style and some very fine instrumental improvisation. To get the full late-1960s San Francisco effect, be sure to turn up your stereo just short of blowing the speakers.

In the early 1970s, the Dead moved in the direction of a simplified, country-oriented sound. Two outstanding albums illustrate this trend: *Workingman's Dead* (1970) and *American Beauty* (1970). These were the Dead's first albums to reach the Top 30. Garcia had picked up the pedal steel guitar, lending a real country flavor to these albums. A reliance on acoustic instruments suggested their dramatic shift away from the psychedelic rock of the late 1960s.

*Blues for Allah* (1975), the Dead's most successful album commercially, is a good album, with even a touch of jazz influence. There were several personnel changes during the 1970s, but the basic nucleus of the band (Garcia, Lesh, Weir, and Kreutzmann) remained intact (McKernan died in 1973 at the age of twenty-seven). Later albums revealed a variety of approaches, including the horns, strings, and vocal choruses of *Terrapin Station* (1977), the all-acoustic double album *Reckoning* (1981), and its companion electric double album *Dead Set* (1981).

The Dead's fans were a flexible and tolerant bunch, as their heroes moved through psychedelia, country rock, blues, folk, jazz, acoustic rock, electric rock, and even horns, strings, and choruses. In their free-spirited, idealistically anticommercial way, the Dead are prime examples of late-1960s San Francisco. The band enjoyed something of a renaissance in the late 1980s with a number 6 album (*In the Dark*) and a Top 10 single ("Touch of Grey"). The death of Jerry Garcia in August 1995 was a traumatic moment for the band and its devoted followers. After several years, the band was revived in 2003 (called The Dead) and continued to tour.

## JANIS JOPLIN

San Francisco in the late 1960s was full of transplants and honest-to-goodness characters. Janis Joplin was both. Born in Port Arthur, Texas (1943), she grew up amidst blues, gospel, and country styles. A natural free spirit, Janis left Port Arthur and headed for San Francisco to sing in a few folk clubs and bars. Shortly, she returned to Texas to attend the University of Texas at Austin. Though she stayed there only one year, she did get some more experience singing in local bars. Judging from those early performances, one concludes that Janis was heavily into black R & B styles; her renditions of "Nobody Knows You When You're Down and Out" and "St. James Infirmary" sound authentically black.

Meanwhile Chet Helms, also from Texas, was busy promoting concerts at San Francisco's Avalon Ballroom. Helms became the manager for a recently organized San Francisco band called Big Brother and the Holding Company. In 1966, he convinced Janis to return to San Francisco as the band's female lead singer. Following an unsuccessful first album, the band got its big break in 1967 at the Monterey International Pop Festival. Janis's natural voice was already raw and strong, but faced with the necessity of overcoming the powerful rock band, she truly began to scream and shout her lyrics. The group's Monterey performance was greeted with unanimous praise. Dylan's manager, Albert Grossman, became Janis's manager, and Columbia Records offered a recording contract.

In 1968, Big Brother's first Columbia album, *Cheap Thrills*, rose to number 1 and stayed there for eight weeks. "Piece of My Heart" hit the singles charts, eventually peaking at number 12. Other songs of interest on this album are Janis's version of Big Mama Thornton's "Ball and Chain" and George Gershwin's "Summertime."

Rumors of the breakup of Big Brother began circulating in late 1968. The idea was planted in Janis's mind that she was the real star and Big Brother was holding her back (an idea not without some truth). She announced her separation from Big Brother and went solo at the beginning of 1969. Big Brother, by the way, had no more hit singles; in fact, their highest-ranking album after Janis left landed at number 134. Janis's *I Got Dem Ol' Kozmic Blues Again* was released in mid-1969 and moved to number 5 on the album charts. The album's title song "Kozmic Blues," is a good example of Janis's powerful, sandpaper-raw voice; her soul-like vocal style is also evident on "Try (Just a Little Bit Harder)."

By the beginning of 1970, Janis was busy creating a truly top-notch band, which she called Full-Tilt Boogie. Since Big Brother, each of her bands seemed better than the previous one, and Full-Tilt Boogie was no exception. Their performance on

Janis Joplin (*Source:* Michael Ochs Archive, Ltd.)

Janis's last album, *Pearl,* is very strong indeed. *Pearl* was recorded mostly during the late summer of 1970. But before it could be released, Janis was found dead in her Hollywood hotel. The victim of a heroin overdose, she was only twenty-seven at the time of her death (October 4, 1970). *Pearl* was released after her death; it hit number 1 and stayed there for nine weeks. "Me and Bobby McGee" was released as a single, and it became Janis's only Top 40 hit, holding the number 1 position for two weeks.

Janis Joplin's musical style places her squarely in mainstream rock, but her roots in R & B and gospel are evident in almost every song. Recall what you read in the musical close-up in Chapter 9, "Soul and Motown," about the gospel-oriented soul singer; then listen, if you can, to Janis's version of "Summertime" on *Cheap Thrills.* Granted, Janis is white, but her vocal style has virtually every characteristic of the soul singer. Sometimes she sings straight-ahead, blues-derived mainstream rock ("Move Over," from *Pearl,* is a strong example). But from that same album, "My Baby" clearly shows gospel roots: the triple meter; the chord movement from I up to IV and on to V; the cadence on the title, which moves from IV back to I; the gospel-style acoustic piano and organ—these elements all create a gospel feeling. If Janis had replaced the words "My Baby" with "My Sweet Lord," the latter would fit quite naturally. For a monumental example of the blues derivation, listen to the live version of "Ball and Chain" on *Janis Joplin's Greatest Hits;* it is a truly remarkable performance that, in a way, tells you everything there is to know about Janis.

Janis was unique. She was a white soul singer; she was a female mainstream rock singer (along with Grace Slick, a prototype in that regard). Her sandpaper voice was like no other. Although the official medical reason for her death was a heroin overdose, one almost feels that she died of old age, having crammed at least one lifetime into her twenty-seven years. She lived life at its fastest possible pace, with no holds barred and full speed ahead. She dressed like a cheap hooker; her hair was usually unkempt; she had a rough complexion and occasional difficulties with plumpness. She was not attractive in the usual sense, certainly not possessing the simple beauty of her counterpart Grace Slick. She was rarely without her bottle of Southern Comfort; she reportedly used every drug San Francisco could provide. In the words of her own song, she was determined to "Get It While You Can" (*Pearl*).

Janis left one remarkable song that may become a classic. "Mercedes Benz" (*Pearl*) is an a cappella vocal solo in which Janis puts her tongue squarely in her cheek and does a song of "great social and political import." She takes potshots at upper-class values, from color televisions to Porsches. Her cackling laughter at the end reminds us that she was truly one of a kind. In a business where everybody copies everybody, Janis was an original and has never been replicated.

## OTHER SAN FRANCISCO GROUPS

The Airplane, the Dead, and Joplin—these were the most prominent artists from the late-1960s San Francisco scene. But of course, there were many others. Table 10–1 summarizes some of them. Several bands formed in the late 1960s in San Francisco would have their biggest impact in the early 1970s. We shall mention them here and then discuss them more fully in later chapters. These would include the Steve Miller Band, Santana, Tower of Power, Creedence Clearwater Revival, and Sly and the Family Stone.

### Table 10–1

| Band | Comments |
| --- | --- |
| Charlatans | 1965–1968; a prototype for later San Francisco bands; repertoire of folk songs and blues; concept was more visual than musical; no hit singles, but in many ways, "got the ball rolling." |
| Quicksilver Messenger Service | 1965–1975; talented lead guitarist John Cipollina played lengthy improvisations rivaling those of the Grateful Dead; series of moderately successful albums 1968–1970. Good example: "The Fool" (*Quicksilver Messenger Service*). |
| Country Joe McDonald and the Fish | Began in 1965 as a folk duo; overtly political protest songs; grew to a quintet and went electric; crazy costumes and humorous stage act; became known for pro-drug songs and Vietnam protest songs. Major appearance at Woodstock; since 1970, Country Joe has had little impact as a soloist. |
| Moby Grape | Premiered at Fillmore in 1966; triple guitar front line. First album and five singles released in 1967 (none made the Top 40, possibly because of reaction against Columbia's glitzy promotion, which smacked of overkill). Second album, *Wow*, included second disc with lengthy instrumental improvisation (with "guests" Al Kooper and Mike Bloomfield). Continued into 1970s (with changing personnel), but peak of popularity was over. |

## *ACID ROCK OUTSIDE SAN FRANCISCO*

San Francisco was the psychedelic center, to be sure, but there were bands in other parts of the country who shared the characteristics of San Francisco acid rock. One thinks of groups such as the Fugs, the Blues Magoos, and the Vanilla Fudge. And the style was also developed by second-wave British invasion groups such as Small Faces, Traffic, and Pink Floyd.

Indeed, after the Summer of Love in 1967, when the San Francisco scene hit its apex, the scene began to unravel in 1968. Crime, drugs, and racial tensions took their toll. The city government banned live performances in the Panhandle, a strip of grass and trees adjacent to Haight–Ashbury where many live concerts had been held. But the most disintegrating effect came from the new "dropout" immigrants who flowed into the city. As *BAM* writer Blair Jackson describes it,

> Somewhere along the line . . . the Haight started to lure droves of young people who were less interested in the utopian ideals that had originally been the source of the neighborhood's strength, and more focused on the idea of being able to take drugs, eat for free, listen to rock and roll, and further the sexual revolution. The Haight–Ashbury culture had encouraged young people to "drop out" of conformist society, and a regrettable by-product of that battle cry was that some people took it as their cue to drop out altogether, ceasing to offer their energy toward the furtherance of the new order. (Jackson 1983, 77)

But what had begun in San Francisco would have its effect elsewhere. Two of the more important non–San Francisco bands of the late 1960s were Jim Morrison and the Doors and the Jimi Hendrix Experience.

### Jim Morrison and the Doors

Jim Morrison was born in Melbourne, Florida, in 1943. At the age of twenty, he enrolled in the film department at UCLA; soon, however, he moved to the Venice Beach culture and began taking LSD regularly. While still at UCLA, he met keyboard player Ray Manzarek (born in Chicago in 1943). The two became friends and decided to start their own band, with Morrison as lead singer and Manzarek playing piano, organ, marimba, and sometimes bass. They recruited two Los Angeles musicians, jazz drummer John Densmore and guitarist Robbie Krieger.

Soon the Doors, as they called themselves, were hired as the house band at the famous Whiskey-à-Go-Go. Signing with Elektra Records in 1966, they released their first album, *The Doors,* in early 1967. Played primarily on the new "progressive FM" stations, the album was a success, rising to number 2. The album contained a long (nearly seven minutes) version of a song by Krieger called "Light My Fire." A shorter single version was released and became a number 1 hit by mid-1967.

The Doors' musical style was blues-based mainstream rock. Morrison's flat baritone voice had a dark sound quality; his vocal lines were usually in a very narrow range and were quite repetitive, frequently emphasizing the interval between the tonic scale degree and the minor third degree. For example, note the similarity between the basic melodic lines of "Light My Fire," "Love Her Madly," "Riders on the Storm," "Moonlight Drive," "Hello, I Love You," and others. The minor keys used in many Doors tunes also result in a darker sound. Add to this the lyrics, which are often centered around death, violence, darkness, and a menacing kind of sex, and the picture is anything but upbeat. Musically, Manzarek's keyboard solos are perhaps the Doors' strongest point.

The second album, *Strange Days*, was another success (a number 3 album) and contained two hit singles, "People Are Strange" (number 12 in 1967) and "Love Me Two Times" (number 25 in early 1968). It also contained the eleven-minute "When the Music's Over." *Waiting for the Sun* (1968) became the Doors' only number 1 album and contained the number 1 single, "Hello, I Love You."

By 1969, the inherent seeds of destruction had begun to manifest themselves. Morrison had developed a serious problem with alcoholism, to go along with his drug habit. His stage performances were erratic, even as he tried to incorporate more theatrical antics. The low point came in March 1969 at a Miami concert. As a song broke down in the middle, Morrison simply stood there, too drunk to know what to do. After a few moments of stunned silence, the audience heard Morrison ask if they wanted him to expose himself; he proceeded to unzip his pants and fulfill his promise. He was arrested for indecent exposure and public drunkenness.

The next Doors album, *The Soft Parade*, was an oddity. The sound of an acid rock group doing soft rock, complete with brass, strings, and backup vocals, was strange indeed. The album made the Top 10, and "Touch Me" rose to number 3 as a single.

With *Morrison Hotel* (1970), the band returned to its mainstream rock sound, but there were no hit singles. Morrison's last album, *L.A. Woman* (1971), hit the Top 10 and yielded two Top 20 singles, "Love Her Madly" and "Riders on the Storm."

Beset by legal and physical problems, Morrison moved to Paris for rest and recuperation. It was there that he died on July 3, 1971; he was found in a bathtub, the victim of a heart attack. He was twenty-seven years old. The Doors issued several more albums before disbanding in 1973.

Jim Morrison (Photograph by Michael Montfort) (*Source:* © 1993 Michael Montfort/Michael Ochs Archive, Ltd.)

## The Jimi Hendrix Experience

There are some interesting connections between Jimi Hendrix and Bob Dylan. First, neither will be remembered primarily as a great vocalist. In fact, Hendrix had not done much singing until he heard Dylan; then he decided that if Dylan could get away with singing, so could he. Second, Hendrix's only Top 40 hit single came in 1968 with "All Along the Watchtower" (number 20), a Dylan song. Finally, just as Dylan almost single-handedly transformed the lyrics of rock music, so Hendrix exerted a tremendous influence on post-1968 rock guitar styles.

Jimi Hendrix was born in Seattle on November 27, 1942, into a middle-class family. He began his musical career playing backup guitar for various black artists such as Little Richard, Ike and Tina Turner, Wilson Pickett, and Jackie Wilson, on the "chitlin' circuit." He arrived in New York in 1964 to back the Isley Brothers and King Curtis and to play recording sessions. In 1965, Hendrix formed his own band, calling it Jimmy James and the Blue Flames. They worked in various Greenwich Village clubs while waiting for a break.

The break came in an unexpected way. Chas Chandler, former bassist with the Animals, encouraged Hendrix to go to England to seek his fame and fortune. He did so in September 1966; there he recruited British musicians Noel Redding (bass) and Mitch Mitchell (drums), forming a rock trio known as the Jimi Hendrix Experience. The group was an immediate success, scoring several major hits on the British charts ("Hey Joe," "Purple Haze," and "The Wind Cries Mary").

In those early days, Hendrix played a heavy dose of blues, some soul songs, and a few originals. He had begun to experiment with feedback, fuzz tone, and other electronically generated or modified sounds. He used only his Stratocaster guitar, an amplifier, and a Maestro fuzz box.

The Experience frizzed their hair, adopted psychedelically appropriate costumes, and prepared to invade America. Their debut was at the Monterey Pop Festival of June 1967. Appearing on the last of five concerts, they had the bad luck of following the Who, a hard-driving British band that had practically drained the audience with its frantic, mainstream rock. But Hendrix played his guitar with his teeth and behind his back; he caressed his guitar and attacked it in a sexually suggestive way. After a rocking version of Dylan's "Like a Rolling Stone" and a driving version of the Troggs' "Wild Thing," he drenched his guitar in lighter fluid and set it on fire (shades of Jerry Lee Lewis). To put it mildly, he succeeded in getting America's attention.

*Are You Experienced?* had already been released in this country (summer 1967) and had risen to number 5. The hard, raw, blues-based mainstream rock contained on this album was unlike anything else on the market at this time, except possibly for a few of the harder San Francisco bands and some of the second-wave British invasion bands. But the guitar sounds were utterly unique. Hendrix was left-handed, but instead of using a left-handed model, he played a right-handed guitar upside down. Some of his unusual effects resulted from the use of extreme volume, thus overloading his sound system; but he also used a fuzz box for distortion, a Uni-Vibe (which simulated rotating speakers), a wah-wah pedal, and the guitar's toggle switch and tremelo bar for special effects. Groups like the Dead, the Who, and the Yardbirds were using similar techniques, but Hendrix seemed to use them with more control for deliberate musical effect. Although one can hear these and other effects throughout the *Are You Experienced?* album, a prime example is "Third Stone from the Sun." It is similar in concept to "Feedback" on the *Live/Dead* album.

Hendrix's finest album was his third album, *Electric Ladyland*, released in August 1968. It became Hendrix's only number 1 album and contained "All Along the Watchtower," his only single hit. But beyond this, *Electric Ladyland* included several highly experimental works that expanded upon ideas encountered in earlier albums. For example, the album's first cut, "And the Gods Made Love," uses tape speed manipulation to create a successful, though brief, electronic composition. "Voodoo Chile" contains excellent playing by drummer Mitchell, guest organist Stevie Winwood, and Hendrix. The bluesy vocal shows the full range of Hendrix's voice, from a Dylanesque style to a full shouting style.

There are many delights on *Electric Ladyland*. There is an interesting thread of unity running through the double album, as several songs are begun on one side and returned to on a later side. For example, the album ends with "Voodoo Child (Slight Return)," which is related to the earlier "Voodoo Chile." Also, "Rainy Day, Dream Away" begins on side 3 as a gentle rock song with a hint of jazz feeling; it seems to be interrupted, only to return on side 4 as "Still Raining, Still Dreaming," this time with a harder rock feeling. One can hear an old-fashioned twelve-bar blues on "Come On (Part I)," and Hendrix's infinite modifications of guitar timbres on "Gypsy Eyes." Although others were experimenting with some of the same effects, rarely were such effects integrated as successfully into the fabric of the accompaniment as they are in "Burning of the Midnight Lamp."

But if you can only listen to one cut on *Electric Ladyland*, listen to "1983" (which imperceptibly flows into "Moon, Turn the Tides"). This long song shows all sides of Hendrix's art. There are fine solos by drummer Mitchell and bassist Redding;

Jimi Hendrix (*Source:* Michael Ochs Archive, Ltd.)

tasteful use of the flute (played by Chris Wood) adds to the ethereal timbre. There are moments of driving rock, countered by peaceful moments of nicely refined electronic effects; echo is added just when needed for maximum effect. Overall, it is a classic.

*Electric Ladyland* shows that Hendrix was well ahead of his time and was a far more creative musician than his reputation as being a flamboyant, drug-influenced, sexually explicit performer would suggest. Indeed, Hendrix himself began to feel that his stage antics were cheapening his act and detracting from his more serious musical abilities. He began to resent his fans' expectations of him; but as he attempted to play it "straight," many fans were dissatisfied, apparently being more impressed by theatrics than by music. Hendrix disbanded the Experience in 1969 and retreated to upstate New York (more shades of Dylan?). However, he did appear at Woodstock, providing a spectacular version of "The Star-Spangled Banner." On New Year's Eve 1969–70, he and his new band, the Band of Gypsys (including bassist Billy Cox and drummer Buddy Miles), appeared at the Fillmore East. This group lasted only a short while, and Hendrix seemed uncertain of his future direction.

He opened his own studio, Electric Ladyland, in New York during 1969 and began recording his next album. There were problems, however; one came in early 1970 at Madison Square Garden, where Hendrix simply stopped playing in the middle of a set; he wandered offstage, apparently lost in his own mind.

They say things happen in threes. Certainly the rock world was shaken by three tragedies within ten months of one another. The three "J's" Jimi, Janis, and Jim— all died between September 18, 1970, and July 3, 1971, all at the age of twenty-seven. Hendrix died in London from inhalation of vomit resulting from barbiturate intoxication. There was insufficient evidence to determine whether his taking an overdose of sleeping pills was accidental or intentional. An autopsy revealed eighteen times the recommended dosage of Vesparax, plus tranquilizers, amphetamines, depressants, and alcohol.

When listening to Hendrix, the contemporary listener may be tempted to say, "Hey, what's the big deal? I've heard lots of recent guitarists who do all that stuff and more!" But that is exactly the point. Hendrix set new styles, new ways of making music with his instrument. Granted, many have followed in his path; and some have built upon his style, taking it even further. But without Hendrix, the others may never have happened.

Hendrix has become almost deified by later rock enthusiasts, especially guitarists. Although he belongs with the somewhat dated psychedelic or acid rock era, he is an important link in a line that runs from the 1950s mainstream rockers to the Stones and their followers, through Hendrix and the other acid rockers, and on into the harder rock and heavy metal of the 1970s and 1980s. Regrettably, some (not all) of the later bands grasped only the superficial and most accessible of Hendrix's developments and left the more subtle and refined elements unused. According to John Morthland, "The Seventies heavy metal bands, with their emphasis on volume, monolithic riffs and droning guitars, owe something to Hendrix, but none have shown even a small fraction of either his finesse or imagination" (Miller 1980, 302).

*MUSICAL CLOSE-UP:*
*THE ART OF IMPROVISATION*

We have referred to the concept of musical improvisation at various times throughout this book. Especially with some of the British blues-based bands (e.g., the Yardbirds) and the San Francisco bands (e.g., the Grateful Dead), and of course with Hendrix, we have encountered styles of rock in which improvisation is a central element. Instrumental improvisation was to become an important factor in most rock styles from the 1970s on. Therefore, we should take a closer look at the practice of musical improvisation.

The dictionary tells us that to improvise is "to compose, or simultaneously compose and perform, on the spur of the moment and without any preparation."* Essentially this means that a musician is improvising anytime he or she makes up something to play on the spot or spontaneously adds to or changes what was previously written or planned. Taken literally, this can mean anything from the most minute change all the way to an entire piece that is made up on the spot. Thus, improvisation is a continuum, running from a one-note (or one-rhythm) change to total freedom:

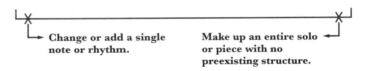

**Change or add a single**     **Make up an entire solo**
**note or rhythm.**             **or piece with no**
                                    **preexisting structure.**

### The Improvisation Continuum

In the classical music tradition, the performer strives to reproduce as faithfully as possible the exact notes and rhythms written by the composer. Even in classical music, however, performers sometimes add their own dynamics, phrasings, and tempo variations; these types of changes, which are usually preplanned, are considered interpretations rather than improvisations. Incidentally, there are some classical styles that call for real improvisation (e.g., certain music from the baroque and early classical periods, as well as some twentieth-century styles). Nevertheless, it has been the popular music traditions that have relied most heavily upon improvisation. Gospel, C & W, rock, and every subcategory of jazz lie somewhere along our improvisational continuum. C & W, for example, has been relatively conservative; it would lie somewhere on the left end of the continuum.

On the other hand, jazz has been the most adventuresome style where improvisation is concerned. Especially since the mid-1940s, there has been an increasing emphasis on freer improvisation in jazz. This trend reached its ultimate in the 1960s, when some jazz performers experimented with "free jazz." In this style, there was almost no preplanning; performers simply played whatever came to mind

*Webster's *New World Dictionary*, second college ed. (New York: Simon and Schuster, 1984).

at the moment, with little regard for traditional structure or even what the other players were playing. This style comes very close to the right extreme of our improvisational continuum.

For the first ten years of rock and roll's history, improvisation certainly existed, but it was rather conservative. Because many of the players could not read music, the songs and arrangements were made up in their heads. Once set, there was an attempt to perform the song more or less the same way each time. Inevitably, no two performances would ever be exactly the same; performers could make small internal changes with each performance. Thus, there was improvisation, but it was rather limited. When one thinks of early rock-and-roll improvisation, one thinks of Chuck Berry, Little Richard, and Jerry Lee Lewis. The least improvisational early rock styles were the soft rock styles and, of course, Motown. But once more, we must stress that even these were, to some extent, improvisational.

However, it is with some of the British blues-based bands, such as the Yardbirds, and the psychedelic rock bands, such as the Dead, that rock improvisation crosses over the imaginary center point on our continuum. When Eric Clapton took off on one of his thirty-minute "rave-ups," rock approached the level of improvisation known in jazz since the early 1940s. When the Dead performed one of their thirty-minute pieces without benefit of a previously agreed-upon structure, they moved to a new level of rock improvisation. On *Electric Ladyland*, we hear Jimi Hendrix moving ever closer to the right side of the improvisational continuum, at times approaching the rock equivalent of free jazz. As we move further into the 1970s with jazz rock, art rock, and heavy metal, we will be dealing more and more with the concept of improvisation.

One by-product of this increasing emphasis on improvisation is the enhanced status of the instrumentalist. Prior to the mid-1960s, *the* rock-and-roll star was the singer; instrumentalists were usually considered the necessary accompanimental baggage. Even with Berry, Little Richard, and Lewis, we tend to think first of their singing "Johnny B. Goode," "Tutti Frutti," and "Great Balls of Fire." Frankly, it is difficult to name many rock stars prior to 1965 whose reputation was built on playing rather than singing. However, since the mid-1960s, the skillful instrumental improviser has gradually ascended to the level of the rock singer (still not as frequently, of course). One rather quickly thinks of guitarists such as Clapton, Hendrix, Jeff Beck, John McLaughlin, Pete Townshend, and Eddie Van Halen; or keyboardists such as Keith Emerson and Rick Wakeman; and even drummers such as Carl Palmer, Billy Cobham, and Danny Seraphine. Certainly the rock singer still dominates the scene, but at least the truly gifted instrumentalist can now hope to receive appropriate recognition and not necessarily be condemned to a place just behind the spotlight.

This musical close-up is entitled "The Art of Improvisation." Improvisation is truly an art; like most arts, it involves some rather indefinable elements (sometimes called "inspiration" or "intuition"), as well as some relatively scientific, objective elements. In some ways, improvisation is the ultimate musical expression, because it combines the skills of both the performer and the composer. The improviser must think (or feel) what to play and then play it, all within a split second. It is a difficult thing to do and a difficult thing to teach. Like any other skill, one can learn the objective rudiments of the skill but not be able to add the intuitive element.

So what are the rudiments of improvisation? What do good improvisers (rock, jazz, or whatever) need to know and what are they doing when they improvise? First, they must have total technical mastery of their instrument (and this can include voice, by the way). It does no good whatsoever to have the greatest musical inspiration of all time and then not be able to play it.

Second, the improviser must have an absolutely solid feeling for rhythm. Rhythm must be internalized; that is, the improviser needs to be able to feel the rhythm inside and automatically. If he or she must count the rhythm or think what part of the measure is happening (i.e., what beat he or she is on), the improvisation is doomed.

Third, the improviser must thoroughly understand chords and scales—that is, the way musical pitches are organized vertically and horizontally. These two terms— *vertical* and *horizontal*—may be a bit confusing to the nonmusician. Vertical organization refers to musical sounds that occur simultaneously—that is, chords (see below).

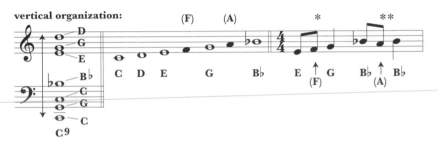

The chord shown above happens all at once; it contains five different pitches (C-D-E-G-B♭). If the improviser is thinking vertically, he or she automatically knows that those five notes will "work" in whatever line is improvised. The "in-between" notes (F and A) can work too; for example, they could be used as "passing" notes between two chord tones (*) or as a "neighbor" to a chord tone (**).

Horizontal organization refers to a musical line, such as a melody, that unfolds note by note in time. Scales organize musical pitch material in a horizontal way.

Thus, if an improviser knows that the collection of pitches shown in measure 1 is the scale used for a certain song, he or she is fairly safe creating an improvisational line using those pitches (such as the line in measure 2). Even so, the improviser needs to be thinking vertically and rhythmically, because *how* those notes are placed within the measure can determine whether they sound "right" against the prevailing chord.

Styles in improvisation change just like everything else. In some styles, vertical thinking predominated; players primarily thought in terms of chords and shaped improvisational lines to fit chords. More recently, players have leaned toward the horizontal (or "linear") approach, thus allowing the scale and melodic line to take precedence over the chord. The latter approach often leads to a more dissonant sound, because the horizontally conceived line may take the player outside of the notes of the prevailing chord.

It is really a rather amazing process. The effective improviser must unerringly feel the rhythm, know the chord progression (vertical thinking) and the appropriate scale (horizontal thinking), dream up something interesting that "fits," and then be able to play it, all instantaneously. But there is still one more complication. The improviser should not just be thinking note to note, beat to beat, and chord to chord. The best improvisers also have some overall idea about the shape of their total solo. Is it to be a structured length (e.g., sixteen bars or thirty-two bars), or is it open-ended ("nod when you are through")? Knowing that, what does one do within that time frame? One can start on low pitches, move to higher pitches, and then end low; or one can start low and gradually move upward toward the end in a straight line; or one can envision a series of peaks. What about dynamics? Does one start softly and build volume to the end, or start loudly, get softer in the middle, and then build to a big finish? Then there are considerations of rhythmic activity. One can begin with sparse rhythmic activity (just a few notes per bar) and build to a flurry of notes at the end, or begin with a burst, calm down in the middle, and end with another burst. There are all sorts of possibilities within each parameter, and when one combines all of the possibilities, the options are almost limitless. Sometimes a player will take one short musical idea (called a motive) and work over and over with that one motive, playing it on different pitches as the chords change, fragmenting it, extending it, changing its rhythm or accents, or even inverting it (changing the direction of the notes).

Shaping one's improvisation is as important as playing the right scale or chord or rhythm. Nothing is worse than a solo that "goes nowhere"—one that aimlessly wanders from beginning to end with a lot of meaningless notes in between.

Far too many rock fans "tune in" to the singer and the lyrics and "tune out" during the instrumental break. It is as though the instrumentalists are just playing to fill space between the vocals. In a good band, some of the most exciting music happens not during the vocals but during the instrumental improvisation. Begin to pay careful attention to such solos. Is the player "on" rhythmically? Is the soloist really in harmony with the chords the others are playing? Or if the solo seems to be dissonant at times, is it intentional ("outside" playing) or unintentional (mistakes)? Can you hear motives being developed (sequenced, fragmented, inverted, repeated, etc.)? And is there direction to the solo or is the player just playing notes? Improvisation is an art. It is difficult, but it is also fun. Most players live for their creative moment in the spotlight—their solo. Perhaps you now have a better idea of what goes into a really good improvisation. Perceptive listening is almost as difficult as good improvising. It takes practice. But if you try, you will be surprised at how rewarding it is to really appreciate a great improvisation.

# 11

# Jazz Rock

## OVERVIEW: A TALE OF SIBLING RIVALRY AND ITS RESOLUTION

Imagine a small family consisting of a mother, a father, and a teenager named Fred. Fred has been the pride and joy of his family for some thirteen years. He has had all of the attention and love of his parents lavished upon him. He has grown through all of the stages of childhood and is now quite a sophisticated, intelligent, and "cool" kid.

Then one day a newcomer appears on the scene: a cute, cuddly, baby sister. Suddenly Fred is no longer the center of attention. In fact, it seems as though he has been forgotten altogether. Everyone devotes more time and attention to baby Susie. Dad busily records Susie's first steps, first words, first everything on miles of videotape. It is not hard to imagine a rather ample supply of jealousy and resentment on Fred's part. After all, this gurgling little brat does not have one tenth of Fred's intelligence, sophistication, or coolness!

Yet some years later, perhaps because Fred and Susie both come from the same roots, they find that they have much in common. In fact, as they become young adults, they find that they have much to share with each other.

No analogy is perfect, but Fred and Susie are a lot like jazz and rock. Both jazz and rock have a similar black parentage. Jazz is half a century older than rock but went through the same growing pains. By the time rock was born, jazz had become a quite sophisticated style of music. Baby rock and roll was starting all over again, with twelve-bar blues, simple and basic rhythms, and illiterate musicians. Yet it was getting all of the attention, shoving jazz off the radio and out of the record stores.

The typical jazz player of the mid-1950s resented rock for two basic reasons—one musical and one financial. First, compared with jazz, rock was a musical infant.

242

Jazz players were often superb technicians on their instruments; most early rock players could barely play three chords. Jazz rhythms, harmonic structures, improvisations, and forms had evolved to a high level of sophistication; rock was basic, simple, and musically mundane. The jazzman had every right to look condescendingly down his musical nose. But to add insult to injury, rock and roll was lifting money right out of the jazzman's pocket. More and more, the jobs at the schools, the country clubs, and the recording studios went to youngsters who could play what was selling: rock and roll.

Conversely, the rockers had no interest in jazz. It was "old people's music." Rock was easier and more fun to play and listen to; besides, it was the big moneymaker. And so the two siblings split. Each was disparaging of the other. It would be some years later that they would find a mutual alliance.

By the late 1960s, a new, young generation of musicians was hitting the scene. Typically they had been born in the mid- to late 1940s. By the time they became a part of the professional music world, rock was no longer some "new kid on the block," to be accepted or rejected; it was just there. They had grown up with rock. However, for the best of these musicians, rock was sometimes boring and musically confining. Their musical appetites yearned for new, more challenging sounds and more sophisticated demands, yet still in a style closely related to rock. The answer: Blend the best of jazz and rock.

Beginning around 1966, several bands appeared with the intent of mixing rock with an older blues band style that included horns. Examples of such bands were the Blues Project, the Paul Butterfield Blues Band, and the Barry Goldberg Blues Band. Typically, these bands added a "horn line" (trumpets and saxes) that played riffs, patterns, and interludes drawn from the style of black bands from the 1940s and 1950s. These early bands were the progenitors of the jazz rock style.

In their third album, *Resurrection of Pigboy Crabshaw* (1967), the Butterfield Blues Band included horns (trumpets and saxes). One member of the Butterfield band, guitarist Mike Bloomfield, went on to the Electric Flag, another early model of the jazz rock band. The Electric Flag had evolved from the earlier Barry Goldberg band and consisted of Goldberg, Bloomfield, drummer Buddy Miles, and a changing membership that totaled between eight and ten players, including three horns. The Flag lasted only a year and a half. Their first album, *A Long Time Comin'* (1968), gives a good idea of their style. If you can find it, listen to "Killing Floor" from that album. It is a twelve-bar blues and illustrates how the horns were integrated into the fabric of the song.

Of more long-lasting importance was the Blues Project. It came originally out of the folk music scene in Greenwich Village. As was the rage in 1965, the band turned electric and played the new folk rock sound. But they also played an electrified blues style. The membership vacillated from the beginning in 1965 through 1968, while they released several moderately successful albums. Along with the usual instrumentation, the Project included flute and saxophone. As it became apparent that the group was dissolving, two of its members, Al Kooper and Steve Katz, recruited two colleagues from a recent Café au Go Go (New York City) jam session—drummer Bobby Colomby and bassist Jim Fielder—and formed a new band. They added four horn players and called their new band Blood, Sweat, and Tears.

## BLOOD, SWEAT, AND TEARS

Al Kooper was no newcomer to the music business. He was from Brooklyn (born in 1944) and had been around music most of his life. At thirteen, he had been a member of the Royal Teens when they recorded the novelty hit "Short Shorts" (number 3 in 1958). He reemerged as coauthor of a number 1 song in early 1965, "This Diamond Ring," recorded by Gary Lewis and the Playboys. Kooper sang and played keyboards; he recorded in the mid-1960s with Dylan and in the later 1960s with Moby Grape, Tom Rush, and in a "super session" with Mike Bloomfield and Stephen Stills.

Kooper and Katz's first recruit was drummer Bobby Colomby (born in New York City in December 1944). He was raised in a family of jazz aficionados and from the age of fifteen played both jazz and rock drums. Jim Fielder was born in Denton, Texas (1947), but grew up in southern California. He played briefly with the Mothers of Invention and the Buffalo Springfield before joining Blood, Sweat, and Tears.

For the horn line, the first recruit was Fred Lipsius who, in addition to alto sax and clarinet, played piano and arranged. The native New Yorker (born in 1943) had studied at Boston's Berklee College of Music before joining a Canadian big band for a year. When the call came from Bobby Colomby to join the jazz rock fusion experiment, Fred was studying classical music and arranging. He helped recruit the balance of the horn section. Dick Halligan was hired as a trombone player but later proved invaluable on flute, keyboards, and as an arranger. Dick was born in Troy, New York (1943), and had earned a master of arts degree from the Manhattan School of Music; his orientation was more toward classical and jazz styles, but he too was fascinated by Kooper's experimental concept. Randy Brecker and Jerry Weiss, both trumpeters, rounded out the original eight-man lineup.

Appearing at the Café au Go Go in Greenwich Village, the new Blood, Sweat, and Tears met with immediate critical and popular approval around New York City. Their first album, *Child Is Father to the Man* (1968), had moments of brilliance that foreshadowed subsequent sounds; but it was an uneven album, revealing the tensions already present between those in the band who favored rock and those who leaned more toward jazz. The "Overture" that opens the album is a pseudoclassical arrangement, including a few tunes from the balance of the album, all "accompanied" by incongruous laughter. "I Love You More than You'll Ever Know" presents a rather bluesy Kooper vocal; it contrasts strongly with a bossa nova jazz arrangement of Harry Nilsson's "Without Her." Two of the album's better cuts are Kooper's "My Days Are Numbered" and Randy Newman's "Just One Smile." Near the end of the latter song, the band breaks into a genuine polyphonic texture that nicely offsets the melody-and-accompaniment texture of the balance of the song. More bluesy singing by Kooper may be heard in "Somethin's Goin' On" (also some fine "dirty" sax work by Lipsius). The strains of the "Overture" are heard at the end of the album, now titled "Underture."

B, S, & T's first album rose to number 47 on the album charts and contained no Top 40 single hits. The tensions within the group culminated in Kooper's, Brecker's, and Weiss's departure. The rest of the band decided to try again. To replace Weiss and Brecker, Lew Soloff and Chuck Winfield were added. Soloff, born in Brooklyn in 1944, had earned his bachelor's degree from the Eastman School of Music in

Blood, Sweat, and Tears (*Source:* Michael Ochs Archive, Ltd.)

Rochester, New York. Chuck Winfield (born in Monessen, Pennsylvania, in 1943) had received his bachelor's and master's degrees from the Juilliard School of Music in New York City. Both trumpeters were steeped in classical background. To replace Kooper, Dick Halligan moved to keyboards (his position on trombone being taken by new member Jerry Hyman); that left only the significant problem of a lead singer. Numerous singers were auditioned until Colomby and Katz remembered David Clayton-Thomas, a Canadian singer who had sung in New York with a group called the Bossmen, a blues-oriented group that had earned five gold records in Canada over a ten-year period. Clayton-Thomas joined the new nine-man Blood, Sweat, and Tears lineup in 1968, and they started recording their next album.

*Blood, Sweat, and Tears* exploded to the number 1 position in early 1969. Three hits came from the album: "You've Made Me So Very Happy," "And When I Die," and "Spinning Wheel"—all reaching the number 2 position. B, S, & T received an unprecedented ten Grammy nominations, eventually winning three awards.

"Spinning Wheel," by Clayton-Thomas, the album's biggest hit, reveals a bit of what jazz rock was about. It begins with a distinctive jazz chord (an augmented ninth chord). Out of that chord comes a gentle rock song; but at the instrumental break, the rock beat gives way to a jazz beat, complete with a jazz "walking bass" and Lew Soloff's jazz-style solo. The rock beat returns as Clayton-Thomas reenters. The song fades on a curious calliopelike sound over an accompanying vamp that alternates 9/8 and 6/8 meters.

Perhaps the most revealing cut on the album is the lengthy "Blues—Part II," essentially an "introduction" to the band, featuring solos by various members. Halligan's solo is an impressive working out of a motive stated at the outset: a series of rising perfect fourths (an interval created by playing a note, such as C, then skipping two notes [D and E], and then playing the next note [F]). He develops the motive by transposing it, fragmenting it, extending it, and inverting it. Near the end of his solo, Halligan builds a chord from a series of perfect fourths and makes a rhythmic vamp out of the chord. The band joins him briefly before Jim Fielder enters with a jazzy bass solo. Colomby solos next—a clean, technically impressive solo. After a brief "comment" by the band, Fielder sets up a rock bass line over which Lipsius sets a jazzlike sax solo. Next, Fielder initiates a familiar rock bass line, one that was used by various other groups, including Cream and Iron Butterfly. As the full band harmonizes this bass line, Lipsius changes to a rock sax solo. Finally, it is Clayton-Thomas's turn. He enters in a relaxed, cavalier style, making the subsequent rise to a big finish even more effective. Accompanied by a steadily rising pattern that begins in the bass and organ but is eventually doubled by trumpets, Clayton-Thomas gradually heightens his vocal emotionality, ending in a pure shouting style. "Blues—Part II" is a real musical journey, with a collection of extremely talented musicians as tour guides.

Odd meters (five beats, seven beats, etc.) and changing meters had been a part of jazz since the 1950s. Except for a few experiments by the Beatles and the Byrds, such metric experiments had not become common in rock. However, jazz rock groups were inclined toward such metric deviations. Steve Katz's "Sometimes in Winter" is basically in quadruple meter. But at the bridge section, the meter changes to 9/8 (in effect doubling the speed of the beat and making nine beats per measure), then back to quadruple, then again back to 9/8, followed by a measure of triple meter (3/4) before finally returning to 4/4. The horns join in a brief chorale at this point, accompanied by a running bass line; the chorale ends in a five-beat measure on another jazz harmony (a major ninth chord with a lowered fifth).

All in all, *Blood, Sweat, and Tears* is an exceptionally strong album. But as we saw with another blended style, folk rock, "purists will be purists." Some hard rockers felt that the jazz rock fusion was too cerebral, too tight, and too sophisticated to be "real" rock. However, B, S, & T opened up a whole new audience for rock. Jazz fans and some of the more open-minded classical listeners could find music to respect and enjoy in B, S, & T. Those rock fans who were willing to listen (fortunately record sales suggest there were many) discovered that they could enjoy a well-played, technically more sophisticated style of rock.

In late 1969, B, S, & T undertook a major tour that included fifty-five performances in nearly every major U.S. city, and many colleges and universities. One of their final performances was at the Fillmore East in New York City. Also among the dates on this tour was a precedent-setting engagement at Caesar's Palace on the Las Vegas "strip." The big Vegas hotels had avoided rock acts until earlier in 1969, when the International Hotel had booked Elvis Presley. B, S, & T's three-day engagement at Caesar's Palace broke the house attendance record set by Frank Sinatra. But the hard-core rock counterculture was aghast that a rock band would stoop to play to such an overtly "upper-crust" audience (the Beatles' 1963 Royal Command Performance had apparently slipped their minds). The reaction reveals that these "rock fans" were not really viewing rock as music but as a sociocultural symbol. As Clayton-Thomas put it, "We didn't change our show for them [the Las Vegas audience]. We're playing our music the same way. It's not diluted one bit from the early days at the Café au Go Go or the early days of the Fillmore East or West" (Wise 1971). Nevertheless, some of the same people who had applauded B, S, & T earlier now howled in derision, even though the music had not changed.

*Blood, Sweat, and Tears 3* (1970) revealed no lessening of quality from its predecessor. It yielded two more single hits, "Hi-De-Ho," by Gerry Goffin and Carole King, and "Lucretia MacEvil," by Clayton-Thomas. The latter is a strong rock piece flavored by jazz harmonies. It is followed by "Lucretia's Reprise," which begins with a jazz rock vamp based on the previous song's chord progression; Clayton-Thomas shouts a vocal improvisation before Lew Soloff enters with a particularly impressive trumpet solo. There is an effective version of James Taylor's "Fire and Rain" and a creative arrangement by Lipsius and Colomby of "Forty Thousand Headmen," a song composed by Traffic's Winwood and Capaldi. In the latter song, themes by classical composers Bartók ("Ballad" from *Fifteen Hungarian Peasant Songs*) and Prokofiev (*Lieutenant Kijé Suite*) and jazz pianist Thelonious Monk ("I Mean You") are artfully interwoven. Clayton-Thomas's vocal versatility is best shown in "Lonesome Suzie" as he covers the range from a soft, tender timbre to a full shouting style (including a falsetto). "Somethin' Comin' On" shows off Fred Lipsius in a fascinating sax solo; notice the effective transition to Halligan's organ solo.

But the masterpiece of *B, S, & T 3* is "Symphony for the Devil/Sympathy for the Devil," a stunningly creative arrangement of the Jagger–Richard song. This version ranks high among the finest achievements in rock music and will be the subject of the musical close-up at the end of this chapter.

There was one personnel change prior to *Blood, Sweat, and Tears 4* (1971); Jerry Hyman was replaced by Dave Bargeron, who played low brass instruments (trombone, bass trombone, tuba, baritone). Dave holds a degree in music education from Boston University. The hard-rocking "Go Down Gamblin'" was the only Top 40 hit from this album. Except for two songs, "John the Baptist (Holy John)," coauthored by Al Kooper, and "Take Me in Your Arms (Rock Me a Little While)," by the Isley Brothers, all songs on *B, S, & T 4* are originals by members of the band. A fun piece on the album is the Dixieland-oriented "Mama Gets High."

Ever since the late 1940s, jazz players had been extending the upper range of their horns. So of course the jazz–rock horn lines followed suit with upper-range playing. Note the trumpet break on "Go Down Gamblin'," for example, as the top note reaches above high C. But a particularly impressive example is Dave Bargeron's solo on "Redemption." Beginning a short motive near the bottom of the trombone range, he moves it up octave by octave until he reaches the upper end of the trumpet's range, reaching high C above the treble clef. Granted, it is virtually a "squeal," but it is typical of jazz players' fascination with brass upper range.

As we discovered with more creative groups, such as the Beach Boys, the Beatles, and the Byrds, there are often small creative ideas worked into songs with such subtlety that one hardly notices. For example, on "Lisa, Listen to Me," as the instrumental break ends, Clayton-Thomas returns to the chorus. But as he sings the vocal line, the horn line imitates what he sings two beats later; the result is a brief but effective polyphony between the two lines. Why bother with this sort of added complexity? B, S, & T could have simply used the same accompaniment they had used on the first two choruses. But that is the creative mind at work: "This time, let's do it differently."

The bottom fell out beginning in 1971. Clayton-Thomas left in hopes of establishing a solo career. Having little success, he returned to the band in the mid-1970s, but by then it was too late. Lipsius and Halligan, the band's most talented arrangers, also left, and by 1973, Katz and Winfield also departed. Through the 1970s there were several lead singers and a dizzying number of changes of instrumental personnel. The band swung like a pendulum between a more progressive jazz style and a heavier rock style. Album sales plummeted; the group's identity was gone. To be sure, there are some fine moments on some of their 1970s albums, but the "magic" of *B, S, & T 2, 3,* and *4* was gone.

## CHICAGO

One of the awards given to Blood, Sweat, and Tears as a result of its second album was *Billboard*'s Trendsetter Award for 1970. It was an appropriate award, for B, S, & T did indeed represent a concept that, in a variety of formats, persisted through the 1970s and on into the 1980s. In the beginning, most jazz rock bands were simply variations on the B, S, & T format. But one of these groups proved to have staying power long after B, S, & T and the others had fallen by the wayside. Chicago's continuing popularity is matched only by a handful of performers in the history of rock. They had at least one Top 40 hit every year in the 1970s and eight hit singles in the 1980s. By 2000, Chicago could claim eighteen gold albums and thirteen platinum albums; from those albums came twenty Top 10 singles, including five that reached number 1. Few rock groups can claim that kind of success for over three decades.

The seven founding members of Chicago were all from the Windy City except for Robert Lamm, who moved there as a teenager. All were born between 1944 and 1948 and were close friends when they formed their first group in 1967, the Missing Links (later the Big Thing), and began playing in clubs throughout the Midwest. A college friend, James William Guercio, had moved to Los Angeles, where he was associated with Columbia Records as a record producer. Following his successful work with B, S, & T, he summoned his old friends to Los Angeles. They became the house band at the Whisky-à-Go-Go and signed a Columbia contract under their new name, Chicago Transit Authority. The original CTA lineup included Lamm on keyboards, Peter Cetera on bass, Terry Kath on guitar, and Danny Seraphine on drums; the horn line consisted of Lee Loughnane on trumpet, James Pankow on trombone, and Walter Parazaider on flute and saxophones. Cetera, Kath, and Lamm alternated as lead singers.

Columbia released *Chicago Transit Authority* in the spring of 1969. Several songs ("Questions 67 and 68," "Beginnings," and "Does Anybody Really Know What Time It Is?") were not immediate successes, but made the Top 30 later (1971).

*Chicago Transit Authority* is a double album (unusual for a first album). The opening cut, "Introduction," is similar in concept to "Blues—Part II," by B, S, & T. Beginning with a strong vocal and instrumental ensemble, it moves to a rapid-fire series of changing meters:

$$\left|\frac{4}{4}\left|\frac{6}{8}\right|\frac{7}{8}\right|\frac{6}{8}\left|\frac{6}{8}\right|\frac{7}{8}\left|\frac{6}{8}\right|\frac{6}{8}\left|\frac{7}{8}\right|\frac{6}{8}\left|\frac{3}{4}\right|$$

Not only is the tempo fast, but the 6/8 measures alternate between a feeling of 3 + 3 and 2 + 2 + 2, further obscuring the meter. The original key of G minor is lost as a series of sequences moves through several implied keys before finally settling back into G minor for a trombone solo by Pankow. Loughnane follows with a trumpet solo in G major, complete with jazz-oriented harmonies. A guitar solo brings back both G minor and the rock feeling; the horn line returns to lead to the closing vocal. No "blended" form can ever hit directly in the middle between two styles. B, S, & T probably landed slightly to the jazz side of jazz rock, whereas Chicago lay more to the rock side.

When Chicago Mayor Richard Daley initiated a lawsuit, the band was forced to shorten its name to Chicago. *Chicago II* was released in early 1970 and contained two Top 10 singles, "Make Me Smile" and "25 or 6 to 4." "Colour My World," a plaintively beautiful and simple song featuring a flute solo by Parazaider, was released later on the flip side of "Beginnings" and became popular in its own right (number 7 in 1971). *Chicago III* (early 1971) was the third consecutive double album; it rose to number 2 and contained the hit singles "Free" and "Lowdown."

*Chicago IV* (number 3 in late 1971) was a four-record boxed set containing live recordings from the band's concert at Carnegie Hall. What followed was an amazing string of five consecutive number 1 albums, beginning in 1972 with *Chicago V* and going through 1975 with *Chicago IX*, a greatest hits album. Only the Beatles, Elton John, and Paul McCartney have matched or exceeded that winning streak in the history of rock. All told, *Chicago V* through *VIII* contained nine Top 30 hits, including six in the Top 10. During this period the band's sound was very consistent. The only personnel change was one addition, Brazilian percussionist Laudir de Oliveira in 1974 (on *Chicago VII* and subsequent albums).

Perhaps the most interesting album is *Chicago VII* because it diverges from the typical Chicago sound. For the first time there were "outsiders" on a Chicago album.

Chicago, rock group (*Source:* Michael Ochs Archive, Ltd.)

Appearing on this album were producer Guercio (acoustic guitar and bass), the Pointer Sisters, and Beach Boys Carl and Dennis Wilson and Al Jardine. The album also explores (lightly) electronic keyboards, including the ARP synthesizer and the Mellotron. The different sounds of *Chicago VII* are heard immediately on side 1. "Prelude to Aire" begins with bongos and tom-toms; Parazaider's rhythmically complex solo is accompanied by increasingly sophisticated cross-rhythms in percussion and the sounds of a Mellotron. "Aire" features the more typical Chicago horn line, but in a fast 7/8 meter, complete with syncopations; at the guitar solo, the meter changes to 7/4 (half as fast as 7/8). The song ends with complicated ensemble patterns back in 7/8. "Devil's Sweet" opens with soprano sax improvisations over chords built in perfect fourths. After some rather ethereal sounds on percussion, there is a lovely duet for flügelhorn and soprano sax. The meter is 6/8 and is full of syncopation. A delicate solo on drums, using wire brushes, provides a transition to the next section, written in duple meter (the 2/4 is reinforced by Seraphine) but with its bass line and horn ensemble in triple meter (3/4). Finally, a somewhat more normal rock sound emerges featuring guitar and synthesizer; a drum solo leads back to the earlier soprano sax improvisations and the opening soprano sax–flügelhorn duet. All in all, side 1 of *Chicago VII* is the most adventurous and complex music on any of the Chicago albums.

In Chapter 14, "The Continuing Fragmentation of Rock," we will see that by the mid-1970s jazz rock fusion had entered a new phase. The style associated with B, S, & T and earlier Chicago was "out"; a newer style featuring more adventurous jazz influences was "in." On side 1 of *Chicago VII*, the band seems to be experimenting with the more contemporary style. On subsequent albums, they returned to their more familiar sound.

Side 2 continues the experimentation of side 1. "Italian from New York" begins with bongos and ARP synthesizer (set in a sequencer pattern); chords built in fourths are set into an accompanying vamp, with five beats per measure. "Hanky Panky," after a syncopated introduction, settles into a pure jazz trombone solo by Pankow. The album begins to return somewhat closer to normalcy with "Lifesaver"; it has a pounding piano beat (in 4/4 meter) and more typical Chicago horn lines. It also provides the album's first vocals. The true Chicago fan must have breathed a massive sigh of relief as the last cut on side 2, "Happy Man," began. Pete Cetera's vocal over a bossa nova-style beat is a far cry from hard rock, but at least it approached the more familiar Chicago style.

Sides 3 and 4 of *Chicago VII* settle down to the more familiar Chicago sound. "(I've Been) Searchin' So Long" is one of Chicago's best songs, starting calmly but building to a big finish with Cetera's shouting vocal improvisations, active string lines, powerful bass lines, and high brass. "Mongonucleosis" is a strong Latin rock piece that may remind us of Buffalo Springfield songs like "Uno Mundo" and, of course, Santana. "Wishing You Were Here" is a beautiful song, profiting from the instantly recognizable Beach Boys harmonies. "Call on Me" is absolutely dead center typical Chicago in every way (it was the biggest hit on this album).

*Chicago VII* is a strong album; whatever the Chicago fan likes, it can be found somewhere on this album. The album reveals the real versatility, creativity, and technical mastery of this band.

The members of the band had been close friends since their early school days; they were like a family. It was a particularly painful shock, then, when Terry Kath accidentally shot himself in January 1978 (he was thirty-one years old); he was replaced by Donnie Dacus.

There was a momentary dip in Chicago's popularity at the turn of the decade. *Chicago XIV* and *XV* (a greatest hits album) failed to make the Top 30. But with *Chicago 16*, the band regained its former strength with "Hard to Say I'm Sorry," which became a number 1 single (their only previous number 1 hit had been "If You Leave Me Now" from *Chicago X*). The albums *Chicago 17* and *18* (1984 and 1986, respectively) sustained the group's popularity and moved away from the jazz rock style toward a purer mainstream rock style.

Probably a central reason for Chicago's remarkable longevity was the stability of its personnel. Six of the original seven members were still with the band as of 1986; although there had been additions and "guest artists" (e.g., Beach Boys, Pointer Sisters, and Maynard Ferguson), the basic nucleus remained intact. Of all of the jazz rock bands of the late 1960s to early 1970s, Chicago alone survived into the 1990s, with four of the original members still performing. Albums such as *Night and Day* (1995), *The Heart of Chicago* (1997), and *Chicago 25* (1998) were moderately successful.

## OTHER JAZZ ROCK GROUPS

Following in the footsteps of B, S, & T and Chicago were many bands that combined basic rock instrumentation with horn lines of varying descriptions. Some achieved impressive musical results, but most failed to achieve significant commercial success. One that did find its way onto the charts was Chase. Bill Chase had played lead trumpet with Woody Herman's big band for a few years before organizing his own jazz rock band. The nine-man band, Chase, took a slightly different approach to the typical jazz rock horn line: it consisted of four trumpets. This emphasis on trumpets—especially in the high range—gave Chase a distinctive sound. Their first album, *Chase*, was released in 1971 and yielded the hit single "Get It On," a hard-rocking tune in the best B, S, & T and Chicago tradition. On another of this album's songs, "Reflections," Chase used a tape delay echo effect on his trumpet solo; the delay was such that he ended up playing a duet with himself.

By the time of their third album, *Pure Music* (1974), the band contained only one original member—Bill Chase himself. The album moved to the more jazz-influenced jazz rock fusion of the mid-1970s; there was little of the strong rock feeling of some of the earlier Chase cuts. *Pure Music* was Chase's last album. On August 9, 1974, Chase and three other band members were killed in a plane crash.

Other bands to follow B, S, & T's and Chicago's lead were Dreams (which included original B, S, & T member Randy Brecker and his brother Mike), White Elephant (a seventeen-member band that also included both Breckers), and Symphonic Metamorphosis (a band made up of eight members of the Detroit Symphony).

By about 1972 the first phase of jazz rock was over (except, of course, for Chicago). But the jazz influence had added new concepts to rock and reinforced a few previous ideas. Jazz brought with it a set of more complex chords, odd meters, changing meters, and complex superimposed rhythms and syncopations. Although some more adventurous rock groups had already experimented with such devices, the jazz influx carried such techniques to new levels of complexity. The concept of the lengthy and complex instrumental improvisation had already been tried by Hendrix, the San Francisco bands, and some British blues-based groups. The jazz influence reinforced this concept and added new sophistication to it. Finally, most previous rock groups had considered horns representative of "old" music and, if used at all, were better reserved for background chords or intermittent punctuations. With jazz rock it became more evident that horns could take their place on the front lines with the lead guitar. Sometimes the jazz rock groups would move smoothly between a rock style and a jazz style; at other times, the rock beat and bass line would underlie a jazz-style solo.

In summary, the new jazz influence added still more musical ideas to the fabric of rock. Just as it had done with the folk and gospel influences earlier, rock absorbed new ideas and broadened as a style. Although such external influences are sometimes decried by rock "purists," one must remember that any style that refuses to assimilate the best of new ideas tends to become insular and stagnant. Rock's ability to integrate stylistic devices from coexisting sources is one of its strengths—and a primary reason why it continues to be a living, evolving, and dynamically vital style.

## MUSICAL CLOSE-UP:
### AN ANALYSIS OF "SYMPHONY FOR THE DEVIL/SYMPATHY FOR THE DEVIL" (BLOOD, SWEAT, AND TEARS)

In the musical close-up at the end of Chapter 7, "The British Invasion," we analyzed a song by the Rolling Stones called "Sympathy for the Devil." It is an effective rock song, but it is relatively simple musically. There were only four chords in the entire six-minute song; the form was simple and repetitive; there was little or no change in the meter, beat, or rhythmic texture; there were only a few changes in timbre and no key changes; the melody was simple and repetitive. This is not to say that the piece is "bad"; in fact, it is quite appropriate to the Stones' style and, as such, is very effective.

On *Blood, Sweat, and Tears 3* there is an "arrangement" of "Sympathy for the Devil" that so utterly transforms the original song that, for all practical purposes, a new composition has been created. Dick Halligan's arrangement in fact seems to require a new title—hence "Symphony for the Devil/Sympathy for the Devil." To help you understand what a talented arranger can do when he or she takes a rather simple song and transforms it into a creative landmark, we will undertake a rather thorough analysis of the B, S, & T version of "Sympathy." To do this, we must tolerate some rather technical material, but we will attempt to keep it understandable to the nonmusic theorist.

The B, S, & T version is nearly eight minutes long and is in three major sections, entitled "Emergence," "Devil's Game," and "Submergence." The Rolling Stones tune actually appears only in the "Devil's Game" section. "Emergence" and "Submergence," then, consist of entirely new material. The figure below shows a diagram of the overall form:

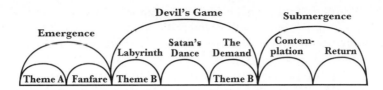

In "Emergence," we are presented with a musical theme that we shall call theme A. This twenty-note theme is shown below.

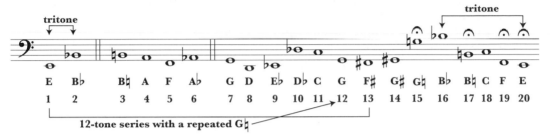

Theme A emerges from the dark, low range of the trombone, bass guitar, and piano (as if the Devil were hesitantly crawling out of some trap door from hell). First we hear notes 1 and 2 of theme A. These two notes are significant. The interval between E and B♭ (notes 1 and 2) is a tritone—that is, it consists of three whole steps. Because the tritone has some unique acoustic characteristics, it was nicknamed many centuries ago *diabolus in musica*—"the Devil in music." What better way to begin a song about the Devil than with the tritone.

After notes 1 and 2, theme A starts over, giving us notes 1 through 6; then it starts over again, this time rushing, with no regular beat, from note 1 to note 15. There is a pause before moving to notes 16 through 20 (with some more pauses). Theme A ends where it began, on E.

Throughout this century, some classical composers have sought to avoid key centers. One way to achieve this was to compose a series of pitches in which all twelve different notes were used with no repetition (thus avoiding emphasis on any one note). Once devised, this series of pitches was used over and over to generate the balance of the composition. Theme A has eleven different pitches before it repeats G (notes 7 and 12); the very next note (F♯) would be the twelfth different pitch. Thus, the first thirteen notes of theme A are like a twelve-note series with one repeated note; notes 14 to 20 are not composed by any "system," but are simply the result of Halligan's intuition. Interestingly, the highest note in theme A is B♭ from it, theme A descends to the final note, E—thus outlining another B♭ to E tritone.

After this darkly ominous presentation of theme A, the celesta plays a sequence that repeats notes 2 through 6 and ends on notes 7 and 8 (transposed to fit the last part of the sequence):

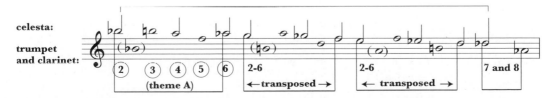

Notice that the celesta sequence is "accompanied" by accent notes at the beginning of each pattern (trumpets and clarinet); these notes are B♭, B♮, and A—notes 2 to 4 of theme A. Returning to the low register, the trombone, bass, piano, and trumpet finish theme A from notes 9 through 20 (untransposed). As the last note (E) is held in the bass, various pitches are added, creating a rather dissonant chord; but the pitches are not random; they are notes 1 through 8 of theme A.

As this chord releases, a series of four descending drumrolls enters. As they increase in volume, the Devil prepares to speak. A brass fanfare is appropriate, but not a "pretty" one. Instead, the brass play a brief but dissonant fanfare, the notes of which are drawn from theme A (notes 1 through 15).

Part 2, "Devil's Game," begins with a section called "Labyrinth." As the Devil introduces himself, we are introduced to theme B, the tune of the Rolling Stones' "Sympathy for the Devil." You may recall that there were six phrases in each chorus of the original song. "Labyrinth" begins with the first chorus, but instead of using the same accompaniment throughout, B, S, & T devised a slightly different accompaniment for each phrase:

Chorus I:
   Phrase 1: "Please allow me"—voice; guitar on first beat of each bar
   Phrase 2: "I've been around"—add piano (E) on third beat of each bar
   Phrase 3: "I was around"—add syncopated bass guitar
   Phrase 4: "Made damn sure"—add syncopated drum notes
   Phrase 5: "Pleased to meet you"—full beat and accompaniment
   Phrase 6: "what's confusing you"—suspend accompaniment in second bar

In the last two measures of the sixth phrase, an organ melody carries us into the second chorus. The notes of the organ melody are from theme A:

The second chorus is not set in the same way as the first chorus. For example, the phrase 1 accompaniment includes organ chords; phrase 2 adds brass chords, each of which starts softly and gets louder; and the bass line falls an octave as phrase 3 begins. As the second chorus ends, the horns provide a transition to the third chorus (where do these notes come from?):

Note the meter changes in this transition.

The third chorus is accompanied by an interesting interplay between the horn line and the electric guitar. The horns play a chord at the beginning of each measure; even though the chords descend within each phrase, the overall pattern rises from phrase to phrase. The guitar is also gradually working up to a high note near the end of the fourth phrase.

In phrase 5, between the words "guess my name" and "what's confusing you," notice the horn line (again from theme A):

Clayton-Thomas finishes the third chorus unaccompanied.

"Satan's Dance" is, in effect, an instrumental break midway through the piece. It consists of three internal sections: (1) a polyphonic section based on fragments of theme A, (2) a sax solo, and (3) a brief fugue on theme A. The opening polyphonic section begins with a five-note motive derived from theme A:

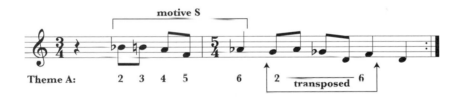

For ease of reference, we will call this motive (notes 2 through 6 of theme A) motive S (for "Sympathy"). After motive S is introduced, it generates a falling sequence that is imitated at a delay of one beat (by keyboards). Then the same thing is done again, but by two muted trumpets and trombone, creating a three-way descending imitative sequence. Next the piano plays a short interlude based on notes 12 through 15 of theme A:

This is followed by a rising sequence, again with imitation, accompanied by rising chords in the horns. At the top of this rising pattern, motive S returns. Finally, Halligan inverts motive S; that is, where the original motive goes up, the inverted motive goes down, and vice versa:

original motive S: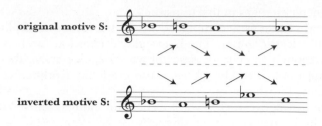

inverted motive S:

Using inverted motive S, Halligan creates another rising sequence, played in imitation (delayed by one beat) on keyboards. This leads to an improvised sax solo, which is accompanied by wild-sounding drums and dissonant brass chords. The horn players produce a series of squeals as the solo comes to an end.

"Satan's Dance" ends in a fugue—a polyphonic technique in which a theme (called a subject) is first presented alone and is then imitated successively by other voices or instruments at different pitch levels. This little fugue begins with theme A (notes 1 through 15), but not at its original pitch level; interestingly, it is transposed up a tritone (the Devil again):

Theme A:  1   2 3   4   5   6   7   8   9   10   11   12   13 14 15
(transposed)

This subject (played by low brass) is imitated beginning in the sixth measure by trumpet. This is accompanied by the continuation of the lower brass line, creating a two-part (and eventually a three-part) polyphonic texture. Finally, in the eleventh measure of the fugue, the second occurrence of the subject (in trumpet) ends, and the third entry occurs, this time in the low range of the piano and bass. But this time the subject is extended to become the full theme A and is played at its original pitch:

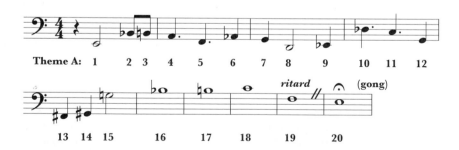

Theme A:  1   2 3   4   5   6   7   8   9   10   11   12

13   14   15        16        17        18        19        20

Over this bass presentation of theme A, the upper lines continue playing countermelodies. As theme A reaches notes 16 to 20, the rhythmic values are lengthened (this is called augmentation); the beat slows down (ritard). As note 20 is reached, a gong is struck.

The fourth chorus is set still differently from the earlier choruses. The lyrics begin in a whisper; the organ accompanies these whispers by building up a huge chord one note at a time. The notes, beginning with the low E, are notes 1 through 12 of theme A. As the chord gets louder with each added note, the whispers increase in volume, finally reaching a loud, full voice as the Devil demands sympathy and courtesy or he will "lay your soul to waste." The climax of the fourth chorus is reached as the organ chord and the spoken lyrics reach their highest volume; suddenly they stop, and the Devil sarcastically says, "Pleased to meet you!" As the accompaniment reenters (on "hope you guess my name"), the instruments begin dropping out successively until nothing is left but the bass. The fourth chorus has created its own little arch, beginning with one bass note and whispers, building to a climax, and ending with a solo bass line.

It is time for the Devil to return; "Submergence" depicts this process. First there is "Contemplation." We hear theme A much as we did in the beginning, starting with notes 1 and 2, then notes 1 through 6, and finally notes 1 through 15. However, theme A stops on note 15; then there is a free "spinning" round and round notes 13 through 15, as they get louder and faster, then softer and slower (a mini-arch). The piano's damper pedal is held down throughout "Contemplation," creating a kind of blur. If the Devil emerged to the sounds of theme A played forward, it is only reasonable that he submerge while theme A is played backward. Thus, in "Return," theme A begins on note 15 and moves backward to note 1 (played by celesta). Trombone, bass, and piano play notes 6 through 1, then notes 2 and 1 (the tritone again). Finally, after a pause, the Devil shuts the trap door to hell behind him as note 1 of theme A sounds one more time.

In an interview with Bruce Cook for the *National Observer,* Steve Katz provided the following understatement: "We've got a thing worked out on the Rolling Stones' 'Sympathy for the Devil' that should really be good" (Wise, 1971). Arranger Halligan has illustrated creative use of every parameter of music: form, timbre, harmony, rhythm, melody, volume, and texture. Although this version is based on the Stones' original material and must therefore be considered an "arrangement," perhaps you can see that it is virtually a new composition. To compare the original version with the B, S, & T version would be like comparing IBM's most sophisticated computer system with a pocket calculator; each has its place, and we may use and enjoy both, but let us understand and appreciate the difference.

# 12

# Art Rock

## OVERVIEW: ROCK AS A "LEGITIMATE" MUSICAL VOCABULARY

Prior to the mid-1960s, rock and roll was generally considered a simple, mundane, and musically inconsequential style that appealed almost exclusively to teenagers. However, the Beatles and others demonstrated that rock could be something more. Using the musical language of rock, an adventurous musical mind could create music of greater substance, music that could challenge our minds and force us to broaden our perspectives. After all, rock and roll is a musical language; and like all languages, it can be used to articulate substantive ideas as well as mindless trivia.

In the late 1960s, the creative minds in rock began to expand. Some artists began to explore more folk styles; some moved toward country and western; others ventured into jazz; and still others developed new electronic techniques. In each case, rock as a style was enriched. It grew and expanded. There was an exciting realization that rock, as a musical language, was flexible and could communicate all kinds of nonverbal expressions. It not limited to two and a half minutes of "walk–talk" lyrics over three basic chords.

We have already met some of these pioneers: the Beatles, the Byrds, Dylan, Aretha Franklin, Jimi Hendrix, and Blood, Sweat, and Tears. To some musicians the question occurred, Just how far can rock really go? Can the musical language of rock be used to create "major" works of art, comparable to those of the classical tradition? Why not? After all, symphonies are made out of melodies, rhythms, chords, timbres, textures, and forms; why can't rock-style melodies, rhythms, chords, and so on be used to create similar works? It was just a matter of time before creative musical minds would try to answer the question.

If earlier attempts to expand rock and roll's horizons by means of blending it with folk, gospel, or jazz styles had created storms of criticism, the attempts to combine rock with classical music brought on a virtual monsoon. Words like "self-conscious" and "pretentious" were hurled with abandon. The critics assumed the worst motives on the part of the new musical explorers, accusing them of "lame affectations of a cultured sensibility" and of seeking "to dignify their work, to make it acceptable for upper-class approbation" (Miller 1980, 347–348). The rock musicians who explored the new ground of "art rock" or "classical rock" were risking condemnation by the hard-core rock establishment. Ironically, that establishment, which prided itself on rock's inherent rebelliousness, could be quite intolerant when some rock musicians ventured into new areas.

Let us identify the following six typical approaches to bringing together classical elements and rock elements:

1. *Quote a classical excerpt in the midst of a rock song.* This is probably the most simplistic and superficial approach to a rock–classical confluence. Simply quoting a motive, theme, or passage in the midst of a rock song may be "cute," but it hardly constitutes a true blending of styles.

2. *Use a classical melody as the basis of a rock song.* Again, this approach simply borrows a melody from the classical repertoire and then builds a rock piece around it. This often occurred in pop music. No real stylistic blending takes place; the result is simply a rock song with a borrowed tune.

3. *Create a series of rock songs conceived as units in a larger form.* Such attempts are often called suites or song cycles. If the songs are not unified in some way, this can, in fact, merely be the pretense of classicism. However, if there is some discernible thematic unity or development within the set, the results can be satisfying.

4. *Adapt a full classical work to a rock-style performance.* Here a greater part of the classical work is "borrowed": the form, the chords, the melodies, and the internal development as the classical composer intended it. These elements are then transformed by rock instrumentation, texture, and rhythmic interpretation. If done well, this method does offer a true mixture of styles.

5. *Create a work for rock group and classical ensemble.* This, too, can be quite successful. Here a rock group performs as a partner with a symphony orchestra or other classically oriented ensemble. Often musical material is presented in a "straight" version by the orchestra and is then used as the basis of further elaboration, in a rock style, by the rock group. Sometimes the two units come together to create a total blend.

6. *Using the musical language of rock, create an extended work modeled after a classical form.* This is the most challenging approach and the one which, if done well, is the most successful. Length is not the criterion. A long rock piece is just that: a long rock piece. But if there is thematic development and purposeful structure, the result can indeed be comparable to classical models, simply using a different musical language. The most impressive achievements in art rock lie within this category.

The discussions that follow concentrate on the fifth and sixth approaches, with occasional references to the fourth.

# ROCK WITH ORCHESTRA

### The Moody Blues

Most art rock explorations came from British bands. The first major effort was by the Moody Blues, a band formed around 1964 as a blues-based band. They debuted at the Marquee Club, where the Stones and many other British bands had received their initial exposure. After an early blues-oriented hit, "Go Now!" (number 10 in 1965), two of the original members departed. With the addition of Justin Hayward and John Lodge, the band purchased a Mellotron and changed musical directions. They issued *Days of Future Passed* in mid-1968; it became their first successful album in the United States, rising to number 3. "Tuesday Afternoon (Forever Afternoon)" hit the U.S. charts (number 24), as did "Nights in White Satin" upon its reissue in 1972 (number 2).

*Days of Future Passed* was recorded with the London Symphony Orchestra and was a concept album. Although important as a prototype, *Days of Future Passed* was a pleasant but rather superficial attempt at rock–classical confluence. There is no real simultaneous interaction between the orchestra and the band and no real blending of styles. The orchestra provides an overturelike beginning, "The Day Begins," that presents some of the themes of later songs. Thereafter, the orchestra provides smooth transitions between the band's songs. At times, the Mellotron provides an orchestra-like accompaniment for the band. Most of the rock songs are in a rather soft style, except for "Peak Hour." The orchestra's music, though well orchestrated, adheres to a late-nineteenth-century style. Therein lies one of the pitfalls of many rock-with-orchestra experiments. Often the rock musician's idea of "classical" music really refers to styles that are fifty to 100 years old. The result, therefore, is a curiously anachronistic blend between up-to-date rock and an out-of-date "classical" style.

The Moody Blues' popularity ebbed and flowed throughout the 1970s and on into the 1980s. They enjoyed peak popularity in the early 1970s with albums like *A Question of Balance* (number 3 in 1970), *Every Good Boy Deserves Favour* (number 2 in 1971), and *Seventh Sojourn* (number 1 in 1972), and again in 1981 with *Long Distance Voyager* (number 1). Their use of Mellotron became an identifying feature, as did their sophisticated melodies, harmonies, and vocals.

### Deep Purple

The next significant effort in the direction of rock with orchestra came from a second-wave British invasion band whose hard rock style would come to be called "heavy metal." Deep Purple was founded by guitarist Ritchie Blackmore in 1968. While living in Hamburg, Blackmore recruited four other British rockers for his new band. Their first single, a hard-rocking song called "Hush," hit the number 4 position on the U.S. charts. Their first two albums, *Shades of Deep Purple* and *The Book of Taliesyn*, also sold well. In September 1969, Deep Purple (now consisting of Blackmore, keyboardist Jon Lord, vocalist Ian Gillan, bassist Roger Glover, and drummer Ian Paice) gathered to perform Lord's "Concerto for Group and Orchestra" with the Royal Philharmonic Orchestra, conducted by Malcolm Arnold. The live recording, made in the Albert Hall, was released as Deep Purple's fourth album.

Lord's "Concerto" is in three large movements (fast-slow-fast), as is typical of the classical concerto. The orchestral style is more contemporary than that of the Moody Blues' orchestra, but still seems to be a compendium of early twentieth-century idioms. Deep Purple maintains its hard rock sound almost throughout this work. There are even "cadenzas"—virtuoso solos (often improvised)—that typify the classical concerto. The second movement includes voice, rather unusual for the concerto, which is an instrumental form. For the most part Lord's themes are presented by the orchestra in a "straight" style and are then interpreted by the band in a rock style. The third movement is by far the most successful, for it is here that the two ensembles and styles begin to mesh, approaching the kind of rock–classical confluence that is usually the goal of such attempts.

In 1970, Lord fulfilled a BBC commission to write another work for rock group and orchestra. Beginning as a Deep Purple project, it soon grew beyond that. The resulting *Gemini Suite* is a six-movement work for rock soloists and orchestra. Each movement is centered around a different soloist, three of whom—Lord, Glover, and Paice—were members of Deep Purple; the other three soloists were guitarist Albert Lee and vocalists Tony Ashton and Yvonne Elliman. In *Gemini Suite,* Lord's orchestral writing is much more sophisticated and there is some excellent rock playing. There is a closer interaction between the soloists and the orchestra, at times providing a very effective partnership. The first movement, "Guitar," is based on the motive of an ascending minor third (e.g., C up to E♭) and an ascending major triad. You can hear these motives being developed throughout the movement, which features some excellent work by guitarist Albert Lee. The second movement, "Piano," combines elements of classical music, rock, and jazz. The third movement, "Drums," begins with some very tight coordination between the orchestra and drummer Ian Paice; soon, of course, there is an extended drum solo after which the orchestra returns with a marchlike section.

Deep Purple (*Source:* Michael Ochs Archive, Ltd.)

"Vocals" begins with a beautifully lyrical string melody; Elliman sings two solo verses (accompanied by orchestra). After a short orchestral interlude, Ashton enters with a solo vocal before being joined by Elliman in a duet based on her earlier vocal melody. The bass guitar movement begins with the bass underlying the orchestra before breaking into a solo cadenza. When the orchestra reenters there is a brief dialogue before the movement ends quietly. In the sixth and final movement, "Organ," the orchestral writing is more contemporary in style, and the interaction between the organ, accompanied by bass and drums, and the orchestra is quite successful as they "trade off" passages. Overall, *Gemini Suite* is a successful step in the direction of rock–classical integration.

Deep Purple's primary impact came in the early 1970s with albums like *Fireball, Machine Head, Who Do We Think We Are!, Made In Japan, Burn,* and *Stormbringer.* Their biggest single hit, "Smoke on the Water" (number 4 in 1973), was an early classic of the hard rock, heavy metal trend of the 1970s. From mid-1973 on, a series of personnel changes hit the band, and their popularity waned; they disbanded in 1976. However, in 1984, they reunited to produce a number 17 album *Perfect Strangers.*

**Procol Harum**

Procol Harum's album *Live in Concert with the Edmonton Symphony Orchestra* (1972) became the group's highest-ranking album (number 5) and their only gold album. Begun in 1962 as the Paramounts, a blues-based band from London, Procol Harum's first single, "A Whiter Shade of Pale" (1967), reached number 5 in the United States. After several personnel changes there was a series of successful albums in the late 1960s and early 1970s.

For the Edmonton performance (November 1971) the band drew upon songs released on earlier albums; the songs were orchestrated and given a larger orchestral context. The most ambitious effort was "In Held 'Twas In I," a nineteen-minute work that had first appeared on the *Shine On Brightly* album. Lyricist Keith Reid provided texts that were often surrealistic, melancholy, and introspective. With "In Held 'Twas In I" Reid takes us on a journey from self-pity and depression, through madness, to an exalted reaffirmation of faith. The orchestra basically provides an accompanying setting for the series of songs in the set and is thus confined to fleshing out the somewhat ponderous, serious rock style of the band's music. Certainly the orchestral style is not as contemporary as the best moments of *Gemini Suite,* nor is the band as hard rocking as Deep Purple. Nevertheless, "In Held 'Twas In I" is a thought-provoking sample of early 1970s art rock.

There were, of course, others who explored the rock-with-orchestra format, such as the New York Rock Ensemble, the Electric Light Orchestra, the Mothers of Invention, and Emerson, Lake, and Palmer. Several of these groups will be discussed in subsequent sections of this chapter.

## ROCK OPERAS AND THEATRICAL WORKS

The works to be discussed in this section all involve music and a theatrical concept. Where the theatrical aspect includes acting, costuming, and scenery, we can use the term *opera.* However, where the intent is a concert presentation—but still with the elements of specific characters, represented by soloists or chorus, and a developing story line—we shall use the more generic term *musical theater.*

In 1967, the relatively conservative world of Broadway was stunned by a "rock musical" called *Hair.* With book and lyrics by Gerome Ragni and James Rado and music by Galt MacDermot, *Hair* was a celebration of the new Aquarian Age and the revolutionary freedom of the psychedelic hippie generation. The popularity of *Hair* (it ran on Broadway for 1,729 performances) was aided to some degree by the notoriety surrounding its nude scene. The rock music of *Hair* was in a soft rock style, but was certainly revolutionary enough for Broadway. "Aquarius/Let the Sunshine In" became a number 1 hit in 1969 for the Fifth Dimension.

Although opera is generally considered a classical form, there is nothing in its definition that dictates a particular musical style. In the simplest terms, an opera is just a play in which most or all of the dialogue is sung instead of spoken. Early in this century, ragtime pianist–composer Scott Joplin had composed several operas using ragtime as the predominant musical style (e.g., *Treemonisha*). In 1935, George Gershwin had used jazz as the basis of his opera *Porgy and Bess.* It seemed only a matter of time before someone used rock as the musical basis of an opera.

## The Who

The Who can be traced back to the late 1950s, when Pete Townshend (born in London in 1945) and classically trained John Entwistle (London, 1946) were members of a Dixieland band. Getting together with guitarist/singer Roger Daltry (London, 1944), they called themselves the Detours at first, and then the Who. Soon they replaced their earlier drummer with Keith Moon (London, 1947), a former member of a British surfing group. They adopted a "mod" image, a new name (the High Numbers), and identified with the same blues-based milieu that produced the Rolling Stones and the Yardbirds. After their first release flopped, they returned to the earlier name, the Who, and cultivated their mod image with flashy new clothes.

The Who gained major popularity in England during 1965 and 1966, placing four singles in the British Top 10. One of these, "My Generation," used a stuttering vocal to enunciate a rebellious teenage theme, ending with the hook line, "Hope I die before I get old." Their anti-establishment image was enhanced quite by accident when, at a 1965 performance, Townshend inadvertently broke the neck of his guitar on a low ceiling; he lost his temper and smashed it to pieces. Keith Moon followed suit by busting up his drum set; noting the frenzied crowd reaction, they decided to keep the instrument-smashing routine as the climax of their act.

The Who's debut album, *The Who Sing My Generation* (1966), contained the title hit plus several rather derivative works, including James Brown's "Please, Please, Please" and a Beatle-like follow-up to "My Generation," called "The Kids Are Alright." But there was also a very strong instrumental called "The Ox," which featured excellent rock drums, piano, and guitar (including an early experiment with feedback).

While producing their second album, *Happy Jack* (1967), a problem arose; the material was ten minutes short of a full album. To fill the gap, Townshend composed a long song with a story line and characters. He called the resulting "A Quick One While He's Away" a "miniopera." Although the Who had been popular in England since 1965, they had failed to make the first British invasion of America.

Their American breakthrough came in June 1967 at the Monterey Pop Festival. Their music made a strong impression, and their next release, the psychedelically oriented "I Can See for Miles," made the Top 10 in the United States. Their next album, a concept album called *The Who Sell Out*, ended with another miniopera called "Rael."

By 1969, the Who had established themselves as an important British mainstream rock band, but rather undistinguished from all the others except perhaps for their flamboyant stage act. It was Townshend's habit to play his guitar with rapid, wind-mill strokes (originally designed to cover his technical limitations) amidst acrobatic leaps, knee drops, and, of course, ultimate instrument smashing. Daltrey vigorously pranced all over the stage, whirling the microphone in the air; Moon pounded the drums, threw sticks in the air, and habitually smashed his set at the end of concerts. Entwistle stood solemnly still throughout.

In 1969, the Who released *Tommy*, a ninety-minute "rock opera." It was created primarily by Townshend, with some material by Moon and Entwistle. Destined to become one of the most acclaimed rock albums since *Sgt. Pepper*, *Tommy* rose to number 4, initiating a series of Top 5 albums for the band. Tommy is the story of a deaf, dumb, and blind boy who triumphs by virtue of his incredible ability as a pinball "wizard." Regarding the plot, Brock Helander calls it "a bizarre and elaborate tale of lost innocence, redemption, and contrition" (Helander 1982, 625). Writer Dave Marsh calls it "skimpy, muddled, silly" (Miller 1980, 290). The music is certainly more restrained and sophisticated than the Who's previous music, but it bears little resemblance to classical music. In general, *Tommy* does not go beyond earlier adventures by groups such as the Byrds, the Beach Boys, Hendrix, and the Beatles. Nevertheless, the concept itself—a ninety-minute theatrical presentation that develops a story line (however vaguely) through the use of characters, based upon a rock musical style—was impressive. *Tommy* captured the imagination of critics and fans alike. It was performed in its entirety in London and in New York (at the Metropolitan Opera House, no less). There was a symphonic version, a stage production, a ballet performance, a brass-band version, and eventually a film version. Although hard-core Who fans shudder at the thought, the likelihood exists that rock history will eventually remember the Who primarily as the band that created *Tommy*.

Townshend, eager to follow up on *Tommy*, began a new project called *Lifehouse*, using a science fiction theme. Although *Lifehouse* was abandoned, several songs for the project were included on the album *Who's Next* (1971). Possibly the Who's strongest "non-opera" album, this album contains consistently excellent mainstream rock singing and playing and well-integrated electronic sounds (the latter resulting from Townshend's new fascination with the synthesizer).

In 1973, *Quadrophenia* was released as Townshend's second full-length rock opera. If schizophrenia refers to a double personality, "quadrophenia" refers to a four-way split. Apparently the reference was to the four very different personalities within the Who. Entwistle was the classically trained stoic; Moon was the flamboyant wild man; Daltrey was the good-time rock-and-roll shouter; Townshend was the thinking, articulate member, consumed with serious rock aspirations and the Indian spiritualism of Meher Baba. The four musical themes of *Quadrophenia*'s four sides seem to reflect this disparate foursome. The plot, if one can call it that, is even more obscure than *Tommy*'s, but the music is more mature. *Quadrophenia* became a number 2 album.

The Who (*Source:* Michael Ochs Archive, Ltd.)

Severe problems overtook the band by the end of the decade. In 1978, years of alcoholism and drug abuse caught up with Keith Moon; he died of an overdose of Heminevrin on September 7, 1978. At a performance at Cincinnati's Riverfront Stadium on December 3, 1979, eleven people were killed in the crush of fans outside of the stadium. Compounding the band's problems, Townshend went on a year long binge of alcohol, cocaine, and heroin. In 1981, he actually fell asleep on stage—not what fans expected from one of rock's most athletic guitarists!

Townshend managed to keep the Who together, although all continued to pursue individual projects. *Face Dances* (1981) hit the Top 5 and *It's Hard* (1982) made the Top 10. With Daltrey, Entwistle, and Townshend officially "middle-aged," only Moon made good on the wish, "Hope I die before I get old."

### Other Rock Operas and Musicals

Another major rock opera of the early 1970s was *Jesus Christ Superstar*. With lyrics by Tim Rice and music by Andrew Lloyd Webber, *Superstar* opened in New York in October 1971 and ran for 720 performances. Centering on the last week of Christ's life, the plot was familiar and the music was strong. The "Overture" presented many of the opera's themes; the individual songs varied from the lovely ballad "I Don't Know How to Love Him" to the mainstream rock song "Superstar." In between were powerful songs like "I Only Want to Say" and humorous songs like "King Herod's Song." Virtually all of the dialogue was sung, often to very effective music.

Other rock musicals and rock operas include *Godspell* (1971), *Joseph and the Amazing Technicolor Dreamcoat* (1971), *The Wiz* (1975), *Evita* (1978), and *Grease* (1972). *Grease,* when it closed in April 1980, was the longest-running Broadway show to date, with a total of 3,388 performances.

### Rick Wakeman and Yes

Keyboardist Rick Wakeman (born in West London in 1949) had entered the Royal Academy of Music at the age of sixteen to study piano and clarinet. By the time he joined Yes (August 1971), the band had already released three albums.

Yes had been formed back in 1968 by vocalist Jon Anderson and bassist Chris Squire. Performing often at the Marquee Club in London, they were heard by Ahmet Ertegun and subsequently signed by Atlantic Records. When Wakeman joined in 1971, he introduced multiple keyboards to the band's sound (acoustic piano, electric piano, organ, Mellotron, clavinet, harpsichord, and synthesizer). Yes had already become known for its long, complex instrumental cuts, and with Wakeman's influence, the band's reputation for "progressive" rock grew stronger. The next album, *Fragile* (number 4 in 1972), yielded the group's only major hit of the 1970s, "Roundabout" (number 13).

*Close to the Edge* (1973) contained only three songs, one of which consumed one entire side of a disc. The live triple album, *Yessongs* (1973), was elaborately packaged and adorned with otherworldly cover art by Roger Dean. Anderson's clear, high voice, Wakeman's excellent keyboard work, and solid musicianship by Squire, guitarist Steve Howe, and drummer Alan White made Yes one of the most appealing rock bands of the 1970s. Four of the five members of Yes had at least some classical training (all except Anderson). For *Tales from Topographic Oceans* (1974), Anderson and Howe based their lyrics on the shastric scriptures by guru Paramhansa Yogananda. This rather experimental album continued Yes's consistent ability to sell albums; but shortly after the release of the album, Wakeman left the group to pursue individual projects.

In 1972–73, using various backup musicians, Wakeman had produced an album called *The Six Wives of Henry VIII*, which featured his multikeyboard work. The nine keyboards—two Mellotrons, two Minimoog synthesizers, organ, acoustic piano, electric piano harpsichord, acoustic harpsichord, and ARP synthesizer—were further modified with other electronic devices (e.g., fuzz and wah-wah pedals, and echo unit). But his most ambitious work came with *Journey to the Centre of the Earth* (1974). Performed live at London's Royal Festival Hall, the production included the London Symphony Orchestra, the English Chamber Choir, narrator, and rock band. Based on the Jules Verne classic, the text is shared by a narrator, a chorus, and two vocalists. A symphonic introduction opens the first part, called "The Journey." After a soft rock song by the band, the orchestra and chorus lead to a narration; brief instrumental passages punctuate and interpret the narrator's words, eventually leading to "Recollection," another soft rock vocal. The pattern of narration and instrumental depiction continues until the final song, "The Forest." A brief segment of Grieg's "In the Hall of the Mountain King" is interjected before the work comes to a Hollywood-style closing.

Wakeman followed *Journey* with yet another attempt at a major work for orchestra, rock band, narrator, and chorus. *The Myths and Legends of King Arthur and the Knights of the Round Table* was given its premiere as a pageant on ice at the London Empire Pool in May 1975. Similar in concept to *Journey*, *King Arthur* is generally less prone to slip into naive clichés and involves moments of more authentic rock style. "Sir Lancelot and the Black Knight" is an interesting combination of shouting

Rick Wakeman (*Source:* Michael Ochs Archive, Ltd.)

vocal, rock, chorus, synthesizer, and orchestra; it may be the best achievement in either of Wakeman's two major works, although "Merlin the Magician" is also a fascinating blend of many diverse elements. Overall, *King Arthur* is a significant advance in the integration of musical styles and media, compared with *Journey. Journey* and *King Arthur* are not operas, but they are a type of musical theater, telling stories and involving characters through a variety of performance forces.

Wakeman rejoined the band in 1976, but by 1980 he and Anderson had both left Yes. Anderson went on to some fascinating work with Greek composer–keyboardist Vangelis, before returning to Yes for the 1983 album *90125*. Yes's biggest hit, "Owner of a Lonely Heart" (number 1), came in 1904.

### Genesis

Genesis had begun in 1967 as a songwriter's collective made up of four students at England's Charterhouse School. By 1971, Genesis had grown to a quintet, including singer Peter Gabriel and drummer Phil Collins. Building a reputation as a "progressive" rock band in England and with a small following in the United States, the band emphasized Mellotron and other electronic keyboards as well as visuals and theatrics in live performance. In 1974, they signed with Atlantic Records and released the double album *The Lamb Lies Down on Broadway*. It moved to number 41 on the album charts, and it was the beginning of their increasingly successful career.

*The Lamb* is a surrealistic description of the adventures of Rael as he confronts the modern civilization of New York City. The "story" unfolds in a series of songs, all performed by Genesis alone (no orchestra, chorus, or narrator). The style has little to do with classical music, adhering to a sophisticated rock style that involves heavy use of electronics. However, the concept is theatrical in that a story, complete with characters and commentary, is developed. On Genesis' subsequent tours, they were able to duplicate the album in live performance, with Gabriel portraying Rael with a series of costume changes.

Peter Gabriel left the band in mid-1975, and Phil Collins took over the role of lead singer. Eventually reduced to a trio, the group achieved its greatest success in the 1980s with three gold albums and two platinum albums, as well as a series of Top 40 hits. Meanwhile, Peter Gabriel released six solo albums through the mid-1980s, each achieving Top 50 status. Collins left the band in 1996, finding success with albums such as *Dance Into the Night* (number 23 in 1996). He won an Oscar in 1999 for "You'll Be in My Heart," a song he wrote for Disney's animated film *Tarzan*.

### On the Classical Side

The confluence of rock and classical music need not always come from the rock side of the spectrum. Several composers whose background is more closely identified with classical music have incorporated rock styles into major productions. Perhaps the most publicized of these works was *Mass* by Leonard Bernstein. Commissioned to write a work for the dedication of the John F. Kennedy Center for the Performing Arts in Washington, D.C., Bernstein created a theater piece loosely based upon the Roman Catholic mass. In addition to orchestra and chorus, there is a boys choir, a pipe organ, a rock organ, and rock and jazz ensembles. Interspersed throughout the *Mass* are several songs in various rock styles. Related works include Lalo Schifrin's *Rock Requiem* and the Electric Prunes' *Mass in F Minor*. For the adventurous listener, there is *Elephant Steps*, with music by Stanley Silverman and text by Richard Foreman. This surrealistic opera is for "pop singers, rock singers, orchestra, rock band, electronic tape, raga group, tape recorder, gypsy ensemble, and elephants." Using advanced contemporary classical styles, Silverman manages several rather convincing rock episodes in this somewhat eccentric but interesting work.

## NONTHEATRICAL ART ROCK BY UNACCOMPANIED ROCK GROUPS

In the overview of this chapter we outlined six typical approaches to the confluence of rock and classical music. The sixth approach is to create an extended work modeled on a classical form using the musical language of rock. Rock operas and theater pieces fall into this category (granted, there is often some overlap between approaches). But there remains a subcategory of the sixth approach that we have not discussed. This involves the unaccompanied rock group (not aided by orchestra, chorus, etc.) creating an extended work related to a classical model, but not an overtly theatrical work. "Symphony for the Devil/Sympathy for the Devil," by Blood, Sweat, and Tears, falls into this category. This is probably the most demanding assignment in the area of art rock. Accordingly, in considering such works, we shall meet several of the most talented groups in the history of rock.

### Emerson, Lake, and Palmer

More than any other person, Keith Emerson has persistently and successfully pursued the concept of art rock. An incredibly talented keyboardist, Emerson (born in 1944) first became known with a group called the Nice. Formed in 1967 as a backup group for singer Pat Arnold, the Nice began touring on their own later that year. Originally a quartet, it soon evolved into a trio featuring Emerson's multiple keyboards instead of the more usual lead guitar. The Nice's second album, *Ars Longa Vita Brevis* (1969), featured an extended work in four movements and suggested future directions for the Nice and Emerson. In late 1969, the band toured the United States to promote their album *Five Bridges Suite*. Side 1 contained the five-movement title work, an excellent example of Emerson's versatility and technique as he moves fluently from rock to jazz to a Bach-like classical style. Accompanied by the Sinfonia of London Orchestra, it is a good example of art rock. Side 2 contained a rock with orchestra adaptation of Jean Sibelius's "Intermezzo," from the *Karelia Suite,* as well as rock interpretations of the third movement of Tchaikovsky's Sixth Symphony, and a unique combination of Dylan's "Country Pie" and fragments from Bach's Brandenburg Concerto No. 6. The last Nice album with Emerson, *Elegy* (1971), contained an extended rock version of Bernstein's "America," from *West Side Story.* For a dazzling display of Emerson's improvisations with the Nice, listen to "She Belongs to Me" (a Dylan song) as performed at the Fillmore East (released on Columbia album P11635, *Nice,* 1973).

It was at a performance at the Fillmore West that Emerson made the acquaintance of guitarist–vocalist Greg Lake, who was there performing with his group King Crimson. The next year, Emerson and Lake recruited drummer Carl Palmer, thus creating Emerson, Lake, and Palmer (ELP). ELP debuted in August 1970 at the Isle of Wight Festival and in 1971 released their first two albums, *Emerson, Lake, and Palmer* (number 18) and *Tarkus* (number 9). "The Three Fates" from the first album is in three parts, the first being a solo on pipe organ, the second a piano solo, and the third a work for the entire trio. As would increasingly be the case with ELP, the work is almost impossible to classify stylistically, owing to the effective blend of classical, jazz, and rock elements. That, of course, is the ultimate goal of a blended style—to be so perfectly blended that the contributing elements are barely distinguishable. "Tank" (same album) features the talents of Carl Palmer; he frequently connected his drums to a synthesizer to modify the sound (an effect that may be heard near the end of his solo in "Tank"). The remarkable keyboard work of Emerson, the clean drumming of Palmer, and the coordination between all three represented a new level of sophistication in rock music. Listen carefully to "The Barbarian" or "Take a Pebble" from that first album to hear how tightly coordinated the trio was.

Side 1 of *Tarkus* contains a seven-part series of songs that comprises the title work. Especially interesting is "Eruption" (the first part of the suite); "Bitches Crystal" on side 2 is impressive for its variety of combined styles and fine playing. "Are You Ready Eddy?" is an ELP-ized version of Jerry Lee Lewis–style 1950s rock. A major effort in the field of art rock came with ELP's third album, *Pictures at an Exhibition* (1972). The work on which the album was based was written in 1874 by Russian composer Modest Mussorgsky. The suite represents the composer's impressions as he strolls through an art exhibition. The "Promenade" theme recurs as he moves from painting to painting; the other segments of the work reflect the paintings he sees. ELP's album adapts a significant amount of the original work, including "Promenade," "The Gnome," "The Old Castle," "The Hut of Baba Yaga," and "The Great Gate of Kiev." There are also some added movements by ELP: "The Sage," "The Curse of Baba Yaga," and "Blues Variation." For the most part, Mussorgsky's themes, rhythms, harmonies, textures, and internal forms are preserved in the ELP version.

Emerson, Lake, and Palmer, rock group (*Source:* Michael Ochs Archive, Ltd.)

The next album, *Trilogy* (1972), rose to the number 5 position. In the midst of "The Endless Enigma" (parts 1 and 2) lies a most impressive fugue, fully developed in classical form and performed impressively by Emerson (assisted by Lake). There is another electronic rock adaptation of a classical work—this time, the "Hoedown" from *Rodeo,* by contemporary American composer Aaron Copland. Two impressive art rock compositions on this album are "Trilogy" and "Abaddon's Bolero."

But it is with *Brain Salad Surgery* (1973) that ELP really "put it all together." As with the Beatles on *Sgt. Pepper,* it is as if ELP draws together all earlier ideas into one consummate album. There is the rock adaptation of a classical work, this time the challenging fourth movement of Argentine contemporary composer Alberto Ginastera's First Piano Concerto, featuring Emerson and Palmer; there is the "cute" piece, "Benny the Bouncer," reminiscent of "Are You Ready Eddy?" and parts of "The Sheriff" (*Trilogy*); there is the "normal" (for ELP) song, "Still . . . You Turn Me On"; there is the spiritualistic "Jerusalem," which recalls "The Only Way" and "Infinite Space (Conclusion)," from *Tarkus.* But the masterpiece of *Brain Salad Surgery* is "Karn Evil 9." This work will be discussed in more detail in the musical close-up at the end of this chapter. Suffice it to say here that this three-movement work fulfills the goals of the sixth approach described in the overview of this chapter: an extended work for a rock group using a classical model but the musical language of rock. "Karn Evil 9" is one of the most impressive achievements in the history of rock.

Touring America in 1974, ELP amazingly managed to re-create "Karn Evil 9" in live performance. They hauled thirty-six tons of equipment with them, including six

Keith Emerson (Photograph by Allen Olivio.) (*Source:* ©Allen
Olivio/Courtesy of London Features International Ltd.)

Moog synthesizers, two organs, an electric piano, and a Steinway grand piano for
Emerson; with Palmer's drum set, synthesizer, timpani, gongs, chimes, and so on,
moving the band around for four months was quite a project.

After the tour, the trio began developing individual interests, resulting in the
double album *Works, Volume 1* (1977). Side 1 contains Emerson's Piano Concerto
No. 1, a three-movement work modeled on the classical piano concerto but
using Emerson's highly personalized blend of classical, jazz, and rock idioms.
Side 2 belongs to Greg Lake, whose songs are accompanied by orchestra and
chorus. Carl Palmer is featured on side 3; his cuts include references to classical
works by Prokofiev and Bach, plus a remake of "Tank." Side 4 consists of the
trio's extended version of Copland's famous "Fanfare to the Common Man"
and the original extended piece, "Pirates." A follow-up album, *Works, Volume 2*
(1977), was less impressive, as was *Love Beach* (1978–79). After a live album and a
greatest hits album were released, ELP seemed to disappear as an entity, with
each member following other interests. However, in the mid-1980s, ELP reappeared with a new "P"—drummer Cozy Powell—and a new album on the
charts. By 1992, Carl Palmer was back with Emerson and Lake for a very strong
album entitled *Black Moon*.

### Frank Zappa

You may have noticed that every band discussed thus far in this chapter has been
British. Indeed, art rock was primarily a British development. However, it was left

to an American band to provide what many feel is both the best and worst in art rock. If that sounds contradictory, wait until you meet the leader of this band. He is a study in inconsistency and self-contradiction. Among the adjectives that describe Frank Zappa are creative, enigmatic, erratic, puerile, pseudointellectual, unique, sophomoric, genius, and (above all) iconoclastic. That last word, according to Webster's, refers to a person "who attacks or ridicules traditional or venerated institutions or ideas regarded by him as erroneous."* Zappa goes well beyond that definition; he attacks or ridicules everything. The following list of Zappa "targets" was assembled while listening to a few minutes of one of his albums:

| | |
|---|---|
| Jews | Jeff Beck |
| Catholics | rock groups (all) |
| hippies | police |
| Beatles | politicians |
| homosexuals | the middle class |
| blacks | the lower class |
| women | the upper class |
| men | Frank Zappa |

By listening to a full hour of Zappa, one could multiply the list by a factor of 10.

Frank Zappa was born in Baltimore on December 21, 1940; he and his family moved to California around 1950, and by 1956 they had settled in Lancaster. He studied music during his brief college career and played with various local bands. Zappa's early musical enthusiasms were for R & B and contemporary classical music, especially Stravinsky and Varèse. Edgard Varèse (1883 to 1965) was an early experimenter in rhythmic complexity, the use of unpitched percussion, atonality (music not in a traditional key), and electronic music. Generally considered a pioneer who was slightly ahead of his time, Varèse became Zappa's musical idol.

Following a few scrapes with the law and some difficulties with his parents, Frank moved to Los Angeles in 1964. There he joined with Ray Collins (vocals), Jim Black (drums), and Roy Estrada (bass) in a band called the Soul Giants; Zappa increasingly became the leader and changed the name to the Mothers of Invention.

Becoming an underground favorite in the Los Angeles of 1965, the Mothers eventually landed a booking at the Whisky-à-Go-Go. Their "freaky" music, looks, and behavior gained them considerable notoriety. Signing with MGM/Verve Records in late 1965, they released their first album, *Freak Out!*, in mid-1966. It was a double album and is often mentioned as the first real concept album, coming a full year before *Sgt. Pepper*. However, the "concept" is rather elusive, unless it is, as David Walley says, "a living testament to L.A. freakdom" (Walley 1972, 60).

*Webster's New World Dictionary, second college ed. (New York: Simon and Schuster, 1984).

Rock musician, avant-garde composer and writer Frank Zappa (1940–1993) in concert. (*Source:* Images, Peter Gould / Getty Images, Inc.)

*Freak Out!* is an amazingly creative album, especially for 1965–66. Many Zappa fans still believe it is his finest album. The first disc contains relatively "normal" songs, although all are touched by Zappa's musical eccentricity and verbal iconoclasm. "Who Are the Brain Police" is miles away from anything being done in pop music then. Several parodies of 1950s soft rock ("Go Cry on Somebody Else's Shoulder" and "Wowie Zowie") reveal Zappa's perfect understanding of that style, and his ability to re-create it with tongue-in-cheek humor. "Motherly Love" suggests the off-color side of Zappa, a characteristic that would increasingly manifest itself on subsequent albums.

If the first disc of *Freak Out!* seemed rather strange, the second disc must have sounded like the epitome of the album's title. There are three extended pieces, the first ("Trouble Every Day") being a serious commentary on the racial riots in Watts. "Help, I'm a Rock" is a good first glimpse into Zappa's approach to art rock. Many contemporary classical composers have concentrated on timbre and improvisation as generative elements in their compositions. They have avoided the "old" concerns with keys, melodies, traditional chords, and metrically organized rhythms. Much of "Help, I'm a Rock" sounds disorganized and even chaotic—like a real "freak-out." However, the work is quite structured; Zappa does a good job of creating a work that is structured to sound unstructured. One reason that this "song" sounds so "freaky" is that it is in a style that is unfamiliar to many people. Unless the listener has heard a good bit of avant-garde "classical" music, "Help, I'm a Rock" sounds like a work by people who have become deranged.

The song begins normally enough with guitar and drums vamping in triple meter. The first section includes nonsense language and various groans, squawks, and other vocal sounds followed by a mini-explosion. The vamp returns and the voices superimpose the repeating words, "Help, I'm a rock" and "Help, I'm a cop," interrupted by Zappa's seemingly improvised monologue. More nonsense vocals, sheeplike bleatings, and another monologue follow. The triple meter vamp is interrupted by a second major section, which features some female heavy breathing and various vocal noises that at times sound like simulated birdcalls. The third section is one of Zappa's finest works: "It Can't Happen Here." This "song" within a "song" may sound quite disorganized, but it really does create a structured form.

A:    "It can't happen here"—nonmetric, nontonal vocal expanding this lyric
B:    "Who could imagine"—(1) "freak out in Kansas" (followed by improvisation on "Kansas") (2) "freak out in Minnesota" (followed by improvisation on "Minnesota")
C:    instrumental section—piano and drums in a fragmented, nontonal, pointillistic style
B:    "Who could imagine"—"freak out in Washington, D.C." (followed by improvisation on "D.C.")
A:    "It can't happen here"—enters underneath previous section, but begins to dominate
D:    "I remember"—metric; three phrases
A:    "It couldn't happen here"—brief return
E:    Suzy Creamcheese—dialogue with semifictional Zappa character
A:    "It can't happen here"—brief return; filtered voices

This is a unique form that combines two common classical forms: the arch form and the rondo. The first five sections create a form that proceeds to a center point and then doubles back on itself (hence the term *arch form*):

$$
\begin{array}{ccc}
 & \text{C} & \\
\text{B} & & \text{B} \\
\text{A} & & \text{A}
\end{array}
$$

Then Zappa begins alternating the A section with new material—the principle behind the classical rondo form. There are many points of interest as the Mothers work with various vocal timbres. For example, note the improvisation on "Minnesota." As one singer repeats "mi-mi-mi-mi-mi," and so on, he changes the timbre almost as if an electronic filter were being applied. Also listen to the female voice in the "I remember" section (D). After the third phrase, she sings "bop-bop-bop" on widely scattered pitches; gradually these are shortened to become mere "clicks" (listen carefully because this happens quickly). Each time one listens to "It Can't Happen Here," one can hear new sounds within the texture that one had not noticed before.

We have taken a little extra time with "Help, I'm a Rock" because it provides considerable insight into Zappa's style of art rock. Unlike Jon Lord, Rick Wakeman, and so many others, Zappa was familiar with the most up-to-date experiments in classical music. His interest in nonmetrical, atonal music was right in line with many classical composers; his use of vocal improvisation and concentration on timbre and texture, often without traditional melody and harmony, was thoroughly contemporary. As we mentioned earlier, when many rock musicians and listeners think of "classical music," they think of Bach, Mozart, Beethoven, and Tchaikovsky; but those composers lived and worked over a century ago. For art rock to be a truly contemporary creation, one should be trying to blend contemporary rock with contemporary classical sounds. Zappa's understanding of Stravinsky, Varèse, Stockhausen, and Cage allowed him to approach this challenge more successfully than most others.

The final work on *Freak Out!* is "The Return of the Son of Monster Magnet," a side-long work that extended many of the concepts initially approached in "Help, I'm a Rock." Zappa also used tape speed variations and backward sounds (real or simulated).

Some mid-1960s listeners to *Freak Out!* must have assumed that the Mothers had to be stoned on drugs to create such weird music. However, Zappa was vehemently opposed to drug abuse and was even a teetotaler where alcohol was concerned. In a letter to the *Free Press* (October 7, 1966), Zappa said that "the sort of high you really want is a spiritual high and you are bullshitting yourself if you trust any chemical and/or agricultural short-cut to do it for you" (Walley 1972, 65).

The *Freak Out!* album was made by five Mothers: Zappa, Collins, Black, Estrada, and guitarist Elliot Ingber. From this point forward, the personnel of the Mothers was constantly changing, but the force of Zappa's personality provided all the consistency that was needed.

Of Zappa's numerous creative albums of the late 1960s through the early 1970s, two deserve special comment. *Uncle Meat* (1969) began as music for a movie that was never finished. By this time, there were ten Mothers; they could play any combination of over two dozen instruments. In some ways, *Uncle Meat* brings together all of the elements of Zappa's prior work in the way that *Sgt. Pepper* did for the Beatles and *Brain Salad Surgery* did for Emerson, Lake, and Palmer. Electronic effects are expanded, there is spoken monologue, 1950s rock parody, contemporary "classical" music, jazz effects, improvisation—everything that Zappa had tried earlier came together in *Uncle Meat*. Like most Zappa albums, *Uncle Meat* is meticulously assembled. Producer Tom Wilson called Zappa "a painstaking craftsman, and in some ways it's a pity that the art of recording is not developed to the extent where you can really hear completely all the things he's doing" (Walley 1972, 64). Referring to the care with which the multiple layers are assembled and with which the seemingly kaleidoscopic chaos is created, Zappa said, "These things are so carefully constructed that it breaks my heart when people don't dig into them and see all the levels that I put into them" (Walley 1972, 80). Among the better cuts on *Uncle Meat* are "Dog Breath, in the Year of the Plague" and "Dog Breath Variations" on side 1, "The Uncle Meat Variations" and "Prelude to King Kong" on side 2, "Project X" on side 3, and all the "King Kong" segments on side 4. Parts of *Uncle Meat* use up to forty overdubbed tracks; electronic manipulations are used to modify normal sounds (e.g., on "Dog Breath," clarinets are sped up to sound like trumpets). Like much of Zappa's work, *Uncle Meat* (most of which was done in late 1967 and early 1968) is years ahead of its time.

The live album, *Fillmore East, June 1971*, contains a miniopera about an aspiring rock group whose first hit was moving up the charts. The story line deals with their experiences with some groupies and ends with a more or less authentic presentation of the imaginary band's hit single, "Happy Together" (actually a number 1 hit for the Turtles in 1967). Two of the new Mothers were Mark Volman and Howard Kaylan, formerly lead singers with the Turtles. Some of the musical themes on the *Fillmore* album go back to the *Lumpy Gravy* album; some of the lyric material can be traced back to *Absolutely Free*. The lyrics on the *Fillmore* album range from sexually implicit (e.g., "I've got the thing you need, I am endowed beyond your wildest, Clearasil-splattered fantasies") to explicit (e.g., "My dick is a monster").

It was this trend toward pubescent humor that increasingly detracted from Zappa's stature through the 1970s. Brock Helander notes Zappa's "penchant for puerile themes" and his "tendency toward cheap vulgarity" (Helander 1982, 655). Ken Tucker accurately observes that Zappa

> spent the decade of the 1970s consolidating his reputation as an ornery oddball whose talents were, depending on your point of view, either squandered or used to decidedly avant-garde ends. Much of the goodwill Zappa had accumulated with the public and critics in the 1960s for his hard-edged, adventurous music dissipated in the 1970s as Zappa began to emphasize sophomoric humor. (Ward, Stokes, and Tucker 1986, 619)

Tucker further concludes that "Zappa's work came to seem schizophrenic" (Ward, Stokes, and Tucker 1986, 619).

As one surveys Zappa's post–1970 work, one is tempted to paraphrase an old poem: "When he was good, he was very very good/And when he was bad, he was horrid." By 1976 Zappa had stopped referring to the ever-changing lineup as the Mothers of Invention and simply recorded under his own name. For all practical purposes, Zappa's effective leadership within the music scene declined severely. Referring to Zappa's triple album, mail-order package of 1982, writer Ken Tucker comments that "the title suggested what many of his once-and-future fans felt" (Ward, Stokes, and Tucker 1986, 619). The title was *Shut Up 'n' Play Yer Guitar*. Frank Zappa died in 1993.

**Summary of Art Rock**

The goals of the art rock movement remain largely unfulfilled; the admittedly difficult object of achieving a satisfactory blend of classical music and rock has proven to be most elusive. The many attempts seem to be undermined by several factors.

1. Many art rockers had a naive and outdated notion of classical music vis-à-vis what it has become in the twentieth century. Thus, their products were combinations of current rock and centuries-old classical style. Deep Purple, for example, played some true mainstream rock in their attempts at confluence, but the classical element was woefully outdated. On the other hand, Zappa's classical style was quite contemporary, but many would note that as the classical elements ascend in his works, the rock elements recede; thus rarely, if ever, did he achieve a true balance.

2. Some groups unnecessarily softened their rock style, supposedly to blend more effectively with their outdated notion of the classical style. Some of the work by Rick Wakeman and the Moody Blues illustrates this pitfall.

3. The transient nature of rock undermines the long-term developmental process that is usually necessary to achieve an ultimate musical goal. Even the greatest classical composers rarely created masterpieces on their first or second try. Jon Lord's *Gemini Suite* is better than his earlier Concerto; Wakeman's *King Arthur* is an advance over his *Journey*. But rock styles change rapidly, and the creators–performers move on to the next thing, often leaving the previous style unfulfilled.

The art rock trend receded as the 1970s progressed, but it did not end. In Chapter 14, "The Continuing Fragmentation of Rock," we shall look briefly at some experimental groups who kept the art rock idea alive.

## MUSICAL CLOSE-UP:
## AN ANALYSIS OF "KARN EVIL 9," BY EMERSON, LAKE, AND PALMER

During the mid-1970s, "Karn Evil 9" was played in a shortened version on many "progressive FM" radio stations. As a result, many listeners became familiar with some segments of this work, but only a minority had really listened carefully and thoughtfully through its entire thirty-minute length. Unless one gives full attention from beginning to end, one is likely to miss both the ideological point and the total musical value.

"Karn Evil 9" is in three movements, called "Impressions." Thus, the macroform is like that of a classical concerto, with the usual three movements: fast, slow, fast. The "First Impression" is in two parts. Let us begin by looking closely at part 1 of "First Impression."

The lyrics of part 1 set the scene quite effectively; the following key words and phrases create a general impression:

| | |
|---|---|
| cold and misty morning | age of power |
| seeds have withered | silent children shivered |
| jackals for gold | suffering in silence |
| betrayed | hurt |
| beat | terrible |
| survival | no compassion |
| sorrow | helpless |
| refugee | |

In fact, "cold" and "sorrow" are used twice. Our impression may be vague, but we certainly get the feeling that whatever or whenever this place is, it is rather bleak and dreary, filled with little of the joy in life. But there is a ray of hope. Our hero promises us repeatedly that he will "be there." He tells us that he will come "to heal their sorrow, to beg and borrow, fight tomorrow." Whatever the problems are with this mysterious society, our hero promises to rectify them.

Musically, part 1 of "First Impression" consists of an introduction, three verses (interrupted by an instrumental break), and a codetta. A coda is a closing section of a major work, comparable to an introduction at the beginning; a codetta is a "small coda" that closes an internal section of a piece. The introduction is brief, but notice how tightly the trio is coordinated. Listen carefully to Palmer's drums; you will find that he is changing his patterns with every measure, perfectly reinforcing the accents and rhythmic patterns of Emerson's line; then listen to Lake's bass line and you will find that he is doing the same. This is analogous to what goes on in a symphony orchestra. The percussion section and the cellos and basses do not simply play continuous patterns throughout; each measure and note is carefully set into the changing fabric of the total sound.

Each of the three verses divides into two internal sections (A and B); part A contains new lyrics each time (verse 1—"Cold and misty morning"; verse 2—"Suffering in silence"; verse 3—"There must be someone"). But in each case an obvious descending series of pitches announces a kind of refrain (part B) on the words "I'll be there." Short instrumental interludes follow verses 1 and 2; the music of these interludes expands upon the musical material of the introduction (some of which is also used to tie the phrases of the verses together).

The second interlude (between verses 2 and 3) is interrupted by an instrumental break. Again notice the tight coordination within the trio. As the break ends, the music of the interrupted interlude returns and leads into verse 3. Notice also that the instrumental accompaniment is slightly different for each verse, thus avoiding the "easy" way of playing the same thing under each verse. The descending series of pitches that has previously announced the "I'll be there" refrain carries lyrics this time ("Can't you see"). After the refrain there is a short codetta as our hero promises to heal the sorrow, beg, borrow, and fight tomorrow. The following diagram presents a graphic representation of part 1 of "First Impression."

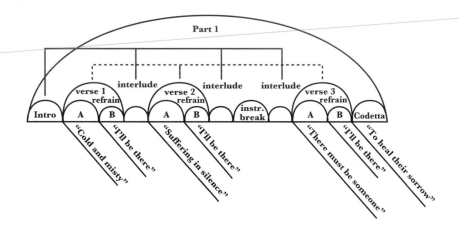

To provide a bit more insight into this mysterious society, part 2 provides an analogy. ELP compares their imaginary society to a carnival sideshow. At carnival sideshows we see unusual, freakish exhibits—things we do not see as a normal part of our lives. There may be a two-headed calf, a 400-pound fat man, a tattooed lady, a sword swallower, a fire eater—all things we do not encounter every day. So what do we see at ELP's sideshow? After a typical carnival barker welcomes us to the show, he points out a row of bishops' heads in jars and a bomb inside a car. Possibly the bishops symbolize organized religion; apparently the society of which ELP speaks does not include organized religion in its normal everyday life. Perhaps the bomb represents terrorism, humanity's spectacular cruelty to itself. ELP is not confining itself to the good or the bad traits of humanity; they are simply pointing out characteristics of the human experience, both good and bad. Next we are shown a real speciality: some tears (could these represent human emotion?). And so it goes, as we are shown laughter (human emotion and joy), a ragtime band (music), a stripper (human sexuality and sensuality), Jesus (faith), and grass (natural phenomena). The world ELP is describing is totally devoid of the characteristics—good and bad—that make humans human. Thanks to their carnival analogy, we have a sharper picture of the bleak society they are telling us about.

Part 2 of "First Impression" begins with a fast introduction in 7/4 meter. After a section that features a series of changing meters, a repeating A♮ is played in the lowest synthesizer "voice"; this note pounds away as Emerson plays a melodic line and then a chord progression over it. This is a *pedal point*—a note that continues to sound as the chords above it change; it will return later in part 2.

Part 2 consists of seven verses. The basic form of each verse is AAB: two 4-measure phrases each with new words followed by a 4-measure refrain on the words "Roll up! See the show!" Separating the second phrase and the refrain of each verse is a 2-measure transition that "announces" the refrain (similar to the procedure used in part 1). A short transition, usually 3 measures long, connects the verses to each other. Verses 1, 2, and 3 proceed according to the basic form; the short transition between verses is different each time (after verse 1, a drumroll; after verse 2, a series of organ glissandi, first descending and then ascending; after verse 3, a series of descending drumrolls).

An instrumental break follows verse 3. After a series of descending guitar scales, the trio builds to a big cutoff, leaving only a synthesizer "bouncing" around some high As (the same pitch, only higher, that was the pedal point at the end of the introduction). The upper pedal point fades and then resumes (in the "old" days, one needed to flip the record at this point). After resuming, the pedal point becomes the only accompaniment to the beginning of verse 4 ("Welcome back, my friends"). The form of verse 4 is shortened to AA (the second phrase adds organ accompaniment). Instead of the usual "Roll up!" refrain, we hear new music to the words "Come inside, the show's about to start." This bridge section has a form similar to the verses; because it is new music, we will designate its form as CCD. The D in this case is a new refrain on the words, "You've gotta see the show." Verse 5 is shortened to just one phrase (A) before moving directly to the bridge, which is also shortened from CCD to CD (omitting its second phrase).

Another instrumental break begins with Emerson's improvisation but soon leads to the theme Lake had played in the earlier instrumental break (the one interrupted by the record flip). This time, instead of ending with the pedal point, the break ends with Palmer's drum solo. This drum solo becomes the only accompaniment for the beginning of verse 6. Verse 6 follows the basic form of verses 1, 2, and 3 (but note the addition of old-fashioned piano as Lake sings about Alexander's ragtime band). The full accompaniment enters on the second phrase of verse 6.

Verse 7 begins with the two phrases of the basic AAB verse form. But instead of the "Roll up!" refrain, we hear new music for the words, "Come and see the show," creating a coda. The instrumental section of this coda includes material taken from the introduction, nicely framing part 2. A series of ominous chords leads to the final cadence of "First Impression." The diagram of Part 2 presents a graphic representation of this part of the "First Impression." The lines above the arches show how internal material is related.

"Second Impression" is entirely instrumental. It is largely "through-composed"— that is, it consists of a series of ever-changing musical sections carrying us forward. We can designate these as sections A, B, C, D, and E; however, there are some

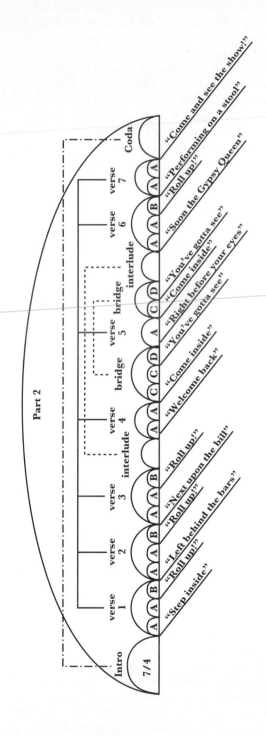

melodic and rhythmic motives that tie together the various sections. Section A features acoustic piano; notice especially several two-note motives in the upper range of the piano; they go by fast, but pick them out if you can:

As Emerson's dazzling solo concludes, section B begins with a repeating bass pattern and a Latin flavor. The fiestalike environment culminates in a series of acoustic piano figures, syncopated chords, and a strong cadence on D major.

Section C provides a real contrast, taking us from the fun and hilarity of the earlier sections to a very pensive and "impressionistic" section. Here motive T becomes very important. We hear it first as ascending chords on the piano:

Throughout this section we hear motive T, sometimes in its original form (descending) and sometimes inverted (ascending). There are strange, rather ephemeral sounds accompanying motive T; these sounds may be produced by plucking, brushing, or otherwise playing on the strings inside the piano. Because there is no steady rock beat in section C, it seems as if time were somehow suspended and we were floating aimlessly. The real clue to the meaning of section C, and indeed the entire "Second Impression," is suggested by a steady clicking sound that enters as the piano plays a series of runs followed by more statements of motive T. Time is passing; the clicking represents the seconds ticking away. Motive T sounds like the ticktock of a clock. We are being transported through time (musically) to the society ELP tried to describe in "First Impression."

After a brief section D on acoustic piano (opening with the same motive that began section C, by the way), we again arrive at a cadence on D major. Section E is a fast boogie-woogie featuring acoustic piano.

"Third Impression" thrusts us into the midst of ELP's imaginary society of the future. Our hero is there to do battle. After assuring us that he will act as our knight in shining armor, he bravely announces that no one in his "army" will yield to the enemy. But even as he speaks, we encounter the enemy, a computer, who warns our hero, "Danger! Stranger! Load your program. I am yourself." Our hero is not intimidated. He says that no computer can stand in his way; only human blood can settle this ultimate battle. He calls upon all the guardians of a "new clear" (nuclear?) dawn to join him as the maps of war are drawn. With that, our hero engages the computer in a musical war.

As the musical representation of the furious battle ends, our hero returns to report on the results. He tells us that we can rejoice in a great victory and assures us that our young warriors have not died in vain. In fact, he says that there is no need to memorialize the dead with flowers on their graves because their names have all been stored permanently in a computer.

Our hero has lost but does not know it. He thinks that he has won, but in fact he, too, has become consumed by the inhuman technology of the computerized society. After all, we do not need flowers to remember our dead; the computer has their names all safely stored in its memory tapes. Our pathetic hero says proudly, "I am all there is"; but the victorious computer tells him that he has been allowed to live. Our hero argues that the computer, after all, was created by humans to do good things. The computer simply replies that there was no choice; its creation was inevitable. It asks, "I'm perfect! Are you?"

"Third Impression" begins with an introduction that includes military-like "horn calls" played on synthesizer. Verse 1 is in two parts (A and B), beginning respectively with the words "Man alone" (A) and "Fear that rattles" (B). A brief interlude leads to verse 2, again with internal parts A ("Man of steel") and B ("Walls that no man thought would fall").

A bridge section of new material begins with the words "No man yields who flies in my ship." It is in this section that the computer "speaks" for the first time. The computer's words are appropriately preceded by a fanfare played by synthesizer. The computer's words throughout the "Third Impression" are apparently generated by human speech fed into the synthesizer, which modifies the incoming signal to create an odd timbre.

The battle itself is represented by a lengthy and technically impressive instrumental break. ELP begins with an appropriately marchlike section in a square-cut 4/4 meter. After yet another pedal point section on A♮, there is a typical ELP rock improvisation featuring organ. Timpani notes and drumrolls cut off the improvisation; swirling sounds begin in the low range of the organ. A slow buildup leads to an effective tension-building section as high-range chords move in rising and falling patterns, creating dissonance against the bass as they steadily move toward their peak. A series of synthesizer "whoops" leads to organ chords and a drum solo, which announce the end of the battle and our hero's return to tell us of his "victory."

His victory statement is set to a new theme. The electronically modified computer words alternate with his protestations. The computer has the "last word," but ELP must figure out how to end their large work. They arrive at the most appropriate coda imaginable. As the final synthesizer chord fades, a sequencer pattern begins. Of all instruments, the sequencer is the most automatic—and perhaps the least human. The sequencer is an electronic instrument that, when programmed, triggers a sequence of pitches, rhythms, timbres, and volume levels on the synthesizer. Once one has programmed the desired pattern into the sequencer, it takes over. It will cycle the programmed pattern forever (or until someone "pulls its plug"). It really is a "music machine." ELP starts the sequencer and then moves the resulting synthesizer sequence back and forth from channel to channel; as the sequence itself gets faster and faster, so does the left-to-right-to-left movement. Finally the sequence becomes almost a blur as it whips back and forth from speaker to speaker. Suddenly it ends. Only silence remains.

"Karn Evil 9" is an exceptionally fine example of the sixth approach to art rock. There is no string quartet and no orchestra—just a talented trio of rock performers.

The musical language is the language of rock. Yet, in its concept, it is more like classical music than a rock song. It is a serious work of large proportions, designed to develop a central thought through a series of internal movements and sections. Appropriate music is created to serve each section as the central idea unfolds. The music is technically demanding; the playing is superb. Every measure is tightly coordinated and fulfills its role in the total scheme. It qualifies on every count as an artistic creation, realized through the language of rock—in other words, art rock.

# 13

# Mainstream Rock

## OVERVIEW: THE DECADE OF NONDIRECTION

The 1950s were revolutionary years for popular music. Through a unique blend of R & B, C & W, and pop, a new musical phenomenon was born: rock and roll. The musical, social, and economic effects of this revolution were tremendous. Although many people participated in this revolution, one giant figure—Elvis Presley—bestrode this revolution like a colossus.

The 1960s began with a fragmented music market, exemplified by a variety of contradictory trends. But again, a musical revolution took place. The Beatles overwhelmed all previous trends, gathering together the diverse elements of pop music into their multifaceted style. They expanded the concept of rock and roll and set precedents for much that would follow. With this expanded concept, rock was blended with other styles to create folk rock, soul music, jazz rock, and art rock. Mainstream rock, which had nearly disappeared in the early part of the decade, was rejuvenated by the British bands of the mid-1960s and split into two related but separate styles: the harder, blues-based style of the Rolling Stones and their followers, and the more refined, expansionist style of the Beatles and their followers. The counterculture of the United States pursued the harder mainstream style, creating its own "psychedelic" or "acid" rock. Thus, just as the 1950s had given birth to rock and roll, the 1960s gave birth to a series of important substyles and witnessed a rebirth of mainstream rock. And again, just as Presley had dominated the 1950s, the Beatles became the giant symbol of the 1960s.

As the new decade of the 1970s dawned, one wondered what exciting new trends, what revolutionary styles, what new musical giants would appear. But such anticipations were soon crushed. The Beatles, musical and spiritual leaders of a generation, announced that they were disbanding; millions of fans reacted almost as if there had been a death (which, in a way, there had been). Then, during a Vietnam War protest at Kent State University, National Guard troops fired into a group of protesters, killing four students. For all practical purposes, those shots ended the student protest movement of the 1960s. The counterculture was shocked even further by the deaths of Jimi Hendrix, Janis Joplin, and Jim Morrison—all between September 1970 and July 1971. Coming on the heels of the disillusioning violence at Altamont in December 1969, all of these events seemed to let the air out of the balloon. The youth movement of the 1960s was over.

When a person is stunned by a series of personal tragedies, it is not uncommon for that person to withdraw into himself or herself. Such life-altering blows can change an extroverted, adventurous, aggressive free spirit into an introverted, apathetic, withdrawn cynic. Within a span of eighteen months, the youth movement absorbed the deaths at Altamont and Kent State, the deaths of Hendrix, Joplin, and Morrison, and the symbolic death of the Beatles. Stunned and disheartened, a generation withdrew. There would be no exciting new trends, no revolutionary styles, no musical giants in the 1970s to match those of the 1950s and 1960s. Instead there would be fragmentation, reaction, and continuation.

Several overriding factors characterize the 1970s. We must discuss these factors individually, but, in fact, they were interdependent. The first, and perhaps the primary factor, was the fragmentation of the market. We saw a similar phenomenon in the early 1960s, but it was soon corrected by the overwhelming presence of the Beatles. But the fragmentation of the 1970s would not be overcome. Its roots lay in the new mentality of the 1970s: "Me first!" The youth generation of the 1960s had addressed itself to society as a whole. It worried about war between nations, inequality between races, the relationship between humanity and the environment, and the roles of men and women. However, by the end of the decade, a new self-orientation had begun to grow as the focus turned toward self-realization and self-fulfillment. People wanted to "find themselves" and explore their own consciousness, to learn "who they were." With the tragedies of 1969 to 1971, this trend became dominant. The attitude became one of "to hell with society; I must take care of me." Students of the 1970s were less concerned with world peace and racial equality, and more concerned with acquiring the skill needed to get a job and make money. As a byproduct of this withdrawal process and the new "me-ism," there seemed to be a reaction against the heavy complexities of the 1960s. Many youth of the 1970s were tired of the heavy issues, the obscure texts, and the intricate complexities of 1960s rock. Instead of the experimentation of the Beatles and the sophistication of jazz rock and art rock, many went "back to the basics" and embraced the simpler styles of disco, country-oriented rock, and hard rock.

Society fragmented into hundreds of subcategories of self-interest groups. The relative simplicity of the old demographics—male and female, youth and adult, black and white, lower, middle, and upper class—fragmented into a complex array of demographic clusters. The sellers of products and services responded accordingly. A specially designed product or service was made available for each minicategory within the society. As John Naisbitt wrote in *Megatrends*, we moved from an "either/or" society to a "multiple option" society. Naisbitt points out that the automobile industry offered 752 different models, including 126 different "subcompacts";

there were over 200 brands of cigarettes; a store in Manhattan specialized in light bulbs, offering 2,500 different types. By the end of the decade, instead of three television networks, cable systems offered the viewer over forty choices. Grocers offered not just mustard but everything from peanut mustard to all-natural, salt-free Arizona champagne mustard (Naisbitt 1982, 241). There were magazines for every conceivable minigroup; the book stores were stuffed with self-help books on everything from diets to how to make a million dollars.

The music industry was no different. Radio discovered the concept of "formatting," that is, programming certain styles of music for a specific audience who typically purchased a predictable set of advertised products. Naisbitt (1982, 239) provides a partial list of such formats:

| | | |
|---|---|---|
| album-oriented rock | disco | country rock |
| easy-listening pop | punk rock | rock country |
| big-band jazz | rhythm and blues | progressive rock |
| progressive jazz | oldies but goodies | |

To this list could be added Top 40, classical music, ethnic music, Christian programming, talk radio, and all news. Record stores carefully segregated their products into bins labeled reggae, punk, disco, heavy metal, jazz, classical, soul, folk, easy listening, rock, and so on.

The world waited for the next Presley or Beatles, but slowly began to realize that that was no longer possible. The music market (indeed, society as a whole) was so fragmented that no one person or group could possibly cut across all those radio formats, all those record bins, and all those demographic minigroups. For a while, each new artist was hailed as the new giant—for example, Elton John, Peter Frampton, and the Bee Gees. But in such a fragmented market there simply could not be such a figure.

If the fragmentation of the "me decade" was a central factor, a secondary factor within the music world was the consolidation of power within the record industry. As Ken Tucker points out, "By the end of the 1970s, the rock market would be controlled by just six major companies: CBS, Warner Communications, Polygram, RCA, MCA, and Capitol-EMI" (Ward, Stokes, and Tucker 1986, 521). The huge music conglomerates were big business; music was not an art, it was a product, like a pencil sharpener or an electric toothbrush. The formula was simple: Identify a viable (monied) submarket through sophisticated market research; determine what that submarket was willing to buy; design a product that met those criteria; create the product; and mass-produce it and mass-market it. Thus, the 1970s music industry sold some hard rock, some soft rock, some neo-folksingers, some neo-country, some neo-jazz-rock, some art rock, some disco, some punk, some heavy metal— each to a clearly defined segment of the market. Each fragment of the society was given the product it wanted. The corporate philosophy was solid: Do not get too experimental or innovative because it might not sell; stick to the proven product. People are not comfortable with that which they do not understand, that which is too new. So continue with what they know, understand, and like.

As a result, we shall find that most of the musical categories to be considered in Chapters 13, 14, and 15 are basically continuations of earlier initiatives. If there was one characteristic that cut across almost all the fragments of the 1970s music scene, it was the explosion of electronic technology. The synthesizer and its various electronic spin-offs permeated virtually every style. There were multiple synthesizers, multiple electronic keyboards, and, of course, electric guitars in every rock group, no matter which subcategory. Sound reproduction at live concerts reached incredible heights of sophistication. And recording studio technology allowed the artists and producers a seemingly unlimited spectrum of possibilities. The rock historian of the twenty-first century may look back at the bewildering kaleidoscope of styles in the 1970s and, finding little to tie it all together, simply call it the decade of electronic rock.

We have already discussed some of the artists whose initial impact came in the 1960s but who continued into the 1970s—groups like the Rolling Stones; Chicago; Emerson, Lake, and Palmer; the Who, and the Dead. Having already discussed their work beyond the 1960s, we shall confine our attention to artists whose principal impact first came in the 1970s and 1980s. The fragmentation phenomenon was so pervasive that if one lists 100 bands, one is tempted to devise seventy-five categories. Although some fit nicely into defined categories, many developed individual styles that elude simple categorization. In order to bring some order to the bewildering array of artists, we will concentrate on mainstream styles in Chapter 13 and survey various "combination" styles in Chapter 14. We will devote Chapter 15 to a discussion of heavy metal and Chapter 16 to dance music. Several of these styles, in turn, fragment into substyles. Quite a few bands straddle two or even three categories. A few seem to fit no category but their own. The reader is, therefore, cautioned to consider these categories merely as aids in structuring the total discussion, and to avoid considering the artists discussed therein to be rigidly pigeonholed. With that caveat, let us plunge squarely into the mainstream.

## MAINSTREAM TRENDS OF THE 1970S

### The British Keep Coming

By 1967, the first British invasion had run its course, with only the Beatles and Stones continuing to have major impact on the U.S. charts. But in the last two years of the 1960s, a host of new British bands launched a second invasion. We have already met a number of these "second-wave" bands— the Who, the Moody Blues, Procol Harum, Emerson, Lake, and Palmer, Deep Purple, Genesis, and Yes—whose peak popularity came in the 1970s.

The rock mainstream entered the 1970s as a two-way split; running parallel to this dual mainstream was the primarily British art rock trend. In the course of the 1970s, these would fragment even further. Some of the bands that began as hard-rocking, blues-based mainstream bands (the "Stones side") veered off toward art rock; they became known as progressive rock bands. On the other hand, some bands of similar derivation increased the "hardness" of their brand of mainstream rock and evolved into "heavy metal" bands. Heavy metal developed into a major rock style—one that continued strongly through the 1980s and even into the 1990s and beyond. We shall devote the entirety of Chapter 15 to this important style. Still others on the harder side of the mainstream took a rather odd turn toward "glitter rock" or "glam rock"—essentially a visual or theatrical (not musical) distinction. And finally, some rebelled against *everything* and developed the "punk" trend. The other side of the mainstream (the less strident "Beatles side") also fragmented, although somewhat less dramatically. A number of these groups also drifted toward art rock, joining in the so-called progressive rock trend; others moved toward a more commercially popular sound (Top 40 oriented); and a few steered a course right down the center. Let us begin with the late 1960s to early 1970s British second-wave bands and see where they lead us.

When last we spoke of Eric Clapton, he was a member of the Yardbirds, a British blues-based band that stressed lengthy improvisational solos. Prior to that, Clapton had been with John Mayall's Bluesbreakers. Clapton's interest in blues and improvisation continued in his next group, Cream, formed in 1966. One of the first rock trios, Cream enjoyed a successful but brief career for slightly over two years. Their second album, *Disraeli Gears* (late 1967), includes several examples of their improvisational solos. As was the case with other improvisatory groups of the late 1960s, the band would establish a basic riff and then, using the riff as a foundation, superimpose a series of long improvisational solos. "Sunshine of Your Love" (number 5 in 1968) contains one of the most familiar (and oft-imitated) riffs in rock. Cream's repertoire included original songs as well as older American blues material. The double album *Wheels of Fire* (number 1 in 1968) offers several good illustrations of Cream's use of the twelve-bar blues (note especially "Politician" and "Crossroads"). Internal tensions led to the dissolution of the band in late 1968.

Following the breakup of Cream, Clapton formed two short-lived bands: Blind Faith (1969) and Derek and the Dominoes (1970 to 1972). Tortured by a severe drug problem and an on-and-off love affair with Patti Harrison (George's wife)—whom he eventually married—Clapton retreated from the limelight for a while. He returned in 1974 with the number 1 album *461 Ocean Boulevard*, issued under his own name. It contained the number 1 single hit, "I Shot the Sheriff," a reggae-style song composed by Bob Marley. Through the 1970s, 1980s, and 1990s, Clapton continued to record under his own name; he continues to be considered one of rock's most influential guitarists.

One of England's finest keyboard players was Stevie Winwood (born in Birmingham, England, in 1948). Having played with the Spencer Davis Group in his midteens, Winwood formed his own group, Traffic, in late 1967. A talented collection of musicians, Traffic was besieged by breakups, reorganizations, and constant personnel shifts. Winwood left briefly in 1969 to join Blind Faith, but returned after that band's dissolution. Traffic's finest album came in 1970 with *John Barleycorn Must Die* (number 5). Especially impressive was the strong playing of Winwood and the always tasteful work of woodwind player Chris Wood. Much of the material written by Winwood and drummer Jim Capaldi was quite creative and included touches of jazz and folk elements in addition to rock. Following the release of *When the Eagle Flies* (1974), which featured more excellent keyboard work by Winwood, the group disbanded. Winwood experienced significant solo success in the mid-1980s with the triple-platinum *Back in the High Life* (number 3 in 1986), which included two Top 10 singles: the Grammy-winning "Higher Love" (number 1; featuring Chaka Khan) and "The Finer Things" (number 8). In 1988 came a number 1 album, *Roll With It*, that included three hit singles: the title track (number 1), "Don't You Know What the Night Can Do?" (number 6), and "Holding On" (number 11). Capaldi and Winwood reunited, however, to release *Far From Home* in 1994.

Rod Stewart was born in London in 1945 to Scottish parents. In his late teens, he began singing with a number of the early British blues-based bands. In early 1967, he helped form the Jeff Beck Group with Beck and bassist–guitarist Ron Wood; in his two years with Beck, Stewart gained initial exposure to a wide audience in England and the United States. By 1970, a British mainstream band, Small Faces, was on the verge of disbanding; instead they reorganized as Faces and acquired the services of Ron Wood and Rod Stewart. Stewart had already signed as a solo artist with Mercury Records, so he pursued a dual career as a soloist and as a member of Faces. However, Stewart's solo career gradually overshadowed the group's work, and Faces disappeared by the mid-1970s.

Stewart's second album, *Gasoline Alley* (1970), made the U.S. Top 30 and was the real beginning of his solo success. It was a hard-rocking album with clear blues roots. Stewart's hoarse, raspy voice was distinctive and seemed just right for the shouting tradition of blues-based mainstream rock. Stewart's follow-up album, *Every Picture Tells a Story* (1971), became a number 1 album and contained the hit single "Maggie May" (number 1 in 1971). He developed a flamboyant and spectacular stage act, complete with flashy costumes and his distinctive wild blond hairstyle.

Following *Never a Dull Moment* (number 2 in 1972), Stewart's popularity seemed to decline for several years. However, in 1975, he reemerged with the successful *Atlantic Crossing* album, which made the U.S. Top 10. Although it is sometimes felt that Stewart's post–1975 work falls short of his earlier blues-based classics, he continued to be an important rock personality well into the 1990s and beyond. In the late 1990s, after having a cancerous nodule removed from his thyroid gland, Stewart released a series of significantly mellower recordings, including *Human* (2001) and a series of recordings of jazz standards and show tunes in a series entitled *The Great American Songbook* (*It Had to Be You*, 2002; *As Time Goes By*, 2003; and *Stardust*, 2004).

### The Gentler Side of the British Mainstream

As we have mentioned, the harder side of the British mainstream of the 1970s fragmented into basic hard rock, heavy metal, glitter rock, and punk–new wave. Meanwhile, there was also the continuation of the somewhat less outrageous, less deafening, less shock-oriented side of the mainstream.

One of the most successful of these mainstream groups began on the harder, blues-based side and crossed over to the softer side in the mid-1970s. The nucleus of Fleetwood Mac was formed in 1967 by former members of John Mayall's Bluesbreakers. Soon, several other veterans of Mayall's group were added. The resulting quartet—Jeremy Spencer, Peter Green, Mick Fleetwood, and John McVie— debuted as Green's Fleetwood Mac at the British National Jazz and Blues Festival in August 1967. As appropriate for a late-1960s British blues-based band, Fleetwood Mac included songs by Elmore James, Howlin' Wolf, and Sonny Boy Williamson (plus several blues-based originals) on their first album, *Fleetwood Mac* (1968). As would be the case for the balance of the 1960s, the band would enjoy considerable popularity in England but remain virtually unknown in the United States.

The transition from a strong blues base to a softer style began in the early 1970s as a result of various personnel changes (including the addition of McVie's wife Christine on keyboards and vocals). The first album with the new quintet was *Future Games* (1971). The old blues sound was now in the past, and the newer Fleetwood Mac emphasized ballads and more refined harmonies. Through the early 1970s, there were more personnel changes; albums sold moderately well, but none reached the U.S. Top 30.

By 1974, the band had survived legal difficulties, more personnel changes, and moved to Los Angeles. There they recruited the duo of Stevie Nicks (vocals) and Lindsey Buckingham (guitar and vocals). The initial album featuring the new lineup (Fleetwood, two McVies, Nicks, and Buckingham) indicated that the transformation from the harder to the softer side of the rock mainstream was complete. *Fleetwood Mac* (1975) was a commercial success, becoming their first number 1 album and producing three Top 40 hits. The follow-up album, *Rumours* (1977), was even bigger, as it held the number 1 position for thirty-one weeks and turned platinum with over fourteen million copies sold. Again there were three hit singles, including the number 1 song "Dreams." With three songwriters contributing to the new repertoire (Nicks, Buckingham, and Christine McVie), there was no dearth of good material. The solid vocal harmonies, which included two female voices, and the excellent musicianship of the entire band accounted for their brilliant success. The *Rumours* album suggests the versatility of the band as they move from the mainstream rock style of "Don't Stop" and "Go Your Own Way" to the soft rock sound of "Dreams." There is a liberal dose of folk rock style and even frequent touches of country sounds.

The McVie divorce and the personal separation of Nicks and Buckingham did not damage the group's professional work. The double album *Tusk* was released in 1979; it carried the earlier-evidenced versatility of the group toward a true eclecticism. Buckingham was the primary force behind *Tusk*; he ventured into several rather eccentric experiments (e.g., "Not That Funny") that undoubtedly puzzled a few of Fleetwood Mac's fans. *Tusk* also yielded three Top 40 hits.

As the 1980s began, the individual members of Fleetwood Mac increasingly pursued individual projects. The most successful was Stevie Nicks, who enjoyed seven Top 40 hits in the early 1980s.

One of those promptly anointed as the Presley or Beatles of the 1970s was Elton John. Although he was enormously successful, he certainly was far short of being the influential phenomenon across all markets that such status would require. Elton John presents yet another case in which the student of rock history must be cautious; the rock establishment's "party line" has generally condemned John as being banal, mechanical, and slickly commercial. On the other hand, rock historian Charles Brown went so far as to say that "Elton John epitomizes the best of 1970s music" (Brown 1987, 148). The truth, again, may lie somewhere in between.

Elton John was born Reginald Dwight in Middlesex, England, in 1947. He began playing piano at the age of four and won a scholarship to London's Royal Academy of Music at the age of eleven. Later joining the band Bluesology, Elton began a period of some six years knocking around the nether regions of the British music business. Finally, thanks to a massive PR effort by Uni Records, "Your Song" (from Elton's second album, *Elton John*, 1970) entered the U.S. charts and rose to the Top 10 in early 1971. The music to "Your Song" was written by Elton, but the lyrics were by Bernie Taupin. The team of John and Taupin wrote virtually all of Elton's music until they split up in 1976.

Elton's peak period was from late 1971 through early 1976. Beginning with *Madman Across the Water,* he released nine albums, seven of which went to number 1. Along with the album sales, there were over a dozen Top 20 hits, including five number 1 songs. Of particular interest is the *Honky Chateau* album, which deemphasized the huge string arrangements and featured more guitar-oriented rock. "Honky Cat" and "Rocket Man" were taken from this album. Also notable was "Crocodile Rock" from *Don't Shoot Me, I'm Only the Piano Player;* it is a clever piece of nostalgia on the late 1950s soft rock sound (compare it with Paul Anka's "Diana"). "Saturday Night's Alright for Fighting" is a strong example of Elton's mainstream rock style; on songs such as this, he would jump up and down at the piano and generally put on quite an athletic show, recalling the antics of Little Richard and Jerry Lee Lewis. "Bennie and the Jets" features some very fine piano work by Elton plus some strong falsetto singing. Elton's version of "Lucy in the Sky with Diamonds" was appropriately recorded with the assistance of Dr. Winston O'Boogie (John Lennon).

In 1974, Elton signed an eight million dollar contract with MCA Records (the largest contract in rock history until Stevie Wonder topped it in 1975 with his thirteen million dollar Motown contract). In 1975, Elton starred in the movie version of

*Tommy.* But in 1976 he announced his "retirement" and disbanded his backup group. That year he and Taupin recorded their final album together, *Blue Moves*. Elton's retirement was short-lived; in 1978 he released *A Single Man,* yet another platinum album. Since then, Sir Elton John has continued to record, and his albums and singles continue to sell well. In 1997, he and Bernie Taupin reunited to remake "Candle in the Wind," a song originally written as a tribute to Marilyn Monroe. The new version was created for and performed at the funeral of Princess Diana. This recording may be the highest selling single of all time; U.S. sales reached 11 million in the first month. Elton also had great success with soundtracks for *The Lion King* and *The Road to El Dorado*. In the 1990s and beyond the turn of the new century, his albums continued to enjoy considerable success, with many of them certified as gold, platinum, and even multiplatinum.

Elton John (*Source:* Michael Ochs Archive, Ltd.)

Before leaving the British mainstream, we must illustrate how desperately everyone was expecting the next giant of rock and roll. Mention the name of Peter Frampton now and you are likely to get a shrug of the shoulders or simply a blank look. But for a period of slightly less than two years, from 1976 to 1977, Frampton was being mentioned in the same breath as Presley and the Beatles. After all, the 1970s were half over and there had been no true "king."

Frampton was a singer–guitarist who had played with a group called the Herd in the late 1960s and with Humble Pie (a hard rock band) in the early 1970s. Pursuing a generally undistinguished solo career, Frampton suddenly burst on the scene with a tremendously successful live double album, *Frampton Comes Alive!* (1976). *Alive* zoomed to number 1 and stayed there for ten weeks; it turned platinum and eventually sold over fifteen million copies. The song "Do You Feel Like We Do" featured a "voice box," a device that routes the electric guitar signal through a tube into the singer's mouth, thus allowing the mouth to shape the guitar timbre into "words."

Frampton went from being just another British rocker to the Presley–Beatles of the 1970s almost overnight. He was suddenly a superstar, playing to packed stadiums. The follow-up album, *I'm in You* (1977), reached only number 2, and although it was certified as platinum, it did not come close to the sales records established by *Alive!*. Frampton played the role of Billy Shears in the movie *Sgt. Pepper's Lonely Hearts Club Band*—an embarrassing film according to both critics and fans. Following a severe automobile accident, Frampton attempted to pick up where he had left off, but it was not to be. Another candidate for Giant of the Seventies bit the dust after a grand total of two Top 10 albums.

## Mainstream Rock in the States

For each British mainstream fragment—harder mainstream, softer mainstream, heavy metal, glitter rock, and punk–new wave—there was an American parallel. Generally speaking, the American mainstream rock groups tended to be less hard than their British counterparts. To begin this discussion, we must return to San Francisco and meet a group called Creedence Clearwater Revival (CCR). CCR shared very little in common with their Bay Area colleagues of the late 1960s. Their "good ol' boy," Deep South sound was largely determined by their acknowledged leader, John Fogerty.

Formed originally as a high school group in 1959, the Blue Velvets played 1950s-style rock and roll. With the British invasion, they became the Golliwogs, hoping to capitalize on the British image. Finally, in late 1967, they changed their name to Creedence Clearwater Revival and released a remake of an old 1950s hit, "Suzie Q." (sung by Dale Hawkins, number 27 in 1957); it moved to number 11 in 1968.

CCR consisted of John Fogerty (guitar, vocals, keyboards, and harmonica), brother Tom Fogerty (guitar, piano, vocals), Stu Cook (bass and piano), and Doug Clifford (drums). Their second album, *Bayou Country* (1969), by its very title, fostered the deep southern image. From the album came a monster hit, "Proud Mary" (number 2 in 1969). Fogerty's black enunciation reinforced the southern image of the group. *Willy and the Poorboys,* possibly CCR's most representative album, illustrates CCR's typical styles: There is good time rock and roll with "It Came Out of the Sky"; the deep southern sound is obvious in "Down on the Corner," "Cotton

American rock group Creedence Clearwater Revival. From left to right; Doug Clifford, Tom Fogerty, Stu Cook and John Fogerty (*Source: Getty Images, Inc.*)

Fields," and "The Midnight Special"; songs like "Feelin' Blue" and "Side o' the Road" are very bluesy, although by adhering to one basic chord throughout, they sound like the first phrase of a twelve-bar blues repeated over and over; "Effigy" is about as San Francisco–ish as CCR ever got. The southern sound was sometimes closer to rockabilly ("Suzie Q."), and at other times closer to the black blues sound. An interesting melding of styles may be heard in the Motown hit "I Heard It Through the Grapevine," in which CCR preserves the original's basic melody and harmonies but adds a lengthy guitar improvisation.

CCR's popularity continued into the early 1970s. However, by 1971, Tom Fogerty had grown uncomfortable with his younger brother's dominance; he left the band. John yielded to the desires of Cook and Clifford to have more creative input; thus, on *Mardi Gras*, Fogerty contributed only three songs. The music was softer and revealed stronger country influences. The album was CCR's first not to reach the Top 10 since their very first album. In October 1971, they disbanded. Following the breakup, John Fogerty released a series of six solo recordings between 1973 and 1998, including *Centerfield* (number 1 in 1985) and *Blue Moon Swamp* (1997), which only reached number 37 but earned a Grammy for Best Rock Album.

Another San Francisco band that succeeded in 1970s mainstream rock was the Doobie Brothers. Formed in San Jose in 1969, the Doobies endured a bewildering series of personnel changes throughout their career. Normally using a lineup of two guitars, bass, and two drums, the band played a strong style of mainstream rock. Their first album, *Toulouse Street* (1972), included the popular anthem, "Listen to the Music" (number 11 in 1972). The unique voice of Tom Johnston, plus the strong vocal harmonizations, established the band's appeal. As with many U.S. bands, the Doobies were not as hard as their mainstream British counterparts, falling more to the softer side of the mainstream, combining good vocals, good harmonies, and clean playing with sophisticated recording production.

A good sample of early 1970s Doobie Brothers may be heard on *The Captain and Me* (number 7 in 1973). Especially appealing are "Long Train Running" (number 8) and "China Grove" (number 15). The sound of the band changed somewhat in 1975, when Tom Johnston fell ill with bleeding ulcers; he continued intermittently with the band, but, by early 1977, he had left the band permanently.

With the loss of their lead singer and chief songwriter, a new Doobie sound emerged with the title song from the 1976 album, *Takin' It to the Streets*. Having added the ex–Steely Dan guitarist Jeff Baxter in 1974, they now added another former member of Steely Dan, keyboardist–vocalist Mike McDonald. The harmonies became more sophisticated and even a bit jazz oriented. McDonald proved to be a valuable contributor as a songwriter to replace Johnston. However, personnel changes constantly plagued the band, and by 1982 the Doobies had passed their peak of popularity.

Sometimes associated with the late 1960s San Francisco scene, Steve Miller probably belongs more to the American mainstream of the 1970s. Raised in Dallas, the young Miller formed a strong liking for black R & B. After attending the University of Wisconsin, Miller moved to Chicago, where he played with local bluesmen such as Muddy Waters and several white blues enthusiasts such as Paul Butterfield, Mike Bloomfield, and Barry Goldberg. Following the migration to San Francisco, Miller formed his own band in 1966. Playing the San Francisco concert halls and generally participating in the Haight–Ashbury scene, Miller never really joined the true acid rock style, remaining more in the blues-based rock mainstream.

Miller's big break came in late 1973 with his ninth album *The Joker;* the album hit number 2 and the title song rose to number 1. Miller's popularity ebbed and flowed through the balance of the 1970s, but in 1982 he hit big again with *Abracadabra* (number 3); the title song became Miller's third number 1 single. Miller's mainstream style showed his blues roots, sometimes colored by touches of country and even vestiges of the old San Francisco sound. Generally, he maintained a position on the softer side of the American mainstream rock style of the 1970s.

It is no doubt becoming apparent how fragmented rock really was in the 1970s. Even the fragments fragmented as each artist (or group) within a given style sought to establish an individual identity. Black music also fragmented, as various artists moved in different directions. One of the first stylistic directions evolved in San Francisco, as Sylvester Stewart combined soul music with psychedelic rock to create a style called "psychedelic soul." Stewart was born in Dallas in 1944 but soon moved with his family to northern California. There he and his siblings sang in a gospel group, The Stewart Four. Sly, as he became known, played guitar and drums as well as organ and piano.

In 1966, he organized the Stoners, and by 1967, the band had evolved into the seven-member Sly and the Family Stone (the membership was biracial and included Sly's sister Rose and his brother Fred). Success first came in 1968 with *Dance to the Music;* the album fared poorly, but the title song made the Top 10. Their fourth album, *Stand!*, became Sly's first truly successful album (number 13 in 1969), yielding four hit singles, including the number 1 "Everyday People." Reinforcing the band's popularity was their appearance at Woodstock in August 1969. The *Woodstock* film

Sly Stone (*Source:* Michael Ochs Archive, Ltd.)

enhanced the group's popularity, especially with their sensational performance of "I Want to Take You Higher."

Sly's style combined many elements. At its foundation was a basically funky beat and bass line; horns added a jazzy element reminiscent of the old Memphis and Stax–Volt soul sound; some of the guitar work and the band's relatively loose performance style were associated with the San Francisco psychedelic sound, as were some of their drug-oriented lyrics; more often the lyrics dealt with black-oriented and youth-oriented themes. Of particular interest was the vocal format. There were frequently two or three lead singers on a given song; juxtaposition of a female voice and two distinctly different male voices created a unique sound. Although almost any Sly song will reveal the group's style, one of the best examples is their early "Dance to the Music." It contained most of the stylistic characteristics that made Sly and the Family Stone popular.

By 1971, Sly's hard-won success began to lead to his demise. A contributing factor, according to Jack McDonough, was Sly's "eccentric, unpredictable, and irresponsible behavior, prompted, all reports agreed, by an extreme fondness for cocaine" (McDonough 1985, 207). Sly began showing up late or not at all for important concerts; in Chicago, a riot resulted from his nonappearance. The late 1971 album, *There's a Riot Goin' On*, reached number 1 and certainly carried ironic implications. But the end was near. *Fresh* (1973) was Sly's last Top 10 album, and "If You Want Me to Stay" was his last major hit (number 12). Subsequent albums fared less well; a disco-flavored album failed to make the Top 200 and a solo album reached only number 45. The late 1979 album *Back on the Right Track* proved only that Sly was not (it reached number 152).

Before leaving San Francisco we must mention one other band that began in the 1970s and endured to become a major act of the 1980s. Journey began in 1973 with two former members of Santana—keyboardist Gregg Rolie and guitarist Neal Schon—as its nucleus. Journey's first three albums, which emphasized their instrumental work, were not big sellers. Things began to change in 1977 when lead singer Steve Perry was added. His unique and powerful voice gave Journey a truly distinctive sound and was largely responsible for the success of their fourth album, *Infinity* (number 21 in 1978). Having survived numerous personnel changes, Journey entered the 1980s with only two of its original members (Schon and bassist Ross Valory).

In the early 1980s, Journey became firmly established as an important mainstream rock band. Their album *Frontiers* (number 2 in 1983), which yielded four hit singles, is an interesting album, as side 1 contains milder material whereas side 2 reflects a style that is closer to hard rock and heavy metal. Such diversity typified

Journey, a talented band that could produce ballads like "Open Arms" and "Faithfully" without sounding like a soft rock group; they could also move to the other extreme and sound like a heavy metal band (but far more artistic than most) in songs like "Edge of the Blade." In between was a hard mainstream rock style that featured Perry's strong high voice (always perfectly controlled, even when he was shouting or screaming), Schon's superb guitar breaks, and solid musicianship by the rest of the band.

Leaving San Francisco we move back to the South, where rock and roll was born. Other than the soul recordings in Memphis and Muscle Shoals, rock had left its birthplace. Most rock of the 1960s had come from places like Detroit, Los Angeles, San Francisco, Philadelphia, New York City, Liverpool, and London. However, in the early 1970s there was an effort to get "back to the basics" of southern rock and roll. In 1969, Duane and Gregg Allman (born in Nashville in 1946 and 1947, respectively) formed a band that would initiate the southern rock trend. Duane continued playing guitar sessions behind other artists such as Wilson Pickett, Aretha Franklin, Boz Scaggs, Delaney and Bonnie, and Eric Clapton's Derek and the Dominoes. The band's real breakthrough came when Phil Walden, formerly Otis Redding's manager, began Capricorn Records in Macon, Georgia, and released the Allman Brothers Band's live album, *At Fillmore East* (1971). The blues-based rock style was evident on songs like "In Memory of Elizabeth Reed" and the side-long "Whipping Post" (or listen to "Midnight Rider" from the earlier *Idlewild South* album).

The first tragedy to strike the Allman Brothers was the death of Duane in a motorcycle accident in late October 1971. *Eat a Peach* (1972) contained Duane's last recordings; the double album reached number 4 on the album charts. His leadership and guitar talents were sorely missed. Slightly over one year later, the band's bassist, Berry Oakley, was killed in a motorcycle accident near the site of Duane's death.

The band managed to produce a new album, *Brothers and Sisters*, in 1973; it became the Allman Brothers Band's first and only number 1 album. A good example of the southern blues rock is "Southbound," a traditional twelve-bar blues that displayed a perfect blending of R & B and rock. An earlier example of the Allman Brother's twelve-bar blues rock is "Statesboro Blues," from the *Fillmore* album; like "Southbound," it contains a "black" shouting vocal. "Jessica" is a good straight-ahead southern rock tune, revealing some very strong playing.

By 1976 the band had fragmented. After several years, Gregg Allman reassembled a band and released several albums in the late 1970s and early 1980s that were moderate sellers.

The Allman Brothers were a real key to the beginning of the southern rock sound. Their work in the period from 1970 to 1973 established the return of rock to its southern R & B roots. Following in their footsteps was Lynyrd Skynyrd, a band whose roots can be traced back to the mid-1960s in Jacksonville, Florida. The Allman Brothers Band had been a sextet with two drummers (like the Doobies) and a dual lead guitar format. Lynyrd Skynyrd added a third lead guitar, becoming a rock septet.

Lynyrd Skynyrd established a strong reputation as a live performance band, partially as a result of their tour with the Who in 1973. Their peak popularity dates from the Top 10 hit "Sweet Home Alabama" (1974) through 1977, during which time three of their four albums made the Top 10. Taking the Allman Brothers' blues-based sound and adding a slightly harder rock sound, the band achieved a unique style. However, tragedy was to end it all in 1977 when the band's charter plane crashed, killing vocalist Ronnie Van Zant and two other band members and injuring others. Three days before the crash, *Street Survivors* had been released; it reached number 5 on the album charts, the highest ranking of any Skynyrd album.

An interesting compilation album released in late 1982 is *Best of the Rest;* it contains lesser-known cuts from earlier albums plus two unreleased songs recorded at Muscle Shoals. There are good examples of twelve-bar blues rock songs such as "I've Been Your Fool," "Call Me the Breeze" (from *Second Helping*), and "T for Texas" (from *One More from the Road*, 1976). "I'm a Country Boy" illustrates the black style vocal from the R & B tradition over an insistent hard rock riff; there are even some nice country rock sounds on a song like "I Never Dreamed" (from *Street Survivors*). And of course, there is some good strong southern rock, as in "Double Trouble" (from *Gimme Back My Bullets*, 1976).

Continuing our survey of the American mainstream of the 1970s, we move from the South to the Midwest. The group Kansas is sometimes considered to be a progressive or art rock band, based on the fact that the band prominently included violin and that the musical form of some of their compositions extended well beyond a simple verse-chorus structure. Indeed, there are moments when the classical training of several of Kansas's members can be discerned (e.g., "Lonely Wind" and "Journey from Mariabronn," especially with the latter's meter changes and modal tunes). However, more often the overall sound is that of a sophisticated form of mainstream rock.

The six members of Kansas were fine players and singers. Their rock sound was solid; their harmonies (vocal and instrumental) were well conceived and well performed. From Topeka, Kansas, they formed their band in 1971. Kansas experienced their greatest success between 1976 and early 1978 with the albums *Leftoverture* (number 5 in 1976), which contained the masterful "Carry On Wayward Son" (number 11 in 1977), and *Point of Know Return* (number 4 in 1977), which included the number 6 hit "Dust in the Wind." Through the late 1970s and early 1980s Kansas produced a series of moderately popular albums, including the number 10 album *Monolith*, the band's first self-produced recording, and several more Top 40 hits. In 1983, the group disbanded, but just three years later three of the original members joined with Steve Morris, guitarist for the jazz-fusion group Dixie Dregs, and released two albums that did not sell well. Success proved elusive after the initial period of success in the late 1970s. Even when the original members of Kansas reconvened (substituting Billy Greer on bass) in 2000 to release *Somewhere to Elsewhere*, the audience did not materialize.

The problem of categorization continues when we move up to Chicago and encounter Styx. We shall include them in this discussion of mainstream rock of the 1970s, although some writers would place them in the progressive rock category; yet their biggest hit, "Babe," came close to a style of soft rock.

In early 1975, *Styx II*, which had been released back in 1973, finally entered the Top 20, and the single "Lady" simultaneously hit the Top 10 (number 6). The 1977 album *The Grand Illusion* became a smash hit and was the first of a series of five platinum albums. Along with the albums came a series of successful singles, including five Top 10 hits and the number 1 song "Babe" (1979). Styx's mainstream style could lean toward a harder sound at times, and toward a softer sound at other times;

there were even occasional touches of progressive rock. Taken overall, their style is a good representation of American mainstream rock of the late 1970s to early 1980s. A song like "Suite Madame Blue" (from *Caught in the Act,* 1984) provides an interesting sample of the various sounds of Styx.

Tying the British and American mainstream together was Foreigner, an international band formed by three New Yorkers and three Londoners. Formed in 1976 by guitarist Mick Jones (formerly with Spooky Tooth) and Ian McDonald (formerly with King Crimson), they signed with Atlantic Records and released their first album, *Foreigner,* in 1977. As with Journey and Styx, Foreigner is capable of moving from a hard rock mainstream norm toward the edges of heavy metal on one side, or toward the softer side for contrast. Interestingly, their two most successful singles, "Waiting for a Girl Like You" and "I Want to Know What Love Is," were among Foreigner's softer rock sounds. After several successful albums and singles in the late 1970s, the band shrunk from a sextet to a quartet. Their 1981 album *4* was a monster hit, becoming Foreigner's only number 1 album. Foreigner achieved their first number 1 single in early 1985 with "I Want to Know What Love Is" (from the *Agent Provocateur* album).

## MAINSTREAM ROCK IN THE EIGHTIES

### Bruce Springsteen

With all of the fragmentation, subcategories, cross-fertilizations, and individualized styles of the 1970s and 1980s, a rather understandable question could be posed: Whatever happened to just plain mainstream rock? Amidst all the hyphens and adjectives, was there anything left that consisted of a gutsy singer, a drummer, some guitarists, a piano player, and maybe a saxophonist playing good old dead-center rock and roll? The answer was "yes," but it was a rather well-kept secret until the 1980s.

Like Michael Jackson, Bruce Springsteen achieved superstar status in the 1980s; and like Jackson, he was no overnight sensation. Both had paid their dues through years of work in the music industry. Springsteen was born in 1949 in Freehold, New Jersey. As a teenager, he worked in a series of bands in the New Jersey and New York City (Greenwich Village) area. In 1972, he finally caught the attention of John Hammond, the A & R (artists and repertoire) representative for Columbia Records. Hammond, as we saw in the case of Dylan, had a penchant for spotting unique, nontraditional vocalists—those with a rough and raw basic sound.

Springsteen's first Columbia album, *Greetings from Asbury Park, New Jersey* (1973), was a slow seller, not appearing on the charts until 1975 and then rising only to number 60. Springsteen toured in 1973 as an opening act for Chicago, but his appeal was limited to certain rock critics and a cult of ardent fans in the Northeast. For his 1974 tour, Springsteen formed what was to become his excellent backup band, the E Street Band. The first real turn in Springsteen's career came with the release of *Born To Run* in 1975. Accompanied by a massive PR campaign (over $200,000 worth), the album broke the Top 5; the title song also broke the Top 40 charts, peaking at number 23.

With *Born To Run,* Springsteen became known to a much wider public. Side 2, especially, revealed the multifaceted appeal of Springsteen's music. The title song was mainstream rock (true of most Springsteen); note especially the instrumental break, featuring the excellent playing of saxophonist Clarence Clemons. This is not art rock, jazz rock, folk rock, or any other kind of mixed rock; it is quintessential, dead-ahead rock and roll. Springsteen's raw, unsophisticated voice, as with Dylan, Joplin, Hendrix, and others, is either loved or hated; one must decide whether to accept it or reject it on its own terms. The lyrics are typical Springsteen: references to the frustrations, confusions, dreams, and disappointments of the average working-class person. The themes of unemployment, social issues, the difficulties of Vietnam veterans, and the rage and frustration of being unable to beat "the establishment" pervade almost all of Springsteen's songs. In that way, he is related to the heritage of the folk rock trend of the 1960s—one of the few remnants of that sentiment in the 1970s and 1980s.

"Meeting Across the River" is a relatively rare example of Springsteen in a softer mode. The trumpet obbligato played by Randy Brecker adds a nice touch to this haunting song. Although generally ignored, "Jungleland" may be the most interesting song on *Born To Run*. Moving nicely out of "Meeting Across the River," "Jungleland" begins quietly with piano and strings. Springsteen sets the scene: the street life of New York City and New Jersey after dark. In the second verse, the tension builds and the textures gradually thicken. As Springsteen reaches the title line, "Jungleland," the full E Street Band enters and the subsequent verse conforms to Springsteen's typical mainstream rock style. A strong instrumental break, once again, reveals the strong musicianship of the backup band. After several verses, the rock beat slows to half speed for Clemons' mournful sax solo. As the beat resumes, Clemons continues to drive the song toward its conclusion. But there is yet another interruption as the energy dissipates; the beat stops and the texture thins to acoustic piano. Springsteen reenters in a style similar to the opening verses. For the final verse, the tempo quickens and slows, reflecting the meaning and mood of the text. The music throughout "Jungleland" is skillfully manipulated to fit the text—the ultimate goal of any music-and-text configuration.

Just as things seemed to have broken through for Springsteen, legal problems arose. Spending much of his time touring, Springsteen returned to the studio in 1980 to record some four dozen songs. From these sessions came *The River* (1980), Springsteen's first number 1 album. This strong double album produced a number 5 single ("Hungry Heart") and launched Springsteen into his 1980s superstar status.

With this newfound success, Springsteen took a potentially dangerous step with his next album, *Nebraska* (1982). This rather odd album was all acoustic and was recorded at his home on a four track cassette recorder. Beyond that, the songs are rather brooding and introspective. The album sold anyway, moving to number 3 on the album charts.

But Springsteen's biggest impact came in 1984 with *Born in the U.S.A.* The title song became a popular anthem of the mid-1980s, even though it reached only number 9 on the single charts. The album reached number 1 and yielded two other singles, "Dancing in the Dark" (number 2) and "Cover Me" (number 7). Springsteen has yet to achieve a number 1 single. "Born in the U.S.A." was interpreted by many as being a patriotic song. However, as with many Springsteen songs, there is an underlying conflict between the promise of the American Dream, with its high ideals and comfortable affluence, and the stark disappointment felt by many who, for one reason or another, fail to realize the dream.

Rock and roll super-star Bruce Springsteen in concert in Miami, Florida (*Source*: Getty Images, Inc.)

In 1986, Springsteen released a five-record boxed set called *Bruce Springsteen and the E Street Band Live: 1975–85*. It contains ten sides of high-quality live recordings made over a ten-year period. What is revealed is a mainstream rock star who has maintained his own unique style, disregarding the transient ebbing and flowing of rock-related substyles. One single, "War," from the *Live* album, reached the Top 10. Springsteen's final album of the 1980s was *Tunnel of Love*. This album reached the number 1 position and yielded two Top 10 hits ("Brilliant Disguise" and the title song, "Tunnel of Love"). In late 1989, Springsteen split from his longtime associates, the E Street Band. Throughout the 1980s and 1990s, "the Boss" remained true not only to his own musical principles, but to the historic principles of mainstream rock and roll: to express popular sentiments in a hard-driving, uncomplicated, but musically proficient style. His recordings during the 1990s, though critically acclaimed, sold less well than his earlier work. A reunion tour with the E-Street Band reinvigorated both the artist and his audience. Springsteen produced one of the most austere and poignant artistic responses to the tragedy of 9/11 in his double-platinum album *The Rising* (2002).

## U2

Springsteen, Michael Jackson, and Madonna (we will discuss these last two in Chapter 16, "Dance Music") proved to be the superstars of the early 1980s (and beyond). In the last half of the decade, two rock groups emerged to achieve superstar impact. The first of these was an Irish rock group, U2. Formed in 1976 by drummer Larry Mullen, the quartet paid its dues for four years by opening for other bands and touring England and Ireland. A CBS contract produced a commercially unsuccessful EP. Finally, in 1980, Island Records signed the band to a contract.

Two early albums (*Boy* and *October*) fared poorly. In 1983, *War* rose to the number 12 position, but the next album, *Under a Blood Red Sky* (a live album), peaked at number 28. By 1984, U2 had created a relatively small, but devoted audience. *The Unforgettable Fire* again rose to number 12 and produced one minor hit, "Pride (In the Name of Love)."

U2's less than spectacular success in the early 1980s becomes somewhat understandable if one listens to these early albums. They are not bad, but neither do they distinguish themselves from the sea of average mainstream rock bands vying for attention. *The Unforgettable Fire* provided the first solid hints that U2 was capable of better things. For example, both the title song and "A Sort of Homecoming" are strong, well-performed mainstream rock songs. The haunting "4th of July" evokes a New Age feeling (more about New Age later). "Bad" (no relation to Michael Jackson's song) has a repetitive, minimalistic accompaniment. However, lead singer Bono's vocal abilities are severely taxed in songs like "Promenade" and "MLK."

Indeed, U2 has no musical "star." Lead singer Bono (Paul Hewson) is unusually candid about his own talents. Thus, in one interview he said, "I can't really work out why anyone would buy a U2 record. When I listen to it, I just hear all the mistakes. . . . But I don't like the way I've sung on any of the records. I don't think I'm a good singer, but I think I'm getting to be a good singer" (Bronson 1988, 673). In the macho, egotistical world of the self-aggrandizing rock star, such remarks are quite rare.

In a *Time* interview, Larry Mullen recalled pulling the band's personnel together: "Adam [bass guitarist Adam Clayton] just *looked* great. He talked like he could play, used all the right words, like 'gig.' I thought this guy *must* know how to play. Then Bono . . . arrived, and he meant to play the guitar, but he couldn't play very well, so he started to sing. He couldn't do that either" (Bronson 1988, 666).

With all of that, how could this rather undistinguished group become superstars of the late 1980s? The story begins to unfold in 1987 with the release of *The Joshua Tree*. Recall what we said earlier about bands that are able to keep their membership intact for a period of years. By 1987, U2 had been together for eleven years with no change of membership. The results were a new tightness for the band and noticeably stronger performance skills for each individual. The album not only achieved the number 1 position (for nine weeks) but was awarded a Grammy as "Album of the Year." Two number 1 singles ("With or Without You" and "I Still Haven't Found What I'm Looking For") came from *The Joshua Tree*. U2 was finally established as an important rock band of the 1980s.

One big album does not equate to superstardom (remember Peter Frampton?). In 1988, U2 followed with another number 1 album, *Rattle and Hum*. This double album was a sound track from their concert/documentary film of the same name. Comparing an early album such as *Under a Blood Red Sky* with *Rattle and Hum* provides a real lesson in the remarkable improvement that time and perseverance can yield to a band that stays together and "pays its dues" over the years. There are tight, solid, and powerful performances of mainstream rock songs, such as "Helter Skelter" and "Hawkmoon." There is a moving performance of "I Still Haven't Found What I'm Looking For," complete with a strong gospel feel. And even when Bono's voice is fully exposed, as on "Love Rescue Me," the lead singer comes through with a strong, steady tone and reliable intonation. *Rattle and Hum* adds the talents of other stars like B. B. King ("When Love Comes to Town"), Bob Dylan ("Love Rescue Me"), Brian Eno ("Heartland"), George Pendergrass and Dorothy Terrell ("I Still Haven't Found What I'm Looking For"), and the Memphis Horns ("Angel of Harlem" and "Love Rescue Me"). Overall, *Rattle and Hum* provides a fascinating musical tour.

Like Springsteen, U2 often incorporates social, political, and even spiritual messages in their songs. For example, "Pride (In the Name of Love)" and "MLK" are tributes to Martin Luther King; "Silver and Gold" is a song protesting apartheid; "God Part II"—dedicated to John Lennon—questions many forms of hypocrisy in society.

U2's success continued throughout the 1990s with albums such as *Achtung Baby* (number 1 in 1991), *Zooropa* (number 1 in 1993), the multiplatinum *All That You Can't*

*Leave Behind* (number 3 in 2000), and *How to Dismantle an Atomic Bomb* (2004). These albums yielded an impressive series of single hits and several Grammy Awards.

### Huey Lewis and the News

One of the more interesting entries on the gentler side of the 1980s mainstream was Huey Lewis and the News. Lewis and his band accumulated a decade of experience in the United States and England while playing a variety of styles, from punk and new wave to disco. Lewis's first album, *Picture This* (1982), moved to number 13 and produced one Top 10 hit. But it was the follow-up album that brought Lewis to the forefront as a 1980s rock star. *Sports* hit number 1 in 1983 and yielded four Top 10 hits: "Heart and Soul" (number 8), "I Want a New Drug" (number 6), "The Heart of Rock and Roll" (number 6), and "If This Is It" (number 6). They continued their success with "The Power of Love," the theme from the popular movie *Back to the Future.*

Lewis followed *Sports* with another number 1 album, *Fore!*, which contained five Top 10 hits, including two number 1s ("Stuck With You" and "Jacob's Ladder"). His last album of the decade was *Small World* (1988), a particularly creative album that included some brilliant work by the Tower of Power horn section (see Chapter 14), jazz saxophonist Stan Getz, and Bruce Hornsby.

In some ways, Lewis's success is surprising. A level-headed, intelligent, and content family man, he is a stark contrast to the sex, drugs, and violence trend of much 1980s rock. He is almost a nostalgic throwback to the earlier days of rock and roll. In the words of Christopher Connelly, "Videos of the News have become a wel-

Huey Lewis (*Source:* Courtesy of Hulex Corporation)

come oasis of normality in the broken-glass and leather-bikini world of MTV" (McDonough 1985, 161). He projects the image (apparently genuine) of just a good guy playing and singing some good old rock and roll. In that sense, he could be considered a toned-down version of Bruce Springsteen. In the case of both performers, it would seem that "the heart of rock and roll is still beating."

### Female Stars

The 1980s found more women in mainstream rock than in any previous decade. One of the most remarkable comebacks in rock history was achieved by Tina Turner. After disappearing from the charts for a full decade, Tina Turner reappeared in the mid-1980s as a "new" star. Her album *Private Dancer* moved to number 3 in 1984 and yielded three Top 10 hits, including the number 1 song, "What's Love Got To Do With It." Sporting a punk-like hairstyle and emphasizing her still-sexy legs, Tina capitalized on the new video trend, even as she turned fifty years old in 1988.

New female stars also appeared and were well received by the rock audience. From the New York City punk–new-wave scene came Blondie, a male quintet plus lead singer Debby Harry. The band produced a series of hits from 1979 to 1981, beginning with "Heart of Glass" (number 1 in 1979). Also coming from a punk background, Joan Jett and the Blackhearts hit the top spot in 1981–82 with "I Love Rock'n'Roll." Jett's cover version of "Crimson and Clover" (originally by Tommy James and the Shondells in 1969) also reached the Top 10. Pat Benatar, a classically trained singer, produced three consecutive Top 5 albums from 1980 to 1982. Her strong vocals placed her in the rock mainstream, where she produced a Top 10 hit in 1980, "Hit Me with Your Best Shot."

## MAINSTREAM ROCK BEYOND THE EIGHTIES

In the history of rock and roll, several artists have retained a high degree of popularity across multiple decades. This is no small feat when one considers the number of new artists appearing each year and the high level of competition inherent in the popular music market. Classic rock acts that maintained a musical presence at the beginning of the twenty-first century include the Rolling Stones, Aerosmith, and the Eagles (primarily through the solo recordings of Don Henley). As time inevitably marched on, some of these artists, undoubtedly considered revolutionaries during the 1960s and 1970s, tended to become more mellow. This observation might apply to artists such as Eric Clapton, Sting, Elton John, and the Eagles.

Other musicians exhibited a similar move toward this softer, more adult-oriented sound as their musical style matured, but balanced this musical shift by continuing to produce a significant amount of material that retained the rebellious, energetic, and often loud aspects of rock and roll. As a result, artists like Bruce Springsteen, Rod Stewart, Paul McCartney, and Billy Joel managed to retain their maturing fans from earlier decades while attracting a whole new audience of post-boomers.

As part of the process of musical maturation, several rock artists turned toward classical music as a creative outlet. We have already mentioned Paul McCartney's *Give My Regards to Broad Street* (1984). In 1991, McCartney premiered his first classical composition, *Liverpool Oratorio*, receiving a lukewarm reception. In 2000, following the death of his wife after a battle with breast cancer, he released *A Garland for Linda* (number 7, Classical), a collection of modern classical pieces including one of his own entitled "Nova." Elvis Costello's *The Juliet Letters* (1993) represents an ambitious effort consisting of a song cycle created in collaboration with England's Brodsky Quartet. The album's concept, inspired by an article telling of letters addressed to Juliet Capulet (the character from Shakespeare's play), is based on a set of poems penned by Costello and his collaborators. In addition, Costello collaborated with Burt Bacharach on the soundtrack for *Grace of My Heart* (1996), resulting in a Grammy nomination for the song "God Give Me Strength." Elton John turned to composing film soundtracks for animated features such as *The Lion King* (1994; including the Academy Award–winning Best Original Song "Can You Feel the Love Tonight") and *The Road to El Dorado* (1999), in addition to collaborating with Tim Rice on the Broadway musical version of Verdi's *Aida* (1999). In 2001, Billy Joel released *Fantasies & Delusions: Music for Solo Piano* (debuted at number 1 on the Classical chart). Credited to "William Joel," performed by virtuoso Richard Joo, and recorded in Vienna at the famous Mozartsaal in the Vienna Konzerthaus, it reveals an earnest attempt by a veteran rock and roller to communicate with his audience via classical music, using only a solo piano.

This trend toward rock artists reaching outside their typical musical vocabulary and finding a place in "serious" art music is likely to continue and provides the potential for some highly interesting and eclectic future recordings, though it should be noted—as was a common theme in Chapter 12, "Art Rock"—that most of these artists maintain an outdated concept of "classical music."

## Eric Clapton

Because he serves as a prime example of a mellowing rock legend and because his acoustic version of "Layla" (1992) allows a direct comparison with his performance on the original recording (a hit for Derek and the Dominoes in 1970), the following discussion focuses on Eric Clapton. Beginning his career as a premiere blues-rock guitarist with bands like the Yardbirds and John Mayall's Bluesbreakers, and later establishing a new definition for the word *loud* in his power trio Cream, Eric Clapton serves as a particularly good example of the mellowing rock legend. He became a guitar superstar by the age of 21, developing a cultlike following of musical disciples. It was not uncommon to see graffiti proclaiming "Clapton is God" in London during the late 1960s. Playing with bands as varied as Cream, Derek and the Dominoes (with guitar legend Duane Allman), Blind Faith, and John Lennon's Plastic Ono Band, Clapton was much in demand as a guitarist. He contributed lead solos to recordings by the Beatles and Frank Zappa and released a series of impressive solo recordings beginning with his self-titled album in 1970.

Just prior to his thirtieth birthday and after an almost two-year retreat from the public eye, during which he overcame a severe heroin habit, Clapton's musical style changed markedly. From the screaming electric guitar played at extremely high volume levels evolved a much more relaxed, easygoing style, as exemplified in his cover version of Bob Marley's "I Shot the Sheriff." Both the single and the album on which it was included, *461 Ocean Boulevard*, reached number 1 in 1974.

In 1992, Clapton appeared on MTV's *Unplugged* series, performing acoustic versions of many of his songs, including Derek and the Dominoes' classic tune,

"Layla." A comparison of the version released in 1970 to the revised version of 1992 provides an excellent example of the contrast between Clapton's early and more recent musical styles. The high-energy rock feeling of the early recording is replaced by a relaxed, laid-back musical feel. What are the specific musical elements that make this later recording sound so different? First of all, the overall instrumentation changed, replacing the two screaming rock guitars of Clapton and Duane Allman with acoustic guitar and acoustic piano. Clapton's vocal style is much lighter on the *Unplugged* performance, resulting in a more mature, introspective sound in contrast to the youthful rebellion apparent in the Derek and the Dominoes recording. Most noticeable, however, is the complete absence of the prominent guitar riff that pervades the original version.

**Layla Guitar Riff**

Why is such a memorable aspect of the original tune left out of the cover version? This question leads us to a discussion of the most changed musical aspect of Clapton's later recording, the rhythm. Most obvious is the significant change in tempo. The original recording was much faster, falling somewhere between 114 to 120 beats per minute, depending on which section one listens to. In contrast, the *Unplugged* version remains at a steady 93 beats per minute throughout. Listen carefully to both versions of "Layla," concentrating on how the beats are subdivided. If you focus your attention on the drummer's hi-hat cymbal in the original version or the tambourine part in the later recording, it is possible to determine an interesting difference between the two. In the verses of the original recording, the beat is divided in half (duple subdivision), while the beat in the choruses, where the word *Layla* enters, is divided into four (quadruple) subdivisions. In contrast, the MTV performance incorporates a triple subdivision of the beat, often with only the first and third notes of this subdivision being played. The resulting long-short, long-short rhythm is sometimes referred to as a "shuffle beat" and is associated with a more relaxed musical style.

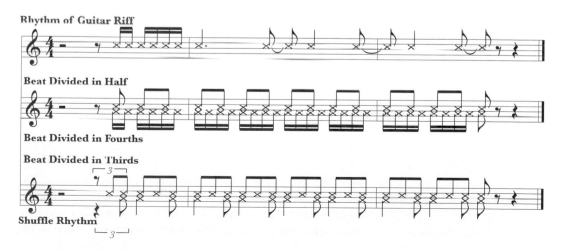

**Rhythm of Guitar Riff**

**Beat Divided in Half**

**Beat Divided in Fourths**

**Beat Divided in Thirds**

**Shuffle Rhythm**

If we look closely at the rhythm of the guitar riff from the Derek and the Dominoes recording, we can determine immediately why this musical signature of the original was not incorporated into the later version. In fact, because of the beat subdivision, it could not have been used without destroying the underlying shuffle rhythm. The guitar riff requires that each beat be divided into fourths rather than thirds. Therefore, Clapton chose to use the melody and harmony of the original, while altering both the timbre and rhythm for this remake of his classic tune. The recording of his MTV session earned Clapton nine Grammy nominations. He was actually awarded six Grammys, including Record of the Year, Song of the Year, and Best Pop Vocal Performance, Male for "Tears in Heaven" (number 2, 1992), a song inspired by the tragic death of his four-year-old son. Following a brief reunion with his fellow band members for Cream's induction into the Rock and Roll Hall of Fame, Clapton returned to his roots, releasing a collection of classic blues tunes entitled *From the Cradle* (number 1 in 1994), which won a Grammy for Best Traditional Blues Album and has since become the best-selling traditional blues recording in history (George-Warren and Romanowski, 2001).

In 1996, Clapton's single "Change the World" (a number 5 hit produced by Babyface) was recorded for the movie *Phenomenon* and debuted at number 9, the highest debut position ever attained by Clapton. After a brief electronica stint with T.D.F., collaborating with keyboard player Simon Climie (*Retail Therapy* in 1997), Clapton released *Pilgrim* (number 4 in 1998). This album represented his first recording of mostly original songs since the late 1980s. *Riding with the King* (2000) was a collaboration between Clapton and one of his greatest influences, B. B. King, resulting in another Grammy for Best Traditional Blues Album. After releasing *Reptile* in 2001, a rather mixed bag of cover songs and originals, Clapton recorded another homage to one of his primary musical influences. *Me & Mr. Johnson* (2004) included Clapton's interpretations of nearly half of the 29 songs premier blues legend Robert Johnson wrote and recorded during his brief lifetime. Like the recording made with B. B. King, one can hear the respect and admiration Clapton has for his predecessors and the important role their musical influence played in his artistic development.

In addition to his musical activities, Clapton founded the Crossroads Centre in 1998, a facility for drug and alcohol rehabilitation, located on the southeast shore of Antigua in the Caribbean. In 1999, he auctioned 100 guitars from his collection to raise money and to garner attention for his continuing personal crusade against drug addiction, an affliction about which he knew a great deal from first-hand experience.

## MUSICAL CLOSE-UP:
### A LOOK AT ROCK LYRICS

Technically speaking, lyrics are not a musical element. Nevertheless, throughout the history of music, words and music have had an inseparable and intimate relationship. After all, the most natural (and cheapest) instrument is the human voice. And if a person sings, it is quite likely that he or she will sing words. Music alone is a powerful communicative tool, but its communication is nonverbal. The addition of words provides a more specific form of communication—one that is more readily comprehensible to the average listener. A given piece of music may make us feel sad in a general way, but the words tell us what there is to be sad about (the loss of a love relationship, for example).

In spite of the importance of the guitar, drums, and various types of keyboards, rock has been, above all, vocal music. The overwhelming number of artists discussed in this book were singers (granted, most also played one or more instruments). In some cases, rock songs began with the music, the words being added to fit; but just as often, a song originated with a poem (lyrics) to which music was added. It works both ways.

Early rock lyrics were usually about boy–girl romantic situations or about good times. Sex was rarely involved, and when it was, the references were implicit. Among the most popular 1950s rockers, Little Richard came the closest to suggestive lyrics (e.g., "Good Golly Miss Molly" and "Long Tall Sally"). Some songs spoke of teenage life in the 1950s, usually expressing sympathetic understanding and a symbolic pat on the back (e.g., "School Days" by Chuck Berry and "Yakety Yak" by the Coasters).

The 1960s brought about major changes in rock lyrics. Although the surfers were still concerned with boy–girl romance and good times (add sun, surf, and cars to the list) and the dance craze focused (obviously) on dancing, the rising folk music trend brought a sense of seriousness to rock lyrics. Social and political issues were addressed by folk singers and the subsequent folk rockers. It was at this point that the music (including the lyrics) ceased being merely a mirror of society and began to be an active *agent of change* in society. The folkies and folk rockers wished not to reflect society, but to *promote change* in that society. They quite correctly understood that the music and words combination was a powerful agent for change. Their lyrics pointed the way to what they believed could be a better way of life—life without war, violence, racial prejudice, and environmental pollution.

By 1967, rock lyrics had made steady and impressive progress from the "walk-talk," "arms-charms" lyrics of the 1950s to the thought-provoking lyrics of Dylan, the Beatles, the Byrds, and others. But around 1967, further changes began to take place. Prior to 1967, the subject of drugs had been regarded as taboo where song lyrics were concerned. Occasional references to drugs were accomplished by means of the double entendre. Songs like "Eight Miles High" and "Lucy in the Sky with Diamonds" created controversy but were excused because of the possibility of an innocent alternative meaning. (These and other uses of double entendre have been discussed in earlier chapters.)

But in 1967, songs like "White Rabbit" by the Jefferson Airplane and "A Day in the Life" by the Beatles began to appear. The old double entendres were seen as being hypocritical; drug references were no longer implicit; they became explicit. It was at this point that rock took a significant step as it moved across the line from the innocent and the occasionally suggestive double entendre to the blatant enunciation of taboo topics.

Since the late 1960s, explicit references to drugs have become rather common in rock lyrics. Because the drug culture utilizes an ever-changing jargon of its own, many rock song references are perfectly clear to the initiated but pass right by the non-drug-oriented listener. Thus, while Country Joe McDonald sang overt drug songs like "Acid Commercial," others resorted to drug jargon in songs like "Along Comes Mary" (the Association), "Proud Mary" (CCR), and "Lady Jane" and "Jumpin' Jack Flash" (the Rolling Stones). The drug references functioned in a dual capacity: They *reflected* the drug-oriented segment of the rock community that produced the songs, but because of the wide distribution of the music, they also *spread* the pro-drug message to a broader spectrum of society that otherwise might not have been tantalized by drugs. So to the oft-asked question, did rock music merely reflect the growing use of drugs in the 1960s and 1970s or was it an active agent in that trend, we must answer yes, it did both.

And what of the other major taboo: sex? Again, the music of the late 1960s edged ever closer to overt and explicit sexual references. In British rock, the Rolling Stones led the way toward more explicit references to sex; on this side of the Atlantic, the "credit" must go to Frank Zappa. The latter's *Fillmore East* album (1971) contained explicit sexual lyrics, although couched in Zappa's typical dirty joke context. More menacing was a song on the Stones' *Goats Head Soup* (1973). Originally entitled "Starfucker," the song includes references to vaginal deodorant, "pussy," and "giving head to Steve McQueen." Ahmet Ertegun insisted on the change of title to "Star Star."

Granted, there had always been "underground" groups that had produced sexually explicit songs, but Zappa and the Stones were frontline superstars. Once the barriers were broken, the trend was unstoppable. The level of sexual explicitness remained more or less constant through the 1970s and intensified in the 1980s. Particularly noticeable were two new aspects in sexual rock lyrics: (1) the combination of sex and violence (often using the latter as a metaphor for the former), and (2) the fascination with "deviant" sexual behavior. Let us look briefly at these two subtrends.

Songwriters have used many different metaphors when referring to sex. They have described the innocence and springlike beauty of sex with references to "the birds and the bees"; referring to the thrill and excitement of sex, they have written of "bells and fireworks" and even "thunder and lightning" (the title of a 1972 hit for Chi Coltrane). But, in the 1980s, more violent metaphors became common. Songs by Mötley Crüe, Kiss, the Who, AC/DC, Judas Priest, Dokken, and even Marvin Gaye describe the male sex organ as a gun, a knife, a sword, a steel rod, or a pipe; Kiss and AC/DC refer to the female sex organ as a cake to be cut or butter to be sliced; ejaculation is the act of shooting the gun; and semen consists of bullets. Granted, some of the songs could be interpreted as references to sex or violence. But it is the virtual equation of the two, so that one is uncertain which is intended, that alarms many observers.

The second subtrend in sexual lyrics has been the drift toward forms of sex other than the normal male–female variety. Leading the way here was Prince, who sang of incest ("Sister"), masturbation ("Jack U Off"), group sex ("When You Were Mine"), and oral sex ("Head"). Songs like Judas Priest's "Eat Me Alive" give two for the price of one—violence *and* oral sex. There are songs that combine sex and the occult and songs reveling in sadomasochism. The uses of explicit language to describe more or less "normal" sex are simply too numerous to mention; and, of course, there are examples of songs that, using nonverbal utterances (sighs, moans, screams, etc.), are musical depictions of the sex act (e.g., Prince and Donna Summer). We've certainly come a long way from "I Want to Hold Your Hand."

Drugs and sex were not the only themes to find increasingly explicit expression in rock lyrics of the 1970s and 1980s. Themes of rebellion took a variety of forms. One can say, of course, that rock and roll, even in its earliest forms, was inherently rebellious. Certainly one factor in rock's appeal to the 1950s teenager was that Mom and Dad usually did not like it. The more adult society decried the music of Presley, Lewis, and Little Richard, the more teens liked it. It became their music and helped create a youth society—a social and economic entity unto itself. In a subtle sense, this was a type of rebellion. But the lyrics of those early rock songs were rarely overt in their rebellion. In the 1960s, folk, folk rock, and other socially oriented styles criticized existing society and offered "a better way"; these songs represented a more positive type of rebellion (in fact, a better word might be *reform*).

Perhaps in part because of the disillusionment of the 1960s youth movement, the rebellion of the 1970s and 1980s grew increasingly angry and negative. AC/DC's "School Daze" provides a stark contrast to Chuck Berry's "School Days." Whereas Berry suggested that at three o'clock students lay down their educational burdens and swing down to a malt shop to dance, AC/DC screams at them to burn down the school. School itself is referred to as a "juvenile prison" and a "homework hellhouse." Negative views of education had been expressed earlier by Pink Floyd in "Another Brick in the Wall—Part II" when they said, "We don't need no education/We don't need no thought control/No dark sarcasms in the classroom/Teacher, leave them kids alone."

Songs by Kiss and Mötley Crüe reinforced a violent and angry form of rebellion against school, parents, and other authority figures. Twisted Sister angrily shouted, "We're not gonna take it anymore!" and disparagingly characterized adult (parental) society as being "condescending," "trite," "jaded," and "boring." They added, "We don't want nothing, not a thing from you," and "If that's your best, your best won't do." Just as Ozzy warned, "Do what you will to try and make me conform/But I'll make you wish you had never been born." Twisted Sister shouted at parents, "Just you try and make us!"

The violent sentiments of the metal bands were carried to even further extremes by some rappers (specifically the "gangsta" rappers to be discussed in Chapter 17, "Rap and Hip-Hop"). For these rappers, the targets of their violent lyrics were less likely to be parents and education as was the case with the metal bands. Gangsta rappers aimed their hostility at women, the police, and white people in general. As with the other themes discussed in this close-up, the lyrics were extremely explicit in their references to acts of violence and sexual organs and acts.

Once again, it must be noted that such sentiments can be seen as reflections of normal teenage rebellion; but there is also the possibility that the open defiance and angry hostility expressed in such songs may have the effect of intensifying normal (and even healthy) teenage rebellion, turning it into something far more destructive.

Another form of rebellion that has grown steadily in rock lyrics is the trend toward the occult and, in its most extreme form, satanism. Although one can trace satanic references back to songs like "Sympathy for the Devil" and "Lucretia MacEvil," such references were rather innocuous and, in fact, painted a distinctly unflattering image of the Devil. However, by the 1980s, some groups were not merely referring to the Devil but were openly proselytizing for satanism. Venom's album notes make their position clear: "We are possessed by all that is evil; the death of you, God, we demand. We spit at the virgin you worship, and sit at Lord Satan's right hand." Similar messages may be received from groups such as Mercyful Fate, Exciter, Slayer, Megadeth, Iron Maiden, AC/DC, and King Diamond. Although some of the satanic groups simply used this rather extreme form of rebellion as a sales gimmick, others seem to be genuinely devoted to their messages.

Another theme that has caused increasing concern is that of suicide. There had been a brief fascination with death in a few songs of the late 1950s and early 1960s (e.g., Mark Dinning's "Teen Angel" of 1960, the Shangri-Las' "Leader of the Pack" of 1964, and Jan and Dean's "Dead Man's Curve," also from 1964). Suicide had been specifically referred to in Jody Reynold's morose song of 1958, "The Endless Sleep." But, by the 1980s, teen suicides had tripled in a thirty-year period and had become the second leading cause of death among people under age twenty-five. Compounding the concern, an alarming number of teens had committed suicide while listening to suicide-oriented rock songs. One of the most oft-cited of such songs is Ozzy Osbourne's "Suicide Solution," which contains the lines, "suicide is the only way out," and "why don't you kill yourself 'cause you can't escape the Master Reaper." (The early heavy metal group Blue Oyster Cult used that same reference in their song "Don't Fear the Reaper.") Similar sentiments are expressed in songs by Pink Floyd, AC/DC, Black Sabbath, and Metallica. As you would expect, in most cases the bands and their defenders offer alternative interpretations for the lyrics. However, to a depressed, potentially suicidal sixteen-year-old, the most obvious message is the one grasped. And of course, the old argument is presented that these songs merely *reflect* the increasing occurrence of suicide among today's youth. But, again, that may only be half the truth; the other half is that repetitive listening to suicide songs while in a depressed mental state (often further beclouded by alcohol or drugs or both) may be just the reinforcing factor needed to push a given teenager over the edge. Thus the music, while reflecting a societal trend, may simultaneously reinforce or extend that same trend.

The five aforementioned themes—drugs, sex, violent rebellion, satanism, and suicide—have raised concerns about the effects of the more explicit rock lyrics on teenagers. Groups such as the National Parent Teacher Association and the Parents Music Resource Center communicated such concerns to the recording industry and also attempted to alert parents and teenagers to the potential dangers. With the concurrence of educators and psychiatrists armed with considerable research, they suggest that some (not all) rock lyrics may have gone so far that they have become potentially dangerous to the impressionable minds of teens and preteens. We will return to this premise in Chapter 19, "An Overview and An Editorial."

What is virtually unarguable is that rock lyrics have changed dramatically over rock's first five decades. By the turn of the century, one could truthfully say that there was no topic that was taboo to the rock lyricist; the language of those lyrics had virtually no limitations on explicitness. The innocence of the 1950s and the idealism of the 1960s were, for the most part, gone. A song like Madonna's "Material Girl," with its proud statement of purely materialistic values, would have been received with total revulsion twenty years earlier (1965); in 1985, it reached number 2 on the charts.

Much of the concern over explicit lyrics has centered on heavy metal and rap bands, and indeed, they seem especially prone to such antisocial lyrics. But we must point out that not all heavy metal and rap bands produce such lyrics, and some other artists have produced some of the most explicit lyrics (e.g., Prince and Marvin Gaye). Furthermore, not all rock-and-roll lyrics deal explicitly or implicitly with drugs, sex, violent rebellion, satanism, and suicide. Many songs never touch upon any of these topics. We have dealt with these topics because some are relatively new to rock in the 1970s (e.g., satanism and suicide), and some were new in their level of explicitness (sex, drugs) and vehemence (rebellion).

# 14

# The Continuing Fragmentation of Rock

## OVERVIEW: SUBSTYLES OF THE 1960S EVOLVE INTO THE 1970S AND BEYOND

With the arrival of the Rolling Stones and the Beatles, rock's mainstream divided into a harder side and a gentler side. Although one can discern those two basic trends in mainstream rock in the 1970s and beyond, the fact is that even these two basic branches of the mainstream fragmented into a plethora of individualistic styles.

In the 1960s, we also saw a dramatic expansion of rock in at least two ways. First, due mostly to the Beatles, the musical language of rock became more sophisticated and creative. Second, artists began to look outside of rock for styles that could be combined with rock to create entire new styles. Thus we saw the emergence of folk-rock, jazz-rock, art-rock, and soul music. In the 1970s and 1980s, we will see that these combination styles continued to develop, although several of them acquired new names. Thus jazz-rock transformed into fusion music. The folk-rockers became known as singer-songwriters. Art rock evolved into progressive rock. And country rock was, in some cases, called progressive country. An exception seemed to be soft rock, which continued its unswerving existence from its inception with Pat Boone and Elvis Presley straight into the new century.

Two styles that were new in the 1970s and developed dramatically in the 1980s were heavy metal and rap. We will discuss these two styles separately in Chapters 15 and 17. Both of these new styles (each in its own way) were strongly anti-establishment. We mentioned the "me decade" of the 1970s in the Overview in Chapter 13. If anything, this self-absorption was compounded in the 1980s—called by some the "Decade of Greed." Instead of rebelling against the establishment as the youth of the 1960s did, the youth of the 1970s and 1980s were more likely to tend to their own interests and pursue success within the establishment. Of course in any decade there are those—especially among the youth—who rebel against the norm. For them, heavy metal and rap were the perfect expressions of anger and frustration with the establishment.

In the mid-1970s, the Watergate crisis resulted in a heightened distrust of the government and the American political system. In the midst of the Presidential campaign of 1974, a group of political "dirty tricksters" broke into Democratic headquarters at the Watergate Hotel in Washington, D.C. Although some were initially content to dismiss the action as "politics as usual," the scandal intensified as it became evident that the break-in was planned and/or sanctioned by high level officials within the Nixon administration. The sordid affair eventually resulted in the President's resignation from office.

For young people who were by nature skeptical of the government and politics, the Watergate crisis alienated them even further. They were angry and frustrated with the "establishment." Heavy metal rock music seemed to be a perfect expression of their anger.

From 1980 through 1988, the White House was occupied by President Ronald Reagan, a conservative Republican. His Vice President, George Bush Sr., succeeded him as President from 1988 through 1992. During the Reagan years, the economy expanded and, aside from several small skirmishes, there was a period of peace. Those who functioned within the system flourished. However, there were those who felt disenfranchised. This especially included many African-Americans. The rise of rap music (or hip-hop) became an expression of their anger.

And so as is almost always the case, society and music reflected each other. Those who were content to work within the system to enhance their own hopes and dreams tended to be rather nonrebellious. They were content as well with the continuation of musical styles that were simply extensions of the past (even with new names). Thus it is not surprising that mainstream rock, jazz-rock (fusion), folk-rock (singers/songwriters), art rock (progressive rock), country-rock (progressive country), and soft rock flourished.

But for those who were disaffected by the Watergate crisis of the 1970s and those who did not benefit during the Reagan years, heavy metal and rap became the favored musical styles.

Let us continue our survey of the 1970s and beyond by looking at the various combination styles that continued out of the 1960s. Even though these styles were essentially continuations, we will see as we did with the mainstream styles that each style fragments into an array of distinct sounds and artists.

## ART ROCK EVOLVES INTO PROGRESSIVE ROCK

The type of art rock represented by Jon Lord's *Concerto* and *Gemini Suite* and Rick Wakeman's *Journey* and *King Arthur* receded after the mid-1970s; the rock opera concept also faded by that time. What remained were groups such as Yes and Emerson, Lake, and Palmer, who relied on the musical language of rock to create longer, more complex works that they hoped could be taken as seriously as classical works. To distinguish such groups from the earlier rock with orchestra and rock opera advocates, the term *progressive rock* took the place of art rock.

The progressive rock groups of the 1970s were not only from England and the United States, but from several other European countries as well. As with most 1970s styles, there was a considerable range of styles within the category of progressive rock.

## Pink Floyd

The roots of Pink Floyd lie in London's blues-based rock community of the 1960s. The band was formed in 1965 from the remnants of several previous groups. By early 1966, Pink Floyd was appearing at the Marquee Club; later that year they moved to the Sound/Light Workshop, where they presented what was reportedly England's first rock with lights show. Their debut album, *The Piper at the Gates of Dawn* (released in the United States in late 1967 as *Pink Floyd*), was critically acclaimed but rose only to number 131 in the United States. The group's creative leader, Roger "Syd" Barrett, became increasingly affected by psychological problems reportedly intensified by drug abuse; he left the band in 1968.

Pink Floyd produced a series of moderately successful albums through the early 1970s. Their live performances utilized elaborate state-of-the-art sound systems and elaborate stage props (e.g., a sixty-foot inflatable octopus). But the turning point came in 1973 with *The Dark Side of the Moon*. Having become associated with the psychedelic rock trend, and with their space-oriented lyrics, the band found themselves established as progressive rock superstars with this album, which was produced by Alan Parsons. *Dark Side*, which required some nine months to produce, not only became a number 1 album but became the longest-running chart album in history, remaining on the charts for 741 weeks; that is over fourteen years. This archetypal British progressive rock album deals with alienation, paranoia, and lunacy (literally). The heavy use of electronics was typical of Pink Floyd; although the album was rather dark and brooding, there were rock songs like "Time" and "Money" (the latter made the Top 40—number 13 in 1973). The song "Us and Them" shows the influence of producer Parsons (compare to the later "Time" by the Alan Parsons Project); "Brain Damage," a song about insanity, foreshadows later trends in heavy metal lyrics. There are touches of jazz (note the sax work on "Us and Them"), soul (e.g., "The Great Gig in the Sky"), and pure electronic experimentation ("On the Run").

Pink Floyd's success continued through the mid- and late-1970s. The tour that promoted *The Wall* (number 1 in late 1979 to early 1980) involved such elaborate logistics that there were only three performances (London, New York City, and Los Angeles). Singing of alienation and loneliness (as usual), Pink Floyd gradually assembled, brick by brick, a thirty-foot high stage-wide wall between themselves and the audience; it toppled (of course) just before the end of the show. Also utilizing extra singers and instrumentalists, film, elaborate lighting, and more giant plastic inflatables, *The Wall* tour was among the most elaborate in rock history. In spite of internal squabbles, lawsuits, and personnel changes, Pink Floyd produced several number 1 albums in the 1990s (*The Division Bell* in 1994 and *P.U.L.S.E.* in 1995). A major tour in 1994 included a performance of *The Dark Side of the Moon* in its entirety.

## King Crimson

One of the leading British progressive rock groups of the 1970s was King Crimson. The ever-changing personnel of this band included a number of prominent 1970s rock musicians: Greg Lake (ELP), Ian McDonald (Foreigner), Bill Bruford (Yes and Genesis), John Wetton (Asia and Uriah Heep), and Boz Burrell (Bad Company). The guiding force of King Crimson was Robert Fripp (born in Wimbourne, Dorset, in 1946). The band first gained attention at the July 1969 Hyde Park concert with the Rolling Stones. Their first album, *In the Court of the Crimson King*, was critically acclaimed and achieved surprising success (number 25 in the United States). The album contained five extended pieces and revealed the art rock creativity of Fripp.

King Crimson established a wide following in England and Europe, but a relatively small (but loyal) following in the United States. *Larks' Tongues in Aspic* (1973) is a fascinating album, especially for its extended works, including the title song (parts 1 and 2), "Exiles," "Easy Money," and "The Talking Drum." Throughout, the band's sound changes often and dramatically. There are moments of genuine hard rock, experiments with minimalism, changing meters, sound effects, interesting violin and viola work, and electronics. It is thoughtful music, utilizing a wide spectrum of sound resources in a diverse variety of styles. As such, *Larks' Tongues* provides a good perspective on the state of British progressive rock in the mid-1970s.

In late 1974, Fripp finally disbanded King Crimson. He later joined with Brian Eno to create several albums exploring the minimalist concepts that would be developed later by new wave and new age groups. Fripp's fascination with electronics led to the development of "Frippertronics," a style that involved creating a tape delay system through the use of two tape recorders and guitar. Although many bands happily answered to the phrase "progressive rock" in the 1970s, few truly deserved that title more than King Crimson.

As often happens after such groups are "disbanded" or certain artists "retire," King Crimson sprang to life again in 1981 with a new sound and new personnel. New to the group were guitarist Adrian Belew (who had recorded with Zappa, Bowie, and the Talking Heads), bassist Tony Levin (who had recorded previously with Peter Gabriel), and drummer Bill Bruford (formerly with Yes). A series of impeccably produced recordings followed, revealing the high level of musical skill inherent in the band. These albums included *Discipline* (1981), *Beat* (1982), and *Three of a Perfect Pair* (1984). In 1994, the band was augmented with additional performers and continued to release new recordings that contained both new material and live performances of older songs.

## Jethro Tull

Jethro Tull was usually grouped with the other British progressive rock bands of the 1970s. However, in retrospect, Tull seems far less consistently innovative and musically sophisticated than King Crimson, ELP, Yes, and Pink Floyd. Beginning in Blackpool, the group moved to London in 1967 to make its mark on the blues-based rock scene. Ian Anderson (flute, sax, guitar, and vocals) grew into the leadership role, moving the band's sound away from its blues base toward the new progressive rock sound.

Tull found a more receptive audience in the United States than in their native England. Their *Thick as a Brick* (1972) established the band in the ranks of progressive rock, inasmuch as it consisted of one album-long work as opposed to a collection of individual cuts. Anderson's flute solos shifted between sounds of rock, jazz, and classical music. The next album, *Living in the Past*, yielded a popular single (the title song) that may be the first hit single in quintuple meter since Dave Brubeck's "Take Five" of 1961. The concept album, *A Passion Play* (1973), was critically scorned but rose to number 1 anyway. Several albums from 1974 through 1977 sold well in the United States. Even though the group continued to release recordings into the 1990s and beyond, they were never able to regain the impact they enjoyed in the late 1970s.

## Other British Art Rockers

British leadership in art rock and progressive rock continued throughout the 1970s. In addition to the bands mentioned thus far, one could include the Electric Light Orchestra (ELO), Soft Machine, Gentle Giant, and Henry Cow. Of these, the most popular by far was ELO. Soft Machine and Gentle Giant produced some very sophisticated progressive rock but failed to have major commercial impact. Henry Cow may have been one of the most innovative and creative of these bands, but they remain largely unknown. To the adventurous listener who is interested in off-the-beaten-track art rock, music by Soft Machine, Gentle Giant, and especially Henry Cow can open up a new world of musical experience.

An offshoot of the progressive rock trend was the movement toward heavily electronic rock, characterized by a strong reliance on synthesizers and related electronic keyboards. Later called synthe-pop, techno-rock, or electro-pop, such music combined rock elements with the most advanced resources in musical high tech. Certainly many of the art rock groups mentioned thus far helped initiate this trend. One of the most successful early ventures into this branch of art rock was made by Mike Oldfield (born in Essex, England, in 1953). In 1972, he released the impressive solo album *Tubular Bells*. Oldfield played a wide variety of instruments on the album, which was an impressive recording achievement as well, utilizing over forty tracks and countless overdubs. An excerpt from the forty-nine-minute work was used as the theme for the movie *The Exorcist*, thus guaranteeing the album's success.

## Progressive Rock in Europe

Several German groups enjoyed success in the field of heavily electrified progressive rock. Passport was perhaps the best; purely instrumental, Passport relied primarily on the saxophone and keyboards of Klaus Doldinger. Combining elements of rock and jazz with a strong dose of tasteful electronic keyboards, Passport provided much enjoyable music, even though their albums were not big sellers (the 1974 album *Looking Thru* gives a good sample of their work). Triumvirat, another German group, sounded remarkably like Emerson, Lake, and Palmer. Kraftwerk succeeded in a way neither Passport nor Triumvirat did: they achieved a Top 30 single, "Autobahn" (number 25 in 1975). Their first album released in the United States contained the side-long version of "Autobahn," created almost exclusively by electronic sound sources; it rose to number 5 on the U.S. album charts.

Gradually, progressive rock spread from England to other European countries. One of the best was the band led by guitarist Terje Rypdal in Norway. Rypdal's band shifted smoothly between a progressive rock style and jazz–rock fusion. Rypdal's 1974 album *Whenever I Seem to Be Far Away* is a good example of his work. From Holland came Focus, another band that moved deftly between progressive rock and jazz–rock fusion. Focus was formed in 1969 by organist and flutist Thijs Van Leer, a graduate of the Amsterdam Conservatorium. Featuring the fine guitar work of Jan Akkerman, Focus was capable of a variety of styles, as illustrated on *Focus 3* (1973), a double album. "Love Remembered" is a hauntingly beautiful soft rock song with jazz overtones, somewhat similar to parts of Pink Floyd's *Dark Side of the Moon* and much of the Alan Parsons Project's work. "Carnival Fugue" is a particularly interesting work that begins like a classical fugue but soon moves to a jazz–rock fusion style. *Hamburger Concerto* (1974) places the band more clearly in the progressive rock category; the title work, a six-movement suite (not really a concerto in the classical sense), contains classical references and is a more or less successful attempt at "serious" rock. The 1973 album *Hocus Pocus* reached number 9 on the album charts.

## JAZZ ROCK EVOLVES INTO FUSION

The first phase of the jazz–rock trend was typified by groups like Blood, Sweat, and Tears, Chicago, and Chase—groups that combined horn lines with basic rock instrumentation. As the 1970s began, a new style of jazz–rock was born; to distinguish this newer approach from the older B, S, & T–Chicago style, the newer sound became known as "fusion music." The seminal album in this trend came in 1970 with *Bitches Brew,* a double album by jazz trumpeter Miles Davis. Among the musicians on this album were many of the key figures in the fusion trend of the mid- and late-1970s: John McLaughlin, Chick Corea, Wayne Shorter, Bennie Maupin, and Joe Zawinul. To Davis's rather austere style of jazz were added electric guitar, electric bass, electronic keyboards, and modified rock beats and bass lines. Whereas B, S, & T and Chicago essentially added jazz elements to their rock style, Davis added rock elements to his jazz style.

To the average listener, *Bitches Brew* presented a forbidding sound. The songs were long (usually a full side) and sounded like rather aimless, disjointed improvisations, containing few or no "tunes" and no simple jazz or rock beats. But Davis had started some of the best musical minds in jazz and rock thinking. Several would take his basic, uncompromising style and modify it to create a popular style of jazz–rock fusion for the 1970s.

### John McLaughlin

One such person was John McLaughlin, generally regarded as one of the premier guitarists of the 1970s. In 1971, he assembled a band consisting of himself, Czechoslovakian keyboardist Jan Hammer, drummer Billy Cobham, bassist Rick Laird, and violinist Jerry Goodman. The group, known as the Mahavishnu Orchestra, established itself as a popular jazz–rock fusion group with *Birds of Fire* (1973). McLaughlin took Miles Davis's basic ideas and moved them closer to the progressive rock style. Cobham's drum patterns, though complex and technically demanding, were still recognizable rock beats; similarly, Laird's bass patterns were derived from more

THE CONTINUING FRAGMENTATION OF ROCK

familiar rock style bass lines. As McLaughlin, Hammer, and Goodman played tunes and improvisations over these drum and bass foundations, the results were less foreign to the typical rock listener. At times, Mahavishnu moved closer to jazz, creating a true jazz–rock fusion; at other times, they moved closer to rock, giving the impression of a progressive rock band. The band's playing was virtuosic at times, as they moved through various meters and technically impressive solos. Mahavishnu's *Apocalypse* (1974), recorded with the London Symphony Orchestra conducted by Michael Tilson Thomas and produced by George Martin, was an effective essay in art rock. In 1974, McLaughlin disbanded the Mahavishnu Orchestra (it was reformed for a brief two-year period beginning in 1984).

## Weather Report

Another alumnus of *Bitches Brew* was keyboardist Joe Zawinul, formerly pianist and composer with Cannonball Adderley's jazz group. Joining with soprano saxophonist Wayne Shorter (also a Davis alumnus), Zawinul formed Weather Report, one of the most influential of the 1970s fusion bands. Like the Mahavishnu Orchestra, Weather Report modified the *Bitches Brew* concepts, making their sound more palatable for a larger audience. But unlike Mahavishnu, which moved toward progressive rock, Weather Report leaned toward jazz. Although Weather Report could certainly play straight-ahead jazz and incorporate recognizable rock influences, they could also effect an ethereal, delicate sound, characterized by tinkling bells and otherworldly electronics. Most often their songs (which rarely included vocals) were structured around several melodic motives, one or more bass patterns, and an accompanying riff; from there the musicians improvised. Weather Report's albums ranked consistently high for a jazz-oriented group. The band continued as an influential jazz ensemble into the mid-1980s. Recall that *Chicago VII* reflected the newer fusion style of the mid-1970s, especially the sound of Weather Report.

## Jazz-Oriented Fusionists

Through the 1970s a number of jazz artists moved toward the fusion style by adding electric bass, electronic keyboards, and rock-derived bass lines and rhythms. One of the most successful was Herbie Hancock. He had played piano with earlier Miles Davis groups and had established himself in the 1960s as a formidable jazz pianist (his funky "Watermelon Man" was especially popular). His album *Head Hunters* (1974) revealed an appealing fusion style and rose to number 13, an unusually high ranking for a jazz-oriented record. Hancock emphasized electronic keyboards, complete with filters, wah-wah pedals, and synthesizer modifications. The follow-up album, *Thrust,* equaled the chart position of *Head Hunters;* listen to "Actual Proof" from *Thrust* to get a good idea of Hancock's fusion style.

Jazz keyboardist Chick Corea (yet another *Bitches Brew* alumnus) also moved into the fusion sound, producing a series of moderately successful albums from 1976 to 1978. One of the most popular jazz pianists of the 1960s was Ramsey Lewis. Lewis had actually enjoyed a number 5 single in 1965 (his funky "The 'In' Crowd"). In the mid-1970s, he turned toward the new electronic jazz–rock fusion sound. As an example, listen to "Tambura," an especially good cut from his *Sun Goddess* album.

## Santana

Through the 1970s and 1980s others have pursued the second-phase jazz–rock fusion trend as initiated by Miles Davis's *Bitches Brew*. One thinks of Oregon, Spyro Gyra, and Julian Priester. But there were fusion groups whose roots were not with Davis's *Bitches Brew*. Santana, for example, had begun back in early 1967 as a blues band. Leader Carlos Santana was born in Autlán, Jalisco, Mexico, in 1947. He moved with his family to San Francisco in 1962. After working with Michael Bloomfield (Electric Flag) and Al Kooper (B, S, & T), Santana added percussionists Mike Carabello and Jose "Chepito" Areas and emphasized Latin and African rhythms. Appearing at Woodstock in 1969 as a virtually unknown band, Santana electrified the crowd with their "Latin rock." Their debut album, *Santana*, rose to number 4 in 1969 and yielded a Top 10 hit, "Evil Ways."

In the early 1970s, Santana became one of the most popular bands not only in the United States but, because of their international tours, in the world. The band had two number 1 albums and three Top 20 hits. Meanwhile, Carlos Santana recorded an album with drummer Buddy Miles that moved closer to the jazz–rock fusion style. When Santana reorganized for their next album, *Caravanserai* (1972), there was a decided turn toward jazz–rock fusion. Although the album sold well (number 8), the "new" sound undoubtedly disconcerted many Santana fans. Certainly there was still the technically proficient guitar work of Carlos Santana and the solid keyboard work of Gregg Rolie; but the old Latin rock sound was less evident.

With *Amigos* (1976), Santana returned to a Latin-oriented style. By that time, Carlos Santana was the only remaining original member of the band. Subsequent albums through the mid-1980s sold well, although of equal interest have been Carlos's recordings outside of his own band with a variety of other artists, such as John McLaughlin, Alice Coltrane, Herbie Hancock, Wayne Shorter, Tony Williams, Willie Nelson, and Booker T. Jones.

After *Blues for Salvador* (1988) won a Grammy, Santana's popularity ebbed for almost ten years. However, in 1999 Santana returned with a vengeance. *Supernatural* reached number 1 and sold over 15 million copies (21 million worldwide). "Smooth" spent twelve weeks at the number 1 position and "Maria, Maria" also reached number 1. The album received nine Grammy Awards. Santana was back! He has continued to release recordings (*Divine Light* in 2001 and *Shaman* in 2002) and has established a humanitarian organization called the Milagro Foundation to serve underrepresented and underprivileged children around the world in the areas of health, education, and the arts.

## Earth, Wind, and Fire

From a musical perspective, one of the finest bands of the 1970s was Earth, Wind, and Fire, formed in 1970 by Maurice White (born in Memphis in 1941). White had worked as a session drummer at Motown and Chess Records before touring with jazz pianist Ramsey Lewis for three years. Earth, Wind, and Fire (E, W, & F) was a large band, consisting of Maurice White and his brothers Verdine (bass) and Fred (percussion), plus six other musicians. The early *Last Days and Time* (1972), although it only reached number 87, was a musically impressive album. Of particular interest on this album is "Power," a seven-minute cut that begins and ends with a kalimba, an African "thumb piano" in which a series of tuned metal tongues are fixed to a resonating board or box. A strong rhythmic vamp is established over which the very talented Ronald Laws improvises a soprano sax solo; after a guitar solo, the rhythm breaks for a multilayered section for flutes. The insistent beat returns for a brief keyboard solo that fades back into the kalimba as the song ends.

E, W, & F's next few albums fared progressively better, culminating in their first number 1 album, *That's the Way of the World* (1975). The title song reached number 12 and "Shining Star" became the band's first number 1 single. Established as one of the most popular black bands of the 1970s, E, W, & F placed a series of eight consecutive albums in the Top 10, while enjoying six Top 10 singles.

Listening to any of E, W, & F's mid-1970s albums gives a good impression of the band's style. *Gratitude* (1975–76), *Spirit* (1976), and *All 'n All* (1977) reveal a talented band that both sings and plays with equal musicality. Vocals are smooth and well harmonized. In contrast with Maurice White's lyrical baritone voice, there is frequent use of falsetto (usually by Philip Bailey). Rhythms are rock-based but are far more complex than mainstream rock patterns; the tight coordination among drums, bass, rhythm guitar, and keyboards is not unlike the best of the fusion groups. E, W, & F's horns are used in a variety of ways, from the short, punctuating style of the 1960s Memphis–Stax–Volt horns to a genuine jazz–rock fusion style. The song "Magic Mind" from *All 'n All* shows their mature style of the mid-1970s. There is the solid, insistent accompaniment pattern played by drums, bass, and rhythm guitar; there are solid vocal harmonies including falsetto; particularly impressive are horn sections, such as the one near the end of the song, which is rhythmically quite complex as a result of its multilayered construction. On the same album listen to the jazz vocals on "Runnin'." Earth, Wind, and Fire set a high standard for horn-dominated, jazz-influenced music of the 1970s. Maurice White stopped touring with the band in the mid-1990s and revealed (just prior to the band's induction into the Rock and Roll Hall of Fame in 2000) that he had been diagnosed with Parkinson's disease. Despite the challenges, he continued to be actively involved as a producer, songwriter, and studio vocalist.

**Tower of Power**

Somewhat similar stylistically to E, W, & F was a San Francisco band called Tower of Power. Troubled by constant personnel changes, Tower of Power never achieved the commercial success of E, W, & F but certainly produced a high caliber of music. Growing out of the East Bay Area, with its multiethnic, working-class industrial society, Tower of Power became an alternative to the psychedelic sound of the Haight–Ashbury society. Formed in 1967 by Emilio Castillo, the band first adopted a Motown-derived image and sound. Several early albums sold only moderately well. In 1973, lead singer Rufus Miller was replaced by the talented Lenny Williams. Williams's smooth, soulful vocals seemed to make the difference. Tower of Power's next three albums featured Williams, and all three made the Top 30.

The black sound came primarily from the lead singer's style but was reinforced by the funky rhythmic foundation and the Memphis–Stax–Volt-derived horn lines. The horn line consisted of three saxes (and other woodwinds) and two brass (sometimes two trumpets, sometimes trumpet and trombone). One of Tower of Power's finest albums was *Back to Oakland* (1974). The opening and closing theme of this album,

"Oakland Stroke," shows the herky-jerky style of the band as complex rhythmic patterns are distributed throughout the ensemble. On the other hand, the sublime blend of Williams's voice and the Tower of Power horns is best illustrated on "Just When We Start Makin' It" (also note Chester Thompson's fine organ solo). The rhythmically complex accompaniment patterns in "Can't You See (You Doin' Me Wrong)" create a jittery sound beneath Williams's smooth vocal line. The Motown-derived emphasis on baritone sax is evident in "Squib Cakes," a particularly strong jazz–rock fusion song that features excellent solos by Bruce Conte (guitar), Mic Gillette (flügelhorn), Lenny Pickett (tenor sax), and Chester Thompson (organ).

**Other Fusion Artists**

We have mentioned Jeff Beck before—as a member of the Yardbirds in the mid-1960s (he replaced Eric Clapton). After leaving the Yardbirds, Beck formed his own group in 1967. His first two albums, *Truth* and *Beck-ola*, featured Rod Stewart as lead vocalist. In 1975, Beck issued *Blow by Blow*, which would prove to be his biggest-selling album (number 4). Beck's reputation as one of rock's finest guitarists was firmly established well before the release of *Blow by Blow*, but with this album he gained additional respect as he moved out of the rock mainstream into jazz–rock fusion. Featuring Beck's quartet (guitar, keyboards, bass, and drums), *Blow by Blow*, produced by George Martin, was a thoroughly impressive album. Several follow-up albums continued the fusion sound, with Jan Hammer supplying excellent keyboard work. Beck remained one of rock's most creative guitarists well into the 1980s.

Coming from still a different direction was Chuck Mangione. Classically trained at the Eastman School of Music, Mangione formed an excellent jazz quartet featuring his own work on flügelhorn. Accompanied by the Rochester Philharmonic Orchestra, Mangione produced a live album, *Friends and Love* (1971). Combining classical concepts with jazz and softer rock elements, Mangione's style evolved into a kind of art–jazz–rock–pop style. Always tasteful and accessible, Mangione brought a comfortable jazz sound to a wide audience. His most successful album, *Feels So Good* (number 2 in 1977), produced a Top 5 hit (the title song).

On the outer edges of jazz–rock fusion is Steely Dan. Leaning toward the rock side of the fusion style, this band reveals subtle jazz influences combined with the gentler side of the rock mainstream. The two key members of Steely Dan were bassist Walter Becker (New York City, 1950) and keyboardist Donald Fagen (Passaic, New Jersey, 1948). They formed Steely Dan in 1972 as a quintet. Their third album, *Pretzel Logic* (1974), reached the Top 10 and contained their biggest hit, "Rikki Don't Lose That Number" (number 4).

Steely Dan recorded their next album with the assistance of extra session musicians. *Katy Lied* (1975) revealed more obvious jazz influences (for example, listen to "Doctor Wu," with jazz saxophonist Phil Woods). *The Royal Scam* (1976) also utilized numerous extra players and had a clearer jazz–rock fusion sound. Steely Dan's last two studio albums, *Aja* (number 3 in 1977) and *Gaucho* (number 9 in late 1980) were not only big sellers but yielded four single hits. Steely Dan was something of an enigma; they had a unique sound that, even though often characterized as jazz–rock fusion, was nothing like Chicago, Mahavishnu, Santana, Weather Report, and so on. With an ever-changing membership, a sophisticated and enigmatic style, and an unalterable aversion to touring, it is amazing that they achieved such commercial success. In the early 1980s, Becker and Fagen went their separate ways, with Fagen gaining considerable respect for his solo album *The Nightfly* in 1982.

After over ten years, Becker and Fagen reunited for a national tour in 1993. Although they continued to record separately, they joined again to release *Two Against Nature* in 2000. The album won three Grammy Awards, including Album of the Year.

## THE SINGER–SONGWRITERS OF THE 1970S

The first explosion of folk rock had dissipated by 1968; however, from the prototypes established by Dylan, Baez, the Byrds, Simon and Garfunkel, Buffalo Springfield, and others came a number of major new acts of the 1970s. Some stayed more or less in the folk rock vein, but with some significant modifications; others veered off toward a country-oriented style; and still others moved closer to a pop-oriented or softer sound; and one or two even flirted with jazz. As was the case with art rock/progressive rock and jazz rock/fusion, the 1970s performers were given a new stylistic appellation to distinguish them from their 1960s progenitors. The term *singer–songwriter* became the acknowledged categorical term for these 1970s latter-day folk rock performers.

Once again the term *singer–songwriter* must be considered a loose and ill-defined term. According to Janet Maslin, "the term singer/songwriter . . . was always more of a catchall than a legitimate musical genre" (Miller 1980, 339). Indeed, the term implies nothing at all about style but merely tells us that a person composes and performs songs. In retrospect, the term seems to distinguish a group of performers more for what they were not than for what they were. In other words, "singer–songwriter," in the popular usage of the term, usually referred to a musician who (obviously) composed and sang his or her own songs (very often as a solo act) in a post–Dylan folk or folk rock style, and who was not oriented toward mainstream rock, art rock, jazz rock, soul, or disco. And even with that broad definition, one can think of a few exceptions.

As we saw when we traced Dylan, Baez, and Simon and Garfunkel into the 1970s, several changes took place as the style evolved. First, the lyrics changed from a focus on the world's problems (war, racial equality, the brotherhood of humankind, etc.) to a focus on the self. As Maslin notes, "The form's clearest hallmark became a self-absorption complete enough to counterbalance the preceding era's utopian jive" (Miller 1980, 339). Second, in many cases (not all), the folk rock trend toward electronic rock increased dramatically. The 1970s singer–songwriter happily utilized the latest advancements in studio technology, electronic keyboards, and synthesizers. Let us begin our survey of 1970s singer–songwriters with one of the most talented of them all: Joni Mitchell.

### Joni Mitchell

Born in 1943 in Alberta, Canada, Joni Mitchell was raised in Saskatoon, Saskatchewan. After marrying folk singer Chuck Mitchell, she moved to Detroit (1966) and toured the East Coast with her husband. After the breakup of her marriage, she moved to New York City, where she became a part of the folk music scene. Signed to Reprise Records, her first four albums (1968 to 1971) sold progressively well and revealed a developing talent for more refined musicianship and inventive melodies. Her lyrics focused on themes of romantic love and the experience of lost love.

Switching to Asylum Records, Mitchell hit her commercial peak with *Court and Spark*, which rose to number 2 in 1974 and yielded a major hit with "Help Me" (number 7). "Help Me" exemplifies Mitchell's songwriting ability at its best. The melodic line is wide-ranging and inventive; rhythmic interest comes not only from the occasional metric changes but from the rhythmic inflections of the melody, which often conflict with the established meter; the harmonic material is quite sophisticated and shows a relation to jazz. Mitchell's clear, pitch-perfect voice is evident in this and other songs on *Court and Spark*. Of particular note is the decidedly jazzy song "Twisted." Mitchell's performance perfectly depicts the mental distortion that is the song's subject—including the overdubbed duet on the schizophrenic final lines.

Subsequent albums found Mitchell drifting further toward a jazz-influenced style. The double album *Don Juan's Reckless Daughter* (1977–78) firmly broke with her pop-folk past; using jazz musicians from Weather Report, she included the side-long "Paprika Plains," accompanied by full symphony orchestra. The 1979 album *Mingus* went all the way to jazz. In preparation for some eighteen months, the album began as a collaboration with jazz great Charles Mingus, but became a memorial when Mingus died in early 1979. Two of the album's songs are Mitchell's, but four are Mingus's music and Mitchell's words. Fusion greats Wayne Shorter, Herbie Hancock, and Jaco Pastorius are among the musicians on this remarkable album. Mitchell's success, both commercial and critical, continued into the 1990s with *Night Ride Home* (1991), *Rubulent Indigo* (1994), and *Taming the Tiger* (1998).

## Carole King

The other leading female singer–songwriter of the 1970s (other than Baez, of course) was Carole King. A member of the famous Brill Building group of songwriters, King (with and without her husband, Gerry Goffin) had written a staggering number of hit songs for other artists since the early 1960s, including the Shirelles; the Drifters; Bobby Vee; the Everly Brothers; Steve Lawrence and Eydie Gorme; Little Eva; Herman's Hermits; the Animals; B, S, & T; the Monkees; Aretha Franklin; and the Byrds. By the late 1960s, she had dissolved the songwriting team and divorced Goffin.

King's second solo album, *Tapestry* (1971), became a monster hit. It reached number 1 and held that position for fifteen weeks; it eventually stayed on the charts for 302 weeks and was the biggest-selling pop album in history up until that time. "It's Too Late," backed with "I Feel the Earth Move," became number 1 hits. Other strong songs on this album were "You've Got a Friend," "Smackwater Jack," and "(You Make Me Feel Like) A Natural Woman."

Subsequent albums sold well but lacked the magical impact of *Tapestry*. *Wrap Around Joy* (number 1 in 1974) was a particularly strong album and even hinted at a slight bend toward jazz, although not so pronounced as Joni Mitchell's. The hit single "Jazzman" (number 2 in 1974) featured a sax solo by the L.A. Express's Tom Scott. King's albums since 1977 sold less well.

King's style emphasized simple piano accompaniments and a pop or soft rock musical style. If her basic style was affected by any other style at all, it might have been a light touch of funk–soul–gospel (e.g., "We Are All in This Together," from *Wrap Around Joy*).

## James Taylor

James Taylor (born in Boston in 1948) was raised in an affluent and musical family. His early attempts at a recording career were not successful, so he moved to London, where he impressed Paul McCartney and Peter Asher, signing with Apple Records in 1968. His first album, *James Taylor*, did not fare well, although it contained several good songs (e.g., "Something in the Way She Moves" and "Carolina on My Mind"). Asher managed to negotiate a new contract for Taylor with Warner Brothers and produced his next album, *Sweet Baby James* (1970). It was a great success (number 3) and yielded the major hit "Fire and Rain" (number 3 in 1970). Taylor sang in a soft folk rock style with perhaps just a touch of country influence. A morose look at the depression of lost love, "Fire and Rain" exemplifies the inward turn and self-orientation of the singer–songwriter trend of the 1970s. Taylor's follow-up album, *Mud Slide Slim and the Blue Horizon* (1971), rose to number 2 and contained Carole King's "You've Got a Friend." Even this relatively positive and outgoing song sounded sad and introspective in Taylor's version.

In 1972, Taylor married singer Carly Simon. Recorded at his home in Martha's Vineyard, *One-Man Dog* (1972) reached the Top 5 and contained the attractive (but sad-sounding) "Don't Let Me Be Lonely Tonight," with excellent sax work by Michael Brecker. Others assisting Taylor on this album included Carole King and Linda Ronstadt. *Gorilla* (1975), a refreshing album, actually had a brighter, more upbeat sound, as exemplified by "Mexico" and the Holland-Dozier-Holland song "How Sweet It Is" (number 5 in 1975).

In the late 1970s, Taylor recorded with other artists including Simon and Garfunkel and wife Carly Simon. Taylor became one of the style setters among the post–Dylan softer singer–songwriters. Unlike some of the others, he never turned toward the heavily electronic sound or to jazz or the mainstream side of rock. A somewhat uncharacteristic R & B-style song, "Steamroller" was included on his *Greatest Hits* album (late 1976) and is interesting primarily because it was so out of character for Taylor. Taylor has continued to record and perform. His album *Hourglass* (number 9 in 1997) won a Grammy for Best Pop Album.

## Jim Croce

Jim Croce's songs were usually as upbeat and positive as Taylor's were morose and depressing. Ironically, Croce's own story became one of the saddest of the 1970s. Croce was born and raised in Philadelphia. Signed to Capitol Records, he and his wife Ingrid released a duet album in 1969 that did not sell well. However, with the help of some friends, Croce found himself given a second chance by ABC Records. With good production and strong backup musicians, Croce's *You Don't Mess Around with Jim* moved to number 1. The title song made the Top 10, and "Operator" made the Top 20, firmly establishing Croce as a bona fide member of the 1970s singer–songwriter trend.

Croce's vocal timbre was unique; among all of the singer- songwriters of the time, Croce's voice was one that was easily and instantly recognizable. His enunciation was perfectly clear, but he had a peculiar brogue all his own. Croce's songs were well constructed musically, had appealing melodies, and often had a lilting rhythm that reflected his upbeat attitude. There were the "character" songs (e.g., "You Don't Mess Around with Jim," "Rapid Roy," and "Bad, Bad Leroy Brown") and the plaintively beautiful songs ("Photographs and Memories" and "Time in a Bottle"). Either way, Croce made the listener feel good.

Croce had recorded his third ABC album, *I Got a Name*, in the summer of 1973, but before the album could be released he was killed in a plane crash near Natchitoches, Louisiana (he was thirty years old). Released posthumously, *I Got a Name* became a number 2 album and yielded three top 40 hits. "Time in a Bottle" was also released (from the first ABC album), and it made number 1 in late 1973. In the words of that song, "There never seems to be enough time to do the things you want to do once you find them."

## Cat Stevens

The folk and folk rock trends of the 1960s and the singer–songwriter trend of the 1970s were American phenomena. An important exception was Cat Stevens (born Steve Georgiou, London, 1948). Several early albums and singles did well enough in England but made little impact in the United States. However, *Tea for the Tillerman* (1971) caught on and moved to number 8 on the American charts; the single "Wild World" rose to number 11. The song "Father and Son" is a particularly touching song that is reminiscent of the style of Bob Dylan.

Stevens accompanied himself on acoustic guitar; like Croce, he was unique and instantly recognizable, not only for his vocal timbre but for his enunciation. Most of his songs were rather gentle; even the more rhythmically oriented songs (e.g., "Wild World," "Ready," and "Peace Train") were gentle when compared to mainstream rock.

Stevens released a series of popular albums from 1971 through 1977, which yielded a string of hits, including "Morning Has Broken" (number 6 in 1972) and "Oh Very Young" (number 10 in 1974). In 1974 there was a slight change from acoustic guitar-oriented accompaniments to piano-oriented accompaniments. By 1978, Stevens had turned to the Muslim religion, adopted a new name (Yusef Islam), and dropped out of the music industry. The former musician found his name in the news again in September 2004 when, due to the appearance of his name on a national security "watch list," the plane he was flying on from London to the United States was diverted to Maine and grounded. Islam (Stevens) was questioned and detained prior to being returned to Britain.

## Billy Joel

One of the few 1970s singer–songwriters to persevere into the 1980s and beyond was Billy Joel. Born on Long Island, New York, in 1949, Joel was a classically trained pianist. From 1964 through 1976, Joel knocked around the music business, his only major success coming with *Piano Man* (1974), an album that made the Top 30 and yielded the number 25 hit by the same name. But from 1977 through 1980, Joel released three Top 5 albums (*The Stranger, 52nd Street,* and *Glass Houses*) that yielded three major hit singles, including his first number 1 song, "It's Still Rock and

Roll to Me." These successes propelled Joel headlong into the 1980s, where he found continued success. By the end of 1984, Joel had achieved twenty-two Top 40 hits, including the number 1 "Tell Her About It" and the number 3 "Uptown Girl."

Joel does not fit the post–folk rock singer–songwriter trend in the way that Taylor, Croce, Stevens, Mitchell, and others do. He moved closer to mainstream rock (the softer side) and toward more elaborate production. His refusal to become "typed" into any one style has led to some criticism (recall similar problems with Presley, Dylan, Franklin, and others). For example, on *An Innocent Man* (1982), one can hear a shouting R & B-derived mainstream song like "Easy Money," a doo-wop-oriented song like "The Longest Time," or a ballad-style song like the title song. There is also the 1950s-style soft rock of "This Night" (complete with melodic references to the second movement of Beethoven's Piano Sonata in C Minor, Op. 13—"Pathétique"); there is good time rock and roll in "Tell Her About It," the Four Seasons–like "Uptown Girl," and the Sam Cooke–ish "Careless Talk." There are reminiscences of Jerry Lee Lewis and Little Richard in "Christie Lee" and touches of jazz in the harmonica work of Toots Thielemans on "Leave a Tender Moment Alone." Joel's solid musical background is evident in the flawless construction of his songs and his impressive performance technique.

Joel's success continued into the 1990s with *River of Dreams* (number 1 in 1993). The album's title song reached number 3 on the charts. He also completed several very successful international tours with Elton John (1994 and 1999).

## Crosby, Stills, Nash, and Young

The term *singer–songwriter* usually refers to a soloist; however, before leaving the singer–songwriter trend, we must mention Crosby, Stills, Nash, and Young. Stylistically, they fit into the singer–songwriter trend, even though they were a group. As Brock Helander notes, "More an aggregation of three (and four) individuals than a group, Crosby, Stills, Nash (and Young) created a characteristic sound that the three original members have attempted to maintain, somewhat equivocally, into the late-Seventies" (Helander 1982, 116).

We have met David Crosby (the Byrds), Stephen Stills (Buffalo Springfield), Graham Nash (the Hollies), and Neil Young (Buffalo Springfield) in earlier sections of this book. As the first wave of folk rock dissipated in 1968, Crosby, Stills, and Nash formed their new group after an informal jam session in Los Angeles. Releasing their first album for Atlantic (*Crosby, Stills, and Nash*), the group emphasized excellent vocal harmonies and sociopolitical commentary. All three played guitar, with Stills dubbing in keyboard and bass parts (drums were supplied by Dallas Taylor). All three principals contributed songs to the group's repertoire. The debut album reached number 6 and yielded two moderately successful singles.

Neil Young joined the group in 1969 in time to perform with the group at Woodstock. The addition of Young allowed Stills to move to keyboards and enabled the group to execute rather complex four-part harmonies. There was a firm reliance on acoustic guitar, with only light use of electric guitars and keyboards.

The title song of the quartet's first album *Deja Vu* (number 1 in 1970) provides a good sample of C, S, N, & Y. Tight vocal harmonies change in relatively fast rhythm in its opening moments. After a short vocal solo section, the vocal harmonies reenter, reflecting some jazz influence. Some Beach Boy–like vocal polyphony follows;

Crosby, Stills, Nash, and Young (*Source:* Michael Ochs Archives, Ltd.)

changing to falsetto, the group sings the hook line, "We have all been here before." With its frequent sectional changes, "Deja Vu" is a very effective song ("Carry On" illustrates similar vocal harmonies).

There can be little doubt that C, S, N, & Y was the most sophisticated vocal group of the early 1970s. Their musical style was the natural extension of the work of the Byrds and Buffalo Springfield of the late 1960s. There were even the occasional country-oriented sounds developed by the earlier groups (e.g., "Teach Your Children"). The C, S, N, & Y style occasionally moved toward the gentler side of mainstream rock in songs like "Almost Cut My Hair" and "Woodstock" (the latter composed by Joni Mitchell).

The turbulent lives of the individuals within C, S, N, & Y were bound to lead to instability. A live album, *4 Way Street*, was released in 1971 and also went to number 1. But by that time, the group had gone their separate ways. Each recorded solo albums, often with the assistance of at least one of the other former C, S, N, & Y members. The quartet reunited for a tour in the summer of 1974; a greatest-hits album released that year went to number 1 (rare for a "hits" album). From the mid-1970s on, the group was on-again, off-again, often uniting around political events (e.g., the antinuclear MUSE—Musicians United for Safe Energy—demonstration in 1979, and the Survival Sunday concert in 1980). The band reunited yet again in 1999 to record *Looking Forward* and launch another tour.

## Reggae

As we saw in Chapter 5, "Transition: The Early 1960s," a popular style of Jamaican music—calypso—enjoyed brief popularity in the late 1950s and played a role in the early days of the folk music trend. In the 1970s, a Jamaican musical style reappeared in both the United States and England. Reggae originated in Jamaica in the

Bob Marley (*Source:* Michael Ochs Archives, Ltd.)

mid-1960s. The leader of the reggae trend was Bob Marley (born in St. Ann's Bay, Jamaica, in 1945). Marley's recording career began in the early 1960s, but his first real success came with "Simmer Down" in 1964. Over the next few years, Marley and his Wailing Wailers recorded some thirty songs and became the hottest group on the island. In the early 1970s, the Wailers became known throughout the Caribbean, but it was not until 1972 that they signed with Island Records and began to build an international reputation.

Reggae music is closely tied to the Rastafarian religion, which revered the late emperor of Ethiopia, Haile Selassie (common name: Ras Tafari). Speaking for the deprived and dispossessed classes of Jamaica, reggae music spoke of the dream of an eventual return to the African homeland. The music has a dry, staccato (detached) beat and guitar accompaniment; moderate tempos prevail, and the beat is relatively gentle. The Jamaican dialect colors the lyrics, which often express the political beliefs of the Rastafarians.

Marley's *Natty Dread* (1975) brought the Wailers to the U.S. charts. However, it was not until 1976 that Marley made a major impact with *Rastaman Vibration* (number 8). "War" (from *Rastaman Vibration*) was based upon a speech by Emperor Selassie; "Roots, Rock, Reggae" became a minor hit.

By the late 1970s, reggae's popularity had begun to fade. *Exodus* (number 20 in 1977) was Marley's last Top 40 album; subsequent albums sold moderately, primarily to a relatively small cult following in the United States and England. Marley's dreadlocks (long, tightly braided locks) were imitated by the most devoted reggae fans, especially in reggae's heyday (roughly 1976 to 1978). Bob Marley died of cancer in 1981 at the age of thirty-six; he was given an official funeral by the people of Jamaica, who had also honored him with the nation's Order of Merit one month before his death.

The reggae style was particularly influential in Britain. The Rolling Stones and quite a few of the British punk groups reflected the influence of reggae. In addition, artists as varied as Johnny Nash, Paul Simon, Led Zeppelin, Stevie Wonder, Elvis Costello, the Police, the Clash, and Eric Clapton (Marley's "I Shot the Sheriff") all reflected the reggae influence in particular songs.

## FOLK INFLUENCES IN THE 1980S AND 1990S

Since the beginning of recorded history, folk music (sometimes referred to as "roots music") has provided a common musical experience for members of a given social group. The music of Woody Guthrie and Pete Seeger provided a foundation for much music of the 1960s (the Kingston Trio; Bob Dylan; and Peter, Paul, & Mary) and on into the 1990s (Tracy Chapman and Jewel). During the 1990s and at the beginning of the twenty-first century, there were signs of revitalized interest in these familiar musical influences. The surprise popularity of the soundtrack for the film *O Brother Where Art Thou?* (number 1 in 2001) resulted in a stay of well over a year on the album chart. The first track on the album is a recording of "Po Lazurus," an authentic worksong performed by James Carter and other prisoners working in a chain gang from Camp B at Mississippi State Penitentiary as they chopped wood while singing. The song was captured in a 1959 field recording by folk music historian Alan Lomax. This "various artist" recording juxtaposes such authentic recordings with music from long ago (Harry "Mac" McClintock's 1928 recording of "Big Rock Candy Mountain" and the Stanley Brothers' 1955 recording of "Angel Band"), new recordings by roots artists who have been around awhile (the Fairfield Four, Ralph Stanley, and The Whites), and new renditions of period songs by contemporary artists (Emmylou Harris, Allison Krauss, Gillian Welch, and John Hartford). What appeared to be a "roots revival" as a result of this soundtrack and follow-up releases lasted only a couple of years, but other folk styles continued to exert their influence on popular music.

## Bob Dylan's Reign Continues

In a manner similar to the way in which Santana's commercial revival confirmed the importance of Latin music, the reappearance of Bob Dylan during the 1990s heralded a revitalized interest in folk-influenced music. A new generation of listeners became aware of Dylan's legacy listening to the music of the Wallflowers, a band formed in 1990 by Dylan's son, Jakob. Dylan's *Time Out of Mind* (number 10 in 1997) placed higher on the charts than any album he released since his first recording as a born-again Christian, *Slow Train Coming* (number 3 in 1979). The album earned the songwriter three Grammy awards, including Album of the Year, Best Contemporary Folk Album, and Best Male Rock Vocal Performance for "Cold Irons Bound." Garth Brooks recorded a cover version of "To Make You Feel My Love," another track from *Time Out of Mind*, resulting in a number 1 hit on the Country chart. In 2000, Dylan composed "Things Have Changed" for the *Wonder Boys* soundtrack that was also released on a two-disc anthology later that year. The song not only won a Grammy, but it also earned Dylan's first Oscar for Best Original Song. In 2002, Dylan released *Love and Theft* (number 5), continuing his series of commercially successful and critically acclaimed recordings and winning a Grammy for Best Contemporary Folk Album. He published an autobiography entitled *Chronicles, Volume One* in 2004.

## Tracy Chapman

Other folk-influenced performers and singer-songwriters have continued to carry on the folk music tradition within the popular music industry that began in earnest with the Kingston Trio in the late 1950s. The release of Tracy Chapman's self-titled debut in 1988 and the surprising commercial success of several tracks ("Fast Car" [number 6], "Talkin' 'bout a Revolution," [number 75], and "Baby Can I Hold

You" [number 48]) suggested that, at a time when radio airwaves were pumping out the music of George Michael, Van Halen, Bon Jovi, and the soundtrack from *Dirty Dancing*, the record-buying public was also interested in music that was at once reflective and introspective. Chapman's follow-up album, *Crossroads* (1989), reached number 6, while *Matters of the Heart* (1992) peaked at number 53. Later albums proved successful, though not at a consistently chart-topping level: *New Beginning* (number 4 in 1995) and *Telling Stories* (number 33 in 2000).

### Jewel

The daughter of both members of a folk duo from the 1970s, Jewel Kilcher became one of the most successful female solo artists in the history of rock music. Her recording debut, *Pieces of You* (1995), garnered little attention until over a year following its release date. A steady diet of touring and a resulting set of hit singles in 1996, "Who Will Save Your Soul" (number 11) and "You Were Meant for Me" (number 2), eventually pushed the album to number 4 on the *Billboard* chart, selling over 11 million copies. The third single, "Foolish Games" (number 7), was included in the soundtrack for the film *Batman and Robin*. Jewel's participation in Lillith Fair, an all-female concert tour organized by Sarah McLachlan, placed her in a prominent position during a period when the number of female artists on the album charts surpassed the number of male artists for the first time. Other performers who participated in this important music festival over the years included Shawn Colvin, Sheryl Crow, the Dixie Chicks, Indigo Girls, Queen Latifah, Monica, Liz Phair, and many others. Jewel's follow-up recording, *Spirit* (1998), was not released until almost four years after her first album and debuted at number 3. Though the first single, "Hands," reached number 6, follow-up singles failed to reach the Top 50: "Down So Long" (number 59) and "Jupiter (Swallow the Moon)" (number 51). She continued to record folk-influenced music such as the albums *This Way* (number 9 in 2001) and *0304* (number 2 in 2003), but the sales fell far short of her earlier recordings.

## COUNTRY ROCK AND PROGRESSIVE COUNTRY

### The 1970s

As discussed earlier, C & W was one of the progenitors of rock and roll, and rockabilly emerged as one of the three basic trends of early rock. But by the early 1960s, rockabilly had almost completely died away. For much of the 1960s, the C & W influence in rock was virtually nonexistent. Only near the end of the decade did there appear to be some tentative interest in rekindling the old partnership between C & W and rock. In Chapter 8, "Folk Music and Folk Rock," we noted some country rock explorations by the Byrds, Buffalo Springfield, and Bob Dylan in their late-1960s albums.

As the 1970s began, another surge of interest came from a rather surprising source: San Francisco. The Grateful Dead took a definite turn toward country rock with their 1970s albums *Workingman's Dead* and *American Beauty*. Jerry Garcia was actively involved with a new San Francisco country rock band of the early 1970s known as New Riders of the Purple Sage. The New Riders' albums sold moderately from 1971 through 1974 but tapered off dramatically after that.

Somewhat in the same vein were the Flying Burrito Brothers, whose membership included Chris Hillman and Gram Parsons. This post–Byrds country rock band existed from 1969 through 1975 and released some half-dozen barely successful albums. Somewhat more successful was Pure Prairie League, a Cincinnati band whose albums in the mid-1970s made the Top 40 and were considered important contributions to the country rock style.

## The Eagles and the Band

The most successful of the country rock bands was the Eagles, formed in 1971 in Los Angeles. *Eagles* was released in 1972 and yielded a Top 10 hit, "Witchy Woman." Their third album, *On the Border* (1974), reached the Top 20 and contained the band's first number 1 song, "Best of My Love." The years 1975 and 1976 were peak ones for the Eagles, as their next four albums reached number 1, yielding four more number 1 singles.

As with most of the aforementioned country rock bands, the Eagles moved between mainstream rock, a post–folk rock style, and country rock. Their first number 1 album, *One of These Nights* (1975), illustrates this versatility. Songs such as "After the Thrill Is Gone," "Hollywood Waltz," and "Lyin' Eyes" (number 2) are perfect examples of 1970s country rock. The lead vocals, the backup vocals, the beat, and the instrumental backup all contribute to the country-oriented sound. However, a song such as "Journey of the Sorcerer" moves toward progressive rock; the timbre of the mandolin may recall bluegrass music, but there is no stylistic incorporation of bluegrass. Several songs on the album show little or no derivation from country music (e.g., "Visions," "One of These Nights," and "Too Many Hands"); such songs are nearer the gentler side of mainstream rock.

In the mid-1970s, Bernie Leadon (guitar, banjo, mandolin, steel guitar, and vocals) left the band and was replaced by guitarist-vocalist Joe Walsh. Subsequent albums, beginning with *Hotel California* (1976–77), revealed a drift away from the country rock sound so evident in the Eagles' first four albums. By 1981, founder Glenn Frey (guitar, keyboards, and vocals) called it quits, and so did the Eagles. They reunited in 1994 for a very successful tour and they released a number 1 album, *Hell Freezes Over*. The band was inducted into the Rock and Roll Hall of Fame in 1998. In early 2001, the Eagles' *Their Greatest Hits, 1971–1975* surpassed Michael Jackson's *Thriller* (1983) as the greatest selling album up to that time (28 million and counting). Having sold over 100 million albums total, the Eagles have proven to be one of the most significant forces in the history of rock music.

Among other country rock bands of the 1970s was Bob Dylan's backup group, The Band. Although this group of four Canadian musicians plus one member from Arkansas had been around since the early 1960s, their first recognition (aside from the Dylan connection) came in 1968 with *Music from Big Pink*. Several albums between 1969 and 1976 sold quite well (three albums made the Top 10), and they were among the groups responsible for the reemergence of interest in country-influenced rock.

## The Charlie Daniels and Marshall Tucker Bands

It seems only natural that some of the southern rock bands of the 1970s would turn toward C & W as an influence. Whereas bands like Lynyrd Skynyrd and the Allman Brothers leaned toward R & B influences, other southern bands, like the Charlie Daniels Band and the Marshall Tucker Band, leaned toward C & W influences.

Charlie Daniels was born in Wilmington, North Carolina, in 1936. Early in his career he played in a bluegrass band called the Misty Mountain Boys, and later he played on several Dylan albums, including *Nashville Skyline*. Forming his own band in the early 1970s, Daniels first hit the charts with "Uneasy Rider" (number 9 in 1973).

The Charlie Daniels Band featured Daniels on lead guitar, banjo, violin, and vocals; using the double drummer concept, the band also included a second guitar lead, plus keyboards and bass. Whereas the bands previously discussed were basically rock bands with a country influence, Daniels was a genuine fifty-fifty blend of country and rock. Their first gold album, *Fire on the Mountain* (1974–75), featured several strong country rock songs such as "Long Haired Country Boy" and "The South's Gonna Do It Again" (number 29 in 1975). The latter song is a twelve-bar blues that features Daniels' fiddling; the style is sometimes called southern rock boogie or southern boogie and blues. Southern country rock lyrics often dealt with broken romances (a C & W tradition), alcohol, and gambling, depicting a laid-back good-ol'-boy society. The vocalists' enunciation emphasized southern roots. At times, the music moved toward a purer rock style, as in "No Place to Go."

The Daniels Band toured extensively, playing at sites as varied as the Grand Ole Opry and President Carter's inauguration. They found their biggest success with the *Million Mile Reflections* album (1979), with its hit single "The Devil Went Down to Georgia," which again featured Daniels' virtuosic fiddling.

Similar in concept to the Charlie Daniels Band, the Marshall Tucker Band began in 1970 as the Toy Factory, changing the name by 1972. There is no person named Marshall Tucker in the band; the name supposedly refers to a local piano teacher in their hometown of Spartanburg, South Carolina. Their first three albums were reasonably successful, but in 1975 *Searchin' for a Rainbow* made the Top 20. Performing as many as 300 concerts per year, Marshall Tucker found themselves to be increasingly popular as a live performance and album band but without major impact on the singles charts. In fact, their only Top 40 singles were 1975's "Fire on the Mountain" (number 38) and 1977's "Heard It in a Love Song" (number 14). The former song is a good example of Marshall Tucker's country rock sound, with its steel guitar introduction, gentle country rock beat, and country-oriented vocal. The style is basically country with a light rock influence; note woodwind player Jerry Eubanks's flute line near the middle of the song, adding an interesting timbre that made Tucker's sound unique. Another good example is "Virginia" (also on *Searchin' for a Rainbow*), which uses a rock-derived guitar and bass riff to tie the song together. Of special interest is Eubanks's brief but lovely soprano sax solo.

## Linda Ronstadt

Possibly because of the early precedents set by the Byrds and Buffalo Springfield, most country rock of the 1970s involved groups rather than solo performers. A significant exception was Linda Ronstadt (born in Tucson in 1946). After moving to

Los Angeles, she formed a folk-oriented trio called the Stone Poneys. Things started off well enough; the group's second album yielded a number 13 hit, "Different Drum" (late 1967 to early 1968). But the next few albums failed to have major impact, producing only one moderately successful single, the folksy "Long, Long Time" (1970). Nor had she had much success with her four solo albums.

However, in 1974, she recorded *Heart Like a Wheel*, produced by Peter Asher, who also became her manager. For the balance of the 1970s, Ronstadt was the leading female solo singer on the rock scene. The album yielded a number 2 hit ("When Will I Be Loved") and her first number 1 song ("You're No Good"). Following *Heart Like a Wheel*, Ronstadt's next five studio albums placed numbers 4, 3, 1, 1, and 3, respectively. In that span (1975 through 1980), she placed a dozen songs in the Top 40, including five in the Top 10.

In spite of her folk-oriented beginnings, Ronstadt became known as a country rock singer. Certainly albums such as *Linda Ronstadt* and *Don't Cry Now* reinforced that image (for example, listen to "Silver Threads and Golden Needles" from *Don't Cry Now*). Throughout the 1970s, she continued to perform in a country-influenced style. *Heart Like a Wheel* contained the country-oriented "When Will I Be Loved" and even a version of Paul Anka's "It Doesn't Matter Anymore" (Ronstadt's version of this song was much more "countrified" than Buddy Holly's original pop style version). On *Prisoner in Disguise* (1975), even Smokey Robinson's "Tracks of My Tears" comes out country, as does Neil Young's "Love Is a Rose." Nevertheless, she produced a Top 5 hit in 1975 with Holland-Dozier-Holland's "Heat Wave," in a version that had little to do with country music. And in the 1980s, Ronstadt had incredible success with several albums that recycled old songs from the 1930s and 1940s in lush arrangements backed by bandleader Nelson Riddle. She had even dabbled with the new wave trend by singing several Elvis Costello songs on 1980's *Mad Love*.

## Willie Nelson and Waylon Jennings

Around the edges of country rock were two other types of performer: the country pop singers and the progressive country (or redneck rock) singers. Interest in country rock naturally led to an interest in pure country music. The central figure in this trend was Willie Nelson (born in Abbott, Texas, in 1933). Nelson had moved to Nashville in 1961, where he had some success as a composer of country and pop songs for other artists; and as a performer he placed a few hits on the country charts. But Willie felt that the Nashville country music establishment was too restrictive. One of the first hints that Nelson was a rebel was his introduction of black country singer Charlie Pride on his 1967 tour.

Late in 1969, after his Nashville home had burned, Nelson moved back to Texas. Several years later he initiated his now-famous Fourth of July "picnics"—huge outdoor affairs that drew not only country music fans but young rock fans. Willie dropped the traditional country singer image; instead he wore faded jeans and tee shirts; he grew his hair long and even pigtailed it; he put an earring in his ear and wore a bandanna around his head. By the norms of the traditional country music world, Nelson had become a rebel—an "outlaw." He was a redneck hippie.

In 1975, Nelson released *Red-Headed Stranger;* "Blue Eyes Cryin' in the Rain" moved to number 21 on the pop charts, thus opening the doors for more crossover recordings by other "progressive country" singers: Tompall Glaser, Waylon Jen-

Willie Nelson, country western star, performs at the Reebok Riverstage in New York. (*Source:* AP/World Wide Photos)

nings, Kris Kristofferson, Jessi Colter (Jennings' wife), and Jerry Jeff Walker. RCA's progressive country sampler, *The Outlaws* (1977), brought the music of Nelson and some of the others to a wider audience (it became a platinum album—the first in country music). Willie went on to have several more Top 40 hits in the early 1980s. His *Stardust* album of 1978 featured his versions of old pop favorites from the 1930s and 1940s (something of a precedent for Ronstadt's pop albums of the 1980s).

Waylon Jennings's association with rock was only slightly stronger. Born in Littlefield, Texas (near Lubbock) in 1937, Jennings had played with Buddy Holly on his fateful last tour. Jennings had several country hits during the 1960s, but with the release of *The Outlaws*, he became a national figure. His *Ol' Waylon* album (1977) hit the Top 20 and yielded a Top 30 hit, "Luckenbach, Texas (Back to the Basics of Love)." His 1978 album with Nelson, *Waylon and Willie* ("Mamas, Don't Let Your Babies Grow Up to Be Cowboys"), and his recording of the theme song for the television show *The Dukes of Hazzard* gained further national attention for Jennings. Jennings died in 2002 from diabetes-related conditions.

### Progressive Country

The progressive country movement was more a social phenomenon than a musical one. Nelson's music was firmly rooted in the country tradition. Rock elements were subdued or totally absent. What appealed was Willie's image as a rebel.

In 1980, the film *Urban Cowboy* (starring John Travolta, but including musical appearances by some fourteen country and country rock acts) made the country movement très chic. Suddenly there were people all over the nation wearing boots and broad-brimmed Stetson hats. But the center of the progressive country movement stayed firmly in Austin, Texas, where the Armadillo World Headquarters became to this trend what the Fillmore had been to San Francisco. Huge country ballrooms, such as Gilley's in Houston and Billy Bob's in Fort Worth, capitalized on the urban cowboy trend.

### Glen Campbell and Kenny Rogers

From the softer side of country came singers like Glen Campbell and Kenny Rogers. Campbell was born in Arkansas in 1936. His gentle country pop style first reached national attention in 1967 with a number 5 album, *Gentle on My Mind*, and a Top 30 hit, "By the Time I Get to Phoenix." After hitting what seemed to be a high spot in 1968 and 1969 with songs like "Wichita Lineman" (number 3) and "Galveston" (number 4), Campbell's popularity began to fade. But with the rising interest in country music in the late 1970s, Campbell enjoyed a real comeback (e.g., "Rhinestone Cowboy" of 1975 and "Southern Nights" of 1977). His country ballad style was not far removed musically from that of Nelson and other traditional country singers; however, he did not follow the "outlaw" or rebel image of Nelson and the other progressive country artists.

Kenny Rogers was born in Houston in 1941. Joining with several members of the New Christy Minstrels, he formed Kenny Rogers and the First Edition. They produced their two biggest hits in the late 1960s, "Just Dropped In (To See What Condition My Condition Was In)" and "Ruby, Don't Take Your Love to Town." With their folk and country style (with just a touch of rock), the band continued to have moderate success into the early 1970s. In the mid-1970s, Kenny disbanded the First Edition and pursued a solo career. Emphasizing the country side, he had his first solo hits in 1977 with "Lucille" (number 5—no relation to Little Richard's song). Beginning with "She Believes in Me" (from *The Gambler*), Rogers initiated a long series of Top 20 hits that carried him into the 1980s as one of the most successful country pop artists in the music industry. Like Campbell, he stayed with the softer ballad style and in spite of his graying beard did not follow the Nelson–Jennings "outlaw" image of progressive country.

## The 1980s and 1990s

In the 1980s, crossover artists like Dolly Parton, Kenny Rogers, Eddie Rabbitt, Alabama, and the Oak Ridge Boys created a revived interest in country music within the general rock audience. As a result, sales of recordings by more mainstream country singers increased appreciably during the 1980s. George Strait, Reba McEntire, and Ricky Skaggs are credited with spawning a neotraditionalist movement (Haislop, Lathrop, and Sumrall 1995). The success of crossover artists proved that there was still an audience for traditional country sounds. Songs like Strait's "Ocean Front Property" (number 1 Country chart in 1987) and Skaggs' "Lovin' Only Me" (number 1 Country chart in 1989) revealed an undeniable rock influence in their use of electric guitars, drums, and in their general production quality. Multi-instrumentalist Skaggs even played an instrument called the mandocaster, a five-string instrumental cross between the mandolin and the Telecaster electric guitar. The pop-oriented production of songs like McEntire's "For My Broken Heart" (number 1 in 1991) stretches the boundary normally associated with C & W. However, the basic songs remained steadfastly identifiable as country music, incorporating the characteristic electric guitar twang, the presence of the pedal steel, and recognizable country-influenced vocal stylings.

In the mid-1980s, research by the Country Music Association suggested that fans wanted to hear authentic, traditional country music sung by young performers. Continuing the neotraditionalist movement begun by George Strait and Ricky Skaggs, new artists such as Randy Travis and Dwight Yoakam enjoyed great national popularity. Songs like "On the Other Hand" and "Forever and Ever, Amen" brought Randy Travis to the top of the Country chart in 1986 and 1987, respectively. However, a significant shift was taking place in the music industry, as exhibited in the phenomenal sales of these recordings. During a period when country albums were considered highly successful if they sold a half million copies, sales of Travis's recordings were reaching into the multimillions. Implicit in his sales record is the fact that country music was, by the late 1980s, appealing to an audience larger than that of the traditional country purists.

Undoubtedly, some members of the rock audience had been turned off by recent developments in the alternative music scene and the explicit violence inherent in a high percentage of rap recordings. As a result, they began searching for other musical styles with which they could be comfortable. It was largely this group of disaffected rock music fans who began to listen to country music and, liking what they heard, propelled the new generation of country artists toward an explosion of popularity in the 1990s.

The country crossover phenomenon and the resulting emergence of the C & W neotraditionalist movement set the stage for a musical explosion in the early 1990s. The year 1989 saw the release of a series of debut albums destined to bring country music to an extraordinary new height of popularity. Emerging artists included Clint Black, Garth Brooks, Alan Jackson, Travis Tritt, and Mary Chapin Carpenter. For the purpose of brevity, in the following discussion of country performers, all references to chart positions will refer to the Country chart, unless otherwise specified.

## Garth Brooks

Though Garth Brooks eventually proved to be the most prominent country music artist of the early 1990s, it was Clint Black who initially led the pack of young country singers. After a short period of time, however, it became apparent that Brooks provided the definitive example of country crossover for the decade. Combining elements of rock and country into a series of incredibly successful recordings and a high-energy stage show, Brooks became the top-selling solo artist in history (George-Warren and Romanowski, 2001), selling over 100 million albums. His songwriting ability and charismatic appeal enabled him to transcend the boundaries of the C & W market without alienating his strong base of traditional country music fans.

Born on February 7, 1962, in Yukon, Oklahoma, Troyal Garth Brooks was the son of former country singer Colleen Carroll and an ex-Marine. Originally setting his sights on becoming an athlete at Oklahoma State University, Brooks turned toward a career in country music after failing at the javelin toss. He was so discouraged by the music business on his first trip to Nashville in 1985 that he returned home after only 23 hours. Returning two years later with much more realistic expectations about the music business, Brooks approached and was turned down by almost every label in Nashville. Persistence paid off when he was seen by a Capitol Records executive performing "If Tomorrow Never Comes" at the Bluebird Cafe. The following year, he was signed to Capitol and began his recording career.

Garth Brooks's self-titled debut album (number 2 in 1989) and its four Top 10 singles ("Much Too Young (to Feel This Damn Old)," "If Tomorrow Never Comes," "Not Counting You," and "The Dance") were not enough to eclipse the rising star of Clint Black. It was with the arrival of his second release, *No Fences* (1990), however, that Brooks stepped into the spotlight as the leading proponent of the new generation of country artists. The first sound heard at the beginning of the recording is a distant clap of rolling thunder, as if to inform the listener that what follows is likely to be different from anything that had gone before. As the mysterious song "The Thunder Rolls" unfolds, rock influences are obvious in the drumbeat and rock guitar riffs. Notice the use of the twelve-bar blues form in the verses for "Two of a Kind, Workin' on a Full House." The youthful energy exuded in songs like "Friends in Low Places" or "Two of a Kind . . . " is beautifully balanced by the compassionate sensitivity of "Victim of the Game" and "Unanswered Prayers." Brooks seemed to be equally comfortable in either role, and his fans found this duality extremely appealing. *Ropin' the Wind* (1991) was the first album in history to debut at the number 1 position on both the Pop and Country album charts. On the Country album chart, *Ropin' the Wind* replaced Brooks's own previous album, *No Fences*, which was completing its 41-week reign at the top! This album also began an impressive series of number 1 albums on the Pop chart as well. *Ropin' the Wind* (1991), *The Chase* (1992), and *In Pieces* (1993) all debuted at number 1 on both the Country and Pop album charts. "Against the Grain," the opening song on *Ropin' the Wind*, leaves no doubt about Brooks's musical influences. The initial chord played by electric guitars, bass, and drums sets the rock-based country tone for the album. Garth Brooks's shameless incorporation of distorted rock guitar timbres and a driving backbeat places his musical style well within the boundaries of rock and roll. Listen to "Kickin' and Screamin'" and "The Night Will Only Know" from *In Pieces*, or "The Old Stuff" and "The Fever" from *Fresh Horses* (1995). Such songs are more accurately described as country-influenced rock than rock-influenced country. The verses of "Kickin' and Screamin'" are based on an altered version of the twelve-bar blues form that provided the foundation for so many R & B and mainstream rock tunes.

Brooks's Christmas album, *Beyond the Season* (1992), reached number 2 on both charts and a greatest hits compilation, *The Hits* (1994), was the first of his recent chart-toppers not to debut at number 1. *Fresh Horses* (1995) contained two number 1 singles, "She's Every Woman" and "The Beaches of Cheyenne," in addition to "It's Midnight Cinderella" (number 5), "The Change" (number 19), and "The Fever" (number 23), a cover version of a song by Aerosmith. The sales of this album remained impressive, reaching number 2 on the Pop album chart and selling 4 million copies, but it sold millions less than Brooks's previous releases and did not reach number 1. The resulting "disappointment" caused Brooks to turn down the Favorite Artist of the Year award at the American Music Awards in 1996, saying "he didn't feel he deserved it" (George-Warren and Romanowski, 2001). His next album, *Sevens* (1997), once again reached number 1 on both the Country and Pop charts with help from a limited-edition release (777,777 copies that sold out in a week) and a free concert for a quarter of a million fans in New York City that was simultaneously broadcast live on HBO. Confident that his career was back on track, Brooks made the bold decision to record an album as "Chris Gaines," a fictional Australian rock star. The album was promoted as a "greatest hits collection" and included a wide variety of musical styles, from new wave to R & B. Shunned by his country fans and ridiculed by critics, the album still managed to reach number 2 on the Pop chart and contained his only Hot 100 Top 40 hit: "Lost in You" (number 5 in 1999).

Garth Brooks provides an interesting exception to the image-conscious aesthetic that often drives the popular music industry. His slightly pudgy frame and receding hairline are reminiscent of the characteristics that predestined Bill Haley to be eclipsed by Elvis Presley as rock and roll emerged in the early 1950s. However,

Brooks' consistently creative musical output, energetic stage show, and endearing personality overcame such cosmetic issues. Brooks's high-tech, high-energy stage show, revealing obvious influence of theatrical rock bands like Springsteen, Queen, and Kiss, attracted both country and rock fans to his live performances, consistently selling out 60,000-seat auditoriums.

### Shania Twain

The career of Shania Twain provides the quintessential rags-to-riches story with a sentimental family-oriented twist. Growing up as part of a working class family in northern Ontario, Eileen Twain (Shania's birth name) was poor by American standards. Her mother and stepfather were very supportive of her musical development and, despite their economic condition, always managed to send her to Toronto for voice lessons. Her appearance on a nationally broadcast variety show, *The Tommy Hunter Show*, caught the attention of Mary Bailey, a well-known Canadian country singer who had the connections that eventually landed Shania in Nashville (Dickerson 1998). In 1987, as Twain's career was just taking off, tragedy struck when her parents were both killed in an auto accident. Because Twain's older sister was married with children of her own, Shania took responsibility for raising her three teenage siblings, putting a hold on her musical career until her brothers were old enough to take care of themselves. In 1991, with Bailey's assistance, Twain found herself in Nashville recording a three-song demo that earned her a contract with Mercury Records, the same label that had signed Kathy Mattea a few years earlier. Shortly after arriving in Nashville, the singer changed her name to "Shania" in honor of the Ojibwa heritage of her stepfather. In Ojibwa, the name means "I'm on my way."

Her self-titled debut album (1993) didn't perform well either on the radio or in record sales. Neither of the two singles, "What Made You Say That" and "Dance With the One That Brought You," entered the Top 50. She followed the album with a tour that was largely disappointing in terms of audience reaction. However, it afforded an opportunity for her to be heard by John "Mutt" Lange, former producer of rock bands including Foreigner, AC/DC, and Def Leppard. The two agreed to collaborate on the next album, and Lange made it clear he wanted to record only songs that she had composed. Interestingly, most of the tracks on this album, except one written by the producer himself and an unaccompanied fragment by Twain, were songs that were rejected by Mercury when considering material for the first album. Apparently collaborating on more than just music, Lange and Twain were married before the album was complete. *The Woman in Me* (number 5 in 1995) evidenced a fresh approach to country music, including upbeat energy, powerful rock guitars, and top-notch production standards. The album eventually generated seven hit singles, including "Any Man of Mine" (number 31) and "(If You're Not in It for Love) I'm Outta Here" (number 74), both number 1 C & W hits. In 1997, Twain and Lange succeeded once again with *Come On Over* (number 2), containing an incredible nine hit singles this time, including "You're Still the One" (number 2), "From This Moment On" (number 4), "That Don't Impress Me Much" (number 7), and "Man! I Feel Like a Woman" (number 23). Surpassing sales of 19 million, the album became the best-selling album in country music history.

Shania's critical and commercial success in both pop music and country music is evidenced by the awards she has received. In 1998, she received Grammy Awards for Best Female Country Vocal Performance and Best Country Song for "You're Still the One," a song co-written by Twain and her husband/producer. The following year, at the Country Music Association Awards, she was named Entertainer of the Year. The outlook for her future success appears bright indeed.

### The Dixie Chicks

Taking their name from a classic country rock song by Little Feat ("Dixie Chicken," 1973), the Dixie Chicks released their debut album in 1990 (*Thank Heavens for Dale Evans*). At that time, the group from Lubbock, Texas consisted of sisters Martie and Emily Erwin, Laura Lynch, and Robyn Lynn Macy. Following the 1992 release of *Little Ol' Cowgirl,* Macy left the group to form the group Domestic Science Club, in search of a purer bluegrass sound. Meanwhile, in 1993, the remaining Chicks released a third album (*Shouldn't A Told You That*) and performed at President Clinton's inaugural. In 1995, Lynch left the group and was replaced by Natalie Maines (vocalist), forming the trio that would prove to be one of the most successful country rock acts of the 1990s with Martie on fiddle and mandolin and Emily on guitar, dobro, and banjo.

With the release of *Wide Open Spaces* (number 1 Country album, 1998), the Dixie Chicks attained superstardom. "There's Your Trouble" and "You Were Mine" both entered the Top 40 and, along with the title cut, all three went to number 1 on the Country singles chart. The album eventually sold over 12 million copies. The Dixie Chicks were nominated for a Best New Artist Grammy, which they did not win, but they succeeded in winning both the Best Country Album (*Wide Open Spaces*) and Best Country Performance by a Duo or Group with Vocal ("There's Your Trouble") awards. That same year they won three Country Music Awards: Album of the Year, Top Group, and Top New Group. The release of *Fly* (1999) and the Top 40 singles "Cowboy Take Me Away" and "Without You"—both of which topped the Country singles chart—confirmed that the group's superstar status. This level of success continued unabated with the release of *Home* (number 1 in 2002), containing two more Top 40 singles: "Long Time Gone" and "Landslide," a song composed and originally performed by Fleetwood Mac's Stevie Nicks.

The Chicks became embroiled in a political controversy over a statement Maines made in March of 2003 about being "ashamed" that President Bush was from their home state of Texas. A significant backlash occurred from the group's fan base, as some radio stations refused to play their music and some fans went so far as to destroy their personal copies of the group's CDs. Maines eventually apologized for the remark. The Dixie Chicks' next album, *Top of the World*, was released at the end of 2003 but did not soar to platinum status as had the previous two releases.

### Other Country Artists

The careers of other country stars rivaled that of Garth Brooks. Clint Black, Travis Tritt, Mary Chapin Carpenter, Emmylou Harris, Alan Jackson, Hank Williams Jr., and a plethora of others all played an important role in keeping country music in the spotlight. The progressive country music of the Kentucky Headhunters, k. d.

lang, and Lyle Lovett encouraged a generation of rock enthusiasts to broaden its musical horizons to include C & W. The crossover success of Billy Ray Cyrus's "Achy Breaky Heart" (number 1 Country and number 4 Pop in 1992) succeeded in confirming the position of country music within the mainstream.

As country artists rose to their highest level of popularity since the emergence of rock and roll, country music dance halls flourished. Providing music for such social gathering places presented a certain difficulty with the eclectic mix of the new country audience. One attempt to meet this challenge, Brooks and Dunn's "Boot Scootin' Boogie" (number 1 in 1992), provided a curious blend of musical styles. The club mix version of the song takes the fundamental country sound and dance hall lyrics, adding an unmistakable rock backbeat and synthesizer bass line, not unlike those found in recordings by Madonna or other Pop Dance artists. Even the musical form exhibits close ties to rock and roll. Each verse is sung over a twelve-bar blues in which the final phrase is extended by two measures.

As the 1990s progressed, the fusion of country-folk and rock achieved an overwhelming level of popularity as evidenced by its continued commercial success. However, by the end of the decade, its popularity began to wane. Though artists like Garth Brooks and Shania Twain continued to sell millions of albums and their singles sometimes appeared on the Pop charts, the number of country rock crossovers was noticeably less than in the mid-1990s.

## THE "JAM BAND" PHENOMENON

Following in the footsteps of the Grateful Dead (and their post-Garcia incarnations as The Other Ones and later The Dead) and amassing a similarly devoted fan base, a number of "jam bands" began to hit the scene during the 1980s and 1990s. These groups integrated the sounds of country, folk, bluegrass, rock, jazz and even punk into an eclectic and highly energized musical performance. Like the Dead before them, studio recordings always took a backseat to their live performances and improvisation formed a significant part of their concert performances. Some of the most popular groups that fall into this category include Phish, the String Cheese Incident, and Widespread Panic. Many jam band fans, a nomadic bunch reminiscent of Deadheads, migrated with the bands from city to city on their concert tours. Rather than being frowned upon, as is the case in most concert venues where video cameras and tape recorders are confiscated, bootleg tapes of concert performances were openly traded by fans with the band's permission.

### Phish

The most successful of the jam bands of this period was Phish. Formed at the University of Vermont in 1983 by guitarists Trey Anastasio and Jeff Holdsworth and drummer Jon Fishman, the initial purpose of the group, as it has remained to the present, was simply to play music (i.e., to "jam"). The term *jam* suggests a freedom in the style of performance, as opposed to the highly rehearsed sound of most commercial recordings, allowing for extended sections of improvisation, focusing on expressive communication from a performer to the other players and audience. The energetic sound of such music is one of the primary reasons that both musicians and audiences find jam bands so enjoyable to listen to. In these sometimes lengthy sections of instrumental improvisation, band members drew concurrently from numerous musical traditions, including country, rock, and jazz.

In 1988, Phish recorded their debut, *Junta*, and sold cassette copies at their performances. Not your typical commercial recording, the average track length on this album was almost nine minutes long, with "Union Federal," the longest track, weighing in at 25 minutes! By the time of their second album, *Lawn Boy* (1990), the group had built a significant following and was one of the first bands to utilize the Internet as a means of information dissemination, maintaining contact with their fans, and selling merchandise (including recordings). After signing with Elektra, *A Picture of Nectar* (1992) was their first major label release, followed shortly by reissues of their first two recordings. Beginning in 1993, the band's consistently acclaimed live performances began to translate into placement on the album chart: *Rift* (number 51 in 1993); *Hoist* (number 34 in 1994); *A Live One* (number 18 in 1995); *Billy Breathes* (number 7 in 1996); *Slip, Stitch & Pass* (number 17 in 1997); *The Story of the Ghost* (number 8 in 1998); and *Farmhouse* (number 12 in 2000). A six-disc set, humorously titled *Hampton Comes Alive* (1999)—remember Peter Frampton?—even reached number 120 on the Hot 200 album chart. Phish has never had a Top 40 hit. This is perhaps not surprising given the influence of the Dead who, as you recall, had only one Top 40 hit in their astonishing 30-year career. Phish continued to release numerous recordings into the new millennium. Before a crowd of nearly 70,000 in Coventry, Vermont on August 14 and 15, 2004, following several days of torrential rains, the band played their farewell concert.

## Other Jam Bands

Following the success of Phish, other jam bands began to appear, including Widespread Panic, Disco Biscuits, ekoostic hookah, and Rebecca's Statue. An outgrowth of the jam-band phenomenon, "jam-grass" incorporated a similar emphasis on improvisation, but exhibited a musical sound influenced primarily by mountain music and bluegrass (e.g., *Cornmeal's In the Kitchen*, 2001). Whether this renewed interest in folk-influenced music is simply a fad or a longer-lasting trend remains to be seen. However, at present, interest in such performance-oriented groups appears to be growing stronger.

## The Dave Matthews Band

Though not typically included under the "jam band" rubric, the music of The Dave Matthews Band certainly matches the eclectic mix of musical styles evident in these performance-oriented groups and the group built a fan base of equal magnitude, allowing fans the opportunity to record and freely circulate their performances. Formed in 1991 in Charlottesville, Virginia, the permanent lineup for the group included Matthews (guitar and vocals), LeRoi Moore (woodwinds), Boyd Tinsley (violin), Stefan Lessard (bass), and Carter Beauford (drums). The band's rise to prominence resulted from a combination of superbly crafted studio recordings (*Remember Two Things*, 1993 and *Under the Table and Dreaming*, number 11 in 1994) and their appearance on the 1993 and 1994 H.O.R.D.E. tours and as opening act for

Phish and Blues Traveler. The release of *Crash* (number 2 in 1996) left no doubt that the band had arrived. Matthews and his band exemplified an extremely high caliber of musicianship, as evidenced by their impeccable series of studio recordings and the technical skill inherent in their live performances. Whereas Phish might entertain their audience with an on-stage performance on a vacuum cleaner, Matthews's musical style expanded outward to include not only the influences cited above but to supplement these Western sounds with elements of world music, influenced in this vein perhaps by the adventurous works of artists like Paul Simon, Peter Gabriel, and Sting.

Though almost any recording would suffice to illustrate this integration of musical styles, a particularly good example is evident in the opening tracks of *Before These Crowded Streets* (1998). The brief opening track, "Pantala Naga Pampa" (with its Indian title meaning "There's a python in my pants"), reveals Latin and Caribbean musical influence and segues directly into "Rapunzel" with its staccato and syncopated rhythms verses. The Middle Eastern influence of "The Last Stop" and its unveiled sociopolitical message provide stark contrast to the musical style and delivery of the opening tracks. With "Don't Drink the Water," we return to a more traditional Matthews Band sound.

In the late 1990s, the band returned to their live performance aesthetic, releasing *Live at the Red Rocks 8.15.95* (number 3 in 1997), *Live at Luther College* (with Tim Reynolds; number 2 in 1999), and *Listener Supported* (number 15 in 1999). As a new decade approached, their studio albums proved even more popular: *Before These Crowded Streets* (debuted at number 1 in 1998) and *Everyday* (number 1 in 2001). The band's prolific output continued unabated with *Busted Stuff* (number 1 in 2002), Matthews's first solo album *Some Devil* (number 2 in 2003), and another series of live recordings (*Live at Folsom Field*, 2002; *Central Park Concert*, 2003; and *Live at The Gorge*, 2004).

## SOFT ROCK OF THE 1970S

Just as was true in the 1950s and 1960s, soft rock was immensely popular in the 1970s. And just as all the other trends of the 1970s fragmented into numerous subcategories, so too did soft rock. Generally speaking, as hard rock grew harder (especially with heavy metal and punk rock), soft rock grew softer. Some of the artists discussed in this section sit squarely on the imaginary dividing line between soft rock and pure pop, moving back and forth across the line, depending on which album and which song one is considering. Recall that we consider a song to be soft rock if one or more of rock's basic musical elements is present—for example, a rock-like bass line or a rock-derived rhythmic pattern, no matter how gentle. If there is an absence of such elements, the song is considered pure pop music.

### The Carpenters

The soft rockers of the 1970s were a varied lot, as some came from a rock orientation, others from a folk or singer–songwriter background, a few from C & W, and even some from the soul side. The hottest soft rock act of the early 1970s was the

Carpenters. Richard and Karen Carpenter (born in 1946 and 1950, respectively, in New Haven, Connecticut) were talented musicians. Richard sang and played keyboards; Karen sang and played drums. Their second album, *Close to You* (1970), rose to number 2 and produced their first number 1 hit, "(They Long to Be) Close to You," by Hal David and Burt Bacharach, and a number 2 hit, "We've Only Just Begun." Both songs lie squarely on the soft rock–pop borderline. For example, the bridge of "We've Only Just Begun" has a stronger beat, complete with backbeat brass accents on the second beat and a steady eighth-note tambourine—enough to establish a soft rock sound. But the other sections of the song withdraw these elements and thus lie more in the pop realm. "Close to You" was primarily a pop song, although there was a very light triple division of the beat (listen for the cymbals) in its bridge section. There are a few other very light touches of rock influence: syncopations, a steady quadruple beat with all four beats about evenly stressed, and a few rock-style piano voicings. The Carpenters' lush jazz-like vocal harmonies (e.g., listen to "Love to Surrender") are the result of multitracking, a technique with which Richard had been experimenting for several years.

Their next album, *The Carpenters* (1971), also reached number 2 and yielded three Top 5 songs. Again in "Superstar" the formula included a bridge section with a more pronounced beat; in the other sections, the bass played a dotted quarter and eighth-note pattern ♩. ♪ ♩ under a light but steady duple division of the beat. Many of the Carpenters' songs conform to this pattern: a pop sound with subtle rock elements moving to a harder style (relatively speaking, of course) in the bridge sections. Touches of jazz may be heard in the vocal harmonies (and, for example, in the brief sax solo on "Rainy Days and Mondays"). Karen Carpenter's excellent voice was capable of a variety of subtle changes; she must be considered one of the finest rock or pop singers of the 1970s.

The Carpenters (*Source:* Michael Ochs Archives, Ltd.)

The Carpenters' popularity was consistent through 1975. Beginning in 1976, album sales began to slump. In 1983, Karen died of cardiac arrest resulting from her long struggle with anorexia nervosa. She was thirty-two years old.

## Barry Manilow

In the late 1970s, the biggest name in soft rock was Barry Manilow. Manilow (born in Brooklyn in 1946) began playing the piano as a youngster but preferred jazz to rock and roll. After taking courses at City College of New York, the New York College of Music, and even Juilliard, he found work in the music business composing and performing commercial jingles. In the early 1970s, he worked as producer–arranger for Bette Midler. Finally, in 1974, he released a ballad called "Mandy"; the song climbed to number 1 by early 1975. His next album, *Tryin' to Get the Feeling* (1975), rose to number 5, with the title song making the Top 10 and "I Write the Songs" reaching number 1. These two songs provide good insight into Manilow's style. A fine singer in the soft rock–pop style, Manilow often began songs very quietly, with little accompaniment. Gradually the texture thickened as full orchestra and backup voices were added. Near the end, full production resources were used to build a big finish. Notice especially the drum part; from the outset, there is typically a subtle backbeat on the second and fourth beats. But as the song nears its big finish, the backbeat becomes quite exaggerated, usually with considerable echo.

Manilow did not compose "I Write the Songs." In fact, the song (composed by Bruce Johnston) had been recorded earlier by the Captain and Tennille and by David Cassidy. The lyrics, of course, refer to neither the singer nor even the song's composer, but to music as a concept. Indeed, "I Write the Songs" is an eloquent

acknowledgment of music's role in human society, as it makes the world sing, cry, dance, take a chance, and feel love. Another effective ode to music's interactions with human behavior is "Beautiful Music" (music by Manilow, lyrics by Marty Panzer). Midway through the song, Manilow moves as close to the gentler side of mainstream rock as he ever does (listen also to "A Nice Boy Like Me" to hear Manilow at his "rockiest"). For the balance of the 1970s, Manilow was the premier figure in soft rock. By 1990, he had enjoyed over two dozen Top 40 hits, including eleven in the Top 10.

Popular American singer Barry Manilow, previously both an advertising jingle composer and accompanist of comedienne Bette Midler, during a concert at Wembley Arena, London. (Getty Images, Inc.)

**Neil Diamond**

Neil Diamond (born in Coney Island, New York, in 1941) is a singer–songwriter who has been a successful member of the music industry for forty years. Starting as a staff writer for several publishing houses, he had seen several of his compositions hit the charts ("Sunday and Me" by Jay and the Americans; "I'm a Believer" and "A Little Bit Me, a Little Bit You" by the Monkees; "The Boat That I Row" by Lulu; and "Kentucky Woman" by Deep Purple).

Beginning with "Cherry, Cherry" (1966), Diamond, the performer, had a series of Top 20 hits through the late 1960s. It was "Sweet Caroline" (number 4 in 1969) that initiated his greatest period of popularity (at least until his "comeback" in the early 1980s). He achieved six Top 10 hits between 1969 and 1974, including the number 1 hits "Cracklin' Rosie" and "Song Sung Blue." Diamond's strong voice, usually accompanied by full orchestra and vocal backup with very professional production, created a popular soft rock style. On occasion, a rock-derived beat and a rock bass line provided the necessary hint of rock to justify the label "soft rock" (e.g., on "Sweet Caroline" and "Longfellow Serenade").

Even in the late 1970s, when his solo Top 10 hits stopped coming, Diamond was never far from the top of the charts. A resurgence of Diamond's popularity resulted from his film debut in *The Jazz Singer*. The sound track album reached number 3 and produced three Top 10 hits. "America" (from *The Jazz Singer*) qualifies as soft rock; the album's other songs are in a pop style (although the bridge section of "Love on the Rocks" may cross the line back into soft rock).

**Olivia Newton-John**

Moving from a harder style to a softer style is fairly common (e.g., Bobby Darin, Buddy Holly, Fats Domino, and even Elvis Presley). But moving the other way is both rare and difficult. Nevertheless, the somewhat odd career of Olivia Newton-John includes such a shift. Born in Cambridge, England, in 1947, Olivia launched her career with television and local pub appearances. Her version of Dylan's "If Not for You" hit the U.S. charts in 1971 and moved as far as number 25. But in 1973 she cut "Let Me Be There"; in early 1974 it peaked at number 6 and earned Olivia a Grammy for best female country vocal. That is why we used the word *odd* in reference to her career. Somehow this pretty girl born in England and raised in Australia became identified as a country music singer! She followed with two Top 5 hits in 1974, including her first number 1 song, "I Honestly Love You." Her success with soft "country-style" ballads led to her being named 1974's Female Vocalist of the Year by the Country Music Association (her competition included "real" country singers Loretta Lynn, Tammy Wynette, Dolly Parton, and Tanya Tucker). Many country fans and artists were enraged; some of the artists pulled out of the CMA and formed the Association of Country Entertainers.

In any event, Olivia followed in 1975 with two more Top 5 songs, including the number 1 "Have You Ever Been Mellow." The year 1978 brought the beginning of a major change in her career. Appearing in the 1950s nostalgia film *Grease*, Olivia portrayed Sandy, a demure, ponytailed innocent who, at the end of the plot, is transformed into a leather-jacketed, sexy "chick" in tight pants. The sound track album

Olivia Newton-John (*Source:* Michael Ochs Archives, Ltd.)

moved to number 1 and included three hit singles. The number 1 "You're the One That I Want" was a genuine rock song, lying between soft rock and the gentler side of the mainstream.

It seemed as though Sandy's transformation in *Grease* was replicated in Olivia's career. The new Newton-John released *Totally Hot*, with its hit single, "A Little More Love" (number 3 in late 1978). Appearing in the 1980 film *Xanadu*, she had two hit singles from its sound track album. The image change became complete with the controversial "Physical" in 1981. The song, from the gentler side of mainstream rock, utilized the old double entendre trick: Was it about the physical fitness craze or just plain sex? Whichever it was (if not both), the song became Olivia's fifth number 1 hit. Musically, most of Olivia's post-*Grease* songs are rock; the softer elements include the elaborate production and Olivia's soft pop voice (and her image). Certainly she lies closer to the mainstream than the Carpenters, Manilow, and Diamond.

## SOFT ROCK CONTINUES TO EVOLVE

### Lionel Richie

One of the most successful acts on the softer side of rock was Lionel Richie. Lead singer of the Commodores throughout the 1970s, Richie began moving away from the Commodores in 1981. He wrote and recorded the theme from the movie *Endless Love* and saw it move to number 1. Of over fifty Motown hits (on various labels), "Endless Love," a duet sung by Richie and Diana Ross, remained at the top longer than any (nine weeks). It was the first of four number 1 songs for Richie between 1981 and 1984.

Richie's work with Kenny Rogers and then Diana Ross tended to pull him further away from his "team of brothers," the Commodores. By 1983, they had recorded their first album without Richie (*Commodore 13*), and the split was complete. Meanwhile, Richie had released his first solo album, *Lionel Richie* (number 3 in 1982), which yielded three top 5 singles, including the number 1 hit "Truly."

Richie's first number 1 album, *Can't Slow Down* (late 1983), produced an amazing five Top 10 singles, including two number 1 songs, "All Night Long (All Night)" and "Hello." Although Richie's biggest successes have been in the soft rock ballad style, he sometimes moves to a moderate or fast beat—always with a funky dance beat (sometimes close to disco). The Jamaican influence in "All Night Long" was an interesting stylistic touch (note, for example, Richie's affected Jamaican enunciation and the nonsense syllable section—supposedly an old Jamaican chant).

Richie continued into the mid- and late-1980s as a major figure in the music industry, writing songs, performing, recording, and producing for himself and others. In 1985, he was coauthor (with Michael Jackson) of "We Are the World," a song (and video) produced by Quincy Jones to focus attention on, and raise money for, the underfed in Africa. The recording included a star-studded list of performers, including Harry Belafonte, Ray Charles, Bob Dylan, Waylon Jennings, Billy Joel, Willie Nelson, Steve Perry, Smokey Robinson, Kenny Rogers, Diana Ross, Paul Simon, Bruce Springsteen, Tina Turner, Stevie Wonder, and many others (including, of course, Jackson and Richie).

Richie's 1986 album, *Dancing on the Ceiling*, became his second consecutive number 1 album. Although it proved to be his last of the decade, Motown pulled a string of successful singles from the album, including "Say You, Say Me" (number 1), "Dancing on the Ceiling," "Love Will Conquer All," "Ballerina Girl," and "Se La."

## Pop Divas of the 1980s and 1990s

Several female singers found tremendous success in the field of 1980s soft rock. After Whitney Houston's first hit single in 1985 ("You Give Good Love"), she reeled off ten Top 10 hits before the end of the decade, including a remarkable seven consecutive number 1 hits, breaking the old record of six in a row established by the Beatles and the Bee Gees. Her two albums, *Whitney Houston* (1985) and *Whitney* (1987), held the number 1 position for fourteen and eleven weeks, respectively.

Paula Abdul's success came near the end of the decade with three consecutive number 1 hits in 1988 and 1989 ("Straight Up," "Forever Your Girl," and "Cold Hearted"). After one number 3 song ("It's Just the Way that You Love Me"), she began the 1990s with three more consecutive chart-toppers. Her first album, *Forever Your Girl*, hit number 1 in 1989 and held that spot for ten weeks.

A new crop of solo female artists emerged in the 1990s representing a wide array of musical styles. According to Dickerson (1998, 17), "1996 was a landmark year. It was the year female solo artists out-charted their male counterparts on the Top 20 charts for the first time in history." Of the artists scoring Top 20 hits that year, 61 percent were female, and the following year the percentage fell only slightly to 60 percent.

On the "pop" end of the spectrum were Christina Aguilera, Jessica Simpson, and Britney Spears (see Chapter 16). These artists often spoke openly of their Christian faith and espoused the virtue of virginity, a dramatic departure from the Madonna-esque "bad girl" image of the previous decade. Interestingly, as they espoused such values, these same performers often dressed in extremely revealing and sexually explicit clothing, presenting quite a contradiction between the verbal and visual messages communicated to their listening audience. However contradictory, the combination of sweet girl and sex kitten proved very effective commercially.

## Mariah Carey

A vocalist of incredible technical ability, Mariah Carey experienced a rise to stardom and commercial success rivaled by only a handful of her predecessors. Exhibiting a multioctave vocal range, her recordings reveal both a sultry ballad singer and virtuoso vocal technician. In addition to her impressive vocal technique, Mariah was actively involved in writing and producing her recordings.

An association with Brenda K. Starr proved to be the catalyst for Carey's meteoric rise to fame when Starr met Columbia Records executive Tommy Mottola at a social gathering and presented him a copy of Carey's demo tape. After playing the tape in his car as he left, Mottola returned to the party immediately to meet Carey. Signing Mariah to Columbia subsidiary CBS Records, Mottola took a personal interest in the development of her career. The support of one of the top executives at Columbia and Carey's phenomenal musical talent resulted in a level of success reserved for only a small number of artists since the beginning of rock and roll.

Carey's vocal style reveals heavy R & B and gospel influences. Listen, for example, to "Vision of Love" from her debut album. Carey's vocal delivery in "Vision of Love" is heavily blues inflected, especially in its use of blue notes throughout (see p. 220). Her melismatic style of singing is similar to that of Aretha Franklin's gospel recordings, discussed at the end of Chapter 9, "Soul and Motown." The difference between Mariah and her predecessors is in her incredible vocal range and willingness to use it completely, as exhibited in the final chorus of the song. As Carey sings a variation of the melody on one track of the recording, she harmonizes with herself on a second track, incorporating her extreme high pitch range (up to three octaves above middle C). We have talked in earlier chapters about the male falsetto voice. Female vocalists do not exhibit a falsetto voice in the same manner. As a result, to produce extremely high pitches, the singer creates a whistle by pushing air between the vocal chords (Miller 1986). The resulting sound, Mariah Carey's uppermost register, is called a "whistle tone." The song concludes with an extended melisma (at one point with no instrumental accompaniment), incorporating obvious blues and gospel influences.

Carey's debut album reached number 1 in 1990 and contained four number 1 hit singles: "Vision of Love," "Love Takes Time," "Someday," and "I Don't Wanna Cry." Critical acclaim was quick to follow, as she was awarded two Grammy Awards in 1991 (Best New Artist and Best Female Vocalist). Her second album, *Emotions* (1991), also reached number 1, yielding a second series of hit singles: "Emotions" (number 1), "Can't Let Go" (number 2), and "Make It Happen" (number 5). With this album Carey made history, becoming the first artist whose initial five singles all went to number 1. In fact, eight of her first ten singles would eventually reach the top of the chart. Her *Unplugged* recording produced a number 1 cover of "I'll Be There," a number 1 hit for the Jackson Five in 1970. After marrying Mottola, almost twice her age, Carey continued her commercial success with *Music Box* (number 1 in 1993), resulting in three more Top 10 hits: "Dream Lover" (number 1), "Hero" (number 1), and "Without You" (number 3). Following a number 2 duet ("Endless Love") with Luther Vandross in 1994, she released *Daydream*, containing the number 1 hits "Fantasy" and "One Sweet Day." The latter, featuring 1990s vocal group Boyz II Men, held the number 1 position for 16 weeks and is listed by Whitburn (2000, 814) as the number 1 hit in *Billboard* Hot 100 history from 1955 to 1999. *Daydream* debuted at number 1 and made Carey the first female in the history of rock music to have three albums with sales of over 8 million copies each.

In 1997, the singer divorced Mottola and released *Butterfly* (number 1 in 1997), revealing evidence of hip-hop influence as clearly demonstrated in the song "Honey," a collaborative effort with rap artists Ma$e and the Lox. "My All," a second number 1 hit from the same album, followed in 1998. Her next release, *#1s*, was a greatest hits collection containing all thirteen of her chart-topping singles to date and four new cuts, including "When You Believe," a duet with Whitney Houston that appeared in the animated motion picture *The Prince of Egypt. Rainbow* (number 2 in 2000), containing the number 1 hit "Heartbreaker," provided an appropriate end to the decade in which Mariah dominated the charts and became its best-selling female artist. Her interest in infusing the upbeat musical style of her recordings with elements of hip-hop continued with vocal appearances by a variety of rap artists, including Jay-Z and Snoop Dogg.

In 2001, Carey signed an 80 million dollar multirecord deal with Virgin Records (the largest ever to date), announcing that her first release would be a soundtrack to a film (*Glitter*) in which she would play the starring role. At the time, there seemed to be little risk involved in such a plan but, as is often the case in the music industry, even the best-laid plans sometimes go astray. Mariah was not the only artist to flounder during this year of falling record sales. According to *Rolling Stone* magazine (February 14, 2002, 21), it was ". . . the kind of year the music business would just as soon forget . . . the most dramatic year of decline since the disco boom went bust in the late Seventies." As a result of the dismal commercial performance of *Glitter* (although it reached number 7 in 2001) and declining record sales, Carey and Virgin parted ways, with the record company paying off $28 million of the contracted amount. The release of *Charmbracelet* (number 3 in 2002) on Carey's own label (a subsidiary of Island/Def Jam), though far from a commercial failure, was not received with the multiplatinum success of her earlier recordings.

## Other Soft Rock Sounds

Soft rock continued into the 1980s with groups like Air Supply and the Alan Parsons Project. The former (from Australia) combined lush instrumental backgrounds, highly professional production work, and strong vocals. The Alan Parsons Project stayed basically in the area of soft rock, but often veered toward art rock.

A rather interesting phenomenon in the world of late 1980s soft rock was the popularity of some extremely young teen groups. The most successful of these was the quintet New Kids on the Block. The New Kids were between the ages of eleven and fifteen when the group was formed in 1984 by producer Maurice Starr. Several years earlier, Starr had gathered some thirteen- to fifteen-year-olds from Boston into a reasonably successful group called the New Edition. This group managed to place six hits in the Top 40 between 1984 and 1988. Based on that success, Starr had high hopes for the New Kids. He was not disappointed. Their 1989 album *Hangin' Tough* rose to number 1 and yielded five Top 10 hits, including two number 1s ("I'll Be Loving You" and "Hangin' Tough"). The New Kids became the hottest soft rock group of the late 1980s, especially with the younger rock fans. Their style alternated between soft ballads (four out of ten cuts on *Hangin' Tough*) and a techno-dance style much like Madonna's. Starr played or programmed all of the instruments on the album.

The New Kids followed with a re-release of an earlier album (self-titled), followed by a Christmas album (1989). As the decade turned, the New Kids released another number 1 album, *Step By Step* (1990), which yielded several more single hits (including the number 1 title song). In 1990, Maurice Starr introduced yet another Boston group between ages eleven and thirteen, Perfect Gentlemen. They proceeded to produce a Top 10 hit, "Ooh La La (I Can't Get Over You)." The New Kids, New Edition, and other "packaged" acts of the late 1980s were harbingers of the Boy Bands (and Girl Bands) of the 1990s, to which we will return in Chapter 16.

## New Age Music

Before we move past soft rock, we must note the advent of the softest style of music to hit the popular market since the mid-1950s—so-called New Age music. As yet, this style is only vaguely defined. The musical origins of New Age music seem to be within that branch of new wave music that tended toward the minimalist trend in classical music. Precedents can be found in some music by Brian Eno and Robert Fripp. There is certainly a relation to the synthe-pop or techno-rock groups of the 1970s (e.g., Passport and Kraftwerk) as well as classical electrominimalists, such as Philip Glass and Steve Reich.

A good example of electronic New Age music might be Tangerine Dream. This German group, headed by Edgar Froese and Chris Franks, emphasizes electronic keyboards of all sorts. The music is usually rather quiet and serene, bathing the listener in waves of shimmering electronic sounds and repetitive, overlapping patterns (a hallmark of the minimalists). For a sample, listen to *Tangram* (1980). Do not expect short, cute, three-minute ditties; Tangerine Dream, in the tradition of art rockers, usually opts for side-long works that gradually unfold in a stream-of-consciousness idiom.

Another group that has been dubbed "New Age" is the Mannheim Steamroller. Similar in general concept to Tangerine Dream, Steamroller produced a series of albums named *Fresh Aire I, II, III*, and so on. Steamroller existed well before the term *New Age* became chic; when the term came into vogue, it seemed to fit groups such as Tangerine Dream and Mannheim Steamroller, which previously had been wandering around without a stylistic pigeonhole.

Not all New Age music is heavily electronic. Its gentle, soothing waves also can be accomplished with acoustic instruments or combinations of electronic and acoustic instruments. Leading this field in the late 1980s was the Windham Hill Record Company, a California label that grossed over $25 million in 1985 and grew steadily thereafter. By 1986, Windham Hill accounted for 15 to 20 percent of the billings for its distributor, A&M Records. Quiet, almost Muzak-like, Windham Hill records (and others similar in concept) surround the listener with a soft, soothing sound environment. Several of the more well-known names in this style are pianist George Winston and guitarist Will Ackerman (cofounder of Windham Hill). Although there is some derivation from rock, New Age is essentially antirock in most ways. Where rock has historically been stimulative music, most New Age music is sedative in nature. It seems to offer the antidote for the loud, screaming tension, the driving beat, and the shock mentality of much rock and roll (especially heavy metal, punk rock, and harder mainstream rock). But it may be more than a reaction against rock; it may also be a reaction against the stressful tensions and fast-paced tempo of life in the 1980s.

Also derived from the new-wave trend, but leading in a different direction, were the Police, a British trio headed by lead singer Sting (born Gordon Sumner in 1951). Originally formed in 1977, it was not until 1980 that major success came with their third album, *Zenyatta Mondatta* (number 5). The Police's peak came in 1983 with *Synchronicity*, their first number 1 album. The album included mainstream rock in the form of the title song (parts 1 and 2), some reggae references ("Walking in Your Footsteps"), some punk rock ("Mother"), some soft rock (the number 1 song "Every Breath You Take"), and even a touch of jazz rock ("Tea in the Sahara"). *Synchronicity* had something for everyone. As was often the case with the Police, the lyrics were quite introspective and intellectually oriented; hints of New Age philosophy appeared in various songs on the album. In the mid-1980s, Sting sought to establish himself as an actor, quite apart from the Police. Having appeared in *Quadrophenia* in 1979, and *Brimstone and Treacle* in 1982, he starred in *The Bride* in 1984. His musical career as a solo artist also is quite impressive, with six Top 10 albums (*The Dream of the Blue Turtles* in 1985 and . . . *Nothing Like the Sun* in 1987). He also produced six Top 20 singles before the end of the decade. Sting's successes continued into the 1990s with albums such as *Ten Summoner's Tales* (number 2 in 1993), *Mercury Falling* (number 5 in the 1996), *Brand New Day* (number 9 in 2000), and *Sacred Love* (number 3 in 2003).

Table 14–1 summarizes several more important soft rock acts of the 1970s.

## MUSICAL CLOSE-UP:
### COUNTRY OR ROCK?

Country music re-emerged as one of the most commercially successful musical styles during the late 1980s and early 1990s. Admittedly, it had never disappeared completely from the popular music scene. The 1950s rockabilly style of Buddy Holly and the southern rock bands of the 1970s are just two examples of rock music that exuded obvious country influence. However, the C & W that played such an important role in the careers of many early rock stars (e.g., Bill Haley, Elvis Presley, and Jerry Lee Lewis) bears only a faint resemblance to the country music that gained popularity toward the end of the twentieth century.

Referring back to the discussion of C & W in Chapter 2, country music was described as having a well-defined audience: poor whites, primarily in the rural South and Midwest. Country artists were promoted and their recordings were distributed almost exclusively by low-budget, independent record companies. The musical style tended to be fairly consistent. In almost all cases, the simple, singable melodies and lyrics were of prime importance. Most songs were based on diatonic harmonies (frequently no more than three or four chords) and basic, straightforward rhythms. Singers often incorporated an affected nasality in their vocal production,

## Table 14–1

| Name | Typical Hits | Comments |
|---|---|---|
| John Denver | "Take Me Home Country Roads" (no. 2, 1971); "Rocky Mountain High" (no. 9, 1973); "Sunshine on My Shoulder" (no. 1, 1974) | Folk background (played and sang with Chad Mitchell Trio for four years). Peak popularity from 1971 through 1976. Folk roots flavored by light touches of C & W and soft rock. |
| Osmonds (also Donny Osmond, and Donny and Marie) | "One Bad Apple" (no. 1, 1971); "Go Away Little Girl" (Donny Osmond, no. 1, 1971) | Began with Alan, Wayne, Merrill, and Jay Osmond. Soon added Donny, Marie, and Jimmy. Usually a quintet, they placed ten songs in Top 40 from 1971 to 1976. As a soloist, Donny had twelve Top 40 hits in the same period. Later in the 1970s, Donny and Marie became a duet, hosting a successful national television show. By the end of 1978, the total Osmond family had created thirty-two Top 40 hits. |
| Roberta Flack | "The First Time Ever I Saw Your Face" (no. 1, 1972); "Killing Me Softly with His Song" (no. 1, 1973); "Feel Like Makin' Love" (no. 1, 1974) | Soul background; early experience in church music. University-trained musician; worked as a school teacher and as a club pianist. Style has elements of soul with influences of jazz and soft rock. Many successful duet releases with Donny Hathaway. |
| America | "A Horse with No Name" (no. 1, 1972); "Ventura Highway" (no. 8, 1972); "Tin Man" (no. 4, 1974) | Trio (Gerry Beckley, Daniel Peek, Dewey Bunnell) known for good vocal harmonies and enigmatic lyrics. George Martin produced many of their gentle rock hits. |
| Seals & Crofts | "Summer Breeze" (no. 6, 1972); "Diamond Girl" (no. 6, 1973); "Get Closer" (no. 6, 1976) | Duo (Jim Seals and Dash Crofts) from Texas. Members of the Champs ("Tequila") in the late 1950s. Soft rock style with lyrics sometimes reflecting their Baha'i faith (e.g., "Hummingbird" and "East of Ginger Trees"). Occasional touches of country influence. |

sometimes introducing special techniques such as yodeling, falsetto, or allowing the voice to crack with emotion. C & W performers of the 1940s and 1950s played acoustic instruments (acoustic guitars, string bass, etc.) almost exclusively. The pedal steel (slide guitar) and fiddle rounded out the traditional C & W ensemble. Recall that most of the early C & W groups did not use a drummer. As a result, the bass player not only supplied the music's harmonic foundation, but was also responsible for providing the rhythmic drive. Often the bassist would slap the neck of the instrument percussively while playing the notes of a simple bass line. These bass lines normally consisted of the first and fifth notes of the musical scale for each chord of the harmony.

Examples of typical C & W from this early period will serve to confirm these relatively consistent musical characteristics. Eddy Arnold's "Bouquet of Roses" (number 1 Country in 1948) exemplifies the simple melody, three-chord harmony, and uncomplicated rhythm associated with C & W. The presence of the pedal steel and fiddle place this song squarely in the category of country music. The absence of drums is made less noticeable by the acoustic guitar player's emphasis on beats two and four, that is, the backbeat . . . chunk-a CHUNK chunk-a CHUNK. The bass line for this song is a good example of the typical C & W bass line previously illustrated. Arnold's eventual crossover into the Pop market is evident even in the vocal style of his early recordings, incorporating a lead vocal style more closely related to the pop crooners than the nasal style of his fellow C & W artists and a highly trained group of backup singers. The song "Anytime" (also number 1 Country in 1948) reveals another side of Arnold's vocal character. Listen to the manner in which he quasi-yodels from his normal singing voice into a high falsetto pitch and then down into the extreme low range of his voice in the chorus of this song on the word *anytime*.

Kitty Wells' Top 10 single "There's Poison in Your Heart" (number 9 Country in 1955) and Hank Williams's "Your Cheatin' Heart" (number 1 Country in 1953) provide additional support for these same basic C & W musical characteristics. The acoustic instrumentation is identical to Arnold's "Bouquet of Roses." Vocal techniques are typical of those heard in recordings by other C & W artists. Wells's emphasis on consonants (e.g., *r* in the word *heart*), rather than sustaining pitches on vowel sounds, gives her vocal style a less-refined, untrained character. Williams's emotive vocal "cracks" have similar effect, giving the music a comfortable feeling, lacking any semblance of pretense. The manner in which the fiddle and piano take turns carrying on a back-and-forth musical dialogue with the vocalist is a technique often incorporated in C & W.

The love-oriented lyrics for these songs are typical of C & W. "Bouquet of Roses" speaks of a young romantic bringing a gift to his beloved, while both "There's Poison in Your Heart" and "Your Cheatin' Heart" provide examples of the heartache experienced by a jilted lover. The series of harmonic diagrams that follow is provided to confirm the simplicity of the harmonies used in each of these songs. Notice the predominance of three primary chords (I, IV, and V) and the infrequent use of chromatic harmonies (marked with an asterisk).

"Bouquet of Roses"—original key: E♭ major

| I |-----| I | IV | I |-----| V |-----|

| I |-----| I | IV | I |-----| V | I |

"There's Poison in Your Heart"—original key: G major

```
|  I  |  V  |  I  |-----|  V  |-----|  I  |-----|

|  I  |  V  |  I  |-----|  V  |-----|  I  |-----|

|  IV |-----|  I  |-----|  II*7 |-----|  V  |  V7  |
```

"Your Cheatin' Heart"—original key: C major

```
|  I  |-----|  IV |-----|  V  |-----|  I  |-----|

|  I  |-----|  IV |-----|  V  |-----|  I  |-----|

|  IV |-----|  I  |-----|  II*7 |-----|  V  |-----|

|  IV |-----|  I  |-----|  II*7 |-----|  V  |-----|
```

Country music of the 1990s retained several of the musical characteristics associ-ated with C & W, but there were a number of significant changes. With the series of albums released by new country artists at the end of the 1980s, a variety of rock ele-ments became integral to the recordings of this new breed of country star. The fol-lowing discussion will focus primarily on the music of Clint Black and Travis Tritt, but Garth Brooks, Shania Twain, Alan Jackson, Mary Chapin Carpenter, or any number of other artists could have served just as well.

Black's debut album *Killin' Time* (1989) was undoubtedly a country album, evi-denced by the traditional instrumentation (acoustic guitars, fiddle, steel guitar, and harmonica) and his vocal style. The title song opens with what can be described as a blues-influenced rock guitar riff, though the bass line, fiddle parts, and vocal style are pure country. "Better Man" provides an interesting juxtaposition of country and rock styles. The introduction and choruses incorporate a strong rock-influenced backbeat, while during the verses the drummer's style lightens substantially beneath stylistic inflections typically used by country performers. Though rock elements were certainly evident, this debut album was well within the boundaries of country music of the time.

However, the title song from his second release, *Put Yourself in My Shoes* (1990), stretches the definition of country almost to the breaking point. The yodeling vocal line assists in retaining at least a modicum of country sensibility. However, the blues-influenced harmonica introduction and fiddle fills interspersed throughout the song suggest an evolution of musical style. Perhaps the most obvious deviation is in the increased complexity and chromaticism of the harmony, as outlined below:

"Put Yourself in My Shoes"—original key: A major

| | | | | |
|---|---|---|---|---|
| intro: | I VI⁷* | V III* | ♭III* II⁷* | V |
| verse: | V | VI⁷* | I | V |
| | V | VI⁷* | I | V |
| | I | VII* | iii | VI⁷* |
| | V | VI⁷* | ♭III* II⁷* | V |
| chorus: | I | V | I | V |
| | I | V | VI⁷* | II* ♭II* |
| | I | V | I | V |
| | I VI⁷* | V III* | ♭III* II⁷* | V |

Notice the high degree of chromaticism in this piece (identified by the asterisks) in comparison to the C & W songs previously outlined. Such chromaticism was often utilized in pop tunes and soft rock. "Put Yourself in My Shoes" incorporates both traditional country harmonies and relatively adventurous chromatic chord progressions into a single song. Notice that four of the seven chords in the introduction are chords that are outside of the key. High levels of chromaticism can also be found in the last half of the verse and the second and fourth phrases of the chorus. The chord progression for the last phrase of the chorus duplicates the introduction. Listen carefully to the chorus of this song. Compare the bass line present here to that heard in the C & W examples discussed earlier. The presence of a heavier rock-influenced drumbeat frees the bass player to provide a rock-style, quarter-note bass line called a "walking bass line."

Observe also the syncopated rhythms played in the eighth measure of this example and the anticipation (i.e., early arrival) of the D major chord in the ninth measure . . . a slight increase in rhythmic complexity. "Put Yourself in My Shoes"

presents a hybrid song form, consisting of both country and rock characteristics. The vocal style and instrumentation reveal little deviation from what was typically heard on C & W recordings. Especially noticeable is the prominent role retained by the pedal steel. However, the chromatic harmonies, the blues riffs played by both the harmonica and fiddle, the heavy drumbeat heard in the chorus, and the shouting vocal style hinted at in the final chorus reveal a definite rock influence.

Several of Black's later recordings lead one to question whether they can be classified as country at all. Listen carefully, for example, to "Wherever You Go" from *One Emotion* (1994). The electric guitar part throughout is taken directly from mainstream rock and utilizes a performance technique called "bar chords." In the most simple case, as heard in the introduction to this song, the performer plays only the root, the fifth scale degree, and an octave above the root (i.e., using only the three lowest-pitched strings), resulting in the following chord:

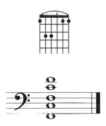

The resulting chord contains the first and fifth scale degrees (an open fifth), but the third degree of the chord is absent. As a result, the tonality is ambiguous, neither major nor minor, accommodating equally well either a major third (A in the chord above), minor third (Ab in the chord above), or a pitch somewhere in between the two (a "blue" note). In addition, this fingering pattern can be moved to any position on the guitar neck to form a chord, requiring only a minimal amount of technical expertise to play any chord of the chromatic scale. Bar chord technique has been utilized to great advantage throughout the history of rock. The opening measures of Deep Purple's "Smoke on the Water" provide a clear musical demonstration of this bar chord technique. With that in mind, listen closely to Black's "Wherever You Go," and notice the distinct contrast between this style of country music and early C & W.

With Travis Tritt, the transformation of country into a subgenre of rock music was complete. "Put Some Drive in Your Country" from Tritt's debut album provides an irrefutable confirmation of this fact. Notice, for example, the distorted rock guitar timbre and the musical texture consisting of multiple rhythmic guitar lines subtly intertwined underneath a sustained electric slide guitar. The resulting sound is reminiscent of 1970s southern rock. In addition, Tritt's shouting-style vocal delivery and the strong, consistent drumbeat including a heavy backbeat further emphasize the rock–country fusion. In the chorus of this song, Tritt's lyrics even state his case explicitly when he references a childhood promise made to himself to combine Southern rock and country.

Rock influences are a consistent feature of Travis Tritt's recordings. Even his ballads exhibit characteristics clearly derived from rock. Listen to "Anymore" (from *It's All About to Change*). Notice that the soft acoustic guitar accompaniment and vocal melody line heard at the beginning gradually build to a powerful rock ballad, adding a solid drumbeat, distorted rock guitars, and culminating in a rock-style electric guitar solo. Gone is the pedal steel break typical of country ballads. In fact, the manner in which this song builds is reminiscent of Led Zeppelin's classic "Stairway to Heaven." "Bible Belt" (featuring Little Feat, one of the premier, though undeservedly lesser-known, southern rock bands of the 1970s) is a straight-ahead rock song with little country influence. Also noteworthy are the rock bass line, driving drumbeat, and shouting vocal style with its bluesy inflection evident throughout this song. The instrumental solos also reveal significant rock influence. The pedal steel characteristic of country music is replaced by an electric slide guitar in the style of Duane Allman, followed by a honky-tonk piano solo in the style of Jerry Lee Lewis. The driving blues-oriented rock style of "Leave My Girl Alone" and "Blue Collar Man" (both from *T-r-o-u-b-l-e*) share more in common with the music of Eric Clapton and Led Zeppelin than with George Strait or Ricky Skaggs. The guitar timbre and performance style incorporated in these songs is derived completely from rock and roll. Notice also that the harmonic structure of "Leave My Girl Alone" is that of the twelve-bar blues. "Blue Collar Man" (co-written by Tritt and Lynyrd Skynyrd guitarist Gary Rossington) is a sixteen-bar blues that simply repeats the first four measures of a basic twelve-bar blues progression. Recall the similar extension incorporated by the Rolling Stones in "19th Nervous Breakdown" (see the Musical Close-Up in Chapter 7, "The British Invasion").

Shania Twain's landmark recording *Come On Over* (1997)—the title itself a double-entendre reference to the musical crossover—contains further evidence that rock music's influence on the new generation of country artists was not short term. The opening synthesized horn riff followed by a Madonna-esque spoken cue ("Let's go, girls . . . ") and distorted rock guitar tracks sets the tone for the album. "Love Gets Me Every Time" initiates a recurrent alternation between, in addition to integration of, rock and country elements. Listen to the brief one-measure rock guitar tremolo followed by three measures of a rock riff then one measure of country fiddle. The following verse structure combines the rock guitar riff with the fiddle part, adding a pedal steel and vocal inflections (not to mention lyric choice, e.g., "gol darn") to shift toward the country side of the stylistic scale. "From This Moment On" shares more in common with the rock ballads of Journey and R & B crossovers of Celine Dion, Peabo Bryson, and Luther Vandross than with its country ancestor, right down to the rock guitar solo accompanied by a repeated sixteenth-note synthesizer pattern. The title track provides an interesting integration of the accordian-dominated zydeco music of New Orleans and Jamaican reggae, along with the typical country and rock elements.

Like Tritt's "Put Some Drive in Your Country," Shania includes her own anthem explicitly touting the musical integration of rock and country: "Rock This Country" (once again, a phrase with double meaning). Opening with straight-ahead rock guitar and a powerful quadruple meter rock drum foundation, listen to the stylistic alternation evident in the recurring chorus section, presenting a musical dialogue between the rock guitar and fiddle, alternating every two measures. An element of consistency is maintained by the continuing rock drumbeat, emphasizing the backbeat. With this recording, there was certainly no doubt that Shania had, in fact, "come over" to rock and roll.

In summary, a quick checklist of musical characteristics will enumerate commonalities and identify significant differences between C & W and country music of the 1990s. As in C & W, the melody and lyrics (frequently love-oriented) retain their position of primary importance. The nasal quality, falsetto, and emotive cracks in the voice often are incorporated into more recent country, though yodeling has been used less frequently. However, later country music often juxtaposes a shouting style of vocals reminiscent of R & B and mainstream rock with traditional country vocal techniques. Many of the more traditional-sounding country songs utilize instrumentation quite similar to that of C & W, though drums are almost always present in these later recordings. The pedal steel and fiddle provide a strong link with the country past. However, many of the rock-influenced country songs dispense with the pedal steel in favor of an electric slide guitar. Wearing a metal or glass cylinder on one finger of the left hand (assuming a right-handed performer), the guitar player slides the cylinder up and down the neck in lieu of pressing the strings into the fingerboard, creating a glissando (sliding pitch) effect. This style of playing was pioneered by early blues guitarist Robert Johnson, mastered by Duane Allman and Dicky Betts of the Allman Brothers Band, and adopted by many other southern rock bands of the 1970s (e.g, the Eagles, the Marshall Tucker Band, and Lynyrd Skynyrd). Contrast the sound of the traditional pedal steel in Garth Brooks's "Two of a Kind, Workin' on a Full House" to the use of the rock-influenced slide guitar in "Thunder Rolls."

The rhythm section in later country music took on a much more prominent role. The drums often propelled the music forward, powerfully emphasizing the backbeat and, at times, introducing tightly synchronized, syncopated rhythms with the bass player. With the drummer providing a consistently solid beat, the bass player was no longer tied to the simple two-beat bass lines found in most C & W of the 1940s and 1950s. In their search for new musical ideas, many bass players gained musical inspiration from rock bass lines. The simple harmonics of C & W were emulated in many recent country songs. Frequently, however, the chord changes incorporated creative alterations and higher levels of chromaticism than those of its predecessor. Finally, it is worth noting that the general production quality of country music recordings increased significantly in the transitional period during the 1980s, rivaling the studio sound quality of major rock artists.

In view of all of the points enumerated previously, it would appear that the role of musical influence has come full circle. As rock music coalesced in the early 1950s, C & W exerted considerable influence on many of the artists, as well as on the music itself. At various stages (rockabilly, southern rock, etc.), country revived its influence on this younger musical sibling. During the final decade of the twentieth century, however, rock music exerted considerable musical influence upon country music. Many musical characteristics of rock became an integral part of the new style of country.

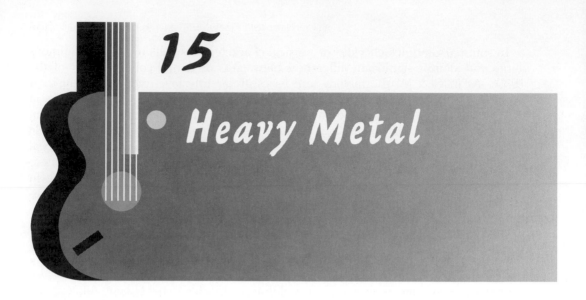

# 15

# Heavy Metal

## OVERVIEW: "WE'RE NOT GONNA TAKE IT ANYMORE"

Writing about heavy metal is like trying to aim at a moving target. The problem is that many heavy metal fans (and some writers) use the term qualitatively rather than as a stylistic designation. As we shall see in the course of this chapter, heavy metal (as a musical style) has certain musical characteristics, just as jazz-rock, R & B, disco, and other styles do. If a given group generally adheres to those musical characteristics, the term applies. Unfortunately, the term loses its meaning if used as a relative term to describe a personal qualitative judgment. If a group plays heavy metal in 1985 and does not change their style, in 1989 they are still heavy metal—even though subsequent groups may have come along that play "heavier" metal.

And what is it, by the way, that the subsequent groups play that makes their music "heavier?" Broadly considered, heavy metal has been a rather static style—not dramatically changed from the mid-1970s to the late 1980s. That is true if we are speaking specifically of the music. What have changed over the years are the lyrics and the extramusical factors (e.g., image and theatrics). The antihero mentality, combined with the post–Alice Cooper shock trend, have created an escalating situation in which each band must be louder, grosser, more rebellious, and more shocking than its predecessors. With each step of this "progression," the most recent groups become "heavy metal" (if the term is used qualitatively), and the "old-timers" slip into a much-derided "softer" category. But the changes are rarely in the music itself. As Ken Tucker puts it, "The most popular 1980s heavy metal acts broke little new ground musically—the whole appeal of heavy metal is that it stays roughly the same" (Ward, Stokes, and Tucker 1986, 608).

For most of the 1970s and 1980s, heavy metal was the hardest of the rock styles. Its appeal was primarily to those whose self-image was that of the angry, macho, anti-establishment rebel. The general profile of the heavy metal fan was that of a thirteen- to eighteen-year-old Hispanic or Anglo male, often from less affluent and turbulent family circumstances. (*Note:* Such demographic profiles may be valid in general, but one must remember that there are also a vast number of exceptions to the general profile.) It is usually assumed that heavy metal consumers found that the musical style somehow reinforced their general displeasure with the society around them. The music helped them act out their anger and frustration with all of the societal institutions that they felt had let them down (e.g., the family, the church, the schools).

Certainly the lyrics were a big part of this angry rebellion. In the Musical Close-Up at the end of Chapter 13, we included violence, suicide, and the occult among the frequent themes of post–1960s rock lyrics. These themes are not uncommon in heavy metal songs. But the anger was not expressed only by the lyrics. As we shall see as we examine the heavy metal style further in this chapter, characteristics of the music itself tend to reinforce the image of the angry young man shaking his fist at all parts of society. Elements such as the extreme volume; the distorted timbres; the screaming vocals; the insistent, repetitive riffs; and the screeching, high-speed solos all seem to reinforce the disaffected youth who has decided that he is "not gonna take it anymore" (in the words of heavy metal band Twisted Sister).

In this chapter, we will trace the evolution of heavy metal from its late-1960s roots into the 1970s, first from the British groups and then from the American groups. We will then discuss three heavy metal bands from the 1980s that seem to typify the style in that decade. Finally, we will see how heavy metal moved through the 1990s and combined with another anti-establishment style—rap—to create yet another blended style.

## BRITISH HEAVY METAL EVOLVES

From the British blues-based bands evolved a harder mainstream rock style. A developmental line can be drawn from groups such as the Rolling Stones, the Yardbirds, and the Who to mainstream groups such as Cream, Blind Faith, Traffic, and Faces. This hard rock mainstream continued through the 1970s and into the 1980s. But branching off from this mainstream was a development that was eventually called heavy metal. Musically, heavy metal began as an exaggeration of the hard rock side of the mainstream. If hard rock was loud, heavy metal was louder; if hard rock was simple and repetitive, heavy metal was simpler and more repetitive; if hard rock singers shouted, heavy metal singers screamed; if hard rockers experimented with electronic distortion and feedback, heavy metalers distorted everything; if hard rock favored long instrumental improvisations, heavy metal offered longer, louder, and more dazzling instrumental solos; if hard rock was *countercultural*, heavy metal would come to specialize in the *anticultural*. One of the prototypes of British heavy metal was Deep Purple. When Jon Lord and his colleagues were not creating works like the *Concerto for Group and Orchestra* and the *Gemini Suite*, the band was developing a harder style of mainstream rock that was an early form of heavy metal.

## Led Zeppelin

The premier British heavy metal band of the 1970s was Led Zeppelin. In 1968 the Yardbirds disbanded; guitarist Jimmy Page recruited Robert Plant (lead vocals and harmonica), John Bonham (drums), and John Paul Jones (bass and keyboards) and renamed the group Led Zeppelin. Signed almost immediately by Atlantic Records, the band released their first album, *Led Zeppelin,* in 1969; it proved to be their least popular album, reaching "only" number 10 on the U.S. charts (their next eight albums ranked either number 1 or 2). Although Zeppelin would eventually place half a dozen singles in the U.S. charts, they never released a single in Great Britain.

Following several tours of the United States, Zeppelin released *Led Zeppelin II* (1969), their first number 1 album. A shortened version of "Whole Lotta Love" became a Top 5 hit, and the band was firmly established. "Whole Lotta Love" (the album cut) gives a good idea of the heavy metal sound in its early years. There is an insistent eighth-note (duple) subdivision of each beat; a strong, low-range guitar riff repeats under each verse; the vocal is high pitched, bordering on the full shouting style. There is guitar distortion and, if played properly, it is loud. A long break in the middle of the song is reminiscent of San Francisco–style electronic experimentation (much feedback and distortion over a continuous beat). A brief guitar solo leads to the return of the basic riff and vocal; a free tempo shouted vocal solo breaks the pattern briefly, but the vocal and riff return and lead to the final fade-out. "Whole Lotta Love" is hard rock—only harder. Another interesting song on this album was "What Is and What Should Be," a song that alternates between sections of heavy metal and "softer" sections. "The Lemon Song," a twelve-bar blues, illustrates the continuing thread from old R & B through the blues-based British bands to early heavy metal.

Led Zeppelin: John Paul Jones, Robert Plant, Jimmy Page, John Bonham (*Source:* AP/World Wide Photos)

*Led Zeppelin III* and *Led Zeppelin IV* continued Zeppelin's popularity. Ironically, their most famous song, "Stairway to Heaven" (from *IV*), was never released as a single. It is a classic of early 1970s hard rock–heavy metal. "Stairway" begins with acoustic guitars and recorders; a modal vocal melody enters and soon keyboards and electric guitars are added to the accompaniment. When drums enter after several choruses, the pattern of increasing intensity becomes obvious. The turning point is a strong guitar solo, carrying the intensity to a new, higher level. When the vocal reenters, it is in a typical high-pitched, shouting heavy metal timbre. The accompaniment turns into a rhythmic riff, and the peak is finally reached. The end is most effective: a simple a cappella vocal phrase that reiterates the hook line.

Zeppelin's preeminence continued through *Houses of the Holy* (1973), *Physical Graffiti* (1975), and *Presence* (1976). Page's fascination with the occult was well known; he had, in fact, moved into the former home of Aleister Crowley, a mystic who has often been linked with satanic religion. Some of Zeppelin's surrealistic lyrics led observers to interpretations ranging from Celtic mythology to druidic symbolism to pure satanism. There have been charges of backward Satanic messages in some songs (e.g., "Stairway to Heaven").

Zeppelin's problems began in 1975, when a series of personal tragedies struck Robert Plant. Zeppelin's 1979 concert, their first live appearance in England since the mid-1970s, was panned by critics. The final blow was the death of drummer John Bonham in September 1980. Led Zeppelin chose not to continue. However, the remaining three band members reunited several times in the 1980s and Jimmy Page and Robert Plant collaborated on *No Quarter* (1994) and *Walking Into Clarksdale* (1998). In 1997, a collection of Zeppelin's live BBC sessions reached number 12 and was certified platinum. In 1999, the recording industry announced that Zeppelin was only the third act in history to achieve four or more diamond-certified albums (ten million copies sold).

## Black Sabbath and Ozzy Osbourne

Going deeper into the British heavy metal sound and the black magic image was Black Sabbath, a quartet from Birmingham, England. Formed in 1969, they called themselves Earth (changed later that year to Black Sabbath). *Black Sabbath* was released in 1970 and was a moderate success. Lead singer John "Ozzy" Osbourne's voice was distinctive: high pitched, screaming, and sometimes on pitch. The lyrics centered on mystical references to the soul, fantasies, insanity, and similar concepts. There were the distorted, repetitive guitar riffs and steady duple subdivisions of the beat that were to characterize heavy metal. The vocal style and the musical ambiance seemed to project attitudes of anger, defiance, and aggression; where most earlier rock styles had been good time, "rockin' and partyin'" music, this music seemed to be clenching its fists until the knuckles turned white.

Although Black Sabbath had no single hits, their albums sold well through the 1970s. Osbourne left the group in 1978 to become a major heavy metal solo act of the 1980s. He was replaced for three albums (1980 to 1983) by Ronnie James Dio.

Osbourne fared well commercially after his split from Black Sabbath. The anti-hero concept first mentioned when we spoke of the Rolling Stones reached new levels with Osbourne; for example, a glance at the cover of *Bark at the Moon* (1983) suggests how far we have "progressed" from the days of Presley or the Beach Boys. The song "Rock 'n' Roll Rebel" (*Bark at the Moon*) is a teenage anthem, but not in the same way as Dylan's "The Times They Are a-Changin'." Ozzy tells parents, "Do what you will to try and make me conform/But I'll make you wish you had never been born," whereas Dylan asked them to "Please get out of the new one [new road]/If you can't lend your hand."

Rather surprisingly, in the early years of the new century Ozzy and his family (wife Sharon, daughter Kelly, and son Jack) starred in a reality show on TV entitled *The Osbournes.* The show was amazingly successful, suggesting once again that what was once "countercultural" is often absorbed into the (more or less) mainstream culture.

The early British heavy metal of 1970 does not sound significantly different from that of 1987. The lyrical messages changed, but the music remained rather static. Ken Tucker seems to have hit upon the reason for this status.

> Heavy metal . . . is the primary music of teenage rebellion and, almost by definition, something a listener outgrows. As such, it is also an ideal commercial proposition, for it bypasses such sticky items as an artist's changing ambitions or inevitably uneven output. In the world of heavy metal, a new set of teens is ever entering the marketplace, and with them arrives the latest set of outrageous stars, whose popularity lasts just about as long as its generation of teens. (Ward, Stokes, and Tucker 1986, 486)

"Bark at the Moon" by Ozzy Osbourne (*Source:* Michael Ochs Archive, Ltd.)

# AMERICAN HEAVY METAL

As was the case in England, some American mainstream bands of the late 1960s turned the power up a bit higher and drifted steadily into heavy metal. In 1968, Steppenwolf had a number 2 hit with "Born to Be Wild"; contained in the song's lyrics was the phrase "heavy metal thunder." The phrase seemed to be an appropriate description for the musical sound and the shortened version of the phrase stuck: heavy metal. Also referred to in its earlier forms as power rock, American heavy metal seems to have developed simultaneously in California and Michigan with groups like Blue Cheer, Iron Butterfly, Steppenwolf, MC5, Grand Funk Railroad, and Alice Cooper. Blue Cheer was a power trio from San Francisco that enjoyed moderate success from 1968 to 1970. Iron Butterfly, formed in 1966 by keyboardist Doug Ingle, moved from San Diego to Los Angeles, where they became the house band at the Whisky-à-Go-Go. The band will be remembered primarily for its seventeen-minute "In-A-Gadda-Da-Vida," released on an album by the same name in 1968. A powerful work, it features a series of solos organized around repetitive bass riffs; "In-A-Gadda-Da-Vida" was in line with the concept of the long instrumental improvisations being developed simultaneously by some of the San Francisco groups and British blues-based bands.

Steppenwolf, formed in Toronto by German-born John Kay, moved to Los Angeles and signed a contract with Dunhill Records. By today's standards, Steppenwolf barely qualifies as heavy metal; they seem to be more of a mainstream hard rock band. They tended to be more sociopolitically oriented and less prone to ultraloud repetitive chords and riffs than the purer heavy metal bands. By 1972, Steppenwolf's popularity had waned and they disbanded. Kay reorganized the band in 1974, but they failed to regain their earlier appeal.

The Michigan influence was first felt with MC5, an early heavy metal band from Detroit. Their initial album, *Kick Out the Jams* (1969), was a live album and contained some profanity, which caused repercussions with some record stores and eventually with the record company itself (Elektra). Moving to Atlantic, MC5 released one more album before disbanding. Far more successful was Grand Funk Railroad, a power trio formed in the mid-1960s in Flint, Michigan. Their appearance in 1969 at the Atlanta Pop Festival created a strong impression. Able to play a strong mainstream rock style or move to a heavy metal style, Grand Funk released a series of eight Top 10 albums from 1970 through 1974. In the meantime, they produced nine Top 40 singles, including two number 1 hits, "We're an American Band" (1973) and "The Loco-Motion" (1974). (For a while—from 1973 to 1975—they dropped the "Railroad" from their name.) As noted earlier, 1970s American hard rock groups were usually not as "hard" as their British counterparts; similarly, the early American heavy metal groups were not as consistently "heavy" as the British heavy metal groups. Often they would venture into a heavy metal style (e.g., Grand Funk's "Sin's a Good Man's Brother" on *Close to Home*), only to retreat to a more mainstream style for the majority of their repertoire.

## Alice Cooper

The Doobie Brothers produced an album in 1974 profoundly entitled *What Were Once Vices Are Now Habits*. One could paraphrase that title in regard to heavy metal: What was once heavy metal is now mainstream rock. As each new heavy metal band "upped the ante" and managed to "out-heavy" its predecessors, that which was formerly considered heavy metal slowly receded to a comparatively "softer" category. With the coming of Alice Cooper, a new brand of heavy metal was initiated, one that added the element of shock. If the Stones had initiated the antihero trend in rock, it was inevitable that someone would take that concept to its "logical" extreme: not simply an avoidance of the traditional hero concept but an active attempt to be as repulsive, disgusting, and perverse as possible (Cooper, of course, predates the punk trend of the later 1970s).

Alice Cooper is the name of the band as well as the stage name of its lead singer, Vincent Furnier. Born in Detroit in 1948, he moved to Phoenix and eventually to Los Angeles. While playing for a memorial birthday party for Lenny Bruce, Cooper was heard by Frank Zappa, who signed the band to a contract with his new Straight Records. Their first two albums, released in the late 1960s, were commercially unsuccessful.

Cooper took his stage name from the story of a sixteenth-century woman who was burned at the stake for witchcraft (he had dreamed that he was her reincarnation). Creating a highly theatrical stage act that consisted of tidbits of violence, the occult, sadomasochism, and animal abuse, Cooper began to achieve local notoriety.

In 1969, while performing at a local Detroit ballroom, Cooper ended the evening's entertainment by throwing several live chickens out into the crowd; the crowd responded by ripping the chickens to shreds. The resulting publicity apparently convinced Cooper that if his music was getting him nowhere, perhaps shock could do it for him.

Cooper's first Warner Brothers album, *Love It to Death* (1971), made the Top 40 and yielded the number 21 hit, "Eighteen"—originally titled "Love It to Death (I'm Eighteen)." This song, a typical teen frustration song, was not particularly "heavy" in terms of heavy metal; but it did feature Cooper's shouting vocal style. *School's Out* (1972) really launched Cooper to national status as America's premier shock rock–heavy metal band. The album reached number 2 and the title song climbed to number 7. "School's Out" remains a good representation of early 1970s American heavy metal: repetitive guitar riffs, power chords, distorted guitar solo, shouted lyrics (in this case, expressing the teen's disgust with education), and a driving beat (especially near the end). It is a forerunner of later heavy metal songs such as "School Daze" by AC/DC and similar works by Pink Floyd and others.

The peak year for Alice Cooper was 1973. *Billion Dollar Babies* became Cooper's first and only number 1 album, yielding three Top 40 singles. Ironically the title song did not chart, possibly because its lyrics were a bit strong for early 1970s radio standards. On the highly publicized *Billion Dollar Babies* tour, Cooper sang the title song while abusing a toy doll—beating, kicking, stabbing, and throwing it, simulating intercourse with it, and decapitating it.

The major tour that promoted his *Welcome to My Nightmare* album (1975) was a full theatrical production, with Cooper in facial makeup, portraying a series of scenes from his "nightmare." Subsequent albums declined in popularity, and Cooper labored through the late 1970s and early 1980s with only moderate success. A comeback tour in 1987 attempted to recreate Cooper's nightmare; he pulled out all of his old tricks: representations of child abuse, abuse of women, sadomasochism, insanity, necrophilia, and murder by strangulation and impalement.

Alice Cooper (Photograph by Byron Samford. (*Source:* Courtesy of *San Antonio Light*)

As Brock Helander notes, "Alice Cooper was one of the first rock groups consciously to dupe the unwitting media into promulgating a totally negative image for commercial gain" (Helander 1982, 103). Cooper was capable of good mainstream rock and roll (e.g., "Under My Wheels"); his "Be My Lover" uncannily resembles the sound of Jagger and the Stones. His occasional attempts at ballads ("Desperado" and "Only Women Bleed") suggest that his shouting vocal style must be preferred over his attempts to really "sing." In all likelihood, Cooper will be remembered for his theatrics and his initiation of the shock rock phenomenon, rather than for his music per se.

## Kiss

As indicated earlier, heavy metal is often a game of one-upmanship. If Cooper could use heavy black makeup around his eyes, Kiss could go all the way to full makeup. With the theatrics and makeup, Kiss (and Cooper, for that matter) drew a connection between heavy metal and the glitter rock trend that was more prominent in England (such American versions of glitter rock, however, were more "macho" in image and avoided the androgynous image of Bowie, for example). Kiss's musical style was pure heavy metal— the heaviest of the American groups up to that time.

Kiss was formed in 1972 by bassist Gene Simmons and established their reputation through their shock rock–heavy metal live performances. In fact, through 1984, only four of their sixteen albums reached the Top 10; they have had only one Top 10 hit ("Beth," in 1976). But, as Brock Helander says, "Kiss . . . endeared themselves to legions of prepubescent fans . . . with gimmicks such as mock blood vomiting, fire breathing, explosions and fireworks, dry ice fogs, and rocket-firing guitars in performance" (Helander 1982, 312). As with Cooper, the success of Kiss resided more in the image and theatrics than in the music.

Sales began to slip in the early 1980s; thus as a possible shot in the arm the band "unmasked" for their 1983 album *Lick It Up.* They enjoyed something of a comeback in the mid-1980s, riding the tide of heavy metal popularity. *Lick It Up* went gold; the follow-up album *Animalize* (1984) went platinum. Kiss's message for the mid-1980s was explicitly sexual (e.g., "Fits Like a Glove" from *Lick It Up,* and "Hot

Rock group Kiss (*Source:* Christ Walter / Retna Ltd. USA)

Blood" from *Animalize*). A discussion of these and similar lyrics may be found in the Musical Close-Up in Chapter 13.

The original members reunited for a performance on MTV in 1996. The reunion led to a tour (the highest grossing concert tour of the year) and the release of *Psycho-circus* (number 3 in 1998). In 2003, Kiss's *Symphony* found the band performing with orchestral accompaniment (much as Metallica had done in 1999). Shortly thereafter, Peter Criss left the band (for a second time) as the remaining members made plans for a "World Domination" tour in 2004.

### Rush

Most critics agreed that heavy metal had all of the musical value of an electric razor. Loudness and grossness sold records to ever-susceptible teenagers, but contributed little to the evolution of rock as a musical style. However, even in the field of heavy metal, there were occasional groups that avoided the show biz theatrics and commercially inspired grossness and concentrated on the music. One of the earliest and most successful of these groups was Rush, a Canadian power trio. Rush's first three albums were not big sellers, although the heavy metal style was in line with the more popular bands; singer Geddy Lee's high screaming vocals compared favorably to those by Cooper, Osbourne, and others. It was not until Rush's fourth album, *2112* (1976), that sales began to improve (this and all subsequent albums have been either gold or platinum). For the balance of the 1970s, Rush attracted a relatively small but loyal following among those who liked the heavy metal style but were turned off by the gimmickry of the more popular bands.

As the 1980s dawned, Rush began to find a bigger market. Previously Rush's only compliance with typical heavy metal messages had been a flirtation with the "darker side"—especially on *Fly by Night* ("By-Tor and the Snow-Dog") and *Caress of Steel* ("The Necromancer"). Pure heavy metal songs, such as "Finding My Way" (*Rush*) and "Anthem" (*Fly by Night*), typified their earlier sound. But through the 1980s, Rush seemed to lessen the "heavy" part of their heavy metal style. This softening, combined with the aforementioned tendency of heavy metal to get progressively heavier, resulted in Rush's gradually finding itself more in the category of sophisticated hard rock (or possibly progressive rock). If one compares *Rush* (1974) with *Grace Under Pressure* (1984), one finds not only a remarkably different image but also a strikingly different musical style. Although vestiges of heavy metal remain, much changed. Lee's voice dropped from his earlier adenoidal screaming range to a more normal singing range; there is a heavy dose of synthesizers; the style adheres more closely to a strong mainstream hard rock style. Rush's success continued into the 1990s and beyond with *Test for Echo* (number 5 in 1996), *Vapor Trails* (number 6 in 2002), and *Feedback* (2004). There were also two live recordings (*Different Stages* in 1998 and *Rush in Rio* in 2003). As evidence of their continuing popularity and critical acclaim, Rush received a Juno award (Canada's Grammy) for Music DVD of the Year for the *Rush in Rio* album.

## HEAVY METAL CONTINUES

In the 1980s, heavy metal had a major impact. There would be a long list of successful heavy metal bands—far more than we can discuss here. We will, therefore, discuss three bands in more detail and then survey some of the others.

### Guns N' Roses

One of the most successful rock bands of the late 1980s, Guns N' Roses was a quintet based in Los Angeles. Their first few releases (including a four-song EP, *Live Like a Suicide*) did not fare well commercially. Their big breakthrough came in 1988 with the album *Appetite for Destruction*. It rose to the number 1 position and stayed there for five weeks. The album produced three Top 10 singles, including the number 1 "Sweet Child o' Mine." The success of the next album, *GN'R Lies*, was somewhat surprising, inasmuch as it was a reissue of the 1986 EP (*Live Like a Suicide*), plus four new tracks. Yet even this eight-song album sold sufficiently to achieve a number 2 ranking ("Patience" was released as a single and reached number 4).

*Lies* is a good album to study because it represents the sound of GN'R before and after their rise to stardom. There is a surprising variety of styles represented between the 1986 and 1988 material. The first two songs (both from 1986) are typical heavy metal, complete with screaming vocal, fast, pounding rhythm, steady duple subdivision of the beat, distorted "power" guitar accompaniment, and defiant lyrics. With the album's third song, "Move to the City," GN'R moves back to a hard rock mainstream style. The difference between late 1980s hard rock and heavy metal can be a rather fine distinction. But in "Move to the City," notice that lead singer Axl Rose lowers his voice range from the high scream of the first two songs. Also notice that the beat is no longer a steady duple subdivision (straight eighth notes), but a more rocking long–short pattern. This difference is also evident on the last of the 1986 songs, "Mama Kin." Here the guitar accompaniment is almost Chuck Berry–like at times.

With the 1988 cuts, there is even more variety. The album's single hit, "Patience," begins with acoustic guitars and whistling. When the vocal begins, one is reminded

Guns N' Roses (Photograph by Neil Zlozower) (*Source:* © 1988 Neil
Zlozower/Michael Ochs Archive, Ltd.)

of the opening verses of Led Zeppelin's "Stairway to Heaven." But unlike "Stairway," "Patience" does not build to a powerful climax. Instead, it continues to
develop in a style quite close to a typical singer–songwriter style of the 1970s (except
perhaps for Rose's more forceful vocal at the end).

"Used to Love Her" is the sort of song that can easily create controversy because
of the lyrics ("Used to love her, but I had to kill her," etc.). In some cases the musical
style of such songs makes the lyric seem frighteningly serious. But in this GN'R
song, one gets the feeling that the band is just kidding. There is a gentle rockabilly
tone that makes the song seem lighthearted. "You're Crazy" continues with a rather
gentle rocking beat. Here, Rose varies from a heavy metal scream to a Zappa-like
vocal style (even the lyrics may remind one of Zappa).

*Lies'* last cut, "One in a Million," again bears some kinship to the older
singer–songwriter style, but is beefed up by a much harder accompaniment. Again,
the lyrics are the type that draw criticism; not only does Axl refer to "police and nig-
gers," but he complains that "immigrants and faggots" are spreading diseases and
speaking unintelligible languages.

Overall, GN'R presents an interesting and varied profile. They have been typed
as heavy metal, but only some of their music actually falls into that category. They
certainly are heavily derivative (not necessarily a put-down, because all musical
styles derive from one or more prior styles—including rock and roll itself). For example, a quick tour through *Lies* suggests images of singer–songwriters, Zappa, Led
Zeppelin, and Chuck Berry.

GN'R drew considerable criticism not only because of some lyrics, but also
because of some of the bad-boy behavior of Axl Rose. To the more common

charges of being vulgar and sexist were added the charges of racism. The band's antics (e.g., late concert starts, cancelled concerts, fistfights, etc.) were reminiscent of the old Rolling Stones bad-boy image. Rose, by the way, married Erin Everly (Don Everly's daughter) in 1990; the marriage lasted three weeks.

Through the 1980s, GN'R performed as a quintet. In addition to Rose, there was Duff McKagan (bass), Steven Adler (drums), and guitarists Izzy Stradlin (Jeffrey Isbell) and Slash (Saul Hudson). In the 1990s, there were fierce squabbles and personnel changes. Although GN'R (with Axl Rose) continued into the new century, the commercial success of the band and the solo projects of its various members provided only a pale reflection of their popularity in the 1980s.

## Van Halen

If one metal band came close to superstar status, it would be Van Halen. Eddie and Alex Van Halen were born in Holland (1957 and 1955, respectively) and emigrated to the United States in 1968. Trained in classical music, they soon turned to rock and roll. After establishing their reputation with hard rock and heavy metal bands in southern California, they signed a recording contract with Warner Brothers with the assistance of Kiss's Gene Simmons.

By that time, Eddie had moved from drums to guitar, whereas brother Alex made the same switch in reverse; Michael Anthony played bass, and David Lee Roth was the lead singer. Van Halen's first five albums (1978 to 1982) each rose progressively higher in the Top 20. But the band's commercial and musical triumph came in late 1983 and early 1984 with *1984* (*MCMLXXXIV*), which rose to number 2 and yielded a monster hit, "Jump" (number 1 in 1984) and two other Top 20 singles. "Jump" was based upon a catchy series of syncopated chords on synthesizer over a pounding, steady eighth-note bass. A harmonically interesting guitar solo and a virtuosic synthesizer solo made "Jump" one of the most popular and musically valid songs to come out of heavy metal in the 1980s.

However, by 1985, tensions between lead singer David Lee Roth and the Van Halens had reached the breaking point. It was generally agreed that Eddie Van Halen had become one of the premier guitarists in rock (not just heavy metal); but it was Roth, with his sexy bad-boy image, who provided the commercial charisma for the group. Roth's solo album, *Crazy From the Heat* (number 15 in 1985), provided a clue that a change was imminent. In the album, Roth displayed convincing versatility and charm in the Beach Boys' "California Girls" (number 15) and the old Louis Armstrong and Al Jolson favorites, "Just a Gigolo/I Ain't Got Nobody." Later in 1985, Roth announced that he was leaving the band. Subsequently, Roth and the Van Halens pursued their individual careers. The replacement of Roth with singer Sammy Hagar certainly did not slow down Van Halen. Both their 1986 album *5150* and their 1988 album *OU812* reached the number 1 position. Van Halen's success continued into the first half of the 1990s with albums such as *F.U.C.K.* (*For Unlawful Carnal Knowledge*) (number 1 in 1991), *Van Halen Live: Right Here, Right Now* (number 5 in 1993), and *Balance* (number 1 in 1995). However, after 1996 and the replacement of Sammy Hagar by Gary Cherone, Van Halen's fortunes ebbed as *Van Halen III* (number 4) was greeted by only moderate success in comparison with earlier recordings. In 2004, along with the release of *Best of Both Worlds* (another greatest hits

Van Halen (*Source:* Michael Ochs Archive, Ltd.)

album plus three new tracks), Van Halen and Hagar reunited to begin work on a new album and promotional concert tour.

Even as the preceding discussion of Van Halen is being read, many readers are no doubt crying, "But they're not heavy metal!" Remember our moving target concept? Even though rock historians such as Joel Whitburn, Ken Tucker, and Charles T. Brown all describe Van Halen as a heavy metal band, today's heavy metal fan is likely to disown the group as having "gone commercial" or "softened up." Again, this is the problem with the term *heavy metal* as a moving target.

### Metallica

Though some metal bands (Queensrÿche and Van Halen, for example) infused their musical world with positivism and encouragement, with Metallica we experience a not so subtle shift toward gloom and doom. Many hard-core heavy metal fans hold Metallica as being the archetypal representative of the heavy metal style of the late 1980s and 1990s. The California-based band was formed by Lars Ulrich (drums) and James Hatfield (vocals) in 1981. Guitarist Kirk Hammett joined the band in 1982, replacing Dave Mustaine (who left Metallica to form Megadeth). Jason Newsted (bass) joined in 1986 after Cliff Burton was killed in a bus crash in Sweden.

Metallica's first charted album, *Ride the Lightning*, was released in 1984 and peaked at number 100. Although the next two albums, *Master of Puppets* (1986) and *The $5.98 E.P.: Garage Days Revisited* (1987), rose only to numbers 29 and 28, respectively, they did sell well enough to be certified platinum (one million units sold).

With . . . *And Justice For All* (1988), Metallica cracked the Top 10 (number 6). Rather unexpectedly, the album produced a number 4 single ("One"). Hard-core heavy metal bands did not place many singles on the charts in the 1980s, because the typical heavy metal song was not considered appropriate for Top 40 format airplay. Normally, for any heavy metal band to have success with a single, the song would need to be toned down several notches. Such is the case with "One," which is about as close to a ballad as Metallica normally comes. Even though the song is performed by a heavy metal band, it has few characteristics of the heavy metal style.

   . . . *And Justice For All* is a good representation of Metallica's style (except, ironically, for the single hit "One"). Musically, there are the requisite pounding, distorted, low guitar riffs, insistent heavy beat (and constant duple subdivision), growling vocals, and "speed metal" guitar solos. A few of the song titles suggest the rather gloomy tone of the album: "Blackened," "Harvester of Sorrow," "The Frayed Ends of Sanity," "To Live is to Die," and "Dyer's Eve." The lyrics reinforce this mood with frequent use of such words as:

| | | |
|---|---|---|
| obscurity | callous | mutilation |
| death | opposition | darkest |
| dead | agitation | expiration |
| deadly | decay (decadence) | cancellation |
| evolution's end | frigid | smouldering |
| blistering | contradictions | darkening |
| terminate (termination) | chill | hypocrisy |
| kill (kills) | violation | |

This list was taken from one song ("Blackened"). Actually, it is one of the more positive songs on the album, concerning itself with the threatening of the environment. The tone of the lyrics (reinforced by the angry, driving music) pounds away at the impending doom of the planet and of humanity. Most of the album's songs are about the miserable ways of society and how they overpower the helpless victim (presumably Metallica's teenaged listeners).

   Metallica obviously pitches its message to angry, rebellious youth who appreciate the band's empathy and reinforcement of their plight. Whether Metallica's music alleviates or exacerbates the "at-risk" youth's problem is a serious question. In their defense, Metallica notes (in "Eye of the Beholder") that "energy derives from both the plus and the negative." If you listen to only one song on . . . *And Justice For All*, try "Dyer's Eve." It represents all of the characteristics of Metallica's style of heavy metal, including the angry/despondent, generation gap/victim lyric.

   Metallica's popularity continued into the 1990s and beyond. *Load* (1996) reached the number 1 position and reflected some influence of grunge and other alternative styles. The band followed with *ReLoad* (number 1 in 1997), and *Garage Inc.* (number 2 in 1998), *St. Anger* (number 1 in 2003), and an EP entitled *Some Kind of Monster* (2004). The 1999 album, *S&M* (number 2), is a live collaboration with the San Francisco Symphony.

## Other Heavy Metal Bands

We have selected three heavy metal bands (Guns N' Roses, Van Halen, and Metallica) as being representative of the various heavy metal styles of the 1980s and 1990s. Needless to say, there were many other heavy metal bands during this period, any of which may be just as appropriate as the aforementioned. For example, other American heavy metal bands that attained prominence in the decade included Mötley Crüe, Twisted Sister, W.A.S.P., Quiet Riot, Queensrÿche, Ratt, Staind, and Slipknot (with their outrageous S&M-style wardrobe). England was home to several bands that were considered leaders in heavy metal: Iron Maiden, Judas Priest, Whitesnake, and Def Leppard. Numerous other countries produced heavy metal bands that achieved significant success on the American charts; for example, AC/DC is from Australia; Krokus is from Switzerland; the Scorpions are from Germany.

With all of the heavy metal bands from the 1970s into the new millennium that typically feature one or two guitarists, one should expect a few real guitar virtuosos to emerge. After all, with the sometimes breakneck tempos, the need for forceful "macho" playing, and the emphasis on extended solos, there is ample opportunity for the potential guitar superstar to develop. So it is that a few real "monster" guitarists have come from the ranks of heavy metal. One thinks of Eddie Van Halen, Randy Rhodes, Jimmy Page, and Steve Vai. Vai is an especially talented guitarist and a creative musician. His early experiences were with Frank Zappa, an influence that is evident in much of his later work. For example, listen to the highly creative (and humorously eccentric) *Flexable*, recorded in 1983 and released in 1988. Later, Vai performed with Alcatrazz (1985), David Lee Roth's band (1986–1988), and Whitesnake (1989).

Perhaps the most impressive guitarist to come from the heavy metal style is Swedish guitarist Yngwie Malmsteen. A former lead guitarist with Alcatrazz, Malmsteen formed his own band called Rising Force. The band's 1988 album managed to reach the number 40 position. Subsequent releases sold to a relatively small, "in-the-know" audience, but did not enjoy the mass popularity necessary to reach the top chart positions.

Many heavy metal bands rely to a greater or lesser degree on the shock factor to gain, or maintain, their reputations. Thus, some have become increasingly overt in their references to sex and drugs; many dwell on extreme forms of rebellion, violence, and depression (including suicide). A fascination with the occult and the macabre has led some bands to satanic themes (Venom, Mercyful Fate, Megadeth).

With the success of heavy metal in the 1980s, many hard rock bands have become "heavier" in some of their songs. And, of course, even heavy metal bands sometimes pull back from the pounding beat, distorted guitar riffs, and screaming vocals. The result is that the line between hard rock and heavy metal became very fuzzy, especially by the late 1980s. Often a given band could be categorized either way, depending on what specific song one considered or what the standards of a given listener might be. As always, precise, rigid definitions and categorizations are elusive when dealing with music.

## Metal Fragments

By the mid-1980s, hardcore began to give way to a heavy metal-based spin-off referred to as thrash metal. Blending elements of 1970s heavy metal bands like Black Sabbath with the speed and intensity of hardcore, the postpunk rock audience (often referred to as "headbangers") was given a raw alternative to the mainstream heavy metal of Van Halen, Bon Jovi, and Def Leppard. Elements of the thrash metal sound can be found in the 1970s recordings of Motörhead, Iron Maiden, Diamond Head, and AC/DC. Because most of these bands originated in England, this movement has sometimes been referred to as the new wave of British heavy metal. Credit for the first full-fledged thrash metal recording goes to Metallica (discussed earlier in this chapter).

Metallica's original guitarist, Dave Mustaine, created an even harder-driving version of thrash metal, forming Megadeth upon his departure in 1985. "Speed metal," as this derivative style was sometimes called, was incorporated by many recent recording artists, including rapper Ice-T's Body Count. "Skin o' My Teeth," "Architecture of Aggression," and "High Speed Dirt" on *Countdown to Extinction* (1992) all serve as excellent examples of speed metal. Notice how the high-volume electric guitars played by Mustaine and Marty Friedman dominate the musical texture, typically subdividing the beat into four equal parts (quadruple subdivision). This insistent rhythm provides an accompanimental foundation that refuses to recede into the background, demanding the listener's constant attention as Mustaine's sinister vocals are heard above the energetic din. The driving rhythm of the guitars is solidly matched by Nick Menza's powerful drumming and completed on the low end by David Ellefson's electric bass. Compare these musical characteristics to the sound of Body Count's eponymous recording and note the similarities of the instrumental accompaniment supporting Ice-T's rapping.

Another derivative style, "death metal," combined the tempo, volume, and heavy metal distortion of speed metal with graphic images of death and destruction. This substyle was exemplified in the music of Carcass, Cadaver, Napalm Death, and Slayer. The popularity of thrash (and speed) metal in the 1990s was evidenced by the success of Metallica's self-titled album (debuting at number 1 in 1991), which resulted in three Top 40 hits, including "Enter Sandman" (number 16). Megadeth followed suit with *Countdown to Extinction* (number 2 in 1992) and *Youthanasia* (number 4 in 1994), while Slayer hit the charts with *Divine Intervention* (number 8 in 1994).

## Nü Metal (Rap Metal)

As we shall see in Chapter 17, "Rap and Hip-Hop," spoken rhymes are not the sole property of African-American performers. One subgenre of rap was primarily occupied by white rappers: the Nü Metal phenomenon, combining heavy metal and rap. A harbinger of this approach can be found in the music of Ice-T's project *Body Count* (1992) with its thrash metal accompaniment providing a foundation for the rapper's spoken social commentary.

Nü Metal dripped with the angst that formed an inherent element of grunge, but dispensed with any pretense of subtlety. Whereas songwriters like Kurt Cobain often looked inside themselves for solutions to the world's problems and exhibited a high degree of tolerance, the lyrics of this hard-driving music were often loaded with misogyny, homophobia, and aggression. The aggression was often aimed at women—most often represented as little more than sex objects—and caused a well-deserved backlash. Other groups used the genre effectively as a platform for political and social commentary.

Clearly fitting into the latter camp, Rage Against the Machine was formed in 1991. Zack de la Rocha and Tom Morella were raised in an environment of activism due to their parents' efforts related to Chicano causes and the plight of the African-American, respectively. The two connected with Brad Wilk (drums) and Tim Commerford (bass), producing a set of recordings that earned them a recording deal with Epic Records. The band refused to sign, however, until they were guaranteed complete creative control over their output, an astonishingly bold demand for new artists. With the release of *Evil Empire* (number 1 in 1996) and *Battle of Los Angeles* (debuting at number 1 in 1999), the audience for this music left no doubt about their desire for more. In 2002, the instrumentalists of Rage merged with Soundgarden lead vocalist Chris Cornell (see Chapter 18) to form Audioslave. The new band released an eponymous CD (number 7) that, on its best tracks, combined the driving rhythms and urgency typical of Rage Against the Machine with the melodicism and vocal power of Cornell's former band.

Following the lead of Rage Against the Machine, Korn opened the door of mainstream music to Nü Metal. Members of the group included Jonathan Davis (vocals), Brian "Head" Welch (guitar), James "Munky" Shaffer (guitar), Reggie "Fieldy" Arvizu (bass), and David Silveria (drums). Though their initial self-titled album received relatively little attention, the band's incessant touring and growing fan base resulted in its follow-up, *Life Is Peachy* (1996), debuting at number 3 on the album chart. With the release of *Follow the Leader* and *Issues* (both debuting at number 1 in 1998 and 1999, respectively), Nü Metal proved a powerful force. *Untouchables* (number 2 in 2002), *Take a Look in the Mirror* (number 9 in 2003), and a greatest hits collection (number 4 in 2004) revealed that Korn's position as a leading band within this genre remained strong.

Korn's influence also assisted Limp Bizkit to attain superstardom. Joined in 1995 by turntable manipulator DJ Lethal (formerly with House of Pain), Limp Bizkit began its rise to prominence. Formed by rapper Fred Durst while making a living in Jacksonville as a tattoo artist, the band's fortunes changed when the singer took the opportunity to provide a demo tape to the members of Korn, who he had just tattooed. Limp Bizkit's initial release, *Three Dollar Bill, Y'all$* (number 22 in 1997), contained a rap–metal cover of "Faith," a song written and originally recorded by George Michael (number 1 in 1987). Upon its release, *Significant Other* (1999) replaced the Backstreet Boys' *Millennium* at the top of the charts, eventually selling over seven million copies. The band's performance at Woodstock '99 was cited by some as the event initiating the "mayhem and hooliganism that ultimately brought the three-day festival down in flames" (George-Warren and Romanowski 2001, 567). *Chocolate Starfish and the Hot Dog Flavored Water* (debuting at number 1 in 2000) was the fastest selling rock recording of the year. In 2001, the band contributed "Take a Look Around" to the soundtrack of *Mission: Impossible 2*. In 2003, they released another album of their own (*Results May Vary*, number 3).

Having proven to be a popular genre with the record-buying public, other rap metal artists followed. Some of the more successful of these include Kid Rock, Staind, System of a Down, and Linkin Park.

## MUSICAL CLOSE-UP:
### METER IN HEAVY METAL AND ALTERNATIVE ROCK

As you recall from our discussion at the beginning of this chapter, the musical style of heavy metal is generally simple and repetitive. There are, however, certain early examples (like the changing meters inherent in Rush's "XYZ" from *Moving Pictures* and the syncopation of Led Zeppelin's "Black Dog" from *Led Zeppelin IV*) that are exceptions to this generalization. As this musical style developed into the 1990s, interesting metrical structures became more commonplace.

To establish the basic premise of this musical close-up, let us briefly review some music by early heavy metal pioneers Black Sabbath and Alice Cooper. With few exceptions, the songs recorded by these bands are in quadruple meter and almost always use a duple subdivision of the beat. Both of the Top 40 singles from Alice Cooper's trio of breakthrough albums, *Love It to Death* (1971), *Killer* (1971), and *School's Out* (1972), exemplify the simplicity of metrical structure typical of this style. Listen to "I'm Eighteen" (number 21) and "School's Out" (number 7) to confirm the consistent meter throughout the song. Note also that these songs provide examples of the two basic types of subdivision, with the former illustrating duple subdivision and the latter illustrating triple subdivision. As further evidence, consider the complete set of tracks on *Killer*, focusing specifically on meter. "Under My Wheels," "Be My Lover," "You Drive Me Nervous," "Yeah, Yeah, Yeah," and the title track are all easily recognizable as quadruple meter with duple subdivision. Even the more theatrical tracks ("Desperado" and "Dead Babies") incorporate metrically consistent rhythms throughout their duration, though a significant amount of variety is provided through the use of musical texture and instrumentation. The single song on this album in which the rhythmic structure does not remain consistent is "Halo of Flies," which uses quadruple meter throughout, but changes from duple to triple subdivision about 5 minutes into the song (at the entrance of strings, leading to a bass ostinato that emphasizes the new subdivision).

Black Sabbath has exerted an influence on almost every heavy metal band (and most "alternative" bands). The driving rhythms and metrical regularity of their recordings, especially the early works with Ozzy Osbourne as vocalist, laid the foundation for this style of rock. Listen to "Paranoid," "Iron Man," "Hand of Doom," "Electric Funeral," "Sweet Leaf," "Lord of This World," or "Supernaut." Any of these could serve as a prototypical example of heavy metal rock (even the ballads) with their use of quadruple meter and duple subdivision. In the rather rare instances in which Black Sabbath songs are in triple meter (e.g., "Solitude"), again the meter is consistent throughout. However, exceptions to this rule exist. For example, the brief introduction to "War Pigs" incorporates triple meter with triple subdivision, but leads into a series of verses and choruses clearly exemplifying quadruple meter with duple subdivision.

As heavy metal music merged with elements of newer alternative trends (see Chapter 18) in the early 1990s, some groups began freely manipulating the solid metrical foundation upon which heavy metal had been built. Some of the most interesting of these experiments can be found on recordings by Soundgarden and Tool. These metrical manipulations come primarily in two varieties: uncommon meters (those other than duple, triple, or quadruple) and complex metrical structures resulting from frequently changing metrical groupings. Both types will be described in detail below with specific examples.

One means of infusing a sense of metrical interest into a song is to base the rhythmic structure on meters that are not divisible by two or three (e.g., 5, 7, 11, etc.). As has been pointed out previously, duple, triple, and especially quadruple meter are by far the most common meters in all rock styles, including mainstream rock and heavy metal. Some interesting examples of the use of uncommon meters include Soundgarden's "My Wave" (five beats per measure; after brief intro) and Tool's "Ticks & Leeches" (seven beats per measure when vocals enter) and "Lateralus" (five beats per measure when vocals enter). Another metrical device is to change the symmetrical subdivisions of a common meter into an asymmetrical pattern. For example, instead of the usual eight subdivisions in quadruple meter (2 + 2 + 2 + 2), the subdivisions could be arranged into a 3 + 3 + 2 pattern. You can hear this pattern in the verses of Tool's "Intolerance." In such cases, the meter is more accurately described as 3/8 + 3/8 + 2/8 rather than the more traditional 4/4. Such metric patterns are sometimes referred to as *complex* or *asymmetrical meters*. The pattern of 3 + 3 + 2, found in "Intolerance," is one of the most commonly used complex patterns incorporated in the music of Tool. You can find a clearly audible occurrence of this pattern in "Disposition."

We have seen the practice of changing meters before (remember examples by the Beatles, the Byrds, Chicago, and others). This technique has been used in classical music since the early twentieth century. Tool's "Schism" provides an excellent, but relatively simple, example of this technique. Following a brief acoustic guitar intro, the meter combines a group of five eighth notes and a group of seven eighth notes, each preceded by a quick ascending arpeggio. Listen carefully to this section until you can hear the pattern. After you have internalized this pattern, notice that, as the vocals sustain the word "communication" (approximately 1:20 into the piece), the metrical pattern shifts ever so slightly. At this point, the meter alternates a group of *six* eighth notes with the same group of seven eighth notes as before. The original meter returns when the vocals return with "I know the pieces fit. . . ." Soundgarden's "Mailman" provides another example of changing meters. Listen to the introduction and first verse of this song and notice that there is a consistent sequence of the following metrical groupings: 8 beats + 8 beats + 7 beats + 6 beats. Yet another example of changing meter can be heard in Marilyn Manson's "Get Your Gunn" (from the *Portrait of an American Family* album). This song alternates between sextuple meter (six beats per measure) in the verse and octuple meter (eight beats per measure) in the chorus.

As an example of a particularly complex metrical structure within a heavy metal context, we will closely examine an excerpt from Tool's "The Grudge" (the opening track on *Lateralus*). The piece opens with a highly syncopated set of interlocking rhythms that, though complex, fit within a "common time" context (quadruple meter with duple subdivision). Approximately one minute into the piece, the lead voice enters, followed by guitar power chords emphasizing every beat. When the musical texture thins abruptly (1:20), the meter changes to quintuple meter, leaving an electric guitar performing a repeating ostinato pattern. The normal grouping of subdivisions in quintuple meter would be 2 + 2 + 2 + 2 + 2. However, with the lyrics "Clutch it like a cornerstone ..." (1:45), the grouping of subdivisions becomes an asymmetrical 3 + 3 + 4. At the lyrics "Saturn ascends ..." (2:10), the meter reverts to the more normal 2 + 2 + 2 + 2 + 2, which remains constant through several changes in the musical texture until the next verse arrives (2:40). At that point the meter reverts to the 3 + 3 + 4 asymmetrical pattern. As this song alternates between a normal grouping of subdivisions (2 + 2 + 2 + 2 + 2) and an asymmetrical grouping (3 + 3 + 4), what we experience is really a shift in accent, since both patterns occupy the space of five beats (10 subdivisions).

It can be enlightening indeed to explore some of the more progressive forms of heavy metal and its various musical progeny. The creative manipulation of rhythmic structure is often an important reason why some songs sound fresh and interesting while others seem mundane and boring.

# 16

# Dance Music

## OVERVIEW: THE SELLING OF ROCK—CHANGES IN THE 1980S AND 1990S

### The Music Video

In January of 2004, the author asked some 80 students in a class on the history of rock to name the five most important current rock music acts. The resulting list suggested 208 different names. Only four names received more than ten votes—Dave Matthews Band, Radiohead, Outkast, and Pearl Jam. This admittedly unscientific survey suggests that the fragmentation of the 1970s continued unabated into the 1980s and beyond (e.g., suggested names included such widely diverse acts as Metallica, Phish, Eminem, Coldplay, and Weezer).

In spite of this bewildering fragmentation of the market, the music industry continued to develop new and more sophisticated ways of delivering and promoting its product. During the 1980s, there were several new developments that transformed the music industry. The first and most important of these was the music video. As we have previously noted, the recording industry and the radio industry have been partners in the promotion of rock music since the mid-1950s. Generally, television was not a major factor in the development of rock. To be sure, there were the appearances by Presley, Lewis, the Beatles, the Stones, and others on variety shows such as Ed Sullivan's and Steve Allen's. And, of course, there were shows like *American Bandstand, Hullabaloo, Malibu U.,* and *Shindig,* which promoted various rock, pop, and folk styles. In the 1960s and 1970s, some variety shows and series featured such performers as the Smothers Brothers, the Monkees, Donny and Marie Osmond, and Sonny and Cher. In England, rock-oriented television shows were more common than they were in the United States.

But in spite of such occasional associations between television and the rock industry, it was radio that was the primary purveyor of rock and roll in all of its forms. But with the coming of cable television in the late 1970s and early 1980s, there was an opportunity for a wide spectrum of specialized television formats: all-news stations, all-weather stations, Christian-oriented stations, all-movie stations, and so on. Why not an all-rock music station? Warner's Nickelodeon channel had experimented with a show called *Popclips,* which featured a "veejay" (video jockey) running a series of music videos—video presentations of pop and rock songs as performed by the original artists. The idea of visual presentations of rock songs was not new (recall the Beatles' promotional film for "All You Need Is Love"—followed shortly by the Stones' "We Love You"). But with the increasing popularity of videotape technology, the idea of transferring the Top 40 radio format to television was inevitable. Thus, on August 1, 1981, an all-rock television channel debuted. Music Television—MTV—was allotted $20 million in start-up costs by its corporate parent, Warner Amex Satellite Entertainment Company. Just as record companies had long provided promotional discs to radio stations for airplay, so they now provided their rock videos to MTV at no cost. The promotional value to the record company and artist was tremendous. Using personable veejays, MTV mimicked the successful radio format of chatter and play, augmented by interviews and news of tours (and, of course, the inevitable contests).

Artists and companies scrambled to create imaginative and technically innovative videos to go along with new releases. That the video often had little to do with the lyrics seemed to be only a minor concern. Video added a new weapon to the arsenal of the record companies in their continuing battle to promote artists and records. Now, if the video itself had enough appeal, it alone could propel a song to popularity. Some bands owed their success largely to the video format (e.g., Duran Duran).

Naturally, the MTV idea spread. Soon, WTBS in Atlanta, another cable station, produced *Night Tracks*—six hours of videos on weekend nights; the USA Network launched *Night Flight* in 1990; and even NBC ran their *Friday Night Videos.* In the early 1980s, rock videos, and MTV specifically, were the hottest new thing in rock. Other music-only cable stations (e.g., Country Music Television, the Nashville Network, Black Entertainment Television, the pay-per-view The Box, and VH-1, the sister channel launched by MTV in 1985 to appeal to an older audience) have challenged MTV's music video monopoly. Even the major networks, vying for the teen market, have programmed music video offerings into weekend late-night time slots. Music video channels have changed, chameleon-like, since their inception to reflect the most recent musical trends, giving each new musical direction and its associated artists an opportunity to be seen by a national audience. Some succeeded in taking advantage of this opportunity (Ice Cube, Nirvana, and Mariah Carey), while others faded away almost as fast as they appeared.

But MTV had its detractors. One complaint was that the network emphasized white rock almost to the exclusion of black rock. This was undoubtedly the result of marketing studies that indicated that cable owners tended to be mostly middle- to upper-class urban whites. So MTV designed its programming to hit its primary audience. But when Michael Jackson became a superstar, appealing to almost every demographic segment of the population, MTV yielded to the pressures of the marketplace and belatedly ran not only Jackson's videos but other black artists' videos as well.

Another criticism of MTV (and music videos in general) had to do with the frequent emphasis on sex and violence. A fascinating study by Barry L. Sherman and Joseph R. Dominick, entitled "Violence and Sex in Music Videos: TV and Rock and Roll," was published in the *Journal of Communication* (winter 1986). Their scientifically validated study noted that about 56.6 percent of the rock videos contained examples of violent acts; they also reported that about 75.9 percent included representations of sexual activities. To be sure, the examples ranged from the most innocent to rather extreme. Such observations may be alarming but should hardly be surprising. After all, the television (and movie) industry discovered many years ago that sex and violence sell. Thus, it seems inevitable that rock videos would follow this time-proven—if questionable—formula for success.

Yet another problem with the new emphasis on music videos stemmed from the fact that *seeing* music in addition to *hearing* it resulted in an overemphasis on the image of rock artists, sometimes at the expense of musical integrity. During the late 1980s, for example, the pop charts were often dominated by pretty faces and well-shaped bodies, rather than innovative musical talents. Compare the sound of Paula Abdul and Janet Jackson (examples of the former) to recordings by Aretha Franklin and Luther Vandross (examples of the latter). The culmination of this tendency was realized late in 1989 with revelations concerning Milli Vanilli, whose *Girl You Know It's True* album won the 1989 Grammy Award for Best New Artist. Rob Pilatus (an out-of-work dancer and model) met Fabrice Morvan (a gymnast) in a Los Angeles disco. After an unsuccessful attempt at stardom, the two singers accepted a proposal from Frankie Farian, a producer at his own studio in Munich. For $4,000 each, plus royalties, Pilatus and Morvan, sporting dreadlocks and clothing that revealed their well-defined musculature, lip-synched to vocal tracks sung by Charles Shaw, a U.S. Army veteran (Romanowski and George-Warren 1995). Once the reality of this artistic deception came to the public's attention, and after both Pilatus and Farian confirmed the truth of these rumors, an embarrassed Grammy committee rescinded the band's award. Lawsuits were filed against Arista Records and various concert promoters, resulting in a settlement that granted purchasers of the recording a rebate of up to three dollars. Over 80,000 claims were filed in response. In 1991, Farian released a recording by the real Milli Vanilli that bombed, lacking the visual excitement generated by Pilatus and Morvan. Rob and Fab, without the musical direction of Farian, released their own self-titled recording in 1993, also failing to attract any significant attention.

The use of lip-synching and ghost artists is not unique to Milli Vanilli. As mentioned in Chapter 6, "The Beatles," Ringo Starr was replaced by a studio drummer on early Beatles recordings (e.g., "Love Me Do" and "P.S. I Love You"). Members of The Monkees sang but did not play any instruments on their early recordings, leaving this task to various studio musicians. The Monkees eventually learned to play instruments well enough to perform their songs in live concerts. More recent acts such as Technotronics and C+C Music Factory have hired models to lip-synch to vocals supplied by less attractive singers (DeCurtis and Henke 1992). The line of demarcation between such enhancement and outright fraud became decidedly blurred during the 1990s.

Major artists performing on international tours were forced to compete with their finely crafted music videos. Because of the physical impossibility of simultaneously performing the complex choreography, exaggerated theatrics, and vocal parts, many of these artists resorted to lip-synching at least portions of their live performance to ensure the perfection expected by the MTV generation. Spontaneity, one of the cornerstones of early rock and roll, was thus cast aside in an effort to please an audience expecting a perfectly executed, visceral, multimedia experience.

Beginning in the mid-1980s, MTV began programming more than just music videos. Attempting to appeal to a larger audience, programming included a game show (*Remote Control*), animated adventures (e.g., *Beavis & Butthead* and *Ren & Stimpy*), *MTV News*, and political coverage (*Choose or Lose*). By 2004, it was sometimes difficult to find music playing on MTV—a fact lamented in Bowling for Soup's nostalgic hit single "1985" (2004). In addition to providing nonmusic programming, MTV expanded beyond merely presenting current musical trends. At times, it became actively involved in influencing the direction of musical evolution. In the late 1980s, *Yo! MTV Raps* played an influential role in the popularization of rap music. MTV then began sponsoring a series of *Unplugged* concerts: performances in which various rock artists disconnected themselves from their powerful amplifiers and electronic instruments to perform, in most cases, entirely on acoustic instruments. Performers included rock-and-roll mainstays like Eric Clapton, Paul McCartney, Sting, Bruce Springsteen, Rod Stewart, Bob Dylan, the Eagles, and Aerosmith, as well as relatively new artists such as Mariah Carey, Nirvana, Hootie and the Blowfish, Alice in Chains, Babyface, Alanis Morissette, Jay-Z, Shakira, and Staind. These performances allowed the audience to hear alternate versions of familiar songs, focusing on the craftsmanship or lack thereof evidenced by the artists' songwriting talent.

Network television also jumped on the proverbial bandwagon, scheduling programs that documented the creation of musical groups, awarding recording contracts and concert tours to the winners. On March 24, 2000, *Making the Band* premiered on ABC. According to the Pazsaz Entertainment Network, the show was "a real-life drama that documents the journey of young bandsmen from their selection in a cross-country talent search to their rise to pop stardom." The self-titled debut album released by O-Town, the band created in the process, was certified platinum in 2001 and contained the hit single "Liquid Dreams" (number 10). For its third season, *Making the Band* moved to MTV. The WB Network responded with *Popstars,* a similarly formatted talent search. The first installment resulted in the creation of a five-member girl group, Eden's Crush, and a debut album titled, not surprisingly, *Popstars* that contained the hit single "Get Over Yourself" (number 8). VH1 also participated in this movement, introducing *Bands on the Run,* a more typical "battle of the bands" type of competition. Each band was given a band van and the opportunity to tour eleven American cities, promoting and playing thirteen shows over an eight-week period. Setting their own ticket and merchandise prices, the goal was to make the most money on the tour. The grand prize consisted of $50,000 in cash, $100,000 in music gear, a video to be placed in heavy rotation on—you guessed it—VH1, and a showcase performance for "A&R heads of major record labels." Flickerstick, a Dallas rock quintet and winners of the competition, found themselves the subject of a bidding war among several major labels. Epic Records signed the band and released a remixed version of their recording *Welcoming Home the Astronauts,* containing the single "Beautiful" (number 25 on the Modern Rock chart).

The process of putting talented individuals together was, of course, nothing new. Examples date back to the girl groups of the 1960s and the formation of The Monkees for television. What was new, however, was the undeniable truth that there was serious money to be made out of making the process of artist selection, image transformation, and developing every aspect of the act into a public spectacle.

## The Compact Disc

Several other developments in the 1980s should be mentioned. Whereas the seven-inch single was the primary medium of rock and roll in the 1950s, the twelve-inch LP album became the dominant medium in the 1960s. Throughout the 1970s, cassette tapes gained in popularity. At first, cassettes were quite unsatisfactory. Sound quality was inferior, and there were frequent mechanical problems. By the end of the 1970s, however, these technical problems had been solved. Cassette tapes of the early 1980s produced a high-quality sound, and the players were every bit as sophisticated as the older reel-to-reel models. By 1983, roughly 50 percent of the total profits from recorded music (some $3.78 billion) came from cassette sales; in 1984, cassette sales surpassed album sales for the first time in history (Ward, Stokes, and Tucker 1986, 596). The trend continued steadily until 1991, when the industry noted the first decline in cassette shipments—from 442 million in 1990 to 360 million in 1991 (down about 18.6 percent).

The decline in cassette sales was related to the growing popularity of compact discs. These small discs not only last longer than any other previous recorded format, but produce a superior sound. By 1991, the industry was shipping over 333 million CDs (up more than 16 percent over 1990). Although this is less than the number of cassettes shipped, the trend was clear: CDs were going up and cassettes were going down. The industry was quite pleased with this trend because CDs cost about three dollars to manufacture (about the same as LPs and cassettes), but the retail price for a CD normally ran between thirteen and seventeen dollars, whereas cassettes retailed for about nine to ten dollars. Speaking of LPs, by the early 1990s they had practically disappeared from the scene. The decline of the LP was dramatic: from 295 million units shipped in 1981 to just under five million in 1991—a decline of over 98 percent. Meanwhile, the shipments of CDs rose from about 800,000 in 1983 to 333 million in 1991. The newest audio medium, DAT (digital audio tape) in a minicassette format, may be the next major trend; however, as of this writing, DATs have been slow to gain a mass audience, perhaps because many listeners have invested in CD players and CD libraries. Nevertheless, the recording industry can hardly complain. In the four years from 1985 through 1988, recorded music sales rose from $4.4 billion to $6.2 billion.

Other developments in the 1980s included the small portable cassette players (often with built-in AM and FM bands). The Sony Walkman™ and similar products became omnipresent. Now the music fanatic could hook the player onto a belt, slap on lightweight headphones, and have music almost anywhere all the time. The larger "boom boxes" or "ghetto blasters" were less favored because of their physical cumbersomeness. But they had the advantage of having speakers, whereas the Walkman types required headphone listening. By the 1990s, the Discman™, the CD parallel to the Walkman, had become equally popular.

## Rock Music Soundtracks

Continuing a trend that began in the mid-1950s, another form of media, the movie soundtrack, has provided a means for record companies and the motion picture industry to advertise their respective products, resulting in a system that is highly profitable to both. The bicycle-riding montage to the accompaniment of "Rain-drops Keep Fallin' on My Head" (number 1 in 1969), inserted into *Butch Cassidy and the Sundance Kid*, provides one of the first examples of a segment of film that was included solely for the purpose of marketing a hit song. Since that time, hit singles have figured prominently in the filmmaking process. Between 1956 and 1958, soundtrack albums for *The King & I*, *Around the World in 80 Days*, *South Pacific*, and *Gigi* all reached the top of the pop album chart. Original cast recordings of Broadway musicals and soundtrack albums for Elvis Presley's and the Beatles' successful films also proved extremely popular. From 1962 to 1963, Leonard Bernstein and Stephen Sondheim's soundtrack from *West Side Story* held the number 1 position on the album chart for 54 weeks, setting a record that still stands.

In most of these cases, the music on the recordings was taken from scenes in the film when the entire cast broke out in song. During these portions of the film, the audience was expected to suspend their belief to an even greater degree than demanded in the typical motion picture experience. This diegetic—or source—music was assumed to be audible to all characters on the screen (Gorbman 1987). At other times, however, music is used for the purpose of setting a mood to highlight the drama of the action taking place. This nondiegetic—or background—music is presumed not to be heard by the characters in the motion picture, but serves to enhance the psychological drama for the audience. Throughout film history, this latter role has most often been fulfilled by hiring a composer to create an appropriate musical score specifically for the given motion picture. In recent film releases, how-ever, it has become commonplace to incorporate preexisting hit singles into the soundtrack. In the context of the motion picture, these songs may be used nondiegetically to set the mood for a scene by appropriately matching the musical style and lyrics of the music to the visual images. It also is possible that music from the soundtrack will be heard by characters in the drama as it emanates from a car radio, blares from the open doors of a nightclub, or plays softly from a bedside radio. In either case, members of the audience who like the music heard in the pro-duction are likely to purchase the soundtrack recording. Looked at from another perspective, individuals who hear a soundtrack recording packed with hit singles will certainly be influenced to attend the film. This kind of mutual promotion has signifi-cantly enhanced profits for both record and film companies.

Popular music soundtracks have been incorporated for a variety of purposes. Music from the past can serve to authenticate the era in which a film is set (*American Graffiti*, 1973; *Wayne's World*, 1992; *Dazed and Confused*, 1993), or to lend a sense of nos-talgia (*The Big Chill*, 1983; *Stand By Me*, 1986). High-energy dance music can bolster cinematic dramas in which dancing itself plays a prominent role (*Flashdance*, 1983; *Footloose*, 1984; *Dirty Dancing*, 1987). Some films incorporate both pop songs and an orchestral score, allowing each musical style to perform the role for which it is most appropriate. *Batman* (1989) provides a good example of this combination, incorporat-ing pop songs by Prince and an orchestral score by Danny Elfman, former member of the progressive rock band Oingo Boingo. One of the most interesting popular music soundtracks in recent years is the various artist collection for *O Brother, Where Art Thou?*. This compilation recording, a surprise Grammy winner for Album of the Year in 2002, contains tracks performed by a variety of artists, including the Stanley Brothers, The Soggy Bottom Boys, and many others.

Perhaps the most obvious manner in which rock music can be incorporated into a soundtrack is to produce a film that chronicles the development of a musical group. Fictional accounts of such bands have proven highly successful with theater audiences (*The Commitments*, 1991; *That Thing You Do*, 1996). In addition, there have been films that attempt to provide at least a quasi-biographical account of real rock-and-roll performers from the past. *La Bamba* (1987), chronicling the life of Latino rocker Richie Valens; the Jerry Lee Lewis feature film *Great Balls of Fire* (1989); and *The Doors* (1991), Oliver Stone's interpretation of the career of Jim Morrison, provide good examples of such films. Given both the record sales and box office success resulting from the association of pop music and the cinema, rock music will certainly continue to be an integral part of the motion picture experience for years to come.

## THE RETURN OF DANCE MUSIC

In the early days of rock, it was just assumed that every song was intended for dancing. Whether it was "Blueberry Hill" or "Great Balls of Fire," people were supposed to dance to rock and roll. This assumption reached a peak in the early 1960s with the dance craze (represented most dramatically by "The Twist"). However, as the 1960s progressed, there were styles that were designed for listening, not dancing. Certainly this was true of the folk music trend. As the music of the Beatles became more experimental—especially with changing meters—dancing became almost impossible. Most of the music of the jazz-rock/fusion and art-rock/progressive rock styles of the late 1960s and 1970s was not intended for dancing.

This is not to say that dancing went away. Motown provided a steady diet of music that emphasized dancing. And there was certainly plenty of other music to dance to in both the 1960s and 1970s. But after the dance craze faded in the mid-1960s, it wasn't until the mid-1970s that a style developed again specifically for dancing. To trace the evolution of disco, we need to go to Philadelphia.

### The Philadelphia Sound

As we have seen earlier, Motown's power receded in the 1970s. Stevie Wonder and Diana Ross were the company's greatest strengths. But as so many others left (e.g., Gladys Knight, the Jackson Five, the Four Tops, and the Miracles), Motown found it difficult to compete in a fragmented rock industry that varied from psychedelic soul to heavy metal to glitter rock. In the early 1970s, a new black-owned company appeared that gave Motown considerable competition. Producer–songwriters Kenneth Gamble and Leon Huff formed Philadelphia International Records and, for a while at least, appeared to have created another Motown. Gamble, Huff, and partner-to-be Thom Bell were experts at providing lush orchestrations for their black vocal groups. In 1972, they produced a major hit with "Back Stabbers," by a quintet from Canton, Ohio, known as the O'Jays, followed by their number 1 hit "Love Train" (1973).

Part of the so-called "Philadelphia sound" was due to the consistently strong backing of a group of studio musicians known as MFSB (Mother, Father, Sister, Brother). In addition to providing the recognizable backing for most of Philadelphia International's vocal acts, MFSB had a major hit of their own with "TSOP (The Sound of Philadelphia)"; it moved to number 1 in 1974 and became the theme song for the popular black-oriented music and dance television show *Soul Train*.

By 1975, Philadelphia International (PI) was grossing over $25 million per year and was second only to Motown among black-owned record companies. But the young company soon encountered rough waters. Gamble and Huff were indicted on payola charges (Huff was eventually cleared and Gamble was assessed a $2,500 fine). Gamble's personal problems, combined with desertions by key staff members and some artists, greatly reduced PI's dreams of Motown-like success. By the late 1970s, PI's influence was greatly reduced; however, the style of Gamble and Huff's music is often cited as a precursor of one of the 1970s most popular trends: disco.

## DISCO

The term *disco* was originally a shortened form of the word *discotheque*—a type of dance hall that had begun in France in the early 1960s. Cabaret owners found it far more economical to hire one disc jockey to spin records than to hire a live band; also, a variety of music could be played, some of which was bound to please every customer's taste. During the 1960s, the discotheque concept was adopted in the United States, at first in the form of "underground" clubs. However, the concept caught on, and soon discotheques catering to all segments of society were flourishing all over the country. With the coming of the San Francisco–style concert halls, with their live bands, discos faded out somewhat in the late 1960s and very early 1970s. Soon, however, they reemerged, featuring music that was specifically designed for dancing—a style that became known, naturally enough, as disco music.

The 1970s discos offered a disc jockey armed with two turntables so that he or she could move smoothly from record to record; thus, "the beat never stopped." Adding to this sound environment were an array of pulsing colored lights and flashing strobe lights. The disco music was formatted into twelve-inch discs with one song per side. In the early 1970s, discos played pop and rock music, but they increasingly leaned toward the danceable black sound of Philadelphia International and similar styles. The music of the O'Jays, the Spinners, the Stylistics, the Temptations, Stevie Wonder, and Marvin Gaye was the typical fare of the early 1970s discos.

By early 1974, several artists released records specifically designed for the new disco scene. The Hues Corporation's "Rock the Boat" and George McCrae's "Rock Your Baby" both reached number 1 in 1974. "Rock Your Baby" was written and produced by two engineers at TK Studios in Hialeah, Florida: Harry Wayne Casey and Richard Finch. Soon forming their own nine-member band, Casey and Finch released more disco songs under the name KC and the Sunshine Band. They scored four number 1 hits in the three years from 1975 through 1977. KC's music featured a simple but insistent rhythm track that never varied from the first measure to the last. The vocal line typically consisted of short unison phrases more in the nature of repeating patterns than a true melody in the traditional sense. Lyrics were simple and repetitive to the point of absurdity (e.g., "Wrap Your Arms Around Me" repeats the title twenty-nine times in its three minutes and forty-seven seconds—or once every seven seconds). A horn line was also simple and repetitive and was used to punctuate the vocal line. The rhythm was the all-important point (a solid 4 beats per bar), and all else was subservient to it.

In 1975, the disco style exploded on the national scene. Led by Studio 54 in New York City, discotheques opened everywhere—either glitzy new constructions or rejuvenated old clubs, barns, or ballrooms. Some reports estimate that there were 10,000 discos in North America at the height of the disco craze, with some 200 to 300 in New York City alone.

One of the biggest disco hits of 1975 was "The Hustle" by Van McCoy. With its gentle sound, infectious beat, flute lead, and attractive string countermelody, "The Hustle" was a cut above the average disco song. Hitting the number 1 spot in the summer of 1975, the song spawned variants such as the California hustle, the Latin hustle, the American hustle, the New York hustle, and the tango hustle (shades of the twist). Coupled with the success of KC, Shirley and Company, the Hues Corporation, George McCrae, and others, disco became The Thing even for pop artists such as pianist Peter Nero, jazz flutist Herbie Mann, trumpeter Doc Severinsen, and pop orchestra leader Percy Faith.

## Donna Summer

The next year, 1976, saw the first impact of one of disco's premier artists, Donna Summer. Born LaDonna Gaines in 1948 in Boston, Summer's talent was far from evident in her first hit, "Love to Love You Baby" (number 2 in early 1976). The song featured Summer's breathy vocal enriched by her moaning, groaning, and otherwise emoting the title over and over. Originally a four-minute song, "Love to Love You Baby" was increased to a nearly seventeen-minute version for disco play. Too long for the standard seven-inch single, it was released to the record stores on a twelve-inch disc like the ones used by discotheque disc jockeys. The twelve-inch single soon became a common medium for commercial disco releases and, for that matter, was still around in the late 1990s.

With "Last Dance" (number 3 in 1978) Summer hit upon the style that would make her more than a panting, groaning disco queen. The song begins with a slow balladlike section that builds tension in the listener, who of course knows that "the beat" is coming any minute. Summer reveals a solid, full

American pop singer Donna Summer on stage in New York. (*Source:* Images, Robin Platzer / Getty Images. Inc.,)

voice capable of more than terse come-ons and breathy double entendres. Once this style was established, Summer recorded a series of hits that were legitimate soft rock songs that also happened to be based upon the familiar disco beat. One of her best, "MacArthur Park," became her first number 1 song; between 1976 and 1980, she released ten Top 10 songs, including three number 1s.

### *Saturday Night Fever* and the Bee Gees

If 1975 was the year disco became a national phenomenon, 1977 was the year it became an international rage. Perhaps the most influential factor in this augmentation of disco's popularity was the extremely popular film *Saturday Night Fever*, starring John Travolta. The film's story line concerns a young working-class New York man who becomes a prizewinning disco dancer. The sound track album became a true blockbuster, selling over twenty-five million copies and becoming the biggest selling sound track album of all time. It held the number 1 position for twenty-four weeks (only five albums of any kind have held that position longer). The album included songs by several artists we have already mentioned—KC and the Sunshine Band, MFSB, and Yvonne Elliman. In addition, there was a disco setting by Walter Murphy of the first movement of Beethoven's Symphony No. 5. The number 1 song, "A Fifth of Beethoven," illustrates the fact that virtually any previously composed music could be "discofied" simply by borrowing the melody and harmony and setting it on top of a disco beat and bass line.

There is no doubt that the big winners from *Saturday Night Fever* were the Bee Gees. However, Barry, Maurice, and Robin Gibb were anything but newcomers to the scene in 1977. Born on the Isle of Man, England, in 1946 (Barry) and 1949 (twins Maurice and Robin), the Gibb brothers began singing together as children in Manchester. First hitting the charts in 1967 with "New York Mining Disaster 1941," they produced a series of hits through 1969. The trio almost dissolved at the turn of the decade but soon reunited to produce the number 3 song, "Lonely Days," and their first number 1 song, "How Do You Mend a Broken Heart?"

The years 1973 and 1974 were difficult ones for the Bee Gees; they had no hit singles for the first time since 1967, and their albums fared poorly. But just as it appeared that they would fade as so many others had before them, the new disco style offered salvation. The 1975 album *Main Course* hit the Top 20 and contained the number 1 song "Jive Talkin'." After two more successful albums, plus a live album and greatest hits album (and another half-dozen single hits), the Bee Gees were established as honest-to-goodness disco superstars.

But it was *Saturday Night Fever* that turned the Bee Gees into a household name and led to the inevitable "next Beatles" suggestions. Most of the film's music was written by the brothers; they sang six songs on the double album, three of which became number 1 songs in 1977–78 ("How Deep Is Your Love?," "Stayin' Alive," and "Night Fever"). They followed with three more number 1 songs in 1978–79, making an impressive string of six consecutive number 1s. Following *Saturday Night Fever*, the Bee Gees produced two more number 1 albums. But as the disco mania faded in the early 1980s, so did the Bee Gees, who had become typed as a disco act. In the 1990s, however, the group enjoyed a renaissance, although more so in the United Kingdom and Germany than in the United States.

The Bee Gees (*Source:* Getty Images. Inc.)

Among the other groups that found success in the late 1970s disco surge were Kool and the Gang, the Village People, Tavares, and Chic. By 1980, disco had been adopted by jet-set, upper-class society, and thus became the target of intense ridicule by the rock community. After all, there had been disco songs by Ethel Merman, the Boston Pops Orchestra, and Barbra Streisand; there was even a Mickey Mouse Disco album. It seemed as though everyone had a disco song or album—even Rod Stewart and Elton John. Although one could still go to affluent metropolitan clubs and hear a steady diet of 1980s-style synthesizer-oriented disco (called "techno-dance"), the basic style died an unmourned death around 1980. In the rock establishment, disco became an even more reviled and derided style than soft rock. Nevertheless, in the period from 1975 to 1980, it was an extremely potent force in the music industry.

## MOTOWN KEEPS DANCING

### Michael Jackson

Occasionally we hear of "bubble babies": babies who must stay in an enclosed, sterile environment in order to grow. Michael Jackson's "bubble" was show biz—the stage. Growing up in his insulated world of theaters, studios, microphones, and lights, Michael never learned "the streets" that so many other black performers knew. The Apollo Theater, the Motown and Epic studios—these were his elementary, middle, and high schools. In an industry of ultraworldly people, Michael is a study in almost incredible naïveté.

Jackson's stage image was just the opposite. He appeared to be the singing, dancing, jiving extrovert who was the ultimate example of black funk. Michael Joe Jackson was born in Gary, Indiana, in 1958. The musical Jackson family was headed by
Joe Jackson, who saw to it that his six sons and three daughters knew music. The
three oldest boys—Jackie, Tito, and Jermaine—formed a high school group that
soon expanded with the addition of younger brothers Marlon and Michael. After
several auditions, the group finally impressed Berry Gordy, who later recalled that
he liked their tight vocals and polished performance style.

The Jackson Five's first three albums reached the Top 5 and yielded four consecutive number 1 hits and one number 2 hit, all in slightly over a year (1970). The next
nine Motown albums (through 1976) were not quite as spectacular but nevertheless
yielded ten more Top 40 hits. The natural musicianship of Michael Jackson dominates these recordings. His prepubescent voice was unmistakable (and not easily
duplicated by would-be copycat groups). The songs, arrangements, and production
continued the natural evolution of the Motown sound of the 1960s with little fundamental change.

Young Michael eagerly absorbed all that went on in his (limited) environment. He
noticed that many ex-Motowners struggled when they found themselves out in "the
world" without the company to train, produce, and promote them. So he watched
and listened and absorbed the details of the entire process. When the time came to
leave the nest, he would be ready.

That time came in 1976. All but Jermaine switched to the Columbia-affiliated
Epic Records. The loss of the Jackson Five did not delight Gordy. Motown sued
Columbia for $20 million, but eventually settled for $600,000 and rights to the
group's name.

The Jackson Five (*Source:* Michael Ochs Archive, Ltd.)

And so they became the Jacksons and added younger brother Randy and sisters LaToya and Maureen. Their four studio albums for Epic in the period from 1976 to 1980 sold unevenly. The first two, dominated by Gamble and Huff's "Philadelphia Sound," were unsuccessful, but the last two, *Destiny* and *Triumph,* placed at number 11 and number 10, respectively.

Michael Jackson's solo career has been fabulously successful, flamboyant, and controversial. Perhaps the high point was *Thriller,* Michael's megamonster album of 1982–83. The list of this record's staggering accomplishments recalls similar lists often compiled regarding Presley and the Beatles: over 40 million copies sold (so far); held the number 1 position for thirty-seven weeks (second only to the sound track album from *West Side Story*); yielded seven Top 10 hits, including two number 1s; *The Making of Michael Jackson's "Thriller,"* an hour-long home videocassette, sold over 350,000 copies within six months of its release; and so on. Forever searching for the next Presley or Beatles, the public hastily nominated Jackson as the superstar of the 1980s.

Michael's first important solo album had come in 1979. *Off the Wall,* produced by Quincy Jones, sold over seven million copies and produced four Top 10 songs, including two number 1 hits. The album revealed Michael's versatility as he moved from fast dance-oriented songs to softer ballads. As big an album as *Off the Wall* was (it eventually peaked at number 3), Michael continued to work within the Jacksons. Their album, *Triumph* (1980), was reasonably successful, rising to number 10 by the end of the year.

Even as the Jacksons' promotional tour for *Triumph* ended, Michael and Quincy Jones began planning the follow-up album to *Off the Wall.* The resulting *Thriller* album was released in 1982. The first single hit from the album (reaching number 2 on the charts) was "The Girl Is Mine," which featured Jackson and Paul McCartney.

As 1983 began, a second song from *Thriller,* "Billie Jean," began moving up the charts, reaching number 1 by early March. Michael created the basic rhythm on a drum machine (it was "punched up" by a live drummer). The persistent bass line was added next, creating the interesting chug-chug sound of the song. Michael did the vocal line in one take. The lyrics were heavier than had been typical of previous Jackson songs; they concerned paternity charges resulting from an illicit love affair. The infectious beat, the menacing tone of the vocal and instrumental lines, and the effective video combined to make "Billie Jean" a whopping success.

Following "Billie Jean" up the charts was "Beat It," Michael's updating of the gang dance/rumble scenes from Bernstein's *West Side Story.* The bass and guitar riff from "Beat It" became instantly recognizable; the hard, macho vocal (macho for high-voiced Michael, at least) was appealing, as was the neo-*West Side Story* video. Adding to the unusually hard edge was Eddie Van Halen's guitar solo. By the time "Beat It" ended its three-week stay at number 1, it was becoming clear that *Thriller* was going to be a big album.

On May 16, 1983, NBC aired a two-hour salute to Motown's twenty-fifth anniversary. The show consisted primarily of old film clips, monologues, and updated performances by old Motown favorites. Although much of this nostalgia-oriented show looked backward, one exciting moment was utterly up to date and provided a glimpse of the future. After the Jacksons had run through some earlier hits, Michael took the stage as a solo act (sequined white glove and all). After a few remarks, he launched into "Billie Jean." Gracefully moving through his dance steps, heavily oriented to the break-dancing style, complete with the smooth, backward "moonwalk," Michael clearly established himself in the nation's consciousness as a solo act, distinct from the old Jackson Five. His appeal cut across the demographic lines, reaching the young, their parents, male and female, black and white. He was the superstar of the early 1980s.

By the end of 1983, three more *Thriller* singles had made the Top 10. Early in 1984 the title song made its appearance on the charts, eventually rising to number 4. The song's video was trendsetting; it was a minifilm directed by feature film director John Landis. With elaborate staging, sophisticated visual effects, state-of-the-art theatrical makeup, a miniplot, and lots of Jackson-style dancing, the "Thriller" video established an entire new level for music videos. The song itself had all of the hooks: a uniquely recognizable bass riff, a catchy beat (with strong backbeat), a strong vocal, superior production, and even the eerie voice of horror film star Vincent Price in a closing "rap." In more ways than one, it was a monster.

The much-heralded "Victory Tour" (for the Jacksons' *Victory* album of 1984) fell short of expectations. Ticket prices were high, and people wanted Michael—not the Jacksons. "Michaelmania" had run at fever pitch from late 1982 through 1984. But with no releases in 1985 or 1986, Michael's detractors—of whom there were many—happily pronounced him to be another certified fad. To their chagrin, Michael's new album, *Bad*, was released in 1987 and became another monster hit. It debuted at the number 1 position and stayed there for six weeks. Granted, these numbers pale in comparison to *Thriller*, but so does almost every other album in history (*Thriller* was eventually surpassed as the best-selling album of all time by *The Eagles' Greatest Hits 1971–1975*).

*Bad* is a strong album, producing seven hit singles (including five number 1 hits—the most ever drawn from one album). Produced by master producer Quincy Jones,

*Bad* shows Michael's continued strength in the style of "Beat It" and "Billy Jean." Indeed, most of the songs on *Bad* follow the general style of those earlier hits. An interesting exception is "I Just Can't Stop Loving You," a soft rock ballad sung with female vocalist Siedah Garrett. It is a beautifully written song with a well-shaped melody and appropriate harmonies. Michael's and Siedah's voices are so well-matched that one must pay very close attention to know who is singing at any given moment. It is also interesting to note a general similarity between the first two melodic phrases of this song and the opening phrases of "Home," the final song of the musical *The Wiz*. In the

Michael Jackson performing at Madison Square Garden (*Source:* Hollis / Retna Ltd. USA)

movie version of this musical, this powerful song was performed by none other than Michael's idol, Diana Ross.

Although Michael Jackson did not prove to be the next Presley or Beatles, the rumors of his professional death proved to be "greatly exaggerated." In 1991, he signed a one billion dollar multimedia contract with Sony. Although Michael's recordings fared moderately well at best through the 1990s, he remained a pop icon. He was married several times (including for two years to Lisa Marie Presley), endured several costly court battles, and established an admirable reputation as a philanthropist. Unfortunately, beginning in the 1990s and continuing into the new century, Michael has been repeatedly accused of inappropriate behavior with children—a charge he vehemently denies. The impact of these allegations, however, has been significant. Though his recordings continue to sell impressively—*Invincible* (2002) sold over two million copies—the commercial success of his later albums falls far short of his recordings made during the 1970s and 1980s.

### The Commodores

Motown's other big success of the 1970s was the Commodores. The six members of this group met as students at Alabama's Tuskegee Institute; in 1971, they signed with Motown. Originally designed in the Motown tradition of the Temptations, Four Tops, and so on, the Commodores capitalized on the disco trend and made their impact as one of the more lasting of the disco groups. Their peak years were 1976 through 1981, during which time they enjoyed five Top 10 albums and nine Top 10 singles, including number 1 hits "Three Times a Lady" (1978) and "Still" (1979). By 1982, lead singer Lionel Richie had departed to pursue his successful solo career (see Chapter 14). The Commodores eventually regrouped and had moderate success with *Commodores 13* in 1983 and *Nightshift* in 1985.

## OTHER MUSIC FOR DANCING

Among the new stars in the 1980s was a flamboyant new female singer named Cyndy Lauper. Affecting a punk–new wave look (complete with colored hair), she hit hard with her debut album *She's So Unusual* (number 4 in late 1983 too early 1984). In fact, Lauper's first album is the only debut album in history to yield four Top 5 singles. In spite of her punkish image, Lauper stayed in the rock mainstream (the gentler side of it). Her voice has an unusually high-pitched (at time almost squeaky) timbre, reminiscent of some older female stars (e.g., Teresa Brewer).

Janet Jackson was the youngest of the nine Jackson children and made her singing debut at the age of seven in Las Vegas with her famous brothers. Her first hit single came at the age of twenty ("What Have You Done For Me Lately"). She followed with numerous hit singles, including eight number 1 hits by the beginning of the new millennium. During that same period, Janet recorded five number 1 albums. With the release of *Damita Jo* in 2004, Jackson proved that her career was far from over, in spite of (or because of?) a controversial appearance at the Super Bowl that same year (during her televised half-time performance, one of her breasts was exposed).

## Madonna

The most successful female star of the mid- to late-1980s was Madonna (born Madonna Louise Veronica Ciccone, in Detroit in 1959). Having attained a limited reputation as a disco vocalist, she released her first album, *Madonna*, in 1983. The album made the Top 10 and included two Top 10 singles ("Borderline" and "Lucky Star"). These two, along with several single releases ("Everybody" and "Into the Groove"), were style setters in 1980s dance music—a synthesized update of 1970s disco. (We will have more to say about "techno-dance music" later in this chapter.) Madonna's early dance hits have a gentle disco beat provided by a synthesized drum beat and a synthesized bass line. Color is provided by bubbling synthesizers and simulated brass/wind interjections (and sometimes by live backup vocals).

Without question, Madonna's life as a superstar began in late 1984 with the release of *Like a Virgin* (her first number 1 album and single). In spite of some controversy over the hook line, "Virgin" is a well-crafted song, sung convincingly. Except for a slight reduction in overall funkiness, one can easily imagine Michael Jackson singing this song equally well (even down to the little high-pitched "ohs" both singers like to toss in).

The techno-dance style is also evident in Madonna's next hit, "Material Girl." It was not until the release of "Crazy for You" that the real vocal potential of Madonna became apparent. Even the song's writers, John Bettis and Jon Lind, admitted they questioned the choice of Madonna for their ballad. Bettis says his reply was, "'Excuse me? This is for Madonna? Really? Can she sing a song like this?' Jon and I were surprised at the choice of artist at the time, if you want to know the truth" (Bronson 1988, 606). Even producer John Benitez was more accustomed to

the usual dance music production. In spite of all this, Madonna showed convincingly that she could handle the more demanding ballad style of "Crazy for You." The song hit number 1 in May 1985.

Once Madonna broke out of the dance music stereotype, her career was off and running. Her broader talents were explored in films such as *Desperately Seeking Susan, Shanghai Surprise, Who's That Girl?, Bloodhounds of Broadway,* and *Dick Tracy.* Her next number 1 song, "Live to Tell," reinforced her newfound reputation as a talented singer outside of the dance music style.

*True Blue* (1986) was Madonna's second consecutive number 1 album. It yielded three number 1 singles, including "Live to Tell," "Open Your Heart," and the controversial

Madonna (*Source:* Michael Ochs Archive, Ltd.)

"Papa Don't Preach." "Papa" is an interesting combination of a dance music accompaniment under a sensitive story line that portrays an unwed younger mother reporting her situation to her father.

Madonna continued to produce Top 10 hits through 1986 and 1987. The next musical bombshell was the number 1 album *Like a Prayer* (1989). Again, Madonna incited controversy (more due to the video than to the song). Although the ever-present dance accompaniment is there once again, Madonna and her backup singers drive to a relatively soulful climax. That soulful vocal style is also evident in "Express Yourself," another major hit from *Like a Prayer.*

Madonna turned the new decade with *I'm Breathless,* an album of songs from, or inspired by, the movie *Dick Tracy.* Hits like "Justify My Love" and "Rescue Me" continue the techno-dance style under a mostly spoken lyric.

No discussion of Madonna would be complete without a few remarks about her extramusical image. Modeling herself rather obviously after Marilyn Monroe, she unabashedly projected the female-as-sex-object stereotype. Her revealing costumes, sexually suggestive videos, and self-advertised lifestyle left little doubt that she intended to be the female sex icon of the 1980s (and 1990s). The song "Justify My Love" is overtly suggestive, with more sighing and deep breathing than any song since Donna Summer's "Love to Love You Baby." Madonna's flamboyant persona was enhanced even more by her eventful but brief marriage to actor Sean Penn (1985–89). Her appeal was primarily with young teen (and preteen) audiences, among whom she spawned many twelve- and thirteen-year-old look-alikes. In the 1990s, she established a reputation as an actress, most notably for her title role in the movie *Evita.* In 1992, Madonna signed a seven-year, $60 million deal with Time Warner guaranteeing release of all albums, films, and books under her own production company. Her popularity continued unabated into the new century with albums such as *Ray of Light* (number 2 in 1998) and *Music* (number 1 in 2000).

## Prince

One of the more puzzling black acts of the 1980s was Prince. Born Prince Rogers Nelson in Minneapolis in 1960, Prince combined a number of fragments into his enigmatic persona: considerable shock, lots of soul–funk, a touch of glitter (Little Richard style), occasional rap, some folk-like sociopolitical commentary, and even some hints of Michael Jackson. The one overt factor overriding all of these diverse internal elements was sex: Prince sold sex in all of its forms. His album *Dirty Mind* contained songs dealing with incest, oral sex, and group sex. Such subjects were nothing new to Prince, whose earlier albums contained songs like "Soft and Wet" and "I Wanna Be Your Lover," with its line, "I want to come inside you."

*Controversy* (1981) contained the ultimate rap: the full text of the Lord's Prayer. Other attention grabbers were "Sexuality" and "Do Me Baby," one of the more blatant step-by-step descriptions of sexual activity up to its time. And that was only side 1. Side 2 offered "Private Joy," "Ronnie, Talk to Russia" (a quick little ditty urging arms control), "Annie Christian," and "Jack U Off" (no explanation required). *Controversy* (as an album and as a technique) worked.

Prince's next album, *Prince **1999*** (1982), reached the Top 10, and the single "Little Red Corvette" broke through all radio markets to reach number 6. Prince finally reached the top with *Purple Rain* in 1984. The movie was a combination of fantasy and biography; the sound track album moved to number 1—selling over thirteen million copies in its first year—and yielded four Top 10 songs, including two number 1s. With the singles undoubtedly promoting album sales among a wide audience, many first-time Prince fans were probably surprised to hear a song like "Darling Nikki" with its reference to masturbation. Prince accepted the 1984 Oscar for the score to *Purple Rain* and murmured his thanks to God.

Prince's popularity continued throughout the decade with five more albums, including two that reached number 1: *Around the World in a Day* (1985) and *Batman* (1989). Nor did Prince lack success in the singles market, placing sixteen songs in the Top 20, including four number 1 hits ("When Doves Cry," "Let's Go Crazy," "Kiss," and "Batdance"). In 1993, Prince announced that henceforth he would be known as Artist Formerly Known as Prince (AFKAP), later shortened to Artist. One year later, Warner Brothers dropped its distribution deal with Prince. Self-promotion and online distribution proved less effective and, as a result, singles and album sales for this artist were not impressive during the mid-1990s. However, with the release of *Musicology* in 2004, Prince became one of the top touring acts of the year, signaling a resurgence of interest in this talented yet enigmatic performer.

## DANCING THROUGH THE 1990S AND BEYOND

Dance music continues to be an important element in youth culture. Many artists who appeared during the 1980s continued their success into the 1990s and beyond: Madonna, Michael Jackson, Janet Jackson, and Whitney Houston. In addition, the 1990s revealed a number of artists that rivaled, and sometimes surpassed, the potential of these earlier stars. The rubric "dance music" is admittedly quite broad and encompasses a wide array of musical styles. We will focus on three categories, each of which contains a number of subcategories. Pop dance music was driven by the marketing and promotional machines of the major record companies. The beginnings of rave dance music can be found in techno forms dating back to the work of Kraftwerk during the 1970s. Finally, the Latin Invasion was comprised of a rising number of Latin American artists who attained remarkable commercial success in the United States. No longer part of the "world music" genre, this style of dance music found its way into the mainstream of American musical culture. A fourth dance style—rap dance—will be discussed in Chapter 17.

### Pop Dance Music

The Pop music machine just kept right on rolling into the new millennium, though generally declining record sales may give some indication that the public was beginning to tire of such "packaged" acts, producing slick, highly produced pop tunes. The use of the term *pop* may be slightly misleading in this context, because dance music of almost every description was revealing significant R & B influence. Recall that, during the 1940s and 1950s, many white artists and major labels recorded covers of R & B songs by African-American artists. Listening to both versions of these early recordings reveals a significant differentiation in performance style. During the 1990s, however, some white artists were quite accomplished at copying the style and delivery of authentic R & B, including the soulful interpolations, melismatic phrasings, and wide array of timbral variations for expressive purposes.

## 'N Sync

Following in the footsteps of successful boy bands of the 1980s (New Edition, New Kids on the Block, and Menudo), 'N Sync—like the Backstreet Boys before them—became a sensation. The members of 'N Sync, a Florida-based boy band, all came to the group with previous entertainment experience. Chris Kirkpatrick and Joey Fatone, who initiated formation of the band, both worked at Universal Studios in Orlando. Lance Bass had toured with a national children's choir and Justin Timberlake and JC Chavez had both been regulars on the Disney Channel's *The New Mickey Mouse Club,* appearing with costars Christina Aguilera and Britney Spears. By 1995, 'N Sync was being handled by the same forces who had propelled the Backstreet Boys to international success, Lou Pearlman and Johnny Wright. The band appeared at the same European concert venues where the Backstreet Boys had recently performed and were signed to RCA. The band's eponymous debut album received little attention until after their taped concert performance was aired on the Disney Channel. Shortly after the show, the album reached number 2 and yielded one Top 40 single, "I Want You Back" (number 13). Their seasonal album, *Home for Christmas,* reached number 7 and contained the hit single "(God Must Have Spent) A Little More Time On You" (number 8 in 1999). A cover version of this same song by the group Alabama (featuring 'N Sync) reached number 29 that same year.

In 1999, a collaborative effort with Gloria Estefan resulted in a Top 10 single, "Music of My Heart" (number 2), the title song from a motion picture starring Meryl Streep. That same year, the group left RCA for Jive Records, a move about which the rival Backstreet Boys (Jive recording artists themselves) were not at all happy. With 'N Sync's following release, *No Strings Attached* (number 1 in 2000), there was no longer any doubt about which boy band reigned supreme. The almost inconceivable sales record set the previous year by the Backstreet Boys' *Millennium,* which sold 1.1 million copies during its first week, was more than doubled by the new 'N Sync recording, which sold an amazing 2.4 million copies in its first week. The album contained three Top 5 singles: "Bye Bye Bye" (number 4), "This I Promise You" (number 5), and "It's Gonna Be Me" (number 1). Even the release of the Backstreet Boys' *Black & Blue* could not put a damper on the commercial success of 'N Sync's release, which sold consistently well into 2001. Though the rival Backstreet Boys' album sold 1.6 million copies during its first week—surpassing the sales of their record-breaking *Millennium*—when compared to 'N Sync, their performance was second best. 'N Sync's success continued unabated with the release of *Celebrity* (number 1 in 2001). The success of Justin Timberlake's solo debut (*Justified,* 2002) tolled the death knell for the rest of the band. Timberlake and his former *Mickey Mouse Club* costar Christina Aguilera were among Billboard's Top 5 Artists of 2003).

## The Spice Girls

At the same time the boy bands were gaining popularity, a new batch of girl groups was on the horizon. Primary among the girl groups of the 1990s was The Spice Girls, a group of female vocalists from Britain, four of whom answered an ad placed in *The Stage* magazine by Bob and Chris Herbert, who managed the British boy band Take That!. The ad read simply "Wanted: Streetwise, outgoing, ambitious, and dedicated girls to play in a band." All four were hired, but departed shortly thereafter, choosing to pursue their own direction. In 1995, they signed with Virgin Records. Each member of the group was given a nickname by the contributors to *Top of the Pops,* a British teen magazine. These names were assigned based on each singer's personality, looks, or interests: Geri Halliwell became "Ginger Spice," Victoria Beckman became "Posh Spice," Melanie "Mel B" Brown became "Scary Spice," Melanie "Mel C" Chisholm became "Sporty Spice," and Emma Lee Bunton became "Baby Spice." Their first single, "Wannabe," debuted at number 1 in the United Kingdom . . . the first debut single by an all-female group to enter at the top of the British charts. The song became a number 1 hit in the United States in 1997. *Spice,* the group's debut album, reached number 1 in the United Kingdom and was the first debut album ever to enter the American charts at number 1. The album contained three Top 10 hits: "Wannabe" (number 1), "Say You'll Be There" (number 3), and "2 Become 1" (number 4). The response of American fans was not too unlike that garnered by the Fab Four three-and-a-half decades earlier, winning The Spice Girls a series of lucrative endorsements.

The group's second album, *Spiceworld* (number 3 in 1997), was released simultaneously with the opening of their movie of the same name, featuring the single "Spice Up Your Life" (number 18). Ginger Spice left the band in 1998 to pursue a solo career, though her debut recording, *Schizophonic* (number 42 in 1999) was not as successful as her work with her Spice Sisters. The Spice Girls, now a quartet since Halliwell was not replaced, released *Forever* in 2000. Compared to their previous success, this recording was considered a commercial failure and the group members disbursed to pursue solo projects.

### Destiny's Child

Comparisons between Destiny's Child and the Supremes are inevitable. The manner in which focus is primarily given to lead vocalist Beyoncé Knowles is reminiscent of the attention lavished earlier upon Diana Ross with the other vocalists assuming, sometimes unwillingly, a supporting role. The four original members of the group, initially enduring a series of name changes, were Beyoncé Knowles, Kelly Rowland, LeToya Luckett, and LaTavia Roberson. After a loss on *Star Search,* the group, then known as Da Dolls, was signed by Elektra, though their contract was canceled in 1995 when they failed to produce an album. At that time, Matthew Knowles (Beyoncé's father, who had no prior experience in the entertainment industry) took the reigns and landed the group a deal with Columbia in 1997. The quartet, now known as Destiny's Child, released their self-titled debut album (number 67 in 1998), containing the hit single "No, No, No" (number 3 in 1997), a remix by Wyclef Jean of the Fugees. *The Writing's on the Wall* (number 6 in 1999) proved to be the group's breakthrough, including four Top 40 hits: "Bills, Bills, Bills" (number 1), "Bug a Boo" (number 33), "Say My Name" (number 1), and "Jumpin', Jumpin'" (number 3). In an interesting business move, upon turning 18 in 1999, Roberson and Luckett informed Knowles' father that they were terminating their contract with him and were choosing to seek independent management. By early the next year, the pair was no longer part of Destiny's Child, a fact they claimed not to be aware of until seeing the video for "Say My Name," which included their replacements, Tenetria "Michelle" Williams and Farah Franklin. After less than half a year,

Franklin was let go for reportedly missing performances. Destiny's Child—now a trio—recorded the song "Independent Women, Part 1" from the soundtrack for *Charlie's Angels*, and it became a number 1 hit in 2000. Nominated for five Grammys, the group won two awards for "Say My Name." In 2001, the group continued its winning streak with *Survivor* (number 1), containing "Survivor" (number 1) and "Bootylicious" (number 7).

## Rave Dance Music

During the 1980s and 1990s, dance music was a primary form of entertainment, and artists recording this music constituted many of the most commercially successful performers of the period. With the emergence and eventual dominance of the synthesizer, computer-controlled sequencers, digital sampling, and loop-based composition, technology played an integral role in the creation of this music and its performance. Leading directly out of the disco era as that musical phenomenon fizzled in the early 1980s, techno blended the incessant beat of disco with the high energy and "devil may care" attitude of punk. Incorporating segments of previously recorded music, drumbeats, television chatter, and other "found sounds," the music was intentionally repetitive and noisy . . . providing a background for dancing and all-night partying. The style emerged in Detroit, led by DJ Derrick May, and passed to the UK, where associated underground psychedelic dance parties (raves) were very popular during the 1980s.

Contemporaneous with the emergence of techno was another genre of dance music known as house, named after the Warehouse club in Chicago from which it originated. It is possible to consider house music as the "style out of which most dance music since the mid-1980s has developed" (Fulford-Jones 2000, 758). In contrast to disco, out of which it also evolved, house music was not a song-based form. Instead, many early house recordings consisted of a repetitive drum machine rhythm track in quadruple meter, a "relentless" bass drum pounding on every beat, and high hat cymbals emphasizing the off-beats. Bass lines and string parts (reminiscent of those typical of the disco era) were performed on synthesizers. Techno and house music spawned numerous and sometimes difficult to distinguish subgenres, including trip hop (Massive Attack, Tricky, and Portishead), dub (Lee "Scratch" Perry), electronica (Aphex Twin), and trance, an excessively repetitive style that suited its utilitarian purpose as "music to stimulate movement" at rave parties. In 1996, DJ Shadow's trip hop album *Endtroducing* was the first recording to be released that was constructed entirely out of samples (i.e., preexisting music).

Interestingly, many DJs responsible for providing this style of music seemed to be content doing so while retaining relative anonymity, working in dimly lit rave locations surrounded by cables interconnecting sound system, turntables, and often a computer. As the genre became more popular in the early 1990s, however, major labels began to take an interest. Included in the first batch of signed artists were 808 State, the Orb, Messiah, and Moby. Notable among such DJs for shedding his anonymity, Moby began to incorporate a variety of styles into his albums. In addition to the predictable high-speed, repetitive tracks, *Everything Is Wrong* (1995) integrated elements of heavy metal ("All That I Need") and blues-influenced punk

("What Love"). With *Play* (number 45 in 2000), Moby's audience expanded significantly and two Grammy nominations were evidence of growing critical acclaim. On this recording, Moby explored older styles of music, including traditional blues and gospel.

With the blinding pace at which computer technology is advancing from year to year, one can expect to see continuing development of these technology-related dance genres. The latest round of prime movers is led by Kid606 (Miguel Depedro) and Matmos (Martin Schmidt and Drew Daniel). These DJs synchronize the beats of their dance music using laptop computers instead of turntables. Other electronica-related groups worthy of mention include Prodigy, Chemical Brothers, Daft Punk, Chicks on Speed, Basement Jaxx, and Stereo MCs. With a significant number of record labels devoted to the genre—for example, Tigerbeat6 (Kid606's label in Oakland), Schematic (Miami), and Carpark (New York)—America currently leads the way in the production of electronic dance music (Reynolds 2001).

## THE LATIN INVASION

The 1990s brought a new round of Latin artists to the pop music scene. The level of success experienced by many of these performers suggested that "Latin Music" no longer deserved to be considered part of that large umbrella labeled "world music." Rather, the Latin influence had worked its way into the fabric of the American mainstream. Artists whose music assisted in confirming this transition included Ricky Martin, Selena, Jennifer Lopez, Christina Aguilera, Enrique Iglesias, and Marc Anthony. This dance-oriented music, often based on Latin rhythms like the cumbia and salsa, seemed to excite the passions of listeners. There was often a focus on sensuality and it was a music in which the male singers were allowed, if not expected, to be emotionally vulnerable.

If there were any doubt about the musical infusion of Latin culture, final confirmation was provided by the phenomenal return of Carlos Santana with the release of *Supernatural* (number 1 in 1999), containing the hit single "Smooth," which held the number 1 position on the charts for 12 weeks. Built upon the Latin rock sound of Santana's ensemble, the talent of many guest performers (including Dave Matthews, Eric Clapton, Lauryn Hill, Wyclef Jean, and Rob Thomas) provided an eclectic mix resulting in one of the most critically acclaimed and commercially successful albums of all time. The album won nine Grammys and was certified 14 times multiplatinum in America, selling over 21 million copies worldwide.

Setting the Pop music world "stage" for this Latin Invasion was an accomplishment that required a potent superstar, someone to "swarm the beach" of the American popular music scene. Previous attempts had proven moderately successful, but did not provide a foundation for a stylistic influx. Recall that Richie Valens recorded "La Bamba" (number 22 in 1959) as the B-side for his hit single "Donna" (number 2 in 1958) and Julio Iglesias experienced a mild degree of success recording duets with well-established American performers: "To All the Girls I've Loved Before" with Willie Nelson (number 5 in 1984) and "All of You" with Diana Ross (number 19 in 1984). During the 1980s, the role of harbinger was effectively carried out by Gloria Estefan and her band the Miami Sound Machine.

**Gloria Estefan**

Beginning as lead vocalist for a Latin-American-flavored popular music group, the Miami Sound Machine, Gloria Estefan's vocal and songwriting talents have proven highly marketable. Her father, bodyguard to the Cuban president, fled to Miami with his family in 1959 when Gloria was only two years old. In 1975, Gloria Fajardo (Estefan's maiden name) and her cousin auditioned for the Miami Latin Boys, a local wedding band led by keyboardist Emilio Estefan, Jr. Renamed the Miami Sound Machine and performing a mixture of dance and salsa music, the group proved to be one of the most popular in Miami. Three years later, Fajardo married Emilio, becoming Gloria Estefan.

The first recordings of the band were in Spanish, recorded on CBS's Hispanic subsidiary. Initially popular in the Latino market, Miami Sound Machine eventually gained widespread popularity as they began recording songs in English. After scoring a

Gloria Estefan and Miami Sound Machine (*Source:* Sherry Rayn Barnett / Michael Ochs Archive, Ltd.)

popular dance hit in the European market with "Dr. Beat" in 1984, they released their first English-only album, *Primitive Love*, which included three Top 10 hits: "Conga" (number 10), "Bad Boy" (number 8), and the ballad "Words Get in the Way" (number 5). The musicians playing on the recording were different from those touring with the band. Affectionately known as the Three Jerks, Joe Galdo, Rafael Vigil, and Lawrence Dermer composed and recorded most of the songs, while the touring band consisted of Enrique Kiki Garcia (drums), Juan Avila (bass), and Raul Muciano (sax and keyboards). Gloria Estefan, of course, performed both in the studio and onstage. Resigning his role as keyboard player, Emilio Estefan took over management of the group.

By the release of their next album, *Let It Loose* (1987), Estefan's principal role in the group was confirmed as the album was credited to Gloria Estefan and the Miami Sound Machine. Five Top 40 hits resulted from the release of this album, including her first number 1 single, "Anything For You." Following the promotional tour for *Let It Loose*, Estefan began her career as a solo artist, releasing *Cuts Both Ways* in 1989. The two Top 10 singles resulting from her solo debut, "Don't Wanna Lose You" (number 1) and "Here We Are" (number 6), were both ballads, though the high-energy dance tune "Get On Your Feet" reached number 11. Tragically, in the spring of 1990, Estefan sustained a serious injury when her tour bus was hit by a truck while traveling along an icy stretch of highway in Pennsylvania. Her husband and child were injured slightly but she suffered a broken vertebra that required surgical reparation. Her follow-up album, *Into the Light* (1991), contained a song about the accident entitled "Coming Out of the Dark" (number 1). Images often associated with near-death experiences are obvious in both the title of the song and throughout the album. *Hold Me, Thrill Me, Kiss Me* (1994) contained the hit singles "Everlasting Love" (number 27) and "Turn the Beat Around" (number 13). The latter song was featured in *The Specialist*, a film starring Sylvester Stallone.

Maintaining a close connection with her cultural heritage, Estefan frequently recorded Spanish language versions of her songs. The compact disc recording of *Cuts Both Ways* contains two such examples: "Si Voy a Perderte (Don't Wanna Lose You)" and "Oye Mi Canto (Hear My Voice)." She also released an all-Spanish solo album entitled *Mi Tierra* (1993), featuring performances by an impressive list of Cuban musicians, including Tito Puente, Luis Enrique, and Arturo Sandoval.

Gloria Estefan has played an integral role in injecting Latin musical influences into the pop music market, opening the door for a wide variety of artists, including Mellow Man Ace ("Mentirosa" in 1990), Kid Frost ("La Raza" in 1990), Los Del Rios ("Macarena," number 1 in 1996), Mana (*Donde Jugaran los Niños* was certified six times platinum and the group performed on MTV's *Unplugged* series), and a number of others to be discussed in the following sections. Confirmation of Latin music's successful invasion of the American charts came with the Bayside Boys Mix of "Macarena" by Los Del Rios, maintaining the number 1 position in 1996 for 14 weeks.

The official year of the Latin Invasion can be identified as 1999. Though various forces were building prior to that time, the arrival of commercially successful recordings by Ricky Martin (*Ricky Martin*, number 1), Jennifer Lopez (*On the 6*, number 8), Enrique Iglesias (*Bailamos*), Marc Anthony (*Marc Anthony*), Shakira (*Donde Estan los Ladrones*), and Christina Aguilera (*Christina Aguilera*) confirmed the significance of this new subgenre of rock.

### Selena

In 1989, Selena Quintanilla became the first artist signed to EMI's recently established Latin label. Originally attracted by what the label's executives believed to be strong crossover potential, Selena's early success came as lead singer for her group Selena y Los Dinos, including her older siblings Abraham (bass) and Suzette (drums). *Ven Conmigo,* the band's first recording, reached number 1 on *Billboard's* regional Mexican chart in 1991 (Rosen 1996). Selena was not herself fluent in the Spanish language, but she became a superstar in the genre of Tejano music. After transitioning to solo act status, Selena released *Entre a Mi Mundo* and *Selena Live!,* both following the lead of her initial recording by reaching the top of *Billboard's* Mexican chart. In 1993, the latter album earned the singer her first Grammy for Best Latin American Performance. Her next album, *Amor Prohibido* (1994), illustrated a wide variety of musical influences, including Tejano, R & B, and hip-hop. The album went platinum, and the title track won Selena her second Grammy.

Just as crossover success seemed inevitable, tragedy struck the young star. Concurrent with pursuing her musical career, Selena had opened two clothing boutiques. The singer's father had discovered paperwork proving that the manager of her shop in San Antonio, Yolanda Saldivar (founder and former president of Selena's fan club), was embezzling. On March 31, 1995, Selena went to a motel in Corpus Christi to discuss these charges with Saldivar. The conversation turned into an argument and, as she turned to depart, the singer was shot in the back. Still alive, Selena staggered into the lobby and named Saldivar as the shooter. Despite tremendous efforts to save her, including a blood transfusion, Selena died at the hospital later that afternoon, a little more than two weeks before her 24th birthday. In the singer's honor, then-governor George Bush named April 16th "Selena Day." *Dreaming of You* (1995) was released posthumously and entered the *Billboard* chart at number 1, the first Tejano record to ever reach the top of the chart. This album has since sold 3 million copies.

### Ricky Martin

Ricky Martin (born Enrique Martin Morales) began singing and acting at the age of six. In 1984, at the age of twelve, Martin joined the Puerto Rican boy band Menudo. Five years later, the singer was forced to leave the group, having reached the maximum age allowed by the band's dictates. In order to retain its youthful image, Menudo members agreed that no one in the band's rotating lineup could be over 16 years old. Martin's initial major success in America came not as a singer, but as an actor when the performer landed a role on the popular soap opera *General Hospital* in 1994. This enviable role was followed in 1996 by a brief period appearing in the Broadway version of *Les Misérables.* While earning a living primarily as an actor, the singer also released four Spanish-language albums: *Ricky Martin* (1991), *Me Amaras* (1993), *A Medio Vivir* (1995), and *Vuelve* (1998; number 1 on the Latin chart). The single "La Copa de la Vida (The Cup of Life)," from *Vuelve,* was used as the anthem of the 1998 World Cup competition. The song topped the singles chart in over 30 countries (not the United States), selling more than 11 million copies worldwide.

According to George-Warren and Romanowski (2001), "La Copa . . ." became "the biggest selling single in the history of Columbia Records" (p. 614).

Martin performed at the 1999 Grammy awards, where he himself was awarded a Grammy for Best Latin Pop Performance. *Ricky Martin* (number 1 in 1999) was the singer's first recording in English and contained the number 1 megahit "Livin' La Vida Loca," which became one of the best-selling singles since the beginning of *Billboard*'s Hot 100. In 2000, Martin released a follow-up album, *Sound Loaded* (number 4), resulting in only one hit single, "She Bangs" (number 12). It is possible that the appearance of so many Latino (and Latina) artists and the resulting increase in the number of recordings from which to choose had taken a toll on some of those performers who were previously most successful. Of course, with so many singers being welcomed into Hollywood's motion picture industry (Ice Cube, Marky Mark, Jennifer Lopez, etc.), Martin provides another viable candidate, given his previous experience in the field.

The popularity of Latin-influenced music rose substantially during the 1990s and constituted an "invasion" in 1999. Time will determine the extent to which this interest is permanent in the taste of the American record-buying public. The trend continues at present. According to the Recording Industry Association of America, during a period of slumping shipments within the music industry at large, sales of Latin music CDs rose 9 percent during 2001 (Fu 2002).

---

## MUSICAL CLOSE-UP:
## THE ANATOMY OF DISCO

It is indeed stating the obvious to say that the primary musical element in disco is the rhythm. In fact, the rhythmic element is almost the only common ingredient that ties together the multitude of disco songs from the 1975 to 1980 period. Tonal elements  melody and harmony—vary widely. The proof of this is that everything from Beethoven's Fifth Symphony to country songs to jazz tunes were adapted to the disco style simply by setting the respective tunes and harmonies over a disco beat. Texture varied also, from solo voice to three- and four-voice vocal harmonies. A tour through the work of Donna Summer reveals an interesting variety of textures, even within one song, such as "No More Tears (Enough Is Enough)." Forms also varied widely, from short, simple songs to longer, more complex forms.

If there is a secondary factor (behind rhythm), it is timbre. Most disco songs involve singer(s), drums, electric bass, rhythm guitar, strings, and sometimes brass. In fact, string lines consistently accompany the vast majority of disco songs. But these are not the lush string harmonies associated with pop or soft rock. Instead, the disco string line is usually fast moving, providing a busy counterline behind the vocal melody. Sometimes strings punctuate the texture in much the way brass and winds do in some other styles.

But the overriding factor is the rhythm. Because of the format of most discotheques, a wide variety of tempos was considered inappropriate. Using two turntables, the disc jockey simply juxtaposed the end of one song with the beginning of the next, providing a continuous flow of dance music. Wide variances in tempo would have destroyed that flow. Therefore, disco songs lie within a relatively narrow range of tempos. Also, to create the exciting, upbeat ambiance of the clubs, faster tempos were preferred.

Dancing is, of course, a physical activity, and disco music seems to "connect" in some mysterious way with our physical systems. It is difficult to listen to disco music and not feel the urge to move with the beat. There has been some speculation that the typical disco tempo is a multiple (double) of the characteristic human pulse rate (about 60 beats per minute). Such theories suggest that the most appealing disco tunes reinforce our body's "natural rhythm" by conforming to a tempo of about 120 beats per minute. For example, most of Donna Summer's disco songs range from 120 to 130 beats per minute (most often from about 124 to 130). Assuming that the pulse rate is likely to quicken somewhat while dancing, this conforms to the "double pulse rate" theory. But there are also gentler disco songs. For example, most of the songs from *Saturday Night Fever* range from 108 to 114 beats per minute. In reality, there seem to be two distinct tempo groupings for disco: a quicker tempo in the 120 to 130 range, and a more "laid-back" tempo in the 108 to 114 range.

But what of the rhythmic patterns themselves? There seem to be two basic elements common to most disco songs. First, all four beats are hit equally; in other words, the typical rock backbeat normally is missing. The quadruple meter is set by the dry thud of a bass drum. Second, there is a subdivision of each beat into four parts (notated as sixteenth notes). So the basic disco rhythm looks like this:

The underlying subdivision of the beat is often played on hi-hat cymbals (with hard sticks) and reinforced by the rhythm guitar (often with a wah-wah pedal).

If this were all there were to it, the disco beat would indeed be as simple and boring as its detractors claim. But in fact, there is still room for considerable variance. The basic quadruple subdivision is consistently felt, but actual patterns vary. For example, some songs have a pattern that plays the first, third, and fourth subdivisions (skipping number two—although it is still *felt*).

In fact, the "missing" second subdivision may be present in another part of the texture (e.g., in the rhythm guitar or in the string or brass lines). Syncopated patterns can be devised that accent larger patterns (over two or four beats) but that are still dependent upon the quadruple subdivision. For example, "MacArthur Park" (Summer) includes the following patterns.

All of these patterns do not occur simultaneously, of course. But as each one occurs, it reinforces the basic pattern being provided by percussion, bass, and guitar. The bass, in fact, often plays a *duple* subdivision of the beat, providing a level midway between the basic beat and the quadruple subdivision:

None of these patterns is *inherently* "disco." In fact, the brass pattern (brass III above) is similar to one used by Blood, Sweat, and Tears in "Lucretia MacEvil," which of course is not a disco tune. But taken *all together,* with the right instrumentation (timbres) and tempo, the aggregate sound is disco.

Listen to several disco songs. In most cases you will hear the four equal beats and the basic quadruple subdivision (listen for the bass drum and the hi-hat cymbal). But beyond that, there are many other rhythmic layers. What is the bass player doing? How about the rhythm guitar? Listen to the string or brass lines; are they "punching up" the quadruple subdivision? You may begin to hear more than you thought was there!

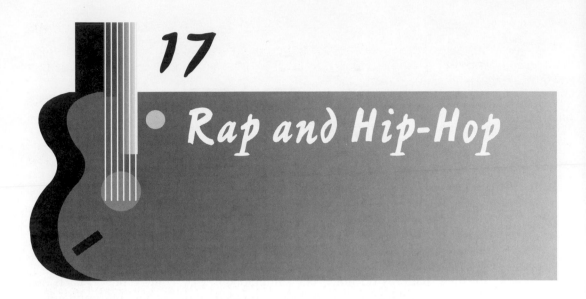

# 17

# Rap and Hip-Hop

## OVERVIEW: TECHNOLOGY, THE INTERNET, AND THE MUSIC INDUSTRY

In earlier chapters, we saw how the explosion of electronic technology affected groups such as Emerson, Lake, and Palmer, Yes, Passport, Kraftwerk, Triumvirat, the Talking Heads, and a host of others. This trend continued unabated throughout the 1970s and 1980s. The technological advances of the 1980s were bewildering. Not only did synthesizers become capable of doing more and more sophisticated operations, but tools such as samplers, sequencers, drum machines, and guitar and wind MIDI (Musical Instrument Digital Interface) controllers made it possible to create complex multilayered compositions electronically. Often one had to listen carefully and with a critical ear to be able to discern the acoustic performances from the electronic.

Perhaps the biggest single event occurred with the creation of the MIDI standard in 1983, a language that allowed electronic sound sources (synthesizers, for example) to interact with computers and/or other synthesizers. The MIDI revolution, along with more powerful, smaller, and user-friendly personal computers, had a tremendous impact on all styles of music. The worst problem created by this trend was that no sooner had one invested money and learning time in one set of tools than newer models would hit the market that rendered previous hardware and software obsolete.

Terms such as *techno-dance* and *techno-rock* were applied in the 1980s to groups whose musical style was centered on electronically generated sounds. Typical of the techno-dance groups was New Order, a group from Manchester, England. If you wondered what happened to disco, listen to a bit of *Substance* (1987). Disco was back but transformed to the timbres of synthesizers and drum machines. The repetitive accompaniment patterns and monotone vocal delivery may remind us of some new-wave bands (like Devo) and some of the minimalists (like Brian Eno). The music may have been a bit monotonous to listen to, but that steady repetitiveness made it perfect for dancing.

Less dance-oriented but heavily electronic was The Cure, another British group. Their albums from the early 1980s made little impact in this country; however, they began to enjoy greater acceptance in the late 1980s, especially with their number 2 album *Disintegration* (1987). This album produced an attractive hit single, "Lovesong" (number 2), which was lighter on the electronics than the rest of the album. The Cure delivers rich and colorful walls of synthesized sound, reminiscent of Tangerine Dream. But, in most cases, there is a stronger and more defined beat. Still, they rarely go all the way to a neo-disco beat and are, therefore, usually described as being techno-rock rather than techno-dance.

Depeche Mode's style and popularity curve was similar to The Cure's. Again, albums from the early 1980s sold rather poorly. However, beginning with the single "People are People," this British band began to receive more recognition. *Music for the Masses* (1987) made the Top 40; *Violator* (1990) reached the Top 10 and produced three Top 30 hits, including "Enjoy the Silence" (number 8). As is so often the case, the single hit was not exactly typical of the general style of the album. In this case, "Enjoy the Silence" moved rather close to the techno-dance style. Like The Cure, Depeche Mode relied heavily on electronically generated and modified sounds over a clearly defined beat, which usually stopped short of the typical techno-dance beat. The result was a type of gentle mainstream rock—but heavy on electronics.

A potential rival to MIDI as the single greatest technological advance in music production during the late 1980s and early 1990s was digital sampling, a process that involves the conversion of sound energy into a series of numbers representing the sound amplitude at discrete intervals of time. The arrival of compact discs in the consumer market made such technology commonplace, a feat that digital audio tape (DAT) had failed to accomplish. In the sampling process, sound energy is passed through an analog-to-digital converter that is responsible for assigning a number to the signal amplitude at any given moment in time. For reasons that are well beyond the scope of this text, it has been determined that in order to reproduce all frequencies audible to the human ear this measurement must be made 44,100 times every second. When these samples are reproduced (i.e., played back), a reverse sequence occurs. A digital-to-analog converter transforms the sequence of numbers into a continuous signal that can then be amplified and sent to a speaker system, resulting in musical sound. Transforming sound energy into a series of numbers in this manner allows the sound to be easily manipulated (e.g., played backward, speeded up, slowed down, combined with special effects, etc.) using the processing capabilities of a computer.

Prior to the arrival of digital sampling, musicians had attempted to recreate sounds of acoustic instruments by "synthesizing" the timbre on a variety of electronic keyboard instruments. This is a difficult process and often led to sounds that shared only a slight resemblance to the sound of the acoustic instrument being modeled. Using digital sampling, however, the sound of acoustic instruments could simply be "recorded" digitally and then "played back" by pressing an assigned key on a synthesizer keyboard. Many recordings of the late 1980s and 1990s incorporated sampling to such an extent that a "new" song may be entirely based on the musical foundation of previous recordings. For example, M.C. Hammer's hit single "U Can't Touch This" (number 8 in 1990) is based on Rick James's "Super Freak" (number 16 in 1981); "Pray" (number 2 in 1990) incorporates the rhythm track from Prince's "When Doves Cry" (number 1 in 1984); and "Pumps and Bumps" (number 26 in 1994) uses samples from George Clinton's "Atomic Dog." Other examples of this sampling technique may be heard in "Ice Ice Baby" by Vanilla Ice (bass line sampled from Queen and David Bowie's "Under Pressure"), "That's the Way Love Goes" by Janet Jackson (samples from James Brown's "Papa Don't Take No Mess"), "Slow Motion" by Color Me Badd (samples from "Spinning Wheel" by Blood, Sweat, and Tears), and "Wildside" by Marky Mark and the Funky Bunch (samples from Lou Reed's "Walk on the Wild Side"). Some songs incorporate a multitude of samples from a variety of songs. For example, "Ain't 2 Proud 2 Beg" by TLC (number 6 in 1992) uses samples from James Brown's "Escape-ism," Kool & the Gang's "Jungle Boogie," Average White Band's "School Boy Crush," Silver Convention's "School Boy Crush," and Bob James's "Take Me to the Mardi Gras." Use of previously recorded music in this way initiated a serious legal debate concerning copyright infringement. It is likely to be a topic that will take many years and a significant amount of litigation to resolve.

### New Technologies and the Internet

The final years of the twentieth century witnessed the death of the cassette tape as a viable medium for distributing commercial recordings. Dominance of the compact disc format and the arrival and eventual ubiquitous presence of the CD recorder sold with most new computer purchases sealed its fate. According to the Recording Industry of America's Yearend Statistics, between the years 1998 and 1999, sales of cassette versions of commercial recordings dropped 22 percent. Commercial cassette tape sales slid another 38.5 percent the following year. Another set of incompatible media formats, the DVD audio disc (DVD-A) and the Super Audio CD (SACD), was on the horizon, poised to acquire significant market share over the course of the next several years.

The most significant technological innovation impacting the commercial music industry during the 1990s was the arrival of file-sharing capabilities via the Internet. Using this technology, brought into the mainstream—there's that word again—by Napster and other similar Web sites, users were able to download digitized versions, typically in compressed MP3 format, of their favorite music or could share selected songs from their recording library with others around the world. In fact, *Spin* magazine declared that the number 1 album of 2001 was "Your Hard Drive" (January, 2002). Many idealistic musicians across the globe saw the Internet as a "great equalizer," giving artists direct access to an audience without the need for an intervening record company. With the dramatic drop in the cost of digital audio workstations (a personal computer with sequencing and digital audio software), artists could produce near studio-quality recordings at a fraction of the cost. In reality, however, the continuing need for marketing and distribution to succeed in the music business impeded the rise of all but a few of these hopefuls.

The response of the recording industry, similar to the reaction when the phonograph, radio airplay of music, and the CD recorder were introduced, was initially one of protectionism. As you might imagine, the potential impact upon the profit margins of major record companies resulted in a major backlash and eventual legal challenges. After a series of contentious confrontations, the record companies decided to buy their way out of the difficulty. BMG purchased Napster and Universal acquired MP3.com. For a brief period, this move proved fairly successful at limiting the amount of file sharing involving copyrighted commercial recordings, though other peer-to-peer software packages (e.g., Gnutella, Kazaa, and Morpheus) realized increased use by former Napster users.

Some artists recognized the potential of this new technology and proved quite savvy at using the new means of direct communication with their audience for the purpose of introducing themselves to the world or enhancing record sales. For example, in their early days (prior to signing with a major label), Phish used the Internet effectively to market their recordings and hawk band merchandise. In association with Sonic Foundry (makers of loop-based music creation software Acid), several artists offered their fans a chance to remix tracks from their recordings (www.acidplanet.com). Participating artists included Madonna ("Ray of Light," "Music," and "Deeper and Deeper"), Boz Scaggs ("Ms. Riddle"), Static-X ("Black and White"), Garbage ("Androgyny"), Debra Soule ("Amen"), and New Order ("Crystal"). Allowing an audience access to the sound files used as a foundation for such hit singles is certainly an innovative and enlightened approach. In a sense, the listener is given the opportunity to become a creator using existing, professionally produced musical materials.

Other artists, including Courtney Love and a coalition organized by Don Henley, began to actively address the inequities inherent in the recording industry concerning the relationship between artists and the corporations that market and distribute their work. According to Don Henley, the primary aim of his coalition was to raise money to wage a legal battle against the major labels to "change the fundamental rules that govern most recording contracts, including copyright ownership, long-term control of intellectual property and unfair accounting practices" (Wild 2002, 17).

During 2004, the success of online music sales initiated another potential paradigmatic shift for the recording companies and their represented artists. Apple's iStore, Real Media's Rhapsody, and even Wal-Mart began offering individual songs in copy-protected digital formats online for between $0.49 and $0.99 each. Entire albums could be purchased for between $4.99 and $9.99. This sales model offered the consumer incomparable convenience and immediate gratification, since one could purchase, download, and playback the recording in a matter of minutes . . . without leaving the house! Around this same time, portable MP3 players (like the iPod and Rio) began to overtake the market previously dominated by Sony Walkman and Discman. Once songs were purchased and downloaded from the Internet or digital files extracted from audio CDs, these songs could be transferred to the portable device and listened to anywhere using a set of headphones. As the technology developed and became more affordable, portable units selling for between $150 and $400 could hold a person's entire recording collection (up to 10,000 songs for a 40GB model!). Following a significant decline in recording sales, availability of digitized sound files on the Internet (both legal and illegal), and major artists threatening to organize a union and take legal action, the recording industry was in a state of crisis.

## RAP'S BEGINNINGS

Although many Americans became aware of rap music in the mid-1980s, the style actually dates back to the late 1970s. It seems to have developed in the neighborhoods of New York City (especially Harlem, the Bronx, and Brooklyn). A graphic description of a typical "block party" of 1977 is provided by Havelock Nelson and Michael Gonzales in their book *Bring the Noise:*

> A crew of soul brothers (Mod Squad afros, bell bottom jeans) troop down the hill with cartons of records, speakers, two turntables, and a mixer. These are the new gangsters in town, aural outlaws controlling the public airwaves. Slammin' their equipment in front of an old street lamp, their hands move slow, hooking wire and mics and testing a Gil Scott Heron drumbeat on a Technics turntable. BOOM/BLAST—"Yo, this be DJ Hollywood rockin' da turntables in da hood." Needles bounce, explode with the sound of the new urban blues. BOOM/BLAST—heavy bass riffs lifted from an ancient Stanley Clarke disc.

> While Hollywood bellows into the mic', turntable assassin Lovebug Starski plays the role of Doc Magic Hands—spinnin' discs, scratchin' records, borrowing this drumbeat, that keyboard riff. "All da ladies in da hood say, 'Yeah!' Fem voices roar and the block party erupts. (Nelson and Gonzales 1991, xvi)

In the late 1970s, such block parties were part of a collection of urban art forms, labeled "hip-hop," emerging in the South Bronx. The term, reputedly first coined by Starski himself, was used to describe the lifestyle, fashions, fast-talking comedy, and cultural expressions of this region of New York City (Toop 2000). The "cultural expressions" referenced include break dancing, graffiti art, freedom writing, double-Dutch jump-roping, and music. During the 1980s, as the significance of break dancing and graffiti receded, the term *hip-hop* became associated primarily with a specific urban musical style. Hip-hop tracks incorporated extant musical sounds, combining these previously recorded segments into a new composition. It is interesting to note that at the same time bands in the punk movement like the Police and the Clash were being influenced by reggae, hip-hop was inspired by Jamaican DJs U-Roy and Lee Perry. Setting up their sound systems in parks, school yards, and abandoned buildings, early hip-hop pioneers (known as "spinners") included Kool Herc, Grandmaster Flash ("The Adventures of Grandmaster Flash on the Wheels of Steel," number 55 R & B in 1981), Afrika Bambaataa ("Planet Rock," number 48 in 1982), Kurtis Blow ("The Breaks," number 87 in 1980), the Fatback Band ("King Tim III (Personality Jock)," 1979) and the Sugar Hill Gang ("Rapper's Delight," number 36 in 1980). Kool Herc began to add masters of ceremony (MCs) to speak over the foundation of these rhythmic grooves, sometimes covering up the silence with handclaps or to provide improvised prosodic displays as the DJ changed records on one or more of his turntables. The addition of an MC evolved into the musical form commonly referred to as "rap." The identity of the MC was an important aspect of the performance, often beginning a rap with a pronouncement (or verbal "tagging") . . . "Yo, we got my homeboy Eazy-E in the house. Compton's definitely in the house . . ." (from the beginning of NWA's "Something Like That" from *Straight Outta Compton*). Spoken rhymes often included references to other rap artists, events, and/or songs, sometimes initiating a back-and-forth dialog from recording to recording.

Hip-hop was created primarily by DJs using turntables rather than by musicians performing on traditional acoustic and/or electronic instruments. A patchwork of musical sounds was woven together to create dance music, often in a manner similar to the technique used by a jazz musician to spontaneously improvise a solo. As in the 1950s, DJs once again ascended to a position of prominence in the world of music. Whereas DJs who were integral to the emergence of rock and roll (e.g., Alan Freed) were responsible for bringing the music of black musicians to a wider audience, however, this new generation of DJs played a significant role in the creation of new music using libraries of preexisting recordings. Some of the favorite musical resources used by early hip-hop DJs included percussion and rhythm tracks from recordings by James Brown, Rufus Thomas, and other soul and funk artists. Many rappers in the 1980s and 1990s incorporated these same sources to create grooves for their own recordings. In 1989, for example, Public Enemy used the rhythmic motif from James Brown's "Funky Drummer" as a basis for "Fight the Power," the theme song for Spike Lee's *Do the Right Thing* (1989). Using two turntables and a mixer, a skilled DJ could create a "seamless blend of beats, riffs and hooks" that eventually came to be used as a foundation for early rap music (Peel 2000, 406). In addition to excerpts from funk recordings, break sections from 1950s and 1960s rock songs and instrumental compositions were frequently used.

DJs developed techniques for adding their own sounds to the accompaniment. In the late 1970s, hip-hop DJs effectively transformed the turntable, a device used primarily to play back recordings, into a musical instrument. "Scratching," as the technique came to be known, was accomplished by quickly pushing and pulling records on the turntable, resulting in a variety of effects: loops (short repeated sections), musical bursts, and backward playback. Some DJs used more than two turntables and developed a technique called "beat mixing," which involved playing back multiple records simultaneously while appropriately adjusting the speed of each recording so that the resulting complex rhythmic pattern would remain synchronized for lengthy periods of time.

There are many examples of dance music recordings that incorporated existing materials into a new context; for example, the use of sections from "Good Times" by Chic (number 1 in 1979) for the Sugar Hill Gang's "Rappers Delight" (number 36 in 1980), Afrika Bambaataa's use of melodies by Kraftwerk and Ennio Morricone for his own "Planet Rock" (number 48 in 1982), or the use of the Rolling Stones' "The Last Time" (number 9 in 1965) for The Verve's "Bitter Sweet Symphony" (number 12 in 1997). Following the advent of the personal computer (PC) and the incredibly fast pace of its evolution, however, the PC soon became the primary workstation for creating complex accompaniment tracks over which MCs would rap. The technique of "borrowing" excerpts from previously recorded material was, almost from the beginning, surrounded by controversy. Many believed that taking brief sections of a composition was well within the poetic license exercised by an artist, while others felt that it was a direct violation of U.S. copyright law. In just one of the many such cases that found its way into the legal system, the hip-hop group De La Soul settled out of court for failing to credit the Turtles after sampling a portion of their recording "You Showed Me" (number 6 in 1969). The band used the excerpt superimposed over a sample from a recording of a French lesson in "Transmitting Live from Mars" from their debut album, *3 Feet High and Rising* (number 24 in 1989).

In its most basic form, rap disposes of melody completely, utilizing instead the rhythmic declamation of a spoken voice (or voices) over a foundation of percussion. Precursors of this declamatory style can be found in the recordings of many soul artists, including Barry White, Isaac Hayes, and Millie Jackson. The lyrical content of rap recordings is often dramatically different from other songs within the rock-and-roll mainstream. Some subgenres of rap frequently incorporate graphic depiction of violence, degrading objectification of women, and sexually explicit lyrics. Initially, rap audiences consisted primarily of young African-American listeners, though during the 1990s teenagers of all ethnic backgrounds accepted the musical style.

One of the first commercially released rap records was "Rapper's Delight" by a Harlem group known as the Sugarhill Gang. Released in 1979, it finally peaked at number 36 in early 1980. By the mid-1980s, most people had heard some rap music, but it was still considered a black underground style, not commercially viable for major recording companies or MTV. Granted, there were a few "cute" raps that did reach the mass audience (e.g., video raps by professional football teams), but the hard-core style was not to have real national exposure until 1984–1986. A few rap albums in this period sold sufficiently to enter the charts: *Run-D.M.C.* (1984), *King of Rock* (1985), and *Raising Hell* (1986) by Run-D.M.C.; *Escape* (1984) by Whodini; and *Licensed to Ill* (1986) by the Beastie Boys.

The real breakthrough year for rap was 1986. *Raising Hell* by Run-D.M.C. reached the number 3 position and yielded a number 4 single, "Walk This Way," and a number 29 hit, "You Be Illin'." "Walk This Way" was an update of a 1977 hit by Aerosmith and adds voice and guitar of Aerosmith members Steve Tyler and Joe Perry. The rock flavor of Run-D.M.C.'s rap version probably accounts for its national chart success. However, hard-core rap purists resented the intrusion of rock into their style. (They also were a bit suspicious of Run-D.M.C. because they were from the comparatively upscale borough of Queens instead of the "real streets" of Harlem, Brooklyn, or the Bronx.) The lesser hit, "You Be Illin'," was more to the taste of the rap purists.

Because of its commercial success, Run-D.M.C.'s *Raising Hell* introduced the rap style to a much broader national audience. The trio featured Daryl McDaniels as the "MC" (the master of ceremonies who delivers most of the raps), Jason Mizell as the "DJ" (master of turntable manipulations), and Joseph Simmons as the drummer /keyboardist. Virtually all rappers have street names; thus, McDaniel was "DMC"; Mizell was "Jam Master Jay"; and Simmons was "Run." The roles of the MC and drummer are obvious. A new element, however, is the work of the DJ, who manipulates discs on turntables to produce rhythmic scratches, backward and forward snatches of sound, and brief samples of chords, words, and riffs from prerecorded discs. Listen to "You Be Illin'" to get an idea of what Jam Master Jay adds with his turntables (this song also contains a piano bass line and a "live" sax part). As further evidence of the connection between rap (even styles other than "gangsta rap") and violence, Jam Master Jay was shot in the head and killed while in the lounge of his recording studio on October 30, 2002.

Later in 1986, a white rap trio, the Beastie Boys, broke into the virtually all-black style with a number 1 album, *Licensed to Ill.* If black rap purists were suspicious of Run-D.M.C. from Queens, they strongly resented these "beige boys" from upper middle-class backgrounds. Adam Yauch ("MCA") and Michael Diamond ("Mike

D") began as Young and Useless, a punk-oriented group. After adding Adam Horovitz ("King Ad-Rock") in 1981, they moved to rap and became the Beastie Boys. Their raps cover a range of topics from sexual promiscuity to drugs and alcohol to political commentary. As with Run-D.M.C., the most commercially successful cut from *Licensed to Ill* was the most rock-oriented single, "(You Gotta) Fight For Your Right (To Party)," which peaked at number 7 in early 1987. In fact, this song is more hard rock than rap. *Licensed to Ill* was the first rap album to hit number 1.

The Beastie Boys' next album, *Paul's Boutique* (number 14 in 1989), was three years in coming as the result of a legal dispute with their record company, Def Jam. The sound of the album was significantly different from their debut, selling far fewer copies and resulting in only one minor hit, "Hey Ladies" (number 36). Another three years passed before their third album, *Check Your Head* (number 10 in 1992), was released. With the release of *Ill Communication* (1994) and *Hello Nasty* (1998) the Beasties returned to the top of the charts, where both albums debuted. In 2004, after another long pause, the Beastie Boys released *To the 5 Boroughs* (also debuting at number 1). Though not prolific in their output, the Beasties continue to chart high with their releases, though the total sales figures have dropped significantly since the 1990s.

The next rapper to achieve a mass audience was L.L. Cool J. Like Run-D.M.C., James Todd Smith was from Queens. His first album, *Radio* (1985), had limited sales. But *Bigger and Deffer* (1987) rose to number 3 and yielded a hit single, "I Need Love." But as with Run-D.M.C.'s "Walk This Way" and the Beastie's "Fight For Your Right," Cool J.'s hit single was not a typical rap song. Instead of being hard rock oriented, "I Need Love" was a "rap ballad." While that may seem like a self-contradictory term, it refers to a rap that has a slow tempo, soft beat, gentle accompaniment, and love-oriented lyrics. Although hard-core rappers intensely dislike the success of such "impure" rap hits, such songs did bring the general concept of the rap style (rhythmically delivered spoken lyrics) to a wide audience and paved the way to success for more "authentic" rap songs. (Speaking of rap combination styles, listen to "The Do Wop" from *Bigger and Deffer*—a fun combination of rap and doo-wop.)

Cool J. enjoyed fairly consistent success after 1987, especially with his album *Walking With a Panther* (number 6 in 1989). By that time, rap had been accepted as a commercially viable style. His success continued through the 1990s with *Mama Said Knock You Out* (number 16 in 1990 and a Grammy winner), *14 Shots to the Dome* (number 5 in 1991), *Mr. Smith* (number 20 in 1995), and *Phenomenon* (number 7 in 1997). L.L. Cool J. is cited as an influence by many rappers who came after and was the first rap artist to perform on MTV's *Unplugged* (1991). In the transition from the 1980s to the 1990s, an explosion of rap artists hit the airwaves and the charts. These would include D.J. Jazzy Jeff and the Fresh Prince, the Fat Boys, Public Enemy, NWA, M.C. Hammer, Ice Cube, and Vanilla Ice. Although we cannot discuss all of these (or others) in detail, we shall at least survey some of the changes represented by a few of these artists.

New York City may have been the birthplace of rap, but other cities contributed to the growth of the style. D.J. Jazzy Jeff and the Fresh Prince were from Philadelphia; Los Angeles produced Eazy E, Ice Cube, and N.W.A. With *Straight Outta Compton* (NWA), a large segment of the public became aware of the deepest, most hard-core style of rap, untouched by hard rock, ballads, doo-wop, or any other softening or blending intended to achieve greater commercial success. This album only reached number 37, but it sold over two million copies. With the *Compton* album, many Americans were confronted by a style they had not heard from L.L. Cool J., Run-D.M.C., the Beastie Boys, or D.J. Jazzy Jeff and the Fresh Prince. One of the original members of NWA, Ice Cube, produced an album (*AmeriKKKa's Most Wanted*) in 1990 that followed the trend set by NWA (perhaps with somewhat more interesting samples of preexisting material). Nelson and Gonzales describe the album as follows:

> From dealers chillin' in front of the projects to rival gangs spraying them with bullets, from the din of children roaming through the streets of shattered glass to a group of pregnant girlies gulping cheap, sweet wine in front of the local 7-Eleven. With an eye that magnifies brutal characters and violent situations, Ice Cube exposes a world that seems on the brink of exploding in the ear of the listener. This is Black Cali, 1990: Welcome to the nightmare (Nelson and Gonzales 1991, 107).

These albums by NWA and Ice Cube established a substyle of rap that has become known as "gangsta rap." We will address the subject of "gangsta rap" in a separate section later in this chapter.

As some rap groups moved further into the angry, defiant style of "gangsta rap," there were others who played more to the mainstream. Often defiled by the purists as being fraudulent, they nonetheless have achieved great commercial success. The most successful of the black rappers at the end of the 1980s was M.C. Hammer (Stanley Kirk Burrell), a product of Oakland, California. His first album *Let's Get It Started* was reasonably successful; but his second album *Please Hammer Don't Hurt 'Em* (1990) was a monster. It reached number 1 and stayed there for nearly half a year. Listening to this album, one can see why the harder rapper can barely tolerate Hammer. His raps are antidrugs, antiviolence, and speak positively to a young black generation. He even included several rap ballads in *Please Don't Hurt 'Em*. Some of the samples (brief borrowed backgrounds) were from prior hits by Rick James, Marvin Gaye, the Jackson Five, Prince, and the Chi-Lites. Several singles from the album moved into the Top 20: "Pray," "Have You Seen Her?" (a ballad), and "U Can't Touch This." Much of Hammer's popularity certainly stemmed from his dancing, as exemplified in his videos.

Following close behind Hammer's popularity was a white rapper, Vanilla Ice (Robert Van Winkle). His album *To The Extreme* (1990) sold more than seven million copies. The hit single "Ice Ice Baby" peaked at number 1—the first rap single to do so. Some black rappers have accused Vanilla Ice of parodying black music; at the very least, he seems to be a rather pale imitation of the real thing and his status as a superstar proved to be fleeting indeed.

By the end of the 1980s, rap was firmly entrenched as a new musical style. Its musical derivation was primarily from James Brown; recall his steady, unchanging vamps, half-sung, half-spoken "hip" lyrics and herky-jerky accompaniments. Recent technological innovations have made the sampling process much easier than it was for the original rappers, who had to have skilled hands on a turntable. Now electronic instruments (samplers) can record the tiniest prerecorded material and allow it to be electronically modified, saved, and mixed in at the touch of a few buttons.

Rap is more of a social phenomenon than a musical one. Other than the rather clever samples, the music of rap tends to be simplistic and repetitive. There is no melody in most cases—only a bass line, a funky beat (often on a drum machine), and some rhymes. But the rhymes are the key element. They range from the usual love topics to intense social commentary (either positive, as with Hammer, or graphically negative).

## RAP COMES OF AGE

In Chapter 2, "The Roots of Rock," black R & B of the late 1940s and early 1950s was described as being the most important musical style leading to the emergence of rock and roll. At that time, it was relatively easy to determine specific musical attributes that distinguished R & B from other contemporaneous musical styles, such as Pop or C & W. Its typical instrumentation, the hard-driving prominence of its rhythmic component, the simple three-chord harmonies common to the twelve-bar blues form, and the shouting vocal style set R & B apart from other musical styles of the time. By the 1990s, such a wide variety of music was being labeled "R & B" that this stylistic descriptor had been rendered practically meaningless. Soulful, but relatively mellow, performers such as Anita Baker, Luther Vandross, and white vocalist Michael Bolton were all labeled R & B artists. At the same time, rappers often lay claim to being R & B artists. Rap music evolved into more than just one of many substyles of black music; it became one of the primary directions of popular music for young audiences of every race.

Along with the multitude of dance recordings, rap music proved to be a potent tool for protest and political activism. Inspiration for this movement was evident in collectives of militant black poets during the late 1960s and early 1970s; for example, the Last Poets in Harlem (New York) and the Watts Prophets (Los Angeles). Following their lead, musician-poet Gil Scott-Heron released "The Revolution Will Not Be Televised" (1973), popularized by a cover version contained on Labelle's *Pressure Cookin'*, which was released the same year. Early rap recordings initiating this trend include Brother D's (with Collective Effort) "How We Gonna Make the Black Nation Rise?" (1985) and Grandmaster Flash and the Furious Five's poignant portrayal of life in the ghetto entitled "The Message" (number 4 R & B in 1982).

One of the most influential politically oriented hip-hop acts of the time was Public Enemy, boasting a dual rapper format with Chuck D (Carlton Ridenhour) as the authoritative political activist and sidekick Flavor Flav (William Drayton). The group also included Terminator X and Professor Griff. In a dramatic visualization of their militant message, the group's backup dancers, known as the Security of the First World (S1W), carried fake Uzis and, as a parody of Motown choreography, performed stiff, martial arts movements. In 1987, these self-proclaimed "prophets of rage" released their debut album, *Yo! Bum Rush the Show*. Though critically acclaimed by hip-hop insiders, the album brought little commercial success. The release of the band's second album, however, was hailed as a tour de force. *It Takes a Nation of Millions to Hold Us Back* (number 42 in 1988) sold over a million copies and contained "Don't Believe the Hype" (number 18 R & B). Chuck D labeled rap music as "CNN for black culture." After recording "Fight the Power" for Spike Lee's film, Public Enemy released *Fear of a Black Planet* (number 10 in 1990). This album addressed controversial topics including white racism ("Burn Hollywood Burn" and "911 is a Joke") and encouraged African-American members of American society to unite ("Brothers Gonna Work It Out" and "War at 33¹/₃"). The band's next two releases,

Public Enemy (*Source:* Lisa Haun / Michael Ochs Archive, Ltd.)

*Apocalypse 91* (number 4 in 1991) and *Greatest Misses* (number 13 in 1992), continued their commercial success. The powerful messages contained in many of these songs provided unity and a clear sense of justice, as well as inspiration for future artists: Run-D.M.C.'s "Hard Times" (1983) and Boogie Down Productions' *Criminal Minded* (1987). Though the lyrics conveyed strong feelings and a passionate belief in correcting the social and economic inequity evident in the treatment of minorities across the United States, the message was not a violent one. Violence, it seems, was left to rappers flooding the airwaves with a new subgenre known as "gangsta rap." Public Enemy's *Muse Sick-N-Hour Mess Age* (number 14 in 1994) contained lyrics criticizing this new style of rap with its extreme portrayal of violence, encouragement of drug use, misogynistic vignettes, and materialism. The manner in which this album entered high on the charts and quickly faded away suggests that the young generation may have found a new set of messengers to listen to, perhaps those about whom Chuck D was speaking.

**Gangsta Rap**

By the mid-1990s, gangsta rap became a dominant subgenre of rap. Best-selling rap artists Ice Cube, Snoop Doggy Dogg, Ice-T, Dr. Dre, Cypress Hill, Scarface, and many others incorporated themes of gang-related violence and explicit porno-graphic depictions into their recordings, often augmenting the musical experience with the addition of extramusical sounds, including gunshots and sirens. Warner Music Division at Time Warner experienced a tremendous backlash as political and social groups like the National Political Congress of Black Women and various police associations forced them to defend—sometimes at great expense—the distribution of this music. Under pressure from such groups, Time Warner removed the song "Cop Killer" from the eponymous debut album by *Body Count,* a project led by rapper Ice-T. This explicit description of an inner-city youth planning the premeditated murder of unsuspecting police officers suggests the depths to which the verbal message of this music had fallen, and the willingness with which major recording companies yielded to profit motives, signifying a flagrant disregard for societal consequences. As a result, lyrics like the following from "Cop Killer" were featured prominently in gangsta rap recordings:

> I got my twelve gauge sawed off,
> I got my headlights turned off,
> I'm 'bout to bust some shots off,
> I'm 'bout to dust some cops off.[1]

In conjunction with the driving beat, heavy metal guitar style, angry attitude, and violent lyrics, gangsta rap successfully managed to pump the adrenaline of a generation of inner-city youth. Rappers who "throw down," to use their own terminology, such gang-related lyrics often claimed to be merely reporting incidents witnessed in their experience of inner-city urban life, not giving their stamp of approval to such actions. However, lyrics detailing graphic violence like the ones cited above certainly serve to fan the fire of hatred far too common in these troubled urban areas, rather than offering solutions to undeniable social and economic problems.

With the rise of successful gangsta rappers on the West Coast (Ice-T, NWA, Ice Cube, Dr. Dre, and others), New York's claim to hip hop preeminence was in question. This rivalry eventually found its way into recordings, with Marian "Suge" Knight (West Coast) and Sean "Puffy" Combs (East Coast) trading threats and insults via their song lyrics. The desire to "dis" (disrespect) other competing groups using the imagery of gang warfare was common among gangsta rappers.

Many of the most successful rap artists rose to popularity as part of an ensemble and then decided to strike out on a solo career. This "splinter phenomenon" is certainly not exclusive to rap music, but has been a common occurrence throughout the history of rock and roll (e.g., Lionel Richie from the Commodores, Sting from The Police, Peter Gabriel from Genesis, Bobby Brown and Bel Biv DeVoe from New Edition). Two rap groups serve as examples of this continuing phenomenon.

## NWA

Formed in 1986, NWA ("Niggaz With Attitude") experienced great commercial success with *Straight Outta Compton* (1989) and *EFIL4ZAGGIN* (number 1 in 1991; the title is "Niggaz 4 Life" backward). The former album resulted in significant controversy due to its inclusion of the track "Fuck the Police," for which distributor Priority Records received a "warning letter" from the FBI. Members of the group who

---

[1]"Cop Killer" written by Ernie Cunnigan and Tracy Marrow. Copyright © 1992 PolyGrams International Publishing, Inc. Ernknecsea Music and Rhyme Syndicate Music. Used by permission. All Rights Reserved.

went on to highly successful solo careers include Ice Cube (O'Shea Jackson), Eazy-E (Eric Wright), and Dr. Dre (Andre Young). As a solo artist, Ice Cube released *AmeriKKKa's Most Wanted* (number 19 in 1990), *Death Certificate* (number 2 in 1991), *The Predator* (debuting at number 1 in 1992), and *Lethal Injection* (number 5 in 1993). During the 1990s, he had a very successful acting career, appearing in films such as *Boyz N the Hood* (1991), *Higher Learning* (1992), *Friday* (1995), *The Players Club* (1998; written by, directed by, and starring Ice Cube), *Anaconda* (1997), *Three Kings* (1999), and *All About the Benjamins* (2002). Eazy-E recorded *Eazy-Duz-It* (1988), *It's On (Dr. Dre) 187um Killa* (number 5 in 1993), and *Str8 Off the Streetz of Muthaphukkin Compton* (number 3 in 1996). Before his death in 1995 (due to complications related to AIDS), Eazy-E played an important role in nurturing the career of Bone Thugs-N-Harmony, producing their double-platinum debut EP. After his departure from NWA, Dr. Dre went on to establish Death Row Records with Marian "Suge" Knight. His solo efforts include *The Chronic* (number 3 in 1993) and *2001* (number 2 in 1999). As producer, Dre worked successfully with Snoop Doggy Dogg, Tupac Shakur, and others. Dr. Dre was also responsible for discovering a white rapper from Detroit named Eminem and produced his highly controversial recordings (we will discuss Eminem later in this chapter).

### The Wu-Tang Clan

Rising from the housing projects of Staten Island, the Wu-Tang Clan provides another example of a rap splinter group. Two cousins, RZA (Robert Diggs) and GZA (Gary Grice), were the group's founders, enlisting the assistance of Ol' Dirty Bastard (Russell Jones), Inspectah Deck (Jason Hunter), Raekwon (Corey Woods), U-God (Lamont Hawkins), Ghostface Killah (Dennis Coles), Method Man (Clifford Smith), and Masta Killa (Elgin Turner). Their debut album, *Enter the Wu-Tang (36 Chambers)* (number 41 in 1993), demonstrated their ghetto-related lyricism infused with references to the martial arts. Interestingly, the group's contract with Loud Records allowed each member freedom to negotiate with other labels for the release of solo project work. Method Man's *Tical* (number 4 in 1994) was the first to take advantage of this arrangement, but many more would follow, including his own *Tical 2000: Judgment Day* (number 2 in 1998) and *Blackout!* (number 3 in 1999). Other solo projects included GZA's *Liquid Swords* (number 9 in 1995) and *Beneath the Surface* (number 9 in 1996), RZA's *RZA as Bobby Digital in Stereo* (number 16 in 1998) and production credit for two albums as a member of Gravediggaz, Raekwon's *Only Built 4 Cuban Linx* (number 4 in 1995) and *Immobilarity* (number 9 in 1999), Ol' Dirty Bastard's *Return to the 36 Chambers: The Dirty Version* (number 7 in 1995) and *Nigga Please* (number 10 in 1999), Ghostface Killah's *Ironman* (number 2 in 1996) and *Supreme Clientele* (number 7 in 2000), Inspectah Deck's *Uncontrolled Substance* (number 19 in 1999), and U-God's *Golden Arms Redemption* (number 58 in 1999). Though group members experienced a significant amount of success as solo artists, they continued to record as the Wu-Tang Clan; for example, *Wu-Tang Forever* (number 1 in 1997), *The W* (number 5 in 2000), *Iron Flag* (2001), and *Disciples of the 36 Chambers* (2004). In November, 2004, Ol' Dirty Bastard died after collapsing suddenly in a New York recording studio just days short of his thirty-sixth birthday. The cause of death was a heart attack due to intoxication by the combined effects of cocaine and Tarmadol.

# OTHER RAPPERS

### Salt-n-Pepa

Interestingly, while gangsta rap was becoming more extreme in its depiction of violence, milder forms of rap were being accepted into the mainstream of popular music. One of the first rap groups to cross over successfully to the pop charts, Salt-n-Pepa, consisted of three female members: Cheryl "Salt" James, Sandy "Pepa" Denton, and Pamela Greene (DJ). The trio, formed in 1985, released *Hot, Cool, and Vicious* the following year, with fellow Sears co-worker Hurby "Luv Bug" Azor acting as manager and producer. The album resulted in three minor R & B singles. Success on the pop charts did not come until a San Francisco DJ at KMEL remixed the B-side of one of these singles, "Push It." The remixed version of the single reached number 19, spending 13 weeks on the charts, and was eventually nominated for a Grammy in 1988. That same year, Greene was replaced as DJ for the group by Deidre "Spinderella" Roper. The most successful song from the two following albums, *A Salt with a Deadly Pepa* (1988) and *Blacks' Magic* (1990), was "Let's Talk About Sex" (number 13 in 1991) from the latter recording. Wanting to play a larger role in the creative process, the women separated from Azor to release *Very Necessary* (number 4 in 1993). It was on this album that the group attained their highest chart success with "Shoop" (number 4) and "Whatta Man" (number 3), a collaboration with the popular female vocal group En Vogue. In the mid-1990s, Salt-n-Pepa adopted the image of tough-rapping divas, as exhibited on "Ain't Nuthin But a She Thing" (number 38 in 1995). However, the role of tough females in rap ultimately fell to Queen Latifah and Sistah Souljah, who rapped forcefully on the subjects of African nationalism and pro-woman activism. As in the title song from Sistah Souljah's *360 Degrees of Power* (1992), strident rhymes against racial oppression often contained explicit antiwhite sentiments.

### Eminem

As mentioned previously, rap music originated as an almost exclusively African-American art form, evolving out of hip-hop culture in the South Bronx. As time went by, however, white rappers appeared on the scene. Early examples of non-black rappers include Vanilla Ice (Robert Van Winkle) and Marky Mark (Mark Wahlberg), though neither of these "white boys" could truly hold a candle to the rap style and verbal gymnastics of contemporaneous black MCs. More authentic sounding white rappers followed, including House of Pain and the Beastie Boys. In the late 1990s, the arrival of Marshall Mathers (a.k.a. Eminem) revealed that rap, gangsta or otherwise, was no longer solely the province of African-American performers.

The appearance of white rappers provides an interesting parallel to the period when rock music emerged in the 1950s. While nonblack rap artists prior to the appearance of Eminem might be seen as purposefully toning down the angst and subject matter of their African-American counterparts to make the style palatable to a wider audience (like Pat Boone covering a tune by Big Joe Turner), Eminem performed rhymes uncensored, emulating the style of his predecessors (like Elvis's comparatively authentic integration of stylistic traits of R & B artists). Though Mathers recording debut, *Infinite* (1997), attracted little attention, the follow-up EP won him a recording contract with

Eminem (*Source:* Michael Ochs Archive, Ltd.)

Interscope and initiated a professional relationship with its influential founder, Dr. Dre. With Dre's assistance, Eminem's second recording was extended into the breakthrough album *The Slim Shady LP* (number 3 in 1999), winning a Grammy for Best Rap Album. A single from the album, "My Name Is" (number 36), was also recognized as the Best Rap Solo Performance that same year. *The Marshall Mathers LP,* debuting at number 1 in 2000 and becoming the fastest selling rap album of all time, proved that Eminem was a force with which to be reckoned within the genre and earned him a second consecutive Grammy for Best Rap Album. His commercial success continued unabated with *The Eminem Show* (number 1 in 2002), *8 Mile* (number 1 in 2002; starred in the movie and performed

soundtrack), and *Encore* (number 1 in 2004). His influence as an artist and talent scout also proved quite effective with several spinoff projects, including Dirty Dozen (D12) and 50 Cent.

The critical and commercial success of Eminem's recordings was second only to the controversy resulting from concern about the themes upon which the rapper expounded. Eminem seemed to shrink from no opportunity to offend or challenge. He freely ranted about guns, drugs, killing, abuse, homosexuality, misogyny, and many other controversial topics, often seeming to promote and encourage violence. Among the loudest voices in protest against his music were gay rights activists, religious groups, women's groups, and even members of his own family. He was sued by his mother for defamation and by his estranged wife (who he "killed" more than once in his recorded narratives). Like many of the other artists discussed in this section, Mathers himself wound up on the wrong side of the law, receiving two years probation for assault and carrying a concealed weapon. The assaulted man allegedly kissed the rapper's wife outside a nightclub.

Why is it that we, both as authors of a rock history text and as the listening public, give attention to such an individual? Simply put, Eminem was, in fact, one of the best MCs rapping during the transition to the new millennium. His rhyming skills and delivery style rivaled many of the best African-American performers of the time, winning him the respect not only of the general public, but of many of his peers in the rap community. Secondly—and this is, admittedly, a slippery slope—the storytelling on Eminem's albums was presented through the eyes of "Slim Shady," a fictional alter ego who has been described as "a homicidal comedian through whom

Mathers enacted his most outrageous and perverse revenge fantasies" (George-Warren and Romanowski 2001, 304). When Eminem narrates for us a tale of riding in the car with his daughter to a drop-off point where they will dispose of the lifeless body of the child's mother (along with two other bodies, implied to be the stepfather and a half brother)—as he does in "'97 Bonnie and Clyde"—we are to believe that this is simply a storyteller stretching the bounds of poetic license for dramatic effect. There is no doubt that the dramatic impact is great, but once again we ask, what of social responsibility?

## NEW JACK SWING

In spite of the controversy surrounding gangsta rap, developments at the end of the 1980s served to bring rap into the mainstream of popular music. Credited largely to the influence of multi-instrumentalist and producer Teddy Riley, a new variety of rap referred to as "New Jack Swing" or "Neo-Soul" evolved out of New York City, merging the hip-hop beat with light rap and traditional R & B vocals. Riley's own group, Guy, had an R & B hit with "Groove Me" in 1988. Singles by the band were selected for inclusion in the soundtracks to two black urban films, *Do the Right Thing* (1989) and *New Jack City* (1991). Members of Guy went their separate ways after releasing *The Future* (1990), which resulted in three Top 10 R & B singles: "Let's Chill" (number 3), "Do Me Right" (number 2), and "D-O-G Me Out" (number 8). Following the group's dissolution, Riley assisted Michael Jackson during the recording of *Dangerous* (1991), stamping that release with his trademark production sound. Listen to "Jam," the opening cut on Jackson's recording, to hear Riley's New Jack Swing influence. The song begins with rhythmically spoken words over a heavy dance beat. Throughout the entire recording, Jackson's vocals seem to take on a more mature, yet desperate, tone. In the middle of the song, following a brief synthesized horn break, there is a straight-ahead rap section, giving way once again to Jackson's vocals.

In 1994, Riley formed Blackstreet and experienced continued success with "Before I Let You Go" (number 7 in 1994) and "No Diggity" (number 1 in 1996). A reunion of Guy resulted in *Guy III* and a hit single, "Dancin'" (number 19 in 1999). Following Riley's lead, other producers, including Jimmy Jam and Terry Lewis and Babyface, picked up on this eclectic and highly lucrative blend of musical styles. Jimmy Jam and Terry Lewis were originally members of The Time and proved integral to the success of Janet Jackson. The production talent of Babyface gained massive critical acclaim as his artistry continued unabated into the late 1990s. He worked with artists including Paula Abdul, Pebbles, TLC, the Jacksons, Whitney Houston, Boyz II Men, and Bobby Brown. His production work and songwriting skill resulted in an amazing twelve Grammy nominations in 1997, tying a record set by Michael Jackson following the release of *Thriller* (1982).

One of the first artists to popularize the New Jack Swing sound, benefiting from Teddy Riley's production skill, was Keith Sweat. Working as a commodities broker on Wall Street, Sweat successfully marketed his own demo, succeeded in finding an interested management company, and eventually signed a record contract. His debut single "I Want Her" (number 5 in 1988) revealed a smooth blend of R & B and hip-hop, becoming the first New Jack Swing hit to receive national attention.

Keith Sweat's vocal style is reminiscent of soul singers about whom you have read in previous pages.

Other rap groups place more importance on the declamatory speaking style and hip-hop rhythms, but still incorporate melodic aspects into the song structures. Former bandmates of Bobby Brown in New Edition, Ricky Bell, Michael Bivins, and Ronnie DeVoe formed Bell Biv DeVoe in 1988. The three had previously served a subsidiary role to primary lead vocalists Brown and Ralph Tresvant, but proved to be a dance music powerhouse when, encouraged by Jimmy Jam and Terry Lewis, the group began producing their own dance music. Bell Biv DeVoe's biggest hits ("Poison" and "Do Me!," both number 3) were culled from their debut album *Poison* (1990). All six members of New Edition, including Bobby Brown and his replacement Johnny Gill, reunited in 1996 to produce *Home Again* (number 1 on both Pop and R & B charts), including the songs "Hit Me Off" (number 3), "I'm Still in Love With You" (number 7), and "You Don't Have to Worry" (number 10). Other examples of this rap–R & B blend may be found in the music of Snap! ("The Power," number 2 in 1990), Marky Mark & the Funky Bunch ("Good Vibrations," number 1 in 1991), Color Me Badd ("I Adore Me Amor," number 1 in 1991), and Arrested Development ("Mr. Wendal," number 6 in 1993).

The successful crossing over of rap music into the mainstream of American popular music was completed by the late 1980s. Signs of such a transition had been on the horizon for some time but, with the collaborative effort of Run-D.M.C. and Aerosmith on a cover version of "Walk This Way" (number 4 in 1986), the crossover was complete, including the all-important acceptance of hip-hop by MTV. Confirmation of the fact came shortly thereafter with the release of the Beastie Boys' *Licensed to Ill*—the first rap album to reach number 1. Vanilla Ice became the most commercially successful white rapper at the time with the release of *To The Extreme* (number 1 in 1990), while the biggest crossover rap artist to date was (M.C.) Hammer, selling 10 million copies of *Please Hammer Don't Hurt 'Em* (number 1 in 1990). Final confirmation that black artists—and rap in particular—had truly been accepted into the mainstream was provided in the October 11, 2003 *Billboard* magazine. That week, on the Hot 100, all Top 10 songs were by black recording stars. All but one—the top position—were by rappers:

| | | |
|---|---|---|
| 1. | "Baby Boy" | Beyoncé (featuring Sean Paul) |
| 2. | "Shake Ya Tailfeather" | Nelly, P. Diddy, & Murphy Lee |
| 3. | "Get Low" | Li'l Jon & the East Side Boyz (featuring Ying Yang Twins) |
| 4. | "Right Thurr" | Chingy |
| 5. | "Frontin'" | Pharrell (featuring Jay-Z) |
| 6. | "Damn!" | YoungBloodz (featuring Li'l Jon) |
| 7. | "P.I.M.P." | 50 Cent |
| 8. | "Into You" | Fabolous (featuring Tamia/Ashanti) |
| 9. | "Stand Up" | Ludacris (featuring Shawnna) |
| 10. | "Where Is the Love?" | Black Eyed Peas |

The evolution of rap produced a wide variety of substyles within this genre of rock. From the raw intensity of gangsta rap to the R & B melodicism of New Jack Swing to the eclectic sounds of jazz-rap (a rap hybrid initiated by the Jungle Brothers and popularized by US3's "Cantaloop"), the characteristic spoken delivery of lyrics was absorbed into the mainstream of contemporary youth culture. According to Arthur Kempton (2003), as we settled into the new millennium, 70 percent of hip-hop sales was attributable to white consumers.

## MUSICAL CLOSE-UP:
### EXPRESSIVE MUSICAL PERFORMANCE: RHYTHMIC DELIVERY OF RAP

Music is a highly expressive form of human communication, filled with subtle nuance and meaningful gestures. The same musical phrase performed by two different artists will never be *exactly* the same. In fact, it is not even possible for the *same* artist—short of using digital sampling—to perform the same phrase twice in precisely the same way. Such exactitude of replication is simply beyond human ability. Subtle changes occur in the pitch, loudness, tone color, and duration of the tones performed. Such changes provide the basis for a "human" performance. The use of the term *imperfect* is sometimes used to describe such alterations, though we believe this to be a misnomer. In fact, subtle changes in these basic musical elements result in *expressive deviations* that add meaning to the musical message . . . often intentionally, sometimes unintentionally. If you want to hear a clear comparison of two performances—one that incorporates expressive deviations ("imperfections") and one that does not—simply select a specific song to use ("Yesterday" by Lennon & McCartney will do as well as any). Listen carefully to the original studio recording by the Beatles and notice—beyond the meaning of the lyrics—the mood, style, and emotion that are communicated by the musical performance. Now, use your favorite Internet search engine to locate a MIDI file of this same song. Listen to this "performance" of the song, in which all note durations are played mechanically exactly as they are represented in the musical score and in which there is little, if any, differentiation in loudness from note to note. The very important element missing from this latter music is the "expressive performance" aspect . . . the human element that gives music its impressive ability to communicate nonverbally.

Have you ever wondered why there is more than one recording of Beethoven's Fifth Symphony or any other classical masterpiece? It is because the "notes on the page" provide only a *guideline* to the performer. Much of the communicative message is added in the performer's interpretive process of changing the notes on the written page into musical sound. Of course, a significant amount of popular music is created and performed without the use of a written score. As revealed by the three *Anthology* releases by the Beatles, the creative process often involves multiple attempts to perform a song—in different keys, at different tempos, and with different interpretations. This is an integral part of the creative process. Listening to a number of live recordings of the same song performed by an artist is another way to observe such expressive differences. Cover versions of popular songs, as a third type of observation, often emphasize differences in expressive style to set them apart from the original recording.

Above, when describing a rapper's style of vocal delivery, we mentioned that the "tones" are altered in expressive ways. The term *tone* might seem inappropriate in this context, since the element of pitch within a melodic framework is typically absent from rap. However, all forms of expressive deviation are available to the rapper—even pitch—through the use of voice inflections. Though these artists do not "sing," in a traditional sense, there is certainly a pitch contour evident in their spoken delivery . . . otherwise, the style would become as boring as listening to someone speak in a monotone. Listen carefully to any of the latest rap singles listed on the *Billboard* Top 40 and see if you can follow the pitch contour of the spoken voice as it moves from low- to high-toned inflection.

In a more general sense, rappers have adopted a variety of styles for rhythmically delivering their rhythms. According to Gioia (2003), the rap artist

> consciously exploits stress-meter's ability to stretch and contract in syllable count. In fact, playing the syllable count against the beat is the basic metrical technique of rap. Like jazz, rap extravagantly syncopates a flexible rhythm against a fixed metrical beat thereby turning a traditional English folk meter into something distinctively African-American. By hitting the metrical beat strongly while exploiting other elements of word music, rappers play interesting and elaborate games with the total rhythm of their lines.

In this musical close-up, we will compare the vocal delivery of several of the most highly respected and commercially successful rap artists: Run-D.M.C., Snoop Dogg, Eminem, and OutKast.

As you learned earlier, one of the first rap groups to reach a mass audience was Run-D.M.C. Often, as a means of providing sonic variety, rap groups include more than one rapper who takes turns filling the role of MC. Run-D.M.C. fits this model, as do NWA, Wu-Tang Clan, the Beastie Boys, and many others. One unique facet of Run-D.M.C.'s rapping technique is that, rather than the typical form of alternating verses or even lines within a verse, Joseph Simmons ("Run") and Darryl McDaniels ("D.M.C.") start and finish one another's lines or create a dynamic musical texture by interlocking words and/or phrases. Perhaps the most dramatic use of this technique is found in the opening lines to "Peter Piper" (the opening track on *Raising Hell*). In the following excerpt, the words or phrases delivered by each rapper are differentiated by the use of plain or boldfaced text, while italicized text represents a phrase intoned by both in unison.

> Now, Peter **Piper** picked **peppers,** but Run rocked **rhymes.**
> Humpty **Dumpty** fell **down,** that's his hard **time.**
> Jack B. **Nimble** was **nimble,** and he was **quick,**
> But Jam **Master** cut **faster,** *Jack's on Jay's dick.*

Though extreme in its application, this kind of alternation is not a new performance technique and, in fact, can be traced back as far as the appearance of *hocket* in the Medieval organum and the Renaissance motet. The two lead rappers perform their energetic rap delivery with a high level of rhythmic precision, never straying too far from the beat.

In contrast, Snoop Dogg's rap delivery is significantly more subdued. In fact, as a quintessential gangsta rapper, the relaxed drawl with which the words of his rhymes are delivered serves to increase the intensity of the meaning of the words. Listen to "Murder Was the Case" (1994), a song from the soundtrack for a documentary film of the same name about Snoop and Dr. Dre. The song was a remix of a track originally released on *Doggystyle* (1993). Note the typically soft, somewhat breathy delivery of the lyrics. He also uses a wide pitch range as portions of the text are delivered in a near falsetto range. Other significant aspects of Snoop's style are exemplified by his more relaxed rhythmic delivery—lagging behind the beat at some points, while rushing ahead slightly at others—and the lax manner of his rhyming structure. Most of the time couplet phrases rhyme, but sometimes they don't. To break up the quadruple meter and duple subdivision feel, the rapper periodically inserts triplet rhythms, providing a subtle lilt to the musical delivery . . . while the text of the song relays a story of Dogg's "murder," awakening from a coma, then incarceration.

With Eminem (Marshall Mathers), all pretense is dropped and the intensity of performance is a direct result of the delivery style. Mathers moves frequently and comfortably from intense, in-your-face machine gun delivery to taking apparent pleasure in mocking rap music . . . his own and that of other artists. As an early example of this artist's rap style, listen to "My Name Is" (on *The Slim Shady LP*). The opening lines—as the title and hook line suggest—"tag" the recording as being performed by alter ego Slim Shady. In particular, notice his use of the high-pitched "chicka-chicka" motive (a recurrent idea used on each of his recordings), a vocal attempt to replicate—parody?—a DJ's turntable scratching technique, a prominent element of many rap recordings. Apart from the meaning of the lyrics and the frequently offensive subject matter, the most consistent rhythmic characteristic is that Eminem's vocal delivery is always ever so slightly behind the beat. This slightly dragging rhythmic sense is an effective technique to increase the level of tension and to enhance the sense of urgency perceived while listening to the music.

Finally, demonstrating a style with audible ties to New Jack Swing, OutKast members Dre (or Andre 3000) and Big Boi present a musical fabric that alternates between catchy melodic hooks and rap. As a result, OutKast represents a hybrid form of rap that utilizes the rap format of a duo of rappers alternating back and forth and, at times, rapping in unison. This rhythmic vocal delivery is contrasted tastefully with melodic hooks. To hear a representative example of this music, listen to "So Fresh and So Clean" (from *Stankonia*). Notice how the syncopated melody of the chorus hook line appears periodically between rapped rhymes that constitute the verses. As you observe the verses, notice how the rhythmic rhyming of both rappers—self-described "mother-funkers"—is delivered with a high degree of precision . . . even the sixteenth-note subdivisions are performed nearly flawlessly, laying right in the groove. Also notice in the rapped verses that a line or couplet rhymed by one rapper or the other is often concluded in unison by both rappers. They also incorporate the hocket technique identified in the discussion of Run-D.M.C.

As you have seen from the discussion above and have heard from the examples mentioned, even without the benefit of beautiful melodies, rap artists have numerous ways in which to embellish an expressive performance: altering the loudness, timbre, duration, and even pitch range of the vocal delivery. The artists chosen to illustrate different approaches in the preceding paragraphs are considered exemplary, but they hardly provide an exhaustive set of examples. With the concepts of "expressive performance" in mind, seek out examples of your own to compare and contrast the approach that various artists take to communicating a musical message via the rhythmic enunciation of their rhymes.

# 18

# Alternative Styles

## OVERVIEW: BOOMERS AND POST-BOOMERS

At the end of World War II, the United States experienced a significant increase in birthrate. This trend continued into the early 1960s. The resulting bulge in population is usually called the "baby boom." Virtually every industry in the nation, including the music industry, carefully followed (and attempted to predict) the movement of the boomers as they moved through the last half of the twentieth century. A noticeable bulge in the population statistics, they are counted not only as numbers, but as dollars. The dollars in the pockets of the boomers have been and will continue to be a major market influence from the 1950s well into the new century.

The boomers were the first generation that was raised almost entirely on rock music. By the turn of the century, the boomers were mostly forty- or fifty-something years old. Although they may have been rebels in the 1960s and 1970s, by the 1980s and 1990s they began to settle down. They were by then doctors, lawyers, professors, and successful business executives. They married (usually several times) and raised families. With the arrival of the twenty-first century, many were beginning to look toward retirement. As is typically the case with the life cycle, many also became more conservative. The boomers continued to be most comfortable with things the way they were and were rather disturbed by the antics of their offspring. They were powerful because of their sheer numbers and economic strength. They were certainly an important element in the election of Presidents Reagan and Bush in the 1980s, and in the congressional and gubernatorial elections of 1994, which saw Republicans win control of both houses of Congress for the first time in four decades—a majority that was sustained into the first decade of the twenty-first century. After eight years of Democratic leadership in the White House, Republican George W. Bush was elected to the Presidency for two terms. As we shall see in this chapter, the economic strength of the boomers continued to be a major determinant in the flow of the music industry into the new century, as older and more mainstream styles of rock once again became big business.

By the early l970s, the boomers had begun having families of their own. As these offspring moved through their teens, from about the mid-1980s until slightly past 2000, they too wielded some economic influence. But if the history of rock music tells us anything, we should expect that the musical tastes of this younger generation—or post-boomers, as we shall call them—will be at odds with the musical preferences of their parents. The post-boomers, as was the case with their parents, were drawn to musical styles that were clearly distinct from their parents's music. In fact, the more distinct—and even repulsive—to their parents, the better. They sought "alternative" styles, which leads us to a closer consideration of that word.

## Anomie and Alternatives

In the late l980s and l990s, certain rock groups and styles were referred to as "alternative rock." Considering the entire history of rock music, this term seems redundant. Indeed, most rock music from its very beginning was "alternative" music. The young audiences in 1955 were fascinated by the music of Fats Domino, Chuck Berry, and Bill Haley, precisely because it represented a real alternative to the pop styles of Tony Bennett, Nat "King" Cole, and Eddie Fisher. The music of Elvis Presley, Little Richard, and Buddy Holly (and many others) continued this alternative style. When mainstream rock seemed to fade in popularity in the early 1960s, the young audiences again went crazy (literally) over the new sounds of the Beatles and the Rolling Stones because it sounded different. It was an exciting new alternative to the soft rock, pop, and rockabilly that had dominated the charts for several prior years (see the Overview in Chapter 5, "Transition: The Early 1960s").

One can trace this fascination with the alternative throughout rock history. Heavy metal, punk rock, gangsta rap—these and other styles can be seen as reactions (or alternatives) to styles that enjoyed mainstream popularity. However redundant it may be in the context of rock history, the term *alternative rock* seemed to have been accepted in the 1990s. This chapter will examine more closely the various substyles of this generic term.

But before moving on and incorporating the term *alternative* into our discussion, let us consider its implications just a bit further. In the early 1960s, we observed a brief period of fragmentation within the music market as seen in Chapter 5. But the overwhelming power of the Beatles—at least temporarily—overcame that fragmentation. However, in the 1970s, the fragmentation resumed with a vengeance (see Chapter 14, "The Continuing Fragmentation of Rock"). *Fragmentation*, of course, is simply a word that describes an explosion of alternatives. Generally speaking, we think of alternatives as being good. After all, it is nice to have a wide array of choices. But is it possible to have too many choices? Can the presence of too many choices virtually paralyze us?

Consider people who have a large and varied collection of recorded music. They come home after a day at work or school and think, "Gee, I think I'll listen to some music." But while perusing their collection of CDs, tapes, and records, they are stymied. A Beethoven symphony would be nice. Or am I more in the mood for the Rolling Stones? Maybe some light jazz would be pleasant. Should I play my CD by

Radiohead or my old Chicago record? "Oh heck; I can't decide. Maybe I'll watch some TV instead."

Perhaps you can re-create similar cases of "decisional paralysis"—"Oh, to heck with it!"—when you are confronted with over 100 TV channels, 200 kinds of wine, dozens of varieties of mustard, or a dizzying array of magazines on the rack. Of course, these decisions (or nondecisions) are not of life-shattering importance.

But what if the multiplicity of choices—alternatives—exists in more important realms, such as values and lifestyles? Easy, you might say. You just figure out what is "good" (meaning healthy, safe, and wise) and what is "bad." But, again, what if society has purged those terms and concepts from our vocabulary and thinking? What if things are no longer "good" or "bad," "right" or "wrong," but merely "alternative?" The implication is that all of those choices are equally acceptable.

In the late 1960s, the boomers seriously questioned the values of "the establishment." Among other things, this led to the antihero phenomenon (see the Overview in Chapter 8, "Folk Music and Folk Rock"). In effect, this resulted in a reversal of traditional values to the extent that good became bad and bad became good. (We will develop this thought further in Chapter 19.) Suffice it to say here that in the intervening decades, there has been an increasing hesitation to render value judgments about what is good or bad, right or wrong, better or worse. This philosophy of egalitarianism—that all things should be equal—was implied in the late 1960s and early 1970s by the phrase, "different strokes for different folks." In other words, what is right for one person may not be right for another. There was no firm definition of what was right; it all depended upon the person or circumstances. All things were relative rather than absolute. In the late 1980s and 1990s, some school districts advocated teaching "situational ethics." This philosophy suggested that there is no absolute right or wrong; instead, what was right or wrong varied according to the situation.

The desire to avoid stigmatizing some individuals or circumstances led to phrases such as "alternative lifestyles" and "alternatively abled." People spoke of alternative medicine and alternative cuisine. And, of course, we had alternative music. Indeed, the word *alternative* became one of the buzzwords of the 1990s.

But as suggested by the preceding anecdote, too many choices among equals (or alternatives) can lead to an inability to make any choice at all. The post-boomers seem to have grown up with little or no guidance regarding values because, after all, if all alternatives are equal, then there is no difference in value (and, hence, no value at all). By extension, there are no standards because all things are simply equal alternatives. There need be no rules because there is no better or worse behavior.

The French have a word that seems to apply in this situation: *anomie*. It refers to a person or society that lacks purpose, identity, or ethical values, thus leading to a feeling of rootlessness. In fact, some writers have referred to the post-boomers as "Generation X"—a generation without an identity.

Adolescent psychiatrists tell us that children and teenagers actually want to know where their boundaries are. They subconsciously need and crave limits, rules, standards, and values, even though they may protest to the contrary. If this is true, we can understand why those without clearly defined boundaries might feel angry and betrayed. In frustration, they push further and further against what they believe to be society's norms, just to see how far they can go before forcing society to say, "Enough!". To witness the results of such a set of circumstances, perhaps we need look no further than the tragedy at Columbine High School on April 20, 1999 and similar "copycat" events that have occurred all too frequently since that time.

Keep this in mind as you read about the excesses evident in some styles of rap music (Chapter 17) and the more extreme styles of alternative rock in this chapter. Are the post-boomers determined to see just how tolerant society will be before it finally lays down some limits? As we consider the music of the post-boomers, note that oftentimes the music and lyrics seem angry. Often, the performers appear to be angry, as do their audiences. Whereas young girls used to sob uncontrollably at performances by Frank Sinatra, Elvis Presley, or the Beatles, now both females and males in the audience often seem to be mad at the world.

Could it be that the availability of too many alternatives has led to a generation severely affected with anomie? The baby boomers protested because they did not like the establishment; their offspring may be protesting because of the lack of an establishment.

## ALTERNATIVE ROCK: THE PROBLEM OF DEFINITIONS

Throughout this text, we have been extremely careful about the use of certain words when they are intended to connote a specific musical style. Pop, mainstream, R & B, and other terms have all maintained an intended distinction one from another, based on specific, identifiable musical characteristics. At the conclusion of the twentieth century, the diversity of musical styles (branches of the rock-and-roll genealogical tree) became so numerous that it makes the previously mentioned fragmentation during the 1960s and 1970s seem minor by comparison. Concurrent with this further division of rock music was a high level of cross-pollination between styles, resulting in a plethora of new stylistic labels for these various hybrids. Many of these subgenres are very difficult, if not impossible, to discriminate (e.g., New Jack Swing, neo-soul, hip-hop, house music, triphop, trance, electronica, rave, techno, speed metal, rap metal, and many others).

In addition, terms that have become familiar from earlier chapters of this text have begun to take on different meanings, often deviating from the manner in which they have been used thus far. The term *rhythm and blues* provides a case in point. This term is no longer used to describe only the branch of the rock music tree that has its roots in the R & B of the 1940s and 1950s, but it is now often used to describe music much different than previously included (e.g., some subcategories of rap are now considered R & B). "Pop," as defined by *Billboard's* online list of "Top Pop Catalog Albums," includes artists as diverse as Creed, Enya, U2, Pink Floyd, Metallica, Dixie Chicks, Miles Davis, Sade, Michael Jackson, 'N Sync, and Celine Dion. Only the latter artist would have been a likely candidate for Pop as defined in earlier chapters and this label would not be appropriate for all of the music she has recorded. Further evidence of the blurring of boundaries can be found by listening to the music itself. The song "Pop" (number 19 in 2001) from 'N Sync's *Celebrity* derived as much from hip-hop and techno dance music as from the musical style after which the song is named. Listen carefully to the final section of the single in which members of the group themselves become a virtual drum machine, providing the dance beat by making vocal sounds that are then heavily processed by the recording engineer.

Use of the term *mainstream,* as if discussing a particular musical style, became particularly problematic at the beginning of the twenty-first century. A quick look at albums attaining multiplatinum status—tangible socioeconomic evidence of mainstream appeal—during the first two months of 2002 provides a glimpse of the diversity of taste inherent in the record-buying public at the time (see Table 18–1). At a time when "alternative" music (Linkin Park), rap and R & B artists ( Ja Rule, Nelly Furtado, Shakira, and Usher), Latin music (Enrique Iglesias), and Christian Rock (Creed and a various artist gospel recording) were all listed alongside the Dave Matthews Band, Nickelback, and Pink Floyd, the meaning of *mainstream* became diluted to the point of being meaningless. As further proof of this fact, it is worth noting that the three best-selling albums of 2001 were Shaggy's reggae crossover *Hotshot,* new age artist Enya's *A Day Without Rain,* and boy band 'N Sync's *Celebrity.* As a result of the evolving definitions of these stylistic labels, the distinction between "mainstream" and "alternative" artists in the present chapter will be based not on musical style, but on artist intent. Mainstream artists of the 1980s and 1990s (discussed in Chapter 13) will include members of the music business who approached their craft in a manner similar to that of a corporation seeking to turn a profit, using music as a commodity. In contrast, artists in the "alternative" category, at least in the

**Table 18–1    Albums Released during 2000 and 2001 that Earned Multiplatinum Certification from the Recording Industry Association of America during January and February of 2002**

| Artist | Album Title | Label | #Sold (millions) |
|--------|-------------|-------|------------------|
| Creed | *Weathered* | Wind-Up Records | 5 |
| Destiny's Child | *Survivor* | Columbia | 4 |
| Enya | *A Day Without Rain* | Reprise | 6 |
| Nelly Furtado | *Whoa, Nelly!* | Dreamworks | 2 |
| Enrique Iglesias | *Escape* | Interscope | 2 |
| Ja Rule | *Pain is Love* | Murder, Inc. | 2 |
| Michael Jackson | *Invincible* | Epic | 2 |
| Linkin Park | *Hybrid Theory* | Warner Bros. | 7 |
| Dave Matthews Band | *Everyday* | RCA Records | 3 |
| Nickelback | *Silver Side Up* | Roadrunner | 3 |
| Pink | *Missundaztood* | Arista | 2 |
| Pink Floyd | *Echoes: The Best of Pink Floyd* | Capitol | 3 |
| Shakira | *Laundry Service* | Epic | 2 |
| Soundtrack | *Coyote Ugly* | Curb | 3 |
| Soundtrack | *O Brother, Where Art Thou?* | Mercury Nashville | 4 |
| Usher | *8701* | Arista | 3 |
| Various Artists | *Songs 4 Worship: Shout to the Lord* | Integrity | 2 |

early years of their professional music careers, actively spurn the trappings of the business side of the industry, seeking rather to express themselves artistically whether there was money to be made or not. This latter approach is quite similar to the "indie" record labels of the 1950s. In fact, many of these artists intentionally chose to associate with an independent record label rather than a major recording conglomerate in an attempt to avoid the corporate money-making machine, as the recording industry is often perceived. Some artists, as in the case of Ani DiFranco, even go so far as to establish their own record labels, marketing and distributing their own recordings. In this sense, the "alternative" approach will be considered a "state of mind" that distinguishes it from the mainstream commercial approach of other artists.

## THE BEGINNINGS OF ALTERNATIVE ROCK: THE 1970S

### Glitter Rock

Since the very beginning of rock, a central theme has been the relationship between the sexes. Whether soft rock and rockabilly artists were singing about love or mainstream artists were implicitly or explicitly singing about sex, the assumption was that both the love and the sex was heterosexual. This is a natural continuation of the traditions in the roots of rock: R & B, C & W, and pop. When an offshoot of the British mainstream varied from this norm, we can begin to use the term *alternative* as defined above. Certainly, glitter (or glam) rockers were expressing their own individuality through their portrayal of androgynous stage characters with little thought for mainstream commercial success.

The unquestioned leader of this early alternative trend was David Bowie, one of the true enigmas of rock. He has been compared to a chameleon—able to change his persona radically and seemingly endlessly. When describing Bowie, most writers speak of his theatricality, his symbolic role, and his complicated psyche. His music is rarely the central focus. And indeed, Bowie was not a great musical innovator; he seemed to be more an actor who used rock music as his medium of communication.

Bowie (born in South London in January 1947) changed his name in 1966 from David Jones to David Bowie in order to avoid confusion with Davy Jones of the Monkees. As a teenager he pursued his talent for art by working for a commercial art company and a London advertising agency; his theatrical abilities carried him into a mime company, avant-garde films, and a few commercials. Looking for his own musical style, he tried being a Dylan-like folksinger, an Anthony Newley–type pop singer, and a member of various local rock bands.

After several unspectacular albums, Bowie opened an Arts Lab in South London, but it folded after about eighteen months. Realizing that to get attention he would need to shock the public, he went back into the studio and produced *The Man Who Sold the World* (1970). It contained some rather morose songs about his bizarre upbringing. The album cover depicted Bowie dressed to resemble either Lauren Bacall (Helander 1982, 49) or a "swishy blunt-cut Beau Brummel" (White 1984, 202). Openly admitting his bisexuality, Bowie soon found his style being referred to as glitter rock or glam rock. He began to project a purposely androgynous image.

Around 1972 he created a "character" named Ziggy Stardust. His first album as Ziggy, *The Rise and Fall of Ziggy Stardust and the Spiders from Mars*, revealed Bowie's ability to shift his musical gears. The opening moments of "Rock 'n' Roll Suicide" sound like Dylan; "It Ain't Easy" reminds us of R & B; and songs like "Star" and "Suffragette City" are good old rock and roll. The Ziggy Stardust tour of the United States in 1972 featured Bowie's own peculiar mixture of bizarre makeup and costumes, elaborate lighting and staging, and camp theatricality.

Bowie reached a peak of popularity in 1974 with *Diamond Dogs* and a live album, *David Live*, his first Top 10 albums. The *Diamond Dogs* tour to the United States included a $250,000 set; midway through the tour, Bowie scrapped it and changed to a stark, plain style. Gone, too, was the orange hair and the deathly white face. *Young Americans*, released in 1975, contained elements of soul, R & B, and even disco ("Fame"). Promoting that album and the follow-up, *Station to Station*, Bowie toured in 1976 with a new image: dressed in black except for a white dress shirt, blond hair slicked back.

After spending nearly a year in Berlin developing his next dramatic shift, Bowie reemerged in early 1977 with the first of three albums recorded in collaboration with art rock composer–performer Brian Eno. These three albums, *Low* (1977), *"Heroes"* (1977), and *Lodger* (1979), experiment with the heavily electronic "minimalist" sound of some late 1970s art rock. By 1980, the true actor in Bowie came to the fore. He had appeared in several earlier films, but with his starring role in *The Elephant Man* (live on tour and on Broadway), he achieved critical acclaim. Bowie's success (and his ever-changing looks) continued into the new century with compact disc releases of his early recordings, new collaborations (Brian Eno and Trent Reznor), innovative use of the Internet for marketing his music, and new releases, including *Hours . . .* (1999), *Heathen* (2002), and *Reality* (2003).

Back in 1976, Bowie had commented, "I consider myself responsible for a whole new school of pretensions" (Miller 1980, 389). Certainly prior to Bowie, rock had prided itself on its rough-and-ready macho image (even Slick and Joplin belted and shouted lyrics in an aggressive, masculine way) and its unpretentious sincerity. But Bowie's theatrical makeup, orange hair, effeminate image,

David Bowie as Ziggy Stardust (*Source:* Michael Ochs Archive, Ltd.)

and fictional stage personae presented a new phenomenon. He was putting on a show; it was not real, it was theater. The effect on other performers such as Elton John, Alice Cooper, Kiss, and Boy George is easily recognized. Although these performers had dramatically different musical styles, all devised costumes or makeup and presented a theatrical show.

A somewhat similar image was projected by Boy George (born George O'Dowd in London in 1961). He combined the androgynous glitter image of David Bowie with a soft rock sound. Complete with female makeup, clothing, and hairstyle, Boy George sang in a soft, gentle voice that kept early fans guessing: Was it a he or a she? His group, the Culture Club, hit its peak popularity in the early 1980s with a series of Top 10 songs in 1983 and 1984, including the number 1 "Karma Chameleon." Gradually pulling back from the androgynous look, Boy George nevertheless saw his career derailed by his severe drug addiction. Other British acts that fell into the glitter rock trend were Mark Bolan's Tyrannosaurus Rex, Gary Glitter, Mott the Hoople, and Roxy Music.

## PUNK MOVEMENTS: A RETURN TO THE BASICS

### Punk I: The British Punks

The fragmented market of the early 1960s included several trends that seemed to be direct contradictions of one another (e.g., folk versus surfing music). And so it was in the 1970s. One of the offshoots of the harder branch of mainstream rock was actually a rebellion against most of the other trends within rock, including soft rock, art rock, jazz fusion, heavy metal, and disco. As was the case with several 1970s rock trends, the focal point of punk rock was not musical but extramusical. As Keith Richard commented, "I don't think there was anything new musically, or even from the PR point of view, image-wise. There was too much image . . . and the music seemed to be the least important thing. It was more important if you puked over somebody" (Shaw 1982, 293).

Punk rock can be considered in one of three ways: (1) as the ultimate rebellion against virtually all forms of post-1960s rock and against society in general; (2) as the ultimate extension of the harder side of mainstream rock initiated by the Stones and other British blues-based bands; or (3) as both of the foregoing. Punk enthusiasts prefer the first explanation because they enjoy their self-image as ultimate rebels. Future rock historians may prefer the second explanation because, indeed, most of the elements of punk rock were simply the reduction ad absurdum of elements present in hard mainstream rock. But it is also possible that the truth is a combination of both explanations.

The harder style of mainstream rock, from the Stones through heavy metal, set itself in opposition to the sophisticated experimentation and artistic ambitions of the post-Beatle branch of mainstream rock. Hard rockers stressed simplicity and repetitiveness; they preferred basic rock and roll; they hoped to shock "straight" society. The punks extended all these characteristics, playing music that was even simpler, more repetitive, and louder; their lyrics were patently gross; their images and antics were far more shocking. While extending these characteristics, they openly rebelled against the long, technically demanding instrumental solos, the serious art rock aspirations, and the wealthy, commercially successful rock star syndrome of many mainstream groups.

The first major British punk group was the Sex Pistols, formed in 1975. Basing their act on several prior "punk" bands from the United States (e.g., the Ramones and the New York Dolls), they played simple, loud rock and roll that reverted to the musical vocabulary of the hardest 1950s style, but with considerably less skill and taste. Lead singer Johnny Rotten had never sung before joining the Pistols. But as Keith Richard said, the music was not really the point. Signed by EMI, the Pistols released a single, "Anarchy in the UK" in 1976; it became a minor British hit. In early 1977, the Pistols appeared on London's *Today* television show; when host Bill Grundy asked Rotten to say something outrageous, he responded with several choice profanities. As a result "Anarchy" became a bigger hit. The Pistols were denounced everywhere, from Parliament to the newspapers, and EMI dropped them like a hot potato. On their twenty-one-date tour, all but three concerts were canceled or stopped in progress.

A&M Records signed the band, now including Sid Vicious (John Ritchie) on bass, and subsequently dropped them—all in one week's time. Finally, Virgin Records signed them to a new contract and released a sarcastic version of "God Save the Queen," which became a major British hit. Their one and only album, *Never Mind the Bullocks, Here's the Sex Pistols,* was released in late 1977. In early 1978, they attempted a U.S. tour, complete with considerable promotional hype. However, the act was a bit too much for American audiences, and the tour was abandoned in San Francisco. Rotten quit (or was fired) and formed a new band, Public Image, Ltd. According to Timothy White, their first album, *First Issue,* "sounded like seven alley cats in a blender with the setting on 'grind'" (White 1984, 225). Lydon, now using

The Sex Pistols (*Source:* Michael Ochs Archive, Ltd.)

his birth name, recorded several more albums before disappearing from the music scene in the early 1980s. The Sex Pistols continued through 1978; but in October, Sid Vicious was charged with murdering his girlfriend, Nancy Spungeon, in Manhattan. He was found dead of an apparent drug overdose in Greenwich Village in early 1979. All four original members (Sid Vicious was not the initial bass player) reunited for a world tour in 1996, resulting in a live recording (*Filthy Lucre Live*, 1996) and a documentary (Julen Temple's *The Filth and the Fury*, 2000).

Sex Pistols performances included vulgar lyrics, shocking on-stage antics (sticking large pins in their bodies or slashing themselves with razor blades and broken bottles), and slapping members of the audience. As a social or psychological phenomenon, the punk trend may be deemed significant; as a musical style, it was important only to see just how bad rock and roll could get. As Lydon himself said later, "The Sex Pistols were a fiasco. A farce" (Miller 1980, 462).

The other major British punk band, the Clash, sounded almost good when compared with the Sex Pistols. Slightly less outrageous than the Pistols in terms of lyrics and antics, the Clash nevertheless carried on the musical style of simple, basic, and repetitive harmonies, simple melodies, basic rhythms, and lots of screaming and distortion. The Clash released their first album, *The Clash*, in 1977. Not unlike the 1960s folkies, the Clash included songs that protested everything: boring jobs, police, America, rock music, violence, and racism. The growing affinity between the punks and reggae music was illustrated in "Police and Thieves" and "White Man in Hammersmith Palais." *London Calling* (1979) made the Top 30 in the United States, as did the single "Train in Vain (Stand by Me)." The band actually broke the Top 10 with the album *Combat Rock* (1982) and a single, "Rock the Casbah."

In addition to the two major punk bands discussed above (Sex Pistols and the Clash), there were many other punk bands that wielded significant influence over musical developments during the following years. One of the most prolific of these groups, The Fall, was a British group from Manchester. Through a series of personnel changes and having shifted through many record companies, the band continued to release a consistent series of recordings from 1979's *Live at the Witch Trials* to *Unutterable* (2000), followed by a bewildering series of compilations and live recordings. Lead vocalist Mark E. Smith, the sole constant in the band's surprisingly long career, serves as a harbinger to the white rappers discussed in Chapter 17. With their tuneful single "Totally Wired" (1981), the band seemed to follow the move of many toward the new wave style. The Mekons and Joy Division are two other British punk bands worthy of mention. Both bands proved to have tremendous staying power, evolving musically from punk (or perhaps post-punk) to heavily electronic dance music. Following the suicide of lead singer Ian Curtis in 1980, Joy Division added a keyboard player and changed their name to New Order. The regrouped band's breakthrough single was "Blue Monday," which hit number 5 on the *Billboard* Dance Chart in 1983.

With the negative publicity received in 1978 to 1979 by the Sex Pistols and other punk bands, some sought to establish a new designation with less negative connotations. Thus, the term *new wave* was widely circulated. As Arnold Shaw notes, one can view new wave as an offshoot of punk, somewhat subtler and less prone to the gruesome, the overtly repulsive, and the sadomasochistic; or new wave may simply be a term coined to escape the criticism and censure heaped upon punk groups (Shaw

1982, 262). As is often the case, the truth may be a bit of both. After all, most bands (and their record companies) can tolerate—and at times even encourage—public outrage, unless it becomes so extreme that customers refuse to buy records and concert tickets. Also, it is understandable that impaling oneself with pins and slicing one's chest open with broken glass begins, after a few performances, to lose its appeal, even to the most devoted of fans and performers.

Thus, beginning in about 1979, many of the revolutionary punk bands, including the Clash, lessened the aggressive tone of their music, making it more palatable and accessible to a wider audience. This change initiated a move toward the new wave style described above. So it was with Elvis Costello (born Declan McManus in 1955). Whether it was due to his doubly nostalgic pseudonym or the gradual American acceptance of punk music, Costello's early recordings were moderately successful (*My Aim Is True,* number 32 in 1977; and *This Year's Model,* number 30 in 1978). Underneath the punk attitude and the new wave musical veneer, his songwriting for these recordings reveals early signs of a skilled craftsman at work. In 1979, he launched his third major album, *Armed Forces,* with an American tour. The album rose to number 10, but in the midst of the tour, an incident occurred that had a transforming effect on Costello. He had been capitalizing on the mean, angry punk image quite successfully; but one night, in a Columbus, Ohio, bar, Costello publicly referred to Ray Charles as a "blind, ignorant nigger" and then went on to make similar comments about James Brown. Chastened severely in the press, Costello was embarrassed by the incident and subsequently apologized. According to Ken Tucker, Costello would "tone down his aggressive demeanor for the rest of the tour, and, indeed, for the next few years" (Ward, Stokes, and Tucker 1986, 569). In some ways, that incident may have been a significant line of demarcation between punk and new wave.

Costello's songwriting talents began to be appreciated once the prohibitive shield of punkdom was penetrated. In fact, several of his songs have been covered by such singers as Linda Ronstadt and George Jones. Costello himself seemed to mellow somewhat, often recording oldies (*Taking Liberties,* 1980) and country-flavored material (*Almost Blue,* 1981). In the mid- to late-1990s, he teamed with pop songwriter Burt Bacharach for several successful albums, one of which (*Painted From Memory,* 1998) resulted in a Grammy award. The two musicians also made a cameo appearance in the movie *Austin Powers: The Spy Who Shagged Me* (1999), performing a cover version of Bacharach and David's "I'll Never Fall in Love Again." Costello continued to record prolifically in a wide range of musical styles. In addition to the collaborations with Burt Bacharach mentioned above, he recorded a collection of piano ballads composed, orchestrated, and conducted by the composer (*North,* 2003); an orchestral composition (*Il Sogno,* 2004); and an album that was nominated for three Grammys in 2004 (*Delivery Man*).

### America's Punk Minimovement

Although the punk movement made its greatest immediate impact in England, its roots lie in a handful of early- to mid-1960s American bands. Two such prototypes were the MC5 and the Velvet Underground. Formed in a suburb of Detroit in 1965, the Motor City Five (MC5) served as a prototype for the American punk band. During a brief three-year period from 1969 to 1971, the band released a series of influential recordings, including *Kick Out the Jams, Back in the USA*, and *High Time*. Also formed in 1965, the Velvet Underground was an eccentric band from New York City. Organized by classically trained pianist Lou Reed, the Underground defies categorization: Not only were they not in the mainstream, they were not in any stream but their own.

Joining with John Cale, a classically trained violist and pianist from South Wales, guitarist Sterling Morrison, female drummer Maureen Tucker, and German-born female singer Nico, Reed christened the new group the Velvet Underground (after the name of a paperback book that was a survey of sadomasochism). They became a part of Andy Warhol's traveling "happenings," called The Exploding Plastic Inevitable.

Signed by MGM Records, the band released *The Velvet Underground and Nico* in 1967. Containing several explicit songs about dope ("I'm Waiting for the Man" and "Heroin") and sadomasochism ("Venus in Furs"), the album received very little radio play and died after reaching the number 171 position. Nico left the group, but the others released a highly experimental second album called *White Light/White Heat* in 1968. The title song was another drug song; "The Gift" consisted of a surrealistic, sexually oriented spoken lyric over a noisy, repetitive accompaniment. "I Heard Her Call My Name" was an early experiment in distortion and feedback; the seventeen-minute "Sister Ray" contained half-sung, half-spoken sexually explicit lyrics over a heavily distorted, repetitive accompaniment. This avant-garde album peaked at number 199. The Underground staggered along for several years before finally disbanding in 1972.

As an anti-commercial, anti-establishment avant-garde band, complete with emphasis on drugs and sex, the Velvet Underground may be cited as an early forerunner of the punk movement. Not far behind was Iggy Pop and the Stooges. James Osterberg (Iggy Pop) was from Ann Arbor, Michigan. In 1967, he formed a quartet

The Velvet Underground (*Source:* Michael Ochs Archive, Ltd.)

that specialized in loud, simple, and repetitive music, which served as a background for Osterberg's outrageous antics. According to Brock Helander, "Over the years, his notoriety grew with deeds such as threatening and vilifying audiences, cutting himself with broken bottles, pouring hot wax over his body, intentionally smashing his teeth, and throwing up, even urinating on audiences and allowing ardent fans to perform fellatio on him" (Helander 1982, 577).

Iggy and the Stooges's debut album was produced by the Velvet Underground's John Cale in 1969. After this and the follow-up album fared poorly, the band went to England to work with David Bowie. Bowie produced their third album, *Raw Power*. Often cited as an archetype, not only of the punk trend but also for the heavy metal style, *Raw Power* reached only number 182 on the charts. By 1974, the band had disintegrated. Several years later, Iggy teamed up with David Bowie again and released several more albums. At the turn of the decade he made another tour, complete with more outrageous antics, to promote his new albums, *New Values* and *Soldier*. Even more than the Velvet Underground, Iggy Pop became the prototype of the punk style of the late 1970s.

If the punk style flourished anywhere in the United States, it was in New York City. Following in the footsteps of the Velvet Underground came Patti Smith, who recited her poetry over the sounds of a drummerless duo or trio of instrumentalists. The Patti Smith Group released four albums during the 1970s, two of which, *Easter* (1978) and *Wave* (1979), made the Top 20. Smith dropped out of the music scene in the early 1980s when she moved to Detroit and married MC5 guitarist Fred "Sonic" Smith. In the late 1980s, she returned to the recording studio and released a series of albums, including the politically scathing election year release of *Trampin'* (2004). From Queens came the Ramones, a quartet that created an early punk image with their torn tee shirts and black leather jackets. The relatively small punk movement in the United States stayed loyal to the Ramones, allowing two of their albums to crack the Top 50 (*Rocket to Russia* in 1977 and *End of the Century* in 1980).

Crossing between the punk movement and the glitter rock trend (an even smaller trend in the United States) were the New York Dolls. Adopting eccentric costumes and sometimes androgynous makeup, the Dolls combined an amateurish primitivism with raw violence. Their brief appearance on the scene yielded two albums in 1973 and 1974.

The two 1970s punk–new wave bands that may claim a significant place in rock history are the Talking Heads, led by David Byrne, and the Police (whose lead singer, Sting, had an extremely successful solo career). Emerging from the New York punk scene in 1977, the Talking Heads led the way from punk to new wave. They avoided the eccentric costumes and onstage antics and drew upon contemporary classical trends to create a more sophisticated style. Their early lyrics often emphasized the struggle between the individual and society.

The Heads's first four albums were produced by Brian Eno, an English art rock musician who had once been a member of Roxy Music. Eno was oriented toward experimentation with the latest in electronic technology—for example, synthesizers, tape manipulation, and computerized keyboards. By the beginning of the 1980s, Eno was forming a bridge to a subcategory of contemporary classical music often called minimalism (also called pattern music and process music). The minimalists created their music by designing a limited number of tonal sequences or patterns of unequal length; then, as these patterns repeated over and over, they created a constantly shifting overall sound. The basic concept of the minimalists's simple, repetitive patterns was naturally appealing to rock musicians (and vice versa). In late 1970s New York City, rock musicians such as Eno, Robert Fripp (also formerly of Roxy Music), and Fred Frith were drawn to the music of minimalist composers like Philip Glass and Steve Reich.

Talking Heads' albums such as *Remain in Light* (1980) illustrate a rock style adaptation of the minimalist principles. When transferred to rock, the patterns were modified to conform to the regular quadruple meter. But one can hear the reliance on steady, unchanging patterns layered throughout the instrumental accompaniment. The result is an elaborate drone effect: It sounds rather robotlike and emotionless, as if some great machine were grinding out the music. For example, in "The Overload" (*Remain in Light*), a steady drone persists throughout; the drum pattern is unchanging; the vocal line is sung as if it were a somber chant; only various electronic sounds color the otherwise unchanging sound environment. In songs like "Once in a Lifetime" and "Houses in Motion," with their reliance on spoken lyrics over a constantly repetitive accompaniment, one is reminded of the old Velvet Underground of the late 1960s. One also hears influences of reggae and other black styles in the music of the Talking Heads (again, "Houses in Motion" is a good example). They even managed a Top 10 hit in 1983 with "Burning Down the House." The Heads continued to evolve through the mid-1980s, and must be considered one of the most musically significant outgrowths of the punk–new wave movement. Lead singer David Byrne continued a highly successful and prolific solo career into the first decade of the twenty-first century.

Also derivative of the punk movement and influenced by the new-wave trend were the Police, a British trio headed by lead singer Sting (born Gordon Sumner in 1951). Originally formed in 1977, it was not until 1980 that major success came with their third album, *Zenyatta Mondatta* (number 5). The Police's peak came in 1983 with *Synchronicity*, their first number 1 album. The album included mainstream rock in the form of the title song (parts 1 and 2), reggae references ("Walking in Your Footsteps"), punk influence ("Mother"), soft rock (the number 1 song "Every Breath You Take"), and even a touch of jazz rock ("Tea in the Sahara"). *Synchronicity* had something for everyone. As was often the case with the Police, the lyrics were quite introspective and intellectually oriented; hints of New Age philosophy appeared in various songs on the album. In the mid-1980s, Sting sought to establish himself as an actor, quite apart from the Police. Having appeared in *Quadrophenia* in 1979 and *Brimstone and Treacle* in 1982, he starred in *The Bride* in 1984. His musical career as a solo artist also is quite impressive, including a series of Top 10 albums between 1985 and 2003: *The Dream of the Blue Turtles* (number 2 in 1985), . . . *Nothing Like the Sun* (number 9 in 1987), *Soul Cages* (number 2 in 1991), *Ten Summoner's Tales* (number 2 in 1993), *Mercury Falling* (number 5 in 1996), *Brand New Day* (number 9 in 2000), and *Sacred Love* (number 3 in 2003). Tracks from these albums produced numerous hit singles during this same period.

Growing out of the new wave movement were groups like Blondie, Pere Ubu, and Devo. The latter (from Akron, Ohio) took the idea of the machinelike, repetitive patterns and created a robotlike sound, using short, clipped vocals and instrumental lines. The result was an antiseptic rock sound, seemingly devoid of emotion—almost as far from soul music as one can get. Pere Ubu (from Cleveland) was similar in some ways, but the "vocals" of David Thomas varied from blunt, choppy declarative phrases and repeating words and phrases to sudden bursts of emotive squawks and shouts. Generally (with the exception of the Talking Heads), new wave seems to have been a brief fad during the transition to the 1980s and has had little long-term impact on the evolution of rock music.

## ALTERNATIVE STYLES

Referring to any musical style as alternative immediately begs the question, "Alternative to what?" Though there are many—present authors included—who would question the validity of using such a broad term to classify music, this particular word has become so widely used in discussions of popular music that its exclusion from a rock history text would be a glaring omission. Therefore, let us attempt to determine what it is exactly that separates alternative music from mainstream rock and roll. Rock music itself began as an alternative to the Pop, C & W, and R & B of the late 1940s and early 1950s. Since that period of emergence, several musical elements have remained relatively consistent throughout the various musical styles and subgenres of rock and roll. Some of the most obvious of these musical elements are the strong backbeat incorporated into most rock songs, the predominance of melody, the relatively simple harmonies, the prominence of homophonic textures and loud volume, and the tendency toward simple, repetitive forms. As in any list of this type, it would take little effort to identify exceptions to each of these consistencies within the pages of this book. For example, many soft rock songs do not incorporate a strong backbeat; the harmonies and musical form of Emerson, Lake, and Palmer's "Karn Evil 9," or Blood, Sweat, and Tears's "Symphony for the Devil" are anything but simple and repetitive; and folk rock musicians of the 1960s and singer–songwriters of the 1970s did not always play their music at high levels of volume. However, when looking back across the entire history of rock and roll, these consistencies do appear to hold true for a majority of rock recordings. Therefore, in a comparative discussion of alternative rock, these musical elements will be useful.

As rock evolved into the 1960s, some artists began veering away from the raw energy and improvisational style of early rock stars. Buddy Holly's experimentation with recording techniques, the more central role of the recording studio in the music of the Beach Boys, and the Beatles's experimental albums took rock music many steps away from the immediacy inherent in the sound of early rockers like Little Richard, Chuck Berry, and Jerry Lee Lewis. It became common for a rock band to spend hundreds of hours in the recording studio, attempting to produce a perfect album. In many cases, each musician was required to play a part over and over in the recording studio, sometimes capturing only a short section on tape at a time, eventually providing a flawless performance. These "perfect takes" were then expertly combined by a recording engineer, with input from the artists and producer(s), resulting in a technically perfect recording, or at least a reasonable approximation of such. Recordings such as Queen's *A Night at the Opera* (1975) took multitracking studio techniques to the extreme, as illustrated in the quasi-operatic section of "Bohemian Rhapsody" (revived in 1992 by its inclusion in the soundtrack for *Wayne's World*).

Claiming that this move toward perfectionism resulted in a sanitized version of rock and roll lacking the spontaneous energy of its roots, the punk movement of the late 1970s was a deliberate attempt to return to the imperfection and excitement inherent in early rock. Following a brief series of raucous recordings between 1975 and the end of the decade, punk rock seemed for the most part to be subsumed by New Wave, its typically less aggressive and less radical musical sibling, appealing to a much wider audience.

The roots of alternative music can be found in the return to the basics of rock considered essential by the punk movement: Keep the music simple, limit the number and length of instrumental solos, and play "with an attitude." This attitude often comes across as an overt expression of anger, both in the lyrical content of the songs and in the behavior of the musicians. Harbingers of these dissenters from the mainstream of rock began to appear in the 1960s; for example, the Velvet Underground (laying a foundation for the punk movement) and Captain Beefheart (eclectic pioneer of art rock). A similar reversion to musical simplicity and overt antisocial behavior was one of the distinctive characteristics in the split between the Beatles and the Rolling Stones during the 1960s (discussed in Chapter 6). Though one of the difficulties inherent in any discussion of alternative music is the wide range of styles subsumed under this heading, it is possible to identify three main trends: post-punk hardcore music, thrash metal, and grunge. Having discussed thrash metal in Chapter 15, we will now take a close look at hardcore and grunge, along with their derivatives, all of which are commonly referred to as "alternative."

## Punk II: Post-Punk Hardcore

A number of bands, both in America and England, refused to follow the new-wave directions encouraged by the corporate complex of the recording industry, developing instead into the hardcore movement of the early 1980s. These hardcore bands form a direct link between punk rock of the late 1970s and the emergent forms of alternative music in the 1980s and 1990s. Formation of the SST record label in southern California provided a means for bands like Black Flag (whose guitarist Greg Ginn had founded the label) and the Minutemen to record and distribute their music without the support of a major recording company. Following in the footsteps of their punk rock progenitors, the hardcore bands took loudness, intensity, tempo, and nihilism to new extremes.

Two premier hardcore bands of the early 1980s, X and Black Flag, served as prototypes for hard rock bands of the post-punk era. Combining the hyperactive guitar banging and pulsating drum rhythms of punk rock with lyrics expressing dark disillusionment and distrust, John Doe (John Nommensen, bass and vocals), Exene Cervenka (Christine Cervenka, vocals), Billy Zoom (Tyson Kindale, guitar), and Don J. Bonebrake formed X in 1977, evolving out of the Los Angeles punk scene. "Nausea," "Sex and Dying in High Society," and "We're Desperate" provide typical examples of the band's sound and message.

In addition to founding SST Records, Greg Ginn (guitar) and Charles Dukowski (bass) added a party animal aesthetic to the nihilistic angst of the hardcore movement. Exuding a feeling of disillusionment, Henry Rollins (Black Flag's vocalist since 1981) professed to be the typical product of a dysfunctional family. In discussing his feelings about life, he said, "I don't know jack shit about love, or about feeling a relationship with a blood relative. That shit means nothing to me" (Szatmary 1996, 277). Such sentiments were expressed musically in songs like "Depression," "Dead Inside," and "Life of Pain" to the accompaniment of loud, distorted guitars and driving rhythms.

A large number of other bands could be included in a discussion of hardcore rock, some of the most prominent of whom were The Germs, Hüsker Dü, the Replacements, Dead Kennedys, Circle Jerks (formed by founding Black Flag vocalist Keith Morris), and Suicidal Tendencies. However, because the hardcore movement served as a bridge between punk music of the 1970s and the alternative movement of the late 1980s, we will turn now to developments relevant to these later musical styles.

## Grunge

The Pixies.   One of the most influential bands of the late 1980s, the Pixies laid the musical foundation upon which Grunge and much of the alternative music that followed are based. Cited as a primary musical influence by Nirvana's Kurt Cobain, the Pixies had but one album that reached the Top 100 (*Doolittle*, number 98 in 1989). Formed in Boston during 1986, Black Francis (born Charles Michael Kitteridge Thompson IV; guitar and vocals), Joey Santiago (guitar), Kim Deal (bass), and David Lovering (drums) began as Pixies in Panoply. In 1987, the band released their debut EP, entitled *Come On Pilgrim*. Their first full-length recording, *Surfer Rosa* was released the following year. A staple of the Pixies' musical style was the use of a soft verse alternating with a hard rocking chorus, a style frequently adopted in the music of Nirvana. Though Pixies recordings continued to be released in the early 1990s (*Bossanova*, 1990 and *Trompe le Monde*, 1991), the high level of tension between band members resulted in a series of solo projects and the eventual breakup of the group. The solo projects by Black Francis and those by Kim Deal (both the Breeders and the Amps) exerted a significant impact upon the burgeoning alternative music scene. In a surprise chain of events, the Pixies reunited for a world tour in 2004. While many rock acts were canceling shows due to hard economic times for the music industry in general, the Pixies performed a series of sold-out tour dates.

Emerging from the Seattle area at the end of the 1980s, grunge proved to be the most commercially successful subgenre of the alternative music scene. Driven by the belief that the basis of artistic freedom was to provide an outlet so musicians could maintain artistic control over their material instead of turning this responsibility over to a major record company, Bruce Pavitt turned an unsuccessful record store venture into a highly successful regional label called Sub Pop Records. Of course, it is likely that many of the bands who found their way to Sub Pop could not have attracted the attention of any major label, due to their raw musical style and the state of the music industry during the 1970s and 1980s. As a result, Pavitt began his career in the recording business by releasing a compilation of music written and performed by regional bands from the Pacific Northwest, entitled *Sub Pop 100*. His next release was an EP (extended play record) by Green River, a local band with a sound that would soon become associated with the Northwest.

Two members of Green River left to form Mudhoney in 1988, one of the earliest grunge bands and Sub Pop's biggest-selling group during these early years. The other two members of Green River formed Mother Love Bone (one of the first Seattle bands to sign with a major label) and later achieved superstardom as Pearl Jam. Musical characteristics of this early form of grunge were closely related to the hardcore sound discussed earlier and, therefore, to the punk music of the 1970s.

The apparent purpose behind grunge and, for that matter, hardcore or thrash metal is not aesthetic beauty of the sort revered by the mainstream pop culture. Rather, the artists fitting into these alternative categories revel in dissonance, the sound that purposely pervades their music at almost every turn, as if challenging the listener to move away from the comfortable place of the familiar, the tried and true. Though the musical characteristics of grunge were often intentionally uncomfortable to listen to, there was an element of tolerance in the message of the lyrics. Songwriters like Kurt Cobain of Nirvana were openly pro-gay and pro-woman. Whereas the lyrics of punk rock commonly spewed messages of hate at the establishment and the world in general, grunge artists tended more toward self-reflection, taking that same intense hatred and turning it inward in a form of self-loathing.

Nirvana.    Though Sub Pop's first real success story came with two EPs by Soundgarden, *Screaming Life* (1987) and *Fopp* (1988), credit for bringing the sound of Seattle grunge to the mainstream rock audience must go to Nirvana. Influenced musically by local punk band the Melvins, Black Flag, San Francisco's Flipper, Black Sabbath, and the Pixies, Kurt Cobain and childhood friend Krist Novoselic formed Nirvana in 1987. The group signed with Sub Pop Records the following year. Typical of the production that went into recordings made by most of their grunge contemporaries, Nirvana's debut album (*Bleach*, 1989) was recorded for a total cost of $606.17 (Romanowski and George-Warren, 1995). "School," "Blew," and their cover of Shocking Blue's "Love Buzz" exemplify the fast-paced rock style of the band. It is the melodicism of the ballad "About a Girl," however, that revealed the underlying talent and songwriting craftsmanship that was to carry Nirvana to a level of success far beyond that attained by the other Seattle bands. Receiving critical acclaim for this project, the band signed a recording contract with David Geffen's DGC label, hoping to deliver the musical style of the Pacific Northwest to a national audience. In 1990, they added drummer Dave Grohl.

Nirvana attained impressive commercial success with the release of *Nevermind* (number 1 in 1991), eventually selling over ten million copies. In addition to successful album sales, two of the songs registered as Top 40 hits: "Smells Like Teen Spirit" (number 6) and "Come As You Are" (number 32). "Smells Like Teen Spirit" was a breakthrough not only for Nirvana, but for the entire alternative music scene. With the release of this single, alternative music was accepted by many white, middle-class post-boomers as the music of their generation. African-American youth had accepted rap music as their own, and now a second segment of the American youth population had a musical style from which teenage anthems began to emerge. "Smells Like Teen Spirit" is the first such song to evolve from the alternative tradition and to make a mark in the mainstream arena of rock and roll, stating explicitly the expectations of the post-boomer generation . . . "Here we are now, entertain us." In 1992, Nirvana released a collection of early singles and outtakes under the title

Kurt Cobain of Nirvana (*Source:* Joe Hughes / Michael Ochs Archive, Ltd.)

*Incesticide.*   Their fourth album (*In Utero,* 1993) confirmed the band's prominent position in the minds of the youth of America, debuting at number 1. Cobain had wanted to call the album *I Hate Life and Want to Die,* but the record company eventually convinced him otherwise. Though this recording resulted in no Top 40 hits, both "All Apologies" and "Heart-Shaped Box" became favorites on AOR radio stations.

Success at the level experienced by Nirvana affects artists in different ways. There are those such as the Beatles, the Rolling Stones, and Van Halen who seem to thrive on attention and economic success as a confirmation of their ability. Others feel differently. Kurt Cobain's level of personal happiness and satisfaction seems to have been inversely related to the level of Nirvana's success in the music business. The greater the heights to which their popularity rose, the more Cobain felt his audience was blind to the anti-establishment message of their music. In response to those who accused him of selling out to the influences of a major label, Cobain replied as follows in the liner notes for *Incesticide* (1992):

> A big fuck you to those of you who have the audacity to claim that I'm so naïve and stupid that I would allow myself to be taken advantage of and manipulated. I don't feel the least bit guilty for commercially exploiting a completely exhausted Rock youth Culture because, at this point in rock history, Punk Rock (while still sacred to some) is, to me, dead and gone.

The need to justify commercial success seems to be a common trait of alternative bands. Emerging as strong adherents of the artistic freedom associated with independent record labels, many alternative bands found themselves a few short years later signed with major labels and selling records at a rate comparable to—sometimes even surpassing—their mainstream rock counterparts.

During a period of time that, by all normal accounts, should have been extremely uplifting for him—unprecedented popularity for the band, his marriage to Courtney Love (vocalist for Hole), and the birth of their healthy baby—Cobain began to show signs of extreme discontent. Beginning in the spring of 1993, his unhappiness was manifested through a series of drug overdoses and a domestic assault incident. Revolver in hand, Cobain threatened to commit suicide in his own home on March 18, 1994. Following this event, he checked into a recovery center at the end of

March, but sneaked away after only two days. One week later, on the eighth of April, he shot himself in the head with a 20-gauge shotgun.

The news of Cobain's death was as devastating to the post-boomers as the earlier deaths of Jimi Hendrix, Janis Joplin, and Jim Morrison had been to the baby boom generation. Nirvana's fans, along with hosts of radio stations and MTV, mourned their loss for weeks following the news of his tragic end. Later that year, *Unplugged in New York* (an album of Nirvana's live appearance on MTV the previous year) debuted at number 1, appropriately capping the career of one of the most significant rock groups of the early 1990s. In 1996, the remaining band members released a second posthumous album entitled *From the Muddy Banks of the Wishkah*. Named after the river flowing through the band members's hometown of Aberdeen, the album contains 16 songs recorded during live performances between 1989 and 1994. The MTV performances and these live recordings were originally intended to be combined into a double album, but the plan was abandoned after Cobain's death.

**Pearl Jam.**    Another group that is widely credited with bringing the Seattle sound to national attention is Pearl Jam. As mentioned previously, bassist Jeff Ament and guitarist Stone Gossard had been members of Green River, one of the earliest proponents of grunge. Following the breakup of that band, the two band mates joined vocalist Andrew Wood to form Mother Love Bone. Wood died of a heroin overdose shortly after the band completed its first album. Adding Mike McCreedy (guitar), Eddie Vedder (vocalist from San Diego), and Dave Krusen (drums), the band began performing under the name Mookie Blaylock in honor of the New Jersey Nets basketball star. Shortly thereafter, they changed their name to Pearl Jam, a reference to what the *Rolling Stone Encyclopedia* refers to as a "psychedelic confection" made by Vedder's half Native American great-grandmother (George-Warren and Romanowski 2001, page 745). Apparently not exhibiting the aversion to major labels shared by some Seattle groups, Pearl Jam signed initially with Epic records and released their debut album (*Ten*, 1992; named after the number on Mookie Blaylock's jersey), which reached number 2 on the charts. Particularly noteworthy examples of Pearl Jam's early musical style are "Even Flow," "Alive," and "Jeremy." In 1992, shortly after Nirvana brought alternative music to mainstream rock radio, Pearl Jam surpassed Nirvana in record sales, combining the riff-heavy guitar sound of 1970s rock with the angst of 1980s post-punk. All the while, however, they continued to provide their listeners with catchy guitar riffs, hook lines, and memorable choruses. Shortly after the release of their debut album, Kusen left the band to be replaced by Dave Abbruzzese. In contrast to the relatively consistent hard rock style of *Ten*, Pearl Jam's second album, *Vs.* (1993, debuting at number 1), reveals an impressive variety of musical styles. Contrast, for example, the hard rock sound of "Go" or "Leash" with the folk influence apparent in both "Elderly Woman Behind the Counter in a Small Town" and "Indifference."

During this period of time, the band made some risky business decisions. Though their rise to popularity was greatly enhanced by MTV hits and their appearance on the second Lollapalooza tour, spurning the accepted conventions of the recording industry, the band refused to release videos to promote *Vs.* In addition, during the promotional tour for the album, Pearl Jam chose to perform in smaller auditoriums and on college campuses, rather than in the stadium settings that had become commonplace for rock concerts. In an incredibly gutsy move, the band canceled the summer portion of their tour because Ticketmaster was pressuring the promoters to charge more than 20 dollars for concert tickets. Pearl Jam took legal action against Ticketmaster for unfair business practices, though the Justice Department eventually ruled in favor of the ticket agency.

After recording their third album, *Vitalogy* (number 1 in 1994), the band fired Abbruzzese and hired Red Hot Chili Peppers drummer Jack Irons. Shrouded in lyrical messages of death and despair, this album provides a soundtrack for the 1990s through the eyes of several post-boomers. Like *Vs.*, this album consists of both heavy rock songs ("Spin the Black Circle" and "Last Exit") and ballads ("Nothingman" and "Better Man"). In addition, however, the band includes some of their most eclectic tunes yet: the funk rhythms and trance-inducing repetitions of "Aye Davanita," the odd two-chord accordion vamp underneath "Bugs," and the art rock-influenced sound collage "Stupid Mop."

With the release of *No Code* (1996), Pearl Jam challenged their association with the grunge movement to an even greater degree. Along with the typical hard rock and punk influences clearly evident in "Hail, Hail" and "Habit," this album reveals a level of musical experimentation beyond that normally associated with alternative—and specifically grunge—bands. From the opening measures of "Sometime," with its soft guitar tone, fretless bass, and rolling thunder, the music promises to be different. A triple meter waltz, "Red Mosquito," alternates dramatically between instrumental sections reminiscent of San Francisco acid rock and verses that take on an almost folk rock or country character. Undoubtedly influenced by Vedder's collaboration with Pakistani vocalist Nusrat Fateh on the soundtrack to the motion picture *Dead Man Walking* (1995), "Who You Are" incorporates droning guitar parts, tribal-sounding drums, and a Buddhist lyric. Pearl Jam recorded an album with Neil Young, *Mirror Ball* (1995), though the name of the band did not appear on the album due to legal complications. Eddie Vedder toured with Hovercraft, his experimental side project. Returning to their hard rock roots, the band released *Yield* (number 2 in 1998) accompanied by the release of their first video since "Jeremy" in 1991.

In the fall of 2000, Pearl Jam made recording history. In one week, they simultaneously released 25 live double albums. Five of these entered the *Billboard* Hot 200 simultaneously: *16/5/00: Spodek, Katowice, Poland* (number 103), *22/6/00: Fila Forum Arena, Milan, Italy* (number 125), *22/6/00: Arena di Verona, Verona, Italy* (number 134), *30/5/00: Wembley Arena, London, England* (number 137), and *26/6/00: Sporthalle, Hamburg, Germany* (number 175). The band continued releasing live recordings from its 2000 tour, reaching a total of 72 releases by mid-2001. The concert from Seattle, Washington on November 11, 2000, a three-CD set, proved the most popular, debuting at number 98 on the charts.

Although hailing from the grunge capital of the world, Pearl Jam moved beyond the boundaries of typical alternative music, revealing the influence of Zeppelin-style 1970s rock and even some Beatlesque experimentation. Confirming these ties with earlier rock and roll, Vedder was the vocalist asked to take the place of Jim Morrison when the remaining members of the Doors reunited for their induction into the Rock and Roll Hall of Fame in 1993.

Riot Grrrl.   As part of the "Women in Rock" thrust that gathered steam during the late 1980s and came to undeniable fruition by the mid-1990s, female performers also found their way into alternative and other punk-influenced musical styles. Unlike many stylistic developments in the study of music, the official establishment of the "Riot Grrrl" phenomenon can be traced to a specific date: August 20, 1991. On this day, indie music fans from the Pacific Northwest swarmed to Olympia, Washington for the International Pop Underground Convention: "Love Rock Girl Style Now." A number of all-female groups—little known outside of the Pacific Northwest—performed for the event, including Heavens to Betsy (Olympia, Washington), Jean Smith (Vancouver, British Columbia), Mecca Normal (British Columbia), and Bratmobile (Eugene, Oregon). The event culminated in what was later to be known as "Riot Grrrl," a revolutionary movement that was inspired by this all-female alternative music but also included activists and writers as well. Early meetings consisted of discussions about music and specific bands performing it, but also more serious issues confronting females, including violence against women and domestic abuse. As a result, "Riot Grrrl meetings were similar to the consciousness-raising sessions held by seventies-era feminists—with the added desire to create music" (Experience Music Project 2002).

There were certainly pioneers from previous decades whose efforts effectively opened the door for this new wave of artists. Suzi Quatro and Joan Jett (and her early all-female band The Runaways) are two examples of female performers of the 1970s and 1980s who performed hard rock music, receiving a significant degree of both critical and commercial success. The Riot Grrrl sound took on a more aggressive feminist tone than the music of these hard rock performers, however. Finding solid roots in the female punk bands of the late 1970s (e.g., the Slits and the Raincoats), Riot Grrrl bands typically adopted a DIY (do-it-yourself) ethic that required no prior musical training. Much like the early punk rock bands, Riot Grrrl spurred female artists to break out of the stereotypical crooning ballad mode, encouraging women to let go of their inhibitions and open themselves to multiples modes of self-expression and creativity. The success of Nirvana's *Nevermind* (number 1 in 1991) focused attention on the Seattle area and assisted in bringing national attention to some of the more successful and deserving Riot Grrrl bands. Bikini Kill and Calamity Jane, for example, both opened shows for Nirvana.

By the summer of 1992, Riot Grrrl was being tauted as the "next big thing" to come from the Pacific Northwest, considered by many at the time to be the hotbed of innovative, energetic musical activity. The Riot Grrrl movement consisted of a group of female entertainers who gathered together for a serious purpose: to support, inform, and empower women. By the mid-1990s, however, many of the original bands had broken up. The movement inspired a wave of female singer–songwriters during the late 1990s, including Ani DiFanco, Jewel, Alanis Morissette, PJ Harvey, Sheryl Crow, Norah Jones, and Sarah McLauchlan . . . music sung by women, for women, primarily about issues important to women. The torch of feminist empowerment was passed from Riot Grrrl to Lilith Fair, McLachlan's touring woman's music festival. Other artists who would be considered members of the Riot Grrrl movement include the Zines, Huggy Bear, Veruca Salt, Elastica, L7, and Sleater-Kinney. One band that would not fit the bill, however, is the Spice Girls (discussed in Chapter 16).

## Pop Punk

As alternative music continued to work its way into the mainstream in the early 1990s, an interesting subgenre emerged from within the punk scene. Maintaining the high energy, punk attitude, and dissonant, distorted guitar sound of it progenitor, some artists began to incorporate melodic hook lines and tuneful choruses, resulting in what is sometimes referred to as "pop punk," an oxymoron if ever one existed. This odd mix of seemingly contradictory musical styles is perhaps best exemplified by the tremendous success of Green Day. Childhood friends in Berkeley, California, Billie Joe Armstrong (guitar and vocals) and Mike Dirnt (bass) formed the band in 1989. After adding John Kiffmeyer on drums, the trio released a series of EPs, two full-length albums (*39/Smooth* in 1990 and *Kerplunk* in 1992), and built a solid following in the Berkeley hardcore music scene before signing with Reprise Records to release its first major label album, *Dookie* (number 4 in 1994). The album won a Grammy for Best Alternative Music Performance and earned Green Day plenty of MTV time, as well as spots on the Lollapalooza tour and at Woodstock '94. The band's easily accessible three-minute song forms with memorable hook melodies facilitated their rise to popularity and the eventual sale of over ten million copies of this album. Though not able to equal the success of their initial major label release, the band has maintained an admirable level of commercial success with *Insomniac* (number 2 in 1995), *Nimrod* (number 10 in 1997), and *Warning* (number 4 in 2000). The latter release revealed a new approach for the band with its folk-influenced sound and higher degree of introspection. With *American Idiot* (number 1 in 2004), Green Day proved they had matured significantly as musicians. Two of the tracks on the album ("Jesus of Suburbia" and "Homecoming") constitute what are essentially multimovement suites, each over nine minutes in length and incorporating an impressive range of musical styles. The title track, overtly political in its message, presents the band's statement in reaction to the confusing and warped environment that constitutes post-September 11 American pop culture.

The energy and commercial viability of this new rock subgenre was taken up in 1992 by another trio, Blink-182, this time from suburban southern California near San Diego. Taking the polished-up punk aesthetic of Green Day and adding a "no girls allowed" mentality, the band augmented their early performances with the addition of wet T-shirt (or wet pants) contests. Blink-182 steadily built a fan base and gradually began to attract significant attention with their series of independent label releases: *Fly Swatter* (1993, EP), *Buddha* (1994), *Cheshire Cat* (1995), *Wasting Time* (1996, EP), and *Dude Ranch* (number 67 in 1997). Major labels began to take notice in 1997 following the band's number 11 hit ("Dammit (Growing Up)") from *Dude Ranch*. After signing with MCA, Blink-182 experienced a high degree of commercial success with *Enema of the State* (number 9 in 1999), containing "All the Small Things" (number 6). The *Mark, Tom and Travis Show* (number 8 in 2000) and *Take Off Your Pants and Jacket* (number 1 in 2001) revealed the band's staying power.

As an earlier revolt against the complexity and loss of spontaneity exhibited in mainstream rock of the 1970s, punk music remained always on the periphery, never attaining widespread appeal relative to that of mainstream rock. In this respect, alternative music has far surpassed the punk movement in terms of commercial success and national attention. Rather than being glossed over and repackaged as a more palatable musical style the way punk elements were incorporated into the creation of new-wave, alternative music—primarily that associated with the Seattle grunge scene and Nü Metal (discussed in Chapter 15)—was accepted "warts and all" into the mainstream of 1990s youth culture.

## INDIE ROCK

Recall that our previous use of the term *indie* has been in reference to the independent record companies during the mid-1950s. In an effort to make a mark in a time when the popular music industry was dominated by the major labels (not much has changed, has it?), independent record labels initially attempted to compete by connecting with a smaller audience to whom they could deliver their product cheaply and efficiently, without the distribution mechanisms available to their corporate competitors. By the 1990s, the term *indie* was being used to refer to music that, in some manner, placed itself in opposition to the mainstream in musical sound, fashion, and/or image. An "indie kid" would typically don clothing that gave a "thrift shop" appearance, Buddy Holly–style dark (sun)glasses, and Converse tennis shoes . . . all readily available at any Urban Outfitters retail store. By adopting this "look," indie kids attempted to convince peers that appearance was not important. It is interesting to note, however, that this specific dress was, in fact, important and played a central role in the social structure of the new indie culture. "The OC Show" on Fox network provided entertainment for the indie culture . . . a set of characters with whom they could closely identify. In addition, the show provided a soundtrack for a generation (available for purchase on CD). Interestingly, the songs played during each episode of every season can be found listed on the show's Web site. Groups that fit into the "indie" category of rock include Weezer and Beck, revealing strong musical influence exerted by Sonic Youth and the Pixies. Dashboard Confessional, Coldplay, Modest Mouse, Jimmy Eat World, and Starsailor are sometimes included in the indie subcategory of "emo" (emotionally-oriented rock).

### Beck

Influenced during his teens by the music of Sonic Youth and Pussy Galore and his upbringing in the bohemian environs of a street musician father and an artist–musician mother, Beck Hansen proved to be the ultimate "indie kid." Eventually, as is often the case with creative musicians saddled with such a stylistic label, he began stretching the boundaries this moniker imposed. After a brief stint in New York City, Beck returned to his southern California birthplace and began performing in a number of artsy coffee shops. Encouraged by Tom Rothrock, owner of Bongload Records, Beck recorded and released "Loser," a strange combination of folk music and rap. The single became a huge regional hit on L.A.'s alternative radio station and initiated a major label bidding war. After signing an agreement with DGC that allowed him to concurrently continue recording for small indie labels, Beck released *Mellow Gold* (number 13 in 1994), including "Loser," which reached number 10 on *Billboard's* Hot 100, his only Top 40 hit during the twentieth century. Choosing to exercise his option, Beck released his next two critically acclaimed albums, *Stereopathetic* and *One Foot in the Grave* (both released in 1994), on independent labels, so the sales generated were not as great as his DGC release.

With *Odelay* (number 16 in 1996), however, Beck returned to the spotlight and received high praise for his efforts. The artist won Grammys for Best Alternative Music Performance and Best Rock Male Vocal Performance ("Where It's At"), while receiving "Album of the Year" recognition from major publications including *Rolling Stone, Spin,* and the *Village Voice.* Later albums, *Mutations* (number 13 in 1998) and *Midnite Vultures* (number 34 in 1999), revealed the depth of Beck's songwriting skills, his versatility as a musician, and confirmed the commercial success of his craft. The latter album is particularly significant in its departure from the sound of previous albums. Sometimes sounding like a Prince clone on this recording, the influence of neo-soul and R & B are evident throughout this self-produced recording. Consider, for instance, the use of falsetto on the tune "Debra" or the Stax-Volt horn section on "Sexx Laws" . . . a dramatic change from the sound of his earlier material. With the release of *Sea Change* (2002), Beck returned to a quieter and more introspective musical style.

## Others

Though Seattle was the epicenter of the grunge movement, the national prominence attained by this music resulted in a proliferation of alternative bands not only from the Pacific Northwest but from all over the United States: Alice in Chains (also from Seattle), Smashing Pumpkins (Chicago), Sonic Youth (New York), Television (New York), Dinosaur Jr. (Amherst, Massachusetts), Soul Asylum (Minneapolis), Pavement (Stockton, California), Stone Temple Pilots (San Diego), Hole with Courtney Love (Los Angeles), and No Doubt with Gwen Stefani (Orange County, California). Showcasing some of the top alternative bands, the annual Lollapalooza concert tour, begun by Jane's Addiction vocalist Perry Farrell, combined the talents of some of alternative music's headliners with up-and-coming artists, allowing fans an opportunity to see their favorites and to be introduced to the next generation of likely stars. A significant number of alternative bands performed at Woodstock '94 and Woodstock '99, the twenty-fifth and thirtieth anniversaries of the 1969 rock festival.

## Punk III: Neo-Punk Propels Rock
## into the New Millenium

With the arrival of *Is This It?* (number 33 in 2001) by The Strokes, there seemed to be a renewed interest in authentic punk rock (i.e., returning to the roots of the movement that initiated Grunge). Forming in 1999, The Strokes were relative latecomers to the revival of the punk aesthetic, though neo-punk of the 1990s (referred to by various names including "post-punk," "garage rock revival," "noise rock," and even "grunge-pop") was slick and clean in comparison to its 1970s precursor. Image, even if an illusion, was a high priority. These bands were willing to spend loads of time and money, if necessary, to ensure that their clothing was vintage and their hair was mussed just right, resulting in the "authentic" look of a punk rock band. In 2003, The Strokes released *Room on Fire,* a critically acclaimed follow-up recording.

During the transition to the twenty-first century, around the same time that The Strokes emerged, a whole group of bands sharing a similar punk aesthetic appeared: The Hives, The Vines, The White Stripes, and Yeah, Yeah, Yeahs. Predating The

Strokes by several years, The Hives provide evidence of how internationally widespread punk-influenced alternative music had become. The band was formed by a group of five school friends in 1993 in the small industrial town of Fagersta, Sweden, influenced primarily by the music of MC5 and Iggy & the Stooges but also deriving their pop stylings from the New Wave trend of the 1980s. The band's image—dressed in sharp suits and ties—placed them in stark contrast to the punk rock image of the 1970s. Interestingly, the band intentionally propagated disinformation about the members's bios; for example, concealing the fact that two members are brothers and claiming their career was masterminded and songs composed by "Randy Fitzsimmons" (whom no one has ever met!). Released in 1997, *Barely Legal* was the group's first full-length release. The recording and the associated U.S. promotional tour received much attention and won over many fans, including Courtney Love of Hole. They continued the success spawned by their aggressive minimalist style with the release of the EP *a.k.a. I-D-I-O-T* (1998) and full-length recordings: *Vendi Vidi Vicious* (1999) containing "Main Offender" and "Hate to Say I Told You So," followed by *Tyrannosaurs Hives* (2004), including "Walk Idiot Walk." The latter album was significantly more polished sounding than the band's previous efforts.

As further proof that punk rock was no longer an isolated U.S.–U.K. phenomenon, the Vines emerged from Sydney, Australia. Craig Nicholls (vocals and guitar) and Patrick Matthews (bass and vocals) met when working together at McDonald's. In the mid-1990s, they began playing covers of tunes by Nirvana and Australian alternative band You Am I. The group's debut album, *Highly Evolved* (number 11 in 2001), was recorded in Los Angeles and released to significant critical acclaim, as a series of singles made it to the airwaves: the title track, "Get Free," "Outtathaway," and "Homesick." The band achieved significant chart success, primarily in Australia and the U.K. The Hives's sophomore effort, *Winning Days* (number 23 in 2004), was one of the most anticipated releases of the year, promoted by their "Australian Invasion" tour. Nicholls's stage antics, always frenetic, became increasingly erratic during this tour and resulted in bassist Matthews walking off stage during a Sydney performance in May 2004. Following that same performance, Nicholls assaulted a photographer. In November, during the court appearance stemming from Nicholls's post-performance behavior, the singer revealed that he has Asperger's syndrome, a form of autism.

Formed in 1997 in Detroit, the White Stripes were an enigmatic, bass-free duo consisting of Jack White (born John Anthony Gillis) and Meg White (born Megan Martha White). Reminiscent of the disinformation campaign of The Hives, Jack and Meg have flamed the fan of uncertainty concerning their relationship. Assumed at various times to be brother and sister or husband and wife, the two musicians contributed significantly to the neo-punk genre in the transition to the new millennium. Typically dressed in red and white outfits, the duo exudes a striking stage presence, while their unique sound—Jack on guitar and vocals, Meg on drums, and no bass—provides an interesting contrast to the typical punk rock instrumentation. In 1997, the Stripes debuted with two single releases, "Let's Shake Hands" and "Lafayette Blues." Released in 1999, their eponymous full-length debut provided a mix of interesting covers (Dylan's "One More Cup of Coffee" and Robert Johnson's "Stop Breaking Down Blues") with the band's own blend of original music. Their second album, *De Stijl* (2000), was named after the Dutch minimalist art movement, cited as a source of inspiration for their own stripped-down, garage band sound. Both *White Blood Cells* (2001) and *Elephant* (2003) were released to widespread critical acclaim. The latter album—using only analog equipment and an eight-track recording system, rather than a typical state-of-the-art digital recording facility—won a Grammy for Best Alternative Album and one of the tracks, "Seven Nation Army," won the Grammy for Best Rock Song (2004).

The Yeah Yeah Yeahs, formed in Brooklyn, New York in 2000, shortly after vocalist Karen O and guitartist Nick Zinner chanced to meet in a bar. The two musicians began writing songs together and added Brian Chase on drums. Like the White Stripes, with whom the Yeah Yeah Yeahs made their initial live performances as an opening act, the band decided not to include a bass player. Their debut EP, *Yeah Yeah Yeahs,* and its follow-up, *Fever to Tell* (2002, including the hit single "Maps"), reveal an interesting blend of quadruple meter dance-oriented beats and a choppy, post-punk sound.

It is too early to tell, in a historical sense, how far reaching will be the effect of bands representing this most recent incarnation of punk-influenced music. The popularity of the bands mentioned above and the sheer number of groups sharing similar musical influences leave little doubt, however, that the infusion of punk elements into the rock mainstream will continue to be an important influence in the foreseeable future.

## PROG ROCK

Amidst all the noise and hubbub of the most basic alternative subgenres, there were some bands who began with the "alternative" mindset, then evolved gradually into music that can rightly be referred to as "high art." Not unlike the music created by art rock performers of the late 1960s and 1970s, these artists once again set about pushing back the boundaries of rock music. Two of the most important of these, Radiohead and Björk, will be discussed at length in the following paragraphs. Other bands that deserve mention in the category include Tool, Nine Inch Nails, Sigur Ros, and God Speed You Black Emperor!

### Radiohead

In 1987, a band named TNT was formed in Oxford, England by boarding school buddies Thom Yorke (vocals and guitar) and Colin Greenwood (bass) with Ed O'Brien (guitar), Phil Selway (drums), and the bassist's younger brother, Jonny (guitar and keyboards). Following a brief period during which the band members disbursed to attend different colleges, the quintet reunited in 1991 as Radiohead. The band quickly built a local following, attracting the interest of Parlophone Records in London. Their debut album, *Pablo Honey* (number 32 in 1993), was a hit both in England and the United States. Undoubtedly influenced by the Seattle grunge movement, the lyrics evidence a similar self-loathing (e.g., "Creep," number 34). Labeled by many critics as a "one-hit wonder," the band silenced the lot with the release of *The Bends* (number 88 in 1995). Though the album sales and chart position were not particularly noteworthy, the band's musical maturation was clearly evident on this fine follow-up recording, garnering praise from many of the same critics who had snubbed their previous work. Like Nirvana before them, the heavy rock sound was balanced, at times, by interesting musical experimentation and, at others, a surprising Beatlesque melodicism; for example, "High and Dry" (number 78).

In 1997, *OK Computer* proved to be the breakthrough album for Radiohead, winning a Grammy for Best Alternative Music recording. Though not intended as a concept album, several songs ("Karma Police" and "Paranoid Android," for example) communicate a concern with the ubiquitous presence of technology in our lives and the implied fear of losing control. "Paranoid Android" provides an excellent example of the band's tight formal structures with adventurous musical elements. Sections of the piece utilize septuple meter (seven beats per measure), changing tempo, polyphonic vocal textures, and the use of changing loudness levels for dramatic effect (e.g., a dramatic crescendo that increases from the relatively soft acoustic guitar sounds heard at the beginning to distorted electric guitars and shouting vocals). There were no Top 40 singles from the album and, reminiscent of the folk-rock trend of the late 1950s and early 1960s, Radiohead's commercial success derived exclusively from album sales.

In the late 1990s, a number of guitar-centric British bands emerged that were obviously influenced by Radiohead's sound (e.g., Travis and Coldplay). Radiohead themselves returned in 2000 with their anxiously awaited *Kid A* (number 1). The album was originally scheduled for a simultaneous premiere via MTV2 and the BBC, but three weeks prior to the scheduled release date, bootleg copies in MP3 format began to appear on the Internet. Despite this fact, however, and what appeared to be an intentional anti-marketing campaign (e.g., no videos for MTV rotation and no singles released), the album shot to number 1. The signature sound of Jonny Greenwood's guitar, so prominent on previous recordings, no longer provided the primary foundation for the accompanimental tracks. Instead, synthesizers and other electronic sounds dominate the musical texture. The album opens with the sound of an electric piano and heavily processed vocal fragments, while the lyrics—once Yorke's vocals enter in earnest—assure us that "Everything [is] in its right place" . . . an interesting commentary on the radical change in the band's sound. Electric guitar sounds are completely absent until the third track, "The National Anthem," when the electric bass guitar provides a driving rock beat. When the electric guitar does appear, it is just as likely to be in the form of feedback providing another layer to be mixed into the complex musical fabric rather than the riffs that made the guitar a central part of a rock ensemble since the time of Chuck Berry's early recordings. In addition, many tracks on *Kid A* contain significantly longer instrumental sections, often providing ambient contrast to the vocal sections instead of inserting a predictable guitar solo into the musical form. "Treefingers"—a song completely without vocals—is an interesting example of an almost four-minute composition that verges on ambient music influenced by the work of Brian Eno. None of the songs from this album were released as singles, and the album was not supported, as was typically the case for rock albums, by extensive promotional touring. *Amnesiac* (2001), containing some tracks recorded during the same sessions as *Kid A*, debuted at number 2 and left no doubt about the band's penchant for musical experimentation. In 2003, the band released yet another critically acclaimed recording, *Hail to the Thief* (number 3).

As mentioned earlier, in addition to their creative musical output, Radiohead provided a model for the manner in which the Internet and even Napster could be used effectively to market and promote commercial releases. About six months before the release of *Kid A*, the band created 15-second video animations ("blips") that they made available to fans via the Internet. Fans were encouraged to trade the clips like "electronic postcards" (Knopper 2001). Given the success of the album upon its release, making these materials available—including MP3 files of some of the tracks—seems to have whetted the appetite of the record-buying public who were ready and willing to purchase the recording once it was available.

## Björk

A very different but equally adventurous approach to the creative process is evident in the music of Icelandic singer Björk Gudmundsdóttir. A performer from an early age, Björk completed her first album when she was eleven years old. The singer experienced significant success in Iceland performing in a hard rock band. In 1984, several members of the band formed KUKL, a band that would later change its name to the Sugarcubes before recording *Life's Too Good* (number 54 in 1988). This album received critical acclaim in both the United States and United Kingdom. A video for the song "Birthday" even managed to work its way into rotation at MTV. After recording several less successful albums (*Here Today, Tomorrow, Next Week!*, *Gling Gio*, and *Stick Around for Joy*) with the band, Björk left in 1993 to pursue a solo career.

Her first release as a solo artist, aptly titled *Debut* (number 61 in 1993), was produced by Nellee Hooper of Soul II Soul. The album contained a single entitled "Human Behavior" that, though it did not reach the Top 40 on the Hot 100 chart, rose to number 2 on the Modern Rock chart. In 1995, Björk released *Post* (number 32), a widely varied collection of songs, revealing the influence of electronica ("Army of Me"), ambient music ("Hyper-ballad"), and even big band jazz ("It's Oh So Quiet"). The singer's unique vocal quality makes her easily identifiable and her stream-of-consciousness lyrics manage to draw the listener into her (rather bizarre) world.

Though the earlier albums provided a strong sense of Björk's creative potential, musicality, and arranging skill, *Vespertine* (number 19 in 2002) left little doubt that she was a force with which to be reckoned. Consisting largely of what can most accurately be described as sonic montages, the singer performs her flowing vocal melodies over a primarily electronic foundation. Some selections ("Cocoon," "It's Not Up to You," and "Heirloom") are highly rhythmic, integrating many interesting sampled source materials into the mix (e.g., electronic pops and clicks, phonograph needle noise, and escaping steam). Add to this unique and highly creative mix the singer's inimitable vocal style and the result is highly interesting and distinctive. She composed the soundtrack and starred in *Dancer in the Dark*, a critically acclaimed motion picture alternating between a dark reality (filmed with only a single camera and no musical score) and the lead character's imaginative fantasy world (filmed with 100 cameras and taking on the character of a Hollywood musical). In a career marked by innovative musical experimentation, Björk's most stunning departure from popular song form yet came with the release of *Medulla* (2004). Built solely out of vocal sounds (sometimes heavily processed), the resulting sonic montage is truly an artistic masterpiece, though the recording presents an undeniable challenge to the listener who yearns to hear a hit single.

An undeniable shift occurred within the realm of rock music during the 1990s. "Alternative" music infiltrated and then dominated the mainstream of popular culture. During the same period, however, many artists continued to stretch the boundaries of rock and roll. It was an exciting decade, the definitive results of which may not be known for many years to come.

## Summary of Punk and Alternative Styles

In its (r)evolutionary path, as we hope has become apparent throughout this text, rock music has been influenced by a wide array of musical styles . . . some closely related to mainstream rock, others vastly different. The punk aesthetic has proven no different. In fact, the initial punk movement of the 1970s—not a dramatic commercial success on its own—found its influence (i.e., simplification of a growing level of complexity) as its musical elements were subsumed into New Wave, a subgenre that did experience a degree of commercial success. The punk movement of the 1980s resulted in the grunge phenomenon, which served to truly bring alternative music into the mainstream of rock. By the time of the neo-punk movement of the 1990s, it was no longer necessary to speak as if the punk movement were separate from the mainstream of rock. In fact, some of the most commercially successful recordings during these years were by artists identified as belonging to one of any number of punk-influenced musical categories. It is still too early to determine the long-term impact of and resulting musical development following the neo-punk movement of the late 1990s and early twenty-first century. However, one thing is not debatable at this point in history: The cyclical infusion of punk elements into the rock and roll mainstream continues to serve as a periodic reminder that rock music, at times, may take itself a little too seriously and move beyond the realm of accessibility and mainstream popular appeal. The punk message is often reflected by a return to the basics from which it emerged. Much as an emergency room physician uses electricity to return animation to a human heart that has stopped beating, the punk aesthetic provides a sense of renewed vigor, frenetic energy, and immediacy to rock music at times when the music appears to be in need of such an infusion.

## MUSICAL CLOSE-UP:
## ALTERNATIVE VIEWS OF ALTERNATIVE ROCK

Have you ever thought to yourself (or perhaps even said), "Life is just too darned complicated!"? Indeed, if one steps back far enough to consider the entirety of human evolution, it does seem that there has been a consistent tendency for us to move from the simple to the complex. As just one example, think about transportation. At first, we needed only to move one foot in front of the other. At some point, we learned that we could save a lot of energy and go farther and faster by riding a horse. Of course, this made things a little more complicated because now we had to tame the horse for riding; we had to teach it when to stop, start, and turn; and we needed to feed the horse and otherwise keep it healthy. Then we learned to hitch one or more horses to some sort of carriage with wheels. Certainly this was more comfortable and could transport many people at once. But again, there was a trade-off, because we needed to keep the carriage and all of its parts in working order. Over one hundred years ago, we learned that we could replace the horse with an engine that could move the carriage. As the automobile evolved over the last hundred years, we encountered still more complicated concerns (e.g., how to provide adequate fuel, how to provide and maintain adequate streets and interstate highways, and what to do when the global positioning system in our car malfunctions!).

You get the idea. Think of any aspect of our existence and you will discern this human characteristic of making our lives more complex. Ironically, it sometimes seems that everything we do to make our lives easier seems to add more difficulty. For example, it is easier to push a button to raise the garage door, but life gets rather difficult when the automatic opener malfunctions.

When the complexities of life begin to overwhelm us, we often yearn for a simpler existence. And so it is with music. Remember the old twelve-bar blues we discussed back in Chapter 2? It was a very simple idea and, in its most basic form, worked well for thousands and thousands of songs. But inevitably, the human tendency to tinker with things had its effect. Over the years, chords were substituted, meters were changed, the AAB lyric and melodic scheme was modified, and there were even measures added or deleted. The same evolution occurred in jazz. Beginning as a rather simple musical style, by the 1940s and 1950s it had become a very sophisticated and complex art form.

Like jazz, rock and roll began as a rather simple style of music. But as we have seen with the Beatles, Brian Wilson, and others, there were ever more creative manipulations to almost every musical element: harmony and tonality, rhythm and meter, timbre, form, and so forth.

As you might expect, this all-pervasive evolution from simplicity to complexity is not an absolutely straight line. At frequent points along the way (whether one is considering the blues, or jazz, or rock, or any other aspect of the human experience), there are those who yearn for a return to simplicity. Their rebellion often takes the form of a "return to the basics" or "return to the roots" movement. And so it was with the punk rockers and those that followed in their footsteps (the various "alternative" rockers discussed in this chapter).

But how are we to evaluate—musically—these alternative styles? Does the product of this rebellion have true musical value or is it simply the noisy ranting of charlatans? As would be particularly appropriate to this chapter, let us consider several alternative answers to these questions.

## Alternative Rock as a Valid Musical Component of Rock History

As stated in the body of the present chapter, the emergence of the mainstream rock sound of Little Richard, Jerry Lee Lewis, Elvis Presley, and other artists in the mid-1950s offered an "alternative" to the sound of Pop artists of the 1940s and early 50s. One of the primary musical distinctions between the earlier forms of music and that of these early rock pioneers was the raw energy inherent in their recordings. In contrast to the carefully arranged instrumental parts and highly trained vocal stylings of the crooners, the R & B–influenced rockers presented a musical style that was—if imperfect in its performance—full of youthful energy and vigor. A similar contrast can be made during the late 1960s if one compares the music of the Beatles and Rolling Stones. The musical style of the Beatles continued to evolve dramatically, resulting in recordings that some (not the present authors) might consider pretentious, while the Stones—after an initial foray into such experimentation—returned to their mainstream rock roots.

Considering the evolution of rock music over the past several decades, one can identify specific musical trends that represented a return to a more basic style. Rock is not, of course, the only musical genre to have experienced such a cyclical pattern of complexity and simplicity. In its long history, classical music has experienced many similar cycles. To focus on only one example, consider the remarkable change from the late Baroque style to the early Classical style. By the end of the Baroque period, complex polyphonic textures were the norm, best exemplified by the fugal compositions of J. S. Bach. The Classicism of Haydn and Mozart was, among other things, a move away from the intricate polyphony of Bach toward simpler textures, singable melodies, and more easily perceived forms. By the end of the Classic Period, however, extreme complexity was again dominant in works such as Beethoven's Ninth Symphony and the *Grosse Fuge*. Similar alternation between simplicity and complexity can be traced right up through the twentieth century and even into the new millennium.

This same cycle of action and reaction has occurred numerous times in the context of rock music. Generally, the punk movements discussed in the present chapter resulted in a return to a rawer, harder-edged sound. This "return to the roots" can be viewed as a valid reaction against two existing trends: the trend toward complexity and the related trend toward technology. Let us look briefly at each of these reactions.

Recall that the transition to the 1960s represented an initial fragmentation of the rock market. The resulting branches of the rock and roll genealogical tree included a variety of musical styles. As the decade proceeded, new styles emerged that were dramatically more complex than those that preceded. Two such examples would include jazz rock (Chapter 11) and art rock (Chapter 12). In comparison to most other subgenres of rock, the music of Blood, Sweat, and Tears, Chicago, Yes, and Emerson, Lake, and Palmer during the late 1960s and early 1970s provided a significant increase in the level of musical complexity. During this same period, the music of Queen, Steely Dan, Pink Floyd, Styx, and others represented a vigorous pursuit of perfectionism in studio recording technique. As a result, some of the highest quality and most innovative recording productions in the history of rock were released during this time. Though many previous artists (Buddy Holly and Brian Wilson, for example) had used the studio as a musical instrument, the level of attention given to every detail of the recording process during the mid-1970s represented a new level of sophistication. One need only listen to the "operatic" section in Queen's "Bohemian Rhapsody" from *A Night at the Opera* (1975) or "Deacon Blues" from Steely Dan's *Aja* (1977) to hear the incredibly high production quality evident in these recordings, incorporating numerous overdubs and retakes. Others who listened to these same recordings at the time felt that rock music had begun to lose its connection with the energy inherent in the immediacy of a live performance. In fact, many early independent label R & B recordings were made by simply hanging a single microphone and capturing a live performance, imperfections and all. The first punk movement was at least partially intended to deflate the balloon of this perfectionist movement, suggesting instead that a do-it-yourself (DIY) aesthetic was more appropriate to rock and roll. Why should the creation and performance of music be reserved for a few highly trained musicians and recording engineers? Punk rockers joyfully celebrated the imperfections of a live musical performance and were more than willing to trade the studio perfection of the bands mentioned above—a sound they believed represented a sanitized and pretentious version of rock—for the energy and immediacy of their own radical musical style. Perhaps it is no coincidence that the Sex Pistols were formed in the same year as the release of Queen's *A Night at the Opera* and their most important recording (*Never Mind the Bollocks, Here's the Sex Pistols*) was released the same year as Steely Dan's *Aja*.

During the 1980s, technology was used to an ever greater extent as a performance tool in popular music. Dance music during this period frequently replaced a live drummer with rhythms "performed" by a drum machine and many of the bass lines and keyboard parts were covered by computer sequencers, rather than performed by live musicians. Even the parts that *were* performed by human hands were typically "quantized"—adjusted temporally to make them more rhythmically accurate—to make the performance more "perfect" than humanly possible. Listen carefully, for example, to Michael Jackson's "Speed Demon" from *Bad* (1987). Following the vocal phrase "speed demon" in the chorus, notice the mechanically perfect performance of the 32nd note runs of the bass synthesizer. Though highly trained musicians possess superb technical skills—and, if anyone could afford to hire such performers during this period, it would have been Michael!—the accuracy with which this musical line is performed (and repeated numerous times without deviation) is simply beyond human capability. Music by many artists during the mid- to late-1980s (Madonna, Prince, George Michael, Stacy Q, and Nu Shooz, for example) incorporated these same technologies. Live performance of certain parts (electric guitar, saxophone, vocals) was often incorporated to balance the lack of expressivity in the technically perfect performances of other parts. Prince, for example, typically used a live drummer *and* a drum machine as a means of getting the best of both worlds: a high degree of rhythmic and metrical accuracy without giving up completely the expressivity inherent in human performance. By the mid-1980s, as described earlier in this chapter, another punk-influenced musical revolution was initiated to counter this move toward computer-based musical performance. This time, the musical infusion arrived from the Pacific Northwest. These "grunge" bands were influenced musically by heavy metal and mainstream bands (Led Zeppelin, Black Sabbath, AC/DC, and Aerosmith), but were also heavily derivative of hardcore punk groups like Black Flag, the Melvins, the Butthole Surfers, and Circle Jerks. Much of the music produced by Sub Pop records during the 1980s was raw and intentionally simplistic. Volume and energy were the prime elements (for example, Mudhoney's "The Rose," Green River's "Hangin' Tree," or Nirvana's "Spank Thru"). However, with Nirvana's *Nevermind* (1991; eventually reaching number 1 fourteen weeks after the album's release, unseating Michael Jackson's *Dangerous* from the top of the chart), the punk aesthetic found a mainstream audience. Other bands, including Soundgarden, Pearl Jam, and Alice in Chains, emerged from the Seattle area to become some of the most popular groups of the 1990s.

Thus, the punk rockers and their progeny can be seen in the larger context of action/reaction. As has been the case throughout music history (and even human history), these rebellions against complexity and technological perfection sought a return to simpler, more "human" values. Taken in this light, they take their legitimate place beside countless others who have tried to balance the scales against the seemingly unstoppable human propensity for increasing complexity and sophistication.

## Alternative Rock as a Form of Musical Charlantanry

The foregoing discussion views much of alternative rock as a legitimate reaction that is comparable to many similar reactions throughout music history. However, one can see this apparent rebellion against complexity in a far different light. After all, there are two very different circumstances that can lead to such a rebellion. First, one may understand and appreciate complexity but consciously opt for a simpler style. Or one may simply be incapable of dealing with the complexity (for one reason or another) and therefore have no choice but to pursue simplicity.

As an example of the former, consider the analogy cited above in classical music. It is true that Haydn and Mozart rebelled against the complex polyphony of Bach and other late Baroque composers. But both Haydn and Mozart were thoroughly schooled in the intricacies of the polyphonic styles that preceded them. They *chose* to develop a very different style. To find a more appropriate parallel to the punk rockers, we would need to identify some Mozart "wanna-be" in Austria of the 1760s whose name and music came and went in a couple of years because it had little or no musical validity. No one could legitimately suggest that Haydn and Mozart wrote in their style because they were incapable of writing complex polyphonic music (in fact, they did so at times). Although they adopted a somewhat simpler texture, their music was extremely sophisticated in other ways.

Far different is the person who adopts a simpler style because he or she really has no choice. He or she simply lacks the talent and sophistication needed to work in a more complex style. In the case of some of the alternative bands (not all, of course), one suspects that their "rebellion" against complexity and perfectionism is nothing more than a convenient rationalization that masks an inability to sing, play an instrument, or work creatively with the musical elements. Their product sells to consumers who, like themselves, are incapable of appreciating anything other than the most basic musical styles. The rock press legitimizes the bands and their simplistic product because to do otherwise would force a value judgment—and remember from the Overview at the beginning of this chapter that in today's egalitarian culture, there is no better or worse, no good and bad; all things have equal value and are simply "alternatives."

Let us return to a question that was posed in the discussion above that viewed alternative rock as a valid countermovement. Articulating part of the alternative philosophy, we asked, "Why should the creation and performance of music be reserved for a few highly trained musicians and recording engineers?" One pretty good answer might be, "Because they know what they are doing!" Let us consider an analogy and see how we feel about it. Suppose we restated our question as follows: "Why should the practice of medicine be reserved for a few highly trained doctors?" Medicine has become incredibly complex and technologically sophisticated. We now have laser surgery and the ability to perform intricate operations that actually replace human hearts, hips, and knees—all monitored closely by elaborate computer hardware and software. What if you or someone you care about were faced with a life-threatening medical emergency? How would you feel if your doctor announced that he or she was a "back to the basics" sort who strongly recommended bloodletting, a few well-chosen leeches, and an old fifteenth-century incantation? That is a type of "alternative medicine" you would probably do well to avoid!

So is alternative rock a valid musical response to the excessive musical and technological complexity of more advanced styles of rock? Or is it just a smokescreen for the musical "wanna-be" (and an audience that is similarly incapable of appreciating more challenging styles)? The answer will probably come with time. Because of the natural tendency of the human race to move from simplicity to complexity, it seems likely that some punk-influenced groups will gradually inch toward greater sophistication, if they are capable of it. Others will stagnate and disappear rather quickly into anonymity.

## A Final Note about Complexity and Simplicity

Before leaving this discussion of complexity and simplicity, we need to be certain that the reader does not draw an erroneous inference. It would be easy to assume that complexity is inherently superior to simplicity. However, that would not be a valid assumption. When we use the terms *complex* and *simple* in this book, we mean to describe—as objectively as possible—the level of creativity demonstrated in the manipulation of the musical elements (as defined in Chapter 2). The music of the Beatles is more musically complex than that of the Rolling Stones. That is simply a fact based on an objective analytical study of the music. But this observation does not imply any kind of value judgment (for example, that the music of the Beatles is "better" than the music of the Rolling Stones). In fact, there is no inherent connection between complexity/simplicity and good/bad. Simple music can be good; complex music can be bad; simple music can be bad; and complex music can be good. "Good" and "bad" are value judgments based on a matrix of personal tastes, backgrounds, educations, and experiences.

Too often we meet people who can appreciate only the complex or only the simple. They thrive on one and denigrate the other. Such people are living only half a life—musically speaking. The truth is that both simple and complex music can have a rewarding function in our lives. There are times when we desire and appreciate the challenges afforded by the more sophisticated music of the Beatles, Blood, Sweat, and Tears, or Emerson, Lake, and Palmer. But there are other times when we crave the simpler, more visceral appeal of Little Richard, the Stones, or James Brown. This is no different than selecting a television show to watch. There are times when you might be ready for a show like *Law and Order*, one that will cause you to think about complicated ethical or legal dilemmas. But there are other times when you just need to "veg out" with a rather mindless sitcom. Both have a function in our lives. It is rather sad to meet someone who can respond only to the complex and is missing the delights of sheer simplicity. Conversely, it is equally sad to know someone who can only deal with the simple, thereby missing the uplifting challenges of the more complex.

In Chapter 7 ("The British Invasion") and Chapter 11 ("Jazz Rock"), we encountered a song titled "Sympathy for the Devil." The original song (by Jagger and Richard) was simple and repetitive. The arrangement by Blood, Sweat, and Tears, however, was remarkably complex. A nonmusical analogy can be made using two technological developments: a supercomputer and a hand-held calculator. One is very complex; the other is relatively simple. But both have practical functions for which the other is ill suited. Thus you would not want America's next space shuttle to be designed and controlled by a hand calculator. Nor do you need to drag a supercomputer along with you to the market to determine which brand of toothpaste is cheaper per ounce. And so it is with the two versions of "Sympathy for the Devil." One is complex; the other is simple. The truly fortunate person is the one who can enjoy each version for what it is. But if you honestly prefer one and find little to like about the other, that is a matter of personal preference and is absolutely your prerogative. What is unfortunate is if you can't tell the difference!

# 19

## An Overview and an Editorial

### OVERVIEW: EIGHT BASIC STATEMENTS

In Chapter 1, "Introduction," we stated the intention that this history of rock and roll would be told as objectively as possible, stating the facts and allowing the reader to draw his or her own conclusions. The evaluative statements made regarding musical content have, it is hoped, been based upon valid musical analysis; and estimates of the relative importance of various performers have been made inasmuch as that seems to be a central task of any historian.

Chapter 19, however, is different. This overview contains a number of subjective evaluations, and the subsequent editorial is highly personalized. It is hoped that the comments therein will prove provocative or instructive; if not, perhaps they will—as was said once before—at least be interesting or entertaining.

Beginning with a mixture of R & B, C & W, and pop music, early rock and roll settled into three basic styles: mainstream rock, rockabilly, and soft rock. In the 1960s, other influences were added (e.g., folk, jazz, gospel, and classical music), resulting in several new substyles. In the 1970s, rock fragmented into a bewildering array of individualized substyles, most of which continued unabated through the 1980s and 1990s and on into the new century. With all of this, can we step back and attempt to draw a series of conclusions that might apply to *all* of the history of rock? Let us try. The eight basic statements that follow seem to apply across the entirety of rock. They are stated in no particular order, except that we will save the most important point for last.

BASIC STATEMENT NUMBER ONE: *Rock and roll may be here to stay, but individual artists and styles are not.* In other words, although rock as a general style may be permanent, its component parts are extremely transitory. Rock and roll is much like the weather: If you don't like it now, wait a while. For every Chicago or Rolling Stones, there are hundreds of performers who are here today and gone tomorrow.

For a number of years, the author conducted a survey in his university classes in rock history. The sole question asked was, "What performer(s) who are popular today will still be popular ten years from now?" The results make the point: The majority of performers named in the 1984 survey were not even mentioned in the 1986 survey. Not only were most of those named in 1984 not popular in 1994, they did not even rate a "mention" just two years later. The individualism of the market is reflected in the fact that out of 100 responses on a given survey, 63 separate artists were named—and few received as many as five votes.

There is one other observation that relates to basic statement number 1: Nothing is as "out" as that which is most recently "out." Very often there is a cycle of popularity to derision to nostalgia. In the aforementioned 1984 survey, Michael Jackson was the biggest vote getter; when his name was mentioned in class in 1986, the responses varied from snickers to outright guffaws. As time passed, the Jackson stigma passed, and Michael became a nostalgia item from the "good old early 1980s." This phenomenon is particularly noticeable with the harder rock styles, especially with heavy metal. The principle in operation here seems to be that the more the appeal of a group is based upon rebellion and shock, the more likely it is to pass from "super in" to "super out." After all, what is outrageously shocking today will be old hat in two years. Which brings us to our next observation.

BASIC STATEMENT NUMBER TWO: *What were once vices are now habits.* The principle of "one-upmanship" is quite powerful within the rock industry. The title of the Doobie Brothers album (i.e., basic statement number 2) makes a profound statement where rock history is concerned. Again, this principle applies with increasing strength in the harder styles, especially where rebellion and shock are major factors. Competition within the rock industry is tremendous. Countless new bands are begun each year in the United States and England (not to mention Japan, Germany, Scandinavia, and elsewhere). All hope to "make it" and see their albums rise to the Top 10 and play to sold-out stadiums.

Unfortunately (or fortunately?) 99 percent will never come close to their dreams. Somehow 1 percent attain success out of all those thousands of bands. Thus, publicity becomes crucial—good or bad matters little (there is an old show biz proverb that all publicity is good publicity). To grab the spotlight from the current stars, a new band must play louder, have more elaborate props, cut bigger holes in their jeans, wear more spikes and chains, shout more obscenities, and bite the heads off more bats than the current groups. If not, they run the risk of being submerged in obscurity forever.

Thus, one-upmanship is a fact of life for many aspiring bands. The only problem is that one-upmanship is a game that no one wins for long. The rules of the game mean another group will soon come along with more powerful amps, even more elaborate props, more revealing costumes, and even more explicit songs. And they will bite the heads off six bats, plus a baby rabbit.

The troublesome result of the one-upmanship game is that it implies a staggering future. If the game continues as it has for the last fifty years, where will rock and roll be by 2020? Just how loud can it get? How sexually explicit? How outrageous? The thinking person must be concerned.

BASIC STATEMENT NUMBER THREE: *Good is bad, and bad is good.* The one-upmanship game would not be a concern if each group were merely trying to play better music, make ever more uplifting statements, and set increasingly better lifestyle examples. This is, in fact, close to the nature of the game in the early and mid-1960s, where love, peace, and racial tolerance were themes. But with the division of the mainstream in the mid-1960s into Beatles and Stones, an interesting change occurred. The Stones represented the antihero concept. Part of their popularity resulted from their being so bad. They acted bad, they sang bad—they were bad. And bad was good. In fact, in black jargon (picked up by nonblack populations), the word *bad,* said with the right inflection, meant "good."

This inversion of traditional evaluative criteria developed through the 1970s, and the message seemed to be that the worse you were, the better you were (and vice versa). Distortion was deliberately added to the music. Thus, rock consumers bought more and more sophisticated stereo systems—presumably as free from any distortion as possible—so they could hear the distortion better. Singers who screamed and shouted out of tune were praised, whereas singers who sang in tune were derided. The "best" or "real" rock groups were those who played with the least sophistication; any attempt to sophisticate the music was condemned as a sellout to commercialism or as a disreputable attempt at musical snobbery.

What may lie at the base of this peculiar inversion of values may be nothing more than sheer laziness. The more sophisticated and complex the music, the more that is required of both the performers and listeners. Some effort must be put forth to perform or listen intelligently to the more sophisticated compositions within any style of music. But it is an effort worth making. There must be something inherent in the finest music that allows it to last for hundreds of years, whereas hack-work totally disappears within a matter of weeks.

But, say some rock writers, "real" rock (meaning simple, three-chord, 4/4 rock) is for the "real" people (the average middle- and lower-income working classes). This is surely the most offensively prejudicial position one can take. It implies that only the privileged socioeconomic classes have the intelligence, inner drive, and discipline to learn to play or listen to the more sophisticated styles of music, and that the "regular guy (or girl)" cannot possibly appreciate more than three chords or four beats. Such a position is not only grossly offensive, it is also dead wrong. Anyone can learn to listen more intelligently to music. One need not know every chord, every metric pattern, or every form to respond to better music (in whatever style). As with anything else (football, baseball, politics, etc.), the more one knows, the more one enjoys.

By the way, the foregoing discussion should not be interpreted to mean that one ought to prefer more sophisticated music and shun simpler music. Musical preference is a complicated issue that profound minds have been grappling with for a long time. There is absolutely nothing wrong with liking simpler styles of music. What is wrong is to disdain more complex styles just because they are more complex. That would be just as bad as disdaining simpler styles just because they are simple. The goal should be to develop a broader taste that can accept and enjoy both simple music and complex music (and everything in between), while recognizing each for what it is. Fortunate is the listener who can enjoy Emerson, Lake, and Palmer or Blood, Sweat, and Tears and appreciate their musical complexities, and then fully enjoy Little Richard or the Rolling Stones, while recognizing their music as being pure and simple fun. In other words, one need not validate one's own musical preference by disparaging other styles.

BASIC STATEMENT NUMBER FOUR: *"My album may be number 1, but I'm not commercial!"* One of the basic ironies in the rock industry is that virtually everyone is striving for commercial success while loudly proclaiming just the opposite. As was mentioned earlier, one of the most damning charges one can make is that a performer has "gone commercial." But rock music is not only a musical phenomenon; it is a commercial enterprise. There need not be a stigma attached to the word *commercial*. The crux of the issue may be whether or not (and to what extent) a group alters its style simply to achieve commercial success. Thus, if a group maintains its style and gradually becomes popular enough to enjoy a wide appeal, they have simply carried their style to a wider audience. That should be a compliment to the musicians and to their earlier fans, validating their musical preference.

More problematic is the case of a band that consciously alters its musical principles solely to achieve commercial success. This rings of hypocrisy and raises embarrassing questions about their musical sincerity. Sometimes it is difficult to know whether such a change is genuine or simply done to make a buck.

As we have seen, the word *commercial* is often slapped onto performers whose talents are versatile enough to enable them to perform in a variety of styles. If a musician has the musical talent to perform convincingly in a variety of styles, he or she should be respected, not condemned. Such condemnation often reflects the narrow-mindedness of the critic more than the lack of integrity of the performer.

In any event, the word *commercial* ought not be used as an evaluative musical term. It means nothing musically; it tells nothing about the harmonies, melodies, forms, and so on. It is an economic term. So beware the next time you hear someone disparage a performer for being "commercial." Try to think (and listen) more deeply than that.

BASIC STATEMENT NUMBER FIVE: *Not all music is art; most of it is simply product.* Have you ever stood in stunned appreciation while some musical whiz sat at a piano and improvised almost any tune you could name? Or have you been amazed at the seemingly mysterious ability of some guitarist to invent tunes and chords at a moment's notice? It is a vestige of nineteenth-century romanticism that we tend to view musical talent with awe and invest it with an aura of mysticism. In earlier centuries, musicians were often viewed merely as skilled technicians, not much different from our modern-day auto mechanics, electricians, or plumbers.

The fact is, only a small percentage of musical talent is mysterious. A much larger percentage is simply the result of plain old hard work. There is a standing joke about composition—that it is 10 percent inspiration and 90 percent perspiration. That is about right. A musician gets a musical idea in the same way one gets ideas about other things—from "somewhere." But then come the pure hard work, discipline, and practice to turn that idea into a full-blown reality.

A true work of art seems to appeal not only to a large number of people but to generations of people over many centuries; it is as though it transcends time. A product, however, is a far more mundane thing. Usually a product begins with someone assessing what will sell, figuring out the technology required to produce it, and then going to work manufacturing it, promoting it, and selling it. Usually such a product serves an immediate function and (as we all know too well) soon wears out or becomes obsolete and is discarded. This process applies to products as varied as automobiles, computers, and electric toothbrushes.

In every century and in every musical style, there have been very few true artists and a large number of musical manufacturers. The former create art; the latter make products. In Mozart's time there were hundreds of hacks who understood the musical language of the time and then went about producing compositions utilizing that language. They knew the skill of creating tunes, chords, and forms that were currently in style. But only a handful of composers of that time had that something "extra" that made their music rise above the level of product to the level of art. Several centuries later we have forgotten the hacks, but we still remember Mozart.

Things are not much different now. Especially in a heavily commercialized industry such as rock music, one can be sure that works of art will be few and far between, whereas 95 percent of what we hear is mere product. Many composers, performers, and engineers have learned the technical skill necessary to manufacture a marketable musical product; hence they go about their business of grinding out those products day after day. Fifty years from now (much less 200), 99 percent will be long gone; only a trace will remain.

So beware when rock musicians attempt to hide behind "artistic freedom." In most cases, they are merely successful manufacturers of a product. As such, they have the same responsibilities to society that manufacturers of automobiles, cigarettes, and lawn mowers have.

But is not artistic freedom necessary for the creation of true art? Well, Bach worked from Sunday to Sunday for the church; he wrote many musical masterpieces within the strict confines of what was acceptable to his employer. Yet he still managed to create musical works that live 300 years later. Was he "free" as an artist? Absolutely not. How far do you think he would have gotten if he had popped a few satanic messages or sexually explicit songs into the Sunday morning church service? Or consider Haydn, who worked for years for an Austrian prince. Each week he had to create chamber music, solo literature, or orchestral music for the court. Because Haydn was a true artist, he created masterpieces within the boundaries imposed upon him. Whether such limitations are set by the church, the state, the employer, or the society as a whole, art can and has flourished within boundaries.

BASIC STATEMENT NUMBER SIX: *The audience for rock is getting both older and younger.* In its beginnings, rock and roll was the music of teens and very young adults (generally seventh grade through college years). But as we entered the 1970s, an inevitable fact became obvious: those 1950s teenagers were entering middle age and they still liked rock. A baby born in 1940 was 15 years old when "Rock Around the Clock" hit number 1; in 1970, that same person turned thirty but very likely still liked Elvis, the Beach Boys, Dylan, and the Beatles. And in 2000, that "baby" was 60 years old and in all probability still liked those artists as well as a few newer ones. Notice the number of "classic rock" and "adult rock" radio stations on your FM dial? Those are aimed at a relatively affluent segment of the population that is roughly 35 to 60 years old. These people are hitting their peak earning years (a fact of considerable interest to radio advertisers), and they want to hear their favorite artists from the 1950s and 1960s, as well as a few of the more conservative acts of the 1970s through 1990s. Indeed, the rock market now extends to 60-year-olds.

The other end of this demographic expansion is with the preteens. The lowering of the age of rock consumerism accelerated with the coming of MTV and other televised rock video formats. It should come as no surprise to anyone that children— little children—like television. Now the seven-, nine-, and 11-year-old has immediate (and free) access to the most up-to-date rock videos. While parents and older siblings are at work, school, or elsewhere, the "latchkey" preteen is left to the electronic babysitter—television. He or she has a choice of cartoons, reruns, game shows, or rap videos. The television rock videos have brought an increasingly younger population into the world of rock and roll. The same can be said about the availability of music via the Internet.

This lowering of the age of pop-music awareness is reflected at rock concerts, where the average age is steadily lowering. Whereas it was not so long ago that the rock concert was the province of those 16 to 24 years old, it is gradually becoming evident that the majority of concertgoers are 12 to 19, with a heavy sprinkling of preteens at most concerts. Whereas in 1957 the typical 12-year-old would only stare in astonishment at older brother's new pink-and-black outfit and greasy ducktail, today's 12-year-old is a carbon copy of the Spice Girls or some other rock model.

Thus, we are saying that the rock market of the early 2000s extends from the early elementary school years to 60-year-olds. True, the teenager is still the center of the market, but to call rock and roll "teen music" is simply no longer accurate.

BASIC STATEMENT NUMBER SEVEN: *Rock is no longer the counterculture—it is the culture.* This statement naturally follows the previous statement. Rock and roll no longer stands as a teen-oriented countercultural phenomenon. It now pervades virtually our entire culture. It cuts across all economic groups, social levels, and ethnic groups. The rock style permeates movie music, music for television, jazz, music at athletic events, church music, and country music. Granted, within rock there are countercultural trends; but as a generic entity, rock so permeates our entire culture that all other styles of music (jazz, classical, pure C & W, etc.) are considered to be on the fringe, admired by small subcultural groups.

BASIC STATEMENT NUMBER EIGHT: *Music, including rock and roll, affects behavior.* Perhaps the most oft-quoted statement in this regard was made by Andrew Fletcher in 1703: "Give me the making of the songs of a nation and I care not who makes the laws." In other words, music may be even more influential in shaping the attitudes and behaviors of a nation than its constitution, legal system, and government. Fletcher was hardly the first to recognize that fact. Socrates' and Plato's mentor, Damon, said that music, "being chaste, has the power of disposing our minds to virtue and, being the contrary, to vice." Centuries later, Martin Luther would say, "Music is one of the greatest gifts that God has given us; it is divine and therefore Satan is its enemy. For with its aid, many dire temptations are overcome; the devil does not stay where music is."

In our own century, anthropologist Alan P. Merriam wrote, "The importance of music, as judged by the sheer ubiquity of its presence, is enormous. . . . There is probably no other human cultural activity which is so all-pervasive and which reaches into, shapes, and often controls so much of human behavior" (Merriam 1964, 218). We have known intuitively for centuries that music can make us feel relaxed, scared, patriotic, ambitious, mad, sad, happy, romantic, and reverent. The ability of music to affect human behavior is the basis of the entire field of music therapy.

In the past few decades, scientists have learned more and more about the ways in which we are affected by music. We know for certain that music affects us both physiologically and psychologically. Various musical stimuli can affect our heartbeat, respiratory rate, glandular secretions, and the production of electricity through the skin. But with all we have learned about the intimate relationship between music and people, there is even more that we do *not* know. Music psychology—an outgrowth of music therapy—is an exciting field of research. In future decades, we are sure to learn much more about how and why we react the way we do to music.

The fact that music is such a powerful tool in manipulating human behavior has been reflected in our society for years. Drums and bugles accompanied armies into battle, partly to spur feelings of patriotism and courage. Film and television producers spend much time, energy, and money ensuring that just the right bit of music accompanies each love scene, horror scene, or chase scene. As Arnold Perris points out, music "reaches the emotions easily, often (always?) ahead of intellectual awareness" (Perris 1985, 6). Perris uses the example of the movie *Jaws*, in which "a melodic motive in the bass arouses our fear of the shark each time we hear it, whether or not the terrifying creature appears before our eyes" (6).

Muzak is carefully programmed throughout the day to calm, stimulate, and otherwise affect the behavior of office workers. Doctors and dentists use music in their waiting rooms to help calm their anxious patients. The ability of music to make repetitive physical tasks easier or even fun has given rise to "jazzercise," in which people congregate to do coordinated calisthenics to pop and rock music. They do 100 jumping jacks and think they are having fun (and pay for the privilege). Doing it without the music would be work.

In the Musical Close-Up in Chapter 13, "Mainstream Rock," we noted the intimate relationship between lyrics and music. Music's ability to help us remember verbal messages has been demonstrated repeatedly by commercial jingles. When an advertiser wants to be sure that a product name, a sales slogan, or even a telephone number becomes lodged in the consumer's mind, he or she turns to music as an aid. Fifty years later, most people who watched television in the 1950s can still recall the product name from an old jingle, "See the U.S.A. in your _____."* They are likely to be able to sing the tune quite accurately. Do such jingles actually affect consumer behavior? Advertisers invest millions each year in the belief that they do.

*Sesame Street* has used this principle for years. Noting that children could reproduce commercial jingles they heard on television, the *Sesame Street* people decided to run "commercials" for the letter j, the number 9, and so on. Thousands of youngsters learned the "advertised" letters and numbers through the repetitive "commercials." Psychologists believe the association of verbal messages with simple and catchy musical phrases helps embed those messages in our minds, ready for instant recall years later.

Certainly rock musicians have understood the power of music to affect human behavior. After all, they see the principle in action as they face thousands of screaming fans in arenas and stadiums night after night. They can "play" the crowd with uncanny insight. Certain songs tend to settle down a crowd, while others can bring the concert to a fever pitch. If they are not careful, artists can create a situation

*Chevrolet

beyond even their own control, as the crowd's animation becomes potentially violent, often threatening the safety of the onstage performers themselves.

The folkies and folk rockers of the 1960s relied heavily on music's ability to affect behavior. Their "message songs" were intended to reinforce and even change people's attitudes toward violence, war, and racial prejudice. David Crosby once remarked, "I figure that the only thing to do was to steal the kids. I still think it's the only thing to do. By saying that, I'm not talking about kidnapping. I'm just talking about changing young people's value systems, which removes them from their parents' world very effectively" (*Rolling Stone* 1971, 410). The acid rockers also knew of music's power. Jimi Hendrix is reported to have said that "you can hypnotize people with music, and when you get people at their weakest point, you can preach to them into their subconscious what we want to say" (Peters and Peters 1984, 76).

On several occasions we have noted that music has the capacity to both reflect society and change it. As composer Roger Sessions noted, "Bach and Mozart and Beethoven did not *reflect* Germany, they helped to create it" (Augros and Stanciu 1984, 139). In his excellent study of the use of music as a force for change, Arnold Perris attempts "to demonstrate that composers in many times and places have consciously used their craft to change the world outside their studio" (Perris 1985, 222). Perris discusses various examples of the use of music in totalitarian societies as an important agent of controlling thought and behavior. Regarding Hitler, he quotes Hellmut Lehmann-Haupt, who said that the dictator "does not think of art as a luxury or a pastime, a pleasant embellishment of life. . . . He has a very healthy respect for it. He knows that there is hardly a better way of getting hold of a person . . . his inner life, the subconscious, hidden personality—than through art" (209). Perris shows how leaders from Saint Augustine to Mao have all understood music's ability to affect human behavior.

But if music possesses such power, there is both good and bad news. The good news is that music can be used to uplift us, to help us learn, and to make us more tolerant. The bad news is that music can also encourage drug abuse, increase violence and rebellion, reinforce suicidal tendencies, and influence our purchasing decisions. Far too many writers on rock get themselves into an embarrassing and untenable position. Their enthusiasm leads them to point with pride to the undeniable effects music has had on clothing, hairstyles, and lifestyles; they praise music for its pivotal role in the civil rights and antiwar movements. Harry Belafonte, a motivating force behind "We Are the World," remarked that "the power of artists is unlimited. . . . There are no boundaries on art; its universal power is absolutely unlimited" (Bronson 1988, 605). But many of the same commentators pull a quick about-face when confronted with potentially negative examples. What about drugs, incest, necrophilia, suicide, violence, degradation of women, satanism, and bestiality? Suddenly the "party line" changes. Music inexplicably becomes impotent; it is *not* considered an influence where these negative behaviors are concerned. Music, such writers would say, is just harmless, good-time entertainment, utterly devoid of any affective power.

The problem is that one cannot have it both ways. If we acknowledge that rock music has had positive effects (as it has), we must also be willing to admit that it has had negative effects (as it has). The person who proudly proclaims "Oh, I listen to the music, but it doesn't affect me" is either hopelessly naive or grossly ill informed.

As people have known for centuries (from Damon to Hendrix), and as scientists have begun to document, music is one of the most powerful tools known to humankind. In Perris's words, "Music is *doing* something to everyone who hears it all the time" (Perris 1985, 6).

## EDITORIAL

Let us review the eight basic statements from the preceding overview:

1. Rock and roll may be here to stay, but individual artists and styles are not.
2. What were once vices are now habits.
3. Good is bad, and bad is good.
4. "My album may be number 1, but I'm *not* commercial!"
5. Not all music is art; most of it is simply product.
6. The audience for rock is getting both older and younger.
7. Rock is no longer the counterculture—it *is* the culture.
8. Music, including rock and roll, affects behavior.

The editorial comments that follow draw in varying degrees upon these eight basic statements.

### How Much Is Too Much?

In its fifty-year history, rock and roll has changed dramatically. Elvis Presley sang about hound dogs and pleaded with his lover not to be cruel. Chuck Berry sang of "school days" and teenage would-be rock and rollers ("Johnny B. Goode"). Elvis bumped his hips; Chuck Berry duck-walked across the stage; Little Richard and Jerry Lee Lewis played the piano every way it could be played.

More recently, Prince tells us that incest is not so bad; Ozzy Osbourne suggests that "suicide is the only way out"; Twisted Sister says to "shoot 'em down with a fuckin' gun"; the Rolling Stones sing "feel the hot cum dripping on your thigh from it"; Venom advises us to "plunge the dagger in her breast . . . sacrifice to Lucifer my Master"; and rapper Ice-T yearns to "dust" (kill) a cop. In concert, W.A.S.P. lead singer Blackie Lawless simulates intercourse using a buzz saw; Slayer simulates the cannibalization of women; Alice Cooper symbolically abuses a baby doll; satanic symbols adorn numerous stage settings. Album covers show meat hooks pressed into nude breasts, chewed-up body parts beneath the blood-drenched mouth of a rock star, and fantastic scenes representing hades. Videos revel in sadomasochism and violence. To paraphrase a popular commercial slogan, "We've come a long way, baby!"

"All a matter of degree," you may say. Little by little, inch by inch, year by year, we have "progressed" from Elvis swiveling his hips through Hendrix humping his guitar and Morrison exposing himself to W.A.S.P. simulating intercourse with a saw blade. Yes, it is just a matter of degree. But when does a difference in degree become a difference in kind? After all, 110 degrees Fahrenheit is simply a difference in degree from 15 degrees; but the former most of us think of as hot and the latter we call cold—opposites in fact. At what point does temperature become "hot" —at 83? at 92? at 100? We are not certain; each of us has a different tolerance for heat. But we would probably all agree that when the thermometer reaches 120 degrees, we are hot. Somewhere, at different degrees along the way, we became hot—we crossed a line.

Has rock and roll, while "progressing" by degrees, crossed a line? Recall five of our basic statements:

1. The one-upmanship principle
2. The inverted values principle
3. The younger rock audience
4. The rock is the culture principle
5. The music affects behavior principle

If these principles continue to operate for the next ten years, as they have for the last fifty, what will rock and roll be like in 2015? What will today's 18-year-old face as he or she attempts to raise a child in the rock culture in the year 2015?

Increasingly, thoughtful observers have begun to wonder just how much is too much. Has the one-upmanship game gone too far? Even though not all agree as to *when* and *where* the line was crossed, many reasonable people agree that things have gotten a bit out of hand. Rock and roll has gradually become something different in kind, not simply different in *degree*. As former Doobie Brothers member Michael McDonald said, "The energy we were trying to create as opposed to the energy people create today and call rock 'n' roll seems like a real dichotomy. This music that was made to make anyone within hearing range feel good is now all of a sudden meant to intimidate" (*Musician*, December 1985, 82). Certainly there is an element of *hatred* and *violence* in much of today's rock that simply has not been present in any style of music previously. Something is different.

A reaction has begun to grow. Whereas rock's critics have traditionally been fundamentalist religious groups, a new segment of the population has become concerned. In June 1984, the National PTA, representing 5.6 million members, adopted a resolution calling upon record companies to advise consumers if their products contained material with explicit language or sexual references and inferences not commonly recommended for all age groups. At the instigation of the Parents' Music Resource Center, a hearing was held before the United States Senate Committee on Commerce, Science, and Transportation on September 19, 1985. Among those testifying were representatives of the PTA, the PMRC, the recording industry, the radio industry, a psychiatrist, a music educator, and performers John Denver, Frank Zappa, and Dee Snider (lead singer of Twisted Sister). The purpose of the hearing was not to foster legislation to control rock music; nor was it antirock, as some writers have erroneously reported (e.g., "Even as the PMRC was mounting its antirock campaign . . . ") (Ward, Stokes, and Tucker 1986, 620). The hearing did attempt to focus attention on a certain segment of the music industry that may have "crossed the line"; it called upon the music industry to clean up its own act and practice some social responsibility. The hearing further encouraged companies to label potentially offensive albums for the purpose of informing the consumer (a standard practice in other segments of the marketplace, from movies to cigarettes to children's toys). Commenting on this topic, Neil Young remarked, "It's a product, it's packaged food for the mind. Why not label it as to content?" (*Washington Post*, September 15, 1985, H-1). You might note that Neil Young is referring to our basic statement number five. Frank Zappa further suggested that lyrics be printed on the outside of albums, a suggestion that met with near unanimous approval. Although some screamed "censorship," that was a false issue. Neither the labeling of the product nor the printing of lyrics qualifies as censorship; in fact, such procedures represent the *increased* dissemination of information, not the suppression of information—in other words, exactly the *opposite* of censorship.

According to basic statement number eight, music, including rock and roll, affects behavior. Will our culture be affected more by Bruce Springsteen, Michael Jackson, Huey Lewis, and Lionel Richie, or by Snoop Dogg, NWA, and Venom? The answer rests with the delicate interplay between the consumer and the industry. If consumers buy more of one and less of the other, the industry will be quick to react. After all, they are merely manufacturing a product to sell. But, to a large extent, the industry can determine what the consumer thinks he or she wants to buy. For example, referring to the selling of Sha-Na-Na, a 1950s-style rock revival group of the 1970s, Neil Bogart of Casablanca Records said, "To build this group, we created a music industry trend. We called it rock 'n' roll revival. With slogans, stickers, buttons, and industry and consumer contests, and even black leather jackets for our promotion staff, we brought back the fifties." Bogart concluded that "talent may be compared to commercial products—the cigarettes you smoke, the TV set you watch, or the car you drive. You select that brand of product that you have been convinced is the one you should buy" (Szatmary 1991, 223–224).

David Szatmary points out the importance of the rock critic in creating the consumer's "free will." He quotes columnist and author Richard Goldstein, who maintained "illusions about the value-free purity of rock until the day in 1969 when my agent informed me that a large music publisher would pay me $25,000 for three presentations on the state of popular music. It was understood that I would favor this company's artists in my reviews" (Szatmary 1987, 171). Some companies provide up to six copies of each new release, worth up to $10,000 per year, to major rock writers (Szatmary 1987, 171). It is simply naive to believe that the rock industry functions with a free-willed consumer purchasing the artistic expressions of an idealistic group of musical creators.

## CAN IT GET BETTER?

Yes. A remarkably valid solution was suggested by none other than Frank Zappa at the Senate hearings in 1985.

> Children in the "vulnerable" age bracket have a natural love for music. If, as a parent, you believe they should be exposed to something more uplifting than "Sugar Walls," support Music Appreciation programs in schools. Music Appreciation costs very little compared to sports expenditures. Your children have a right to know that something besides pop music exists. (U.S. Congress, September 19, 1985)

One of the finest writers on contemporary American culture (and especially on the media and our educational system) is Neil Postman, professor of communication arts and sciences at New York University. In *Teaching as a Conserving Activity*, Postman (1979) suggests that an educational system should serve as a counterbalance to the existing cultural environment. In other words, education should provide what the culture does not. He bravely suggests a curriculum that provides substantive education in areas absolutely essential to the development of human culture. But unlike so many "back-to-basics" prescriptions, Postman wisely includes music and the arts as one of the essentials.

In so considering music a cultural essential, Postman is on absolutely solid anthropological ground. Music has been one of the few consistent characteristics of every society since the beginning of recorded history. No matter how primitive and unsophisticated, no matter what continent, no matter what the ethnic, economic, or social profile, *every* society has had music. Anthropologists have concluded, therefore, that all societies have felt the need for some type of musical expression. It is apparently a necessity of human existence. This anthropological evidence runs exactly counter to the oft-held position that music is a luxury, a nonessential that may be jettisoned from the educational curriculum at the first provocation. How often have you heard some educational reformer angrily demanding that the educational "fluff" be cut out of the curriculum? In most cases, music is cited as one example of "fluff." One can hardly imagine a more historically ill-informed position.

But what kind of music should we teach? Again, Neil Postman has a valid suggestion. Consistent with his philosophy that education should provide a counterbalance to the cultural environment, Postman recommends that schools should stay as far away as possible from contemporary works—especially avoiding products of the popular culture. That idea sounds so reactionary that it is downright revolutionary. But Postman's idea makes good sense. After all, teaching rock and roll to high school students is like teaching Eskimos about ice. Postman argues that the "First Curriculum" (by which he means television and the other electronic media) supplies a glut of information about the contemporary popular culture; hence the "Second Curriculum" (the school curriculum) should provide a counterbalance—that is, it should inform students about alternative artistic products from other (including past) cultures. Thus he is saying almost exactly what Frank Zappa said about the advisability of exposing youth to other styles of music beyond rock and roll.

But we are in the age of relevance; knowledge for knowledge's sake is an unappreciated concept. But relevant to what? Today, most students might reply, "Relevant to making money!" If it applies to operating a computer, running a business, or repairing a DVD player, it is relevant; if it deals with the philosophy of religion, the history of government, or the music of Schubert, it is irrelevant. Worse, it is boring! Remember, Madonna said we are "living in a material world."

Even though we may agree with Postman's idealistic suggestions, we must also face reality. Perhaps the solution lies somewhere in between. For example, perhaps we should study rock and roll; but in doing so, perhaps we should try to distinguish between art and product. What is it about the music of the Beatles that continues to enliven the interest of both the average listener and the musically educated? Why do musical scholars find works by Blood, Sweat, and Tears and Emerson, Lake, and Palmer so fascinating? What was it that these groups (and others) did that seems to set them apart from the others? Maybe the answer has to do with genuine musical creativity—the talent some musicians have to take whatever musical language they prefer (classical, jazz, rock, etc.) and manipulate it (via melody, harmony, form, timbre, rhythm, etc.) in new and imaginative ways. If students can begin to appreciate true musical creativity in rock (and also to recognize the more pervasive musical mundanities), it often follows that they crave further musical stimulation, seeking it out (and finding it) in other styles, such as jazz or classical music. This may not happen in every case, but it happens more often than one might expect.

Rock and roll, just like almost anything else you can name, is neither all good nor all bad. Just because someone criticizes an aspect of rock, he or she should not automatically be labeled "anti-rock." In fact, just the opposite may be true; the criticism may stem from an abiding love of rock music and a belief in its validity as a form of musical expression. Such critics want rock to be the best it can be: a creative musical style that enhances our society rather than debases it.

## WHERE TO NOW?

Trying to forecast trends in the unpredictable music industry is risky business. During the 1990s, rock and roll turned forty years old. Jazz was about that age when it experienced its popular decline, and it was not long after that the "new kid on the block"—rock and roll—took over. Does a similar fate await rock and roll? Will the early 2000s witness the death of rock?

Probably not. One of the points made earlier in this chapter was that rock has become totally integrated into our culture. By now, there is such a multitude of rock styles, each with its own audience, from preteens to folks in their sixties, that it seems highly unlikely that rock will die anytime soon. (For that matter, jazz did not die, it just receded from its position of prominence to a place somewhere in the midst of the musical fabric of our century.)

Like jazz, rock may not *die* in the early 2000s, but there is historical precedent for the emergence of a "new" style that could cause the harder rock styles to decline in their commercial impact. Toward the end of the 1980s, there was a remarkable surge of interest in country and western music. Through the 1990s, a host of new C & W stars emerged: Randy Travis, George Strait, Garth Brooks, Clint Black, and many others. As their style swept across the nation and spread to audiences "raised on rock," it was inevitable that more artists would attempt (again!) to blend country and rock styles. This combination, as we have seen, goes all the way back to the early days of rock and roll (rockabilly). It has come and gone several times in rock's first forty years.

As we have mentioned, the harder rock styles are based to a large degree on the "one-upmanship" principle. Many heavy metal and rap bands have raced pell-mell down a very steep path of explicit sex, graphic violence, anger, depression, and defiance. Coupled with the numbing sameness and a paucity of musical value, this appears to be a path that may well face an eventual dead end. Although there may always be an audience for such music, the early years of the twenty-first century may find a larger number of listeners who have had a stomach full of rock degradation and negativism.

The probability is that the children of the post-boomers will be listening to a musical style that we can hardly imagine. Suppose you had told people in 1946 that in ten years most of the music they were listening to would be obsolete—replaced by a raucous new style called "rock and roll." They would have laughed at you and had no concept of what such music would be like. Just as was true then, the seeds of the next new style are probably around us now, but we are not likely to recognize them.

In spite of our inability to predict the future, we can hazard a few guesses about the music of the early 2000s. Certainly there is no reason to think that the technological trend will slow down; thus it is likely that MIDI instruments, computers, synthesizers, drum machines, samplers, sequencers, and so on will continue to be important in whatever pop styles emerge.

Also, the softer styles of rock seem to have had a consistent appeal throughout the last fifty years, and there is no reason to expect anything different in the future.

And finally, people like to dance. Whether it was swing, the twist, disco, or techno-dance, dance music seems to have a consistent appeal in every era. So we can probably predict that some form of dance-oriented music will continue to be successful well into the 2000s.

Rock has a wonderful, colorful, and exciting history. From Bill Haley and the Comets through Presley, Dylan, the Beatles, the Stones, Motown, Chicago, ELP, Jackson, Springsteen, and Hammer—it is a fascinating story. And it is one that shows no signs of ending any time soon. It is hoped that this and the preceding chapters have given you some perspective on rock's history. Perhaps the next time you hear of an exciting new group or new style, you will have a better idea of how it fits into a larger picture and whence it came.

# Discography

## A BASIC RECORDED LIBRARY OF ROCK AND ROLL

Spending a lot of money on recordings is no problem; anyone can do it. However, the Discography that follows attempts to reduce the seemingly endless possibilities to a manageable collection. Even so, there are approximately 300 entries, equaling an expenditure of between $4,000 and $4,500.

It is hoped that this Discography provides a representative sampling of styles across rock's first fifty years. Needless to say, some hard decisions were made regarding what to include and what to leave out. Of course, no two rock discographers would ever come up with the same list. In this case, there was also the concern that artists and songs discussed in the text were appropriately represented in the Discography.

In trying to keep the list as short (and inexpensive) as possible, some inevitable trade-offs were accepted. First, in a number of cases, greatest hits compilations were listed. While such compilations are a cost-effective way to acquire the "biggies" by a given artist, it must be remembered that some of the given artist's most creative work may not be among the most popular Top 40 hits, but in the "other" tracks of various albums. The authors have attempted to include compilations judiciously, opting for specific albums in cases where the artist's best work might be lost on a greatest hits album.

A second trade-off involves anthologies or compilations (listed separately). Here again, one gains in cost-effectiveness (e.g., why buy an entire album of the Kingsmen when all one wants is "Louie, Louie"). But predictably, most anthologies contain a certain percentage of significant material, plus a balance of "filler" material. Also, there is inevitably some duplication among similar anthologies. Again, there are many anthologies available; those listed were thoughtfully selected for breadth and coordination with the text.

One final note: If your funds are limited, please note the asterisks in the Discography. These selections signify a very basic library of just over 100 items (approximate cost: $1,500), which would seem to be the minimum required to establish a basic sampling of rock's first fifty years. In the cases where multiple recordings are listed for a group or artist, you will find an asterisk to the left of the performers' names and then an asterisk preceding the specific albums that warrant, in the opinion of the authors, this "most significant recording" status. Another option that has recently become available is purchasing individual songs for less than $1 each from a music download service, using a computer-based media player. Two of the most popular options—both free at the time this text was published—are Apple's iTunes (http://www.apple.com/itunes/) and RealPlayer (http://www.real.com/). Though this may be seen as an economic option, it should be considered a "distant second" in terms of purchasing music to build a library. After all, purchasing an entire album, containing both hit singles and album cuts, provides a much broader perspective on the output of any given artist or group. The authors of this text have created an iMix of "must have" singles that can be accessed using iTunes (version 4.5 or later). Simply visit the iMix area of Apple's Music Store, using iTunes, then enter "Stuessy & Lipscomb" into the "Search for:" field. You can download some or all of these items with a click of your mouse and a credit card.

## SELECTED DISCOGRAPHY

AC/DC, *Back in Black*, Epic 80207.

*Aerosmith, *Greatest Hits* (1972–79), Columbia (57367).,*Big Ones*, Geffen 24716.

Air Supply, *The Definitive Collection*, Arista 14611.

*Alice Cooper, *Greatest Hits*, Warner, 78129.

*Allman Brothers Band, *Best of Allman Brothers Band*, Polydor 823–708.

America, *Premium Gold Collection*, EMI 837638.

Animals, *Best of the Animals*, Abkco 4324.

*Baez, Joan, *Diamonds and Rust*, Mobile Fidelity 646 *Hits/Greatest and Others*, Vanguard 79332.

*Beach Boys, *Pet Sounds*, DCC 1035. *The Greatest Hits Vol. 1: 20 Good Vibrations*, EMI 21860. *The Greatest Hits Vol. 2: 20 More Good Vibrations*, EMI 20238.

Beastie Boys, *Ill Communication*, Grand Royal CDP-28599. *Licensed to Ill*, Def Jam 4464.

*Beatles, *Abbey Road*, Capitol 46446. *The Beatles (White Album)*, Capitol 46443. *Sgt. Pepper's Lonely Hearts Club Band*, Capitol 46442. *Please Please Me*, Capitol 46435. *Revolver*, Capitol 46441. *Rubber Soul*, Capitol 46440.

*Beck, *Odelay*, Geffen 24823.

*Beck, Jeff, *Blow By Blow*, Epic 85440.

Belafonte, Harry, *Calypso*, RCA 53801.

*Berry, Chuck, *The Anthology*, chess 112304.

Björk, *Post*, Elektra 61740. *Vespertine*, Elektra 62653.

Black, Clint, *Greatest Hits*, RCA 66671.

Black Sabbath, *Paranoid*, Victor 61711. (See also Osbourne)

*Blood, Sweat, & Tears, *Blood, Sweat, & Tears*, Legacy 63986. *Blood, Sweat, & Tears 3*, Mobile Fidelity 2013. *Blood, Sweat, & Tears 4*, Columbia 66422.

Blondie, *Parallel Lines*, Chrysalis 21192.

Bon Jovi, *Slippery When Wet*, Mercury 538089.

*Boone, Pat, *Pat Boone's Greatest Hits*, MCA 10885.

*Bowie, David, *Ziggy Stardust*, Virgin 21900.

Boy George (see Culture Club).

Boyz II Men, *Cooleyhighharmony*, Motown 6320.

Brooks, Garth, *No Fences*, Capitol 93866

*Brown, James, *20 All Time Greatest Hits*, Polydor 511326.

Buffalo Springfield, *Box Set*, Rhino 74324.

*Byrds, *The Notorious Byrd Brothers*, Legacy 65151. *Greatest Hits*, Sony 9516.

Campbell, Glen, *The Very Best of Glen Campbell*, Capitol 46483.

Carey, Mariah, *#1s*, Columbia CK 69670.

Carpenter, Mary Chapin, *Come On Come On*, Sony 48881.

*Carpenters, *Yesterday Once More*, A&M 75021–6601.

*Charles, Ray, *Ultimate Hits Collection*, Rhino 75644.

Chase, *Chase*, Endorphin 001.

*Checker, Chubby, *Greatest Hits*, Prime Cuts 1334.

Chemical Brothers, *Dig Your Own Hole*, Astralwerks 6180.

Chic, *C'est Chic*, Atlantic 81552.

*Chicago, *Chicago Transit Authority*, Rhino 76171. *Chicago VII*, Chicago Records 3007.

*Clapton, Eric, *461 Ocean Blvd.*, Universal International 9158. *Cream of Clapton*, Polydor/Chronicles 31452 7116. *Unplugged*, Reprise 45024.

Clash, *The Clash*, Sony Japan 520. *London Calling*, Epic 63885.

Coasters, *The Very Best of the Coasters*, Rhino 71597.

Cooke, Sam, *Greatest Hits*, RCA 67605. (See also Soul Stirrers)

Costello, Elvis, *The Very Best of Elvis Costello*, Rhino 76652.

Cream, *The Very Best of Cream*, Polydor/Chronicles 523752.

*Creedence Clearwater Revival, *Chronicle: The 20 Greatest Hits*, Fantasy 2.

*Croce, Jim, *Photographs & Memories*, Atlantic 92570.

*Crosby, Stills, Nash, & Young, *Déjà Vu*, Atlantic 82649.

Culture Club, *Colour By Numbers*, Virgin 86180.

Daniels, Charlie, *Million Mile Reflections*, Columbia 35751.

*Davis, Miles, *Bitches Brew*, Columbia 65774.

*Deep Purple, *Gemini Suite*, Cleopatra 234. *Deepest Purple/The Very Best of Deep Purple*, Warner Brothers 2 3486.

Denver, John, *The Very Best of John Denver*, BMG 67442.

Depeche Mode, *Violator*, Sire 9260812.

Derek & The Dominoes, *Layla*, Polydor 9167.

Devo, *Freedom of Choice*, Warner 3435.

Diamond, Neil, *12 Greatest Hits, Vol. II*, Columbia 38068.

Dixie Chicks, *Wide Open Spaces*, Sony 68195.

DJ Shadow, *Endtroducing*, Mo Wax 124123.

*Domino, Fats, *My Blue Heaven*, Astan 20082 (LP).

Donovan, *Greatest Hits and More*, EMI 1333.

Doobie Brothers, *Best of the Doobies*, Warner 78096.

*Doors, *Best of the Doors*, Elektra 5035 (LP).

*Dr, Dre, *The Chronic*, Death Row 6300.

*Dylan, Bob, *The Essential Bob Dylan, Columbia 85168. *The Freewheelin' Bob Dylan, Columbia ck-8786. The Times They Are a-Changin', Columbia 8905. *Highway 61 Revisited, Sony 90324. Blood on the Tracks, Sony 377.

*Eagles, *Their Greatest Hits, DCC 2051. Hell Freezes Over, Digital Sound 1006.

Electric Light Orchestra, Greatest Hits, Jet 4775002.

Emerson, Keith (and the Nice), Here Come the Nice: Immediate Anthology, CASTL CMETD055.

*Emerson, Lake, & Palmer, *Brain Salad Surgery, Atlantic 19124. *Emerson, Lake, & Palmer, Rhino 72223. Tarkus, Castle 434. *Pictures at an Exhibition, Rhino 72225. Trilogy, Rhino 72226.

*Eminem, *The Eminem Show, Interscope 493290. The Slim Shady LP, Interscope 90287. *The Marshall Mathers LP, Interscope 490629.

Estefan, Gloria, Greatest Hits, Sony 86729

*Everly Brothers, All Time Original Hits, Rhino 75996.

Flack, Roberta, Softly With These Songs: The Best of Roberta Flack, Atlantic 82498.

*Fleetwood Mac, Greatest Hits, Reprise 25801.

Focus, Focus III, Red Bullet 66189.

*Four Seasons, Anthology, Rhino 71490.

Frampton, Peter, Frampton Comes Alive!, Mobile Fidelity 678.

*Franklin, Aretha, Amazing Grace, Atlantic SD2–906. Soul '69, Rhino 71523.

Gaye, Marvin, What's Going On?, Motown 530883.

Genesis, The Lamb Lies Down on Broadway, Virgin 1.

*Grateful Dead, *Live/Dead, Warner 1830. Workingman's Dead, Warner 1869.

Green Day, American Idiot, Reprise. 48777. Dookie, Reprise 45529.

*Guns N' Roses, G N' R Lies, Geffen 24198. *Appetite for Destruction, Mobile Fidelity 699.

*Haley, Bill (and the Comets), Universal Masters Collection, Polygram 112174200088.

Hancock, Herbie, Thrust, Sony 86568.

Harrison, George, All Things Must Pass [boxed edition], Capitol 46688.

Harvey, PJ, Dry, Island 555001.

*Hendrix, Jimi, *Electric Ladyland, MCA 11600. *Are You Experienced?, MCA 11602.

*Holly, Buddy (and the Crickets), The Buddy Holly Collection, MCA 10883.

Houston, Whitney, Whitney: The Greatest Hits, Arista 14626.

Iron Butterfly, In-A-Gadda-Da-Vida, Atco 33250.

Iron Maiden, Number of the Beast, Sony 86210.

Jackson, Janet, Rhythm Nation 1814, A&M 75021–3920.

*Jackson, Michael, HIStory: Past, Present and Future Book 1, Epic 59000. *Thriller, Sony International 504422.

Jackson Five, The Ultimate Collection, Motown 530558.

Jay-Z, Vol. 2: Hard Knock Life, Roc-a-Fella 558902.

*Jefferson Airplane, Surrealistic Pillow, Cloud 9 84791.

Jethro Tull, The Very Best of Jethro Tull, Emi 532614.

Jett, Joan, Fit To Be Tied: Greatest Hits by Joan Jett, Blackheart 31.

*Joel, Billy, Greatest Hits Vols. 1 and 2, Columbia 40121.

*John, Elton, *Greatest Hits, DCC 2013. *Goodbye Yellow Brick Road, Universal International 9107.

*Joplin, Janis, *Cheap Thrills/I Got Dem Ol' Kosmic Blues Again Mama!/Pearl* [boxed set], Sony 64804.

Journey, *Escape/Frontiers/Infinity* [boxed set], Columbia 61387.

Judas Priest, *British Steel,* Columbia ck-36443.

Kansas, *Leftoverture,* Columbia 34224.

*King, Carole, *Tapestry,* Song International 4931805.

King Crimson, *In the Court of the Crimson King,* Discipline Gm 501. *Larks' Tongues in Aspic,* Virgin 849935.

*Kingston Trio, *Story,* EMI 576219.

Kiss, *Lick It Up,* Polygram International 120499.

Lauper, Cyndi, *She's So Unusual,* Song 38930.

*Led Zeppelin, *Led Zeppelin II,* Atlantic 7567–8268–2/4. *Led Zeppelin IV,* Atlantic 11614.

Lennon, John, *Lennon Legend,* Capitol 21954B.

*Lewis, Huey, *Sports,* Mobile Fidelity 509.

*Lewis, Jerry Lee, *25 All-Time Greatest Sun Recordings,* Varese 066129.

Lewis, Ramsey, *Sun Goddess,* Columbia 33194.

Linkin Park, *Hybrid Theory,* Warner Bros. 47755.

*Little Richard, *Good Golly! Ten Greatest Original Hits,* RSP 53314.

L.L. Cool J., *Bigger and Deffer,* Def Jam 527353.

*Lynyrd Skynyrd, *Best of the Rest,* MCA 31006.

McCartney, Paul, *Wingspan,* Capitol 32946.

*Madonna, *The Immaculate Collection,* WEA International 10843.

Mahavishnu Orchestra, *Birds of Fire,* Legacy 66081.

Malmsteen, Yngwie, *Eclipse,* Polydor 843361.

*Mamas & the Papas, *Greatest Hits,* MCA 11740.

Mangione, Chuck, *Greatest Hits,* A&M 540514.

*Manilow, Barry, *Platinum Collection,* Arista 17545.

Mannheim Steamroller, *Fresh Aire 4,* American Gramaphone 5004.

*Marley, Bob, *Legend: The Best of Bob Marley and the Wailers,* Studio One 127.

Marshall Tucker Band, *Searchin' for a Rainbow,* K-Tel 702.

Martin, Ricky, *Ricky Martin,* Sony 69891.

Mathis, Johnny, *16 Most Requested Songs,* Legacy 40217.

*Matthews Band, Dave, *Before These Crowded Streets,* RCA 67660. *Crash,* RCA 66904.

*Mayall, John (and the Bluesbreakers), *Bluesbreakers with Eric Clapton,* Mobile Fidelity 616.

*M.C. Hammer, *Please Hammer Don't Hurt 'Em,* Capitol 92857.

Megadeth, *Countdown to Extinction,* Capitol 98531.

*Metallica, *. . . And Justice For All,* Elektra 60812. *Metallica [Black Album],* Ekektra 61113.

Miami Sound Machine (see Gloria Estefan).

Miller, Steve, *Greatest Hits 1974–78,* DCC 1103.

*Mitchell, Joni, *Court and Spark,* Asylum 1001. *Mingus,* Asylum 505.

Moby, *Play,* V2 Records 27049.

*Moody Blues, *Days of Future Passed,* Polydor 844767.

Morisette, Alanis, *Jagged Little Pill,* Maverick 45901.

Morrison, Jim (see Doors).

Mothers of Invention (see Zappa).

Mötley Crüe, *Theatre of Pain*, Motley/Beyond 78009.

*Nelson, Rick, *A&E Biography: A Musical Anthology*, Capitol 99428.

New Kids on the Block, *Hangin' Tough*, Columbia 40985.

New Order, *Substance: The Singles 1980–1987*, Qwest 25621.

Newton-John, Olivia, *Magic: The Very Best of Olivia Newton-John*, UTV 585233.

*Nirvana, *Nevermind*, Mobile Fidelity 666. *Incesticide*, Geffen 24504.

Notorious B.I.G., *Ready to Die*, Bad Boy 73000.

'N Sync, *Celebrity*, Tombstone 10125.

*NWA, *Straight Outta Compton*, Priority 57112. *Greatest Hits*, Ruthless Records 50561.

Oldfield, Mike, *Tubular Bells*, EMI 850733.

Osbourne, Ozzy, *Bark at the Moon*, Epic 67238.

Outkast, *Stankonia*, La Face 26072.

Parsons, Alan (Project), *The Turn of a Friendly Card*, Arista ArCD-8226.

Passport, *Looking Thru*, Wounded Bird Records 7042.

Pearl Jam, *Vs.*, Sony International 47459.

*Peter, Paul, & Mary, *The Best of Peter, Paul, and Mary: Ten Years Together*, Warner 3105.

Phish, *Junta*, Elektra 61413.

*Pink Floyd, *Dark Side of the Moon*, EMI 679180. *The Wall*, EMI 679182.

*Pixies, The, *Doolittle*, 4AD Records 70905. *Surfer Rosa*, 4AD 78030.

*Platters, *The Best of the Platters*, Ember 3339.

*Police, *Synchronicity*, Interscope 493606.

*Presley, Elvis, *The Sun Sessions*, BMG International 37101. *Worldwide 50 Gold Award Hits*, Vol. I, RCA 56401.

*Prince, *Controversy*, Warner 3601. *The Hits 1*, Paisley Park 45431. *The Hits 2*, Paisley Park 45435–2. *Purple Rain*, Warner Bros. 7599 251102.

Procol Harum, *The Best of Procol Harum*, A&M 75021–3259.

*Public Enemy, *Fear of a Black Planet*, Def Jam 523 446. *It Takes a Nation of Millions to Hold Us Back*, Def Jam 527358.

Queensrÿche, *Empire*, DCC 1138.

*Radiohead, *The Bends*, Capitol 29626. *OK Computer*, Capitol 55229. *Kid A*, Capitol 27753.

Rage Against the Machine, *Rage Against the Machine*, Epic 52959.

Ramones, *Ramones*, Wea International 27421.

Red Hot Chili Peppers, *Blood-Sugar-Sex-Magik*, Warner Bros. 26681.

R.E.M., *In Time*, Warner Bros. 48381. *Eponymous*, Capitol 93457.

Richie, Lionel, *Can't Slow Down*, Motown MOTC-6059.

Rogers, Kenny, *20 Greatest Hits*, Capitol 46106.

*Rolling Stones,. *Their Satanic Majesties Request*, Abkco 8823002. *Exile on Main Street*, Virgin 47864. *Forty Licks*, Abko 40402. *Sticky Fingers*, Virgin 47863.

Ronstadt, Linda, *Greatest Hits*, Asylum 1092.

Ross, Diana (see Supremes).

Run-D.M.C., *Raising Hell*, Profile 16408.

*Rush, *Rush*, Mercury 534 623. *Grace Under Pressure*, Mercury 534 634.

*Santana, *Santana*, Columbia ck-9781. *Supernatural*, Arista 19080. *Caravanserai*, Columbia /Legacy 63595.

Seals & Crofts, *Greatest Hits*, Warner 3109.

Sex Pistols, *Never Mind the Bollocks, Here's the Sex Pistols*, Warner 3147.

Shakur, Tupac, *All Eyez on Me*, Death Row 63008.

*Simon & Garfunkel, *Bookends*, Sony International 95. *Greatest Hits*, Columbia 31350.

Simon, Paul, *Graceland*, Warner Bros. 25447.

Smashing Pumpkins, *Mellon Collie and the Infinite Sadness*, Virgin 40861.

Smith, Patti, *Horses*, Arista ARCD-8362.

Snoop Doggy Dogg, *Doggystyle*, Death Row 63002.

Sonic Youth, *Daydream Nation*, DGC 24515.

Soul Stirrers, *Sam Cooke with the Soul Stirrers*, Specialty 2106 (LP).

Soundgarden, *Superunknown*, A&M 540 198.

*Springsteen, Bruce, *Born in the U.S.A.*, Columbia 38653. *Born to Run*, Sony 64406.

*Steely Dan, *The Very Best of Steely Dan/Reelin' in the Years*, MCA International 19147.

Stevens, Cat, *Greatest Hits*, A&M 546 889.

*Stewart, Rod, *Gasoline Alley*, Mercury 558 059.

*Sting, *Fields of Gold: The Best of Sting 1984–1994*, A&M 540 370.

*Stone, Sly, *Greatest Hits*, Epic 30325.

Strokes, *Is This It?*, RCA 68101.

Styx, *Caught in the Act*, A&M 75021-6514.

*Summer, Donna, *Anthology*, Casablanca/Mercury 518 144.

*Supremes, *The Ultimate Collection*, Motown 530 827.

*Talking Heads, *Remain in Light*, Sire 6095.

Tangerine Dream, *Tangram*, Virgin 11.

Tavares, *Check It Out*, Unidisc 7192. *Hard Core Poetry*, Capitol 11316 (LP).

Taylor, James, *Greatest Hits*, Warner Bros 78094.

Temptations, The, *The Ultimate Collection*, Motown 530562.

Tool, *Aenema*, Volcano 31087

*Tower of Power, *Back to Oakland*, Warner 2749. *Tower of Power*, Warner Bros. 2681.

Tricky, *Maxinquaye*, Island 524089.

Tritt, Travis, *It's All About to Change*, Warner 26589.

*Twain, Shania, *Come On Over*, Mercury 112773.

Twisted Sister, *Stay Hungry*, Atlantic 80156.

*U2, *Achtung Baby*, Polygram 510347. *The Joshua Tree*, Mobile Fidelity 650. *Rattle and Hum*, Polygram 842299. *The Unforgettable Fire*, Universal Japan 9711.

Valli, Frankie (see Four Seasons).

*Van Halen, *1984 (MCMLXXXIV)*, Warner 47741. *Van Halen*, Warner Bros. 47737.

*Velvet Underground, *White Light/White Heat*, Polygram International 9135.

Vicious, Sid (see Sex Pistols).

Wakeman, Rick (also see Yes). *The Myths & Legends of King Arthur & the Knights of the Round Table*, Polygram International 394515.

Weather Report, *Weather Report*, Sony International 9658.

Weezer, *Weezer* [Blue Album], DGC 24629.

Wham!, *Make It Big*, Epic 514.

White Stripes, *Elephant*, V2 27148.

*Who,*Tommy*, Polygram International 9196. *Quadrophenia*, Polygram International 9200. *Who's Next*, Mobile Fidelity 754. *My Generation: The Very Best of the Who*, MCA 11462.

Williams, Hank, *40 Greatest Hits*, Mercury 821233.

Wings (see McCartney).

*Wonder, Stevie, *At the Close of a Century*, Motown 153 992.

Wu-Tang Clan, *Enter the Wu-Tang* (36 Chambers), BMG 2120367.

*Yardbirds, *Ultimate*, Recall 184.

*Yes, *Close to the Edge*, Wea International 6292. *Fragile*, Atlantic 82524. *The Yes Album*, Atlantic 7567826652.

*Zappa, Frank, *Freak Out!*, Video Arts 1203. *Uncle Meat*, Video Arts 1208.


## ANTHOLOGIES

*American Graffiti* (MCA 8001) includes Bill Haley, Del Shannon, Frankie Lymon, Buddy Holly, Diamonds, Beach Boys, Chuck Berry, Platters, Joey Dee, Fats Domino, Flamingos, Silhouettes, Five Satins, Buddy Knox, DelVikings, Big Bopper, Skyliners, Mark Dinning, Spaniels, Booker T. & the MGs, and others.

*Atlantic Blues* (Rhino 82309) four-CD box includes Jimmy Yancey, Professor Longhair, Joe Turner, Meade Lux Lewis, Ray Charles, Dr. John, Stick McGhee, Guitar Slim, Stevie Ray Vaughan, Ike & Tina Turner, B.B. King, LaVern Baker, Wynonie Harris, Esther Philips, Rufus Thomas, Bobby Bland, Aretha Franklin, Howlin' Wolf, Muddy Waters, Freddie King, and others.

*Atlantic Rhythm and Blues: 1947–1974* (Atlantic 82305) seven-CD box includes Stick McGhee, Ray Charles, Joe Turner, LaVern Baker, Clyde McPhatter, Chuck Willis, Coasters, Drifters, Ben E. King, Carla Thomas, Solomon Burke, Booker T. & the MGs, Otis Redding, Sam & Dave, Percy Sledge, Wilson Pickett, Rufus Thomas, Esther Philips, Don Covay, Joe Tex, Brook Benton, King Curtis, Aretha Franklin, Roberta Flack, Donny Hathaway, Les McCann & Eddie Harris, Spinners, and others.

*Dick Clark's #1's 50's to 70's* (Rhino 74350) six-CD box with an eclectic selection of major artists and hits.

*Hair* (RCA 1150): the original Broadway cast recording.

*History of British Rock* (Sire 1CD65471/2) includes Fleetwood Mac, Donovan, Beatles, Chad & Jeremy, Animals, Derek & the Dominoes, Troggs, Dusty Springfield, Billy J. Kramer, Gerry & the Pacemakers, Cilia Black, Searchers, Manfred Mann, Freddie & the Dreamers, Cream, Bee Gees, Peter & Gordon, Kinks, and others.

*Hitsville USA: The Motown Singles Collection 1959–1971* (Motown 636 312) four-CD box featuring virtually every Motown artist and/or group during these years.

*Hitsville USA Volume II: The Motown Singles Collection 1972–1992* (Motown 159 027) four-CD box representing later Motown hits.

*Jesus Christ Superstar* (Decca 11542): the original London studio recording, featuring Ian Gillan (vocalist for Deep Purple) performing the role of Jesus.

*O Brother, Where Art Thou?* (Mercury 170069): the original motion picture soundtrack album.

*Outlaws, The* (SPA 55407) includes Willie Nelson, Waylon Jennings, Tompall Glaser, and Jessi Colter.

\**Saturday Night Fever* (Mobile Fidelity 716) includes Bee Gees, MFSB, Tavares, K.C. & the Sunshine Band, Kool & the Gang, Walter Murphy, Yvonne Elliman, and others.

*Sub Pop 200* (Sub Pop Records 25) includes Nirvana, Soundgarden, Green River, Mudhoney, Screaming Trees, and others.

\**Woodstock* (Atlantic 500) includes Joan Baez, the Who, Jefferson Airplane, Crosby, Stills, Nash, & Young, Country Joe & the Fish, Sly & the Family Stone, Santana, Butterfield Blues Band, Jimi Hendrix, Arlo Guthrie, and others.

## MUSIC DVDS & ROCKUMENTARIES

*The Beatles Anthology* (5-DVD set; Apple C9 7243) is an exhaustive collection of recordings, interviews and performances by the Beatles.

*Don't Look Back* (Docurama NVG-9447) is a documentary about Bob Dylan by D. A. Pennebaker filmed during a three-week concert tour of England during the Spring of 1965.

*Elvis: The Great Performances* (3-DVD set; Rhino R2 976096) captures many defining performances throughout the various periods of Elvis Presley's career.

*Gimme Shelter* (Criterion 99) is a documentary film based on the Rolling Stone tour leading up to and including Altamont.

*History of Rock 'n' Roll* (5-DVD set; Warner 34991) is an exhaustive overview of five decades of rock music, including performances by too many artists to mention and commentary by famous rock musicians who were influenced by the performers you see.

*The Last Waltz* (MGM), a documentary film directed by Martin Scoresese that captures the final concert by The Band; includes guest appearances by Bob Dylan, Eric Clapton, Neil Young, Joni Mitchell, Van Morrison, Muddy Waters, Ringo Starr, Paul Butterfield, and others.

*The Complete Monterey Pop Festival* (3-DVD set; Criterion 167), recorded during the summer of 1967, includes defining performances by Jefferson Airplane, Janis Joplin, The Who, Jimi Hendrix, Simon and Garfunkel, Ravi Shankar, Otis Redding, the Mamas and the Papas, Canned Heat, The Animals, and others.

*Woodstock: 3 Days of Peace & Music* (2-sided DVD; Warner) is a beautiful documentary including performances by Joan Baez, The Who, Jefferson Airplane, Crosby, Stills, Nash, & Young, Country Joe & the Fish, Sly and the Family Stone, Santana, Butterfield Blues Band, Jimi Hendrix, Arlo Guthrie, and others.

# Bibliography

Augros, Robert M., and George N. Stanciu. *The New Story of Science*. Chicago: Gateway Editions, 1984.

Bangs, Lester. *Psychotic Reactions and Carburetor Dung*. New York: Vintage Books, 1988.

Beaujon, Andrew. That Other Rock. *Spin*, pp. 85–87. January, 2002.

Belz, Carl. *The Story of Rock*, 2d ed. New York: Harper Colophon Books, 1972.

Berry, Chuck. *Chuck Berry: The Autobiography*. New York: Simon & Schuster, 1987.

Blake, John. *All You Needed Was Love (The Beatles After the Beatles)*. New York: G. P. Putnam's Sons, Perigee Books, 1981.

Bronson, Fred. *The Billboard Book of Number One Hits*. Rev. ed. New York: Billboard Publications, 1988.

Brown, Charles T. *The Art of Rock and Roll*, 2d ed. Englewood Cliffs, N.J.: Prentice Hall, 1987.

Cash, Johnny. *Man in Black*. Grand Rapids, Mich.: Zondervan Publishing House, 1975.

Charles, Ray, and David Ritz. *Brother Ray: Ray Charles' Own Story*. New York: Dial Press, 1978.

Chuck D. *Fight the Power: Rap, Race, and Reality*. New York: Delacorte Press, 1997.

Cohen, Narney. *Sting: Every Breath He Takes*. New York: Berkley Books, 1984.

Cohn, Nik. *Rock From the Beginning*. New York: Stein & Day, 1969.

Coleman, Ray. *Lennon*. New York: McGraw-Hill, 1984.

Conn, Charles Paul. *The New Johnny Cash*. New York: Family Library, 1973.

Crombie, David. *The Synthesizer and Electronic Keyboard Handbook*. New York: Alfred A. Knopf, 1984.

Crosby, David, and Carl Gottlieb. *Long Time Gone: The Autobiography of David Crosby*. New York: Doubleday, 1988.

Crumbaker, Marge, and Gabe Tucker. *Up and Down With Elvis Presley*. New York: G. P. Putnam's Sons, 1981.

Curtis, Jim. *Rock Eras: Interpretations of Music and Society, 1954–1984*. Bowling Green, Ohio: Bowling Green State University Popular Press, 1987.

Dalton, David. *Janis.* New York: Simon & Schuster (Stonehill Books), 1971.

Dannen, Frederic. *Hit Men.* New York: Vintage Books, 1990.

Davies, Hunter. *The Beatles.* New York: McGraw-Hill, 1968.

DeCurtis, Anthony, and James Henke (with H. George-Warren), eds. *The Rolling Stone Album Guide.* New York: Random House, 1992.

———. *The Rolling Stone Illustrated History of Rock and Roll: The Definitive History of the Most Important Artists and Their Music.* New York: Random House, 1992.

Dickerson, James. *Women on Top.* New York: Billboard Books, 1998.

DiOrio, Al. *Borrowed Time: The 37 Years of Bobby Darin.* Philadelphia: Running Press, 1981.

Dundy, Elaine. *Elvis and Gladys.* New York: Macmillan, 1985.

Dylan, Bob. *Writings and Drawings.* New York: Alfred A. Knopf (Borzoi Books), 1973.

Eisen, Jonathan, ed. *The Age of Rock: Sounds of the American Cultural Revolution.* New York: Vintage Books, 1969.

———. *The Age of Rock 2.* New York: Random House, 1970.

Eliot, Marc. *Rockonomics: The Money Behind the Music.* Rev. ed. New York: Citadel Press, 1993.

Epstein, Brian. *A Cellarful of Noise.* New York: Doubleday, 1964.

Erlewine, Michael, Vladimir Bogdanov, and Chris Woodstra, eds. *All Music Guide to Rock.* San Francisco: Miller Freeman Books, 1995.

Experience Music Project's *Riot Grrrl retrospective: Evolution of Grrl style.* (2002). Retrieved April 20, 2005, from < http://www.emplive.org/explore/riot_grrrl/evolution.asp.

Fernando, S. H. *The New Beats: Exploring the Music Culture and Attitudes of Hip Hop.* New York: Anchor, 1994.

Fong-Torres, Ben, ed. *The Rolling Stone Rock and Roll Reader.* New York: Bantam, 1974.

Friedlander, Paul. *Rock and Roll: A Social History.* Boulder, Colo.: Westview Press, Inc., 1996.

Friedman, Myra. *Buried Alive: The Biography of Janis Joplin.* New York: William Morrow, 1973.

Fu, Lily. *Latin CD Sales Up in 2002.* Retrieved March 17, 2002, from the Grammy Awards Web site: http://grammy.aol.com/news/industry/0313latinsales.html.

Fulford-Jones, Will. House. In S. Sadie (ed.), *The New Grove Dictionary of Music and Musicians,* 2d ed., 11, p. 758. London: MacMillan Publishers, Ltd., 2000.

George-Warren, H., and P. Romanowski, *The Rolling Stone Encyclopedia of Rock & Roll,* 3d ed. New York: Fireside, 2001.

Gillett, Charlie. *The Sound of the City: The Rise of Rock and Roll.* Rev. and exp. ed. New York: Pantheon, 1983.

Gioia, D. (Spring, 2003). Disappearing ink: Poetry at the end of print culture. *The Hudson Review,* 56(1).

Gleason, Ralph J. *The Jefferson Airplane and the San Francisco Sound.* New York: Ballantine, 1969.

Goldman, Albert. *Elvis.* New York: Avon Books, 1981.

———. *The Lives of John Lennon.* New York: William Morrow, 1988.

Goldrosen, Jon. *Buddy Holly: His Life and Music.* Bowling Green, Ohio: Bowling Green University Press, 1975.

Gorbman, Claudia. *Unheard Melodies: Narrative Film Music.* Bloomington, Ind.: Indiana University Press, 1987.

Gore, Tipper. *Raising PG Kids in an X-rated Society.* Nashville: Abingdon Press, 1987.

Gracyk, Theodore. *Rhythm and Noise: An Aesthetics of Rock.* Durham, N.C.: Duke University Press, 1996.

Haislop, Neil, Ted Lathrop, and Harry Sumrall. *Giants of Country Music: Classic Sounds and Stars, From the Heart of Nashville to the Top of the Charts.* New York: Watson-Guptill Publications, 1995.

Hamm, Charles. *Yesterdays: Popular Song in America.* New York: W. W. Norton, 1983.

Harbinson, W. A. *The Illustrated Elvis.* New York: Grosset & Dunlap, 1976.

Harker, Dave. *One for the Money: Politics and Popular Song.* London: Hutchinson & Co., 1980.

Harrington, Richard. Rock with a Capital R and a PG-13. *Washington Post,* H-1, pp. 1, 4. September 15, 1985.

Haynes, Michael K. *The God of Rock.* Linsdale, Tex.: Priority Ministries & Publications, 1982.

Heilbut, Tony. *The Gospel Sound: Good News and Bad Times.* Garden City, N.Y.: Anchor Press, 1975.

Helander, Brock. *The Rock Who's Who.* New York: Schirmer Books, 1982.

Henderson, David. *Jimi Hendrix: Voodoo Child of the Aquarian Age.* Garden City, N.Y.: Doubleday, 1978.

Herman, Gary. *Rock 'n' Roll Babylon.* Philadelphia: Courage Books, 1982.

Hibbard, Don, and Patricia Kaleialoha. *The Role of Rock.* Englewood Cliffs, N.J.: Prentice Hall, 1983.

Hirshey, Gerri. *Nowhere to Run: The Story of Soul Music.* New York: New York Times Books, 1984.

Hodges, Donald A. "The Significance of Music." Unpublished manuscript, 1983.

Hopkins, Jerry. *Elvis: A Biography.* New York: Warner Books, 1972.

———. *Elvis: The Final Years.* New York: St. Martin's Press, 1980.

Humphrey, Clark. *Loser: The Real Seattle Story.* Portland, Ore.: Feral House, 1995.

Jackson, Blair. *Grateful Dead: The Music Never Stopped.* New York: Delilah, 1983.

Jackson, John A. *Big Beat Heat: Alan Freed and the Early Years of Rock and Roll.* New York: Schirmer Books, 1991.

Jancik, Wayne. *The Billboard Book of One-Hit Wonders.* New York: Watson-Guptill Publications, 1990.

Kantner, Larry. Music Business Sings the Blues: Declining Sales Spark New Layoffs. *Rolling Stone,* pp. 21–22. February 14, 2002.

Kelley, Norman. *R&B Rhythm and Business: The Political Economy of Black Music.* New York: Akashic Books, 2002.

Kempton, A. (2003). *Boogaloo: The Quintessence of American Popular Music.* New York: Pantheon Books.

Knopper, Steve. Radiohead: Band of the Year. *Spin,* pp. 69–70. January, 2001.

Kot, Greg. You Say You Want a Revolution. *Chicago Tribune,* February 24, 2002, section 7, p. 1.

———. Cyberspace: It Continues to Be a Bumpy Ride for the Record Industry. *Chicago Tribune,* March 3, 2002, section 7, p. 1.

Leaf, David. *The Beach Boys.* Philadelphia: Courage Books, 1985.

Lennon, John. *In His Own Write and A Spaniard in the Works.* New York: New American Library (Signet Books), 1965.

Lewis, Myra (with Murray Silver). *Great Balls of Fire.* New York: William Morrow, 1982.

Loza, Steve, Ailo Alvarez, Josefina Santiago, and Charles Moore. (1994). Los Angeles Gangsta Rap and the Aesthetics of Violence. *Selected Reports in Ethnomusicology,* 10, pp. 149–161.

Lulow, Kalia. *Barry Manilow.* New York: Ballantine, 1985.

McDonough, Jack. *San Francisco Rock.* San Francisco: Chronicle Books, 1985.

Marcus, Greil. *Ranters and Crowd Pleasers: Punk in Pop Music 1977–92.* New York: Anchor Books, 1993.

Marsh, Dave. *Before I Get Old: The Story of the Who.* New York: St. Martin's Press, 1983.

————. *Born to Run: The Bruce Springsteen Story.* New York: Dell, 1979.

————. *Elvis.* New York: Arlington House, 1982.

Martin, George (with Jeremy Hornsby). *All You Need Is Ears.* New York: St. Martin's Press, 1980.

Martin, Linda, and Kerry Seagrave. *Anti-Rock: The Opposition to Rock 'n' Roll.* New York: Da Capo Press, 1988.

Mason, Michael, ed. *The Country Music Book.* New York: Charles Scribner's Sons, 1985.

Mellers, Wilfrid. *Twilight of the Gods: The Music of the Beatles.* New York: Viking Press, 1973.

Meltzer, Richard. *The Aesthetics of Rock.* New York: Da Capo Press, 1970.

Merriam, A. P. *The Anthropology of Music.* Chicago: Northwestern University Press, 1964.

Miller, Jim E. *The Rolling Stone Illustrated History of Rock and Roll.* Rev. and updated. New York: Rolling Stone Press, 1980.

Miller, Richard. *The Structure of Signing: System and Art in Vocal Technique.* New York: Schirmer Books, 1986.

Murray, Albert. *Stomping the Blues.* New York: Vintage Books, 1982.

Naisbitt, John. *Megatrends: Ten New Directions Transforming Our Lives.* New York: Warner Books, 1982.

Nelson, Havelock, and Michael A. Gonzales. *Bring the Noise: A Guide to Rap Music and Hip-Hop Culture.* New York: Harmony Books, 1991.

Nite, Norm N. *Rock On: The Illustrated Encyclopedia of Rock 'n' Roll. Vol. 1, The Solid Gold Years.* New York: Thomas Y. Crowell, 1978.

————. *Rock On: The Illustrated Encyclopedia of Rock 'n' Roll. Vol. 2, The Years of Change: 1964–1978.* Updated ed. New York: Harper & Row, 1984.

Norman, Philip. *Shout! The Beatles in Their Generation.* New York: Warner Books, 1982.

————. *Symphony for the Devil: The Rolling Stones Story.* New York: Dell, 1984.

Norris, Chris. Eminem: Lunatic Genius, Potty-Mouth, Hatemonger, or All of the Above? Some Thoughts on the Surreal Slim Shady, *Spin,* pp. 60–66. January 2001.

O'Brian, Lucy. *She-Bop: The Definitive History of Women in Rock, Pop, and Soul.* New York: Penguin Books, 1995.

O'Grady, Terence J. *The Beatles: A Musical Evolution.* Boston: Twayne Publishers, 1983.

Orloff, Katherine. *Rock 'n' Roll Woman.* Los Angeles: Nash Publishing, 1974.

Orman, John. *The Politics of Rock Music.* Chicago: Nelson-Hall, 1984.

Peel, Ian. DJ(ii). In S. Sadie (ed.), *The New Grove Dictionary of Music and Musicians,* 2d ed., 23, pp. 406–407. London: MacMillan Publishers, Ltd., 2000.

Perris, Arnold. *Music as Propaganda: Art to Persuade, Art to Control.* Westport, Conn.: Greenwood Press, 1985.

Peters, Dan, and Steve Peters. *Rock's Hidden Persuader: The Truth About Backmasking.* Minneapolis: Bethany House, 1985.

————. *Why Knock Rock?* Minneapolis: Bethany House, 1984.

Porter, Steven Clark. *Rhythm and Harmony in the Music of the Beatles.* Ann Arbor, Mich.: University Microfilms International, 1979.

Postman, Neil. *Amusing Ourselves to Death.* New York: Viking Penguin, 1986.

————. *Teaching As a Conserving Activity.* New York: Delacorte Press, 1979.

Potter, Russell A. *Spectacular Vernaculars: Hip-Hop and the Politics of Postmodernism.* Albany, N.Y.: State University of New York Press, 1995.

Presley, Priscilla Beaulieu (with Sandra Harmon). *Elvis and Me.* New York: G. P. Putnam's Sons, 1985.

Reid, Jan. *The Improbable Rise of Redneck Rock.* Austin, Tex.: Heidelberg Publishers, 1974.

Reynolds, Simon. Laptop Punk and Powerbook Pop. *Spin,* pp. 111–112. August 2001.

Robbins, Ira A. *Trouser Press Record Guide: The Ultimate Guide to Alternative Music.* 4th ed. New York: Collier Books, 1991.

Rolling Stone, editors of, *The Rolling Stone Interviews, Vol. 1.* New York: Warner Paperback, 1971.

————. *The Rolling Stone Interviews, Vol. 2.* New York: Warner Brothers Books, 1973.

Romanowski, Patricia, and Holly George-Warren, eds. *The New Rolling Stone Encyclopedia of Rock and Roll.* Rev. ed. New York: Fireside, 1995.

Rose, T. *Black Noise: Rap Music and Black Culture in Contemporary America.* Hanover, N.H.: Wesleyan University Press, 1994.

Rosen, Craig. *The Billboard Book of Number One Albums: The Inside Story Behind Pop Music's Blockbuster Records.* New York: Watson-Guptill Publications, 1996.

Roxon, Lillian. *Rock Encyclopedia.* New York: Grosset & Dunlap, 1969.

Sanchez, Tony. *Up and Down with the Rolling Stones: The Inside Story.* New York: William Morrow, 1979.

Sauer, Wendy. *Elvis Presley: A Complete Reference.* Jefferson, N.C.: McFarland, 1984.

Scaduto, Anthony. *The Beatles.* New York: New American Library, 1968.

————. *Bob Dylan: An Intimate Biography.* New York: Grosset & Dunlap, 1971.

————. *Mick Jagger: Everybody's Lucifer.* New York: David McKay, 1974.

Schaffner, Nicholas. *The Beatles Forever.* Harrisburg, Penn.: Stackpole Books (Cameron House), 1977.

*Schwann Record and Tape Guide.* New York: ABC Consumer Magazines, Schwann Publications, Summer 1987.

Shaw, Arnold. *Dictionary of American Pop/Rock.* New York: Schirmer Books, 1982.

————. *The Rock Revolution.* London: Collier, 1969.

Shelton, Robert. *No Direction Home: The Life and Music of Bob Dylan.* New York: William Morrow, 1986.

Smith, Joe. *Off the Record: An Oral History of Popular Music.* New York: Warner Books, 1988.

Soocher, Stan. *They Fought the Law: Rock Music Goes to Court.* New York: Schirmer Books, 1999.

Stambler, Irwin. *Encyclopedia of Pop, Rock, and Soul.* Rev. ed. New York: St. Martin's Press, 1989.

Stancell, Steven. *Rap Whoz Who: The World of Rap Music.* New York: Schirmer Books, 1996.

Stuessy, Joe. *The Confluence of Jazz and Classical Music from 1950–1970.* Ann Arbor, Mich.: University Microfilms, 1978.

Szatmary, David P. *Rockin' in Time: A Social History of Rock and Roll.* Englewood Cliffs, N.J.: Prentice Hall, 1987.

————. *Rockin' in Time: A Social History of Rock and Roll,* 2d ed. Englewood Cliffs, N.J.: Prentice Hall, 1991.

————. *Rockin' in Time: A Social History of Rock and Roll,* 3d ed. Upper Saddle River, N.J.: Prentice Hall, 1996.

Taraborrelli, J. Randy. *Call Her Miss Ross.* New York: Birch Lane Press, 1989.

Tobler, John, and Pete Frame. *Rock 'n' Roll: The First 25 Years.* New York: Exeter Books, 1980.

Toop, David. Hip hop. In S. Sadie (ed.), *The New Grove Dictionary of Music and Musicians,* 2d ed., 11, pp. 542–543. London: MacMillan Publishers, Ltd., 2002.

———. Rap. In S. Sadie (ed.), *The New Grove Dictionary of Music and Musicians,* 2d ed., 20, pp. 828–831. London: MacMillan Publishers, Ltd., 2000.

———. *The Rap Attack: African Jive to New York Hip Hop,* 2d ed. London: South End Press, 1991.

Truitt, E. It's the End of the World as Clear Channel Knows It. *Slate,* article posted September 17, 2001. Available at: http://slate.msn.com/default.aspx?id51008314.

U.S. Congress. Senate. Committee on Commerce, Science, and Transportation. Hearing Before the Committee on Commerce, Science, and Transportation: Contents of Music and the Lyrics of Records. United States Senate, 99th Cong., 1st sess., September 19, 1985. Washington, D.C.: U.S. Government Printing Office.

Walley, David. *No Commercial Potential: The Saga of Frank Zappa & the Mothers of Invention.* New York: E. P. Dutton, 1972.

Ward, Ed, Geoffrey Stokes, and Ken Tucker. *Rock of Ages: The Rolling Stone History of Rock and Roll.* New York: Rolling Stone Press, 1986.

Weisbard, Eric (with Craig Marks). *Spin Alternative Record Guide.* New York: Vintage Books, 1995.

Whitburn, Joel. *The Billboard Book of Top 40 Albums.* New York: Billboard Books, 1991.

———. *The Billboard Book of Top 40 Country Hits.* New York: Watson-Guptill Publications, 1996.

———. *The Billboard Book of Top 40 Hits.* 6th rev. ed. New York: Billboard Books, 1996.

———. *The Billboard Book of Top 40 Hits.* 7th rev. ed. New York: Billboard Books, 2000.

———. *Billboard's Top 2000.* Menomonee Falls, Wis.: Record Research, 1985.

———. *Top Pop Albums, 1955–1985.* Menomonee Falls, Wis.: Record Research, 1985.

White, Adam, and Fred Bronson. *The Billboard Book of Number One Rhythm and Blues Hits.* New York: Watson-Guptill Publications, 1993.

White, Charles. *The Life and Times of Little Richard.* New York: Pocket Books, 1984.

White, Timothy. *Rock Lives: Profiles and Interviews.* New York: Henry Holt and Company, 1990.

———. *Rock Stars.* New York: Stewart, Tabori & Chang, 1984.

Wicke, Peter. *Rock Music: Culture, Aesthetics, and Sociology.* Trans. Rachel Fogg. Cambridge, Mass.: Cambridge University Press, 1990.

Wild, David. Musicians Unite Against Record Labels. *Rolling Stone,* January 31, 2002, pp. 17–18.

Williams, Allan, and William Marshall. *The Man Who Gave the Beatles Away.* New York: Macmillan, 1975.

Williams, Don. Bob Dylan: *The Man, the Music, the Message.* Old Tappan, N.J.: Fleming H. Revell, 1985.

Winfield, Betty Houchin and Sandra Davidson, eds. *Bleep! Censoring Rock and Rap Music.* Westport, Conn.: Greenwood Press, 1999.

Wise, Herbert, ed. *Blood, Sweat and Tears.* New York: Amsco Music, 1971.

Woodward, Josef. The Darker Side of Michael McDonald. *Musician,* no. 86, pp. 76–83, 106, December, 1985.

Zimmer, Dave. *Crosby, Stills, and Nash: The Authorized Biography.* New York: St. Martin's Press, 1984.

# Index